Fundamentals of Business Law

Elliot Axelrod
Sandra J. Mullings

Fundamentals of Business Law

Prepared for Law 1101

Edited by David Rosenberg, Elliot Axelrod and Sandra Mullings

Custom Editor:
Liza Rudneva

Sr. Marketing Coordinators:
Lindsay Annett and Sara Mercurio

Custom Production Editor:
Kim Fry

Marketing Manager:
Rob Bloom

Production/Manufacturing Manager:
Donna M. Brown

Rights and Permissions Specialists:
Kalina Ingham Hintz

Developmental Editor:
Brian Coovert

Production Editorial Manager:
Dan Plofchan

Production Coordinator:
Susannah Maynard

The Adaptable Courseware Program consists of products and additions to existing Thomson products that are produced from camera-ready copy. Peer review, class testing, and accuracy are primarily the responsibility of the author(s).

Fundamentals to Psychology
Edited by David Rosenberg, Elliot Axelrod and Sandra Mullings

pg. 000

ISBN 13: 978-0-324-55736-7
ISBN 10: 0-324-55736-1

International Divisions List

Asia (Including India):
Thomson Learning
(a division of Thomson Asia Pte Ltd)
5 Shenton Way #01-01
UIC Building
Singapore 068808
Tel: (65) 6410-1200
Fax: (65) 6410-1208

Australia/New Zealand:
Thomson Learning Australia
102 Dodds Street
Southbank, Victoria 3006
Australia

Latin America:
Thomson Learning
Seneca 53
Colonia Polano
11560 Mexico, D.F., Mexico
Tel (525) 281-2906
Fax (525) 281-2656

Canada:
Thomson Nelson
1120 Birchmount Road
Toronto, Ontario
Canada M1K 5G4
Tel (416) 752-9100
Fax (416) 752-8102

UK/Europe/Middle East/Africa:
Thomson Learning
High Holborn House
50-51 Bedford Row
London, WC1R 4LR
United Kingdom
Tel 44 (020) 7067-2500
Fax 44 (020) 7067-2600

Spain (Includes Portugal):
Thomson Paraninfo
Calle Magallanes 25
28015 Madrid
España
Tel 34 (0)91 446-3350
Fax 34 (0)91 445-6218

Fundamentals of Business Law

Introduction to Law

CHAPTER

1

Law concerns the relations of individuals with one another as such relations affect the social and economic order. It is both the product of civilization and the means by which civilization is maintained. As such, law reflects the social, economic, political, religious, and moral philosophy of society. The laws of the United States influence the lives of every U.S. citizen. At the same time, the laws of each state influence the lives of its citizens and the lives of many noncitizens as well. The rights and duties of all individuals, as well as the safety and security of all people and their property, depend upon the law.

The law is pervasive. It interacts with and influences the political, economic, and social systems of every civilized society. It permits, forbids, and/or regulates practically every known human activity and affects all persons either directly or indirectly. Law is, in part, prohibitory: certain acts must not be committed. For example, one must not steal; one must not murder. Law is also partly <u>mandatory:</u> certain acts must be done or be done in a prescribed way. Taxes must be paid; corporations must make and file certain reports with state authorities; traffic must keep to the right. Finally, law is permissive: individuals may choose to perform or not to perform certain acts. Thus, one may or may not enter into a contract; one may or may not dispose of one's estate by will.

Because the areas of law are so highly interrelated, an individual who intends to study the several branches of law known collectively as business law should first consider the nature, classification, and sources of law as a whole. This enables the student not only to comprehend better any given branch of law but also to understand its relation to other areas of law.

NATURE OF LAW

The law has evolved slowly, and it will continue to change. It is not a pure science based upon unchanging and universal truths. Rather, it results from a continuous effort to balance, through a workable set of rules, the individual and group rights of a society. In *The Common Law*, Oliver Wendell Holmes writes,

> The life of the law has not been logic; it has been experience. <u>The felt necessities</u> of the time, the prevalent moral and political theories, avowed or unconscious, even the prejudices which judges share with their fellowmen, have had a good deal more to do than the syllogism in determining the rules by which men should be governed. The law embodies the story of a nation's development through many centuries, and it cannot be dealt with as if it contained only the axioms and corollaries of a book of mathematics.

Definition of Law

A fundamental but difficult question regarding law is this: What is it? Numerous philosophers and jurists (legal scholars) have attempted to define it. American jurists and Supreme Court Justices Oliver Wendell Holmes and Benjamin Cardozo defined law as <u>predictions</u>

2

of the way that a court will decide specific legal questions. Blackstone, an English jurist, on the other hand, defined law as "a rule of civil conduct prescribed by the supreme power in a state, commanding what is right, and prohibiting what is wrong." Similarly, Austin, a nineteenth-century English jurist, defined law as a general command that a state or sovereign makes to those who are subject to its authority by laying down a course of action enforced by judicial or administrative tribunals.

Because of its great complexity, many legal scholars have attempted to explain the law by outlining its essential characteristics. Roscoe Pound, a distinguished American jurist and former dean of the Harvard Law School, described law as having multiple meanings:

> First, we may mean the legal order, that is, the regime of ordering human activities and relations through systematic application of the force of politically organized society, or through social pressure in such a society backed by such force. We use the term "law" in this sense when we speak of "respect for law" or for the "end of law."
>
> Second, we may mean the aggregate of laws or legal precepts; the body of authoritative grounds of judicial and administrative action established in such a society. We may mean the body of received and established materials on which judicial and administrative determinations proceed. We use the term in this sense when we speak of "systems of law" or of "justice according to law."
>
> Third, we may mean what Mr. Justice Cardozo has happily styled "the judicial process." We may mean the process of determining controversies, whether as it actually takes place, or as the public, the jurists, and the practitioners in the courts hold it ought to take place.

Functions of Law

At a general level the primary function of law is to maintain stability in the social, political, and economic system while simultaneously permitting change. The law accomplishes this basic function by performing a number of specific functions, among them dispute resolution, protection of property, and preservation of the state.

Disputes, which inevitably arise in a society as complex and interdependent as ours, may involve criminal matters, such as theft, or noncriminal matters, such as an automobile accident. Because disputes threaten the stability of society, the law has established an elaborate and evolving set of rules to resolve them. In addition, the legal system has instituted societal remedies, usually administered by the courts, in place of private remedies such as revenge.

The recognition of private ownership of property is fundamental to our economic system, based as it is upon the exchange of goods and services among privately held units of consumption. Therefore, a second crucial function of law is to protect the owner's use of property and to facilitate voluntary agreements (called contracts) regarding exchanges of property and services. Accordingly, a significant portion of law, as well as this text, involves property and its disposition, including the

law of property, contracts, sales, commercial paper, and business associations.

A third essential function of the law is preservation of the state. In our system, law ensures that changes in leadership and the political structure are brought about by political actions such as elections, legislation, and referenda, rather than by revolution, sedition, and rebellion.

Legal Sanctions

A primary function of the legal system is to make sure that legal rules are enforced. **Sanctions** are the means by which the law enforces the decisions of the courts. Without sanctions, laws would be ineffectual and unenforceable.

An example of a sanction in a civil (noncriminal) case is the seizure and sale of the property of a debtor who fails to pay a court-ordered obligation, called a judgment. Moreover, under certain circumstances a court may enforce its order by finding an offender in contempt and sentencing him to jail until he obeys the court's order. In criminal cases, the principal sanctions are the imposition of a fine, imprisonment, and capital punishment.

Law and Morals

Although moral and ethical concepts greatly influence the law, morals and law are not the same. They may be considered as two intersecting circles, as shown in Figure 1-1. The more darkly shaded area common to both circles includes the vast body of ideas that are both moral and legal. For instance, "Thou shall not kill" and "Thou shall not steal" are both moral precepts and legal constraints.

On the other hand, that part of the legal circle which does not intersect the morality circle includes many rules of law that are completely unrelated to morals, such as the rules stating that you must drive on the right side of the road and that you must register before you can vote. Likewise, the portion of the morality circle which does not intersect the legal circle includes moral precepts not enforced by law, such as the moral prohibition against silently standing by and watching a blind man walk off a cliff or foreclosing a poor widow's mortgage.

◆ SEE FIGURE 1-1 Law and Morals

Law and Justice

Law and justice represent separate and distinct concepts. Without law, however, there can be no justice. Although justice has at least as many definitions as law does, justice may be defined as fair, equitable, and impartial treatment of the competing interests and desires of individuals and groups with due regard for the common good.

On the other hand, law is no guarantee of justice. Some of history's most monstrous acts have been committed pursuant to "law." For example, the Nazis acted "legally" under German

◆ FIGURE 1-1 Law and Morals

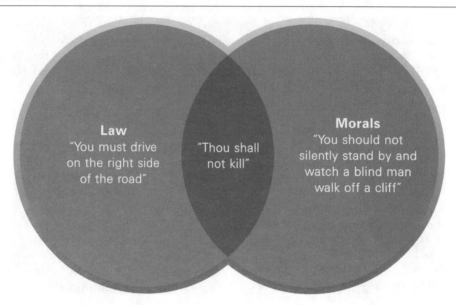

law during the 1930s and 1940s. Totalitarian societies often have shaped formal legal systems around the atrocities they have sanctioned.

CLASSIFICATION OF LAW

Because the subject is vast, classifying the law into categories is helpful. Though a number of classifications are possible, the most useful categories are (1) substantive and procedural, (2) public and private, and (3) civil and criminal.

Basic to understanding these classifications are the terms *right* and *duty*. A **right** is the capacity of a person, with the aid of the law, to require another person or persons to perform, or to refrain from performing, a certain act. Thus, if Alice sells and delivers goods to Bob for the agreed price of $500 payable at a certain date, Alice has the capability, with the aid of the courts, of enforcing the payment by Bob of the $500. A **duty** is the obligation the law imposes upon a person to perform, or to refrain from performing, a certain act. Duty and right are correlatives: no right can rest upon one person without a corresponding duty resting upon some other person or, in some cases, upon all other persons.

◆ SEE FIGURE 1-2 Classification of Law

Substantive and Procedural Law

Substantive law creates, defines, and regulates legal rights and duties. Thus, the rules of contract law that determine when a binding contract is formed are rules of substantive law. This book is principally concerned with substantive law. On the other hand, **procedural law** establishes the rules for enforc-

ing those rights that exist by reason of substantive law. Thus, procedural law defines the method by which one may obtain a remedy in court.

Public and Private Law

Public law is the branch of substantive law that deals with the government's rights and powers in its political or sovereign capacity and in its relation to individuals or groups. Public law consists of constitutional, administrative, and criminal law. **Private law** is that part of substantive law governing individuals and legal entities (such as corporations) in their relations with one another. Business law is primarily private law.

Civil and Criminal Law

The **civil law** defines duties the violation of which constitutes a wrong against the party injured by the violation. In contrast, the **criminal law** establishes duties the violation of which is a wrong against the whole community. Civil law is a part of private law, whereas criminal law is a part of public law. (The term *civil law* should be distinguished from the concept of a civil law *system*, which is discussed later in this chapter.) In a civil action the injured party **sues** to recover **compensation** for the damage and injury he has sustained as a result of the defendant's wrongful conduct. The party bringing a civil action (the **plaintiff**) has the burden of proof, which he must sustain by a **preponderance** (greater weight) of the evidence. Whereas the purpose of criminal law is to punish the wrongdoer, the purpose of civil law is to compensate the injured party. The principal forms of relief the civil law provides are a judgment for money damages and a decree ordering the defendant to perform a specified act or to desist from specified conduct.

◆ FIGURE 1-2   Classification of Law

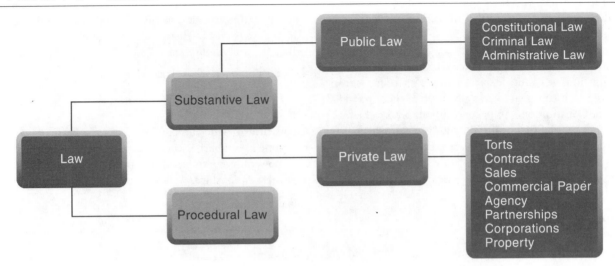

A crime is any act or omission that public law prohibits in the interest of protecting the public and that the government makes punishable in a judicial proceeding brought (**prosecuted**) by it. The government must prove criminal guilt **beyond a reasonable doubt**, which is a significantly higher burden of proof than that required in a civil action. The government prohibits and punishes crimes upon the ground of public policy, which may include the safeguarding of the government itself, human life, or private property. Additional purposes of the criminal law include deterrence and rehabilitation.

◆ SEE FIGURE 1-3 Comparison of Civil and Criminal Law

SOURCES OF LAW

The sources of law in the U.S. legal system are the federal and state constitutions, federal treaties, interstate compacts, federal and state statutes and executive orders, the ordinances of countless local municipal governments, the rules and regulations of federal and state administrative agencies, and an ever-increasing volume of reported federal and state court decisions.

The *supreme law* of the land is the United States Constitution. The Constitution provides that federal statutes and treaties shall be the supreme law of the land. federal legislation and treaties are, therefore, paramount to state constitutions and statutes. federal legislation is of great significance as a source of law. Other federal actions having the force of law are executive

◆ FIGURE 1-3 Comparison of Civil and Criminal Law

	Civil Law	Criminal Law
Commencement of Action	Aggrieved individual (plaintiff) sues	State or federal government prosecutes
Purpose	Compensation Deterrence	Punishment Deterrence Rehabilitation Preservation of peace
Burden of Proof	Preponderance of the evidence	Beyond a reasonable doubt
Principal Sanctions	Monetary damages Equitable remedies	Capital punishment Imprisonment Fines

(handwritten annotations: "OUt Com" next to Burden of Proof; "liable not liable" under Preponderance of the evidence; "Guilhu or not Guilty" under Beyond a reasonable doubt)

orders of the president and rules and regulations of federal administrative officials, agencies, and commissions. The federal courts also contribute considerably to the body of law in the United States.

The same pattern exists in every state. The paramount law of each state is contained in its written constitution. (Although a state constitution cannot deprive citizens of federal constitutional rights, it can guarantee rights beyond those provided in the U.S. Constitution.) State constitutions tend to be more specific than the U.S. Constitution and, generally, have been amended more frequently. Subordinate to the state constitution are the statutes that the state's legislature enacts and the case law that its judiciary develops. Likewise, state administrative agencies issue rules and regulations having the force of law, as do executive orders promulgated by the governors of most states. In addition, cities, towns, and villages have limited legislative powers within their respective municipal areas to pass ordinances and resolutions.

◆ SEE FIGURE 1-4 Hierarchy of Law

Constitutional Law

A **constitution**—the fundamental law of a particular level of government—establishes the governmental structure and allocates power among the levels of government, thereby defining political relationships. One of the fundamental principles

◆ FIGURE 1-4 Hierarchy of Law

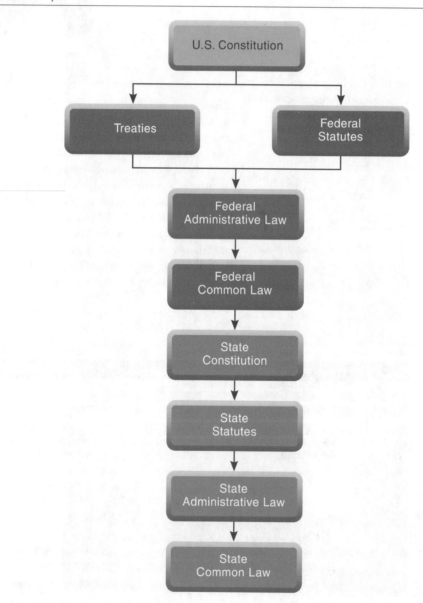

on which our government is founded is that of separation of powers. As detailed in our Constitution, this means that the government consists of three distinct and independent branches: the federal judiciary, the Congress, and the Executive branch.

A constitution also restricts the powers of government and specifies the rights and liberties of the people. For example, the Constitution of the United States not only specifically states what rights and authority are vested in the national government but also specifically enumerates certain rights and liberties of the people. Moreover, the Ninth Amendment to the U.S. Constitution makes it clear that this enumeration of rights does not in any way deny or limit other rights that the people retain.

All other law in the United States is subordinate to the federal Constitution. No law, federal or state, is valid if it violates the federal Constitution. Under the principle of **judicial review**, the Supreme Court of the United States determines the constitutionality of *all* laws.

http: **U.S. Constitution:** http://www.law.cornell.edu/constitution/constitution.table.html
http://findlaw.com/casecode/constitution/
State constitutions: http://www.law.cornell.edu/states/listing.html

Judicial Law

The U.S. legal system is a **common law system**, first developed in England. It relies heavily on the judiciary as a source of law and on the **adversary system** for the adjudication of disputes. In an adversary system the parties, not the court, must initiate and conduct litigation. This approach is based upon the belief that the truth is more likely to emerge from the investigation and presentation of evidence by two opposing parties, both motivated by self-interest, than from judicial investigation motivated only by official duty. Other English-speaking countries, including England, Canada, and Australia, also use the common law system.

In distinct contrast to the common law system are civil law systems, which are based on Roman law. **Civil law systems** depend on comprehensive legislative enactments (called codes) and an inquisitorial method of adjudication. In the **inquisitorial system**, the judiciary initiates litigation, investigates pertinent facts, and conducts the presentation of evidence. The civil law system prevails in most of Europe, Scotland, the state of Louisiana, the province of Quebec, Latin America, and parts of Africa and Asia.

Common Law The courts in common law systems have developed a body of law, known as "case law," "judge-made law," or "common law," that serves as precedent for determining later controversies. In this sense, common law is distinguished from other sources of law such as legislation and administrative rulings.

To evolve steadily and predictably, the common law has developed by application of *stare decisis*. Under the principle of **stare decisis** (to stand by the decisions), courts, in deciding cases, adhere to and rely on rules of law that they or superior courts announced and applied in prior decisions involving similar cases. Judicial decisions thus have two uses: to determine with finality the case currently being decided and to indicate how the courts will decide similar cases in the future. *Stare decisis* does not, however, preclude courts from correcting erroneous decisions or from choosing among conflicting precedents. Thus, the doctrine allows sufficient flexibility for the common law to change.

The strength of the common law is its ability to adapt to change without losing its sense of direction. As Justice Cardozo said, "The inn that shelters for the night is not the journey's end. The law, like the traveler, must be ready for the morrow. It must have a principle of growth."

http: **Federal case law:** http://www.law.cornell.edu/federal/opinions.html
State case law: http://www.law.cornell.edu/opinions.html#state

Equity As the common law developed in England, it became overly rigid and beset with technicalities. Consequently, in many cases the courts provided no remedies because the judges insisted that a claim must fall within one of the recognized forms of action. Moreover, courts of common law could provide only limited remedies; the principal type of relief obtainable was a money judgment. Consequently, individuals who could not obtain adequate relief from monetary awards began to petition the king directly for justice. He, in turn, came to delegate these petitions to his chancellor.

Gradually, there evolved a supplementary system of judicial relief for those who had no adequate remedy at common law. This new system, called **equity**, was administered by a court of chancery presided over by a chancellor. The chancellor, deciding cases on "equity and good conscience," afforded relief in many instances where common law judges had refused to act or where the remedy at law was inadequate. Thus, two systems of law administered by different tribunals developed side by side: the common law courts and the courts of equity.

An important difference between law and equity was that the chancellor could issue a **decree**, or order, compelling a defendant to do or refrain from doing a specific act. A defendant who did not comply with the order could be held in contempt of court and punished by fine or imprisonment. This power of compulsion available in a court of equity opened the door to many needed remedies not available in a court of common law.

Equity jurisdiction, in some cases, recognized rights that were enforceable at common law but for which equity provided more effective remedies. For example, in a court of equity, for breach of a land contract the buyer could obtain a decree of **specific**

performance commanding the defendant seller to perform his part of the contract by transferring title to the land. Another powerful and effective remedy available only in the courts of equity was the **injunction**, a court order requiring a party to do or refrain from doing a specified act. Still another remedy not available elsewhere was **reformation**, where, upon the ground of mutual mistake, contracting parties could bring an action to reform or change the language of a written agreement to conform to their actual intentions. Finally, an action for **rescission** of a contract allowed a party to invalidate a contract under certain circumstances.

Although courts of equity provided remedies not available in courts of law, they granted such remedies only at their discretion, not as a matter of right. The courts exercised this discretion according to the general legal principles, or **maxims**, that they formulated over the years. A few of these familiar maxims of equity are the following: Equity will not suffer a wrong to be without a remedy. Equity regards the substance rather than the form. Equity abhors a forfeiture. Equity delights to do justice and not by halves. He who comes into equity must come with clean hands. He who seeks equity must do equity.

In nearly every jurisdiction in the United States, courts of common law and courts of equity have united to form a single court that administers both systems of law. Vestiges of the old division remain, however. For example, the right to a trial by jury applies only to actions at law but not under federal law and in almost every state to suits filed in equity.

Restatements of Law The common law of the United States results from the independent decisions of the state and federal courts. The rapid increase in the number of decisions by these courts led to the establishment of the American Law Institute (ALI) in 1923. The ALI was composed of a distinguished group of lawyers, judges, and law teachers who set out to prepare "an orderly restatement of the general common law of the United States, including in that term not only the law developed solely by judicial decision, but also the law that has grown from the application by the courts of statutes that were generally enacted and were in force for many years." Wolkin, "Restatements of the Law: Origin, Preparation, Availability," 21 *Ohio B.A.Rept.* 663 (1940).

Regarded as the authoritative statement of the common law of the United States, the Restatements cover many important areas of the common law, including torts, contracts, agency, property, and trusts. Although not law in themselves, they are highly persuasive and frequently have been used by courts in support of their opinions. Because they state much of the common law concisely and clearly, relevant portions of the Restatements are frequently relied upon in this book.

http: **The American Law Institute:** http://www.ali.org

Legislative Law

Since the end of the nineteenth century, legislation has become the primary source of new law and ordered social change in the United States. The annual volume of legislative law is enormous. Justice Felix Frankfurter's remarks to the New York City Bar in 1947 are even more appropriate today:

> Inevitably the work of the Supreme Court reflects the great shift in the center of gravity of law-making. Broadly speaking, the number of cases disposed of by opinions has not changed from term to term. But even as late as 1875 more than 40 percent of the controversies before the Court were common-law litigation, fifty years later only 5 percent, while today cases not resting on statutes are reduced almost to zero. It is therefore accurate to say that courts have ceased to be the primary makers of law in the sense in which they "legislated" the common law. It is certainly true of the Supreme Court that almost every case has a statute at its heart or close to it.

This modern emphasis upon legislative or statutory law has occurred because common law, which develops evolutionarily and haphazardly, is not well suited for making drastic or comprehensive changes. Moreover, courts tend to be hesitant about overruling prior decisions, whereas legislatures frequently repeal prior enactments. In addition, legislatures are independent and able to choose the issues they wish to address, while courts may deal only with issues that arise in actual cases. As a result, legislatures are better equipped to make the dramatic, sweeping, and relatively rapid changes in the law that enable it to respond to numerous and vast technological, social, and economic innovations.

While some business law topics, such as contracts, agency, property, and trusts, still are governed principally by the common law, most areas of commercial law have become largely statutory, including partnerships, corporations, sales, commercial paper, secured transactions, insurance, securities regulation, antitrust, and bankruptcy. Because most states enacted statutes dealing with these branches of commercial law, a great diversity developed among the states and hampered the conduct of commerce on a national scale. The increased need for greater uniformity led to the development of a number of proposed uniform laws that would reduce the conflicts among state laws.

The most successful example is the **Uniform Commercial Code** (UCC), which was prepared under the joint sponsorship and direction of the National Conference of Commissioners on Uniform State Laws (NCCUSL) and the American Law Institute (ALI). (Selected provisions of the Code are set forth in Appendix B of this book.) All fifty states (although Louisiana has adopted only part of it), the District of Columbia, and the Virgin Islands have adopted the UCC. The underlying purposes and policies of the Code are to:

1. simplify, clarify, and modernize the law governing commercial transactions;

2. permit the continued expansion of commercial practices through custom, usage, and agreement of the parties; and

3. make uniform the law among the various jurisdictions.

The NCCUSL has drafted over 200 uniform laws including the Uniform Partnership Act, the Uniform Limited Partnership Act, and the Uniform Probate Code. The ALI has developed a number of model statutory formulations, including the Model Code of Evidence, the Model Penal Code, a Model Land Development Code, and a proposed Federal Securities Code. In addition, the American Bar Association has promulgated the Model Business Corporation Act.

> `http:` **U.S. Code:** http://www4.law.cornell.edu/uscode/
> **State statutes:** http://www.law.cornell.edu/states/listing.html
> **The National Conference of Commissioners on Uniform State Laws:** http://www.nccusl.org
> **Uniform Commercial Code:** http://www.law.cornell.edu/uniform/ucc.html
> **Other Uniform Laws:** http://www.law.upenn.edu/bll/ulc/ulc_frame.htm

Treaties A treaty is an agreement between or among independent nations. Article II of the U.S. Constitution authorizes the president to enter into treaties with the advice and consent of the Senate, "providing two thirds of the Senators present concur."

Only the federal government, not the states, may enter into treaties. A treaty signed by the president and approved by the Senate has the legal force of a federal statute. Accordingly, a federal treaty may supersede a prior federal statute, while a federal statute may supersede a prior treaty. Like statutes, treaties are subordinate to the federal Constitution and subject to judicial review.

> `http:` **Online treaties:** http://www.asil.org/resource/treaty1.htm#sect21

Executive Orders In addition to his executive functions, the president of the United States also has authority to issue laws, which are called **executive orders**. Typically, federal legislation specifically delegates this authority. An executive order may amend, revoke, or supersede a prior executive order. An example of an executive order is the one issued by President Johnson in 1965 prohibiting discrimination by federal contractors on the basis of race, color, sex, religion, or national origin in employment on any work the contractor performed during the period of the federal contract.

Most state governors enjoy comparable authority to issue executive orders.

> `http:` **Executive orders:** http://www.whitehouse.gov/news/orders/

Administrative Law

Administrative law is the branch of public law that is created by administrative agencies in the form of rules, regulations, orders, and decisions to carry out the regulatory powers and duties of those agencies. Administrative functions and activities concern matters of national safety, welfare, and convenience, including the establishment and maintenance of military forces, police, citizenship and naturalization, taxation, coinage of money, elections, environmental protection, the regulation of transportation, interstate highways, waterways, television, radio, trade and commerce, and, in general, public health, safety, and welfare.

To accommodate the increasing complexity of the social, economic, and industrial life of the nation, the scope of administrative law has expanded enormously. Justice Jackson stated that "the rise of administrative bodies has been the most significant legal trend of the last century, and perhaps more values today are affected by their decisions than by those of all the courts, review of administrative decisions apart." *Federal Trade Commission v. Ruberoid Co.,* 343 U.S. 470 (1952). This is evidenced by the great increase in the number and activities of federal government boards, commissions, and other agencies. Certainly, agencies create more legal rules and adjudicate more controversies than all the legislatures and courts combined.

LEGAL ANALYSIS

Decisions in state trial courts generally are not reported or published. The precedent a trial court sets is not sufficiently weighty to warrant permanent reporting. Except in New York and a few other states where selected trial court opinions are published, decisions in trial courts are simply filed in the office of the clerk of the court, where they are available for public inspection. Decisions of state courts of appeals are published in consecutively numbered volumes called "reports." Court decisions are found in the official state reports of most states. In addition, West Publishing Company publishes state reports in a regional reporter, called the National Reporter System, which comprises the following: Atlantic (A. or A.2d); South Eastern (S.E. or S.E.2d); South Western (S.W., S.W.2d, or S.W.3d); New York Supplement (N.Y.S. or N.Y.S.2d); North Western (N.W. or N.W.2d); North Eastern (N.E. or N.E.2d); Southern (So. or So.2d); and Pacific (P., P.2d, or P.3d). At least twenty states no longer publish official reports and have designated a commercial reporter as the authoritative source of state case law. After they are published, these opinions, or "cases," are referred to ("cited") by giving the name of the case, the volume, name, and page of the official state report, if any, in which it is published; the volume, name, and page of the particular set and series of the National Reporter System; and the volume, name, and page of any other selected case series. For instance, *Lefkowitz v. Great Minneapolis Surplus Store, Inc.,* 251 Minn. 188, 86 N.W.2d 689 (1957) indicates that the opinion in this case may be found in

Volume 251 of the official Minnesota Reports at page 188; and in Volume 86 of the North Western Reporter, Second Series, at page 689.

The decisions of courts in the federal system are found in a number of reports. U.S. District Court opinions appear in the Federal Supplement (F.Supp. or F.Supp.2d). Decisions of the U.S. Court of Appeals are found in the Federal Reporter (Fed., F.2d, or F.3d), while the U.S. Supreme Court's opinions are published in the United States Supreme Court Reports (U.S.), Supreme Court Reporter (S.Ct.), and Lawyers Edition (L.Ed.). While all U.S. Supreme Court decisions are reported, not every case decided by the U.S. District Courts and the U.S. Courts of Appeals are reported. Each circuit has established rules determining which decisions are published.

In reading the title of a case, such as *"Jones v. Brown,"* the "v." or "vs." means "versus" or "against." In the trial court, Jones is the **plaintiff**, the person who filed the suit, and Brown is the **defendant**, the person against whom the suit was brought. When a case is appealed, some, but not all, courts of appeal place the name of the party who appeals, or the **appellant**, first, so that *"Jones v. Brown"* in the trial court becomes, if Brown loses and becomes the appellant, *"Brown v. Jones"* in the appellate court. But because some appellate courts retain the trial court order of names, determining from the title itself who was the plaintiff and who was the defendant is not always possible. The student must read the facts of each case carefully and clearly

identify each party in her mind to understand the discussion by the appellate court. In a criminal case, the caption in the trial court will first designate the prosecuting governmental unit and then will indicate the defendant, as in *"State v. Jones"* or *"Commonwealth v. Brown."*

The study of reported cases requires the student to understand and apply legal analysis. Normally, the reported opinion in a case sets forth (a) the essential facts, the nature of the action, the parties, what happened to bring about the controversy, what happened in the lower court, and what pleadings are material to the issues; (b) the issues of law or fact; (c) the legal principles involved; (d) the application of these principles; and (e) the decision.

A serviceable method by which students may analyze and brief cases after reading and comprehending the opinion is to write a brief containing the following:

1. the facts of the case
2. the issue or question involved
3. the decision of the court
4. the reasons for the decision

By way of example, the edited case of *Ryan v. Friesenhahn* is presented after the chapter summary and then briefed using the suggested format.

❧ SEE CASE 1-1

CHAPTER SUMMARY

Nature of Law

✗ **Definition of Law** "a rule of civil conduct prescribed by the supreme power in a state, commanding what is right, and prohibiting what is wrong" (Blackstone)

✗ **Functions of Law** to maintain stability in the social, political, and economic system through dispute resolution, protection of property, and the preservation of the state, while simultaneously permitting ordered change

✗ **Legal Sanctions** are means by which the law enforces the decisions of the courts

Law and Morals are different but overlapping; law provides sanctions, while morals do not

Law and Justice are separate and distinct concepts; justice is the fair, equitable, and impartial treatment of competing interests with due regard for the common good

---

Classification of Law

Substantive and Procedural Law
- *Substantive Law* law creating rights and duties
- *Procedural Law* rules for enforcing substantive law

Public and Private Law
- *Public Law* law dealing with the relationship between government and individuals
- *Private Law* law governing the relationships among individuals and legal entities

Civil and Criminal Law
- *Civil Law* law dealing with rights and duties the violation of which constitutes a wrong against an individual or other legal entity
- *Criminal Law* law establishing duties which, if violated, constitute a wrong against the entire community

Sources of Law	**Constitutional Law** fundamental law of a government establishing its powers and limitations

Sources of Law

Constitutional Law fundamental law of a government establishing its powers and limitations

Judicial Law
- *Common Law* body of law developed by the courts that serves as precedent for determination of later controversies
- *Equity* body of law based upon principles distinct from common law and providing remedies not available at law

Legislative Law statutes adopted by legislative bodies
- *Treaties* agreements between or among independent nations
- *Executive Orders* laws issued by the president or by the governor of a state

Administrative Law body of law created by administrative agencies to carry out their regulatory powers and duties

---

CASE

CASE
1-1

RYAN v. FRIESENHAHN
Court of Appeals of Texas, 1995
911 S.W.2d 113

Rickhoff, J.

This is an appeal from a take-nothing summary judgment granted the defendants in a social host liability case. Appellants' seventeen-year-old daughter was killed in a single-car accident after leaving appellees' party in an intoxicated condition. While we hold that the appellants were denied an opportunity to amend their pleadings, we also find that their pleadings stated a cause of action for negligence and negligence per se. We reverse and remand.

Todd Friesenhahn, son of Nancy and Frederick Friesenhahn, held an "open invitation" party at his parents' home that encouraged guests to bring "bring your own bottle." Sabrina Ryan attended the party, became intoxicated, and was involved in a fatal accident after she left the event. According to the Ryans' petition, Nancy and Frederick Friesenhahn were aware of this activity and of Sabrina's condition.

Sandra and Stephen Ryan, acting in their individual and representative capacities, sued the Friesenhahns for wrongful death, negligence, and gross negligence.* * *

* * *

a. The Petition The Ryans pled, in their third amended petition, that Todd Friesenhahn planned a "beer bust" that was advertised by posting general invitations in the community for a party to be held on the "Friesenhahn Property." The invitation was open and general and invited persons to "B.Y.O.B." (bring your own bottle). According to the petition, the Friesenhahns had actual or constructive notice of the party and the conduct of the minors in "possessing, exchanging, and consuming alcoholic beverages."

The Ryans alleged that Friesenhahns were negligent in (1) allowing the party to be held on the Friesenhahn property; (2) directly or indirectly inviting Sabrina to the party; (3) allowing the party to continue on their property "after they knew that minors were in fact possessing, exchanging, and consuming alcohol"; (4) failing "to provide for the proper conduct at the party"; (5) allowing Sabrina to become intoxicated and failing to "secure proper attention and treatment"; (6) and allowing Sabrina to leave the Friesenhahn property while driving a motor vehicle in an intoxicated state.* * *

b. Negligence Per Se Accepting the petition's allegations as true, the Friesenhahns were aware that minors possessed and consumed alcohol on their property and specifically allowed Sabrina to become intoxicated. The Texas Alcoholic Beverage Code provides that one commits an offense if, with criminal negligence, he "makes available an alcoholic beverage to a minor." [Citation.] The exception for serving alcohol to a minor applies only to the minor's adult parent. [Citation.]

An unexcused violation of a statute constitutes negligence per se if the injured party is a member of the class protected by the statute. [Citation.] The Alcoholic Beverage Code was designed to protect the general public and minors in particular and must be liberally construed. [Citation.] We conclude that Sabrina is a member of the class protected by the Code.

In viewing the Ryans' allegations in the light most favorable to them, we find that they stated a cause of action against the Friesenhahns for the violation of the Alcoholic Beverage Code.

c. Common Law Negligence The elements of negligence include (1) a legal duty owed by one person to another; (2) breach of that duty; and (3) damages proximately caused by the breach. [Citation.] To determine whether a common law duty exists, we must consider several factors, including risk, foreseeability, and likelihood of injury weighed against the social utility of the defendant's conduct, the magnitude of the burden of guarding against the injury and consequences of placing that burden on the defendant. [Citation.] We may also consider whether one party has superior knowledge of the risk, and whether one party has the right to control the actor whose conduct precipitated the harm. [Citation.]

As the Supreme Court in [citation] explained, there are two practical reasons for not imposing a third-party duty on social hosts who provide alcohol to adult guests: first, the host cannot reasonably know the extent of his guests' alcohol consumption level; second, the host cannot reasonably be expected to control his guests' conduct. [Citation.] The Tyler court in [citation] relied on these principles in holding that a minor "had no common law duty to avoid making alcohol available to an intoxicated guest [another minor] who he knew would be driving." [Citation.]

We disagree with the Tyler court because the rationale expressed [by the Supreme Court] in [citation] does not apply to the relationship between minors, or adults and minors. The adult social host need not estimate the extent of a minor's alcohol consumption because serving minors any amount of alcohol is a criminal offense. [Citation.] Furthermore, the social host may control the minor, with whom there is a special relationship, analogous to that of parent-child. [Citation.]

* * *

As this case demonstrates, serving minors alcohol creates a risk of injury or death. Under the pled facts, a jury could find that the Friesenhahns, as the adult social hosts, allowed open invitations to a beer bust at their house and they could foresee, or reasonably should have foreseen, that the only means of arriving at their property would be by privately operated vehicles; once there, the most likely means of departure would be by the same means. That adults have superior knowledge of the risk of drinking should be apparent from the legislature's decision to allow persons to become adults on their eighteenth birthday for all purposes but the consumption of alcohol. [Citations.]

While one adult has no general duty to control the behavior of another adult, one would hope that adults would exercise special diligence in supervising minors–even during a simple swimming pool party involving potentially dangerous but legal activities. We may have no special duty to watch one adult to be sure he can swim, but it would be ill-advised to turn loose young children without insuring they can swim. When the "party" is for the purpose of engaging in dangerous and illicit

activity, the consumption of alcohol by minors, adults certainly have a greater duty of care. [Citation.]

***Accordingly, we find that the Ryans' petition stated a common-law cause of action.

* * *

We reverse and remand the trial court's summary judgment.

Brief of Ryan v. Friesenhahn

Facts

Todd Friesenhahn, son of Nancy and Frederick Friesenhahn, held an open invitation party at his parents' home that encouraged guests to bring their own bottle. Sabrina Ryan attended the party, became intoxicated, and was involved in a fatal accident after she left the party. Sandra and Stephen Ryan, Sabrina's parents, sued the Friesenhahns for negligence, alleging that the Friesenhahns were aware of underage drinking at the party and of Sabrina's condition when she left the party. The trial court granted summary judgment for the Friesenhahns.

Issue

Is a social host who serves alcoholic beverages to a minor liable in negligence for harm suffered by the minor as a result of the minor's intoxication?

Decision

In favor of the Ryans. Summary judgment reversed and case remanded to the trial court.

Reasons

Accepting the Ryans' allegations as true, the Friesenhahns were aware that minors possessed and consumed alcohol on their property and specifically allowed Sabrina to become intoxicated. The Texas Alcoholic Beverage Code provides that a person commits an offense if, with criminal negligence, he "makes available an alcoholic beverage to a minor." A violation of a statute constitutes negligence per se if the injured party is a member of the class protected by the statute. Since the Alcoholic Beverage Code was designed to protect the general public and minors in particular, Sabrina is a member of the class protected by the Code. Therefore, we find that the Ryans stated a cause of action against the Friesenhahns for the violation of the Alcoholic Beverage Code.

In considering common-law negligence as a basis for social host liability, the Texas Supreme Court has held that there are two practical reasons for not imposing a third-party duty on social hosts who provide alcohol to adult guests: first, the host cannot reasonably know the extent of his guests' alcohol consumption level; second, the host cannot reasonably be expected to control his guests' conduct. However, this rationale does not apply where the guest is a minor. The adult social host need not estimate the extent of a minor's alcohol consumption because serving minors any amount of alcohol is a criminal offense. Furthermore, the social host may control the minor, with whom there is a special relationship, analogous to that of parent-child.

QUESTIONS

1. Identify and describe the basic functions of law.
2. Distinguish between law and justice.
3. Distinguish between law and morals.
4. Define and discuss substantive and procedural law.
5. Distinguish between public and private law.
6. Distinguish between civil and criminal law.
7. Identify and describe the sources of law.
8. Distinguish between law and equity.
9. Explain the principle of *stare decisis*.
10. Identify and define four remedies available in equity.

 Internet Exercise Find for the federal government and for your state examples of the following sources of law: (a) constitutional law, (b) judicial law, (c) legislative law, and (d) administrative law. (If such information on your state is not available, choose another state.)

Civil Dispute Resolution

As discussed in Chapter 1, substantive law establishes the rights and duties of individuals and other legal entities while procedural law determines the means by which these rights are asserted. Procedural law attempts to accomplish two competing objectives: (1) to be fair and impartial and (2) to operate efficiently. The judicial process in the United States represents a balance between these two objectives as well as a commitment to the adversary system.

The first part of this chapter describes the structure and function of the federal and state court systems. The second part deals with jurisdiction; the third part discusses civil dispute resolution, including the procedure in civil lawsuits.

The Court System

Courts are impartial tribunals (seats of judgment) established by governmental bodies to settle disputes. A court may render a binding decision only when it has jurisdiction over the dispute and the parties to that dispute; that is, when it has a right to hear and make a judgment in a case. The United States has a dual court system: The federal government has its own independent system, as does each of the fifty states plus the District of Columbia.

THE FEDERAL COURTS

Article III of the U.S. Constitution states that the judicial power of the United States shall be vested in one Supreme Court and such lower courts as Congress may establish. Congress has established a lower federal court system consisting of a number of special courts, district courts, and courts of appeals. The federal court system is staffed by judges who receive lifetime appointments from the president, subject to confirmation by the Senate.

◆ SEE FIGURE 2-1 Federal Judicial System

http: **Information about Federal courts:** http://www.uscourts.gov/about.html

District Courts

The district courts are the general trial courts in the federal system. Most cases begin in a district court, and it is here that issues of fact are decided. The district court is generally presided over by *one* judge, although in certain cases three judges preside. In a few cases, an appeal from a judgment or decree of a district court is taken directly to the Supreme Court. In most cases, however, appeals go to the Circuit Court of Appeals of the appropriate circuit, the decision of which is, in most cases, final.

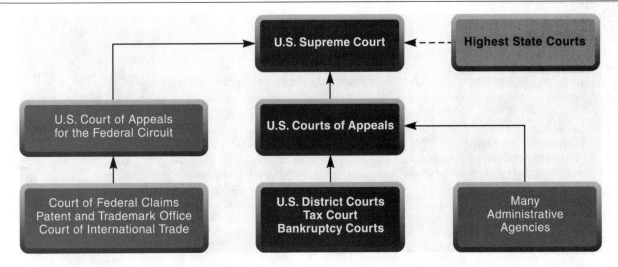

Congress has established 94 judicial districts, each of which is located entirely in a particular state. All states have at least one district, while certain states contain more than one. For instance, New York has four districts, Illinois has three, and Wisconsin has two, while a number of less populated states comprise a single district.

> **http:** **Information about and cases decided by the U.S. district courts:** http://www.law.emory.edu/FEDCTS/
> http://www.law.cornell.edu/federal/districts.html#circuit

Courts of Appeals

Congress has established twelve judicial circuits (eleven numbered circuits plus the D.C. Circuit), each having a court known as the Court of Appeals, which primarily hears appeals from the district courts located within its circuit. In addition, these courts review decisions of many administrative agencies, the Tax Court, and the Bankruptcy Court. Congress has also established the U.S. Court of Appeals for the Federal Circuit, which is discussed in the section on "Special Courts." The United States Courts of Appeals generally hear cases in panels of *three* judges, although in some instances all of the judges of the circuit will sit *en banc* to decide a case.

The function of appellate courts is to examine the record of a case on appeal and to determine if the trial court committed prejudicial error. If so, the appellate court will **reverse** or **modify** the judgment and if necessary **remand** it (send it back) to the lower court for further proceeding. If no prejudicial error exists, the appellate court will **affirm** the decision of the lower court.

> **http:** **Cases decided by the U.S. Courts of Appeals:** http://www.law.emory.edu/FEDCTS/

◆ **SEE FIGURE 2-2** Circuit Courts of the United States

The Supreme Court

The nation's highest tribunal is the United States Supreme Court, which consists of nine justices (a Chief Justice and eight Associate Justices) who sit as a group in Washington, D.C. A quorum consists of any six justices. In certain types of cases, the U.S. Supreme Court has original jurisdiction (the right to hear a case first). The Court's principal function, nonetheless, is to review decisions of the Federal Courts of Appeals and, in some instances, decisions involving federal law made by the highest state courts. Cases reach the Supreme Court under its appellate jurisdiction by one of two routes. Very few come by way of **appeal by right**–cases the Court must hear should a party request the review. In 1988, Congress enacted legislation that almost completely eliminated the right to appeal to the U.S. Supreme Court.

The second way in which the Supreme Court may review a decision of a lower court is by the discretionary **writ of certiorari**, which requires a lower court to produce the records of a case it has tried. Now almost all cases reaching the Supreme Court come to it by means of writs of *certiorari*. The Court uses the writ as a device to choose the cases it wishes to hear. The Court grants writs for cases involving a federal question of substantial importance or a conflict in the decisions of the U.S. Circuit Courts of Appeals. Only a small percentage of the petitions to the Supreme Court for review by *certiorari* are granted, however. The vote of four justices is required to grant a writ.

> **http:** **Information about the U.S. Supreme Court:** http://www.supremecourtus.gov/about/about.html

◆ Figure 2-2 **Circuit Courts of the United States**

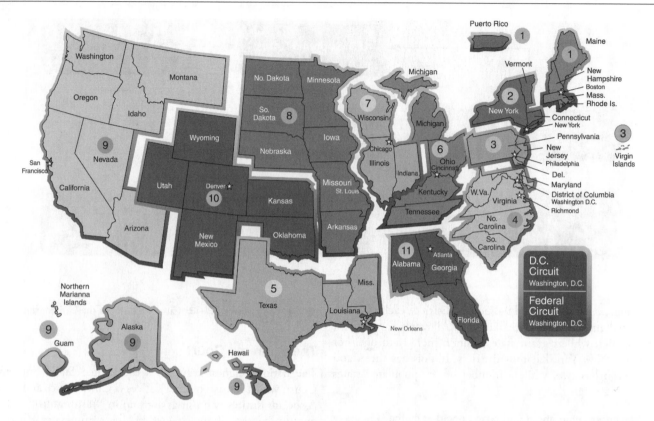

Source: Administrative Office of The United States Courts, January 1983

Special Courts

The special courts in the Federal judicial system include the U.S. Court of Federal Claims, the U.S. Tax Court, the U.S. Bankruptcy Courts, and the U.S. Court of Appeals for the Federal Circuit. These courts have jurisdiction over particular subject matter. The U.S. Court of Federal Claims has national jurisdiction to hear claims against the United States. The U.S. Tax Court has national jurisdiction over certain cases involving Federal taxes. The U.S. Bankruptcy Courts have jurisdiction to hear and decide certain matters under the Federal Bankruptcy Act, subject to review by the U.S. District Court. The U.S. Court of Appeals for the Federal Circuit has nationwide jurisdiction and reviews decisions of the Court of Federal Claims, the Patent and Trademark Office, patent cases decided by the U.S. District Court, the United States Court of International Trade, the Merit Systems Protection Board, and the U.S. Court of Veterans Appeals.

> **http:** **Information about and cases decided by the U.S. Court of Federal Claims:** http://www.uscfc.uscourts.gov/
> **Information about and cases decided by the U.S. Bankruptcy Courts:** http://www.law.cornell.edu/federal/districts.html#circuit

STATE COURTS

Each of the fifty states and the District of Columbia has its own court system. In most states the voters elect judges for a stated term.

◆ See Figure 2-3 State Court System

Inferior Trial Courts

At the bottom of the state court system are the inferior trial courts, which decide the least serious criminal and civil matters. Usually, inferior trial courts do not keep a complete written record of trial proceedings. Such courts, which are referred to as municipal courts, justice of the peace courts, or traffic courts, hear minor criminal cases such as traffic offenses. They also conduct preliminary hearings in more serious criminal cases.

Small claims courts are inferior trial courts which hear civil cases involving a limited amount of money. Usually there is no jury, the procedure is informal, and neither side employs an attorney. An appeal from small claims court is taken to the trial court of general jurisdiction, where a new trial (called a trial *de novo*), in which the small claims court's decision is given no weight, is begun.

◆ Figure 2-3 **State Court System**

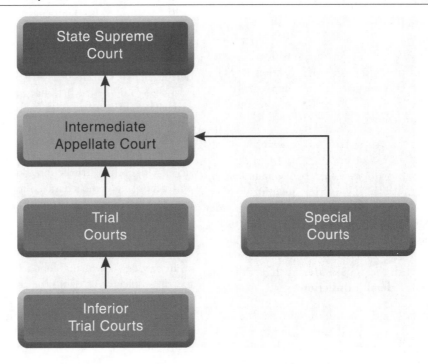

Trial Courts

Each state has trial courts of general jurisdiction, which may be called county, district, superior, circuit, or common pleas courts. (In New York the trial court is called the Supreme Court.) These courts do not have a dollar limitation on their jurisdiction in civil cases and hear all criminal cases other than minor offenses. Unlike the inferior trial courts, these trial courts of general jurisdiction maintain formal records of their proceedings as procedural safeguards.

Special Courts

Many states have special courts that have jurisdiction over particular areas. For example, many states have probate courts with jurisdiction over the administration of wills and estates. Many states also have family courts, which have jurisdiction over divorce and child custody cases. Appeals from these special courts go to the general state appellate courts.

Appellate Courts

At the summit of the state court system is the state's court of last resort, a reviewing court generally called the Supreme Court of the State. Except for those cases in which review by the U.S. Supreme Court is available, the decision of the highest state tribunal is final. Most states also have created intermediate appellate courts to handle the large volume of cases seeking review. Review by such a court is usually by right. Further review is in most cases at the highest court's discretion.

 Information about and cases decided by State courts: http://www.ncsc.dni.us/COURT/SITES/Courts.htm **State court decisions:** http://www.ncsconline.org/ **New York State Court Structure:** http://www.courts. state.ny.us/courts/structure.shtml:

Jurisdiction

Jurisdiction means the power or authority of a court to hear and decide a given case. To resolve a lawsuit, a court must have two kinds of jurisdiction. The first is subject matter jurisdiction. Where a court lacks jurisdiction over the subject matter of a case, no action it takes in the case will have legal effect.

The second kind of jurisdiction is over the parties to a lawsuit. This jurisdiction is required for the court to render an enforceable judgment that affects the rights and duties of the parties to the lawsuit. A court usually may obtain jurisdiction over the defendant if she lives and is present in the court's territory or the transaction giving rise to the case has a substantial connection to the court's territory. The court obtains jurisdiction over the plaintiff when he voluntarily submits to the court's power by filing a complaint with the court.

SUBJECT MATTER JURISDICTION

Subject matter jurisdiction refers to the authority of a particular court to adjudicate a controversy of a particular kind. Federal courts have *limited* subject matter jurisdiction, as set forth in the U.S. Constitution, Article III, Section 2. State courts have jurisdiction over *all* matters that the Constitution or Congress has not given exclusively to the federal courts or expressly denied the state courts.

Federal Jurisdiction

The federal courts have, to the exclusion of the state courts, subject matter jurisdiction over some areas. Such jurisdiction is called **exclusive federal jurisdiction**. Federal jurisdiction is exclusive only if Congress so provides, either explicitly or implicitly. If Congress does not so provide and the area is one over which Federal courts have subject matter jurisdiction, they share this jurisdiction with the State courts. Such jurisdiction is known as **concurrent federal jurisdiction**.

Exclusive Federal Jurisdiction The federal courts have exclusive jurisdiction over federal criminal prosecutions; admiralty, bankruptcy, antitrust, patent, trademark, and copyright cases; suits against the United States; and cases arising under certain federal statutes that expressly provide for exclusive federal jurisdiction.

Concurrent Federal Jurisdiction There are two types of concurrent federal jurisdiction: federal question jurisdiction and diversity jurisdiction. The first arises whenever there is a federal question over which the federal courts do not have exclusive jurisdiction. A **federal question** is any case arising under the Constitution, statutes, or treaties of the United States. For a case to be treated as "arising under" federal law, either federal law must create the plaintiff's cause of action or the plaintiff's right to relief must depend upon the resolution of a substantial question of federal law in dispute between the parties. There is no minimum dollar requirement in federal question cases. When a state court hears a concurrent federal question case, it applies federal substantive law but its own procedural rules.

Diversity jurisdiction arises where there is "diversity of citizenship" and the amount in controversy exceeds $75,000. Then private litigants may bring an action in a federal district court or a state court. **Diversity of citizenship** exists (1) when the plaintiffs are all citizens of a state or states different from the state or states of which the defendants are citizens; (2) when a foreign country brings an action against citizens of the United States; or (3) when the controversy is between citizens of a state and citizens of a foreign country. The citizenship of an individual litigant is the state in which the litigant resides or is domiciled, whereas that of a corporate litigant is both the state of incorporation and the state in which its principal place of business is located. For example, if the amount in controversy exceeds $75,000, then diversity of citizenship jurisdiction would

be satisfied if Ada, a citizen of California, sues Bob, a citizen of Idaho. If, however, Carol, a citizen of Virginia, and Dianne, a citizen of North Carolina, sue Evan, a citizen of Georgia, and Farley, a citizen of North Carolina, diversity of citizenship would not exist because both Dianne, a plaintiff, and Farley, a defendant, are citizens of North Carolina.

The $75,000 jurisdictional requirement is satisfied if the plaintiff makes a good faith claim to the amount in the complaint, unless it is clear to a legal certainty that the claim does not exceed the required amount.

When a federal district court hears a case solely under diversity of citizenship jurisdiction, no federal question is involved, and, accordingly, the federal court must apply substantive state law. The conflict of laws rules of the state in which the district court is located determine which state's substantive law the court will use. (Conflict of laws is discussed later.) Federal courts apply federal procedural rules in diversity cases.

In any case involving concurrent jurisdiction, the plaintiff has the choice of bringing the action in either an appropriate federal court or state court. If the plaintiff brings the case in a state court, however, the defendant usually may have it **removed** (shifted) to a Federal court for the district in which the state court is located.

State Jurisdiction

Exclusive State Jurisdiction The state courts have exclusive jurisdiction over *all other matters* not granted to the federal courts in the Constitution or by Congress. Accordingly, exclusive state jurisdiction would include cases involving diversity of citizenship where the amount in controversy is $75,000 or less. In addition, the state courts have exclusive jurisdiction over all cases to which federal judicial power does not reach. These matters include, but are by no means limited to, property, torts, contract, agency, commercial transactions, and most crimes.

◆ SEE FIGURE 2-4 Federal and State Jurisdiction

◆ SEE FIGURE 2-5 Subject Matter Jurisdiction

Choice of Law in State Courts A court in one state may be a proper forum for a case even though some or all of the relevant events occurred in another state. For example, a California plaintiff may sue a Washington defendant in Washington over a car accident that occurred in Oregon. Because of Oregon's connections to the accident, Washington may choose, under its **conflict of laws rules**, to apply the substantive law of Oregon. Conflict of laws rules vary from state to state.

Stare Decisis in the Dual Court System

The doctrine of *stare decisis* presents certain problems when there are two parallel court systems. Consequently, in the United States, *stare decisis* functions approximately as follows:

◆ Figure 2-4 **Federal and State Jurisdiction**

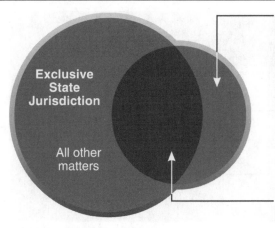

Exclusive State Jurisdiction

All other matters

Exclusive Federal Jurisdiction
1. Federal crimes
2. Bankruptcy
3. Patents
4. Copyright and trademarks
5. Admiralty
6. Antitrust
7. Suits against the United States
8. Specified Federal statutes

Concurrent Jurisdiction
1. Federal questions
2. Diversity of citizenship

1. The United States Supreme Court has never held itself to be bound rigidly by its own decisions, and lower federal courts and state courts have followed that course with respect to their own decisions.
2. A decision of the U.S. Supreme Court on a federal question is binding on all other courts, federal or state.
3. On a federal question, although a decision of a federal court other than the Supreme Court may be persuasive in a state court, the decision is not binding.
4. A decision of a state court may be persuasive in the federal courts, but it is not binding except where federal jurisdiction is based on diversity of citizenship. In such a case the federal courts must apply state law as determined by the highest state tribunal.
5. Decisions of the federal courts (other than the U.S. Supreme Court) are not binding upon other federal courts of equal or inferior rank, unless the latter owe obedience to the deciding court. For example, a decision of the Fifth Circuit Court of Appeals binds district courts in the Fifth Circuit but binds no other federal court.
6. A decision of a state court is binding upon all courts inferior to it in its jurisdiction. Thus, the decision of the supreme court in a state binds all other courts in that state.

7. A decision of a state court is not binding on courts in other states except where the latter courts are required, under their conflict of laws rules, to apply the law of the formerstate as determined by the highest court in that state. For example, if a North Carolina court is required to apply Virginia law, it must follow decisions of the Virginia Supreme Court.

◆ See Figure 2-6 *Stare Decisis* in the Dual Court System

JURISDICTION OVER THE PARTIES

The second essential type of jurisdiction a court must have is the power to bind the parties involved in the dispute. The court obtains jurisdiction over the *plaintiff* when she voluntarily submits to the court's power by filing a complaint with the court. With respect to the *defendant*, a court may meet the requirements for this type of jurisdiction, called **jurisdiction over the parties**, in any of three ways: (1) *in personam* jurisdiction, (2) *in rem* jurisdiction, or (3) attachment jurisdiction. In addition, the exercise of jurisdiction must satisfy the constitutionally imposed requirements of due process: reasonable notification

◆ Figure 2-5 **Subject Matter Jurisdiction**

Types of Jurisdiction	Court	Substantive Law Applied	Procedural Law Applied
Exclusive Federal	Federal	Federal	Federal
Concurrent:	Federal	Federal	Federal
Federal Question	State	Federal	State
Concurrent:	Federal	State	Federal
Diversity	State	State	State
Exclusive State	State	State	State

◆ Figure 2-6 *Stare Decisis* in the Dual Court System

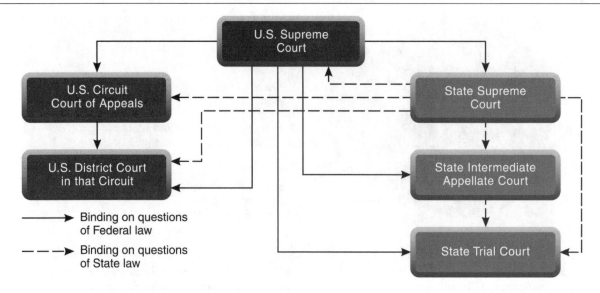

and a reasonable opportunity to be heard. Moreover, the court's exercise of jurisdiction is valid under the Due Process Clause of the U.S. Constitution only if the defendant has minimum contacts with the state sufficient to prevent the court's assertion of jurisdiction from offending "traditional notions of fair play and substantial justice." For a court constitutionally to assert jurisdiction over a defendant, the defendant must have engaged in either purposeful acts in the state or acts outside the state that are of such a nature that the defendant could reasonably foresee being sued in that state. This overriding limitation on jurisdictional power is imposed upon the federal and state courts through the U.S. Constitution.

What notice is due depends on several factors but generally must be "notice reasonably calculated, under the circumstances, to apprise interested parties of the pendency of the action and afford them the opportunity to present their objections."

In Personam Jurisdiction

In personam jurisdiction, or **personal jurisdiction**, is jurisdiction of a court over the parties to a lawsuit, in contrast to jurisdiction over their property. A court obtains *in personam* jurisdiction over a defendant either (1) by serving process on the party within the state in which the court is located or (2) by reasonable notification to a party outside the state in those instances where a "long-arm statute" applies. To *serve process* means to deliver a summons, which is an order to respond to a complaint lodged against a party. (The terms *summons* and *complaint* are explained more fully later in this chapter.)

Personal jurisdiction may be obtained by personally serving a person within a state if that person is domiciled in that state. The U.S. Supreme Court has held that a state may exercise

personal jurisdiction over a nonresident defendant who is temporarily present if the defendant is personally served in that State. Personal jurisdiction may also arise from a party's consent. For example, parties to a contract may agree that any dispute concerning that contract will be subject to the jurisdiction of a specific court.

Most states have adopted **long-arm statutes** to expand their jurisdictional reach beyond those persons who may be personally served within the state. These statutes allow courts to obtain jurisdiction over nonresident defendants whose contacts with the state in which the court is located are such that the exercise of jurisdiction does not offend traditional notions of fair play and substantial justice. The typical long-arm statute permits a court to exercise jurisdiction over a defendant, even though process is served beyond its borders, if the defendant (1) has committed a tort (civil wrong) within the state, (2) owns property within the state and that property is the subject matter of the lawsuit, (3) has entered into a contract within the state, or (4) has transacted business within the state and that business is the subject matter of the lawsuit.

In Rem Jurisdiction

Courts in a state have the jurisdiction to adjudicate claims to property situated within the state if the plaintiff gives those persons who have an interest in the property reasonable notice and an opportunity to be heard. Such jurisdiction over property is called *in rem* jurisdiction, from the Latin word *res*, which means "thing." For example, if Carpenter and Miller are involved in a lawsuit over property located in Kansas, then an appropriate court in Kansas would have *in rem* jurisdiction to adjudicate claims with respect to this property so long as both parties are given notice of the lawsuit and a reasonable opportunity to contest the claim.

Attachment Jurisdiction

Attachment jurisdiction, or **quasi** *in rem* jurisdiction, is jurisdiction over property rather than over a person. Attachment jurisdiction is invoked by seizing the defendant's property located within the state to obtain payment of a claim against the defendant that is *unrelated* to the property seized. For example, Allen, a resident of Ohio, has obtained a valid judgment in the amount of $20,000 against Bradley, a citizen of Kentucky. Allen can attach Bradley's automobile, which is located in Ohio, to satisfy his court judgment against Bradley.

◆ **See Figure 2-7** Jurisdiction

Venue

Venue, which often is confused with jurisdiction, concerns the geographical area in which a lawsuit *should* be brought. The purpose of venue is to regulate the distribution of cases within a specific court system and to identify a convenient forum. In the federal court system, venue determines the district or districts in a given state in which a suit may be brought. State rules of venue typically require that a suit be initiated in a county where one of the defendants resides. In matters involving real estate, most venue rules require that a suit be initiated in the county where the property is situated. A defendant may, however, object to the venue for various reasons.

Civil Dispute Resolution

As mentioned in Chapter 1, one of the primary functions of law is to provide for the peaceful resolution of disputes. Accordingly, our legal system has established an elaborate set of governmental mechanisms to settle disputes. The most prominent of these is judicial dispute resolution, called *litigation*. The rules of civil procedure, discussed in the first part of this section, govern judicial resolution of civil disputes. Judicial resolution of criminal cases is governed by the rules of criminal procedure. Dispute resolution by administrative agencies is also very common.

As an alternative to governmental dispute resolution, several nongovernmental methods of dispute resolution, such as arbitration, have developed. These are discussed in the second part of this section.

CIVIL PROCEDURE

Civil disputes that enter the judicial system must follow the rules of civil procedure. These rules are designed to resolve the dispute justly, promptly, and inexpensively.

To acquaint the student with civil procedure, it will be helpful to carry a hypothetical action through the trial court to the highest court of review in the state. Although there are technical differences in trial and appellate procedure among state and federal courts, the following illustration will provide

◆ **Figure 2-7 Jurisdiction**

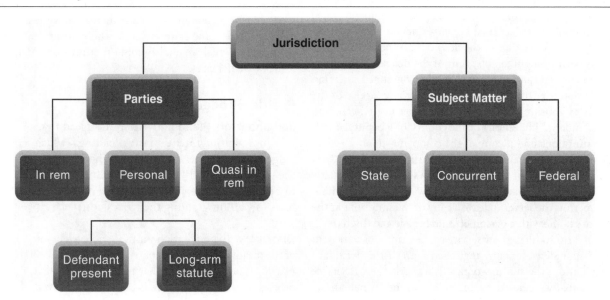

a general understanding of the trial and appeal of cases. Assume that Pam Pederson, a pedestrian, while crossing a street in Chicago, is struck by an automobile driven by David Dryden. Pederson suffers serious personal injuries, incurs heavy medical and hospital expenses, and is unable to work for several months. Pederson desires that Dryden pay her for the loss and damages she sustained. After attempts at settlement fail, Pederson brings an action at law against Dryden. Pederson is the plaintiff, and Dryden the defendant. Each is represented by a lawyer. Let us follow the progress of the case.

| http: | **State civil procedure laws:** http://www.law.cornell.edu/topics/civil_procedure.html |

The Pleadings

The **pleadings** are a series of responsive, formal, written statements in which each side to a lawsuit states its claims and defenses. The purpose of pleadings is to give notice and to establish the issues of fact and law that the parties dispute. An "issue of fact" is a dispute between the parties regarding the events that gave rise to the lawsuit. In contrast, an "issue of law" is a dispute between the parties as to what legal rules apply to these facts. Issues of fact are decided by the jury, or by the judge when there is no jury, whereas issues of law are decided by the judge.

Complaint and Summons A lawsuit commences when Pederson, the plaintiff, files with the clerk of the trial court a **complaint** against Dryden which contains (1) a statement of the claim and supporting facts showing that she is entitled to relief and (2) a demand for that relief. Pederson's complaint alleges that while exercising due and reasonable care for her own safety, she was struck by Dryden's automobile, which was negligently being driven by Dryden, causing her personal injuries and damages of $50,000, for which Pederson requests judgment.

Once the plaintiff has filed a complaint, the clerk issues a **summons** to be served upon the defendant to notify him that a suit has been brought against him. If the defendant has contacts with the state sufficient to show that the state's assertion of jurisdiction over him is constitutional, proper service of the summons establishes the court's jurisdiction over the person of the defendant. The sheriff of the county or a deputy sheriff serves a summons and a copy of the complaint upon Dryden, the defendant, commanding him to file his appearance and answer with the clerk of the court within a specific time, usually thirty days from the date the summons was served. A number of states permit the server to leave a copy of the summons at the defendant's home with a person of "suitable age and discretion." Most long-arm statutes allow service of the summons to be sent to out-of-state defendants by registered mail. If the defendant is a corporation, the statutes typically authorize actual service to the company's general or managing agent. When direct

methods of notifying the defendant are unavailable, service by publication may be allowed.

Responses to Complaint At this point Dryden has several options. If he fails to respond at all, a **default judgment** will be entered against him for the relief the court determines in a hearing. He may make **pretrial motions** contesting the court's jurisdiction over him or asserting that the action is barred by the statute of limitations, which requires suits to be brought within a specified time. Dryden also may move that the complaint be made more definite and certain, or that the complaint be dismissed for failure to state a claim upon which the court may grant relief. Such a motion, sometimes called a **demurrer**, essentially asserts that even if all of Pederson's allegations were true, she still would not be entitled to the relief she seeks, and that, therefore, there is no need for a trial of the facts. The court rules on this motion as a matter of law. If it rules in favor of the defendant, the plaintiff may appeal the ruling.

If he does not make any pretrial motions, or if they are denied, Dryden will respond to the complaint by filing an **answer**, which may contain admissions, denials, affirmative defenses, and counterclaims. Thus, Dryden might answer the complaint by denying its allegations of negligence and stating, on the other hand, that he, Dryden, was driving his car at a low speed and with reasonable care (a **denial**) when his car struck Pederson (an **admission**), who had dashed across the street in front of Dryden's car without looking in any direction to see whether cars or other vehicles were approaching; that, accordingly, Pederson's injuries were caused by her own negligence (an **affirmative defense**) and that, therefore, she should not be permitted to recover any damages. Dryden might further state that Pederson caused damages to his car and request a judgment for $2,000 (a **counterclaim**). These pleadings create an issue of fact regarding whether Pederson or Dryden, or both, failed to exercise due and reasonable care under the circumstances and were thus negligent and liable for their carelessness.

If the defendant counterclaims, the plaintiff must respond by a **reply,** which may also contain admissions, denials, and affirmative defenses.

Pretrial Procedure

Judgment on Pleadings After the pleadings, either party may move for **judgment on the pleadings,** which requests the judge to rule as a matter of law whether the facts as alleged in the pleadings, which for the purpose of the motion are taken to be as the nonmoving party alleges them, form a sufficient basis to warrant granting the requested relief.

Discovery In preparation for trial and even before completion of the pleadings stage, each party has the right to obtain relevant evidence, or information that may lead to evidence, from the other party. This procedure is known as **discovery**. It includes

(1) pretrial **depositions** consisting of sworn testimony, taken out of court, of the opposing party or other witnesses; (2) sworn answers by the opposing party to **written interrogatories**; (3) **production** of documents and physical objects in the possession of the opposing party or, by a court-ordered subpoena, in the possession of nonparties; (4) a relevant court-ordered physical and/or mental **examination**, by a physician, of the opposing party; and (5) admissions of facts obtained by a **request for admissions** submitted to the opposing party. By properly using discovery, each party may become fully informed of relevant evidence and avoid surprise at trial. Another purpose of this procedure is to encourage and facilitate settlements by providing both parties with as much relevant information as possible.

Pretrial Conference Also furthering these objectives is the pretrial conference between the judge and the attorneys representing the parties. The basic purposes of the **pretrial conference** are (1) to simplify the issues in dispute by amending the pleadings, admitting or stipulating facts, and identifying witnesses and documents to be presented at trial; and (2) to encourage settlement of the dispute without trial. (More than 90 percent of all cases are settled before going to trial.) If no settlement occurs, the judge will enter a pretrial order containing all of the amendments, stipulations, admissions, and other matters agreed to during the pretrial conference. The order supersedes the pleadings and controls the remainder of the trial.

Summary Judgment The evidence disclosed by discovery may be so clear that a trial to determine the facts becomes unnecessary. Thus, after discovery, either party may move for a summary judgment, which requests the judge to rule that, because there are no issues of fact to be determined by trial, the party thus moving should prevail as a matter of law. A **summary judgment** is a final binding determination on the merits made by the judge before a trial.

Trial

In all federal civil cases at common law involving more than $20, the U.S. Constitution guarantees the right to a jury trial. In addition, nearly every state constitution provides a similar right. In addition, federal and state statutes may authorize jury trials in cases not within the constitutional guarantees. Under federal law and in almost all states, jury trials are *not* available in equity cases. Even in cases where a jury trial is available, the parties may waive (choose not to have) a trial by jury. When a trial is conducted without a jury, the judge serves as the fact finder and will make separate findings of fact and conclusions of law. When a trial is conducted with a jury, the judge determines issues of law and the jury determines questions of fact.

Jury Selection Assuming a timely demand for a jury has been made, the trial begins with the selection of a jury. The jury selection process involves a *voir dire*, an examination by the parties' attorneys (or, in some courts, by the judge) of the potential jurors. Each party may make an unlimited number of **challenges for cause**, which prevent a prospective juror from serving if the juror is biased or cannot be fair and impartial. In addition, each party has a limited number of **peremptory challenges**, which allow the party to disqualify a prospective juror without showing cause. The Supreme Court has held that the U.S. Constitution prohibits discrimination in jury selection on the basis of race or gender.

Conduct of Trial After the jury has been selected, both attorneys make an **opening statement** concerning the facts that they expect to prove in the trial. The plaintiff and her witnesses then testify upon **direct examination** by the plaintiff's attorney. Each is then subject to **cross-examination** by the defendant's attorney. Thus, in our hypothetical case, the plaintiff and her witnesses testify that the traffic light at the street intersection where Pederson was struck was green for traffic in the direction in which Pederson was crossing but changed to yellow when she was about one-third of the way across the street.

During the trial the judge rules on the admission and exclusion of evidence on the basis of its relevance and reliability. If the judge does not allow certain evidence to be introduced or certain testimony to be given, the attorney may preserve the question of admissibility for review on appeal by making an **offer of proof**. The law does not regard the offer of proof as evidence, and the offer, which consists of oral statements of counsel or witnesses showing for the record the substance of the evidence which the judge has ruled inadmissible, is not heard by the jury.

After cross-examination, followed by redirect examination of each of her witnesses, Pederson rests her case. At this point, Dryden may move for a directed verdict in his favor. A **directed verdict** is a final binding determination on the merits made by the judge after a trial but before the jury renders a verdict. If the judge concludes that the evidence introduced by the plaintiff, which is assumed for the purposes of the motion to be true, would not be sufficient for the jury to find in favor of the plaintiff, then the judge will grant the directed verdict in favor of the defendant. In some states, the judge will deny the motion for a directed verdict if there is *any* evidence on which the jury might possibly render a verdict for the plaintiff. If a directed verdict is reversed on appeal, a new trial is necessary.

If the judge denies the motion for a directed verdict, the defendant then has the opportunity to present evidence. The defendant and his witnesses testify that Dryden was driving his car at a low speed when it struck Pederson and that Dryden at the time had the green light at the intersection.

After the defendant has presented his evidence, the plaintiff and the defendant may be permitted to introduce rebuttal evidence. Once both parties have rested (concluded), either party may move for a directed verdict. By this motion the party contends that the evidence is so clear that reasonable persons could not differ as to the outcome of the case. If the judge grants the motion for a directed verdict, he takes the case away from the jury and enters a judgment for the party making the motion.

If the judge denies the motion, the plaintiff's attorney makes a **closing argument** to the jury, reviewing the evidence and urging a verdict in favor of Pederson. Dryden's attorney then makes a closing argument, summarizing the evidence and urging a verdict in favor of Dryden. Pederson's attorney is permitted to make a short argument in rebuttal.

Jury Instructions The attorneys previously have tendered possible written **jury instructions** on the applicable law to the trial judge, who gives to the jury those instructions he approves and denies those he considers incorrect. The judge also may give the jury instructions of his own. These instructions (called "charges" in some states) advise the jury of the particular rules of law that apply to the facts the jury determines from the evidence.

Verdict The jury then retires to the jury room to deliberate and to reach a **general verdict** in favor of one party or the other. If it finds the issues in favor of the defendant, its verdict is that the defendant is not liable. If, however, it finds the issues for the plaintiff and against the defendant, its verdict will hold the defendant liable and will specify the amount of the plaintiff's damages. In this case, the jury found that Pederson's damages were $35,000. Upon returning to the jury box, the foreman either announces the verdict or hands it in written form to the clerk to give to the judge, who reads the general verdict in open court. In some jurisdictions, the jury must reach a **special verdict** by making specific written findings on each factual issue. The judge then applies the law to these findings and renders a judgment.

Motions Challenging the Verdict The unsuccessful party may then file a written motion for a new trial or for judgment notwithstanding the verdict. The judge may grant a **motion for a new trial** if (1) the judge committed prejudicial error during the trial, (2) the verdict is against the weight of the evidence, (3) the damages are excessive, or (4) the trial was not fair. The judge has the discretion to grant a motion for a new trial (on grounds 1, 3, or 4 above) even if substantial evidence supports the verdict. On the other hand, he must deny the motion for judgment notwithstanding the verdict (also called a judgment n.o.v.) if any substantial evidence supports the verdict. This motion is similar to a motion for a directed verdict, only it is made *after* the jury's verdict. To grant the **motion for judgment notwithstanding the verdict**, the judge must decide that the evidence is so clear that reasonable people could not differ as to the outcome of the case. If a judgment n.o.v. is reversed on appeal, a new trial is *not* necessary, and the jury's verdict is entered. If the judge denies the motions for a new trial and for a judgment notwithstanding the verdict, he enters **judgment on the verdict** for $35,000 in favor of Pederson.

Appeal

The purpose of an appeal is to determine whether the trial court committed prejudicial error. Most jurisdictions permit an appeal only from a final judgment. As a general rule, an appellate court reviews only errors of law. Errors of law include the judge's decisions to admit or exclude evidence; the judge's instructions to the jury; and the judge's actions in denying or granting a motion for a demurrer, a summary judgment, a directed verdict, or a judgment notwithstanding the verdict. Appellate courts review errors of law *de novo*. An appellate court will reverse errors of fact only if they are so clearly erroneous that the court considers them to constitute an error of law.

Assume that Dryden directs his attorney to appeal. The attorney files a notice of appeal with the clerk of the trial court within the prescribed time. Later, Dryden, as appellant, files in the reviewing court the record on appeal, which contains the pleadings, transcript of the testimony, rulings by the judge on motions made by the parties, arguments of counsel, jury instructions, the verdict, posttrial motions, and the judgment from which the appeal is taken. In states having an intermediate court of appeals, such court will usually be the reviewing court. In states having no intermediate courts of appeal, a party may appeal directly from the trial court to the state supreme court.

Dryden, as appellant, is required to prepare a condensation of the record, known as an abstract, or pertinent excerpts from the record, which he files with the reviewing court together with a brief and argument. His **brief** contains a statement of the facts, the issues, the rulings by the trial court which Dryden contends are erroneous and prejudicial, grounds for reversal of the judgment, a statement of the applicable law, and arguments on his behalf. Pederson, the appellee, files an answering brief and argument. Dryden may, but is not required to, file a reply brief. The case is now ready for consideration by the reviewing court.

The appellate court does not hear any evidence; rather, it decides the case upon the record, abstracts, and briefs. After **oral argument** by the attorneys, if the court elects to hear one, the court then takes the case under advisement and makes a decision based upon majority rule, after which the court prepares a written opinion containing the reasons for its decision, the applicable rules of law, and its judgment. The judgment may **affirm** the judgment of the trial court, or, if the appellate court finds that reversible error was committed, the judgment may be **reversed**, or the case may be **reversed and remanded** for a new trial. In some instances the appellate court will affirm the lower court's decision in part and reverse it in part. The losing party may file a petition for rehearing, which is usually denied.

If the reviewing court is an intermediate appellate court, the party losing in that court may decide to seek a reversal of its judgment by filing within a prescribed time a notice of appeal, if the appeal is by right, or a petition for leave to appeal to the state supreme court, if the appeal is by discretion. This petition corresponds to a petition for a writ of *certiorari* in the U.S. Supreme Court. The party winning in the appellate court may file an answer to the petition for leave to appeal. If the petition is granted or if the appeal is by right, the record is certified to the supreme court, where each party files a new brief and argument. Oral argument may be held, and the case is taken under advisement. If the Supreme Court concludes that the judgment of the appellate court is correct, it affirms. If it decides otherwise, it reverses the judgment of the appellate court and enters a reversal or an order of remand. The unsuccessful party may again file a petition for a rehearing, which is likely to be denied. Barring the remote possibility of an application for still further review by the U.S. Supreme Court, the case either has reached its termination or, upon remand, is about to start its second journey through the courts, beginning, as it did originally, in the trial court.

Enforcement

If Dryden does not appeal or if the reviewing court affirms the judgment if he does appeal and Dryden does not pay the judgment, the task of enforcement remains. Pederson must request the clerk to issue a **writ of execution**, demanding payment of the judgment, which is served by the sheriff upon the defendant. If the writ is returned "unsatisfied," Pederson may post bond or other security and order a levy on and sale of specific nonexempt property belonging to Dryden, which is then seized by the sheriff, advertised for sale, and sold at public sale under the writ of execution. If the proceeds of the sale do not produce sufficient funds to pay the judgment, plaintiff Pederson's attorney may institute a supplementary proceeding in an attempt to locate money or other property belonging to Dryden. In an attempt to collect the judgment, Pederson's attorney also may proceed by **garnishment** against Dryden's employer to collect from Dryden's wages or against a bank in which Dryden has an account.

If Pederson cannot satisfy the judgment with Dryden's property located within Illinois (the state where the judgment was obtained), Pederson will have to bring an action on the original judgment in other states where Dryden owns property. Because the U.S. Constitution requires each state to accord judgments of other states **full faith and credit**, Pederson will be able to obtain a local judgment that may be enforced by the methods described above.

◆ SEE FIGURE 2-8 **Stages in Civil Procedure**

ALTERNATIVE DISPUTE RESOLUTION

Litigation is complex, time-consuming, and expensive. Furthermore, court adjudications involve long delays, lack spe-

cial expertise in substantive areas, and provide only a limited range of remedies. In addition, the litigation process offers little opportunity for compromise and often causes or exacerbates animosity between the disputants. Consequently, in an attempt to overcome some of the disadvantages of litigation, several nonjudicial methods of dealing with disputes have developed. The most important of these alternatives to litigation is arbitration. Others include conciliation, mediation, "mini-trials," and summary jury trials.

The various techniques differ in a number of ways, including (1) whether the process is voluntary, (2) whether the process is binding, (3) whether the disputants represent themselves or are represented by attorneys, (4) whether the decision is made by the disputants or by a third party, (5) whether the procedure used is formal or informal, and (6) whether the basis for the decision is law or some other criterion.

Which method of civil dispute resolution–litigation or one of the nongovernmental methods–is better for a particular dispute depends on several factors, including the financial circumstances of the disputants, the nature of their relationship (commercial or personal, ongoing or limited), and the urgency of their need for a quick resolution. Alternative dispute resolution methods are especially suitable where privacy, speed, preservation of continuing relations, and control over the process–including the flexibility to compromise–are important to the parties. Nevertheless, the disadvantages of using alternative dispute mechanisms may make court adjudication more appropriate. For example, except for arbitration, only courts can compel participation and provide a binding resolution. In addition, only courts can establish precedents and create public duties. Furthermore, the courts provide greater due process protections and uniformity of outcome. Finally, the courts are independent of the disputants and are publicly funded.

◆ SEE FIGURE 2-9 Comparison of Adjudication,
Arbitration, and Mediation
Conciliation

| http: | **Information about alternate dispute resolution:** http://www.abanet.org/dispute and http://www.adr.org |

Arbitration

In **arbitration,** the parties select a neutral third person or persons (the arbitrator[s]) who render(s) a binding decision after hearing arguments and reviewing evidence. Because the presentation of the case is less formal and the rules of evidence are more relaxed, arbitration usually takes less time and costs less than litigation. Moreover, in many arbitration cases the parties are able to select an arbitrator with special expertise concerning the subject of the dispute. Thus, the quality of the arbitrator's decision may be higher than that available through the court system. In addition, arbitration normally is conducted

◆ Figure 2-8 **Stages in Civil Procedure**

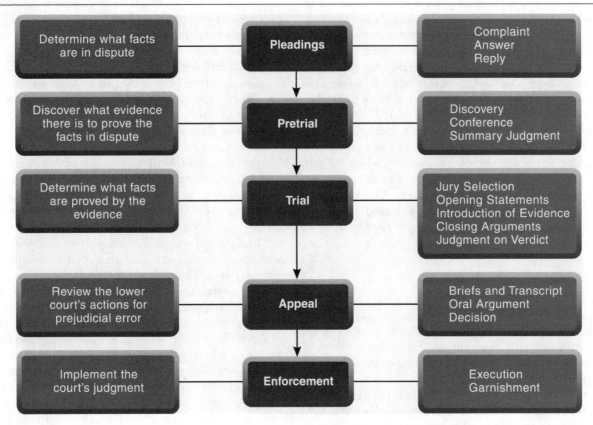

in private, which enables the parties to avoid unwanted publicity. Arbitration is commonly used in commercial and labor management disputes.

Types of Arbitration Arbitration is of two basic types—consensual, which is by far the most common, and compulsory. **Consensual arbitration** occurs whenever the parties to a dispute agree to submit the controversy to arbitration. They may do this in advance by agreeing in their contract that disputes arising out of the contract will be resolved by arbitration. Or, after a dispute arises, they may agree to submit the dispute to arbitration. In either instance, such agreements are enforceable under the Federal Arbitration Act (FAA) and statutes in more than forty states. The great majority of these states have adopted the Uniform Arbitration Act (UAA); the others have adopted substantially similar legislation. (In 2000, the National Conference of Commissioners on Uniform State Laws promulgated the Revised Uniform Arbitration Act to provide state legislatures with a more up-to-date statute to resolve disputes through arbitration. To date, only a few states have adopted the Revised UAA.) In **compulsory arbitration**, which is relatively infrequent, a federal or state statute requires arbitration for specific types of disputes, such as those involving public employees like police officers, teachers, and firefighters.

 Federal Arbitration Act: http://caselaw.lp.findlaw.com/casecode/uscodes/9/toc.html
Revised Uniform Arbitration Act: http://www.law.upenn.edu/bll/ulc/uarba/arbitrat1213.htm

Procedure Usually the parties' agreement to arbitrate specifies how the arbitrator or arbitrators will be chosen. If it does not, the Federal Arbitration Act and state statutes provide methods for selecting arbitrators. Although the requirements for arbitration hearings vary from state to state, they generally consist of opening statements, case presentation, and closing statements. Case presentations may include witnesses, documentation, and site inspections. The parties may cross-examine witnesses and the parties may be represented by attorneys.

The decision of the arbitrator, called an **award**, is binding on the parties. Nevertheless, it is subject to very limited judicial review. Under the Federal Arbitration Act and the Revised UAA grounds for review include (1) the award was procured by corruption, fraud, or other undue means; (2) the arbitrators were partial or corrupt; (3) the arbitrators were guilty of misconduct prejudicing the rights of a party to the arbitration proceeding; and (4) the arbitrators exceeded their powers. Historically, the courts were unfriendly to arbitration; now, however, they favor the procedure.

◆ Fɪɢᴜʀᴇ 2-9 **Comparison of Adjudication, Arbitration, and Mediation/Conciliation**

	Court Adjudication	**Arbitration**	**Mediation/Conciliation**
Advantages	Binding	Binding	Preserves relations
	Public norms	Parties control process	Parties control process
	Precedents	Privacy	Privacy
	Uniformity	Special expertise	Flexible
	Publicly funded	Speedy resolution	
	Compels participation		
Disadvantages	Expensive	No public norms	Not binding
	Time-consuming	No precedent	Lacks finality
	Long delays	No uniformity	No compelled participation
	Limited remedies		No precedent
	Lacks special expertise		No uniformity
	No compromise		
	Disrupts relationships		
	Publicity		

Source: Adapted from Table 4 of *Report of the Ad Hoc Panel on Dispute Resolution and Public Policy,* prepared by the National Institute for Dispute Resolution.

International Arbitration Arbitration is a commonly used means for resolving international disputes. The United Nations Committee on International Trade Law (UNCITRAL) and the International Chamber of Commerce have promulgated arbitration rules which have won broad international adherence. The Federal Arbitration Act has provisions implementing the United Nations Convention on the Recognition and Enforcement of Foreign Arbitral Awards. A number of states have enacted laws specifically governing international arbitration; some of the statutes have been based on the Model Law on International Arbitration drafted by UNCITRAL.

Court-Annexed Arbitration A growing number of federal and state courts have adopted court-annexed arbitration in civil cases where the parties seek limited amounts of damages. The arbitrators are usually attorneys. Appeal from this type of *nonbinding* arbitration is by trial *de novo*.

Many states have enacted statutes requiring the arbitration of medical malpractice disputes. Some states provide for mandatory nonbinding arbitration before bringing a case to court. Other states provide for voluntary but binding arbitration agreements which patients sign before receiving medical treatment.

Conciliation

Conciliation is a nonbinding, informal process in which the disputing parties select a neutral third party (the conciliator) who attempts to help them reach a mutually acceptable agreement. The duties of the conciliator include improving com-

munications, explaining issues, scheduling meetings, discussing differences of opinion, and serving as an intermediary between the parties when they are unwilling to meet.

Mediation

Mediation is a process in which a neutral third party (the mediator) selected by the disputants helps them to resolve their disagreement. In addition to employing conciliation techniques to improve communications, the mediator, unlike the conciliator, proposes possible solutions for the parties to consider. Like the conciliator, the mediator lacks the power to render a binding decision. Mediation is commonly used by the judicial system in such tribunals as small claims courts, housing courts, family courts, and neighborhood justice centers. In 2001 the National Conference of Commissioners on Uniform State Laws promulgated the Uniform Mediation Act, which was amended in 2003. The Act establishes a privilege of confidentiality for mediators and participants. To date two states have adopted it.

http: **Uniform Mediation Act:** http://www.law.upenn.edu/bll/ ulc/ mediat/2003finaldraft.htm

Sometimes the techniques of arbitration and mediation are combined in a procedure called "med-arb." In med-arb, the neutral third party serves first as a mediator. If all issues are not resolved through such mediation, she then serves as an arbitrator authorized to render a binding decision on the remaining issues.

Mini-Trial

A mini-trial is a structured settlement process that combines elements of negotiation, mediation, and trials. Mini-trials are most commonly used when both disputants are corporations. In a mini-trial, attorneys for the two corporations conduct limited discovery and then present evidence to a panel consisting of managers from each company, as well as a neutral third party, who may be a retired judge or other attorney. After the lawyers complete their presentations, the managers try to negotiate a settlement without the attorneys. The managers may consult the third party on how a court might resolve the issues in dispute.

Summary Jury Trial

A summary jury trial is a mock trial in which the parties present their case to an advisory jury. Though not binding, the jury's verdict does influence the negotiations in which the parties must participate following the mock trial. If the parties do not reach a settlement, they may have a full trial *de novo*.

Negotiation

Negotiation is a consensual bargaining process in which the parties attempt to reach an agreement resolving their dispute. Negotiation differs from other methods of alternate dispute resolution in that there are no third parties involved.

CHAPTER SUMMARY

The Court System

Federal Courts
District Courts trial courts of general jurisdiction that can hear and decide most legal controversies in the federal system
Courts of Appeals hear appeals from the district courts and review orders of certain administrative agencies
The Supreme Court nation's highest court, whose principal function is to review decisions of the Federal Courts of Appeals and the highest state courts
Special Courts have jurisdiction over cases in a particular area of federal law and include the U.S. Court of Federal Claims, the U.S. Tax Court, the U.S. Bankruptcy Courts, and the U.S. Court of Appeals for the Federal Circuit

State Courts
Inferior Trial Courts hear minor criminal cases, such as traffic offenses, and civil cases involving small amounts of money; conduct preliminary hearings in more serious criminal cases
Trial Courts have general jurisdiction over civil and criminal cases
Special Courts trial courts, such as probate courts and family courts, having jurisdiction over a particular area of state law
Appellate Courts include one or two levels; the highest court's decisions are final except in those cases reviewed by the U.S. Supreme Court

Jurisdiction

Subject Matter Jurisdiction
Definition authority of a court to decide a particular kind of case
Federal Jurisdiction
- *Exclusive Federal Jurisdiction* federal courts have sole jurisdiction over federal crimes, bankruptcy, antitrust, patent, trademark, copyright, and other specified cases
- *Concurrent Federal Jurisdiction* authority of more than one court to hear the same case; State and Federal courts have concurrent jurisdiction over (1) federal question cases (cases arising under the Constitution, statutes, or treaties of the United States) that do not involve exclusive federal jurisdiction and (2) diversity of citizenship cases involving more than $75,000
State Jurisdiction state courts have exclusive jurisdiction over all matters to which the Federal judicial power does not reach

Jurisdiction over the Parties	**Definition** the power of a court to bind the parties to a suit

Definition the power of a court to bind the parties to a suit
In Personam **Jurisdiction** jurisdiction based upon claims against a person, in contrast to jurisdiction over the person's property
In Rem **Jurisdiction** jurisdiction based on claims against property
Attachment Jurisdiction jurisdiction over a defendant's property to obtain payment of a claim not related to the property
Venue geographical area in which a lawsuit should be brought

Civil Dispute Resolution

Civil Procedure

The Pleadings a series of statements that give notice and establish the issues of fact and law presented and disputed
- *Complaint* initial pleading by the plaintiff stating his case
- *Summons* notice given to inform a person of a lawsuit against her
- *Answer* defendant's pleading in response to the plaintiff's complaint
- *Reply* plaintiff's pleading in response to the defendant's answer

Pretrial Procedure process requiring the parties to disclose what evidence is available to prove the disputed facts; designed to encourage settlement of cases or to make the trial more efficient
- *Judgment on Pleadings* a final ruling in favor of one party by the judge based on the pleadings
- *Discovery* right of each party to obtain evidence from the other party
- *Pretrial Conference* a conference between the judge and the attorneys to simplify the issues in dispute and to attempt to settle the dispute without trial
- *Summary Judgment* final ruling by the judge in favor of one party based on the evidence disclosed by discovery

Trial determines the facts and the outcome of the case
- *Jury Selection* each party has an unlimited number of challenges for cause and a limited number of peremptory challenges
- *Conduct of Trial* consists of opening statements by attorneys, direct and cross-examination of witnesses, and closing arguments
- *Directed Verdict* final ruling by the judge in favor of one party based on the evidence introduced at trial
- *Jury Instructions* judge gives the jury the particular rules of law that apply to the case proves
- *Verdict* the jury's decision based on those facts the jury determines the evidence proves
- *Motions Challenging the Verdict* include motions for a new trial and a motion for judgment notwithstanding the verdict

Appeal determines whether the trial court committed prejudicial error
Enforcement plaintiff with an unpaid judgment may resort to a writ of execution to have the sheriff seize property of the defendants and to garnishment to collect money owed to the defendant by a third party

Alternative Dispute Resolution

Arbitration a nonjudicial proceeding in which a neutral party selected by the disputants renders a binding decision (award)
Conciliation a nonbinding process in which a third party acts as an intermediary between the disputing parties
Mediation a nonbinding process in which a third party acts as an intermediary between the disputing parties and proposes solutions for them to consider
Mini-Trial a nonbinding process in which attorneys for the disputing parties (typically corporations) present evidence to managers of the disputing parties and a neutral third

party, after which the managers attempt to negotiate a settlement in consultation with the third party

Summary Jury Trial mock trial followed by negotiations

Negotiation consensual bargaining process in which the parties attempt to reach an agreement resolving their dispute without the involvement of third parties

---

QUESTIONS

1. List and describe the courts in the federal court system and in a typical state court system.
2. Distinguish between appeal by right and writ of *certiorari*.
3. Distinguish between subject matter jurisdiction and jurisdiction over the parties.
4. Distinguish between exclusive and concurrent federal jurisdiction. Identify the two types of federal concurrent jurisdiction.
5. Define and describe a typical long-arm statute.
6. List and distinguish among the three types of jurisdiction over the parties.

7. Describe the purpose of pleadings.
8. List and explain the various stages of a civil proceeding.
9. Compare and contrast the following: demurrer, judgment on the pleadings, summary judgment, directed verdict, and judgment notwithstanding the verdict.
10. Compare and contrast litigation, arbitration, conciliation, and mediation.

PROBLEMS

1. On June 15, a newspaper columnist predicted that the coast of state X would be flooded on the following September 1. Relying on this pronouncement, Gullible quit his job and sold his property at a loss so as not to be financially ruined. When the flooding did not occur, Gullible sued the columnist in a state X court for damages. The court dismissed the case for failure to state a cause of action under applicable state law. On appeal, the state X Supreme Court upheld the lower court. Three months after this ruling, the state Y Supreme Court heard an appeal in which a lower court had ruled that a reader could sue a columnist for falsely predicting flooding.

   (a) Must the state Y Supreme Court follow the ruling of the state X Supreme Court as a matter of *stare decisis*?

   (b) Should the State Y lower court have followed the ruling of the state X Supreme Court until the state Y Supreme Court issued a ruling on the issue?

   (c) Once the state X Supreme Court issued its ruling, could the U.S. Supreme Court overrule the state X Supreme Court?

   (d) If the state Y Supreme Court and the state X Supreme Court rule in exactly opposite ways, must the U.S. Supreme Court resolve the conflict between the two courts?

2. State Senator Bowdler convinced the legislature of state Z to pass a law requiring all professors to submit their class notes and transparencies to a board of censors to be sure that no "lewd" materials were presented to students at state universities. Professor Rabelais would like to challenge this law as being violative of his First Amendment rights under the U.S. Constitution.

   (a) May Professor Rabelais challenge this law in the state Z courts?

   (b) May Professor Rabelais challenge this law in a federal district court?

3. While driving his car in Virginia, Carpe Diem, a resident of North Carolina, struck Butt, a resident of Alaska. As a result of the accident, Butt suffered more than $60,000 in medical expenses. Butt would like to know, if he personally serves the proper papers to Diem, whether he can obtain jurisdiction against Diem for damages in the following courts:

   (a) Alaska state trial court

   (b) Federal Circuit Court of Appeals for the Ninth Circuit (includes Alaska)

   (c) Virginia state trial court

   (d) Virginia federal district court

   (e) Federal Circuit Court of Appeals for the Fourth Circuit (includes Virginia and North Carolina)

   (f) Virginia equity court

   (g) North Carolina State trial court

4. Sam Simpleton, a resident of Kansas, and Nellie Naive, a resident of Missouri, each bought $85,000 in stock at local offices in their home States from Evil Stockbrokers, Inc. ("Evil"), a business incorporated in Delaware with its principal place of business in Kansas. Both Simpleton and Naive believe that they were cheated by Evil Stockbrokers and would like to sue Evil for fraud. Assuming that no federal question is at issue, assess the accuracy of the following statements:

   (a) Simpleton can sue Evil in a Kansas State trial court.

   (b) Simpleton can sue Evil in a federal district court in Kansas.

   (c) Naive can sue Evil in a Missouri State trial court.

   (d) Naive can sue Evil in a Federal district court in Missouri.

5. The Supreme Court of state A ruled that, under the law of state A, pit bull owners must either keep their dogs fenced or pay damages to anyone bitten by the dogs. Assess the accuracy of the following statements:

   (a) It is likely that the U.S. Supreme Court would issue a writ of *certiorari* in the "pit bull" case.

   (b) If a case similar to the "pit bull" case were to come before the Supreme Court of State B in the future, the doctrine of *stare decisis* would leave the court no choice but to rule the same way as the "pit bull" case.

6. The Supreme Court of state G decided that the U.S. Constitution

requires professors to warn students of their right to remain silent before questioning the students about cheating. This ruling directly conflicts with a decision of the Federal Court of Appeals for the circuit which includes state G.

  (a) Must the Federal Circuit Court of Appeals withdraw its ruling?

  (b) Must the Supreme Court of state G withdraw its ruling?

7. Thomas Clements brought an action to recover damages for breach of warranty against defendant, Signa Corporation. (A warranty is an obligation that the seller of goods assumes with respect to the quality of the goods sold.) Clements had purchased a motorboat from Barney's Sporting Goods, an Illinois corporation. The boat was manufactured by Signa Corporation, an Indiana corporation with its principal place of business in Decatur, Indiana. Signa has no office in Illinois and no agent authorized to do business on its behalf within Illinois. Clements saw Signa's boats on display at the Chicago Boat Show. In addition, literature on Signa's boats was distributed at the Chicago Boat Show. Several boating magazines, delivered to Clements in Illinois, contained advertisements for Signa's boats. Clements also had seen Signa's boats on display at Barney's Sporting Goods Store in Palatine, Illinois, where he eventually purchased the boat. A written warranty issued by Signa was delivered to Clements in Illinois. Although Signa was served with a summons, it failed to enter an appearance in this case. The court entered a default order and, subsequently, a judgment of $6,220 against Signa. Signa appealed. Decision?

8. Mariana Deutsch worked as a knitwear mender and attended a school for beauticians. The sink in her apartment collapsed on her foot, fracturing her big toe and making it painful for her to stand. She claims that as a consequence of the injury she was compelled to abandon her plans to become a beautician because that job requires long periods of standing. She also asserts that she was unable to work at her current job for a month. She filed a tort claim against Hewes Street Realty for negligence in failing properly to maintain the sink. She brought the suit in federal district court, claiming damages of $25,000. Her medical expenses and actual loss of salary were less than $1,500; the rest of her alleged damages were for loss of future earnings as a beautician. Hewes Street moved to dismiss the suit on the basis that Deutsch's claim fell short of the jurisdictional requirement, which then was $10,000, and that the federal court therefore lacked subject matter jurisdiction over her claim. Decision?

9. Vette sued Aetna under a fire insurance policy. Aetna moved for summary judgment on the basis that the pleadings and discovered evidence showed a lack of an insurable interest in Vette. (An "insurable interest" exists where the insured derives a monetary benefit or advantage from the preservation or continued existence of the property or would sustain an economic loss from its destruction.) Aetna provided ample evidence to infer that Vette had no insurable interest in the contents of the burned building. Vette also provided sufficient evidence to put in dispute this factual issue. The trial court granted the motion for summary judgment. Vette appealed. Decision?

10. Mark Womer and Brian Perry were members of the United States Navy and were stationed in Newport, Rhode Island. On April 10, 1978, Womer allowed Perry to borrow his automobile so that Perry could visit his family in New Hampshire. Later that day, while operating Womer's vehicle, Perry was involved in an accident in Manchester, New Hampshire. As a result of the accident, Tzannetos Tavoularis was injured. Tavoularis brought this action against Womer in a New Hampshire superior court, contending that Womer was negligent in lending the automobile to Perry when he knew or should have known that Perry did not have a valid driver's license. Womer sought to dismiss the action on the ground that the New Hampshire courts lacked jurisdiction over him, citing the following facts: (1) he lived and worked in Georgia; (2) he had no relatives in New Hampshire; (3) he neither owned property nor possessed investments in New Hampshire; and (4) he had never conducted business in New Hampshire. Did the New Hampshire courts have jurisdiction?

11. Kenneth Thomas brought suit against his former employer, Kidder, Peabody & Company, and two of its employees, Barclay Perry and James Johnston, in a dispute over commissions on sales of securities. When he applied to work at Kidder, Peabody, Thomas had filled out a form, which contained an arbitration agreement clause. Thomas had also registered with the New York Stock Exchange (NYSE). Rule 347 of the NYSE provides that any controversy between a registered representative and a member company shall be settled by arbitration. Kidder, Peabody is a member of the NYSE. Thomas refused to arbitrate, relying on Section 229 of the California Labor Code, which provides that actions for the collection of wages may be maintained "without regard to the existence of any private agreement to arbitrate." Perry and Johnston filed a petition in a California State court to compel arbitration under Section 2 of the Federal Arbitration Act. Should the petition of Perry and Johnston be granted?

12. Steven Gwin bought a lifetime Termite Protection Plan for his home from the local office of Allied-Bruce, a franchise of Terminix International Company. The plan provided that Allied-Bruce would "protect" Gwin's house against termite infestation, reinspect periodically, provide additional treatment if necessary, and repair damage caused by new termite infestations. Terminix International guaranteed the fulfillment of these contractual provisions. The plan also provided that all disputes arising out of the contract would be settled exclusively by arbitration. Four years later Gwin had Allied-Bruce reinspect the house in anticipation of selling it. Allied-Bruce gave the house a "clean bill of health." Gwin then sold the house and transferred the Termite Protection Plan to Dobson. Shortly thereafter, Dobson found the house to be infested with termites. Allied-Bruce attempted to treat and repair the house, using materials from out of state, but these efforts failed to satisfy Dobson. Dobson then sued Gwin, Allied-Bruce, and Terminix International in an Alabama state court. Allied-Bruce and Terminix International asked for a stay of these proceedings until arbitration could be carried out as stipulated in the contract. The trial court refused to grant the stay. The Alabama Supreme Court upheld that ruling, citing a state statute that makes predispute arbitration agreements unenforceable. The court found that the Federal Arbitration Act, which preempts conflicting state law, did not apply to this contract because its connection to interstate commerce was too slight. Was the Alabama Supreme Court correct? Explain.

http: **Internet Exercise** Find information about the structure and operations of (a) the federal court system and (b) your own state's court system. (If such information about your state is not available, choose another state.)

Business Ethics and the
Social Responsibility of Business

CHAPTER

3

Business ethics is a subset of ethics: there is no special set of ethical principles that applies only to the world of business. Immoral acts are immoral, whether or not a businessperson has committed them. But before a behavior, in business or elsewhere, is judged immoral, special attention must be accorded the circumstances surrounding it. For example, suppose a company discovers a new cost-effective technology that enables it to outperform its competitors. Few would condemn the company for using the technology even if it put one or more competitors out of business. After all, the economic benefits derived from the new technology would seem to so outweigh the social costs of unemployment that it would be difficult to conclude that the business acted immorally.

On the other hand, unethical business practices date from the very beginning of business and continue today. As one court stated in connection with a securities fraud,

> Since the time to which the memory of man runneth not to the contrary, the human animal has been full of cunning and guile. Many of the schemes and artifices have been so sophisticated as almost to defy belief. But the ordinary run of those willing and able to take unfair advantage of others are mere apprentices in the art when compared with the manipulations thought up by those connected in one way or another with transactions in securities.

In the last decade, the almost daily reporting of business wrongs has included, among countless others, insider trading, the Beech-Nut adulterated apple juice scandal, the Bhopal disaster, the Dalkon Shield tragedy, and the savings and loan industry depredations.

Ethics can be broadly defined as the study of what is right or good for human beings. It pursues the questions of what people ought to do, what goals they should pursue. In *Business Ethics*, 5th ed., Richard T. DeGeorge provides the following explanation of ethics:

> In its most general sense *ethics is a systematic attempt to make sense of our individual and social moral experience, in such a way as to determine the rules that ought to govern human conduct, the values worth pursuing, and the character traits deserving development in life*. The attempt is systematic and therefore goes beyond what reflective persons tend to do in daily life in making sense of their moral experience, organizing it, and attempting to make it coherent and unified....Ethics concerns itself with human conduct, taken here to mean human activity that is done knowingly and, to a large extent, willingly. It does not concern itself with automatic responses, or with, for example, actions done in one's sleep or under hypnosis.

Business ethics, as a branch of applied ethics, is the study and determination of what is right and good in business settings. Business ethics seeks to understand the moral issues that arise from business practices, institutions, and decision making and their relationship to generalized human values. Unlike the law, analyses of ethics have no central authority, such as courts or legislatures, upon which to rely; nor do they have clear-cut, universal standards. Despite these inherent limitations, making meaningful ethical judgments is still possible. To improve ethical decision making, it is important to understand how others have approached the task.

Some examples of the many ethics questions confronting business may help to clarify the definition of business ethics. In the employment relationship, countless ethical issues arise regarding the safety and compensation of workers, their civil rights (such as equal treatment, privacy, and freedom from sexual harassment), and the legitimacy of whistle-blowing. In the relationship between business and its customers, ethical issues permeate marketing techniques, product safety, and consumer protection. The relationship between business and its owners bristles with ethical questions involving corporate governance, shareholder voting, and management's duties to the shareholders. The relationship among competing businesses involves numerous ethical matters, including efforts to promote fair competition over the temptation of collusive conduct. The interaction between business and society at large has additional ethical dimensions: pollution of the physical environment, commitment to the community's economic and social infrastructure, and the depletion of natural resources. At the international level, these issues not only recur but couple themselves to additional ones, such as bribery of foreign officials, exploitation of less-developed countries, and conflicts among differing cultures and value systems.

In resolving the ethical issues raised by business conduct, it is helpful to use a seeing-knowing-doing model. First, the decision maker should *see* (identify) the ethical issues involved in the proposed conduct, including the ethical implications of the various available options. Second, the decision maker should *know* (resolve) what to do by choosing the best option. Finally, the decision maker should *do* (implement) the chosen option by developing implementing strategies.

This chapter first surveys the most prominent ethical theories, then examines ethical standards in business, and concludes by exploring the ethical responsibilities of business.

http: **Ethics Resource Center:** http://www.ethics.org
Council for Ethics in Economics: http://www.businessethics.org/
Business for Social Responsibility: http://www.bsr.org
International Business Ethics Institute: http://www.business-ethics.org/
Center for Applied Ethics: http://www.ethics.ubc.ca/resources/business/

LAW VERSUS ETHICS

As discussed in Chapter 1, the law is strongly affected by moral concepts, but law and morality are not the same. Although it is tempting to say that "if it's legal, it's moral," such a proposition is inaccurate and generally too simplistic. For example, it would seem gravely immoral to stand by silently while a blind man walks off a cliff if one could prevent the fall by shouting a warning, even though one is under no legal obligation to do

so. Similarly, moral questions arise concerning "legal" business practices, such as failing to fulfill a promise that is not legally binding; exporting products banned in the United States to third world countries, where they are not prohibited; manufacturing and selling tobacco or alcohol products; or slaughtering baby seals for fur coats. The mere fact that these practices may be legal does not prevent them from being challenged on moral grounds.

Just as it is possible for legal acts to be immoral, it is equally possible for illegal acts to seem morally preferable to following the law. It is, for example, the moral conviction of the great majority of people that those who sheltered Jews in violation of Nazi edicts during World War II and those who committed acts of civil disobedience in the 1950s and 1960s to challenge racist segregation laws in the United States were acting properly and that the laws themselves were immoral.

ETHICAL THEORIES

Philosophers have sought for centuries to develop dependable universal methods for making ethical judgments. In earlier times, some thinkers analogized the discovery of ethical principles with the derivation of mathematical proofs. They asserted that people could discover fundamental ethical rules by applying careful reasoning *a priori*. (*A priori* reasoning is based on theory rather than experimentation and deductively draws conclusions from cause to effect and from generalizations to particular instances.) In more recent times, many philosophers have concluded that although careful reasoning and deep thought assist substantially in moral reasoning, experience reveals that the complexities of the world defeat most attempts to fashion precise, *a priori* guidelines. Nevertheless, reviewing the most significant ethical theories can help to analyze issues of business ethics.

Ethical Fundamentalism

Under **ethical fundamentalism**, or absolutism, individuals look to a central authority or set of rules to guide them in ethical decision making. Some look to the Bible; others look to the Koran or the writings of Karl Marx or to any number of living or deceased prophets. The essential characteristic of this approach is a reliance upon a central repository of wisdom. In some cases, such reliance is total. In others, it occurs to a lesser degree: followers of a religion or a spiritual leader may believe that all members of the group have an obligation to assess moral dilemmas independently, according to each person's understanding of the dictates of certain fundamental principles.

Ethical Relativism

Ethical relativism is a doctrine asserting that individuals must judge actions by what they feel is right or wrong for themselves. It holds that both parties to a disagreement regarding a moral question are correct, because morality is relative. While ethical relativism promotes open-mindedness and tolerance, it has limitations. If each person's actions are always correct for that person, then his behavior is, by definition, moral, and no one can truly criticize it. If a child abuser truly felt it right to molest children, a relativist would accept the proposition that the child abuser was acting properly. As almost no one would accept the proposition that child abuse could ever be ethical, few can truly claim to be relativists. Once a person concludes that criticizing or punishing behavior is, in some cases, appropriate, he abandons ethical relativism and faces the task of developing a broader ethical methodology.

Although bearing a surface resemblance to ethical relativism, situational ethics actually differs substantially. **Situational ethics** holds that developing precise guidelines for navigating ethical dilemmas is difficult because real-life decision making is so complex. To judge the morality of someone's behavior, the person judging must actually put herself in the other person's shoes to understand what motivated the other to choose a particular course of action. In this respect, situational ethics shares with ethical relativism the notion that we must judge actions from the perspective of the person who actually made the judgment. From that point on, however, the two approaches differ dramatically. Ethical relativism passes no judgment on what a person did other than to determine that he truly believed the decision was right for him. Much more judgmental, situational ethics insists that once a decision has been viewed from the actor's perspective, a judgment can be made as to whether or not her action was ethical. Situational ethics does not cede the ultimate judgment of propriety to the actor; rather, it insists that another evaluate the actor's decision or act from the perspective of a person in the actor's shoes.

Utilitarianism

Utilitarianism is a doctrine that assesses good and evil in terms of the consequences of actions. Those actions that produce the greatest net pleasure compared with the net pain are better in a moral sense than those that produce less net pleasure. As Jeremy Bentham, one of the most influential proponents of utilitarianism, proclaimed, a good or moral act is one that results in "the greatest happiness for the greatest number."

The two major forms of utilitarianism are act utilitarianism and rule utilitarianism. **Act utilitarianism** assesses each separate act according to whether it maximizes pleasure over pain. For example, if telling a lie in a particular situation produces more overall pleasure than pain, then an act utilitarian would support lying as the moral thing to do. Rule utilitarians, disturbed by the unpredictability of act utilitarianism and by its potential for abuse, follow a different approach by holding that general rules must be established and followed even though, in some instances, following rules may produce less overall pleasure than not following them. In applying utilitarian principles to developing rules, **rule utilitarianism** thus supports rules that on balance produce the greatest satisfaction. Determining whether telling a lie in a given instance would produce greater pleasure than telling the truth is less important to the rule utilitarian than deciding if a general practice of lying would maximize society's pleasure. If lying would not maximize pleasure generally, then one should follow a rule of not lying, even though telling a lie occasionally would produce greater pleasure than would telling the truth.

Utilitarian notions underlie cost-benefit analysis, an analytical tool used by many business and government managers today. **Cost-benefit analysis** first quantifies in monetary terms and then compares the direct and indirect costs and benefits of program alternatives for meeting a specified objective. Cost-benefit analysis seeks the greatest economic efficiency, given the underlying notion that acts achieving the greatest output at the least cost promote the greatest marginal happiness over less efficient acts, other things being equal.

The primary purpose of cost-benefit analysis is to choose from alternative courses of action the program that maximizes society's wealth. For example, based on cost-benefit analysis, an auto designer might choose to devote more effort to perfecting a highly expensive air bag that would save hundreds of lives and prevent thousands of disabling injuries than to developing an improved car hood latching mechanism that would produce a less favorable cost-benefit ratio.

The chief criticism of utilitarianism is that in some important instances it ignores justice. A number of situations would maximize the pleasure of the majority at great social cost to a minority. Under a strict utilitarian approach, it would, for example, be ethical to compel a few citizens to undergo painful, even fatal medical tests to develop cures for the rest of the world. For most people, however, such action would be unacceptable. Another major criticism of utilitarianism is that measuring pleasure and pain in the fashion its supporters advocate is extremely difficult, if not impossible.

Deontology

Deontological theories (from the Greek word *deon*, meaning "duty" or "obligation") address the practical problems of utilitarianism by holding that certain underlying principles are right or wrong regardless of calculations regarding pleasure or pain. Deontologists believe that actions cannot be measured simply by their results but must be judged by means and motives as well.

Our criminal laws apply deontological reasoning. Knowing that John shot and killed Marvin is not enough to tell us how to judge John's act. We must know whether John shot Marvin in anger, self-defense, or by mistake. Although under any of these motives Marvin is just as dead, we judge John quite differently depending on the mental process that we believe led him to commit the act. Similarly, deontologists judge the morality of acts not so much by their consequences but by the motives that lead to them. To act morally, a person not only must achieve just results but also must employ the proper means.

The best-known deontological theory was proffered by the eighteenth-century philosopher Immanuel Kant. Kant asserted what he called the **categorical imperative**, which has been summarized as follows:

1. Act only according to that maxim by which you can, at the same time, will that it should become a universal law.
2. Act as never to treat another human being merely as a means to an end.

Thus, for an action to be moral, it (1) must possess the potential to be made a consistently applied universal law and (2) must respect the autonomy and rationality of all human beings and avoid treating them as an expedient. That is, one should avoid doing anything that he or she would not have everyone do in a similar situation. For example, you should not lie to colleagues unless you support the right of all colleagues to lie to one another. Similarly, you should not cheat others unless you advocate everyone's right to cheat. We apply Kantian reasoning when we challenge someone's behavior by asking, What if everybody acted that way?

Under Kant's approach, it would be improper to assert a principle to which one claimed personal exception, such as insisting that it was acceptable for you to cheat but not for anyone else to do so. Because everyone would then insist on similar rules by which to except themselves, this principle could not be universalized.

Kant's philosophy also rejects notions of the end justifying the means. To Kant, every person is an end in himself or herself and deserves respect simply because of his or her humanity. Thus, any sacrifice of a person for the greater good of society would be unacceptable to Kant.

In many respects, Kant's categorical imperative is a variation of the Golden Rule. Like the Golden Rule, the categorical imperative reflects the idea that people are, to a certain extent, self-centered. As one writer on business ethics notes, this is what makes the Golden Rule so effective:

> It is precisely this self-centeredness of the Golden Rule that makes it so valuable, and so widely acknowledged, as a guide. To inquire of yourself, "How would I feel in the other fellow's place?" is an elegantly simple and reliable method of focusing in on the "right" thing to do. The Golden Rule works not in spite of selfishness, but because of it. Tuleja, *Beyond the Bottom Line.*

As does every theory, Kantian ethics has its critics. Just as deontologists criticize utilitarians for excessive pragmatism and flexible moral guidelines, utilitarians and others criticize deontologists for rigidity and excessive formalism. For example, if one inflexibly adopts as a rule to tell the truth, one ignores situations in which lying might well be justified. A person hiding a terrified wife from her angry, abusive husband would seem to be acting morally by falsely denying that the wife is at the person's house. Yet, a deontologist, feeling bound to tell the truth, might ignore the consequences of truthfulness, tell the husband where his wife is, and create the possibility of a terrible tragedy. Less dramatically, one wonders whether the world would effect a higher ethical code by regarding as immoral "white lies" concerning friends' appearance, clothing, or choice of spouse.

Social Ethics Theories

Social ethics theories assert that special obligations arise from the social nature of human beings. Such theories focus not only on each person's obligations to other members of society, but also on the individual's rights and obligations within society. For example, **social egalitarians** believe that society should provide all persons with equal amounts of goods and services regardless of the contribution each makes to increase society's wealth.

Two other ethics theories have received widespread attention in recent years. One is the theory of **distributive justice** proposed by Harvard philosopher John Rawls, which seeks to analyze the type of society that people in a "natural state" would establish if they could not determine in advance whether they would be talented, rich, healthy, or ambitious, relative to other members of society. According to Rawls, the society contemplated through this "veil of ignorance" should be given precedence in terms of development because it considers the needs and rights of all its members. Rawls did not argue, however, that such a society would be strictly egalitarian. That would unfairly penalize those who turned out to be the most talented and ambitious. Instead, Rawls suggested that such a society would stress equality of opportunity, not of results. On the other hand, Rawls stressed that society would pay heed to the least advantaged to ensure that they did not suffer unduly and that they enjoyed society's benefits. To Rawls, society must be premised on justice. Everyone is entitled to her fair share in society, a fairness all must work to guarantee.

In contrast to Rawls, another Harvard philosopher, Robert Nozick, stressed liberty, not justice, as the most important obligation that society owes its members. **Libertarians** stress market outcomes as the basis for distributing society's rewards. Only to the extent that one meets the demands of the market does one deserve society's benefits. Libertarians oppose interference by society in their lives as long as they do not violate the rules of the marketplace; that is, as long as they do not cheat others and as long as they honestly disclose the nature of their transactions with others. The fact that some end up with fortunes while others accumulate little simply proves that some can play in the market effectively while others cannot. To libertarians, this is not unjust. What is unjust to them is any attempt by society to take wealth earned by citizens and then distribute it to those who did not earn it.

These theories and others (e.g., Marxism) judge society in

moral terms by its organization and by its method of distributing goods and services. They demonstrate the difficulty of ethical decision making in the context of a social organization: behavior that is consistently ethical from individual to individual may not necessarily produce a just society.

Other Theories

The preceding theories do not exhaust the possible approaches to evaluating ethical behavior, but represent the most commonly cited theories advanced over the years. Several other theories also deserve mention. **Intuitionism** holds that a rational person possesses inherent powers to assess the correctness of actions. Though an individual may refine and strengthen these powers, they are just as basic to humanity as our instincts for survival and self-defense. Just as some people are better artists or musicians, some people have more insight into ethical behavior than others. Consistent with intuitionism is the **good persons** philosophy, which declares that individuals who wish to act morally should seek out and emulate those who always seem to know the right choice in any given situation and who always seem to do the right thing. One variation of these ethical approaches is the "**Television Test**," which directs us to imagine that every ethical decision we make is being broadcast on nationwide television. Adherents of this approach believe an appropriate decision is one we would be comfortable broadcasting on television for all to witness.

ETHICAL STANDARDS IN BUSINESS

This section will explore the application of the theories of ethical behavior to the world of business.

Choosing an Ethical System

In their efforts to resolve the moral dilemmas facing humanity, philosophers and other thinkers have struggled for years to refine the various systems discussed previously. No one ethical system is completely precise, however, and each tends occasionally to produce unacceptable prescriptions for action. But to say that a system has limits is not to say it is useless. On the contrary, many such systems provide insight into ethical decision making and help us formulate issues and resolve moral dilemmas. Furthermore, concluding that moral standards are difficult to articulate and that the boundaries are imprecise is not the same as concluding that moral standards are unnecessary or nonexistent.

Research by noted psychologist Lawrence Kohlberg provides insight into ethical decision making and lends credibility to the notion that moral growth, like physical growth, is part of the human condition. Kohlberg observed that people progress through stages of moral development according to two major variables: age and education. During the first level–the **preconventional level**–a child's conduct is a reaction to the fear of punishment and, later, to the pleasure of reward. Although people who operate at this level may behave in a moral manner, they do so without understanding why their behavior is moral. The rules are imposed upon them. During adolescence–Kohlberg's **conventional level**–people conform their behavior to meet the expectations of groups, such as family, peers, and eventually society. The motivation for conformity is loyalty, affection, and trust. Most adults operate at this level. According to Kohlberg, some people reach the third level–the **postconventional level**– where they accept and conform to moral principles because they understand *why* the principles are right and binding. At this level, moral principles are voluntarily internalized, not externally imposed. Moreover, individuals at this stage develop their own universal ethical principles, and even question the laws and values that society and others have adopted.

Kohlberg believed that these stages are sequential and that not all people reach the third, or even the second, stage. He therefore argued that exploring ways of enabling people to develop to the advanced stage of postconventional thought was essential to the study of ethics. Other psychologists assert that individuals do not pass from stage to stage but rather function in all three stages simultaneously.

Whatever the source of our ethical approach, we cannot avoid facing moral dilemmas that challenge us to recognize and to do the right thing. Moreover, for those who plan business careers, such dilemmas will necessarily have implications for many others: employees, shareholders, suppliers, customers, and society at large.

◆ **SEE FIGURE 3-1** Kohlberg's Stages of Moral Development

Corporations as Moral Agents

Because corporations are not persons but artificial entities created by the State, it is not obvious whether they can or should be held morally accountable. As Lord Chancellor Thurlow lamented two hundred years ago, "A company has no body to kick and no soul to damn, and by God, it ought to have both." Clearly, individuals within corporations can be held morally responsible, but the corporate entity presents unique problems.

Commentators are divided on the issue. Some, like philosopher Manuel Velasquez, insist that only people can engage in behavior that can be judged in moral terms. Opponents of this view, like philosophers Kenneth Goodpaster and John Matthews, Jr., concede that corporations are not persons in any literal sense but insist that the attributes of responsibility inherent in corporations are sufficient in number to permit judging corporate behavior from a moral perspective.

◆ FIGURE 3-1 **Kohlberg's Stages of Moral Development**

Levels	Perspective	Justification
Preconventional (Childhood)	Self	Punishment/Reward
Conventional (Adolescent)	Group	Group Norms
Postconventional (Adult)	Universal	Moral Principles

ETHICAL RESPONSIBILITIES OF BUSINESS

Many people assert that the only responsibility of business is to maximize profit and that this obligation overrides any other ethical or social responsibility. Although our economic system of modified capitalism is based on the pursuit of self-interest, it contains components to check this motivation of greed. Our system has always recognized the need for some form of regulation, whether it be the "invisible hand" of competition, the self-regulation of business, or government regulation.

Regulation of Business

As explained and justified by Adam Smith in *The Wealth of Nations* (1776), the capitalistic system is composed of six "institutions": economic motivation, private productive property, free enterprise, free markets, competition, and limited government. Economic motivation assumes that a person who receives an economic return for his effort will work harder; therefore, the economic system should provide greater economic rewards for those who work harder. Private productive property, the means by which economic motivation is exercised, permits individuals to innovate and produce while securing to them the fruits of their efforts. Jack Behrman, a professor of business ethics, has described how the four other institutions combine with these two to bring about industrialized capitalism:

Free enterprise permits the combination of properties so people can do things together that they can't do alone. Free enterprise means a capitalistic combination of factors of production under decisions of free individuals. Free enterprise is the group expression of the use of private property, and it permits greater efficiency in an industrial setting through variation in the levels and kinds of production.

...The free market operates to equate supply and demand—supply reflecting the ability and willingness to offer certain goods or services, and demand reflecting the consumer's ability and willingness to pay. Price is adjusted to include the maximum number of *both* bids and offers. The market, therefore, is *the* decision-making mechanism outside of the firm. It is the *means* by which basic decisions are made about the use of resources, and all factors are supposed to respond to it, however they wish.

...Just in case it doesn't work out that way, there is one more institution—the *Government*—which is supposed to set rules and provide protection for the society and its members. That's all, said Smith, that it should do: it should set the rules, enforce them, and stand aside. J. Behrman, *Discourses on Ethics and Business*, 25–29.

As long as all these constituent institutions continue to exist and operate in a balanced manner, the factors of production—land, capital, and labor—combine to produce an efficient allocation of resources for individual consumers and for the economy as a whole. To achieve this outcome, however, Smith's model requires the satisfaction of several conditions: "standardized products, numerous firms in markets, each firm with a small share and unable by its actions alone to exert significant influence over price, no barriers to entry, and output carried to the point where each seller's marginal cost equals the going market price." E. Singer, *Antitrust Economics and Legal Analysis,* 2.

History has demonstrated that the actual operation of the economy has satisfied almost none of these assumptions. More specifically, the actual competitive process falls considerably short of the classic economic model of perfect competition:

Competitive industries are never perfectly competitive in this sense. Many of the resources they employ cannot be shifted to other employments without substantial cost and delay. The allocation of those resources, as between industries or as to relative proportions within a single industry, is unlikely to have been made in a way that affords the best possible expenditure of economic effort. Information is incomplete, motivation confused, and decision therefore ill informed and often unwise. Variations in efficiency are not directly reflected in variations of profit. Success is derived in large part from competitive selling efforts, which in the aggregate may be wasteful, and from differentiation of products, which may be undertaken partly by methods designed to impair the opportunity of the buyer to compare quality and price. C. Edwards, *Maintaining Competition.*

In addition to capitalism's failure to allocate resources efficiently, it cannot be relied on to achieve all of the social and public policy objectives a pluralistic democracy requires. For example, the free enterprise model simply does not comprehend or address equitable distribution of wealth, national defense, conservation of natural resources, full employment, stability in economic cycles, protection against economic dislocations, health and safety, social security, and other important social and economic goals. Because the "invisible hand" and self-regulation by business have failed not only to preserve the competitive process in our economic system but also to achieve social goals extrinsic to the efficient allocation of resources, governmental intervention in business has become increasingly common. Such intervention attempts to (1) regulate both "legal" monopolies, such as those conferred by law through copyrights, patents, and trade symbols, and "natural" monopolies, such as utilities, transportation, and communications; (2) preserve competition by correcting imperfections in the market system; (3) protect specific groups, especially labor and agriculture, from failures of the marketplace; and (4) promote other social goals. Successful government regulation involves a delicate balance between regulations that attempt to preserve competition and those that attempt to advance other social objectives. The latter should not undermine the basic competitive processes that provide an efficient allocation of economic resources.

Corporate Governance

In addition to the broad demands of maintaining a competitive and fair marketplace, another factor demanding the ethical and social responsibility of business is the sheer size and power of individual corporations. The five thousand largest U.S. firms currently produce more than half of the nation's gross national product. Statutorily, their economic power should be delegated by the shareholders to the board of directors, who in turn appoint the officers of the corporation.

> In reality, this legal image is virtually a myth. In nearly every large American business corporation, there exists a management autocracy. One man–variously titled the President, or the Chairman of the Board, or the Chief Executive Officer–or a small coterie of men rule the corporation. Far from being chosen by the directors to run the corporation, this chief executive or executive clique chooses the board of directors and, with the acquiescence of the board, controls the corporation. R. Nader, M. Green, and J. Seligman, *Taming the Giant Corporation.*

In a classic study published in 1932, Adolf Berle and Gardner Means concluded that significant amounts of economic power had been concentrated in a relatively few large corporations, that the ownership of these corporations had become widely dispersed, and that the shareholders had become far removed from active participation in management. Since their original study, these trends have steadily continued. The large publicly held corporations–numbering 500 to 1,000–own the great bulk of the industrial wealth of the United States. Moreover, these corporations are controlled by a small group of corporate officers.

Historically, the boards of many publicly held corporations consisted mainly or entirely of inside directors (corporate officers who also serve on the board of directors). During the past

two decades, however, as a result of regulations by the U.S. Securities and Exchange Commission and the stock exchanges, the number and influence of outside directors have increased substantially. Now the boards of the great majority of publicly held corporations consist primarily of outside directors, and these corporations have audit committees consisting entirely of outside directors. Nevertheless, a number of instances of corporate misconduct have been revealed in the first years of this century. In response to these business scandals–involving companies such as Enron, WorldCom, Global Crossing, and Arthur Andersen–in 2002 Congress passed the Sarbanes-Oxley Act. This legislation seeks to prevent these types of scandals by increasing corporate responsibility through imposing additional corporate governance requirements on publicly held corporations.

These developments raise social, policy, and ethical issues about the governance of large, publicly owned corporations. Many observers insist that companies playing such an important role in economic life should have a responsibility to undertake projects that benefit society in ways that go beyond mere financial efficiency in producing goods and services. In some instances, the idea of corporate obligation comes from industrialists themselves. Andrew Carnegie, for example, advocated philanthropy throughout his life and contributed much of his fortune to educational and social causes.

---

http: **Corporate Governance OECD:** http://www.oecd.org/ daf/ corporate-affairs
Corporate Governance Network: http://www. corpgov.net

Arguments against Social Responsibility

Among the arguments opposing business involvement in socially responsible activities are profitability, unfairness, accountability, and expertise.

Profitability As economist Milton Friedman and others have argued, businesses are artificial entities established to permit people to engage in profit-making, not social, activities. Without profits, they assert, there is little reason for a corporation to exist and no real way to measure the effectiveness of corporate activities. Businesses are not organized to engage in social activities; they are structured to produce goods and services for which they receive money. Their social obligation is to return as much of this money to their direct stakeholders as possible. In a free market with significant competition, the selfish pursuits of corporations will lead to maximizing output, minimizing costs, and establishing fair prices. All other concerns distract companies and interfere with achieving these goals.

Unfairness Whenever companies stray from their designated role of profit-maker, they take unfair advantage of company employees and shareholders. For example, a company may support the arts or education or spend excess funds on health and safety; however, these funds rightfully belong to the shareholders or employees. The company's decision to disburse these funds to others who may well be less deserving than the shareholders and employees is unfair. Furthermore, consumers can express their desires through the marketplace, and shareholders and employees can decide independently if they wish to make charitable contributions. In most cases, senior management consults the board of directors about supporting social concerns but does not seek the approval of the company's major stakeholders. Thus, these shareholders are effectively disenfranchised from actions that reduce their benefits from the corporation.

Accountability Corporations, as previously noted, are private institutions that are subject to a lower standard of accountability than are public bodies. Accordingly, a company may decide to support a wide range of social causes and yet submit to little public scrutiny. But a substantial potential for abuse exists in such cases. For one thing, a company could provide funding for causes its employees or shareholders do not support. It could also provide money "with strings attached," thereby controlling the recipients' agendas for less than socially beneficial purposes. For example, a drug company that contributes to a consumer group might implicitly or explicitly condition its assistance on the group's agreement never to criticize the company or the drug industry.

This lack of accountability warrants particular concern because of the enormous power corporations wield in modern society. Many large companies, like General Motors or IBM, generate and spend more money in a year than all but a handful of the world's countries. If these companies suddenly began to vigorously pursue their own social agendas, their influence might well rival, and perhaps undermine, that of their own governments. In a country like the United States, founded on the principles of limited government and the balance of powers, too much corporate involvement in social affairs might well present substantial problems. Without clear guidelines and accountability, the corporate pursuit of socially responsible behavior might well distort the entire process of governance.

There is a clear alternative to corporations engaging in socially responsible action. If society wishes to increase the resources devoted to needy causes, it has the power to do so. Let corporations seek profits without the burden of a social agenda, let the consumers vote in the marketplace for the products and services they desire, and let the government tax a portion of corporate profits for socially beneficial causes.

Expertise Even though a corporation has an expertise in producing and selling its product, it may not possess a talent for recognizing or managing socially useful activities. Corporations become successful in the market because they can identify and meet customers' needs. Nothing suggests that this talent

spills over into nonbusiness arenas. In fact, critics of corporate engagement in social activities worry that corporations will prove unable to distinguish the true needs of society from their own narrow self-interest.

Arguments in Favor of Social Responsibility

First, it should be recognized that even business critics acknowledge that the prime responsibility of business is to make a reasonable return on its investment by producing a quality product at a reasonable price. They do not suggest that business entities be charitable institutions. They do assert, however, that business has certain obligations beyond making a profit or not harming society. Critics contend that business must help to resolve societal problems, and they offer a number of arguments in support of their position.

The Social Contract Society creates corporations and accords them a special social status, including the grant of limited liability, which insulates the owners from liability for debts the organization incurs. Supporters of social roles for corporations assert that limited liability and other rights granted to companies carry a responsibility: corporations, just like other members of society, must contribute to its betterment. Therefore, companies owe a moral debt to society to contribute to its overall well-being. Society needs a host of improvements, such as pollution control, safe products, a free marketplace, quality education, cures for illness, and freedom from crime. Corporations can help in each of these areas. Granted, deciding which social needs deserve corporate attention is difficult; however, this challenge does not lessen a company's obligation to choose a cause. Corporate America cannot ignore the multitude of pressing needs that still remain, despite the efforts of government and private charities.

A derivative of the social contract theory is the stakeholder model for the societal role of the business corporation. Under the **stakeholder model**, a corporation has fiduciary responsibilities to all of its stakeholders, not just its stockholders. Historically, the stockholder model for the role of business has been the norm. Under this theory, a corporation is viewed as private property owned by and for the benefit of its owners–the stockholders of the corporation. The stakeholder model, on the other hand, holds that a corporation is responsible to society at large and more directly, to all those constituencies on which it depends for its survival. Thus, it is argued that a corporation should be managed for the benefit of all of its stakeholders–stockholders, employees, customers, suppliers, and managers, as well as the local communities in which it operates.

◆ SEE FIGURE 3-2 The Stakeholder Model

Less Government Regulation According to another argument in favor of corporate social responsibility, the more

◆ Figure 3-2 **The Stakeholder Model**

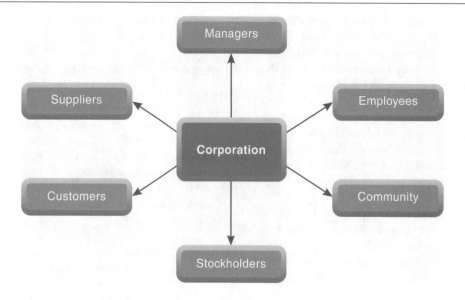

responsibly companies act, the less regulation the government must provide. This idea, if accurate, would likely appeal to those corporations that typically view regulation with distaste, perceiving it as a crude and expensive way of achieving social goals. To them, regulation often imposes inappropriate, overly broad rules that hamper productivity and require extensive record-keeping procedures to document compliance. If companies can use more flexible, voluntary methods of meeting a social norm such as pollution control, then government will be less tempted to legislate norms.

The argument can be taken further. Not only does anticipatory corporate action lessen the likelihood of government regulation, but social involvement by companies creates a climate of trust and respect that reduces the overall inclination of government to interfere in company business. For example, a government agency is much more likely to show some leniency toward a socially responsible company than toward one that ignores social plights.

Long-Run Profits Perhaps the most persuasive argument in favor of corporate involvement in social causes is that such involvement actually makes good business sense. Consumers often support good corporate images and avoid bad ones. For example, consumers generally prefer to patronize stores with "easy return" policies. Even though such policies are not required by law, companies institute them because they create goodwill—an intangible though indispensable asset for ensuring repeat customers. In the long run, enhanced goodwill often leads to stronger profits. Moreover, corporate actions to improve the well-being of their communities make these communities more attractive to citizens and more profitable for business.

CHAPTER SUMMARY

Definitions

Ethics study of what is right or good for human beings
Business Ethics study of what is right and good in a business setting

---

Ethical Theories

Ethical Fundamentalism individuals look to a central authority or set of rules to guide them in ethical decision making
Ethical Relativism actions must be judged by what individuals subjectively feel is right or wrong for themselves
Situational Ethics one must judge a person's actions by first putting oneself in the actor's situation
Utilitarianism moral actions are those that produce the greatest net pleasure compared with net pain

- *Act Utilitarianism* assesses each separate act according to whether it maximizes pleasure over pain
- *Rule Utilitarianism* supports rules that on balance produce the greatest pleasure for society
- *Cost-Benefit Analysis* quantifies the benefits and costs of alternatives

Deontology actions must be judged by their motives and means as well as their results

Social Ethics Theories focus is on a person's obligations to other members in society and also on the individual's rights and obligations within society

- *Social Egalitarians* believe that society should provide all its members with equal amounts of goods and services regardless of their relative contributions
- *Distributive Justice* stresses equality of opportunity rather than results
- *Libertarians* stress market outcomes as the basis for distributing society's rewards

Other Theories

- *Intuitionism* a rational person possesses inherent power to assess the correctness of actions
- *Good Person* individuals should seek out and emulate good role models

---

Ethical Standards in Business

Choosing an Ethical System Kohlberg's stages of moral development is a widely accepted model (see Figure 3-1)

Corporations as Moral Agents because a corporation is a statutorily created entity, it is not clear whether it should be held morally responsible

---

Ethical Responsibilities of Business

Regulation of Business governmental regulation has been necessary because all the conditions for perfect competition have not been satisfied and free competition cannot by itself achieve other societal objectives

Corporate Governance vast amounts of wealth and power have become concentrated in a small number of corporations, which are in turn controlled by a small group of corporate officers

Arguments against Social Responsibility

- *Profitability* because corporations are artificial entities established for profit-making activities, their only social obligation should be to return as much money as possible to shareholders
- *Unfairness* whenever corporations engage in social activities such as supporting the arts or education, they divert funds rightfully belonging to shareholders and/or employees to unrelated third parties
- *Accountability* a corporation is subject to less public accountability than public bodies are
- *Expertise* although a corporation may have a high level of expertise in selling its goods and services, there is absolutely no guarantee that any promotion of social activities will be carried on with the same degree of competence

Arguments in Favor of Social Responsibility

- *The Social Contract* because society allows for the creation of corporations and gives them special rights, including a grant of limited liability, corporations owe a responsibility to our society
- *Less Government Regulation* by taking a more proactive role in addressing society's problems, corporations create a climate of trust and respect that has the effect of reducing government regulation
- *Long-Run Profits* corporate involvement in social causes creates goodwill, which simply makes good business sense

CASES

Throughout this book the authors have included cases dealing with ethical or social issues. Every chapter has at least one case relating to ethical or social issues; in a number of chapters, all of the cases discuss these issues.

QUESTIONS

1. Describe the differences between law and ethics.
2. List and contrast the various ethical theories.
3. Describe cost-benefit analysis and explain when it should be used and when it should be avoided.
4. Explain Kohlberg's stages of moral development.
5. Explain the ethical responsibilities of business.

PROBLEMS

1. You have an employee who has a chemical imbalance in the brain that causes him to be severely emotionally unstable. The medication that is available to treat this schizophrenic condition is extremely powerful and decreases the taker's life span by one to two years for every year that the user takes it. You know that his doctors and family believe that it is in his best interest to take the medication. What course of action should you follow?

2. You have an employee from another country who is very shy. After a time, you notice that the quality of her performance is deteriorating rapidly. You find an appropriate time to speak with her and determine that she is extremely distraught. She informs you that her family has arranged a marriage for her and that she refuses to obey their contract. She further informs you that she is contemplating suicide. Two weeks later, with her poor performance continuing, you determine that she is on the verge of a nervous breakdown; once again she informs you that she is going to commit suicide. What should you do? Consider further that you can petition a court to have her involuntarily committed to a mental hospital. You know, however, that her family would consider such a commitment an extreme insult and that they might seek retribution. Does this prospect alter your decision?

3. You receive a telephone call from a company you never do business with requesting a reference on one of your employees, Mary Sunshine. You believe that Mary is generally incompetent and would be delighted to see her take another job. You give her a glowing reference. Is this right? Explain.

4. You have just received a report suggesting that a chemical your company uses in its manufacturing process is very dangerous. You have not read the report, but you are generally aware of its contents. You believe that the chemical can be replaced fairly easily, but that if word gets out, panic may set in among employees and community members. A reporter asks if you have seen the report, and you say no. Is your behavior right or wrong? Explain.

5. Joe Jones, your neighbor and friend, and you bought lottery tickets at the corner drugstore. While watching the lottery drawing on TV with you that night, Joe leaps from the couch, waves his lottery ticket, and shouts, "I've got the winning number!" Suddenly, he clutches his chest, keels over, and dies on the spot. You are the only living person who knows that Joe, not you, bought the winning ticket. If you sub-

stitute his ticket for yours, no one will know of the switch, and you will be $10 million richer. Joe's only living relative is a rich aunt whom he despised. Will you switch his ticket for yours? Explain.

6. Omega, Inc., a publicly held corporation, has assets of $100 million and annual earnings in the range of $13 to $15 million. Omega owns three aluminum plants, which are profitable, and one plastics plant, which is losing $4 million a year. The plastics plant shows no sign of ever becoming profitable because of its very high operating costs, and there is no evidence that the plant and the underlying real estate will increase in value. Omega decides to sell the plastics plant. The only bidder for the plant is Gold, who intends to use the plant for a new purpose, to introduce automation, and to replace all current employees. Would it be ethical for Omega to turn down Gold's bid and keep the plastics plant operating indefinitely, for the purpose of preserving the employees' jobs? Explain.

7. You are the sales manager of a two-year-old electronics firm. At times, the firm has seemed to be on the brink of failure but recently has begun to be profitable. In large part, the profitability is due to the aggressive and talented sales force you have recruited. Two months ago, you hired Alice North, an honors graduate from State University who decided that she was tired of the research department and wanted to try sales.

Almost immediately after you send Alice out for training with Brad West, your best salesperson, he begins reporting to you an unexpected turn of events. According to Brad, "Alice is terrific: she's confident, smooth, and persistent. Unfortunately, a lot of our buyers are good old boys who just aren't comfortable around young, bright women. Just last week, Hiram Jones, one of our biggest customers, told me that he simply won't continue to do business with "young chicks" who think they invented the world. It's not that Alice is a know-it-all. She's not. It's just that these guys like to booze it up a bit, tell some off-color jokes, and then get down to business. Alice doesn't drink, and although she never objects to the jokes, it's clear she thinks they're offensive." Brad believes that several potential deals have fallen through "because the mood just wasn't right with Alice there." Brad adds, "I don't like a lot of these guys' styles myself, but I go along to make the sales. I just don't think Alice is going to make it."

When you call Alice in to discuss the situation, she concedes the accuracy of Brad's report but indicates that she's not to blame and insists that she be kept on the job. You feel committed to equal opportunity but don't want to jeopardize your company's ability to survive. What should you do?

8. Major Company subcontracted the development of part of a large technology system to Start-up Company, a small corporation specializing in custom computer systems. The contract, which was a major breakthrough for Start-up Company and crucial to its future, provided for an initial development fee and subsequent progress payments, as well as a final date for completion.

Start-up Company provided Major Company with periodic reports indicating that everything was on schedule. After several months, however, the status reports stopped coming, and the company missed delivery of the schematics, the second major milestone. As an in-house technical consultant for Major Company, you visit Start-up Company and find not only that they are far behind schedule but that they had lied about their previous progress. Moreover, you determine that this slippage has put the schedule for the entire project in jeopardy. The cause of Start-up's slippage was the removal of personnel from your project to work on short-term contracts to obtain money to meet the weekly payroll.

Your company decides that you should stay at Start-up Company to monitor their work and to assist in the design of the project. After six weeks and some progress, Start-up is still way behind their delivery dates. Nonetheless, you are now familiar enough with the project to complete it in-house with Major's personnel.

Start-up is still experiencing severe cash flow problems and repeatedly requests payment from Major. But your CEO, furious with Start-up's lies and deceptions, wishes to "bury" Start-up and finish the project using Major Company's internal resources. She knows that withholding payment to Start-up will put them out of business. What do you do? Explain.

9. A customer requests certain sophisticated tests on equipment he purchased from your factory. Such tests are very expensive and must be performed by a third party. The equipment meets all of the industry standards but shows anomalies which cannot be explained.

Though the problem appears to be minor, you decide to inspect the unit to try to understand the test data—a very expensive and time-consuming process. You inform the customer of this decision. A problem is found, but it is minor and highly unlikely ever to cause the unit to fail. Rebuilding the equipment would be very expensive and time-consuming; moreover, notifying the customer that you are planning to rebuild the unit would also put your overall manufacturing procedures in question. What should you do—fix it, ship it, inform the customer?

10. (a) You are a project manager for a company making a major proposal to a Middle Eastern country. Your major competition is from Japan. Your local agent, who is closely tied to a very influential sheik, would receive a 5 percent commission if the proposal were accepted. Near the date for decision, the agent asks you for $150,000 to grease the skids so that your proposal is accepted. What do you do?

(b) What if, after you say no, the agent goes to your vice president, who provides the money? What do you do?

(c) Your overseas operation learns that most other foreign companies in this Middle Eastern location bolster their business by exchanging currency on the gray market. You discover that your division is twice as profitable as budgeted due to the amount of domestic currency you have received on the gray market. What do you do?

http: **Internet Exercise** Internet Exercise Find and identify some Web sites pertaining to business ethics that contain (a) political, social, or economic bias; (b) codes of conduct for companies, associations, or users; and (c) other significant material.

Introduction to
Contracts

CHAPTER 4

It is impossible to overestimate the importance of contracts in the field of business. Every business, whether large or small, must enter into contracts with its employees, its suppliers, and its customers to conduct its business operations. Contract law is, therefore, an important subject for the business manager. Contract law is also basic to other fields of law treated in other parts of this book, such as agency, partnerships, corporations, sales of personal property, commercial paper, and secured transactions.

Even the most common transaction may involve a multitude of contracts. For example, in a typical contract for the sale of land, the seller promises to transfer title to the land, and the buyer promises to pay an agreed-upon purchase price. In addition, the seller may promise to pay certain taxes or assessments; the buyer may promise to assume a mortgage on the property or may promise to pay the purchase price to a creditor of the seller. If attorneys represent the parties, they very likely do so on a contractual basis. If the seller deposits the proceeds of the sale in a bank, he enters into a contract with the bank. If the buyer leases the property, he enters into a contract with the tenant. When one of the parties leaves his car in a parking lot to attend to any of these matters, he assumes a contractual relationship with the proprietor of the lot. In short, nearly every business transaction is based upon contract and the expectations the agreed-upon promises create. Knowing the legal requirements for making binding contracts is, therefore, essential.

DEVELOPMENT OF THE LAW OF CONTRACTS

That law arises from social necessity is clearly true of the law of contracts. The vast and complicated institution of business can be conducted efficiently and successfully only upon the certainty that promises will be fulfilled. Business must be assured not only of supplies of raw materials or manufactured goods, but of labor, management, capital, and insurance as well. Common experience has shown that promises based solely on personal honesty or integrity do not have the reliability essential to business. Hence the development of the law of contracts, which is the law of enforceable promises.

Contract law, like law as a whole, is not static. It has undergone—and is still undergoing—enormous changes. In the nineteenth century virtually absolute autonomy in forming contracts was the rule. The law imposed contract liability only where the parties strictly complied with the required formalities. The same principle also dictated that once a contract was formed it should be enforced according to its terms and that neither party should be lightly excused from performance.

During the twentieth century, contract law experienced tremendous changes. Many of the formalities of contract formation were relaxed. Today, the law usually recognizes contractual obligations whenever the parties manifest an intent to be bound. In addition, an increasing number of promises are now enforced in certain circumstances, even though they do not comply strictly with the basic requirements of a contract. While in the past contract liability was absolute and escape from liability, once assumed, was rare, presently the law allows a party to be excused from contractual duties where fraud, duress, undue influence, mistake, unconscionability, or impossibility is present. The law has expanded the nineteenth century's narrow view of contract damages to grant equitable remedies and restitution as remedies for breach of contract. The older doctrine of privity of contract, which sharply restricted which parties could enforce contract rights, has given way to the current view that permits intended third-party beneficiaries to sue in their own right.

In brief, the twentieth century left its mark on contract law by limiting the absolute freedom of contract and, at the same time, by relaxing the requirements of contract formation. Accordingly, it is now considerably easier to get into a contract and correspondingly less difficult to get out of one.

Common Law

Contracts are primarily governed by state common law. An orderly presentation of this law is found in the Restatements of the Law of Contracts. The American Law Institute adopted and promulgated the first Restatement on May 6, 1932. On May 17, 1979, the institute adopted and promulgated a revised edition of the Restatement—the Restatement, Second, Contracts—which will be referred to as the Restatement. Regarded as a valuable authoritative reference work for more than seventy years, the Restatements have been extensively relied upon and quoted in reported judicial opinions.

The Uniform Commercial Code

The sale of personal property forms a substantial portion of commercial activity. Article 2 of the Uniform Commercial Code (the Code, or UCC) governs sales in all states except Louisiana. (Selected provisions of the UCC are set forth in Appendix B of this text.) A **sale** consists in the passing of title to goods from a seller to a buyer for a price. Section 2–106. A contract for sale includes both a present sale of goods and a contract to sell goods at a future time. Section 2–106. The Code essentially defines goods as movable personal property. Section 2–105(1). **Personal property** is any type of property other than an interest in real property (land). For example, the purchase of a television set, automobile, or textbook is considered a sale of goods. All such transactions are governed by Article 2 of the Code, but, where the Code has not specifically modified general contract law, the common law of contracts continues to apply. Section 1–103. In other words, the law of sales is a specialized part of the general law of contracts, and the law of contracts governs unless specifically displaced by the Code.

Amendments to Article 2 were promulgated in 2003 to accommodate electronic commerce and to reflect development of business practices, changes in other law, and interpretive difficulties of practical significance.

◆ SEE FIGURE 4-1 Law Governing Contracts

http: **Uniform Commercial Code:** http://www.law.cornell.edu/uniform/ucc.html

Types of Contracts Outside the Code

General contract law governs all contracts outside the scope of the Code. Such contracts play a significant role in commercial

◆ FIGURE 4-1 Law Governing Contracts

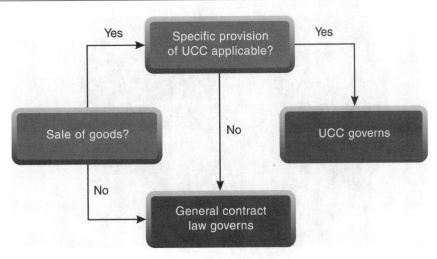

activities. For example, the Code does *not* apply to employment contracts, service contracts, insurance contracts, contracts involving **real property** (land and anything attached to it, including buildings), and contracts for the sale of intangibles such as patents and copyrights. These transactions continue to be governed by general contract law.

◆ SEE CASE 4-1

DEFINITION OF A CONTRACT

A contract is binding agreement that the courts will enforce. Section 1 of the Restatement more precisely defines a contract as "a promise or a set of promises for the breach of which the law gives a remedy, or the performance of which the law in some way recognizes as a duty." The Restatement provides further insight by defining a **promise** as "a manifestation of the intention to act or refrain from acting in a specified way." Restatement, Section 2.

Those promises that meet all of the essential requirements of a binding contract are contractual and will be enforced. All other promises are not contractual, and usually no legal remedy is available for a **breach** (a failure to perform properly) of these promises. The remedies provided for breach of contract (discussed in Chapter 5) include compensatory damages, equitable remedies, reliance damages, and restitution. Thus, a promise may be contractual (and therefore binding) or noncontractual. In other words, all contracts are promises, but not all promises are contracts.

◆ SEE FIGURE 4-2 Contractual and Noncontractual
          Promises

◆ SEE CASE 4-2

REQUIREMENTS OF A CONTRACT

The four basic requirements of a contract are as follows:

1. **Mutual Assent.** The parties to a contract must manifest by words or conduct that they have agreed to enter into a contract. The usual method of showing mutual assent is by offer and acceptance.
2. **Consideration.** Each party to a contract must intentionally exchange a legal benefit or incur a legal detriment as an inducement to the other party to make a return exchange.
3. **Legality of Object.** The purpose of a contract must not be criminal, tortious, or otherwise against public policy.
4. **Capacity.** The parties to a contract must have contractual capacity. Certain persons, such as those adjudicated (judicially declared) incompetent, have no legal capacity to contract, while others, such as minors, incompetent persons, and intoxicated persons, have limited capacity to contract. All others have full contractual capacity.

In addition, though occasionally a contract must be evidenced by a writing to be enforceable, in most cases an oral contract is binding and enforceable. If all of these essentials are present, the promise is contractual and legally binding. If any is absent, however, the promise is noncontractual. These requirements will be separately considered in succeeding chapters.

◆ FIGURE 4-2 Contractual and Noncontractual Promises

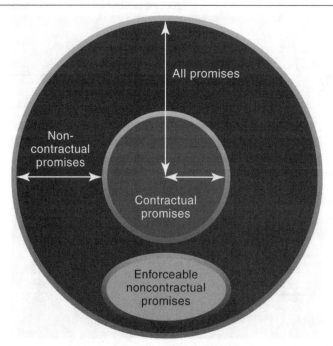

◆ SEE FIGURE 4-3 Validity of Agreements

◈ SEE CASE 4-2

CLASSIFICATION OF CONTRACTS

Contracts can be classified according to various characteristics, such as method of formation, content, and legal effect. The standard classifications are (1) express or implied contracts; (2) unilateral or bilateral contracts; (3) valid, void, voidable, or unenforceable contracts; (4) executed or executory contracts; and (5) formal or informal contracts. These classifications are

not mutually exclusive. For example, a contract may be express, bilateral, valid, executory, and informal.

Express and Implied Contracts

Parties to a contract may indicate their assent either by express language or by conduct that implies such willingness. Thus, a contract may be (1) entirely oral; (2) partly oral and partly written; (3) entirely written; (4) partly oral or written and partly implied from the conduct of the parties; and (5) wholly implied from the conduct of the parties. The first three are known as express contracts, and the last two as implied contracts. Both express and implied contracts are genuine

◆ FIGURE 4-3 Validity of Agreements

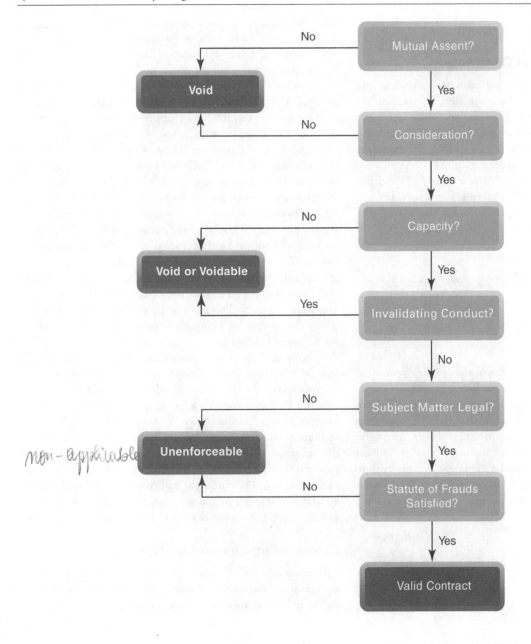

non-applicable

contracts, equally enforceable. The difference between them is merely the manner in which the parties manifest assent.

An **express contract** is therefore one in which the parties have manifested their agreement by oral or written language, or both.

An **implied contract** is one that is inferred from the parties' conduct, not from spoken or written words. Implied contracts are also called implied in fact contracts. Thus, if Elizabeth orders and receives a meal in Bill's restaurant, a promise is implied on Elizabeth's part to pay Bill the price stated in the menu or, if none is stated, Bill's customary price. Likewise, when a passenger boards a bus, a wholly implied contract is formed by which the passenger undertakes to pay the customary fare and the bus company undertakes to provide the passenger transportation.

◆ SEE CASE 4-1

◆ SEE CASE 4-4

Unilateral and Bilateral Contracts

In the typical contractual transaction, each party makes at least one promise. For example, if Ali says to Ben, "If you promise to mow my lawn, I will pay you ten dollars," and Ben agrees to mow Ali's lawn, Ali and Ben have made mutual promises, each undertaking to do something in exchange for the promise of the other. When a contract comes into existence by the exchange of promises, each party is under a duty to the other. This kind of contract is called a **bilateral contract**, because each party is both a *promisor* (a person making a promise) and a *promisee* (the person to whom a promise is made).

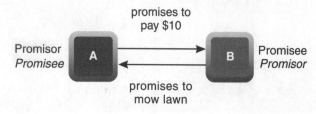

But suppose that only one of the parties makes a promise. Ali says to Ben, "If you will mow my lawn, I will pay you ten dollars." A contract will be formed when Ben has finished mowing the lawn and not before. At that time, Ali becomes contractually obligated to pay ten dollars to Ben. Ali's offer was in exchange for Ben's act of mowing the lawn, not for his promise to mow it. Because he never made a promise to mow the lawn, Ben was under no duty to mow it. This is a **unilateral contract** because only one of the parties made a promise.

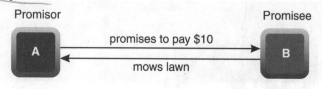

Thus, whereas a bilateral contract results from the exchange of a promise for a return promise, a unilateral contract results from the exchange of a promise either for an act or for a forbearance (refraining) from acting. If a contract is not clearly unilateral or bilateral, the courts presume that the parties intended a bilateral contract. Thus, in the above example, if Ali says to Ben, "I will pay you ten dollars if you will mow my lawn," and Ben replies, "OK, I will mow your lawn," a bilateral contract is formed.

Valid, Void, Voidable, and Unenforceable Contracts

By definition, a **valid contract** is one that meets all of the requirements of a binding contract. It is an enforceable promise or agreement.

A **void contract** is an agreement that does not meet all of the requirements of a binding contract. Thus, it is no contract at all; it is merely a promise or agreement having no legal effect. An example of a void agreement is an agreement entered into by an adjudicated incompetent.

A voidable contract, on the other hand, is not wholly lacking in legal effect. A **voidable contract** is a contract, but because of the manner in which it was formed or a lack of capacity of a party to it, the law permits one or more of the parties to avoid the legal duties the contract creates. Restatement, Section 7. If the contract is avoided, both parties are relieved of their legal duties under the agreement. For instance, through intentional misrepresentation of a material fact (*fraud*), Thomas induces Regina to enter into a contract. Regina may, upon discovery of the fraud, notify Thomas that by reason of the misrepresentation she will not perform her promise, and the law will support Regina. Though not void, the contract induced by fraud is voidable at the election of Regina, the defrauded party. Thomas, the fraudulent party, has no such election. If Regina elects to avoid the contract, Thomas will be released from his promise under the agreement, although he may be liable under tort law for damages for fraud.

A contract that is neither void nor voidable may, nonetheless, be unenforceable. An **unenforceable contract** is one for the breach of which the law provides no remedy. Restatement, Section 8. For example, a contract may be unenforceable because of a failure to satisfy the requirements of the Statute of Frauds, which requires certain kinds of contracts to be evidenced by a writing to be enforceable. Also, the running of the time within which a suit may be filed, as provided in the Statute of Limitations, bars the right to bring a lawsuit for breach of contract. After that period has run, the contract is referred to as unenforceable, rather than void or voidable.

Executed and Executory Contracts

The terms *executed* and *executory* pertain to the state of performance of a contract. A contract fully performed by all of the parties to it is an **executed contract**. Strictly, an executed contract is in the present tense no contract, as all duties under it have been performed; but it is useful to have a term for a completed contract. (The word *executed* is also used to mean "signed," as in to execute or sign a certain document.)

The term **executory**, which means "unperformed," applies to situations where one or more promises by any party to the contract are as yet unperformed or where the contract is wholly unperformed by one or more of the parties. Thus, David and Carla make a contract under which David is to sell and deliver certain goods to Carla in ten days and Carla is to pay the agreed price in thirty days. Prior to the delivery of the goods by David on the tenth day, the contract is wholly executory. Upon David's delivery of the goods to Carla, the contract is executed as to David and executory as to Carla. When Carla duly pays for the goods, the contract is wholly executed and thereby completely fulfilled.

Formal and Informal Contracts

A **formal contract** depends upon a particular form, or mode of expression, for its legal existence. For example, at common law a promise under seal (a particular symbol that serves to authenticate an instrument) is enforceable without anything more. Another formal contract is a negotiable instrument, such as a check, which has certain legal attributes resulting solely from the special form in which it is made. A letter of credit (a promise to honor drafts or other demands for payment) is also a formal contract. Recognizances, or formal acknowledgments of indebtedness made in court, are another example of formal contracts. All other contracts, whether oral or written, are simple or **informal contracts**, as they do not depend upon formality for their legal validity.

PROMISSORY ESTOPPEL

As a general rule, promises are unenforceable if they do not meet all the requirements of a contract. Nevertheless, to avoid injustice, in certain circumstances the courts enforce noncontractual promises under the doctrine of promissory estoppel. A noncontractual promise is enforceable when it is made under circumstances that should lead the promisor reasonably to expect that the promise would induce the promisee to take definite and substantial action or forbearance in reliance on the promise, and the promisee does take such action or forbearance. See Figure 4-2. Section 90 of the Restatement provides:

> A promise which the promisor should reasonably expect to induce action or forbearance on the part of the promisee or a third person and which does induce such action or forbearance is binding if injustice can be avoided only by enforcement of the promise. The remedy granted for breach may be limited as justice requires.

For example, Gordon promises Constance not to foreclose for a period of six months on a mortgage Gordon owns on Constance's land. Constance then expends $100,000 to construct a building on the land. His promise not to foreclose is binding on Gordon under the doctrine of promissory estoppel.

◆ **See Figure 4-4** Contracts, Promissory Estoppel, and Quasi Contracts

◊ **See Case 4-3**

◊ **See Case 4-5**

QUASI CONTRACTS

In addition to implied in fact contracts, there are implied in law, or quasi, contracts, which were not included in the foregoing classification of contracts because a quasi (meaning "as if") contract is not a contract at all. The term *quasi contract* is used because the remedy granted for quasi contract is similar to one of the remedies available for breach of contract.

A quasi contract is *not* a contract because it is based on neither an express nor an implied promise. A **contract implied in law** or **quasi contract** is an obligation imposed by law to avoid injustice.

◆ **Figure 4-4** Contracts, Promissory Estoppel, and Quasi Contracts

	Contract	Promissory Estoppel	Quasi Contract
Type of Promise	Contractual	Noncontractual	None Void Unenforceable Invalidated
Requirements	All of the essential elements of a contract	Detrimental and justifiable reliance	Benefit conferred and knowingly accepted
Remedies	Equitable Compensatory Reliance Restitution	Promise enforced to the extent necessary to avoid injustice	Reasonable value of benefit conferred

For example, Anna by mistake delivers to Robert a plain, unaddressed envelope containing $100 intended for Claudia. Robert is under no contractual obligation to return it. However, Anna is permitted to recover the $100 from Robert. The law imposes a quasi-contractual obligation upon Robert to prevent his unjust enrichment at Anna's expense. The elements of such a recovery are (1) a benefit conferred upon the defendant (Robert) by the plaintiff (Anna); (2) an appreciation or knowledge by the defendant (Robert) of the benefit; and (3) acceptance or retention by the defendant (Robert) of the benefit under circumstances rendering inequitable the defendant's (Robert's) retention of the benefit without compensating the plaintiff for its value.

One court has summarized the doctrine of quasi contract as follows:

> Quasi contracts are not contracts at all, although they give rise to obligations more akin to those stemming from contract than from

tort. The contract is a mere fiction, a form imposed in order to adapt the case to a given remedy....Briefly stated, a quasi-contractual obligation is one imposed by law where there has been no agreement or expression of assent, by word or act, on the part of either party involved. The law creates it, regardless of the intention of the parties, to assure a just and equitable result. *Bradkin v. Leverton*, 26 N.Y.2d 192, 309 N.Y.S.2d 192, 257 N.E.2d 643 (1970).

Not infrequently, courts use quasi contracts to provide a remedy when the parties have entered into a void contract, an unenforceable contract, or a voidable contract that is avoided. In such a case, the law of quasi contracts will determine the recovery permitted for any performance rendered by the parties under the invalid, unenforceable, or invalidated agreement.

◆ **See Figure 4-4** Contracts, Promissory Estoppel, and Quasi Contracts

CHAPTER SUMMARY

Law of Contracts

Definition of Contract a binding agreement that the courts will enforce

Common Law most contracts are governed primarily by state common law, including contracts involving employment, services, insurance, real property (land and anything attached to it), patents, and copyrights

Uniform Commercial Code Article 2 of the UCC governs the sales of goods
- *Sale* the transfer of title from seller to buyer
- *Goods* tangible personal property (personal property is all property other than an interest in land)

Requirements of a Contract

Mutual Assent the parties to a contract must manifest by words or conduct that they have agreed to enter into a contract

Consideration each party to a contract must intentionally exchange a legal benefit or incur a legal detriment as an inducement to the other party to make a return exchange

Legality of Object the purpose of a contract must not be criminal, tortious, or otherwise against public policy

Capacity the parties to a contract must have contractual capacity

Classification of Contracts

Express and Implied Contracts
- *Express Contract* an agreement that is stated in words, either orally or in writing
- *Implied in Fact Contract* a contract in which the agreement of the parties is inferred from their conduct

Bilateral and Unilateral Contracts
- *Bilateral Contract* a contract in which both parties exchange promises
- *Unilateral Contract* a contract in which only one party makes a promise

Valid, Void, Voidable, and Unenforceable Contracts
- *Valid Contract* one that meets all of the requirements of a binding contract
- *Void Contract* no contract at all; without legal effect
- *Voidable Contract* a contract capable of being made void
-  *Unenforceable Contract* a contract for the breach of which the law provides no remedy

Executed and Executory Contracts

- *Executed Contract* a contract that has been fully performed by all of the parties
- *Executory Contract* a contract that has yet to be fully performed

Formal and Informal Contracts

- *Formal Contract* an agreement that is legally binding because of its particular form or mode of expression
- *Informal Contracts* all contracts other than formal contracts

---

Promissory Estoppel

Definition a doctrine enforcing some noncontractual promises

Requirements a promise made under circumstances that should lead the promisor reasonably to expect that the promise would induce the promisee to take definite and substantial action, and the promisee does take such action

Remedy a court will enforce the promise to the extent necessary to avoid injustice

---

Quasi Contracts

Definition an obligation not based on contract that is imposed to avoid injustice

Requirements a court will impose a quasi contract when (1) the plaintiff confers a benefit upon the defendant, (2) the defendant knows or appreciates the benefit, and (3) the defendant's retention of the benefit is inequitable

Remedy the plaintiff recovers the reasonable value of the benefit she conferred upon the defendant

---

CASES

CASE 4-1

Here, the Supreme Court of Idaho reviews a lower court decision which held that there was an implied-in-fact contract in a dispute between companies. The case also illustrates how courts use the "predominant factor" test to determine whether a contract is governed by the UCC.

FOX v. MOUNTAIN WEST ELECTRIC, INC.

Supreme Court of Idaho, 2002
137 Idaho 703, 52 P.3d 848 2002, rehearing denied, 2002
http://caselaw.lp.findlaw.com/data2/idahostatecases/sc/1026/fox8.pdf

Walters, J.

Lockheed Martin Idaho Technical Company ("LMITCO") requested bids for a comprehensive fire alarm system in its twelve buildings located in Idaho Falls. At a prebid meeting, MWE and Fox met and discussed working together on the project. MWE was in the business of installing electrical wiring, conduit and related hookups and attachments. Fox provided services in designing, drafting, testing and assisting in the installation of fire alarm systems, and in ordering specialty equipment necessary for such projects. The parties concluded that it would be more advantageous for them to work together on the project than for each of them to bid separately for the entire job, and they further agreed that Fox would work under MWE. The parties prepared a document defining each of their roles entitled "Scope and Responsibilities."

Fox prepared a bid for the materials and services that he would provide, which was incorporated into MWE's bid to LMITCO. MWE was the successful bidder and was awarded the LMITCO fixed price contract. In May 1996, Fox began performing various services at the direction of MWE's manager. During the course of the project, many changes and modifications to the LMITCO contract were made.

A written contract was presented to Fox by MWE on August 7, 1996. A dispute between MWE and Fox arose over the procedure for the compensation of the change orders. MWE proposed a flow-down procedure, whereby Fox would receive whatever compensation LMITCO decided to pay MWE. This was unacceptable to Fox. Fox suggested a bidding procedure to which MWE objected. On December 5, 1996, Fox met with MWE to discuss the contract. No compensation arrangement was agreed upon by the parties with respect to change orders. Fox left the project on December 9, 1996, after delivering the remaining equipment and materials to MWE. MWE contracted with Life Safety Systems ("LSS") to complete the LMITCO project.

Fox filed a complaint in July 1998 seeking monetary damages representing money due and owing for materials and services provided by Fox on behalf of MWE. MWE answered and counterclaimed seeking monetary damages resulting from the alleged breach of the parties' agreement by Fox.

Following a court trial, the district court found that an implied-in-fact contract existed between the parties based on the industry standard's flow-down method of compensation. The court found in favor of MWE. * * * Fox appeals.

* * *

Implied-in-Fact Contract

* * *

This Court has recognized three types of contractual relationships:

> First is the express contract wherein the parties expressly agree regarding a transaction. Secondly, there is the implied in fact contract wherein there is no express agreement, but the conduct of the parties implies an agreement from which an obligation in contract exists. The third category is called an implied in law contract, or quasi contract. However, a contract implied in law is not a contract at all, but an obligation imposed by law for the purpose of bringing about justice and equity without reference to the intent or the agreement of the parties and, in some cases, in spite of an agreement between the parties. It is a non-contractual obligation that is to be treated procedurally as if it were a contract, and is often refered (sic) to as quasi contract, unjust enrichment, implied in law contract or restitution.

[Citation.]

"An implied in fact contract is defined as one where the terms and existence of the contract are manifested by the conduct of the parties with the request of one party and the performance by the other often being inferred from the circumstances attending the performance." [Citation.] The implied-in-fact contract is grounded in the parties' agreement and tacit understanding. [Citation.] "The general rule is that where the conduct of the parties allows the dual inferences that one performed at the other's request and that the requesting party promised payment, then the court may find a contract implied in fact." [Citations.]

[UCC §] 1–205(1) defines "course of dealing" as "a sequence of previous conduct between the parties to a particular transaction which is fairly to be regarded as establishing a common basis of understanding for interpreting their expressions and other conduct."

* * *

Although the procedure was the same for each change order, in that MWE would request a pricing from Fox for the work, which was then presented to LMITCO, each party treated the pricings submitted by Fox for the change orders in a different manner. This treatment is not sufficient to establish a meeting of the minds or to establish a course of dealing when there was no "common basis of understanding for interpreting [the parties'] expressions" under [UCC §] 1–205(1).

* * * After a review of the record, it appears that the district court's findings are supported by substantial and competent, albeit conflicting, evidence. This Court will not substitute its view of the facts for the view of the district court.

Using the district court's finding that pricings submitted by Fox were used by MWE as estimates for the change orders, the conclusion made by the district court that an implied-in-fact contract allowed for the reasonable compensation of Fox logically follows and is grounded in the law in Idaho. [Citation.]

This Court holds that the district court did not err in finding that there was an implied-in-fact contract using the industry standard's flow-down method of compensation for the change orders rather than a series of fixed price contracts between MWE and Fox.

Uniform Commercial Code

Fox contends that the district court erred by failing to consider previous drafts of the proposed contract between the parties to determine the terms of the parties' agreement. Fox argues the predominant factor of this transaction was the fire alarm system, not the methodology of how the system was installed, which would focus on the sale of goods and, therefore, the Uniform Commercial Code ("UCC") should govern. Fox argues that in using the UCC various terms were agreed upon by the parties in the prior agreement drafts, including terms for the timing of payments, payments to Fox's suppliers and prerequisites to termination.

MWE contends that the UCC should not be used, despite the fact that goods comprised one-half of the contract price, because the predominant factor at issue is services and not the sale of goods. MWE points out that the primary issue is the value of Fox's services under the change orders and the cost of obtaining replacement services after Fox left the job. MWE further argues that the disagreement between the parties over material terms should prevent the court from using UCC gap fillers. Rather, MWE contends the intent and relationship of the parties should be used to resolve the conflict.

This Court in [citation], pointed out "in determining whether the UCC applies in such cases, a majority of courts look at the entire transaction to determine which aspect, the sale of goods or the sale of services, predominates." [Citation.] It is clear that if the underlying transaction to the contract involved the sale of goods, the UCC would apply. [Citation.] However, if the contract only involved services, the UCC would not apply. [Citation.] This Court has not directly articulated the standard to be used in mixed sales of goods and services, otherwise known as hybrid transactions.

The Court of Appeals in *Pittsley v. Houser,* [citation], focused on the applicability of the UCC to hybrid transactions. The court held that the trial court must look at the predominant factor of the transaction to determine if the UCC applies. [Citation.]

The test for inclusion or exclusion is not whether they are mixed, but, granting that they are mixed, whether their predominant factor, their thrust, their purpose, reasonably stated, is the rendition of service, with goods incidentally involved (e.g., contract with artist for painting) or is a transaction of sale, with labor incidentally involved (e.g., installation of a water heater in a bathroom). This test essentially involves consideration of the contract in its entirety, applying the UCC to the entire contract or not at all.

[Citation.] This Court agrees with the Court of Appeals' analysis and holds that the predominant factor test should be used to determine whether the UCC applies to transactions involving the sale of both goods and services.

One aspect that the Court of Appeals noted in its opinion in *Pittsley*, in its determination that the predominant factor in that case was the sale of goods, was that the purchaser was more concerned with the goods and less concerned with the installation, either who would provide it or the nature of the

work. MWE and Fox decided to work on this project together because of their differing expertise. MWE was in the business of installing electrical wiring, while Fox designed, tested and assisted in the installation of fire alarm systems, in addition to ordering specialty equipment for fire alarm projects.

The district court found that the contract at issue in this case contained both goods and services; however, the predominant factor was Fox's services. The district court found that the goods provided by Fox were merely incidental to the services he provided, and the UCC would provide no assistance in interpreting the parties' agreement.

This Court holds that the district court did not err in finding that the predominant factor of the underlying transaction was services and that the UCC did not apply.

* * *

This Court affirms the decision of the district court.

CASE

4-2

Does submission of an application to medical school create a contract between the applicant and the school? The following case considers that question by examining the definition and essential requirements of a contract.

STEINBERG v. CHICAGO MEDICAL SCHOOL

Illinois Court of Appeals, 1976
41 Ill.App 0.3d 804, 354 N.E.2d 586

Dempsey, J.
In December 1973 the plaintiff, Robert Steinberg, applied for admission to the defendant, the Chicago Medical School, as a first-year student for the academic year 1974–75 and paid an application fee of $15. The Chicago Medical School is a private, not-for-profit educational institution, incorporated in the State of Illinois. His application for admission was rejected and Steinberg filed a[n] * * * action against the school, claiming that it had failed to evaluate his application * * * according to the academic entrance criteria printed in the school's bulletin. Specifically, his complaint alleged that the school's decision to accept or reject a particular applicant for the first-year class was primarily based on such nonacademic considerations as the prospective student's familial relationship to members of the school's faculty and to members of its board of trustees, and the ability of the applicant or his family to pledge or make payment of large sums of money to the school. The complaint further alleged that, by using such unpublished criteria to evaluate applicants, the school had breached the contract which Steinberg contended was created when the school accepted his application fee.

* * *

The defendant filed a motion to dismiss, arguing that the complaint failed to state a cause of action because no contract came into existence during its transaction with Steinberg inasmuch as the school's informational publication did not constitute a valid offer. The trial court sustained [ruled in favor of] the motion to dismiss and Steinberg appeals from this order.

* * *

A contract is an agreement between competent parties, based upon a consideration sufficient in law, to do or not do a particular thing. It is a promise or a set of promises for the breach of which the law gives a remedy, or the performance of which the law in some way recognizes as a duty. [Citation.] A contract's essential requirements are: competent parties, valid subject matter, legal consideration, mutuality of obligation and mutuality of agreement. Generally, parties may contract in any situation where there is no legal prohibition, since the law acts by restraint and not by conferring rights. [Citation.] However, it is basic contract law that in order for a contract to be binding the terms of the contract must be reasonably certain and definite. [Citation.]

A contract, in order to be legally binding, must be based on consideration. [Citation.] Consideration has been defined to consist of some right, interest, profit or benefit accruing to one party or some forbearance, disadvantage, detriment, loss or responsibility given, suffered, or undertaken by the other. [Citation.] Money is a valuable consideration and its transfer or payment or promises to pay it or the benefit from the right to its use, will support a contract.

In forming a contract, it is required that both parties assent to the same thing in the same sense [citation] and that their minds meet on the essential terms and conditions. [Citation.] Furthermore, the mutual consent essential to the formation of a contract must be gathered from the language employed by the parties or manifested by their words or acts. The intention of the parties gives character to the transaction, and if either party contracts in good faith he is entitled to the benefit of his contract no matter what may have been the secret purpose or intention of the other party. [Citation.]

Steinberg contends that the Chicago Medical School's informational brochure constituted an invitation to make an offer; that his subsequent application and the submission of his $15 fee to the school amounted to an offer; that the school's voluntary reception of his fee constituted an acceptance and because of these events a contract was created between the school and himself. He contends that the school was duty bound under the terms of the contract to evaluate his application according to its stated standards and that the deviation from these standards not only breached the contract, but amounted to an arbitrary selection which constituted a violation of due process and equal protection. He concludes that such a breach did in fact take place each and every time during the past ten years that the school evaluated applicants according to their relationship to the school's faculty members or members of its board of trustees, or in accordance with their ability to make or pledge large sums

of money to the school. Finally, he asserts that he is a member and a proper representative of the class that has been damaged by the school's practice.

The school counters that no contract came into being because informational brochures, such as its bulletin, do not constitute offers, but are construed by the courts to be general proposals to consider, examine and negotiate. The school points out that this doctrine has been specifically applied in Illinois to university informational publications.

* * *

We agree with Steinberg's position. We believe that he and the school entered into an enforceable contract; that the school's obligation under the contract was stated in the school's bulletin in a definitive manner and that by accepting his application fee—a valuable consideration—the school bound itself to fulfill its promises. Steinberg accepted the school's promises in good faith and he was entitled to have his application judged according to the school's stated criteria.

* * *

[Reversed and remanded.]

CASE
4-3

Does an employee-at will, who is terminated on the day he begins employment, have any recourse against the employer? The following case discusses the circumstances under which an employee might have a claim of breach of contract or a claim based on promissory estoppel.

GORHAM v. BENSON OPTICAL
Court of Appeals of Minnesota, 1995
539 N.W.2d 798

Davies, J.

Appellant contends the district court erred in dismissing his claims for breach of contract, promissory estoppel, and fraud that arose from termination of an at-will employment contract. We affirm summary judgment on the fraud and breach of contract claims, but reverse summary judgment on the promissory estoppel claim and remand for further proceedings.

Facts

In early September 1993, appellant Carl Gorham received a phone call from Ed Iwinski about a job opportunity with respondent Benson Optical. At that time, Gorham earned $38,000 annually working as a store manager for LensCrafters, but indicated he was interested in employment with Benson Optical. Iwinski, who apparently had been offered the job of chief operating officer (COO) for Benson Optical, told Gorham that he was not yet part of the decision-making process on hiring, but would forward Gorham's name to Benson Optical. The next day, Benson Optical's eastern regional manager, Sue Opahle, called Gorham to schedule an interview for an area manager position.

On September 15, 1993, Opahle interviewed Gorham in Chicago. During this interview, Gorham came to believe that Iwinski was effectively Opahle's boss and the COO at Benson Optical.

On September 18, Gorham called Opahle to inquire about the status of his application. Opahle offered him the job of area manager for half of North Carolina and some stores in Florida and Kentucky. She offered him a $50,000 annual salary and discussed relocation. Opahle described the terms of employment over the phone and promised to send a confirming letter and employee packet in two days. Gorham told Opahle that he accepted the position provisionally, and, if he changed his mind, he would notify her within two days. Otherwise, he would give LensCrafters his notice of termination.

When Gorham did not receive the packet on September 20, he called Benson Optical to inquire. Someone in the office called Gorham back, said the packet was in the mail, and reassured him that the deal was finalized so he could give LensCrafters notice. On September 21, Gorham gave LensCrafters his two-week notice of resignation. LensCrafters attempted to keep Gorham in its employment with an offer of a raise, but Gorham declined.

When Gorham received the packet a few days later, it contained two shortcomings, which he called to Benson's attention. Gorham received a corrected letter, which asked that he sign and return it as acceptance of the terms of employment. Gorham signed this letter, but never returned it because he had started having reservations about his employment with Benson Optical.

On about September 30, Iwinski informed Benson Optical's vice president of human resources, Fran Scibora, that he was declining the COO position. Scibora, Opahle, and Benson Optical's chief financial officer, Dominic Sblendorio, immediately contacted Gorham and three other new employees who had been recommended by Iwinski, asking for their reactions to the fact that Iwinski would not be working for Benson Optical. Gorham responded that Iwinski's absence did not change his decision to accept the job. When Gorham asked if Iwinski's departure affected Gorham's job, Scibora assured him that it would not.

Gorham's last day of work for LensCrafters was October 1. On October 3, he flew to Minneapolis for Benson Optical's national sales meeting. On October 4, Scibora, Opahle, and Sblendorio met with Gorham for what they called a "getting to know you" meeting. At the meeting they asked him for the completed employee forms they had sent him; Gorham turned in all the forms except the acceptance letter. The meeting then turned into another interview in which they reviewed Gorham's skills and aptitudes. Scibora finally told Gorham that he did not possess the skills necessary for the area manager position. Gorham had the clear impression that he had been or would be terminated.

This group also met with and terminated three other employees whom Opahle had hired at Iwinski's suggestion. In a letter to Gorham dated October 15, Benson Optical explained that it had terminated his position because Iwinski had declined the job as COO, because of a "change [in] the requirements of the Area Manager's position" and because Gorham's "skills and abilities did not satisfy the requirements for the new direction in which the company is going."

* * *

Analysis

Contract

A party may manifest acceptance of an agreement by written or spoken words, or by conduct and actions. [Citation.] The record establishes that a contract existed here before October 4 because, even though Gorham did not return the acceptance letter to Benson Optical, he demonstrated his acceptance by verbally agreeing to take the job, resigning his former employment, flying to Chicago at his own expense, and reporting for the sales meeting on October 3. He also admitted that, at that time, he considered himself hired.

The hiring letter, however, fell short as a matter of law of guaranteeing Gorham employment for 90 days as he claims. The relevant statement merely informed Gorham that he needed to produce in 90 days or face termination. Because the contract was at-will and there are no issues of fact as to its terms, the district court properly granted summary judgment on Gorham's breach of contract claim.

Promissory Estoppel

Gorham alternatively contends that the district court erred in granting summary judgment for Benson Optical on the promissory estoppel claim. We agree.

The elements of promissory estoppel are:

> A promise which the promisor should reasonably expect to induce action or forbearance * * * on the part of the promisee and which does induce such action or forbearance is binding if injustice can be avoided only by enforcement of the promise.

Restatement of Contracts § 90 (1932), [citation]. [Court's footnote: This provision has remained substantially the same in Restatement (Second) of Contracts § 90 (1981).]

Respondents argue that promissory estoppel is not available when a contract exists. This is true (but with one exception). [Citation.] In *Grouse*, however, the supreme court in effect found an exception to this rule. The exception applies when the contract is of a type that provides no basis for a contract recovery, i.e., an at-will employment contract. [Citation.] Then there is no bar to a promissory estoppel claim.

In *Grouse*, the supreme court applied the doctrine of promissory estoppel to facts very similar to the present case and allowed the plaintiff to recover reliance damages. There, a pharmacy offered a pharmacist a job and, after the pharmacist accepted, resigned his current position, and declined another job offer, the pharmacy hired someone else.* * *

* * *

Significant to this case, the *Grouse* court stated, in dictum: "[U]nder appropriate circumstances we believe section 90 [of the Restatement] would apply even after employment has begun." [Citation.] Gorham presents the specific hypothetical situation the *Grouse* court's dictum addressed—a short time actually on the job. And, independent of the hypothetical and like Grouse himself, Gorham relied on the promise of a new job when he quit his job with LensCrafters and declined any renegotiations with them. Gorham came to Minneapolis to begin work on October 4, believing that he had been hired. Within a day, Benson Optical terminated him. These facts show Gorham's reasonable reliance on Benson Optical's promise of employment, his declining any other job in deference to his new job with Benson Optical, and the injustice to him when, on his first day of "employment," he went through a hostile re-interview process that led to his immediate termination.

We see no relevant difference between Gorham, who reported to the national sales meeting on his first day of employment, and Grouse, who was denied even one day on the job. Both men relied to their detriment on the promise of a new job, only to discover that the opportunity had disintegrated before they ever actually started working. Neither man had a "good faith opportunity to perform his duties." [Citation.] Given these facts, Gorham's claim fits squarely within the spirit of *Grouse* and is entitled to the benefit of promissory estoppel leading to reliance damages.

* * *

The district court erred when it granted summary judgment against Gorham's promissory estoppel claim.

Decision

* * * The doctrine of promissory estoppel allows Gorham to recover good faith reliance damages when Benson Optical terminated him on his first day of employment, after Gorham had detrimentally and reasonably relied on the promise of new employment. Summary judgment on the promissory estoppel claim is reversed and remanded for further proceedings.

CASE
4-4

An implied in fact contract may be formed by the conduct of the parties, rather than by their words. This case illustrates how a court determines whether such a contract was formed, and if so, what its terms are.

WATTS v. COLUMBIA ARTISTS MANAGEMENT INC.
Appellate Division, New York (3rd Dept.), 1992
188 A.D. 2d 799, 591 N.Y.S. 2d 234

CASEY, Justice. Appeal (transferred to this court by order of the Appellate Division, Second Department) from a judgment of the Supreme Court (Weiner, J.), entered May 17, 1991 in Rockland County, upon a decision of the court in favor of defendant.

Plaintiff, a concert pianist, commenced this declaratory judgment action seeking, inter alia, a determination of his liability to defendant, which provides managerial services to performing artists, for services performed by defendant prior to September 1, 1988. Defendant began to provide its services to plaintiff in 1983 when it entered into a contract with Andre Watts Performances Inc. (hereinafter the Corporation), which provided that defendant would act as plaintiff's exclusive agent and that defendant would be compensated for its services by receiving, inter alia, 15% of plaintiff's earnings for American concerts, but defendant would be entitled to no fee if plaintiff was not paid for an engagement. Although the Corporation dissolved in August 1985 and the term of the contract expired September 1, 1986, defendant continued to provide services to plaintiff and plaintiff continued to pay for those services in the manner provided for in the expired contract between defendant and the Corporation. Plaintiff notified defendant in writing on August 9, 1988 that he wished to terminate his relationship with defendant effective September 1, 1988.

When the parties' relationship was terminated, defendant had scheduled a total of 82 engagements for plaintiff for the next two concert seasons. Contracts had been executed as of September 1, 1988 for 48 of the 82 scheduled engagements, and plaintiff performed and was paid for 46 of those 48 engagements. Of the remaining 34 scheduled engagements, for which no contract had been executed as of September 1, 1988, plaintiff performed 33 of them and was paid for 32 of the performances. Defendant claims entitlement to its 15% commission for all 78 of the engagements performed by plaintiff for which he was paid. Plaintiff contends that defendant is entitled to no commission on the 32 engagements for which no contract had been executed prior to September 1, 1988. As to the remaining 46 engagements, plaintiff contends that defendant is entitled only to one half of its usual 15% commission because additional managerial services, including travel arrangements, rehearsal schedules, piano delivery and tuning, receptions, master classes and other details, were required

after September 1, 1988. According to plaintiff, the additional services were performed by another manager retained by plaintiff after September 1, 1988.

At the nonjury trial, plaintiff, an officer of defendant and other witnesses testified. Much of the testimony concerned the managerial services provided to plaintiff in particular and the industry practice in general. Supreme Court found that a contract implied in fact existed between the parties with the same terms and conditions as the expired written contract between the Corporation and defendant, and that defendant was entitled to full commissions for all 78 engagements at issue. Plaintiff appeals from the judgment entered on Supreme Court's decision.

According to plaintiff, Supreme Court erred in "piercing the corporate veil" to bind plaintiff to the terms and conditions of a contract to which he was not a party. Although Supreme Court's decision is not entirely clear on the issue, we read it as finding a separate and distinct contractual relationship between plaintiff and defendant, implied in fact, which arose out of the parties' continued relationship after the Corporation was dissolved and the written contract expired. A contract implied in fact rests upon the conduct of the parties and not their verbal or written words [Citation] Thus, the theories of express contract and of contract implied in fact are mutually exclusive [Citation] Whether an implied-in-fact contract was formed and, if so, the extent of its terms involve factual issues regarding the intent of the parties and the surrounding circumstances [Citation]. We are of the view that the parties' conduct after the expiration of the written contract, including defendant's continued rendition of services, plaintiff's acceptance of those services and plaintiff's payment of commissions in accordance with the terms of the written contract, clearly establish a contract implied in fact with substantially the same terms and conditions as embodied in the expired written contract between defendant and the Corporation [Citations]. The mere fact that plaintiff was not a party to the written contract does not preclude the formation of a new contract, implied in fact, between plaintiff and defendant, with terms and conditions similar to those contained in the written contract.

The remaining question is whether defendant was entitled to full commissions on all 78 engagements booked by defendant prior to

September 1, 1988 for which plaintiff was ultimately paid, as found by Supreme Court, or whether defendant was limited to the recovery of one half of its regular commission on only those 46 engagements for which a contract had been executed prior to September 1, 1988, as plaintiff contends. The evidence establishes that an engagement was booked by defendant when it arranged the date, time and fee for a performance, informed plaintiff of the engagement and was informed by plaintiff that he accepted the engagement. Plaintiff offered evidence that additional management services prior to the execution of a contract are necessary to assure a meeting of the minds between the presenter and plaintiff on the essential terms of the engagement. Defendant offered evidence that the essential terms of date, time and fee were arranged with the booking and that the execution of a contract was largely a formality, involving ministerial details. That plaintiff actually performed 33 of the 34 engagements booked by defendant for which no contract was executed prior to September 1, 1988 tends to support defendant's position. In any event, the terms of the written contract, which were continued by the parties in their new contract implied in fact formed after the expiration of the written contract, contains no reference to the execution of a formal contract with the presenter. Rather, defendant's commission is dependent upon the scheduling of the engagement during the term of the contract and plaintiff's receipt of payment for the engagement. We conclude, therefore, that Supreme Court correctly found plaintiff liable for commissions on all 78 bookings, regardless of whether a contract had been executed prior to September 1, 1988.

We also agree with Supreme Court that defendant is entitled to the full commission on each of the engagements. As previously noted, defendant earned its commission when the engagement was booked and plaintiff received payment for his performance, and it is undisputed that defendant remained ready, willing and able to provide the additional management services which plaintiff contends were necessary before he actually performed the engagements booked by defendant. That plaintiff elected to have those services performed by another manager does not, in the facts and circumstances revealed by the evidence in the record, preclude defendant from receiving the full amount of its commissions. Supreme Court's judgment should, therefore, be affirmed.

ORDERED that the judgment is affirmed, with costs.

CASE
4-5

Here a court applies the doctrine of promissory estoppel to an entertainer's promise to appear in a musical production although no contract had yet been agreed to.

ELVIN ASSOCIATES v. ARETHA FRANKLIN
United States District Court, S.D. New York. 1990.
No. 85 Civ. 5723 (WK).

WHITMAN KNAPP, District Judge.

* * * In early 1984 Ashton Springer, the principal of plaintiff Elvin Associates, began efforts to mount a Broadway musical production about the life and music of Mahalia Jackson, and wrote to defendant Aretha Franklin seeking her agreement to appear in the title role. Franklin called Springer and expressed her strong interest in the production, and told Springer to contact her agents at the William Morris Agency. Springer spoke with Phil Citron and Katy Rothacker of that agency and in several conversations with the latter discussed the basic financial terms of Franklin's engagement to appear. Several proposals and counter-proposals were exchanged, in each instance relayed by Rothacker to Franklin and then back to Springer. Near the end of February 1984, Rothacker called Springer and informed him that his final proposal was acceptable.

In the interim, Springer had already set about making the necessary arrangements to get the production going. He was in frequent consultation with Franklin concerning artistic and production matters, although he negotiated the financial terms of the agreement strictly through her agents. During a conversation about rehearsal and performance dates, Franklin indicated to Springer that there were no other conflicting engagements on her schedule, stating: "This is what I am doing."

After consulting with Franklin, Springer hired George Faison as director-choreographer. In the second week of March, Springer and Faison flew to Detroit to meet with Franklin to discuss various aspects of the production, including rehearsal and performance dates. Franklin agreed on a tentative schedule that called for rehearsals to begin in April and performances to begin in May.

After returning to New York, Springer began negotiating limited partnership agreements with various investors to finance the "Mahalia" production. He also began calling promoters and theaters in various cities in an effort to reserve dates for performances. During discussions with several promoters he learned for the first time that Franklin had recently cancelled several performances, purportedly due to a newly acquired fear of flying. Springer spoke with Citron at William Morris regarding these incidents, and the latter stated that the cancellations resulted from commitments made by prior agents for Franklin without her approval, and reassured Springer that there was no such problem here. Springer also spoke with Franklin, who reassured him that she wanted to do the show and that she would fly as necessary. Springer offered to make alternative arrangements for transportation to the various performance sites, and to alter the performance schedule to accommodate slower forms of transportation. Franklin told Springer that she was uncomfortable traveling more than 200 miles per day by ground transportation, but strongly assured him that she would overcome her fear of flying.

Springer had also in the interim contacted Jay Kramer, his attorney, about the proposed production and the terms he had discussed with Franklin's representatives. Kramer set up a meeting for March 23, 1984 with Franklin's representatives for the purpose of finalizing the agreement. * * * A final draft of the contract was ready for signature as of June 7, the date that Franklin was scheduled to come to New York to begin rehearsals for the show.

Springer had in the intervening weeks made all of the arrangements necessary for rehearsals to begin. He had hired set, lighting and costume designers, stage and technical crew, and had reserved dance studios. Springer was in frequent communication with Franklin during this period, as were Faison and other members of the production staff, concerning such varied matters as the compositions to be performed, the costumes she would wear, and the hiring of her own regular backup singers to be in the chorus. At one point, Franklin sang one of the production songs to Springer over the telephone. At some point during this period, Faison made final determinations as to the compositions to be performed and as to the cast and chorus.

As planned, rehearsals actually began on June 4 without Franklin, and continued for several days. Franklin did not arrive in New York on June 7 and, indeed, never came to New York for the rehearsals. Kramer immediately sought an explanation from Franklin's representatives and was informed that she would not fly. Springer paid the cast through the end of that week, but then suspended the production. He attempted to secure some other well-known performer to fill the title role, but none of the performers whom he contacted would agree to step into the role at that juncture.

On July 18, after having positive discussions with Les Matthews, a Texas financier who purported to be interested in backing the production, Springer wrote to Franklin with a proposal to revive it, whereby rehearsals and opening performances would take place in Detroit, with Franklin covering the excess expense caused by such an arrangement. The terms of Franklin's profit-sharing would be altered to account for the losses and additional costs caused by the suspended production. In August Franklin agreed to sign a draft agreement (doing so only on behalf of Crown Productions) so that Springer could regain some of his lost credibility with potential investors. Franklin's attorney held the signed draft in escrow, release from which was expressly conditioned on Springer's finalization of a performance schedule.

A final performance schedule was never arranged. One of the difficulties Springer encountered was that, due to the collapse of the earlier production, theaters and concert halls were now requiring substantial deposits to reserve particular dates. Springer lacked the capital to make those deposits. Matthews failed to appear for the scheduled closing of the investment agreement in early September, and Springer was unable to

obtain any other financing for the production. He ultimately abandoned this second attempt at mounting the "Mahalia" production.

This lawsuit ensued, with Springer (suing in the name of Elvin Associates) alleging breach of the original agreement to appear in "Mahalia," and Franklin counter-claiming for breach of the second agreement concerning the proposed Detroit-based production. In his pre-trial memorandum, Springer asserted an alternative right to recover on a theory of promissory estoppel.

DISCUSSION

* * * Plaintiff has asserted * * * a right to recover on a theory of promissory estoppel. The elements of a claim for promissory estoppel are: "[A] clear and unambiguous promise; a reasonable and foreseeable reliance by the party to whom the promise is made; and an injury sustained by the party asserting the estoppel by reason of his reliance." Reprosystem, supra, at 264 (quoting Ripple's of Clearview v. Le Havre Associates 88 A.D.2d 120, 452 N.Y.S.2d 447, 449). The " 'circumstances [must be] such as to render it unconscionable to deny' the promise upon which plaintiff has relied." Philo Smith & Co., Inc. v. USLIFE Corporation (2nd Cir.1977) 554 F.2d 34, 36 (quoting Williston on Contracts § 533A, at 801 (3d ed. 1960) (emphasis the court's)).

It is difficult to imagine a more fitting case for applying the above-described doctrine. Although for her own business purposes Franklin insisted that the formal contract be with the corporate entity through which her services were to be "furnished," in the real world the agreement was with her, and we find that she had unequivocally and intentionally committed herself to appear in the production long before day on which it was intended that the finalized agreement with her corporation would be signed.

First, it is clear from the testimony of all of the witnesses that Franklin was enthusiastic about appearing in the production and that at all times during the relevant period gave it the highest professional priority. She early on stated to Springer: "This is what I am doing." Combined with her oral agreement, through her agents, to the basic financial terms of her engagement, her continued expression of this enthusiasm to Springer more than amply afforded Springer a reasonable basis for beginning to make the various arrangements and expenditures necessary to bring the production to fruition.

Second, Franklin could not possibly have assumed that Springer could have performed his obligations to her-which, among other things, included arranging a complicated schedule of performances to commence shortly after her arrival in New York-without committing himself to and actually spending considerable sums prior to her affixing her signature to the contract on the date of such arrival. Throughout the time that he was making those commitments and advancing the necessary sums, she accepted his performance without any disclaimer of her prior promises to him. Indeed, she actively participated in many aspects of the necessary arrangements.

Third, Franklin's expression to Springer of her fear of flying did not, as she has contended, make her promise conditional or coat it with a patina of ambiguity that should have alerted Springer to suspend his efforts to mount the production. Although Franklin rejected Springer's offer to make alternative ground transportation arrangements, her primary reason for doing so was that she was determined to overcome her fear of flying, and it was reasonable for Springer to rely on her reassurances that she would be able to fly. Moreover, it was also entirely reasonable for him to assume that if she could not overcome her fear she would travel to New York by other means, even if it meant spreading the trip over several days. In short, Franklin's fear of flying provides no basis whatsoever for avoiding liability for failing to fulfill her promise, reiterated on several occasions, to appear in "Mahalia." If she could not bring herself to fly, she should have traveled by way of ground transportation. It has not been established that she was otherwise unable to come to New York to meet her obligations.

We conclude that under the circumstances as we have outlined them it would be unconscionable not to compensate Springer for the losses he incurred through his entirely justified reliance on Franklin's oral promises. A determination of the exact amount to be awarded has been reserved for a later trial on damages. * * *

QUESTIONS

1. Distinguish between contracts that are covered by the Uniform Commercial Code and those covered by common law.
2. List the requirements of a contract.
3. Distinguish among (a) express and implied contracts, (b) unilateral and bilateral contracts, (c) valid, void, voidable, and unenforceable contracts, (d) executed and executory contracts, and (e) formal and informal contracts.
4. Explain the doctrine of promissory estoppel.
5. Identify the three elements of an enforceable quasi contract and explain how it differs from a contract.

PROBLEMS

1. Owen telephones an order to Hillary's store for certain goods, which Hillary delivers to Owen. Neither party says anything about the price or payment terms. What are the legal obligations of Owen and Hillary?

2. Minth is the owner of the Hiawatha Supper Club, which he leased during 1972 and 1973 to Piekarski. During the period of the lease, Piekarski contracted with Puttkammer for the resurfacing of the access and service areas of the supper club. The work, including labor and materials, had a reasonable value of $2,540, but Puttkammer was never paid because Piekarski went bankrupt. Puttkammer brought an action against Minth to recover the amount owed to him by Piekarski. Will Puttkammer prevail? Explain.

3. Jonathan writes to Willa, stating "I'll pay you $150 if you reseed my lawn." Willa reseeds Jonathan's lawn as requested. Has a contract been formed? If so, what kind?

4. Calvin uses fraud to induce Maria to promise to pay money in return for goods he has delivered to her. Has a contract been formed? If so, what kind? What are the rights of Calvin and Maria?

5. Anna is about to buy a house on a hill. Prior to the purchase she obtains a promise from Betty, the owner of the adjacent property, that Betty will not build any structure that would block Anna's view. In reliance on this promise Anna buys the house. Is Betty's promise binding? Why or why not?

6. Mary Dobos was admitted to Boca Raton Community Hospital in serious condition with an abdominal aneurysm. The hospital called upon Nursing Care Services, Inc., to provide around-the-clock nursing services for Mrs. Dobos. She received two weeks of in-hospital care, forty-eight hours of postrelease care, and two weeks of at-home care. The total bill was $3,723.90. Mrs. Dobos refused to pay, and Nursing Care Services, Inc., brought an action to recover. Mrs. Dobos maintained that she was not obligated to render payment in that she never signed a written contract, nor did she orally agree to be liable for the services. The necessity for the services, reasonableness of the fee, and competency of the nurses were undisputed. After Mrs. Dobos admitted that she or her daughter authorized the forty-eight hours of postrelease care, the trial court ordered compensation of $248 for that period. It did not allow payment of the balance, and Nursing Care Services, Inc., appealed. Decision?

7. St. Charles Drilling Co. contracted with Osterholt to install a well and water system that would produce a specified quantity of water. The water system failed to meet its warranted capacity, and Osterholt sued for breach of contract. Does the UCC apply to this contract?

8. On March 4, 1970, Helvey brought suit against the Wabash County REMC (REMC) for breach of implied and express warranties. He alleged that REMC furnished electricity in excess of 135 volts to Helvey's home, damaging his 110-volt household appliances. This incident occurred on January 10, 1966. In defense, REMC pleads that the Uniform Commercial Code's Article 2 statute of limitations of four years has passed, thereby barring Helvey's suit. Helvey argues that providing electrical energy is not a transaction in goods under the UCC but rather a furnishing of services that would make applicable the general contract six-year statute of limitations. Is the contract governed by the UCC? Why?

9. In April 1980 Jack Duran, president of Colorado Carpet

Installation, Inc., began negotiations with Fred and Zuma Palermo for the sale and installation of carpeting, carpet padding, tile, and vinyl floor covering in their home. Duran drew up a written proposal that referred to Colorado Carpet as "the seller" and to the Palermos as "the customer." The proposal listed the quantity, unit cost, and total price of each item to be installed. The total price of the job was $4,777.75. Although labor was expressly included in this figure, Duran estimated the total labor cost at $926. Mrs. Palermo orally accepted Duran's written proposal soon after he submitted it to her. After Colorado Carpet delivered the tile to the Palermo home, however, Mrs. Palermo had a disagreement with Colorado Carpet's tile man and arranged for another contractor to perform the job. Colorado Carpet brought an action against the Palermos for breach of contract. Does the UCC apply to this contract?

10. On November 1, 1986, the Kansas City Post Office Employees Credit Union merged into the Kansas City Telephone Employees Credit Union to form the Communications Credit Union (Credit Union). Systems Design and Management Information (SDMI) develops computer software programs for credit unions, using Burroughs (now Unisys) hardware. SDMI and Burroughs together offered to sell to Credit Union both a software package, called the Generic System, and Burroughs hardware. In November 1986, a demonstration of the software was held at SDMI's offices, and the Credit Union agreed to purchase the Generic System software. This agreement was oral. After Credit Union was converted to the SDMI Generic System, major problems with the system immediately became apparent. SDMI filed suit against Credit Union to recover the outstanding contract price for the software. Credit Union counterclaimed for damages based upon breach of contract and negligent and fraudulent misrepresentation. Does the UCC apply to this contract?

11. Richardson hired J. C. Flood Company, a plumbing contractor, to correct a stoppage in the sewer line of her house. The plumbing company's "snake" device, used to clear the line leading to the main sewer, became caught in the underground line. To release it, the company excavated a portion of the sewer line in Richardson's backyard. In the process, the company discovered numerous leaks in a rusty, defective water pipe that ran parallel with the sewer line. To meet public regulations, the water pipe, of a type no longer approved for such service, had to be replaced either then or later, when the yard would have to be redug for such purpose. The plumbing company proceeded to repair the water pipe. Though Richardson inspected the company's work daily and did not express any objection to the extra work involved in replacing the water pipe, she refused to pay any part of the total bill after the company completed the entire operation. J. C. Flood Company then sued Richardson for the costs of labor and material it had furnished. Richardson argued that she only requested correction of a sewer obstruction and had never agreed to the replacement of the water pipe. Is Richardson correct in her assertion? Explain.

12. Insul-Mark is the marketing arm of Kor-It Sales, Inc. Kor-It manufactures roofing fasteners, and Insul-Mark distributes them nationwide. In late 1985, Kor-It contracted with Modern Materials, Inc., to have large volumes of screws coated with a rust-proofing agent. The contract specified that the coated screws must pass a standard industry test and that Kor-It would pay according to the pound and length of the screws coated. Kor-It had received numerous complaints from customers that the coated screws were rusting, but Modern Materials unsuccessfully attempted to remedy the problem. Kor-It terminated its relationship with Modern Materials and brought suit for the deficient coating. Modern Materials counterclaimed for the labor and materials it had furnished to Kor-It. The trial court held that the contract (1) was for performance of a service, (2) not governed by the UCC, (3) governed by the common law of contracts, and (4) therefore, barred by a two-year statute of limitations. Insul-Mark appealed. Decision?

13. In March 1987, William Tackaberry, a real estate agent for Weichert Co. Realtors, informed Thomas Ryan, a local developer, that he knew of property Ryan might be interested in purchasing. Ryan indicated he was interested in knowing more about the property. Tackaberry disclosed the property's identity and the seller's proposed price. Tackaberry also stated that the purchaser would have to pay Weichert a 10 percent commission. Tackaberry met with the property owner and gathered information concerning the property's current leases, income, expenses, and development plans. Tackaberry also collected tax and zoning documents relevant to the property. In a face-to-face meeting on April 4, Tackaberry gave Ryan the data he had gathered and presented Ryan with a letter calling for a 10 percent finder's fee to be paid to Weichert by Ryan upon "successfully completing and closing of title." Tackaberry arranged a meeting, held three days later, where Ryan contracted with the owner to buy the land. Ryan refused, however, to pay the 10 percent finder's fee to Weichert. Weichert sues Ryan for the finder's fee. To what, if anything, is Weichert entitled to recover? Explain.

14. Max E. Pass, Jr. and his wife, Martha N. Pass, departed in an aircraft owned and operated by Mr. Pass from Plant City, Florida, bound for Clarksville, Tennessee. Somewhere over Alabama the couple encountered turbulence, and Mr. Pass lost control of the aircraft. The plane crashed killing both Mr. and Mrs. Pass. Approximately four and a half months prior to the flight in which he was killed, Mr. Pass had taken his airplane to Shelby Aviation, an aircraft service company, for inspection and service. In servicing the aircraft, Shelby Aviation replaced both rear wing attach point brackets on the plane. Three and one half years after the crash, Max E. Pass, Sr., father of Mr. Pass and administrator of his estate, and Shirley Williams, mother of Mrs. Pass and administratrix of her estate, filed suit against Shelby Aviation. The lawsuit alleged that the rear wing attach point brackets sold and installed by Shelby Aviation were defective because they lacked the bolts necessary to secure them properly to the airplane. The plaintiffs asserted claims against the defendant for breach of express and implied warranties under Article 2 of the Uniform Commercial Code ("UCC"), which governs the sale of goods. Shelby Aviation contended that the transaction with Mr. Pass had been primarily for the sale of services, rather than of goods, and that consequently Article 2 of the UCC did not cover the transaction. Does the UCC apply to this transaction? Explain.

http: **Internet Exercise** Find several samples of contracts.

Contract Remedies

When one party to a contract breaches the contract by failing to perform his contractual duties, the law provides a remedy for the injured party. Although the primary objective of contract remedies is to compensate the injured party for the loss resulting from the breach, it is impossible for any remedy to equal the promised performance. To an injured party a court can give as relief what it regards as an equivalent of the promised performance.

This chapter will examine the most common judicial remedies available for breach of contract: (1) monetary damages, (2) the equitable remedies of specific performance and injunction, and (3) restitution. Sales of goods are governed by Article 2 of the Uniform Commercial Code, which provides specialized remedies.

INTERESTS PROTECTED BY CONTRACT REMEDIES

Contract remedies are available to protect one or more of the following interests of the injured party:

1. the **expectation interest**, which is his interest in having the benefit of his bargain by being put in a position as good as the one he would have occupied had the contract been performed;
2. the **reliance interest**, which is his interest in being reimbursed for loss caused by reliance on the contract by being put in a position as good as the one he would have been in had the contract not been made; or
3. the **restitution interest**, which is his interest in having restored to him any benefit that he has conferred on the other party. Restatement, Section 344.

The expectation interest is protected by the contract remedies of compensatory damages, specific performance, and injunction. The reliance interest is protected by the contractual remedy of reliance damages, while the restitution interest is protected by the contractual remedy of restitution.

MONETARY DAMAGES

A judgment awarding monetary damages is the most frequently granted judicial remedy for breach of contract. Monetary damages, however, will be awarded only for losses that are foreseeable, established with reasonable certainty, and unavoidable. The equitable remedies discussed in this chapter are discretionary and are available only if monetary damages are inadequate.

Compensatory Damages

The right to recover compensatory money damages for breach of contract is always available to the injured party. Restatement, Section 346. The purpose in allowing **compensatory damages** is to place the injured party in a position as good as the one she would have occupied had the other party performed under the contract. This involves compensating the injured party for the dollar value of the benefits she would have received had the contract been performed less any savings she experienced by not having to perform her own obligations under the contract. Because these damages are intended to protect the injured party's expectation interest, or the value he expected to derive from the contract, the amount of compensatory damages is generally computed as follows:

> **Loss of value**
> + **Incidental damages**
> + **Consequential damages**
> − **Loss or cost avoided by injured party**
> **Compensatory damages**

Loss of Value In general, loss of value is the *difference between the value of the promised performance* of the breaching party *and the value of the actual performance* rendered by the breaching party.

> **Value of promised performance**
> − **Value of actual performance**
> **Loss of value**

If the breaching party renders no performance at all, then the loss of value is the value of the promised performance. If defective or partial performance is rendered, the loss of value is the difference between the value that the full performance would have had and the value of the performance actually rendered. Thus, where there has been a breach of warranty, the injured party may recover the difference between the value the goods would have had, if they had been as warranted, and the value of the goods in the condition in which the buyer received them. To illustrate, Victor sells an automobile to Joan and expressly warrants that it will get forty-five miles per gallon, but the automobile gets only twenty miles per gallon. The automobile would have been worth $8,000 had it been as warranted, but it is worth only $6,000 as delivered. Joan would recover $2,000 in damages for loss of value.

In addition to loss of value, the injured party may also recover for all other losses actually suffered, subject to the limitation of foreseeability discussed below. These damages include incidental and consequential damages.

Incidental Damages **Incidental damages** are damages that arise directly out of the breach, such as costs incurred to acquire the nondelivered performance from some other source. For example, Agnes employs Benton for nine months for $20,000 to supervise construction of a factory, but fires him without cause after three weeks. Benton, who spends $350 in reasonable fees attempting to find comparable employment, may recover $350 in incidental damages, in addition to any other actual loss he may suffer.

Consequential Damages **Consequential damages** include lost profits and injury to person or property resulting from defective performance. Thus, if Tracy leases to Sean a defective machine that causes him $4,000 in property damage and $12,000 in personal injuries, Sean may recover, in addition to damages for loss of value and incidental damages, $16,000 as consequential damages.

Cost Avoided The recovery by the injured party, however, is reduced by any cost or loss she has avoided by not having to perform. For example, Clinton agrees to build a hotel for Debra for $1,250,000 by September 1. Clinton breaches by not completing construction until October 1. As a consequence, Debra loses revenues for one month in the amount of $10,000 but saves operating expenses of $6,000. She therefore may recover damages for $4,000. Similarly, in a contract in which the injured party has not fully performed, the injured party's recovery is reduced by the value to him of the performance he promised but did not render. For example, Clinton agrees to convey land to Debra in return for Debra's promise to work for Clinton for two years, but she repudiates the contract before Clinton has conveyed the land. Clinton's recovery for loss from Debra is reduced by the value to Clinton of the land.

Nominal Damages

An action to recover damages for breach of contract may be maintained even though the plaintiff has not sustained or cannot prove any injury or loss resulting from the breach. Restatement, Section 346. In such a case he will be permitted to recover **nominal damages**—a small sum fixed without regard to the amount of loss. For example, Edward contracts to sell and deliver goods to Florence for $1,000. Edward refuses to deliver the goods as agreed, and so breaks the contract. Florence, however, is able to purchase goods of the same kind and quality elsewhere for $1,000 without incurring any incidental damages. As a result, although Edward has violated Florence's rights under the contract, Florence has suffered no actual loss. Consequently, if Florence, as she may, should sue Edward for breach of contract, she would recover a judgment for nominal damages only. Nominal damages are also available where loss is actually sustained but cannot be proved with reasonable certainty.

Reliance Damages

As an alternative to compensatory damages, the injured party may seek reimbursement for foreseeable loss caused by his reliance upon the contract. The purpose of **reliance damages** is to place the injured party in a position as good as the one he would have held, had the contract *not been made*. Reliance damages include expenses incurred in preparing to perform, in actually performing, or in forgoing opportunities to enter into other contracts. An injured party may prefer damages for reliance to compensatory damages when he is unable to establish his lost profits with reasonable certainty. For example, Donald agrees to sell his retail store to Gary, who spends $50,000 acquiring inventory and fixtures. Donald then repudiates the contract, and Gary sells the inventory and fixtures for $35,000. Neither party can establish with reasonable certainty what profit Gary would have made; Gary, therefore, may recover from Donald as damages the loss of $15,000 he sustained on the sale of the inventory and fixtures plus any other costs he incurred in entering into the contract. An injured party may choose reliance damages instead of compensatory damages when the contract is itself unprofitable. In such a case, however, if the breaching party can prove with reasonable certainty the amount of the loss, it will be subtracted from the injured party's reliance damages.

Damages for Misrepresentation

The basic remedy for misrepresentation is rescission (avoidance) of the contract, though when appropriate, the courts also will require restitution. At common law, an alternative remedy to rescission is a suit for damages. The Code liberalizes the common law by not restricting a defrauded party to an election of remedies; that is, the injured party may both rescind the contract by restoring the other party to the *status quo* and recover damages or obtain any other remedy available under the Code. UCC Section 2–721. In most states, the measure of damages for misrepresentation depends upon whether the misrepresentation was fraudulent or nonfraudulent.

Fraud   A party induced by fraud to enter into a contract may recover general damages in a tort action. A minority of states allows the injured party to recover, under the "**out-of-pocket**" rule, general damages equal to the difference between the value of what she has received and the value of what she has given for it. The great majority of states, however, under the "**benefit-of-the-bargain**" rule, permits the intentionally defrauded party to recover general damages that are equal to the difference between the value of what she has received and the value of the fraudulent party's performance as represented. The Restatement of Torts provides the fraudulently injured party with the option of either out-of-pocket or benefit-of-the-bargain damages. Section 549. To illustrate, Emily intentionally misrepresents the capabilities of a printing press and thereby induces Melissa to purchase the machine for $20,000. The value of the press as delivered is $14,000, but if the machine had performed as represented, it would be worth $24,000. Under the out-of-pocket rule, Melissa would recover $6,000, whereas under the benefit-of-the-bargain rule, she would recover $10,000.

In addition to a recovery of general damages under one of the measures just discussed, consequential damages may be recovered to the extent they are proved with reasonable certainty and to the extent they do not duplicate general damages. Moreover, where the fraud is gross, oppressive, or aggravated, punitive damages are permitted.

◈ SEE CASE 5-1

Nonfraudulent Misrepresentation   Where the misrepresentation is negligent, the deceived party may recover general damages—under the out-of-pocket measure—and consequential damages. Restatement of Torts, Section 552B. Some states, however, permit the recovery of general damages under the benefit-of-the-bargain measure for negligent misrepresentation. Where the misrepresentation is neither fraudulent nor negligent, however, the Restatement limits damages to the out-of-pocket measure. Section 552C.

Punitive Damages

Punitive damages are monetary damages in addition to compensatory damages awarded to a plaintiff in certain situations involving willful, wanton, or malicious conduct. Their purpose is to punish the defendant and thus discourage him and others from similar wrongful conduct. The purpose of allowing contract damages, on the other hand, is to compensate the plaintiff for the loss that he has sustained because of the defendant's breach of contract. Accordingly, the Restatement provides that punitive damages are *not* recoverable for a breach of contract unless the conduct constituting the breach is also a tort for which the plaintiff may recover punitive damages. Restatement, Section 355.

◈ SEE CASE 5-1

Liquidated Damages

A contract may contain a **liquidated damages** provision by which the parties agree in advance to the damages to be paid in event of a breach. Such a provision will be enforced if it amounts to a reasonable forecast of the loss that may or does result from the breach. If, however, the sum agreed upon as liquidated damages bears no reasonable relationship to the amount of probable loss that may or does result from breach, it is unenforceable as a penalty. (A penalty is a contractual provision designed to deter a party from breaching her contract and to punish her for doing so.) Restatement, Section 356, Comment a states,

> The parties to a contract may effectively provide in advance the damages that are to be payable in the event of breach as long as the provision does not disregard the principle of compensation. The enforcement of such provisions for liquidated damages saves the time of courts, juries, parties and witnesses and reduces the expense of litigation. This is especially important if the amount in controversy is small. However, the parties to a contract are not free to provide a penalty for its breach. The central objective behind the system of contract remedies is compensatory, not punitive.

By examining the substance of the provision, the nature of the contract, and the extent of probable harm to the promisee that a breach may reasonably be expected to cause, the courts will determine whether the agreed amount is proper as liquidated damages or unenforceable as a penalty. If a liquidated damage provision is not enforceable, the injured party nevertheless is entitled to the ordinary remedies for breach of contract.

To illustrate, Reliable Construction Company contracts with Equerry to build a grandstand at Equerry's racecourse at a cost of $1,330,000, to have it completed by a certain date, and to pay Equerry, as liquidated damages, $1,000 per day for every day's delay beyond that date in completing the grandstand. The stipulated sum for delay is liquidated damages and not a penalty because the amount is reasonable. If, instead, the sum stipulated had been $10,000 per day, it would obviously have been unreasonable and therefore a penalty. Provisions for liquidated damages are sometimes found in contracts for the sale of a business, in which the seller agrees not to reenter the same business within a reasonable geographic area and time period. Actual damages resulting from the seller's breach of his agreement would ordinarily be difficult to ascertain, and the sum stipulated, if reasonable, would be enforced as liquidated damages.

❧ SEE CASE 5-2

Limitations on Damages

To accomplish the basic purposes of contract remedies, the law imposes the limitations of foreseeability, certainty, and mitigation upon monetary damages. These limitations are intended to ensure that damages can be taken into account at the time of contracting, that damages are compensatory and not speculative, and that damages do not include loss that could have been avoided by reasonable efforts.

Foreseeability of Damages   A contracting party is generally expected to consider foreseeable risks when entering into the contract. Therefore, compensatory or reliance damages are recoverable only for loss that the party in breach had reason to foresee as a *probable* result of such breach when the contract was made; conversely, the breaching party is not liable for loss that was not foreseeable when the parties entered into the contract. The test of foreseeability is *objective*, based upon what the breaching party had reason to foresee. Loss may be deemed foreseeable as a probable result of a breach by following from the breach (a) in the ordinary course of events or (b) as a result of special circumstances, beyond the ordinary course of events, which the party in breach had reason to know. Restatement, Section 351(2). Moreover, "[a] court may limit damages for foreseeable loss by excluding recovery for loss of profits, by allowing recovery only for loss incurred in reliance, or otherwise if it concludes that in the circum-

stances justice so requires in order to avoid disproportionate compensation." Restatement, Section 351(3).

The leading case on the subject of foreseeability of damages is *Hadley v. Baxendale*, decided in England in 1854. In this case, the plaintiffs operated a flour mill at Gloucester. Their mill was compelled to cease operating because of a broken crankshaft attached to the steam engine that furnished power to the mill. It was necessary to send the broken shaft to a foundry located at Greenwich so that a new shaft could be made. The plaintiffs delivered the broken shaft to the defendants, who were common carriers, for immediate transportation from Gloucester to Greenwich, but did not inform the defendants that operation of the mill had ceased because of the nonfunctioning crankshaft. The defendants received the shaft, collected the freight charges in advance, and promised to deliver the shaft for repairs the following day. The defendants, however, did not make delivery as promised; as a result, the mill did not resume operations for several days, causing the plaintiffs to lose profitable sales. The defendants contended that the loss of profits was too remote, and therefore unforeseeable, to be recoverable. Nonetheless, the jury, in awarding damages to the plaintiffs, was permitted to take into consideration the loss of these profits. The appellate court reversed the decision and ordered a new trial on the ground that the plaintiffs had never communicated to the defendants the special circumstances that caused the loss of profits, namely, the continued stoppage of the mill while awaiting the return of the repaired crankshaft. A common carrier, the court reasoned, would not reasonably have foreseen that the plaintiffs' mill would be shut down as a result of delay in transporting the broken crankshaft.

On the other hand, if the defendants in *Hadley v. Baxendale* had been informed that the shaft was necessary for the operation of the mill, or otherwise had reason to know this fact, they would be liable for the plaintiffs' loss of profit during that period of the shutdown caused by their delay. Under these circumstances, the loss would be the "foreseeable" and "natural" result of the breach.

Should a plaintiff's expected profit be extraordinarily large, the general rule is that the breaching party will be liable for such special loss only if he had reason to know of it. In any event, the plaintiff may recover for any ordinary loss resulting from the breach. Thus, if Madeline breaches a contract with Jane, causing Jane, due to special circumstances, $10,000 in damages where ordinarily such a breach would result in only $6,000 in damages, Madeline would be liable to Jane for $6,000, not $10,000, provided that Madeline was unaware of the special circumstances causing Jane the unusually large loss.

Certainty of Damages   Damages are not recoverable for loss beyond an amount that the injured party can establish with reasonable certainty. Restatement, Section 352. If the injured party cannot prove a particular element of her loss with reasonable certainty, she nevertheless will be entitled to recover the portion of her loss that she can prove with reasonable certainty. The certainty requirement creates the greatest challenge for plaintiffs seeking to recover consequential damages for lost profits on related transactions. Those attempting to prove lost profits caused by breach of a contract to produce a sporting event or to publish a new book experience similar difficulties.

◆ SEE CASE 5-3

Mitigation of Damages Under the doctrine of mitigation of damages, the injured party may not recover damages for loss that he could have avoided with reasonable effort and without undue risk, burden, or humiliation. Restatement, Section 350. Thus, if James is under a contract to manufacture goods for Kathy, and Kathy repudiates the contract after James has commenced performance, James will not be allowed to recover for losses he sustains by continuing to manufacture the goods, if to do so would increase the amount of damages. The amount of loss that James could reasonably have avoided is deducted from the amount that would otherwise be recoverable as damages. On the other hand, if the goods were almost completed when Kathy repudiated the contract, completing the goods might mitigate the damages, because the finished goods may be resalable whereas the unfinished goods may not. UCC Section 2–704(2).

Similarly, if Harvey contracts to work for Olivia for one year for a weekly salary and is wrongfully discharged by Olivia after two months, Harvey must use reasonable efforts to mitigate his damages by seeking other employment. If, after such efforts, he cannot obtain other employment of the same general character, he is entitled to recover full pay for the contract period that he is unemployed. He is not obliged to accept a radically different type of employment or to accept work at a distant place. For example, a person employed as a schoolteacher or accountant who is wrongfully discharged is not obliged, in order to mitigate damages, to accept available employment as a chauffeur or truck driver. On the other hand, if Harvey made no attempt to find substitute employment, his damages would be reduced by the wages he reasonably could have earned had he accepted available comparable employment.

REMEDIES IN EQUITY

At times, damages based on the expectation interest, reliance interest, or restitution interest will not adequately compensate an injured party. In these cases, equitable relief in the form of specific performance or an injunction may be available to protect the injured party's interest.

The remedies of specific performance and an injunction are not a matter of right but rest in the discretion of the court.

Consequently, they will not be granted where:

1. there is an adequate remedy at law;
2. it is impossible to enforce them, as where the seller has already conveyed the subject matter of the contract to an innocent third person;
3. the terms of the contract are unfair;
4. the consideration is grossly inadequate;
5. the contract is tainted with fraud, duress, undue influence, mistake, or unfair practices;
6. the terms of the contract are not sufficiently certain; or
7. the relief would cause unreasonable hardship.

A court may grant specific performance or an injunction despite a provision for liquidated damages. Restatement, Section 361. Moreover, a court will grant specific performance or an injunction even though a term of the contract prohibits equitable relief, if denying such relief would cause unreasonable hardship to the injured party. Restatement, Section 364(2).

Another equitable remedy is **reformation**, a process whereby the court "rewrites" or "corrects" a written contract to make it conform to the true agreement of the parties. The purpose of reformation is not to make a new contract for the parties but rather to express adequately the contract they have made for themselves. The remedy of reformation is granted when the parties agree on a contract but write it in a way that inaccurately reflects their actual agreement. For example, Acme Insurance Co. and Bell agree that for good consideration Acme will issue an annuity paying $500 per month. Through a clerical error, the annuity policy is issued for $50 per month. A court of equity, upon satisfactory proof of the mistake, will reform the policy to provide for the correct amount—$500 per month. In addition, as discussed in Chapter 14, where a covenant not to compete is unreasonable, some courts will reform the agreement to make it reasonable and enforceable.

Specific Performance

Specific performance is an equitable remedy that compels the defaulting party to perform her contractual obligations. Ordinarily, where a seller breaches her contract for the sale of personal property, the buyer has a sufficient remedy at law. If, however, the **personal property** contracted for is rare or unique, this remedy is inadequate. Examples of such property would include a famous painting or statue, an original manuscript or a rare edition of a book, a patent, a copyright, shares of stock in a closely held corporation, or an heirloom. Articles of this kind cannot be purchased elsewhere. Accordingly, should the seller breach her contract for the sale of any such article, money damages will not adequately compensate the buyer. Consequently, in these instances, the buyer may avail herself of the equitable remedy of specific performance.

Although courts of equity will grant specific performance in connection with contracts for the sale of personal property only in exceptional circumstances, they will always grant it in cases involving breach of contract for the sale of **real property**. The reason for this is that every parcel of land is considered unique. Consequently, if the seller refuses to convey title to the real estate contracted for, the buyer may seek the aid of a court of equity to compel the seller to convey the title. Most courts of equity will likewise compel the buyer in a real estate contract to perform at the suit of the seller.

Courts of equity will not grant specific performance of contracts for personal services. In the first place, enforcing such a decree may be difficult if not impossible. In the second place, it is against the policy of the courts to force one person to work for or to serve another against his will, even though the person has contracted to do so, in that such enforcement would closely resemble involuntary servitude. For example, if Carmen, an accomplished concert pianist, agrees to appear at a certain time and place to play a specified program for Rudolf, a court would not issue a decree of specific performance upon her refusal to appear.

❖ See Case 5-4

Injunctions

The **injunction**, as used as a contract remedy, is a formal court order enjoining (commanding) a person to refrain from doing a specific act or to cease engaging in specified conduct. A court of equity, at its discretion, may grant an injunction against breach of a contractual duty where damages for a breach would be inadequate. For example, Clint enters into a written contract to give Janice the right of first refusal on a tract of land he owns. Clint, however, subsequently offers the land to Blake without first offering it to Janice. A court of equity may properly enjoin Clint from selling the land to Blake. Similarly, valid covenants not to compete may be enforced by an injunction.

An employee's promise of exclusive personal services may be enforced by an injunction against serving another employer as long as the probable result will not be to deprive the employee of other reasonable means of making a living. Restatement, Section 367. Suppose, for example, that Allan makes a contract with Marlene, a famous singer, under which Marlene agrees to sing at Allan's theater on certain dates for an agreed fee. Before the date of the first performance, Marlene makes a contract with Craig to sing for Craig at his theater on the same dates. Although, as already discussed, Allan cannot secure specific performance of his contract by Marlene, a court of equity will, on suit by Allan against Marlene, issue an injunction against her, ordering her not to sing for Craig.

Where the services contracted for are not unusual or extraordinary, the injured party cannot obtain injunctive relief. His only remedy is an action at law for damages.

❖ See Case 5-5

RESTITUTION

One remedy that may be available to a party to a contract is restitution. **Restitution** is the act of returning to the aggrieved party the consideration, or its value, which he gave to the other party. The purpose of restitution is to restore the injured party to the position he occupied before the contract was made. Therefore, the party seeking restitution must return what he has received from the other party.

Restitution is available in several contractual situations: (1) as an alternative remedy for a party injured by breach; (2) for a party in default; (3) for a party who may not enforce a contract because of the statute of frauds; and (4) for a party wishing to rescind (avoid) a voidable contract.

Party Injured by Breach

A party is entitled to restitution if the other party totally breaches the contract by nonperformance or repudiation. Restatement, Section 373. For example, Benedict agrees to sell land to Beatrice for $60,000. After Beatrice makes a partial payment of $15,000, Benedict wrongfully refuses to transfer title. As an alternative to damages or specific performance, Beatrice may recover the $15,000 in restitution.

Party in Default

Where a party, after having partly performed, commits a breach by nonperformance or repudiation that discharges the other party's duty to perform, the party in default is entitled to restitution for any benefit she has conferred in excess of the loss she has caused by her breach. Restatement, Section 374. For example, Nathan agrees to sell land to Lilly for $60,000, and Lilly makes a partial payment of $15,000. Lilly then repudiates the contract. Nathan sells the land to Murray in good faith for $55,000. Lilly may recover from Nathan in restitution the part payment of the $15,000 *less* the $5,000 damages Nathan sustained because of Lilly's breach, which equals $10,000.

Statute of Frauds

A party to a contract that is unenforceable because of the statute of frauds may, nonetheless, have acted in reliance upon the contract. In such a case, that party may recover in restitution the benefits she conferred upon the other in relying upon the unenforceable contract. In most states, the party seeking restitution must not be in default. Thus, if Wilton makes an oral contract to furnish services to Rochelle that are not to be performed within a year, and Rochelle discharges Wilton after three months, Wilton may recover as restitution the value of the services he rendered during the three months.

Voidable Contracts

A party who has rescinded or avoided a contract for lack of capacity, duress, undue influence, fraud in the inducement, nonfraudulent misrepresentation, or mistake is entitled to restitution for any benefit he has conferred upon the other party. Restatement, Section 376. For example, Samuel fraudulently induces Edith to sell land for $60,000. Samuel pays the purchase price, and Edith conveys the land. Discovering the fraud, Edith may disaffirm the contract and recover the land as restitution. Generally, the party seeking restitution must return any benefit that he has received under the agreement; however, as discussed in Chapter 9 (which deals with contractual capacity), this is not always the case.

◆ SEE FIGURE 5-1 **Contract Remedies**

LIMITATIONS ON REMEDIES

Election of Remedies

If a party injured by a breach of contract has more than one remedy available to him, his manifesting a choice of one of them, such as bringing suit, does not prevent him from seeking another remedy unless the remedies are inconsistent and the other party materially changes his position in reliance on the manifestation. Restatement, Section 378. For example, a party who seeks specific performance, an injunction, or restitution may be entitled to incidental damages for delay in performance.

Damages for *total breach*, however, are inconsistent with the remedies of specific performance, injunction, and restitution. Likewise, the remedy of specific performance or an injunction is inconsistent with that of restitution.

With respect to contracts for the sale of goods, the Code rejects any doctrine of election of remedies. Thus, the remedies it provides are essentially cumulative, including all of the available remedies for breach. Whether one remedy precludes another depends on the facts of the individual case. UCC Section 2–703, Comment 1.

◆ SEE CASE 5-1

Loss of Power of Avoidance

A party with a power of avoidance for lack of capacity, duress, undue influence, fraud, misrepresentation, or mistake may lose that power if (1) she affirms the contract; (2) she delays unreasonably in exercising the power of disaffirmance; or (3) the rights of third parties intervene.

Affirmance　A party who has the power to avoid a contract for lack of capacity, duress, undue influence, fraud in the inducement, nonfraudulent misrepresentation, or mistake will lose that power by affirming the contract. Affirmance occurs where the party, with full knowledge of the facts, either declares his intention to proceed with the contract or takes some other action from which such intention may reasonably be inferred. Thus, suppose that Pam was induced to purchase

◆ FIGURE 5-1 **Contract Remedies**

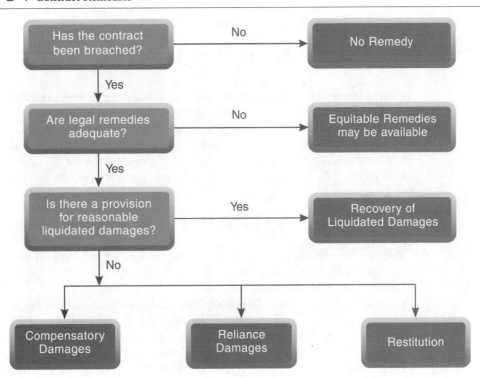

a ring from Sally through Sally's fraudulent misrepresentation. If, after learning the truth, Pam undertakes to sell the ring to Janet or else does something that is consistent only with her ownership of the ring, she may no longer rescind the transaction with Sally. In the case of incapacity, duress, or undue influence, affirmance is effective only after the circumstances that made the contract voidable cease to exist. Where there has been fraudulent misrepresentation, the defrauded party may affirm only after he knows of the misrepresentation. If the misrepresentation is nonfraudulent or a mistake is involved, the defrauded or mistaken party may affirm only after he knows or should know of the misrepresentation or mistake.

Delay   The power of avoidance may be lost if the party who has the power does not rescind within a reasonable time after the circumstances that made the contract voidable have ceased to exist. Determining a reasonable time depends upon all the circumstances, including the extent to which the delay enables the party with the power of avoidance to speculate at the other party's risk. To illustrate, a defrauded purchaser of stock cannot wait unduly to see if the market price or value of the stock appreciates sufficiently to justify retaining the stock.

Rights of Third Parties   The intervening rights of third parties further limit the power of avoidance and the accompanying right to restitution. If A transfers property to B in a transaction that is voidable by A, and B sells the property to C (a good faith purchaser for value) before A exercises her power of avoidance, A will lose the right to recover the property.

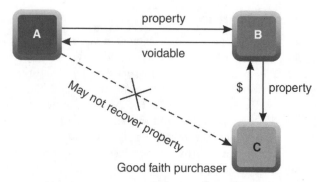

Good faith purchaser

Thus, if C, a third party who is a good faith purchaser, acquires an interest in the subject matter of the contract before A has elected to rescind, no rescission is permitted. Because the transaction is voidable, B acquires a voidable title to the property. Upon a sale of the property by B to C, who is a purchaser in good faith and for value, C obtains good title and is allowed to retain the property. As both A and C are innocent, the law will not disturb the title held by C, the good faith purchaser. In this case, as in all cases where rescission is not available, A's only recourse is against B.

The one notable exception to this rule is the situation involving a sale, *other than a sale of goods*, by a minor who subsequently wishes to avoid the transaction, in which the property has been retransferred to a good faith purchaser. Under this special rule, a good faith purchaser is deprived of the protection generally provided such third parties. Therefore, the third party in a transaction not involving goods, real property being the primary example, is no more protected from the minor's disaffirmance than is the person dealing directly with the minor.

CHAPTER SUMMARY

Monetary Damages

Compensatory Damages contract damages placing the injured party in a position as good as the one he would have held had the other party performed; equals loss of value minus loss avoided by injured party plus incidental damages plus consequential damages
* *Loss of Value* value of promised performance minus value of actual performance
* *Cost Avoided* loss or costs the injured party avoids by not having to perform
* *Incidental Damages* damages arising directly out of a breach of contract
* *Consequential Damages* damages not arising directly out of a breach but arising as a foreseeable result of the breach

Nominal Damages a small sum awarded where a contract has been breached but the loss is negligible or unproved

Reliance Damages contract damages placing the injured party in as good a position as she would have been in had the contract not been made

Damages for Misrepresentation
* *Benefit-of-the-Bargain Damages* difference between the value of the fraudulent party's performance as represented and the value the defrauded party received
* *Out-of-Pocket Damages* difference between the value given and the value received

Punitive Damages are generally *not* recoverable for breach of contract

Liquidated Damages reasonable damages agreed to in advance by the parties to a contract

Limitations on Damages
- *Foreseeability of Damages* potential loss that the party now in default had reason to know of when the contract was made
- *Certainty of Damages* damages are not recoverable beyond an amount that can be established with reasonable certainty
- *Mitigation of Damages* injured party may not recover damages for loss he could have avoided by reasonable effort

Remedies in Equity

Availability only where there is no adequate remedy at law
Types
- *Specific Performance* court decree ordering breaching party to render promised performance
- *Injunction* court order prohibiting a party from doing a specific act
- *Reformation* court order correcting a written contract to conform with the original intent of the contracting parties

Restitution

Definition of Restitution restoration of the injured party to the position she was in before the contract was made
Availability
- *Party Injured by Breach* if the other party totally breaches the contract by nonperformance or repudiation
- *Party in Default* for any benefit conferred in excess of the loss caused by the breach
- *Statute of Frauds* where a contract is unenforceable because of the statute of frauds, a party may recover the benefits conferred on the other party in reliance on the contract
- *Voidable Contracts* a party who has avoided a contract is entitled to restitution for any benefit conferred on the other party

Limitations on Remedies

Election of Remedies if remedies are not inconsistent, a party injured by a breach of contract may seek more than one
Loss of Power of Avoidance a party with the power to avoid a contract may lose that power by
- affirming the contract
- delaying unreasonably in exercising the power of avoidance
- being subordinated to the intervening rights of third parties

---

CASES

CASE
5-1

The following case discusses remedies, including rescission and punitive damages, that may be available to a victim of fraud in a contract for the purchase of real property.

MERRITT v. CRAIG
Court of Special Appeals of Maryland, 2000
130 Md.App. 350, 746 A.2d 923, certiorari denied, 359 Md. 29, 753 A.2d 2

Davis, J.
In the fall of 1995, during their search for a new residence, appellants [Benjamin K. and Julie S. Merritt] inspected Craig's property located at Pergin Farm Road in Garrett County

[Maryland]. After viewing the residence, appellants advised Craig that they were interested in purchasing the property; however, their offer was contingent upon a satisfactory home inspection. On November 5, 1995, appellants, their inspector, and appellee's husband Mark Craig conducted an inspection of the basement area of the residence, during which there was an examination of cistern and water supply pipes. The examination revealed that the cistern had been used to store a water supply reserve, but was not currently utilized.

The inspector advised appellants that the system he had observed was one which utilized a submersible pump in the well from which water flowed to a pressure tank in the basement. The pressure tank distributed water through the internal piping system of the house. There were also two water lines that entered into the basement area. One of the lines came from an 800-foot well that was located on the property, and the other line came from a well located on the adjacent property. The well located on the adjacent property supplied water to both appellants' residence and a guest house owned by Craig. The existence of the adjacent well was not disclosed to appellants.

On December 2, 1995, a contract of sale for the property was executed between appellants and Craig, along with a "Disclosure Statement" signed by Craig on June 9, 1994, and acknowledged by appellants on November 2, 1995, affirming that there were no problems with the water supply to the dwelling. Between November 5, 1995 and June 1996, Craig caused the water line from the guest house to appellants' residence to be cut, and the cistern reactivated to store water from the existing well on appellants' lot. On May 18, 1996, Craig's husband advised Dennis Hannibal, one of the real estate agents involved in the deal, that he had spent $4,196.79 to upgrade the water system on appellants' property and to restore the cistern and remove appellants' house from the second well on Craig's guest house property. On June 14, 1996, appellants and Craig had settlement on the property. Later that afternoon, Craig's husband, without appellants' knowledge, excavated the inside wall of appellants' house and installed a cap to stop a leaking condition on the water line that he had previously cut.

Subsequently, appellants, while attempting to fill a water bed, noticed that the water supply in their well had depleted. On July 13, 1996, appellants met with Craig to discuss a solution to the water failure problem, believing that Craig was responsible for cutting a water line to their house. Appellants agreed with Craig to conduct a flow test to the existing well and contribute money for the construction of a new well. On October 29, 1996, the well was drilled and produced only one half gallon of water per minute. On December 13, 1996, appellants paid for the drilling of a second well on their property, but it failed to produce water. In January 1997, appellants contacted a plumber, Robert Warnick, who confirmed that the line from the guest house well to appellants' residence had been cut flush with the inside surface of the basement wall and cemented closed. Appellants continued to do further work on the house in an effort to cure the water problem.

On February 11, 1997, appellants brought suit against Craig and other appellees in the Circuit Court for Garrett County, seeking rescission of the deed to the property and contract of sale, along with compensatory and punitive damages. During the course of the trial, the judge dismissed appellants' claim for rescission on the ground that they had effectively waived their right to rescission. * * * At the close of trial, the jury returned a verdict in favor of appellants and awarded compensatory damages in the amount of $42,264.76. Appellants were also awarded punitive damages in the amount of $150,000. Subsequently, appellants filed a motion to alter or amend the judgment requesting the court to grant rescission of the contract of sale and the deed, which the circuit court denied on June 17, 1998. Craig moved for judgment notwithstanding the verdict on May 8, 1998, which was also denied by the circuit court. Following the circuit court action, this appeal ensued.

* * *

* * * Under Maryland law, when a party to a contract discovers that he or she has been defrauded, the party defrauded has either "a right to retain the contract and collect damages for its breach, or a right to rescind the contract and recover his or her own expenditures," not both. [Citations.] "These rights [are] inconsistent and mutually exclusive, and the discovery put[s] the purchaser to a prompt election." [Citation.] "A plaintiff seeking rescission must demonstrate that he [or she] acted promptly after discovery of the ground for rescission," otherwise the right to rescind is waived. [Citations.] * * *

In the case *sub judice* [before the court], appellants claim that they were entitled to a rescission of the subject contract of sale and deed and incidental damages. Appellants also claim that they were entitled to compensatory and punitive damages arising from Craig's actions. Appellants, however, may not successfully rescind the contract while simultaneously recovering compensatory and punitive damages. Restitution is "a party's unilateral unmaking of a contract for a legally sufficient reason, such as the other party's material breach" and it in effect "restores the parties to their precontractual position." [Citation.] The restoration of the parties to their original position is incompatible with the circumstance when the complaining party is, at once, relieved of all obligations under the contract while simultaneously securing the windfall of compensatory and punitive damages beyond incidental expenses.

* * *

In sum, although whether appellants promptly repudiated the contract was not squarely before the court, we are not persuaded by appellees' assertion that appellants did not seek rescission in a timely fashion. We hold that, under the facts of this case, appellants must elect the form of relief, i.e., damages or rescission * * *

* * *

We hold that * * * the appellants are entitled to be awarded punitive damages resulting from Craig's actions. A "[p]laintiff seeking to recover punitive damages must allege in detail in the complaint the facts that indicate the entertainment by defendant of evil motive or intent." [Citation.] The Court of

Appeals has held that "punitive damages may only be awarded in such cases where 'the plaintiff has established that the defendant's conduct was characterized by evil motive, intent to injure, ill will or fraud. * * *'" [Citation.] In cases of fraud that arise out of a contractual relationship, the plaintiff would have to establish actual malice to recover punitive damages. [Citation.] Finally, we have stated that "actual or express malice requires an intentional or willful act (or omission) * * * and 'has been characterized as the performance of an act without legal justification or excuse, but with an evil or rancorous motive influenced by hate, the purpose being to deliberately and willfully injure the plaintiff.'" [Citation.]

* * *

The jury believed that the representations made by Craig were undertaken with actual knowledge that the representations were false and with the intention to deceive appellants. * * * Moreover, the record reflects that the jury could reasonably infer Craig's intention to defraud appellants by her representation in the Disclosure Statement that there were no problems with the water supply, and by subsequently making substantial changes in the water system by cutting off a water line which supplied water to appellants' residence immediately after appellants' inspector examined the system. Therefore, we hold that the circuit court was not in error in finding facts from the record sufficient to support an award of punitive damages.

Craig also challenges the punitive damages award on the basis that the amount of the award was excessive.* * *

In the case at hand, the trial judge undertook the appropriate review of the jury's award. It is clear from the court's comments at the hearing that the court's decision not to disturb the jury's verdict was based on the evidence presented at trial and was not excessive. * * * Craig's conduct toward appellants was reprehensible and fully warranted punitive damages. Her conduct in willfully misrepresenting the condition of the water system in the Disclosure Statement, coupled with her actions and those of her husband in interfering and diverting the water flow subsequent to the inspection and sale of the property, constitute egregious conduct. As a result of Craig's conduct, appellants were forced to employ extreme water conservation practices due to an insufficient water supply and they attempted to ameliorate the problem by having two new wells drilled on the property which proved to be unproductive. Moreover, the lack of water supply to appellants' property clearly reduced its market value. * * *

* * *

* * * Consequently, should appellants seek compensatory and punitive damages on remand, appellants' actual knowledge, coupled with the intent to deceive, is a sufficient factual predicate for submission of punitive damages to the jury.

Judgement of the circuit court reversed; case remanded for further proceedings consistent with this opinion.

CASE
5-2

This case illustrates the factors a court will consider in determining whether a liquidated damages clause in a contract is enforceable.

WESTHAVEN ASSOCIATES, LTD. v. C.C. OF MADISON, INC.

Court of Appeals of Wisconsin, District Four, 2002
257 Wis.2d 789, 652 N.W.2d 819
http://www.wisbar.org/res/capp/2002/01-1953.htm

Lundsten, J.

C.C. of Madison, Inc. (Cost Cutters) rented space in a mall owned by Westhaven Associates, Ltd. (Westhaven). Cost Cutters breached its lease by vacating, and Westhaven sought to enforce various lease provisions. The parties dispute whether stipulated damages provisions in the lease are reasonable, and thus enforceable liquidated damages provisions, or unreasonable, and thus unenforceable penalty provisions. Following the terminology used in the seminal case on this topic, [citation], we use the term "stipulated damages" to mean the damages specified in the lease and "liquidated damages" to mean reasonable and enforceable stipulated damages. The parties also dispute whether the lease permits Westhaven to recover attorneys' fees it incurred in its attempt to enforce various lease provisions against Cost Cutters.

* * *

Background

Westhaven owns the Westhaven Village Shopping Center (Shopping Center). On July 28, 1997, Cost Cutters entered into a lease with Westhaven. Cost Cutters leased about 17% of the available rentable space in the Shopping Center. The lease term was ten years.

On October 9, 1999, Cost Cutters closed its store without Westhaven's approval. At this time, the lease rate was $49.58 per day. Before the parties entered into the lease on July 28, 1997, the Shopping Center's occupancy rate was 71%. The Shopping Center's occupancy rate fluctuated after the parties signed the lease, dropping to 53% in October 1999 prior to Cost Cutters' departure. By March 2000, the occupancy rate increased to 72%. From February 1, 2000, forward, Cost Cutters did not pay rent. In accordance with the lease, Westhaven attempted to find a new tenant for the Cost Cutters space. The space remained vacant until it was leased to a third party beginning December 1, 2000. Westhaven then sued Cost Cutters * * * .

Westhaven sought relief under paragraph 14.00 of the lease entitled "Default by Tenant." * * *

* * * There was no dispute that under this paragraph Westhaven was entitled to the lease rate of $49.58 for each day between October 9, 1999, when Cost Cutters vacated, and December 1, 2000, when the space was sublet. * * *

In addition, * * * paragraph 14.00 permits Westhaven to seek stipulated damages under paragraphs 3.02 and 8.00(n) of the lease. Paragraph 3.02 requires Cost Cutters to pay Westhaven $20 per day if Cost Cutters fails to keep its premises open for business during "normal business hours." Westhaven argued that it was entitled to $20 per day for each violation of paragraph 3.02 from October 14, 1999, to November 30, 2000. Paragraph 8.00(n) of the lease requires Cost Cutters to pay a sum equal to Cost Cutters' normal daily rent for each day Cost Cutters fails to keep its premises open for business during specified "minimum hours." Westhaven argued that it was entitled to an amount equal to the daily rent for each violation of paragraph 8.00(n) from October 14, 1999, to November 30, 2000.

Both parties sought summary judgment. * * * Cost Cutters * * * argued that paragraphs 3.02 and 8.00(n) (collectively the "failure to do business" provisions) are unenforceable penalty provisions.

* * * [T]he circuit court ruled that the "failure to do business" provisions contained in paragraphs 3.02 and 8.00(n) were unreasonable and, therefore, unenforceable.

* * * Westhaven * * * appeals the circuit court's determination that the "failure to do business" provisions were unenforceable.

Discussion

* * *

A stipulated damages provision will be enforced if it is reasonable under the totality of the circumstances. [Citation.] The court looks at several factors to determine reasonableness: * * * Essentially, we must look at both the "harm anticipated at the time of contract formation and the actual harm at the time of breach." [Citation.] The factors are not meant to be mechanically applied, and courts may give some factors greater weight than others. [Citation.]

* * *

The first factor we examine when determining the reasonableness of a stipulated damages provision is whether the parties intended the provision to provide liquidated damages or to provide a penalty. As explained in [citation], this factor is "rarely helpful" because the parties' intent has "little relevance to what is reasonable in law." * * *

* * *

The second factor used to determine the reasonableness of a stipulated damages provision examines whether the damages can be estimated *at the time of contracting*. The third factor examines whether the stipulated damages provisions are a reasonable forecast of the *harm caused by the breach*. * * *

Although the second and third factors both use a prospective-retrospective approach, the fact remains that they require two distinct inquiries: the reasonableness of the stipulated damages provision at the time of contracting and the reasonableness of the provision when compared with actual damages after a breach. [Citations.] We first address whether the "failure to do business" provisions were reasonable at the time of contracting.

* * *

As tenants vacate, a shopping center receives less customer traffic, potentially causing other tenants to vacate or go out of business [as well as decreasing the value of the landlord's property]. These consequential damages are often difficult to prove, but that does not prevent sophisticated parties from including consequential damages when estimating the damages at the time of contracting. [Citation.]

* * *

Cost Cutters has failed to persuade us that the "failure to do business" fees were an unreasonable estimation of Westhaven's damages. Cost Cutters did not, for example, present expert testimony that the stipulated damages provisions were unusually harsh as compared with stipulated damages provisions found in other multi-tenant retail commercial leases. To the contrary, in this case Cost Cutters' president, in his deposition testimony, admitted that similar "failure to do business" provisions are common in leases with other shopping malls.

Next, we turn to the question whether the stipulated damages are reasonable in light of the actual damages caused by the breach. [Citation.] As stated above, it is incumbent on Cost Cutters to persuade us that the damages it must pay under the contract do not reasonably relate to the actual harm suffered by Westhaven. Cost Cutters fails to meet this burden.

* * *

Cost Cutters * * * argues that because the occupancy rate at the Shopping Center was low before Cost Cutters departed and actually rose after Cost Cutters left, it is obvious that Westhaven suffered no harm as a result of Cost Cutters' departure. The occupancy rate just prior to Cost Cutters' departure was 53%. About five months later, occupancy had risen to 72%. However, we are not persuaded by the occupancy rate information. Simply because the occupancy rate rose after Cost Cutters' breach does not mean that the breach caused Westhaven no harm. Based on the record before us, the most reasonable inference is that occupancy would have been even higher had Cost Cutters remained in the Shopping Center. When a mall has a low occupancy rate, it does not follow that the mall suffers no harm when a significant tenant vacates. * * *

* * *

We conclude that Cost Cutters has failed to meet its burden of persuasion. Cost Cutters has not shown that the stipulated damages provisions in the lease were unreasonable under the totality of the circumstances.

* * *

Judgment reversed and cause remanded with directions.

McLaughlin, J.

This case involves a closely held cable television corporation that imploded just as it was about to launch its flagship channel.

CASE
5-3

A party seeking to recover damages for breach of contract must prove the existence and amount of such damages with reasonable certainty. The following case illustrates the difficulties faced by a plaintiff who seeks to recover damages for lost profits.

SCHONFELD v. HILLIARD
United States Court of Appeals, Second Circuit, 2000
218 F.3d 164

In 1988, brothers Russ and Les Hilliard formed International News Network, Inc. ("INN") to distribute a British news and information channel in the United States (the "Channel"). Prior to this ambitious venture, the Hilliard brothers owned small midwestern cable television companies with an aggregate of only 66,000 subscribers.

To secure large-scale expertise and prestige, INN brought in Reese Schonfeld, a founder and former President of Cable News Network ("CNN")—initially as a consultant, and later as a shareholder—to help INN negotiate with the British Broadcasting Corporation (the "BBC") for a programming license. INN also retained Daniels & Associates ("Daniels"), the nation's leading financial services company for the cable industry, to prepare a business plan and to drum up investors.

In February 1994, the Hilliards and Schonfeld executed a written Shareholders' Agreement whereby each became a one third shareholder in INN in return for a $10,000 capital contribution. In addition, the Hilliards, who had each already lent $300,000 to INN, agreed to lend up to another $350,000 to INN if necessary to meet its obligations to the BBC. In lieu of a further cash contribution, Schonfeld agreed to invest his time and effort.

The Shareholders' Agreement confirmed the parties' understanding that INN itself would not operate the Channel. Instead, INN would invest in a yet-to-be-formed operating entity. INN's shareholders, if they chose, could increase their personal stakes in the Channel by making additional cash investments in the separate operating entity. The agreement said nothing about the percentage of profits that INN, or any other equity investor, would receive from the Channel's operation.

* * *

The final piece of the puzzle fell into place on March 4, 1994, when the BBC granted INN a 20-year exclusive license to distribute its news and information programming in a 24-hour format, commencing not later than February 1995 (the "March Supply Agreement"). The agreement provided for INN's assignment of the benefits and privileges of the agreement to the yet-to-be-formed operating entity upon written consent of the BBC, whose consent would not be unreasonably withheld. The BBC retained its right, however, to withhold consent to any delegation of INN's duties under the contract.

* * *

In October 1994, the FCC promulgated a new rule allowing cable operators to charge an increased per channel monthly rate for up to six new channels as of January 1, 1995. To take advantage of this window of opportunity, INN asked the BBC to accelerate the launch date of the Channel.

INN and the BBC signed an "Interim Agreement," effective December 14, 1994, in which the BBC agreed to provide provisional programming as early as possible, and to develop an "Americanized" programming format to become available to INN no later than December 31, 1995 under a revised 20-year supply agreement (the "December Supply Agreement"). In consideration for the interim programming feed, INN agreed to pay the BBC approximately $20 million in installments beginning January 3, 1995. The BBC retained the right to terminate the Interim Agreement if, by January 31, 1995, INN had failed to get letters indicating an intent to carry the Channel from cable systems with an aggregate of at least 500,000 subscribers. The December Supply Agreement also: (1) capped INN's initial capital contribution to the operating entity at 15%; and (2) gave the BBC a nondilutable 20% equity interest in the operating entity.

According to three witnesses—Richard Blumenthal (INN's attorney), Schonfeld and Mark Young (a representative of the BBC)—Russ Hilliard repeatedly promised orally that he and his brother would personally fund the Interim Agreement. These promises were allegedly made to induce Schonfeld and the BBC to abandon the March Supply Agreement and enter into the Interim and December Supply Agreements despite the fact that INN did not yet have the cash available to make the necessary payments to the BBC. Schonfeld and Blumenthal testified in depositions that the Hilliards said they planned to invest up to $20 million in the operating entity as financing for the BBC payments. However, there is no oral or written agreement memorializing the precise amount promised, or defining the liabilities and remedies of the parties in the event of the Hilliards' failure to fund.

By mid January 1995, the Hilliards had provided none of the promised funding and INN was in default under the Interim Agreement. In February 1995, the parties met in New York to discuss the situation. Russ Hilliard did not deny that he and his brother had promised to fund the Interim Agreement. He claimed, however, that funding had been withheld because INN was having difficulty obtaining cable operator support. Rather than suing the Hilliards and INN for breach of contract, the BBC offered a chivalrous solution: in exchange for the dissolution of both the Interim and December Supply Agreements, the BBC agreed to release the Hilliards and INN from any and all claims arising out of their breach of the oral agreement and Interim Supply Agreement.

Schonfeld alleges that the Hilliards never really intended to fund the Interim Agreement themselves. He claims that, all along, they had been unsuccessfully attempting to get the money from William Bresnan, the CEO of Bresnan Communications (which is 80% owned by TCI Cable). Russ Hilliard has admitted in deposition testimony that: (1) the funds he had promised were supposed to come from Bresnan or TCI, not from himself and his brother; and (2) he knew the BBC would never have signed the Interim Agreement had it known the truth (i.e., would never have agreed to make the Interim Agreement contingent on funding from Bresnan or TCI).

In April 1995, Schonfeld commenced this diversity action in the United States District Court for the Southern District of New York * * * on behalf of INN for: * * * breach of contract. * * *

In a nutshell, Schonfeld alleged that the Hilliards induced him and INN to abandon the March Supply Agreement and enter into the Interim and December Supply Agreements by falsely representing their intention to personally fund the Interim Agreement. He alleged that the Hilliards' breach of this oral agreement to fund led directly to INN's breach of the Interim Agreement and subsequent loss of the December Supply Agreement.

* * *

To establish lost profit damages, Schonfeld relied on: (1) INN's Business Plan; * * * (3) the BBC's, the Hilliards' and Schonfeld's "belief" that the proposed operating entity would be profitable; and (4) the reports and deposition testimony of two damage experts—Donald Curtis and William Grimes.

* * *

* * * the district court held that Schonfeld could not prove, with reasonable certainty, the existence or amount of damages for lost profits. * * *

* * *

Accordingly, the district court granted summary judgment * * *

Plaintiff, Schonfeld, now appeals, * * * .

* * *

In an action for breach of contract, a plaintiff is entitled to recover lost profits only if he can establish both the existence and amount of such damages with reasonable certainty. [Citation.] "[T]he damages may not be merely speculative, possible or imaginary." [Citation.] Although lost profits need not be proven with "mathematical precision," they must be "capable of measurement based upon known reliable factors without undue speculation." [Citation.] Therefore, evidence of lost profits from a new business venture receives greater scrutiny because there is no track record upon which to base an estimate. [Citation.] Projections of future profits based upon "a multitude of assumptions" that require "speculation and conjecture" and few known factors do not provide the requisite certainty. [Citation.]

The plaintiff faces an additional hurdle: he must prove that lost profit damages were within the contemplation of the parties when the contract was made. [Citation.] "The party breaching the contract is liable for those risks foreseen or which should have been foreseen at the time the contract was made." [Citation.] Where the contract is silent on the subject, the court must take a "common sense" approach, and determine what the parties intended by considering "the nature, purpose and particular circumstances of the contract known by the parties * * * as well as what liability the defendant fairly may be supposed to have assumed consciously." [Citations.]

* * *

Here, the district court concluded that the Channel was a new entertainment venture. * * * The operating entity's profits, the court noted, "were purely hypothetical, stemming from the sale of untested programming to a hypothetical subscriber base, sold to advertisers at a hypothetical price and supported by hypothetical investors and carriers." [Citation.] After reviewing the seemingly endless list of assumptions upon which Schonfeld's expert relied in determining lost profits, the court held that Schonfeld could establish neither the existence nor the amount of lost profits with reasonable certainty. The court also concluded that lost profits were not within the contemplation of the parties. We fully agree with the district court's analysis.

* * *

Subject as they are to the changing whims and artistic tastes of the general public, claims for profits lost in unsuccessful entertainment ventures have received a chilly reception in the New York courts. [Citations.] Curtis believes he adjusted his profit figures to take such factors into account by providing for a 25% variance on the projected cash flows of the operating entity. In his deposition, he stated that he chose the 25% variance based on his experience with the cable industry. However, Curtis failed to establish that this variance would adequately account for any inaccuracies in the revenue and expense assumptions discussed above as well as any changes in consumer demand for British-style news reporting.

Indeed, Curtis failed to account for the effects of any general market risks on the Channel's probability of success. These risks include: (1) the entry of competitors; (2) technological developments; (3) regulatory changes; or (4) general market movements. As the district court correctly noted, "[f]ailure to control for adverse market conditions allows the false inference that plaintiff's venture was an assured success." [Citation.] Therefore, the court properly held that Schonfeld failed to establish a foundation for the existence of lost profits.

* * *

Finally, Schonfeld maintains that he adduced sufficient evidence to establish that liability for lost profits was within the parties' contemplation at the time the Hilliards promised to fund the Interim Agreement. * * *

* * *

* * * Schonfeld is not seeking profits that would have accrued under the alleged oral agreement to fund, or even under the Interim Agreement. Rather, Schonfeld wants to recover lost profits that INN or a nonexistent operating entity might have received from the operation of the Channel. Further, the profitability of the Channel was highly uncertain when the Hilliards promised to fund the Interim Agreement. Nor did they exercise "near exclusive control" over the profitability of the venture. In light of "the nature, purpose and particular circumstances of the contract known by the parties," by orally promising to provide up to $20 million to fund the Interim Agreement, the Hilliards cannot "be supposed to have assumed" liability for approximately $269 million in lost profits that might have been garnered in the future by a nonexistent operating entity. [Citation.]

* * *

For all the foregoing reasons, we affirm the district court's grant of summary judgment dismissing all claims insofar as they seek damages for lost profits.

CASE
5-4

This case discusses the requirements for awarding the remedy of specific performance for a breach of contract and applies them to a failure to give screen credit for making a motion picture.

TAMARIND LITHOGRAPHY WORKSHOP v. SANDERS

Court of Appeal of California, Second District, 1983
143 Cal.App.3d 571, 193 Cal.Rptr.409

Stephens, J.

The essence of this appeal concerns the question of whether an award of damages is an adequate remedy at law in lieu of specific performance for the breach of an agreement to give screen credits. Our saga traces its origin to March of 1969, at which time appellant, and cross-complainant below, Terry Sanders (hereinafter "Sanders" or "appellant"), agreed in writing to write, direct and produce a motion picture on the subject of lithography for respondent, Tamarind Lithography Workshop, Inc. (hereinafter referred to as "Tamarind" or "respondent").

Pursuant to the terms of the agreement, the film was shot during the summer of 1969, wherein Sanders directed the film according to an outline/treatment of his authorship, and acted as production manager by personally hiring and supervising personnel comprising the film crew. Additionally, Sanders exercised both artistic control over the mixing of the sound track and overall editing of the picture.

After completion, the film, now titled the "Four Stones for Kanemitsu," was screened by Tamarind at its tenth anniversary celebration on April 28, 1970. Thereafter, a dispute arose between the parties concerning their respective rights and obligations under the original 1969 agreement. Litigation

ensued and in January 1973 the matter went to trial. Prior to the entry of judgment, the parties entered into a written settlement agreement, which became the premise for the instant action. Specifically, this April 30, 1973, agreement provided that Sanders would be entitled to a screen credit entitled "A Film by Terry Sanders."

Tamarind did not comply with its expressed obligation pursuant to that agreement, in that it failed to include Sanders' screen credits in the prints it distributed. As a result a situation developed wherein Tamarind and co-defendant Wayne filed suit for declaratory relief, damages due to breach of contract, emotional distress, defamation and fraud.

Sanders cross-complained, seeking damages for Tamarind's breach of contract, declaratory relief, specific performance of the contract to give Sanders screen credits, and defamation. Both causes were consolidated and brought to trial on May 31, 1977. A jury was impaneled for purposes of determining damage issues and decided that Tamarind had breached the agreement and awarded Sanders $25,000 in damages.

The remaining claims for declaratory and injunctive relief were tried by the court. The court made findings that Tamarind had sole ownership rights in the film, that "both

June Wayne and Terry Sanders were each creative producers of the film, that Sanders shall have the right to modify the prints in his personal possession to include his credits." All other prayers for relief were denied.

It is from the denial of appellant's request for specific performance upon which appellant predicates this appeal.

* * *

The availability of the remedy of specific performance is premised upon well established requisites. These requisites include: A showing by plaintiff of (1) the inadequacy of his legal remedy; (2) an underlying contract that is both reasonable and supported by adequate consideration; (3) the existence of a mutuality of remedies; (4) contractual terms which are sufficiently definite to enable the court to know what it is to enforce; and (5) a substantial similarity of the requested performance to that promised in the contract. [Citation.]

It is manifest that the legal remedies available to Sanders for harm resulting from the future exhibition of the film are inadequate as a matter of law. The primary reasons are twofold: (1) that an accurate assessment of damages would be far too difficult and require much speculation, and (2) that any future exhibitions might be deemed to be a continuous breach of contract and thereby create the danger of an untold number of lawsuits.

There is no doubt that the exhibition of a film, which is favorably received by its critics and the public at large, can result in valuable advertising or publicity for the artists responsible for

that film's making. Likewise, it is unquestionable that the nonappearance of an artist's name or likeness in the form of screen credit on a successful film can result in a loss of that valuable publicity. However, whether that loss of publicity is measurable dollarwise is quite another matter.

By its very nature, public acclaim is unique and very difficult, if not sometimes impossible, to quantify in monetary terms. * * *

* * *

We return to the remaining requisites for Sanders' entitlement to specific performance. The need for our finding the contract to be reasonable and supported by adequate consideration is obviated by the jury's determination of respondent's breach of that contract. The requisite of mutuality of remedy has been satisfied in that Sanders had fully performed his obligations pursuant to the agreement (i.e., release of all claims of copyright to the film and dismissal of his then pending action against respondents). [Citation.] Similarly, we find the terms of the agreement sufficiently definite to permit enforcement of the respondent's performance as promised.

* * *

In conclusion, the record shows that the appellant is entitled to relief consisting of the damages recovered, and an injunction against future injury.

CASE
5-5

The following case discusses the availability of injunctive relief for the breach of a restrictive covenant in a contract for personal services.

MADISON SQUARE GARDEN CORP., ILL. v. CARNERA
United States Court of Appeals, Second Circuit, 1931
52 F.2d 47

Chase, J.
Suit by plaintiff, Madison Square Garden Corporation, against Primo Carnera, defendant. From an order granting an injunction against defendant, defendant appeals.

On January 13, 1931, the plaintiff and defendant by their duly authorized agents entered into the following agreement in writing:

1. Carnera agrees that he will render services as a boxer in his next contest (which contest, hereinafter called the "First Contest," shall be with the winner of the proposed Schmeling-Stribling contest, or, if the same is drawn, shall be with Schmeling, and shall be deemed to be a contest for the heavyweight championship title; provided, however, that, in the event of the inability of the Garden to cause Schmeling or Stribling, as the case may be, to perform the terms of his agreement with the Garden calling for such contest, the Garden shall be without further liability to Carnera) exclusively under the auspices of the Garden, in the

United States of America, or the Dominion of Canada, at such time, not, however, later than midnight of September 30, 1931, as the Garden may direct. * * *

9. Carnera shall not, pending the holding of the First Contest, render services as a boxer in any major boxing contest, without the written permission of the Garden in each case had and obtained. A major contest is understood to be one with Sharkey, Baer, Campolo, Godfrey, or like grade heavyweights, or heavyweights who shall have beaten any of the above subsequent to the date hereof. If in any boxing contest engaged in by Carnera prior to the holding of the First Contest, he shall lose the same, the Garden shall at its option, to be exercised by a two weeks' notice to Carnera in writing, be without further liability under the terms of this agreement to Carnera. Carnera shall not render services during the continuance of the option referred to in paragraph 8 hereof for any person, firm or corporation other than the Garden. Carnera shall, however, at all times be permitted to engage in sparring exhibitions in which no deci-

sion is rendered and in which the heavyweight championship title is not at stake, and in which Carnera boxes not more than four rounds with any one opponent. * * *

Thereafter the defendant, without the permission of the plaintiff, written or otherwise, made a contract to engage in a boxing contest with the Sharkey mentioned in paragraph 9 of the agreement above quoted, and by the terms thereof the contest was to take place before the first contest mentioned in the defendant's contract with the plaintiff was to be held.

The plaintiff then brought this suit to restrain the defendant from carrying out his contract to box Sharkey, and obtained the preliminary injunction order, from which this appeal was taken. Jurisdiction is based on diversity of citizenship and the required amount is involved.

The District Court has found on affidavits which adequately show it that the defendant's services are unique and extraordinary. A negative covenant in a contract for such personal services is enforceable by injunction where the damages for a breach are incapable of ascertainment. [Citations.]

The defendant points to what is claimed to be lack of consideration for his negative promise, in that the contract is inequitable and contains no agreement to employ him. It is true that there is no promise in so many words to employ the defendant to box in a contest with Stribling or Schmeling, but the agreement read as a whole binds the plaintiff to do just that, providing either Stribling or Schmeling becomes the contestant as the result of the match between them and can be induced to box the defendant. The defendant has agreed to "render services as a boxer" for the plaintiff exclusively, and the plaintiff has agreed to pay him a definite percentage of the gate receipts as his compensation for so doing. The promise to employ the defendant to enable him to earn the compensation agreed upon is implied to the same force and effect as though expressly stated. * * * [Citations.]

As we have seen, the contract is valid and enforceable. It contains a restrictive covenant which may be given effect. Whether a preliminary injunction shall be issued under such circumstances rests in the sound discretion of the court. [Citations.] The District Court, in its discretion, did issue the preliminary injunction and required the plaintiff as a condition upon its issuance to secure its own performance of the contract in suit with a bond for $25,000 and to give a bond in the sum of $35,000 to pay the defendant such damages as he may sustain by reason of the injunction. Such an order is clearly not an abuse of discretion.

Order affirmed.

QUESTIONS

1. Explain how compensatory and reliance damages are computed.
2. Define
   (a) nominal damages,
   (b) incidental damages,
   (c) consequential damages,
   (d) foreseeability of damages,
   (e) punitive damages,
   (f) liquidated damages, and
   (g) mitigation of damages.
3. Define the various types of equitable relief and discuss when the courts will grant such relief.
4. Explain how restitutionary damages are computed and identify the situations in which restitution is available as a contractual remedy.
5. Identify and explain the limitations on contractual remedies.

PROBLEMS

1. Edward contracted to buy 1,000 barrels of sugar from Marcia. Marcia failed to deliver, and because Edward could not buy any sugar in the market, he was compelled to shut down his candy factory.
   (a) What damages is Edward entitled to recover?
   (b) Would it make any difference if Edward had told Marcia that he wanted the sugar to make candies for the Christmas trade and that he had accepted contracts for delivery by certain dates?
2. In which of the following situations is specific performance available as a remedy?
   (a) Mary and Anne enter into a written agreement under which Mary agrees to sell and Anne agrees to buy for $10 per share 100 shares of the 300 shares outstanding of the capital stock of the Infinitesimal Steel Corporation, whose shares are not listed on any exchange and are closely held. Mary refuses to deliver when tendered the $1,000.
   (b) Modifying (a) above, assume that the subject matter of the agreement is stock of the United States Steel Corporation, which is traded on the New York Stock Exchange.
   (c) Modifying (a) above, assume that the subject matter of the agreement is undeveloped farmland of little commercial value.
3. James contracts to make repairs to Betty's building in return for Betty's promise to pay $12,000 upon completion of the repairs. After partially completing the repairs, James is unable to continue. Betty hires another builder, who completes the repairs for $5,000. The building's value to Betty has increased by $10,000 as a result of the

repairs by James, but Betty has lost $500 in rents because of the delay caused by James's breach. James sues Betty. How much, if any, may James recover in restitution from Betty?

4. Virginia induced Charles to sell his boat to her by misrepresentation of material fact upon which Charles reasonably relied. Virginia promptly sold the boat to Donald, who paid fair value for it and knew nothing concerning the transaction between Virginia and Charles. Upon discovering the misrepresentation, Charles seeks to recover the boat. What are Charles's rights against Virginia and Donald?

5. Copenhaver, the owner of a laundry business, contracted with Berryman, the owner of a large apartment complex, to allow Copenhaver to own and operate the laundry facilities within the apartment complex. Berryman subsequently terminated the five-year contract with Copenhaver with forty-seven months remaining. Within six months, Copenhaver placed the equipment into use in other locations. He then filed suit, claiming that he was entitled to conduct the laundry operations for an additional forty-seven months and that through such operations he would have earned a profit of $13,886.58, after deducting Berryman's share of the gross receipts and other operating expenses. Decision?

6. Kerr Steamship Company sent a telegram to the Philippines through the Radio Corporation of America. The telegram, which contained instructions for loading cargo on one of Kerr's ships, was mislaid and never delivered. Consequently, the ship was improperly loaded and the cargo was lost. Kerr sued the Radio Corporation for $6,675.29 in profits lost on the cargo because of the Radio Corporation's failure to deliver the telegram. Should Kerr be allowed to recover damages from Radio? Explain.

7. Daniel agreed to erect an apartment building for Steven for $2 million, Daniel to suffer deduction of $2,000 per day for every day of delay. Daniel was twenty days late in finishing the job, losing ten days because of a strike and ten days because the material suppliers were late in furnishing materials. Daniel claims that he is entitled to payment in full (a) because the agreement as to $2,000 a day is a penalty and (b) because Steven has not shown that he has sustained any damage. Discuss each contention and decide.

8. Sharon contracted with Jane, a shirtmaker, for 1,000 shirts for men. Jane manufactured and delivered 500 shirts, which were paid for by Sharon. At the same time, Sharon notified Jane that she could not use or dispose of the other 500 shirts and directed Jane not to manufacture any more under the contract. Nevertheless, Jane proceeded to make up the other 500 shirts and tendered them to Sharon. Sharon refused to accept the shirts, and Jane then sued for the purchase price. Decision?

9. Stuart contracts to act in a comedy for Charlotte and to comply with all theater regulations for four seasons. Charlotte promises to pay Stuart $800 for each performance and to allow Stuart one benefit performance each season. It is expressly agreed that "Stuart shall not be employed in any other production for the period of the contract." During the first year of the contract, Stuart and Charlotte have a terrible quarrel. Thereafter, Stuart signs a contract to perform in Elaine's production and ceases performing for Charlotte. Charlotte seeks

(a) to prevent Stuart from performing for Elaine, and (b) to require Stuart to perform his contract with Charlotte. What result?

10. On March 1, Joseph sold to Sandra fifty acres of land in Oregon, which Joseph at the time represented to be fine black loam, high, dry, and free of stumps. Sandra paid Joseph the agreed price of $40,000 and took from him a deed to the land. Subsequently discovering that the land was low, swampy, and not entirely free of stumps, Sandra nevertheless undertook to convert the greater part of the land into cranberry bogs. After one year of cranberry culture, Sandra became entirely dissatisfied, tendered the land back to Joseph, and demanded from Joseph the return of the $40,000. Upon Joseph's refusal to repay the money, Sandra brings an action against him to recover the $40,000. What judgment?

11. Linda induced Sally to enter into a purchase of a stereo amplifier by intentionally misrepresenting the power output to be sixty watts at rated distortion when in fact the unit delivered only twenty watts. Sally paid $450 for the amplifier. Amplifiers producing twenty watts generally sell for $200, whereas amplifiers producing sixty watts generally sell for $550. Sally decides to keep the amplifier and sue for damages. How much may Sally recover in damages from Linda?

12. On April 1, Conrad and Owen executed a contract under which Conrad agreed to build a specified house on Owen's land for $700,000. The contract provided that Owen was to make periodic payments to Conrad as different phases of construction were completed, with the last payment of $70,000 due 5 days after completion of the house. The contract further provided that the house was to be completed by August 1 and included the following provision: "If Conrad is late in completing the construction of the house, the purchase price is to be reduced by $3,000 for each and every day after August 1." Conrad constructed the house according to the contract, except that it was completed 5 days after August 1. Owen made all scheduled payments except for the final payment of $70,000. Although Owen could not prove any monetary damages caused by Conrad's delay, Owen offered to make a final payment of $55,000 to Conrad, after deducting $15,000 for the 5 day delay. Conrad rejected Owen's offer and sued Owen for $70,000. How much, if anything, will Conrad recover from Owen? Explain.

13. Millie, a famous singer, entered into a contract to perform at Tanya's night club during the month of December. Tanya advertised that Millie would be performing at Tanya's nightclub and obtained many advance reservations from customers for the performance. In November, Raisa, the owner of another nightclub, convinced Millie to breach her contract with Tanya and to perform at Raisa's nightclub instead during the month of December. On November 15, Millie told Tanya that she would not be available to perform at Tanya's nightclub as planned. When Tanya found out that Millie would be performing at Raisa's nightclub instead, Tanya became furious and immediately called her lawyer.

(a) Tanya sues Millie, demanding specific performance of the contract. Discuss.

(b) Tanya seeks an injunction against Millie, to stop her from performing at Raisa's nightclub during December. Discuss.

(c) Tanya sues Millie for breach of contract and demands damages. What damages, if any, may Tanya recover?

(d) Does Tanya have any action for damages against Raisa? Discuss.

http: **Internet Exercise** Compare the provisions governing remedies for breach of contract contained in the Principles of European Contract Law with the provisions of the U.S. common law.

Mutual Assent

Although each of the requirements for forming a contract is essential to its existence, mutual assent is so basic that frequently a contract is referred to as the agreement between the parties. The Restatement, Section 3, provides this definition: "An agreement is a manifestation of mutual assent on the part of two or more parties." Enforcing the contract means enforcing the agreement; indeed, the agreement between the parties is the very core of the contract.

The manner in which parties usually show mutual assent is by **offer** and **acceptance**. One party makes a proposal (offer) by words or conduct to the other party, who agrees by words or conduct to the proposal (acceptance). A contractual agreement always involves either a promise exchanged for a promise (*bilateral contract*) or a promise exchanged for an act or forbearance to act (*unilateral contract*), as manifested by what the parties communicate to one another.

An implied contract may be formed by conduct. Thus, though there may be no definite offer and acceptance, or definite acceptance of an offer, a contract exists if both parties have acted in a manner that manifests (indicates) a recognition by each of them of the existence of a contract. It may be impossible to determine the exact moment at which a contract was made.

To form the contract, the parties must manifest their agreement objectively. The important thing is what the parties indicate to one another by spoken or written words or by conduct. The law applies an **objective standard** and is, therefore, concerned only with the assent, agreement, or intention of a party as it reasonably appears from his words or actions. The law of contracts is not concerned with what a party may have actually thought or the meaning that he intended to convey, even if his subjective understanding or intention differed from the meaning he objectively indicated by word or conduct. For example, if Leslie seemingly offers to sell to Sam her Chevrolet automobile but intends to offer and believes that she is offering her Ford automobile, and Sam accepts the offer, reasonably believing it was for the Chevrolet, a contract has been formed for the sale of the Chevrolet. Subjectively, there is no agreement as to the subject matter, but objectively there is a manifestation of agreement, and the objective manifestation is binding.

The Code's treatment of mutual assent is covered in greater detail in Chapter 7.

Offer

An offer is a definite proposal or undertaking made by one person to another which manifests a willingness to enter into a bargain. The person making the proposal is the **offeror**. The person to whom it is made is the **offeree**. Upon receipt, the offer confers on the offeree the power of acceptance, by which the offeree expresses her willingness to comply with the terms of the offer.

The communication of an offer to an offeree does not of itself confer any rights or impose any duties on either of the parties. The offeror, by making his offer, simply confers upon the offeree the power to create a contract by accepting the offer. Until the offeree exercises this power, the outstanding offer creates neither rights nor liabilities.

An offer may take several forms: (1) It may propose a promise for a promise. (This is an offer to enter into a bilateral contract.) An example is an offer to sell and deliver goods in thirty days in return for the promise to pay a stipulated amount upon delivery of the goods. If the offeree accepts this offer, the resulting contract consists of the parties' mutual promises, each made in exchange for the other. (2) An offer may be a promise for an act. (This is an offer to enter into a unilateral contract.) A common example is an offer of a reward for certain information or for the return of lost property. The offeree can accept such an offer only by the performance of the act requested. (3) An offer may be in the form of an act for a promise. (This is an offer to enter into an "inverted" unilateral contract.) For example, Maria offers the stated price to a clerk in a theater ticket office and asks for a ticket for a certain performance. The clerk can accept this offer of an act only by delivery of the requested ticket, which amounts, in effect, to the theater owner's promise to admit Maria to the designated performance.

ESSENTIALS OF AN OFFER

An offer need not take any particular form to have legal validity. To be effective, however, it must (1) be communicated to the offeree, (2) manifest an intent to enter into a contract, and (3) be sufficiently definite and certain. If these essentials are present, an offer that has not terminated gives the offeree the power to form a contract by accepting the offer.

Communication

To have the mutual assent required to form a contract, the offeree must have knowledge of the offer; he cannot agree to something of which he has no knowledge. Accordingly, the offeror must communicate the offer, in an intended manner, to the offeree.

For example, Andy signs a letter containing an offer to Bonnie and leaves it on top of the desk in his office. Later that day, Bonnie, without prearrangement, goes to Andy's office, discovers that Andy is away, notices the letter on his desk, reads it, and writes on it an acceptance which she dates and signs. No contract is formed because the offer never became effective; Andy never communicated it to Bonnie. If Andy had mailed the letter, and it had gone astray in the mail, the offer would likewise never have become effective.

Not only must the offer be communicated to the offeree, but the communication must also be made or authorized by the offeror. For instance, if Joanne tells Karlene that she plans to offer Larry $600 for his piano, and Karlene promptly informs Larry of this proposal, no offer has been made. There was no authorized communication of any offer by Joanne to Larry. By the same token, if Lance should offer to sell his diamond ring to Ed, an acceptance of this offer by Dianne would not be effective, because Lance made the offer to Ed, not to Dianne.

An offer need not be stated or communicated by words. Conduct from which a reasonable person may infer a proposal in return for either an act or a promise amounts to an offer.

An offer may be made to the general public. No person, however, can accept such an offer until and unless he has knowledge that the offer exists. For example, if a person, without knowing of an advertised reward for information leading to the return of a lost watch, gives information that leads to its return, he is not entitled to the reward. His act was not an acceptance of the offer because he could not accept something of which he had no knowledge.

Intent

To have legal effect an offer must manifest an intent to enter into a contract. The intent of an offer is determined objectively from the words or conduct of the parties. The meaning of either party's manifestation is based upon what a reasonable person in the other party's position would have believed. The courts sometimes consider subjective intention in interpreting the parties' communications.

Occasionally, a person exercises her sense of humor by speaking or writing words that—taken literally and without regard to context or surrounding circumstances—a promisee could construe as an offer. The promisor intends the promise as a joke, however, and the promisee as a reasonable person should understand it to be such. Therefore, it is not an offer. Because the person to whom it is made realizes or should realize that it is not made in earnest, it should not create a reasonable expectation in his mind. No contractual intent exists on the part of the promisor, and the promisee is or reasonably ought to be aware of that fact. If, however, the intended jest is so successful that the promisee as a reasonable person under all the circumstances believes that the joke is in fact an offer, and so believing accepts, the objective standard applies and the parties have entered into a contract.

A promise made under obvious excitement or emotional strain is likewise not an offer. For example, Charlotte, after having her month-old Cadillac break down for the third time in two days, screams in disgust, "I will sell this car to anyone for $10.00!" Lisa hears Charlotte and hands her a ten-dollar bill. Under the circumstances, Charlotte's statement was not an offer, if a reasonable person in Lisa's position would have recognized it merely as an overwrought, nonbinding utterance.

It is important to distinguish language that constitutes an offer from that which merely solicits or invites offers. Such proposals, although made in earnest, lack intent and are therefore not deemed offers. As a result, a purported acceptance does not bring about a contract but operates only as an offer to accept. These proposals include preliminary negotiations, advertisements, and auctions.

◆ SEE CASE 6-1

Preliminary Negotiations If a communication creates in the mind of a reasonable person in the position of the offeree an expectation that his acceptance will conclude a contract, then the communication is an offer. If it does not, then the communication is a preliminary negotiation. Initial communications between potential parties to a contract often take the form of preliminary negotiations, through which the parties either request or supply the terms of an offer that may or may not be given. A statement that may indicate a willingness to make an offer is not in itself an offer. If Terri writes to Susan, "Will you buy my automobile for $3,000?" and Susan replies "Yes," no contract exists. Terri has not made an offer to sell her automobile to Susan for $3,000. The offeror must manifest an intent to enter into a contract, not merely a willingness to enter into negotiation.

Advertisements Merchants desire to sell their merchandise and thus are interested in informing potential customers about the goods, the terms of sale, and the price. But if they make widespread promises to sell to each person on their mailing list, the number of acceptances and resulting contracts might conceivably exceed their ability to perform. Consequently, a merchant might refrain from making offers by merely announcing that he has goods for sale, describing the goods, and quoting prices. He is simply inviting his customers and, in the case of published advertisements, the public, to make offers to him to buy the goods. His advertisements, circulars, quotation sheets, and merchandise displays are *not* offers because (1) they do not contain a promise and (2) they leave unexpressed many terms that would be necessary to the making of a contract. Accordingly, his customers' responses are not acceptances because he has made no offer to sell.

Nonetheless, a seller is not free to advertise goods at one price and then raise the price once demand has been stimulated. Although, as far as contract law is concerned, the seller has made no offer, such conduct is prohibited by the Federal Trade Commission as well as by legislation in many states.

Moreover, in some circumstances a public announcement or advertisement may constitute an offer if the advertisement or announcement contains a definite promise of something in exchange for something else and confers a power of acceptance upon a specified person or class of persons. The typical offer of a reward is an example of a definite offer, as was shown in *Lefkowitz v. Great Minneapolis Surplus Store, Inc.* In this case, the court held that a newspaper advertisement was an offer

because it contained a promise of performance in definite terms in return for a requested act.

◆ SEE CASE 6-2

Auction Sales The auctioneer at an auction sale does *not* make offers to sell the property that is being auctioned but invites offers to buy. The classic statement by the auctioneer is, "How much am I offered?" The persons attending the auction may make progressively higher bids for the property, and each bid or statement of a price or a figure is an offer to buy at that figure. If the bid is accepted—this customarily is indicated by the fall of the hammer in the auctioneer's hand—a contract results. A bidder is free to withdraw his bid at any time prior to its acceptance. The auctioneer is likewise free to withdraw the goods from sale *unless* the sale is advertised or announced to be without reserve.

If the auction sale is advertised or announced in explicit terms to be **without reserve**, the auctioneer may not withdraw an article or lot put up for sale unless no bid is made within a reasonable time. Unless so advertised or announced, the sale is with reserve. A bidder at either type of sale may retract his bid at any time prior to acceptance by the auctioneer. Such retraction, however, does not revive any previous bid.

Definiteness

The terms of a contract, all of which the offer usually contains, must be reasonably certain so as to provide a court with a basis for determining the existence of a breach and for giving an appropriate remedy. Restatement, Section 33. It is a fundamental policy that contracts should be made by the parties and not by the courts; accordingly, remedies for breach must have their basis in the parties' contract.

However, where the parties have intended to form a contract, the courts will attempt to find a basis for granting a remedy. Missing terms may be supplied by course of dealing, usage of trade, or inference. Thus, uncertainty as to incidental matters will seldom be fatal so long as the parties intended to form a contract. Nevertheless, the more terms the parties leave open, the less likely it is that they have intended to form a contract. Because of the great variety of contracts, the terms essential to all contracts cannot be stated. In most cases, however, material terms would include the subject matter, price, quantity, quality, terms of payment, and duration.

◆ SEE CASES 6-3, 6-4, AND 6-5

Open Terms With respect to agreements for the sale of goods, the Code provides standards by which omitted terms may be determined, provided the parties intended to enter into a binding contract. The Code provides missing terms in a number of instances, where, for example, the contract fails to specify the price, the time or place of delivery, or payment terms. Sections

2–204(3), 2–305, 2–308, 2–309, and 2–310. The Restatement, Section 34, has adopted an approach similar to the Code's in supplying terms the parties have omitted from their contract.

Under the Code, an offer for the purchase or sale of goods may leave open particulars of performance to be specified by one of the parties. Any such specification must be made in good faith and within limits set by commercial reasonableness. Section 2–311(1). **Good faith** is defined as honesty in fact in the conduct or transaction concerned. Section 1–201(19). **Commercial reasonableness** is a standard determined in terms of the business judgment of reasonable persons familiar with the practices customary in the type of transaction involved and in terms of the facts and circumstances of the case.

If the price is to be fixed otherwise than by agreement and is not so fixed through the fault of one of the parties, the other party has an option to treat the contract as cancelled or to fix a reasonable price in good faith for the goods. However, where the parties intend not to be bound unless the price is fixed or agreed upon as provided in the agreement, and it is not so fixed or agreed upon, the Code provides in accordance with the parties' intent that no contractual liability exists. In such case the seller must refund to the buyer any portion of the price she has received, and the buyer must return the goods to the seller or, if unable to do so, pay the reasonable value of the goods. Section 2–305(4).

Output and Requirements Contracts   A buyer's agreement to purchase the entire output of a seller's factory for a stated period, or a seller's agreement to supply a buyer with all his requirements for certain goods, may appear to lack definiteness and mutuality of obligation. Such an agreement does not specify the exact quantity of goods; moreover, the seller may have some control over her output and the buyer over his requirements. Nonetheless, under the Code and the Restatement such agreements are enforceable by the application of an objective standard based upon the good faith of both parties. Thus, a seller who operated her factory for eight hours a day before entering an output agreement cannot operate her factory twenty-four hours a day and insist that the buyer take all of the output. Nor can the buyer expand his business abnormally and insist that the seller still supply all of his requirements.

DURATION OF OFFERS

An offer confers upon the offeree a power of acceptance, which continues until the offer terminates. The ways in which an offer may be terminated, *other than by acceptance*, are through (1) lapse of time; (2) revocation; (3) rejection; (4) counteroffer; (5) death or incompetency of the offeror or offeree; (6) destruction of the subject matter to which the offer relates; and (7) subsequent illegality of the type of contract the offer proposes.

Lapse of Time

The offeror may specify the time within which the offer is to be accepted, just as he may specify any other term or condition in the offer. He may require that the offeree accept the offer immediately or within a **specified** period, such as a week or ten days. Unless otherwise terminated, the offer remains open for the specified period. Upon the expiration of that time, the offer no longer exists and cannot be accepted. Any subsequent purported acceptance will serve as a new offer.

If the offer states no time within which the offeree must accept, the offer will terminate after a **reasonable** time. Determining a "reasonable" period of time is a question of fact, depending on the nature of the contract proposed, the usages of business, and other circumstances of the case (including whether the offer was communicated by electronic means). Restatement, Section 41. For instance, an offer to sell a perishable good would be open for a far shorter time than an offer to sell undeveloped real estate.

❧ See Case 6-6

Revocation

An offeror generally may withdraw an offer at any time before it has been accepted, even though he has definitely promised to keep it open for a stated time. To be effective, notice of revocation of the offer must actually reach the offeree before she has accepted. If the offeror originally promises that the offer will be open for thirty days, but after five days wishes to terminate it, he may do so merely by giving the offeree notice that he is withdrawing the offer. Notice, which may be given by any means of communication, effectively terminates the offer when **received** by the offeree. A very few states, however, have adopted a rule that treats revocations the same as acceptances, thus making them effective upon dispatch. An offeror, however, may revoke an offer made to the general public only by giving to the revocation publicity equivalent to that given the offer.

Notice of revocation may be communicated indirectly to the offeree through reasonably reliable information from a third person that the offeror has disposed of the goods which he has offered for sale or has otherwise placed himself in a position which indicates an unwillingness or inability to perform the promise contained in the offer. Restatement, Section 43. For example, Jane offers to sell her portable television set to Bruce and tells Bruce that he has ten days in which to accept. One week later, Bruce observes the television set in Carl's house and is informed that Carl had purchased it from Jane. The next day Bruce sends to Jane an acceptance of the offer. There is no contract, because Jane's offer was effectively revoked when Bruce learned of Jane's inability to sell the television set to him because she had sold it to Carl.

Certain limitations, however, restrict the offeror's power to revoke the offer at any time prior to its acceptance. These limitations apply to the following five situations.

Option Contracts An option is a contract by which the offeror is bound to hold open an offer for a specified period of time. It must comply with all of the requirements of a contract, including *consideration* being given to the offeror by the offeree. (Consideration is discussed in Chapter 11.) For example, if Ann, in return for the payment of $500 to her by Bobby, grants Bobby an option, exercisable at any time within thirty days, to buy Blackacre at a price of $80,000, Ann's offer is irrevocable. Ann is legally bound to keep the offer open for thirty days, and any communication by Ann to Bobby giving notice of withdrawal of the offer is ineffective. Bobby is not bound to accept the offer, but the option contract entitles him to thirty days in which to accept.

Firm Offers Under the Code The Code provides that a *merchant* is bound to keep an offer to buy or sell **goods** open for a stated period (or, if no time is stated, for a reasonable time) not exceeding three months, if the merchant gives assurance in a **signed writing** that the offer will be held open. Section 2–205. The offeror must use the language of a 'firm offer,' promising not to revoke the offer and not merely stating that the offer will terminate on a certain date. The Code, therefore, makes a merchant's written promise not to revoke an offer for a stated period enforceable even though no consideration is given the offeror for that promise. For offers in which the offeror has stated that the offer will be open for three months or less, the offer will irrevocable for the period stated. Where the offer has stated a period greater than three months, the offer becomes revocable at the end of the third month. A **merchant** is defined as a person (1) who is a dealer in goods of a given kind, (2) who by his occupation holds himself out as having knowledge or skill peculiar to the goods or practices involved, or (3) who employs an agent or broker whom he holds out as having such knowledge or skill. Section 2–104.

❧ See Case 6-7

Firm Offers under GOL § 5-1109 New York State law extends the scope of firm offers beyond that provided by the Code. General Obligations Law § 5-1109 provides, as does UCC 2-205, that an offer will be irrevocable, even though there is no consideration, if the offeror has made a signed written promise that the offer will be irrevocable. GOL § 5-1109 applies to offers other than those covered by the Code. For example, a signed and written firm offer for the sale of a home would be covered by the GOL rule since the Code does not apply to the sale of real estate.

Similarly, a signed and written firm offer for the sale of an automobile by a non-merchant would be covered by the GOL rule since UCC 2-205 applies only to offers for sales of goods by merchants.

GOL § 5-1109, unlike UCC 2-205, does not provide for a maximum period of irrevocability. Thus the offeror will be bound to keep the offer open for the period stated, even if that period is more than three months. If the offer does not state the period of time for which the offer will be irrevocable, the offer will be irrevocable for "a reasonable time."

Statutory Irrevocability Certain offers, such as bids made to the state, municipality, or other governmental body for the construction of a building or some other public work, are made irrevocable by statute. Another example is preincorporation stock subscription agreements, which are irrevocable for a period of six months under many state incorporation statutes.

Irrevocable Offers of Unilateral Contracts Where an offer contemplates a unilateral contract, that is, a promise for an act, injustice to the offeree may result if revocation is permitted after the offeree has started to perform the act requested in the offer and has substantially but not completely accomplished it. Traditionally, such an offer is not accepted and no contract is formed until the offeree has *completed* the requested act. By simply commencing performance, the offeree does not bind himself to complete performance; nor, historically, did he bind the offeror to keep the offer open. Thus, the offeror could revoke the offer at any time prior to the offeree's completion of performance. For example, Linda offers Tom $300 if Tom will climb to the top of the flagpole in the center of campus. Tom commences his ascent, and when he is five feet from the top, Linda yells to him, "I revoke."

The Restatement deals with this problem by providing that where the performance of the requested act necessarily requires the offeree to expend time and effort, the offeror is obligated not to revoke the offer for a reasonable time. This obligation arises when the offeree begins performance. If, however, the offeror does not know of the offeree's performance and has no adequate means of learning of it within a reasonable time, the offeree must exercise reasonable diligence to notify the offeror of the performance.

Promissory Estoppel As discussed in the previous chapter, a noncontractual promise may be enforced when it is made under circumstances that should lead the promisor reasonably to expect that the promise will induce the promisee to take action in reliance on it. This doctrine has been used in some cases to prevent an offeror from revoking an offer prior to its acceptance. The Restatement provides the following rule:

> An offer which the offeror should reasonably expect to induce action or forbearance of a substantial character on the part of the offeree before acceptance and which does induce such action or forbearance is binding as an option contract to the extent necessary to avoid injustice. Restatement, Section 87(2).

Thus, Ramanan Plumbing Co. submits a written offer for plumbing work to be used by Resolute Building Co. as part of Resolute's bid as a general contractor. Ramanan knows that Resolute is relying on Ramanan's bid, and in fact Resolute submits Ramanan's name as the plumbing subcontractor in the bid. Ramanan's offer is irrevocable until Resolute has a reasonable opportunity to notify Ramanan that Resolute's bid has been accepted.

❧ SEE CASE 4-5

Rejection

An offeree is at liberty to accept or reject the offer as he sees fit. If the offeree decides not to accept it, he is not required to reject it formally but may simply wait until the offer terminates by the lapse of time. Through a **rejection** of an offer, the offeree manifests his unwillingness to accept. A communicated rejection terminates the power of acceptance. From the effective moment of rejection, which is the **receipt** of the rejection by the offeror, the offeree may no longer accept the offer. Rejection by the offeree may consist of express language or may be implied from language or from conduct.

Counteroffer

A **counteroffer** is a counterproposal from the offeree to the offeror that indicates a willingness to contract but upon terms or conditions different from those contained in the offer. It is not an unequivocal acceptance of the original offer and, by indicating an unwillingness to agree to the terms of the offer, it operates as a rejection. It also operates as a new offer. For instance, assume that Jordan writes Chris a letter stating that he will sell to Chris a secondhand color television set for $300. Chris replies that she will pay Jordan $250 for the set. This is a counteroffer which, upon **receipt** by Jordan, terminates the original offer. Jordan may, if he wishes, accept the counteroffer and thereby create a contract for $250. If, on the other hand, Chris states in her reply that she wishes to consider the $300 offer but is willing to pay $250 at once for the set, she is making a counteroffer which does *not* terminate Jordan's original offer. In the first instance, after making the $250 counteroffer, Chris may not accept the $300 offer. In the second instance she may do so, as the manner in which she stated the counteroffer did not indicate an unwillingness to accept the original offer, and Chris therefore did not terminate it. In addition, a mere inquiry about the possibility of obtaining different or new terms is not a counteroffer and does not terminate the offer. For example, in response to an offer for the sale of a book for $25, the potential buyer might say, "Would you take $20?" This is not a counteroffer, but an inquiry.

Another common type of counteroffer is the **conditional acceptance,** which purports to accept the offer but expressly makes the acceptance conditional upon the offeror's assent to additional or different terms. Nonetheless, it is a counteroffer

and terminates the original offer. The Code's treatment of acceptances containing terms that vary from the offer are discussed later in this chapter.

❧ SEE CASE 6-8

Death or Incompetency

The death or incompetency of either the offeror or the offeree ordinarily terminates an offer. Upon his death or incompetency the offeror no longer has the legal capacity to enter into a contract; thus, all his outstanding offers are terminated. Death or incompetency of the offeree likewise terminates the offer, because an ordinary offer is not assignable (transferable) and may be accepted only by the person to whom it was made. When the offeree dies or ceases to have legal capability to enter into a contract, no one else has the power to accept the offer. Therefore, the offer terminates.

The death or incompetency of the offeror or offeree, however, does *not* terminate an offer contained in an option.

Destruction of Subject Matter

Destruction of the specific subject matter of an offer terminates the offer. The impossibility of performance prevents a contract from being consummated and thus terminates all outstanding offers with respect to the destroyed property. Suppose that Martina, owning a Buick automobile, offers to sell the car to Worthy and allows Worthy five days in which to accept. Three days later the car is destroyed by fire. On the following day, Worthy, without knowledge of the car's destruction, notifies Martina that he accepts her offer. There is no contract. Martina's offer was terminated by the destruction of the car.

Subsequent Illegality

One of the four essential requirements of a contract, as previously mentioned, is legality of purpose or subject matter. If performance of a valid contract is subsequently made illegal, the obligations of both parties under the contract are discharged. Illegality taking effect after the making of an offer but prior to acceptance has the same effect: the offer is legally terminated.

Acceptance

The acceptance of an offer is essential to the formation of a contract. Once an acceptance has been given, the contract is formed. An acceptance can only be made by an offeree. Acceptance of an offer for a bilateral contract requires some overt act by which the offeree manifests his assent to the terms of the offer, such as speaking or sending a letter, a telegram, or other explicit or implicit communication to the offeror. If the offer is for a unilateral contract, the offeree may refrain from acting as requested or may signify acceptance through performance of the requested act with the intention of accepting. For example, if Joy publishes an offer of a reward to anyone who returns the diamond ring which she has lost (a unilateral contract offer), and Steven, with knowledge of the offer, finds and returns the ring to Joy, Steven has accepted the offer. If, however, Steven returns the ring to Joy but in doing so disclaims the reward and says that he does not accept the offer, there is no contract. Without the intention of accepting the offer, merely doing the act requested by the offeror is not sufficient to form a contract.

A late or defective acceptance does not create a contract. After the offer has expired, it cannot be validly accepted. A late or defective acceptance, however, does manifest the offeree's willingness to enter into a contract and therefore constitutes a new offer. To create a contract based upon this offer, the original offeror must accept the new offer by manifesting his assent.

COMMUNICATION OF ACCEPTANCE

General Rule

Because acceptance manifests the offeree's assent to the offer, the offeree must communicate this acceptance to the offeror. This is the rule as to all offers to enter into bilateral contracts. In the case of an offer to enter into a unilateral contract, however, notice of acceptance to the offeror is usually not required. If, however, the offeree in a unilateral contract has reason to know that the offeror has no adequate means of learning of the performance with reasonable promptness and certainty, then the offeree must make reasonable efforts to notify the offeror of acceptance or lose the right to enforce the contract. Restatement, Section 54.

Silence as Acceptance

An offeree is generally under no legal duty to reply to an offer. Silence or inaction, therefore, does *not* indicate acceptance of the offer. By custom, usage, or course of dealing, however, silence or inaction by the offeree may operate as an acceptance.

Thus, the silence or inaction of an offeree who fails to reply to an offer operates as an acceptance and causes a contract to be formed where by previous dealings the offeree has given the offeror reason to understand that the offeree will accept all offers unless the offeree sends notice to the contrary. Another example of silence operating as an acceptance occurs when the prospective member of a mail-order club agrees that his failure to return a notification card rejecting offered goods will constitute his acceptance of the club's offer to sell the goods.

Furthermore, if an offeror sends unordered or unsolicited merchandise to a person stating that she may purchase the goods at a specified price and that the offer will be deemed to have been accepted unless the goods are returned within a stated period of time, the offer is one for an inverted unilateral contract (i.e., an act for a promise). This practice led to abuse, however, which has prompted the federal government as well as most states to enact statutes which provide that in such cases the offeree-recipient of the goods may keep them as a gift and is under no obligation either to return them or to pay for them.

❧ See GOL § 5-332

Effective Moment

As previously discussed, an offer, a revocation, a rejection, and a counteroffer are effective when they are *received*. An acceptance, on the other hand, is generally effective upon **dispatch**. This is true unless the offer specifically provides otherwise, the offeree uses an unauthorized means of communication, or the acceptance follows a prior rejection.

Stipulated Provisions in the Offer If the offer specifically stipulates the means of communication the offeree is to use, the acceptance, to be effective, must conform to that specification. Thus, if an offer states that acceptance must be made by registered mail, any purported acceptance not made by registered mail would be ineffective. Moreover, the rule that an acceptance is effective when dispatched or sent does not apply where the offer provides that the offeror must receive the acceptance. If the offeror states that a reply must be received by a certain date or that he must hear from the offeree or uses other language indicating that the acceptance must be received by him, the effective moment of the acceptance is when the offeror receives it, not when the offeree sends or dispatches it.

Authorized Means Historically, an authorized means of communication was the means the offeror expressly authorized in the offer, or, if none was authorized, it was the means the offeror used. For example, if in reply to an offer by mail, the offeree places in the mail a letter of acceptance properly stamped and addressed to the offeror, a contract is formed at the time and place that the offeree mails the letter. This assumes, of course, that the offer at that time was open and had not been terminated by any of the methods previously discussed. The reason for this rule is that the offeror, by using the mail, impliedly authorized the offeree to use the same method of communication. It is immaterial if the letter of acceptance goes astray in the mails and is never received.

The Restatement, Section 30, and the Code, Section 2–206(1)(a), both now provide that where the language in the offer or the circumstances do not otherwise indicate, an offer to make a contract shall be construed as authorizing acceptance in any **reasonable** manner. These provisions are intended to allow flexibility of response and the ability to keep pace with new modes of communication.

❧ See Case 6-9

◆ Figure 6-1   Offer and Acceptance

	Time Effective	Effect
Communications by Offeror		
• Offer	Received by offeree	Creates power to form a contract
• Revocation	Received by offeree	Terminates offer
Communications by Offeree		
• Rejection	Received by offeror	Terminates offer
• Counteroffer	Received by offeror	Terminates offer
• Acceptance	Sent by offeree	Forms a contract
• Acceptance after prior rejection	Received by offeror	If received before rejection forms a contract

Unauthorized Means When the offeree uses an unauthorized method of communication, the traditional rule is that acceptance is effective when and if received by the offeror, provided that he receives it within the time during which the authorized means would have arrived. The Restatement, Section 67, provides that if these conditions are met, the effective time for the acceptance relates back to the moment of dispatch.

Acceptance Following a Prior Rejection An acceptance sent after a prior rejection is not effective when sent by the offeree, but is only effective when and if the offeror **receives** it before he receives the rejection. Thus, when an acceptance follows a prior rejection, the first communication to be received by the offeror is the effective one. For example, Anna in New York sends by mail to Fritz in San Francisco an offer that is expressly stated to be open for one week. On the fourth day, Fritz sends to Anna by mail a letter of rejection that is delivered on the morning of the sixth day. At noon on the fifth day, however, Fritz had dispatched a telegram of acceptance that is received by Anna before the close of business on that day. A contract was formed when Anna received Fritz's telegram of acceptance, as it was received before the letter of rejection.

◆ See Figure 6-1 Offer and Acceptance

VARIANT ACCEPTANCES

A variant acceptance—one that contains terms different from or additional to those in the offer—receives distinctly different treatment under the common law and the Code.

Common Law

An acceptance must be *positive* and *unequivocal*. In that it may not change, add to, subtract from, or qualify in any way the provisions of the offer, it must be the **mirror image** of the offer. Any communication by the offeree which attempts to modify the offer is not an acceptance but is a counteroffer, which does not create a contract. For example, in response to an offer of employment at $8.00 an hour, the offeree responds, "I accept. I will work for you for $9.00 an hour." The offeree has made a counteroffer, not an acceptance.

Code

The Code modifies the common law "mirror image" rule, by which the acceptance cannot vary or deviate from the terms of the offer. This modification is necessitated by the realities of modern business practices. A vast number of business transactions use standardized business forms. For example, a merchant buyer sends to a merchant seller on the buyer's order form a purchase order for 1,000 dozen cotton shirts at $60.00 per dozen with delivery by October 1 at the buyer's place of business. On the reverse side of this standard form are twenty-five numbered paragraphs containing provisions generally favorable to the buyer. When the seller receives the buyer's order, he agrees to the quantity, price, and delivery terms and sends to the buyer on his acceptance form an unequivocal acceptance of the offer. However, on the back of his acceptance form, the seller has thirty-two numbered paragraphs generally favorable to himself and in significant conflict with the buyer's form. Under the common law's *mirror image* rule, no contract would exist, for the seller has not accepted unequivocally all the material terms of the buyer's offer.

The Code in Section 2–207 attempts to alleviate this **battle of the forms** by focusing upon the intent of the parties. If the offeree expressly makes her acceptance conditioned upon assent to the additional or different terms, no contract is formed. If the offeree does not expressly make her acceptance conditional upon the offeror's assent to the additional or different terms, a contract is formed. The issue then becomes whether the offeree's different or additional terms may become part of the contract. If both offeror and offeree are merchants, such *additional* terms may become part of the contract, provided they do not materially alter the agreement and are not objected to either in the offer itself or within a reasonable period of time. If both parties are not merchants or if the additional terms materially alter the offer, then the additional terms are merely construed as proposals to the contract. *Different* terms proposed by the offeree will not become part of the contract unless the offeror accepts them. The courts are divided over what terms a contract includes when those terms differ or conflict. Some courts hold that the offeror's terms govern; other courts, holding that the terms cancel each other out, look to the Code to provide the missing terms. Some follow a third alternative and apply the additional terms test to different terms. (See Figure 7-4 in Chapter 7.)

To apply Section 2–207 to the example above: because both parties are merchants and the acceptance was not conditional upon assent to the additional or different terms, (1) the contract will be formed without the seller's different terms unless the buyer specifically accepts them, (2) the contract will be formed without the seller's additional terms unless (a) the buyer specifically accepts them or (b) they do not materially alter the offer and the buyer does not object, and (3) depending upon the jurisdiction, either (a) the buyer's conflicting terms are included in the contract or (b) the Code provides the missing terms, as the conflicting terms cancel each other out, or (c) the additional terms test is applied.

CHAPTER SUMMARY

Offer

Essentials of an Offer	**Definition** indication of willingness to enter into a contract
	Communication offeree must have knowledge of the offer and the offer must be made by the offeror to the offeree
	Intent determined by an objective standard of what a reasonable offeree would have believed
	Definiteness offer's terms must be clear enough to provide a court with a basis for giving an appropriate remedy
Duration of Offers	**Lapse of Time** offer remains open for the time period specified or, if no time is stated, for a reasonable period of time
	Revocation generally, an offer may be terminated at any time before it is accepted, subject to the following exceptions
	• *Option Contract* contract that binds offeror to keep an offer open for a specified time
	• *Firm Offer* a merchant's irrevocable offer to sell or buy goods in a signed writing ensures that the offer will not be terminated for up to three months
	• *Statutory Irrevocability* offer made irrevocable by statute
	• *Irrevocable Offer of Unilateral Contract* a unilateral offer may not be revoked for a reasonable time after performance is begun
	• *Promissory Estoppel* noncontractual promise that binds the promisor because she should reasonably expect that the promise will induce the promisee (offeree) to take action in reliance on it
	Rejection refusal to accept an offer terminates the power of acceptance
	Counteroffer counterproposal to an offer that generally terminates the original offer
	Death or Incompetency of either the offeror or the offeree terminates the offer
	Destruction of Subject Matter of an offer terminates the offer
	Subsequent Illegality of the purpose or subject matter of the offer terminates the offer

Acceptance of Offer

Requirements	**Definition** positive and unequivocal expression of a willingness to enter into a contract on the terms of the offer
	Mirror Image Rule except as modified by the Code, an acceptance cannot deviate from the terms of the offer

Communication of Acceptance

▷**General Rule** acceptance effective upon dispatch unless the offer specifically provides otherwise or the offeree uses an unauthorized means of communication

Stipulated Provisions in the Offer the communication of acceptance must conform to the specification in the offer

Authorized Means the Restatement and the Code provide that unless the offer provides otherwise, acceptance is authorized to be in any reasonable manner

Unauthorized Means acceptance effective when received, provided that it is received within the time within which the authorized means would have arrived

Acceptance Following a Prior Rejection first communication received by the offeror is effective

✗**Defective Acceptance** does not create a contract but serves as a new offer

---

CASES

CASE

6-1

This case concerns the use of the objective standard when analyzing the manifestation of mutual assent (offer and acceptance).

CITY OF EVERETT v. ESTATE OF SUMSTAD
Supreme Court of Washington, 1981
95 Wn.2d 853, 631 P.2d 366

DOLLIVER, J.

The City of Everett commenced an . . . action against the seller (the Sumstad Estate) and the buyer (Al and Rosemary Mitchell) of a safe to determine who is entitled to a sum of money found in the safe. Both the Estate and the Mitchells moved for summary judgment. The trial court entered summary judgment in favor of the Estate. The Court of Appeals affirmed. [Citation.]

Petitioners, Mr. and Mrs. Mitchell, are the proprietors of a small secondhand store. On August 12, 1978, the Mitchells attended Alexander's Auction, where they frequently had shopped to obtain merchandise for their own use and for use as inventory in their business. At the auction the Mitchells purchased a used safe with an inside compartment for $50. As they were told by the auctioneer when they purchased the safe, the Mitchells found that the inside compartment of the safe was locked. The safe was part of the Sumstad Estate.

Several days after the auction, the Mitchells took the safe to a locksmith to have the locked compartment opened. The locksmith found $32,207 inside. The Everett Police Department, notified by the locksmith, impounded the money.

* * * The issue is whether there was in fact a sale of the safe and its unknown contents at the auction. In contrast to the Court of Appeals, we find that there was.

A sale is a consensual transaction. The subject matter which passes is to be determined by the intent of the parties as revealed by the terms of their agreement in light of the surrounding circumstances. [Citation.] The objective manifestation theory of contracts, which is followed in this state [citation] lays stress on the outward manifestation of assent made by each party to the other. The subjective intention of the parties is irrelevant.

A contract has, strictly speaking, nothing to do with the personal, or individual, intent of the parties. A contract is an obligation attached by the mere force of law to certain acts of the parties, usually words, which ordinarily accompany and represent a known intent. If, however, it were proved by twenty bishops that either party, when he used the words, intended something else than the usual meaning which the law imposes upon them, he would still be held, unless there were some mutual mistake, or something else of the sort. [Citation.]

As stated in Washington Shoe Mfg. Co. v. Duke [citation]

> The apparent mutual assent of the parties, essential to the formation of a contract, must be gathered from their outward expressions and acts, and not from an unexpressed intention.

The inquiry, then, is into the outward manifestations of intent by a party to enter into a contract. We impute an intention corresponding to the reasonable meaning of a person's words and acts. [Citation.] If the offeror, judged by a reasonable standard manifests an intention to agree in regard to the matter in question, that agreement is established. [Citation.]

* * *

In the case before us, . . . the Mitchells were aware of the rule of the auction that all sales were final. Furthermore, the auctioneer made no statement reserving rights to any contents of the safe to the estate. Under these circumstances, we hold reasonable persons would conclude that the auctioneer manifested an objective intent to sell the safe and its contents and that the parties mutually assented to enter into that sale of the safe and the contents of the locked compartment.

* * *

This matter is remanded to the trial court for entry of the summary judgment in favor of the Mitchells.

CASE 6-2

LEFKOWITZ v. GREAT MINNEAPOLIS SURPLUS STORE, INC.

Supreme Court of Minnesota, 1957
251 Minn. 188, 86 N.W.2d 689

Murphy, J.

This is an appeal from an order of * * * judgment award[ing] the plaintiff the sum of $138.50 as damages for breach of contract.

This case grows out of the alleged refusal of the defendant to sell to the plaintiff a certain fur piece which it had offered for sale in a newspaper advertisement. It appears from the record that on April 6, 1956, the defendant published the following advertisement in a Minneapolis newspaper:

> Saturday 9 AM Sharp
> 3 Brand New
> Fur Coats
> Worth to $100.00
> First Come First Served
> $1 Each

On April 13, the defendant again published an advertisement in the same newspaper as follows:

> Saturday 9 AM
> 2 Brand New Pastel
> Mink 3–Skin Scarfs
> Selling for $89.50
> Out they go
> Saturday. Each...$1.00
> 1 Black Lapin Stole
> Beautiful,
> worth $139.50...$1.00
> First Come First Served

The record supports the findings of the court that on each of the Saturdays following the publication of the above-described ads the plaintiff was the first to present himself at the appropriate counter in the defendant's store and on each occasion demanded the coat and the stole so advertised and indicated his readiness to pay the sale price of $1. On both occasions, the defendant refused to sell the merchandise to the plaintiff, stating on the first occasion that by a "house rule" the offer was intended for women only and sales would not be made to men, and on the second visit that plaintiff knew defendant's house rules.* * *

The defendant contends that a newspaper advertisement offering items of merchandise for sale at a named price is a "unilateral offer" which may be withdrawn without notice. He relies upon authorities which hold that, where an advertiser publishes in a newspaper that he has a certain quantity or quality of goods which he wants to dispose of at certain prices and on certain terms, such advertisements are not offers which become contracts as soon as any person to whose notice they may come signifies his acceptance by notifying the other that he will take a certain quantity of them. Such advertisements have been construed as an invitation for an offer of sale on the terms stated, which offer, when received, may be accepted or rejected and which therefore does not become a contract of sale until accepted by the seller; and until a contract has been so made, the seller may modify or revoke such prices or terms. [Citations.]* * *

On the facts before us we are concerned with whether the advertisement constituted an offer, and, if so, whether the plaintiff's conduct constituted an acceptance.

* * *

The test of whether a binding obligation may originate in advertisements addressed to the general public is "whether the facts show that some performance was promised in positive terms in return for something requested."

* * *

Whether in any individual instance a newspaper advertisement is an offer rather than an invitation to make an offer depends on the legal intention of the parties and the surrounding circumstances. [Citations.] We are of the view on the facts before us that the offer by the defendant of the sale of the Lapin fur was clear, definite, and explicit, and left nothing open for negotiation. The plaintiff, having successfully managed to be the first one to appear at the seller's place of business to be served, as requested by the advertisement, and having offered the stated purchase price of the article, was entitled to performance on the part of the defendant. We think the trial court was correct in holding that there was in the conduct of the parties a sufficient mutuality of obligation to constitute a contract of sale.

* * *

Affirmed.

This case concerns the need for definiteness and certainty in the terms of a contract.

DOMBROWSKI v. SOMERS
Court of Appeals of New York, 1977
41 N.Y. 2d 858

MEMORANDUM. By this action plaintiff seeks compensation for housekeeping chores rendered pursuant to an alleged oral agreement between herself and the decedent, Edward Vogel, whose household she was sharing.

Three witnesses testified that they heard Vogel say he would "take care of" plaintiff. None recalled any reference to a specific date. The claim itself was not filed until 18 months after the decedent's death.

The words to "take care of", in the context of this record, are too vague to spell out a meaningful promise. Even if they were not, standing alone, they would be legally insufficient to support a finding that there was a contract to compensate plaintiff during her lifetime rather than one to do so by bequest. In the latter case, an enforceable agreement would be required to be in writing.... In short, plaintiff has not met her burden of proof as a matter of law....

Accordingly, the order of the Appellate Division is reversed and the complaint dismissed.

In the following case, the court applies the rules regarding definiteness and certainty of contractual terms to an interesting set of facts.

TRIMMER v. VAN BOMEL
Supreme Court of New York (N.Y. Co.), 1980
107 Misc. 2d 201, 434 N.Y.S. 2d 82

GREENFIELD, Judge. The complex and varied relationships between men and women, when they come to an end, oft leave a bitter residue and a smoldering irritation for which the salve, often the only soothing balm, is cash. It is a poor substitute for love, affection or attention, but for many its satisfactions are longer lasting. "Ordinarily, alimony is the end product of the fission of matrimony by acrimony." More recently, the termination of informal "live-in" relationships has given rise to claims for "palimony." Now, in this case, a man who claims to have been the constant companion of an elderly wealthy widow, who changed his life style from genteel poverty to luxury at her behest, sues at the breakup of their relationship for what may be called, for want of a better term, "companiomony".

Plaintiff is a 67-year-old gentleman, who was earning a modest but respectable living as a travel tour operator, when a person on one of his tours, the defendant, Mrs. Catherine Bryer Van Bomel, a wealthy widow with assets stated to be in excess of $40,000,000, began making demands on his time, and allegedly agreed to support him in luxurious fashion, if he would devote all his time and attention to her. He gave up his business career, in which he admits he was earning no more than $8,900 a year and became the ever-present companion of Mrs. Von Bomel. He moved to larger quarters and modified his wardrobe to suit her tastes. He accompanied her to lunch and dinner, escorted her to the theatre and parties, and traveled with her on her trips to Europe. All this was at the lady's expense, of course. He also acted as her confidante and her friends became his friends.

For five years his life was constantly dominated by the needs, whims and desires of Mrs. Van Bomel. She spent money lavishly on him. Apart from taking care of his rent and his travel expenses, she had his suits hand tailored in Italy and in London, presented him with two Pontiacs and a Jaguar and gave him a monthly stipend. All in all, she expended well over $300,000 for his personal needs. Then, suddenly, it all came to an end. Accustomed to a life of luxury, and now without the means to attain it, plaintiff sues his former benefactress for $1,500,000.

In the first cause of action, plaintiff seeks recovery on an alleged express oral agreement, pursuant to which he agreed to give up his business and render services to the defendant, in return for which defendant would pay and provide (a) all his costs and expenses incurred in connection with the performance of his services, (b) all his costs and expenses for sumptuous living during the time the services were rendered, and (c) to pay "within a reasonable time" an amount sufficient to pay for all his costs and expenses for sumptuous living for the rest of his life. The plaintiff further alleges that he fully performed the agreement on his part and that the defendant, in part performance, paid all his costs and expenses during the period of rendition of services, but has failed and refused to provide plaintiff with a sum sufficient to maintain him on a standard of "sumptuous living" for the remainder of his life, which sum plaintiff contends would be $1,500,000.

In his second cause of action, which sounds in quantum meruit, plaintiff alleges that he performed the various services for defendant for a five-year period and gave up pursuit of his separate business career. For the agreed and reasonable value of his services on the second cause of action, he seeks $1,500,000.

Defendant has moved for summary judgment . . . contending that the action is without merit and that the purported agreement is too vague and indefinite to be enforceable; that defendant's obligations under the alleged agreement are illusory; that the agreement is void for lack of consideration and that plaintiff has already been paid far in excess of the value of any purported services.

Defendant had previously moved for summary judg-ment… and a denial of the motion at that time was affirmed by the Appellate Division. Plaintiff misconstrues the nature of that prior order, since, in clarification, the Appellate Division specifically held that its affirmance of the denial of summary judgment was "without prejudice to renewal thereof after the conclusion of pretrial procedures herein." The Appellate Division specifically noted: "We do not pass upon the merits of plaintiff's claims or defendant's position with respect thereto at this time". Depositions having been concluded, defendant has moved again for summary judgment. That right to renew in these circumstances is predicated not upon the allegation of new or additional material, but upon the completion of discovery. There is now a complete record before the court containing the entire recollections of both plaintiff and defendant, the only parties to the alleged agreement.

While there have been a number of cases dealing with lawsuits by one partner in a nonmarital relationship seeking to recover against the other on the basis of an express or implied agreement the court in this case is not confronted with the public policy considerations which compel the judiciary to uphold the institution of marriage and to distinguish its consequences from less formal and less permanent living arrangements. No meretricious relationship appears to be here involved. At best, plaintiff may be regarded as a companion and paid escort, and not as a substitute mate. These cases are instructive, however, as to which type of agreements may be enforceable and whether recovery is to be permitted on a theory of implied contract or quantum meruit.

In this state, cases of unmarried persons living together who thereafter seek financial recovery frequently run afoul of the theory that a contract founded upon an agreement to live together as man and wife will not be enforced. While one may not claim compensation for having been a paramour, if there are services rendered which are nonsexual in nature and do not arise directly from such a relationship, then such services may be deemed separable, and form the basis for compensation….

The extramatrimonial case involving a claim for the value of services rendered which has received the most publicity to date is *Marvin v Marvin*. In that case the California Supreme Court had reversed the dismissal of Michelle Marvin's complaint as a de facto spouse, and remanded the matter for trial to determine whether or not she was entitled to recovery on an express or implied contract. It was not the holding of the California court that a mistress was entitled to "palimony". At Trial Term, the court found that the allegations that there had been an explicit contract to compensate the plaintiff were not borne out by the facts. Nevertheless, the court, exercising its equitable powers, decided to award the sum of $1,000 per week for a two-year period to enable the plaintiff, who had allegedly given up her budding career, to rehabilitate herself. Interestingly, on the same day that Michelle Marvin was awarded "severance pay" by the California trial court, in New York the female companion of rock star Peter Frampton was cut off without compensation….

The most recent case in this State dealing with extramarital contracts is *Morone v Morone*. In that case, as here, two causes of action were alleged — the first based upon implied contract and the second alleging an explicit oral "partnership agreement". The concept of an implied contract to compensate for services was declared by the court "to be conceptually so amorphous as practically to defy equitable enforcement". Nevertheless, the court concluded that the allegations of an express contract that the woman would furnish domestic services and the man was to have full charge of business transactions and that the "net profits" from the partnership were to be shared equally, set forth an enforceable cause of action. Evidently, "housewifely" services are to be distinguished from such other services as may be rendered during the course of a living-together relationship. When the "tainted" consideration for such contracts is removed, the claim for recovery in extramarital cases stands in precisely the same posture as in this case.

In this case, the services for which plaintiff seeks compensation on a quantum meruit basis, like those in a quasi-marital relationship, arise out of the nature of the relationship of the parties to one another. The services involved — to devote time and attention to the defendant, to allow her wishes to prevail concerning his deportment, habits and associations and to act as companion, to accompany defendant to restaurants, to travel with her, to accept gifts and jewelry, clothing and motor cars from her are of a nature which would ordinarily be exchanged without expectation of pay. As Judge Meyer noted in *Morone v Morone*: "As a matter of human experience personal services will frequently be rendered by two people…because they value each other's company or because they find it a convenient or rewarding thing to do…. For courts to attempt through hindsight to sort out the intentions of the parties and affix jural significance to conduct carried out within an essentially private and generally noncontractual relationship runs too great a risk of error. Absent an express agreement, there is no frame of reference against which to compare the testimony presented and the character of the evidence that can be presented becomes more evanescent. There is, therefore, substantially greater risk of emotion-laden afterthought, not to mention fraud, in attempting to ascertain by implication what services, if any, were rendered gratuitously and what compensation, if any, the parties intended to be paid."

As to personal services between unmarried persons living together or unmarried persons whose actions flow out of mutual friendship and reciprocal regard, there is very little difference. An implied contract to compensate for those things which are ordinarily done by one person for another as a matter of regard and affection should not, under these well-established principles, be recognized in this State. Plaintiff has already received $300,000 from the defendant during the course of their relationship. What further "obligation" can be implied?

The claims of friendship, like the claims of kinship, may be many and varied. To imply an obligation by a wealthy friend to compensate a less wealthy companion for being together, dining together, talking together and accepting tokens of regard stretches the bond of friendship to the breaking point. The implied obligation to compensate arises from those things which, in normal society, we expect to pay for. An obligation to pay for friendship is not ordinarily to be implied — it is too crass. Friendship, like virtue, must be its own reward.

Accordingly, the second cause of action, founded in implied contract, must be dismissed.

The first cause of action, however, alleges an express agreement to pay the plaintiff. For the purposes of this motion for summary judgment, the court must accept as true plaintiff's allegation that defendant agreed to set up a fund which would permit plaintiff to live for the remainder of his life in the sumptuous style to which he had become accustomed. While defendant denies that there were specific conversations about setting up a fund, she does admit having discussions from time to time about making finances available to the plaintiff. She denies, however, and the plaintiff's testimony in his deposition confirms, that no specific dollar amounts were ever specified, no time for performance was ever set and no conditions as to the manner of payment were given, nor was anything ever said about what would happen if the relationship between the parties terminated. Thus, the principal issue presented is whether such an agreement as alleged in the complaint, and as expanded upon in plaintiff's deposition, can be regarded as enforceable. While there is no public policy bar to such an agreement, as an alleged express oral contract, its validity must be tested exactly the same as other contracts. Such a contract is not conceptually invalid....

All courts would agree with the doctrine, although not necessarily the application, that as a basic premise of contract law "'It is a necessary requirement in the nature of things that an agreement in order to be binding must be sufficiently definite

to enable a court to give it an exact meaning' (1 Williston, Contracts [3d ed], § 37)." In Dombrowski v Somers, a unanimous Court of Appeals found that an alleged oral agreement, pursuant to which the decedent said that in return for plaintiff's services he would "take care of" the plaintiff, was too vague to spell out a meaningful promise.

The question in this case is whether an alleged agreement by defendant to pay an amount sufficient to take care of all of plaintiff's "costs and expenses for sumptuous living and maintenance for the remainder of his life" as amplified by plaintiff's testimony, will enable the court to award plaintiff a judgment in a specific sum of dollars. It is clear from the pre-trial depositions of both parties, that no specific dollar amount, or approximate dollar amount, of any alleged fund was ever discussed. No facts are presented which would tend to establish a meeting of minds as to the definition of "sumptuous living." In his 237-page bill of particulars, plaintiff asserted that the defendant had agreed "to provide and set up for him a fund, either by giving him a block of stock or cash, or both, which would take care of all his living expenses in the same expensive style for the rest of his life." Plaintiff is alleging, in essence, a contract of employment, but as reference to his own testimony indicates, there was no specification as to the length of the term, the amount of the compensation, the terms of the payment, the nature of the duties, the manner in which the employment could be terminated and the method of computing "severance pay." Plaintiff's deposition indicates that there was no specific time at which the alleged agreement was worked out, but rather that it developed as part of numerous conversations over an extended period of time, and it is clear that he commenced his "employment" long before any such agreement to take care of him for the rest of his life was discussed.

With respect to the alleged promise of the defendant to set up a "fund" to take care of his needs for "sumptuous living," no specifics were ever discussed....

Nor, admittedly, was there ever any discussion about what was necessary for the plaintiff's living expenses either at that time or at some point off in the future....

What we are talking about, then, at best is "a fund" in some unspecified amount to be set up on some unspecified date in some unspecified manner, and that it was wholly in the discretion of the defendant. The agreement boils down to these words, "She would do it in some way."

Plaintiff has attempted to overcome the inherent vagueness of this "agreement" by trying to spell out, after the fact, what amounts he deems to be required for "sumptuous living." What is "sumptuous" to one person may be merely adequate to another, of course.

"Sumptuous" is defined as involving great expense; costly, lavish, magnificent (Webster's Dictionary, p 1825,...)

Moreover, sumptuous living "cannot be computed from anything that was said by the parties or by reference to any document, paper or other transaction" nor would it be provable by evidence of custom. Nor, for that matter, could defendant be required to account since no partnership agreement is alleged and additionally, defendant's vast holdings were accumulated before she had ever met plaintiff. Essentially, then the amount was left subject to the will of the defendant or for further negotiation. Courts cannot aid parties who have not specified the terms of their own agreements....

Plaintiff calculates that since he was given an average of $71,672 (tax free) by Mrs. Van Bomel during their five-year relationship, that this is the sum he should be given for the rest of his life. That is how he comes to the $1,500,000 set forth in the ad damnum. One million five hundred dollars in six-month certificates would give him $180,000 a year and that same sum in tax-free municipals would produce well over $100,000 per year, in which case the principal would be left intact. It appears clear that we are dealing with an alleged agreement which is too vague in any of its material terms to be deemed enforceable. No amount being specified, no time having been set forth, no mechanics for the payments having been spelled out and there being no specification as to what had to be done to qualify or disqualify the plaintiff for the payments, what we have, at best, is some vague but legally unenforceable reassurance that plaintiff "would be taken care of."

Since plaintiff alleges an express agreement which is to be governed by the law applicable to all contracts, it is instructive to compare the kind of agreement upon which plaintiff relies with other, more detailed contracts which the courts have nevertheless found to be unenforceable. Thus, in Brause v Goldman, where negotiations had progressed to a point of much greater detail than what was involved here, the court found that many of the essentials of an agreement were lacking. In that case, the court declared: "When the wording...exchanged between the parties reveal no present intent to form a binding contract, but rather to continue negotiations with the possible ultimate meeting of minds deferred until some future time, either party may withdraw with impunity prior to that time...."

Further, "The absence of any of the essential elements of an agreement is a bar to its enforcibility." The court found that even though there were memoranda of agreement prepared after oral negotiations, there was no indication as to the date on which the arrangement was to be commenced nor as to the method of payment, nor as to the rights of the parties in the event of various contingencies coming to pass. The Appellate Division declared, "It is not for the court to dictate such terms to the parties, for its function is to enforce agreements only if they exist, and not to create them by the imposition of such terms as it considers reasonable."

In essence, if the relationship between the plaintiff and defendant was that of employer and employee rather than that of friends or benefactress and protege, then clearly it was an employment relationship terminable at will. Plaintiff recognized that he would be rendering services at the pleasure of Mrs. Van Bomel, and that could be for months, for years or on into the indefinite future. Plaintiff testified, "The discussion was that I was to start doing this for her. There was no time limit put on it... I knew that if she decided that she would like to terminate my employment with her, she could do that. She had a perfect right to do that." Would a defendant be bound by a commitment to put up a fund of $1,500,000 for someone who rendered "services" to her for a matter of months by accompanying her to restaurants such as Lutece and the Palm Court? Plaintiff would accompany the defendant to lunch two or three times weekly. He agreed that the defendant never imposed any restrictions upon his activities. For these companionable social activities, it cannot be said that defendant, or her estate, is to be bound for the rest of plaintiff's life.

In an agreement terminable at will, and with no clear bounds and parameters set forth, an alleged obligation which would continue and survive beyond the termination of employment must appear with specificity. What if the relationship had been terminated for "cause?" Suppose plaintiff had been disloyal or discourteous or had secretly embezzled some of defendant's funds, would the agreement to take care of him for life continue nevertheless? Since this relationship was terminable at will, and the relationship had come to an end, this court can see no legal basis upon which the defendant can be compelled to continue lavishing her favors and her bounty upon the plaintiff. There are no guarantees in life, and good fortune, to be enjoyed while it lasts, does not invariably bring with it a life-long annuity. It was defendant who decided to get plaintiff tickets for the Royal Enclosure at Ascot, to buy him fabrics in London to be tailored in Rome. It was defendant who took pleasure in seeing that plaintiff's shoes came from Gucci and his accessories from Saks. When the relationship is terminated, the law does not compel... the dead relationship to continue.

Accordingly, defendant is entitled to summary judgment on the first cause of action as well as the second. The complaint should be dismissed.

*In the following case, the court determines whether the parties have reached
agreement on all material terms and thus have an enforceable contract.*

ANSORGE v. KANE
Court of Appeals of New York, 1927 244 N.Y. 395

POUND, Judge. The main point is simply stated. Defendant owned real property in Flushing, New York. Plaintiff desired to purchase it. Through her agent the parties came together March 25, 1925, and made a memorandum of purchase and sale which describes the property and acknowledges the receipt of $500 as binder thereon and then provides:

"The price is $32,625; payable $12,625 cash; balance of $20,000 to remain on 1st mortgage for five years. The sum to be paid on signing of contract on March 26th, 1925, to be agreed on. The balance of cash payment on passing of title on May 26th, 1925."

The parties never agreed on the sum to be paid on signing the contract. When the owner refused to sign a contract or execute a deed the court below ordered specific performance at the suit of the purchaser. That the parties had not agreed was held immaterial. It was said that the agreement in substance was that the balance of the cash payment would be payable when title passed unless the parties in the interim agreed otherwise....

Appellant contends that the scheme or plan of the parties was left incomplete by the failure to name the sum to be paid when the contract was signed; and that until the sum was named the contract was unenforceable.... The memorandum states the price to be paid but it does not state all the terms of payment.... The fundamental question here presented is whether there was any contract; any actual meeting of minds on all the material elements of the agreement.

If a material element of a contemplated contract is left for future negotiations, there is no enforceable contract.... The price is a material element of any contract of sale and an agreement to agree thereon in the future is too indefinite to be enforceable....

The terms of payment may be no less material. Is this memorandum in effect an agreement to convey the property described if the parties can agree upon the amount to be paid on the signing of the contract but for no sale if they do not agree? Or is the agreement on the sum to be paid on signing the contract a minor and non-essential detail of the transaction? That is the question before us.... The memorandum was on its face a mere binder. The formal contract was to be prepared and executed on the next day. As a part of the agreement was left to future negotiations, the contract was embryonic. It never reached full time. It was not for nothing that the parties provided that a sum should be agreed on to be paid on the signing of the contract; nor was it a minor matter for the owner whether nothing should be paid when the contract was signed and she should wait two months for her money, or whether she should receive a substantial sum, the stronger to bind the agreement, on which she also might receive interest, or even a greater increment, if she had her hands on it. In this connection we observe that the broker demanded that his full commission of ten per cent be paid on the signing of the contract which further suggests that the down payment had more than theoretical importance to the vendor.

The parties had decided to purchase and sell. They had agreed on the purchase price. They had not agreed on the terms of payment. The law implies nothing as to such terms as it does in cases where the rate of interest and date of maturity of a mortgage are not stated...or where it appears that an agreement is to take effect and be acted upon before the details reserved for future agreement, such as time of delivery, are settled, when an implication may arise that, in the event of a failure to agree, the terms shall be such as are reasonable or customary.... The amount to be paid on the signing of the contract was an important element of the complete contract. It was left open. The contract was never completed. The transaction was destitute of legal effect. Specific performance is, therefore, impossible. . . .

The judgment of the Appellate Division and that of the Special Term should be reversed and the complaint dismissed.

If the duration of an offer is not specified, it expires in a "reasonable time." The following case illustrates that a court will consider the particular circumstances in determining whether acceptance has been made in a reasonable time.

22 WEST MAIN STREET, INC. v. BOGUSZEWSKI

Appellate Division, New York (4th Dept.), 1970
34 A.D. 2d 358, 311 N.Y.S. 2d 565

DEL VECCHIO, Justice. Plaintiff appeals from an order of Special Term denying its motion for summary judgment in an action to compel specific performance of a real estate contract.

There is no dispute about the events which preceded this action.

On February 21, 1968 defendant executed an offer to purchase approximately 4.9 acres of land in the Village of Fredonia for $7,000. The offer stated that the closing was to be held at the offices of the attorneys for the defendant 'on or before March 22, 1968 or as soon thereafter as abstracts can be brought to date'. There was no acceptance by plaintiff until March 26, 1968 (four days after the closing date specified in the offer), when the seller crossed out the closing date of March 22, 1968, inserted the date 'April 10, 1968' and signed the acceptance portion of the offer. On April 2, 1968 the seller's attorneys wrote to defendant's attorney enclosing the executed purchase offer, the abstract of title, a copy of a proposed deed and other papers relating to the premises. Receiving no reply, plaintiff's attorneys wrote on five subsequent occasions requesting that a closing date for the transfer be set. Defendant's counsel did not respond directly to any of these letters but did send plaintiff's attorneys a copy of a letter sent to defendant by his attorney on July 5 in which the latter advised that since the client was unwilling to close the transaction he was no longer representing him in the matter and enclosing a bill for his services. He also advised that the abstract of title and the proposed deed description were being returned to the seller's attorneys. By letter to defendant dated July 26 plaintiff tendered a deed and set August 5 as a date for closing. When the tender was not accepted plaintiff commenced this action for specific performance.

After service of the pleadings which put in issue the making of the contract plaintiff served on defendant a notice to admit the execution by him of the purchase offer, the genuineness of his signature thereon and the fact that the offer was not withdrawn prior to acceptance. When no response to the notice was served plaintiff moved for summary judgment on the basis of the notice and an affidavit and supporting papers setting forth the facts recited above.

It is plaintiff's contention that its execution of the acceptance of defendant's purchase offer on March 26, 1968 created a binding contract between the parties which it is now entitled to enforce. Defendant takes the position that the acceptance on March 26 was not an acceptance of a viable offer but was merely a counter offer which was never accepted by the buyer. . . .

Upon the undisputed facts there was never a contract entered into by the parties. The act of the plaintiff in signing the acceptance of the purchase offer on March 26 was too late to constitute an acceptance of defendant's offer to buy made one month and five days prior thereto.

The offer executed on February 21 did not contain any express time limit on its duration. In that circumstance the offer remained open for a reasonable time. "Where an offer specifies the time of its duration, it must of course by accepted within the time limited; where, however, no time is specified for the offer's duration, it is the general rule that it must be accepted within a reasonable time." . . . . The circumstances surrounding the offer, or usage or custom of trade, may also raise an implied limitation on the offer. (9 N.Y.Jur., Contracts §24.) Here, the original offer to buy contained a proposed closing date one month after the offer. The inclusion of the closing date of March 22 is compelling evidence that acceptance of the offer, if it were to occur, must happen before that date, else the closing date would be an impossibility. A similar case is Hamilton v. Patrick, . . . in which the court said:

> "The proposal itself implies the necessity of acceptance on or before that day. It is therein proposed that the deed should be executed and delivered to the plaintiff 'on or before March 1, 1885, at which date said money shall be paid.' Acceptance must precede any obligation to perform, and of necessity must be made so as to admit of performance as proposed. Any subsequent acceptance would imply a contract different from the terms proposed." . . .

The reasonable time for duration of the offer was not longer than the one month within which the offeror hoped to complete the transaction. An acceptance which occurred four days after the proposed closing date and one month and five days after the tender of the offer is clearly beyond a reasonable period of duration. The late acceptance was merely a counter offer which must in turn be accepted by the original offeror to create a contract. (1 Williston on Contracts, 3d ed. §§ 92, 93; Restatement, Law of Contracts, § 73; . . ..) Since there was never any acceptance by defendant of plaintiff's counter proposal, there was no contract between the parties to be enforced.

The order should be modified to grant summary judgment to defendant dismissing the complaint.

This case illustrates the operation of the three-month limitation on the irrevocability of firm offers under UCC § 2-205 and also how revocation may occur by conduct.

CASE
6-7

NORCA CORPORATION v. TOKHEIM CORPORATION
Appellate Division, New York (2d Dept.), 1996
227 A.D. 2d 458, 643 N.Y.S. 2d 139

MEMORANDUM BY THE COURT. In an action, inter alia, to recover damages for breach of contract, the plaintiff appeals from an order and judgment (one paper) of the Supreme Court, Nassau County (Alpert, J.), entered April 11, 1995, which, inter alia, granted the respective motions of the defendants for summary judgment dismissing the complaint. ORDERED that the order and judgment is affirmed, with costs.

If a firm offer is made for a specified period which is in excess of three months, the offer is subject to revocation at the expiration of the three month period (see, Uniform Commercial Code § 2-205, Official Comment 3; [Citations]). An offer may be terminated by indirect revocation . . . . An offeror need not say "revoke" to effectuate a revocation . . . . Where an offeror takes "definite action inconsistent with an intention to enter into the proposed contract," such action is considered a valid revocation (Restatement [Second] of Contracts § 43; see also, 1 Farnsworth, Contracts § 3.17, at 250 [1990]).

In the instant case, the defendant Saint Switch, Inc. (hereinafter Saint Switch), agreed to purchase the assets of

the manufacturing pump division of the defendant Tokheim Corporation. On April 14, 1993, Saint Switch offered, on Tokheim Corporation letterhead, to sell fuel pumps to the appellant. The offer was firm until July 31, 1994. On August 18, 1993, more than three months after the original offer was made, Saint Switch forwarded to the appellant a new offer stating different price terms for the fuel pumps. On November 4, 1993, the appellant attempted to accept the original offer made on April 14, 1993.

We find that the offer made by Saint Switch on August 18, 1993, revoked its earlier offer made on April 14, 1993. The offer made on August 18, 1993, was inconsistent with the original offer in that it had a different price term . . . . In addition, it was made prior to any effective acceptance on the part of the appellant . . . . Accordingly, the Supreme Court properly granted the respective motions of the defendants for summary judgment.

The appellant's remaining contentions are without merit.

This case concerns the definition and effect of a counteroffer under the common law rules.

CASE
6-8

GIANNETTI v. CORNILLIE
Court of Appeals of Michigan, 1994
204 Mich.App. 234, 514 N.W.2d 221

HOOD, J. Defendants were the copersonal representatives of their mother's estate. In that capacity, they listed her home for sale with a real estate agent. Plaintiffs [Patrick and Anne Giannetti] offered $155,000 for the home and submitted a $2,500 deposit. Defendants counteroffered to sell the home for $160,000.

Upon receiving the counteroffer, plaintiffs orally inquired whether certain items could be included with the home. Defendants declined. Plaintiffs then purportedly accepted the counteroffer, but changed the mortgage amount from $124,000 to $128,000 and initialed the change. The real estate agent did not submit this modification for defendants' approval, but, rather, told defendants that plaintiffs had accepted their counteroffer. Defendants signed all the necessary . . . papers for the sale of the property. However, before the closing, defendants sought to rescind the deal. Plaintiffs declined and sued for specific performance.

Defendants' main argument is that the trial court clearly erred in finding that there was a contract where defendants never agreed to plaintiffs' change in the mortgage amount. We reluctantly agree.

As argued by defendants, "[a]n offer is a unilateral declaration of intention, and is not a contract. A contract is made when both parties have executed or accepted it, and not before. A counterproposition is not an acceptance." [Citations.] An acceptance must be "unambiguous and in strict conformance with an offer." [Citation.] "[A] proposal to accept, or an acceptance, upon terms varying from those offered, is a rejection of the offer, and puts an end to the negotiation, unless the party who made the original offer renews it, or assents to the modification suggested." [Citation.] Thus, "[a]ny material departure from the terms of an offer invalidates the offer as made and results in a counter proposition, which, unless accepted, cannot be enforced." [Citation.]

Plaintiffs argue that the modification of the mortgage amount did not vitiate their purported acceptance because the mortgage amount, unlike the purchase price, was not a material term of the contract. We disagree.

* * * In other words, before the change, plaintiffs were obligated to buy the property if they obtained a mortgage for $124,000; after the change, no obligation to buy arose unless they obtained a $128,000 mortgage. Thus, the modification had the legal effect of widening the door through which plaintiffs could escape the contract and it was therefore material. [Citation.]

* * *

Reversed.

The following case deals with the reasonableness of the means of acceptance used by the offeror.

CASE
6-9

DEFEO v. AMFARMS ASSOCIATES

Appellate Division, New York (3rd Dept.), 1990
161 A.D. 2d 904. 557 N.Y.S. 2d 469

WEISS, Justice. Appeal from an order of the Supreme Court (Rose, J.), entered July 14, 1989 in Tioga County, which, inter alia, granted defendant's motion for summary judgment dismissing the complaint.

In 1986 defendant listed its farm located in the Town of Candor, Tioga County, for sale with W.D. Seeley Real Estate. On September 5, 1987 defendant received an offer from plaintiffs submitted through the broker. It rejected the offer on September 7, 1987 and submitted a counteroffer in which the sale price was increased and certain conditions which defendant found objectionable were deleted. This counteroffer was made through the broker with instructions that the sale would have to proceed promptly. A month later, on October 5, 1987, plaintiffs submitted another offer with an acceptable price, but again included the objectionable conditions. On October 9, 1987 defendant rejected this offer and, using the same form, countered by deleting and initialing the objectionable conditions. In this final counteroffer, a new additional term appeared in handwriting: "13. Offer valid to Oct. 17, 1987 at 1700 hours." Peculiarly, the parties claim to be unaware who inserted the clause. This counteroffer was forwarded directly by defendant's attorney . . . to plaintiffs' attorney by Federal Express overnight delivery. Thereafter, plaintiffs' attorney contacted defendant's attorney by telephone on October 13, 1987 and another of defendant's partners on October 15, 1987. The parties dispute the contents of these communications. In the meantime, on October 13, 1987, defendant received a purchase offer with a higher price from third parties through a different real estate broker which it accepted on October 16, 1987. On that very same day, plaintiffs accepted the October 9, 1987 counteroffer and sent it to Seeley Real Estate by certified mail, which Seeley received on October 19, 1987. Defendant denied the effectiveness of acceptance. Supreme Court granted summary judgment dismissing the complaint seeking specific performance, holding that since the offer had been transmitted to plaintiffs' attorney by Federal Express, acceptance sent by mail to the listing real estate broker was unauthorized and ineffective to accept the offer. The court found that since plaintiffs failed to timely communicate acceptance before the offer expired, no binding contract was formed and plaintiffs were not entitled to specific performance. This appeal followed.

The reasonableness of the manner in which an offer is accepted must be viewed under the circumstances in which the offer had been made, with speed and reliability being relevant factors (Restatement [Second] of Contracts § 65; see, 1 Williston, Contracts § 83, at 273 [Jaeger 3d ed.]). Here, the transmission using Federal Express overnight delivery invited acceptance by similar dispatch . . . and plaintiffs' acceptance by mail, particularly to an agent who had been uninvolved in the negotiations of the moment and who had lost contact with the parties, was not invited especially in view of defendant's expressed concern with time. The receipt of the acceptance by the broker two days after the appointed day was not operative (Restatement [Second] of Contracts § 67).

Order affirmed, with costs.

QUESTIONS

1. Identify the three essentials of an offer and discuss briefly the requirements associated with each.
2. Identify and discuss briefly seven ways by which an offer may be terminated other than by acceptance.
3. Compare briefly the traditional and modern theories of definiteness of acceptance of an offer as shown by the common law "mirror image" rule and by the rule of the Uniform Commercial Code.
4. Discuss the five situations limiting an offeror's right to revoke her offer.
5. Explain the various rules that determine when an acceptance takes effect.

PROBLEMS

1. D Corporation entered into a written employment agreement with E on September 1, which provided in part that employment would commence on the following January 1 and "will continue for a period of time to be mutually agreed upon." One month before January 1, D Corporation notified E that it had changed its mind and would not employ E. In E's action against D Corporation for breach of contract, D Corporation contends that there is no contract. Judgment for whom? Explain.

2. On April 15, S wrote to B offering to sell a piece of land that S owned for $50,000. The letter, which was signed by S, stated that the offer would expire on July 30.

On April 20, S received a better offer from X. S called B and told him that he was withdrawing his offer to B.

On April 25, B called S and told him that he was accepting S's offer of April 15. S said that it was too late to accept the offer.

In an action by B against S for breach of contract, judgment for whom? Explain.

3. On May 1, B, a retail wine seller, sent a letter to S offering to buy 50 cases of Chateau Le Pew wine at $100 a case. The letter, which was signed by B, stated that it was a firm offer for 30 days. S received the offer on May 2. By May 10, however, the price of wine was dropping and B wrote to S saying, " I am sorry but I hereby withdraw the offer." S received this letter on May 12.

On May 15, S called B and told him that he accepted B's offer of May 1. B claimed that the offer had been withdrawn and refused to accept delivery of the wine.

In an action by S against B for breach of contract, judgment for whom? Explain.

4. On July 1, S, a steel manufacturer, telephoned B and offered to sell B six carloads of steel at $600 a ton. B said, "That's a lot of steel! Would you promise to keep your offer open for 10 days so that I can think about whether I can use that much?" S replied, "Sure. I promise to keep the offer open for 10 days."

On July 6, S sent a letter to B that stated, "I hereby revoke my offer of July 1." B received this letter on July 7.

On July 8, B called S and said that he was accepting S's offer of July 1. S refused to deliver the steel, claiming that he had validly revoked the offer. In an action by B against S for breach of contract, judgment for whom. Explain?

5. M offered to sell P a parking lot for $35,000. The offer was in writing and signed by M and provided that any acceptance by P must be within 5 days. On the fourth day, M accepted a better offer from D and transferred the parking lot to D on that day. Unaware of this sale, P telephoned M on the fifth day and accepted M's offer. In an action by P against M for breach of contract, judgment for whom?

6. Ames, seeking business for his lawn maintenance firm, posted the following notice in the meeting room of the Antlers, a local lodge: "To the members of the Antlers—Special this month. I will resod your lawn for two dollars per square foot using Fairway brand sod. This offer expires July 15."

The notice also included Ames's name, address, and signature and specified that the acceptance was to be in writing.

Bates, a member of the Antlers, and Cramer, the janitor, read the notice and became interested. Bates wrote a letter to Ames saying he would accept the offer if Ames would use Putting Green brand sod. Ames received this letter July 14 and wrote to Bates saying he would not use Putting Green sod. Bates received Ames's letter on July 16 and promptly wrote Ames that he would accept Fairway sod. Cramer wrote to Ames on July 10, saying he accepted Ames's offer.

By July 15, Ames had found more profitable ventures and refused to resod either lawn at the specified price. Bates and Cramer each brought an appropriate action against Ames for breach of contract. Decisions as to the respective claims of Bates and Cramer?

7. S, a merchant, wrote to B: "August 1, I offer to sell you one Desktop Computer, Model A, price $3,000. This is a firm offer for 30 days from the above date." signed S.

On August 10, B received a letter from S: "I hereby revoke my offer of August 1." signed S.

On August 17, B wrote to S: "I hereby accept your offer of August 1."

(a) Is there a contract? Explain.

(b) Assume that S's offer stated that it was a firm offer for four months, and that on November 15, B mailed an acceptance. Is there a contract? Explain.

(c) Assume that S's offer stated that it was a firm offer for four months, and that on November 14, B received a letter from S, dated November 12. "I hereby revoke my offer of August 1." On November 15, B mailed an acceptance. Is there a contract? Explain.

8. On March 1, S sent a signed letter to B and offered to sell the piano in his home to B for $400, and stated that he would keep his offer open for 4 months. On April 1, S sold the piano to T, his cousin for $500, without informing B that he did so. On June 10, B wrote S stating that he accepted S's offer. S immediately notified B that he could not sell him the piano because he had already sold it to T. B sues S for breach of contract. Judgment for whom? Explain.

9. Alpha Rolling Mill Corporation, by letter dated June 8, offered to sell Brooklyn Railroad Company 2,000 to 5,000 tons of fifty-pound iron rails upon certain specified terms, adding that, if the offer was accepted, Alpha Corporation would expect to be notified prior to June 20.

Brooklyn Company, on June 16, by telegram, referring to Alpha Corporation's offer of June 8, directed Alpha Corporation to enter an order for 1,200 tons of fifty-pound iron rails on the terms specified. The same day, June 16, Brooklyn Company, by letter to Alpha Corporation, confirmed the telegram. On June 18, Alpha Corporation, by telegram, declined to fill the order.

Brooklyn Company, on June 19, telegraphed Alpha Corporation: "Please enter an order for 2,000 tons rails as per your letter of the eighth. Please forward written contract. Reply." In reply to Brooklyn Company's repeated inquiries regarding whether the order for 2,000 tons of rails had been entered, Alpha denied the existence of any contract between Brooklyn Company and itself. Thereafter, Brooklyn Company sued Alpha Corporation for breach of contract. Decision?

10. On September 15, S wrote to B as follows: "I offer to sell you Blackacre for $200,000, all cash, closing on November 1. Please advise as soon as possible. (Signed) S."

On October 1, B mailed his acceptance to S, unaware that S had died on September 30 When B learned of S's death on October 5, B insisted that the Estate of S nevertheless deliver the deed to Blackacre in exchange for B's certified $200,000 check. X, the Executor of S's Estate, refused to do so.

(a) In an action by B against the Estate of S for breach of contract, judgment for whom? Explain.

(b) If S's offer was a valid irrevocable offer for 30 days, would your answer to (a) be different? Explain.

11. On October 1, B received the following letter from S: "I understand that you are interested in buying a pick-up truck, I will sell you mine for $10,000 all cash, and will have it ready for delivery to you on November 15. (Signed) S".

Later that day B telephoned S and inquired: "Can I have 20 days to think over your offer?" S replied: "O.K., you have an irrevocable option for 20 days. Write to me when you decide."

On October 6, B wrote S: "I am still very much interested in your offer. I'm a little short of cash at the moment and would like to know if you would consider taking $5,000 cash and my 30-day note for the other $5,000? (Signed) B." S did not reply.

On October 10, without B's knowledge, S sold and delivered the truck to T for $11,000 cash.

On October 15, B wrote S: "I have decided to accept your offer and will pay you $10,000 in cash when I pick up the truck on Nov.15. (Signed) B." S wrote back: "The truck is sold." B sues S for damages for breach of contract. Judgment for whom? Explain.

12. On May 1, S, a textile manufacturer, mailed to B, a merchant, a written and signed offer to sell 1,000 bolts of blue denim at $40 per bolt. Each bolt would contain 25 square yards. The offer stated "this offer will remain open for 10 days from the above date (May 1) and it will not be withdrawn prior to that date."

Two days later, S, noting a sudden increase in the price of blue denim, changed his mind. After making great personal efforts to contact B, S sent B a letter revoking the offer of May 1. The letter was mailed on May 4 and received by B on May 5. B chose to disregard the letter of May 4. Instead, she continued to watch the price of blue denim rise.

On May 9, B mailed a letter accepting the original offer. The letter was sent by registered mail and was properly addressed and contained the correct postage. However, it was not received by S until May 12, due to a delay in the mail. B demanded delivery of the goods according to the terms of the offer of May 1, but S has refused, claiming there is no contract

(a) Is there a contract? Explain.

(b) If S was not a merchant, would there be a contract? Explain.

13. S, a wholesale fruit dealer, sent the following letter to B, a fruit merchant: "Feb. 1, offer 1,000 boxes of Los Angeles, San Gabriel oranges, at $10.60 per box, F.O.B. Los Angeles: March delivery. Unless I receive your acceptance by 2 P.M. on Feb. 4, I will dispose of them elsewhere. (Signed S)." S's letter was received by B on Feb. 2, at 3 P.M.

At 1 P.M. on Feb. 2, S mailed B the following letter. "I regret to inform you that I am compelled to withdraw my offer dated Feb. 1." S's second letter was not received by B until Feb. 3.

Meanwhile at 5 P.M. on Feb. 2, B mailed the following letter to S: "I accept your offer dated Feb. 1. (Signed B)." Because of a severe snowstorm, which disrupted all means of communication, B's letter was not delivered to S until 4 P.M. on Feb. 4.

(a) Is there a contract between S and B? Explain.

(b) Assume that the words "Unless I receive your acceptance by 2 P.M. on Feb 4 I will dispose of them elsewhere" were not included in S's Feb. 1 letter to B. Is there a contract between S and B? Explain.

14. S offered to sell to B a ten-acre tract of commercial property for $750,000. S's letter indicated the offer would expire on March 1 at 3:00 P.M. and that any acceptance must be received in her office by that time.

On February 28, B decided to accept the offer and mailed an acceptance at 4:00 P.M. B indicated in his letter that in the event the acceptance did not arrive on time, he would assume there was a contract if he did not hear anything from S by March 10. The letter arrived on March 2. S never responded to B's letter.

In an action by B against S for breach of contract, judgment for whom? Explain.

15. On March 10, S sent a written offer to B to sell 3,000 tons of steel rails on certain specified terms. B received this letter on March 11. On March 25, B telegraphed his acceptance which reached S at 3 P.M. on that day. On the same day, March 25, at 2 PM., S mailed B a revocation of his March 10 offer, which B received the following day. Is there a contract? Explain.

16. On May 1, Melforth Realty Company offered to sell Greenacre to Dallas, Inc. for $1,000,000. The offer was made by telegraph and stated that the offer would expire on May 15. Dallas decided to purchase the property and sent a registered letter to Melforth on May 10, accepting the offer. Due to unexplained delays in the postal service, Melforth did not receive the letter until May 22. Melforth wishes to sell Greenacre to another buyer, who is offering $1,200,000 for the tract of land. Has a contract resulted between Melforth and Dallas?

17. S, a manufacturer, sent to B, a retail merchant, an offer to sell 100 television sets for $30,000, terms C.O.D. B wrote to S: "I accept your offer, and will pay you 30 days after delivery. (Signed B)." S tendered delivery of the TV sets to B and demanded cash on delivery. B refused to pay on delivery, and S withheld delivery. S then sued to recover damages for breach of contract.

(a) Judgment for whom? Explain.

(b) Assume that B's letter read as follows: "I accept your offer provided that you agree that payment is due 30 days after delivery." Is there a contract if S made no reply? Explain.

18. Scott, manufacturer of a carbonated beverage, entered into a contract with Otis, owner of a baseball park, whereby Otis rented to Scott a large signboard on top of the center field wall. The contract provided that Otis should letter the sign as Scott desired and would change the lettering from time to time within forty-eight hours after receipt of written request from Scott. As directed by Scott, the signboard originally stated in large letters that Scott would pay $100 to any ballplayer hitting a home run over the sign.

In the first game of the season, Hume, the best hitter in the league, hit one home run over the sign. Scott immediately served written notice on Otis instructing Otis to replace the offer on the signboard with an offer to pay fifty dollars to every pitcher who pitched a no-hit game in the park. A week after receipt of Scott's letter, Otis had not changed the wording on the sign. On that day, Perry, a pitcher for a scheduled game, pitched a no-hit game while Todd, one of his teammates, hit a home run over Scott's sign.

Scott refuses to pay any of the three players. What are the rights of Scott, Hume, Perry, and Todd?

19. Jeff says to Brenda, "I offer to sell you my IBM PC for $900." Brenda replies, "If you do not hear otherwise from me by Thursday, I have accepted your offer." Jeff agrees and does not hear from Brenda by Thursday. Does a contract exist between Jeff and Brenda? Explain.

20. The Thoelkes were owners of real property located in Orange County, which the Morrisons agreed to purchase. The Morrisons signed a contract for the sale of that property and mailed it to the Thoelkes in Texas on November 26. The next day the Thoelkes executed the contract and placed it in the mail addressed to the Morrisons' attorney in Florida. After the executed contract was mailed but before it was received in Florida, the Thoelkes called the Morrisons' attorney in Florida and attempted to repudiate the contract. Does a contract exist between the Thoelkes and the Morrisons? Discuss.

21. Lucy and Zehmer met while having drinks in a restaurant. During the course of their conversation, Lucy apparently offered to buy Zehmer's 471.6-acre farm for $50,000 cash. Although Zehmer claims that he thought the offer was made in jest, he wrote the following on the back of a pad: "We hereby agree to sell to W. O. Lucy the Ferguson Farm complete for $50,000, title satisfactory to buyer."

Zehmer then signed the writing and induced his wife Ida to do the same. She claims, however, that she signed only after Zehmer assured her that it was only a joke. Finally, Zehmer claims that he was "high as a Georgia pine" at the time but admits that he was not too drunk to make a valid contract. Decision?

22. Lee Calan Imports advertised a used Volvo station wagon for sale in the *Chicago Sun-Times*. As part of the information for the advertisement, Lee Calan Imports instructed the newspaper to print the price of the car as $1,795. However, due to a mistake made by the newspaper, without any fault on the part of Lee Calan Imports, the printed ad listed the price of the car as $1,095. After reading the ad and then examining the car, O'Brien told a Lee Calan Imports salesperson that he wanted to purchase the car for the advertised price of $1,095. Calan Imports refuses to sell the car to O'Brien for $1,095. Is there a contract? If so, for what price?

23. On May 20 cattle rancher Oliver visited his neighbor Southworth, telling him, "I know you're interested in buying the land I'm selling." Southworth replied, "Yes, I do want to buy that land, especially as it adjoins my property." Although the two men did not discuss the price, Oliver told Southworth he would determine the value of the property and send that information to him, so that Southworth would have "notice" of what Oliver "wanted for the land." On June 13, Southworth called Oliver to ask if he still planned to sell the land. Oliver answered, "Yes, and I should have the value of the land determined soon." On June 17, Oliver sent a letter to Southworth listing a price quotation of $324,000. Southworth then responded to Oliver by letter on June 21, stating that he accepted Oliver's offer. However, on June 24 Oliver wrote back to Southworth, saying, "There has never been a firm offer to sell, and there is no enforceable contract between us." Oliver maintains that a price quotation alone is not an offer. Southworth claims a valid contract has been made. Who wins? Discuss.

Internet Exercise Go to several retail and auction Web sites, and determine who is the offeror and the offeree. What are the terms of the offer? When can the offer be revoked?

Introduction to Sales and Leases

Sales are the most common and important of all commercial transactions. In an exchange economy such as ours, sales are the essential means by which the various units of production exchange their outputs, thereby providing the opportunity for specialization and enhanced productivity. An advanced, complex, industrialized economy with highly coordinated manufacturing and distribution systems requires a reliable mechanism for ensuring that *future* exchanges can be entered into today and fulfilled at a later time. Because practically everyone in our economy is a purchaser of both durable and consumable goods, the manufacture and distribution of goods involve numerous sales transactions. The law of sales establishes a framework in which these present and future exchanges may take place in a predictable, certain, and orderly fashion with a minimum of transaction costs.

Until the early 1900s, sales transactions were completely governed by general contract law. In 1906, the Uniform Sales Act was promulgated and eventually adopted by thirty-six states. By the end of the 1930s, however, dissatisfaction with this and other uniform commercial statutes brought about the development of the Uniform Commercial Code (UCC). Article 2 of the Code deals with transactions in sales and has been adopted in all of the states (except Louisiana) plus the District of Columbia and the Virgin Islands. The UCC appears in Appendix B. Amendments to Article 2 and 2A were promulgated in 2003 to accommodate electronic commerce and to reflect development of business practices, changes in other law, and interpretive difficulties of practical significance.

Leases of personal property, which are of great economic significance, exceed $100 billion annually. Leases range from a consumer's renting an automobile or a lawn mower to a Fortune 500 corporation's leasing heavy industrial machinery. Despite the frequent and widespread use of personal property leases, the law governing these transactions had been patched together from the common law of personal property, real estate leasing law, and the UCC (Articles 2 and 9). Although containing several applicable provisions, the UCC did not directly relate to leases. Some courts have held, nevertheless, that the UCC is applicable to leases of goods because a lease is a transaction in goods; other courts have refused to apply the Code to leases because actual title to the goods never passed. Still other courts have applied the Code to lease by analogy. Even in states where Article 2 was extended to leases, which provisions were to be applied remained unclear. In any event, no unified or uniform statutory law governed leases of personal property for most of the twentieth century.

To fill this void, the drafters of the Code approved Article 2A—Leases in 1987 and subsequently amended the Article in 1990. An analogue of Article 2, the new Article adopts many of the rules contained in Article 2. Article 2A is an attempt to codify in one statute all the rules governing the leasing of personal property. South Dakota has enacted the 1987 version of Article 2A while the District of Columbia and all the other states except Louisiana have adopted the 1990 version.

This section of the book covers both the sale and the lease of goods. All of the chapters will cover Article 2A in addition to Article 2 by stating the Article 2A section number wherever Article 2A's provision is either identical or essentially the same as the Article 2 provision. Where Article 2A significantly deviates from Article 2, both rules will generally be discussed. This chapter will discuss the nature and formation of sales and lease contracts as well as the fundamental principles of Article 2 and Article 2A.

http: **Uniform Commercial Code, Article 2:** http://www.law. cornell.edu/ucc/2/overview.html
Uniform Commercial Code, Article 2A: http://www.law. cornell.edu/ucc/2A/overview.html
Uniform Law Commissioners: http://www.law.upenn. edu/ bll/ulc/ulcframe.htm
United Nations Commission on International Trade Law: http://www.uncitral.org/en-index.htm

Nature of Sales and Leases

The law of sales, which governs contracts involving the sale of goods, is a specialized branch of both the law of contracts (discussed in other chapters) and the law of personal property. This section will cover the definition of sales and lease contracts and the fundamentals of Article 2 and Article 2A.

◆ SEE FIGURE 7-1 Law of Sales and Leases

DEFINITIONS

Goods

Goods are essentially defined as movable, tangible personal property. For example, the purchase of a bicycle, CD player, or this textbook is considered a sale of goods. "Goods" also include the unborn young of animals, growing crops, and, if removed by the seller, timber, minerals, or a building attached to real property. Section 2–105(1). Under Article 2A, minerals cannot be leased prior to their extraction. Section 2A–103(1)(h).

Sale

The Code defines a sale as the transfer of title to goods from seller to buyer for a price. Section 2–106. The price can be money, other goods, real estate, or services.

Lease

Article 2A defines a lease of goods as a "transfer of the right to possession and use of goods for a term in return for consideration, but... retention or creation of a security interest is not a lease." Section 2A–103(1)(j). A transaction within this definition of a lease is governed by Article 2A, but if the transaction is a security interest disguised as a lease, it is governed by Article 9. Categorizing a transaction as a lease has significant implications not only for the parties to the lease but for third parties as well. If the transaction is deemed to be a lease, then the residual interest in the goods belongs to the lessor, who need not file publicly to protect this interest. On the other hand, if the transaction is a

◆ FIGURE 7-1 Law of Sales and Leases

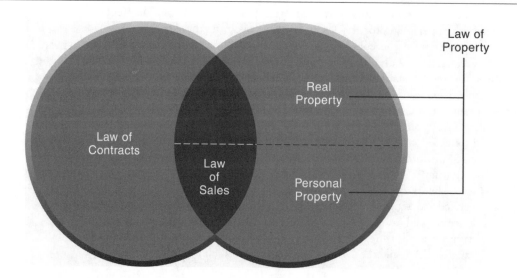

security interest, then the provisions of Article 9 regarding enforceability, perfection, priority, and remedies apply.

Consumer Leases Article 2A affords special treatment for consumer leases. The definition of a consumer lease requires that (1) the transaction meet the definition of a lease under Article 2A; (2) the lessor be regularly engaged in the business of leasing *or* selling goods; (3) the lessee be an individual, not an organization; (4) the lessee take the lease interest primarily for a personal, family, or household purpose; and (5) the total payments under the lease do not exceed $25,000. Section 2A–103(1)(e). Although consumer protection for lease transactions is primarily left to other state and federal law, Article 2A does contain a number of provisions that apply to consumer leases and that may *not* be varied by agreement of the parties.

Finance Leases A finance lease is a special type of lease transaction generally involving three parties instead of two. Whereas in the typical lease situation the lessor also supplies the goods, in a finance lease arrangement the lessor and the supplier are separate parties. The lessor's primary function in a finance lease is to provide financing to the lessee for a lease of goods provided by the supplier. For example, under a finance lease arrangement a manufacturer supplies goods pursuant to the lessee's instructions or specifications. The party functioning as the lessor will then either purchase those goods from the supplier or act as the prime lessee in leasing them from the supplier. In turn, the lessor will lease or sublease the goods to the lessee. Comment g to Section 2A–103. Because the finance lessor functions merely as a source of credit, she typically will have no special expertise as to the goods. Due to the limited role the finance lessor usually plays, Article 2A treats finance leases differently from ordinary leases.

◆ SEE CASE 7-1

Governing Law

Though sales transactions are governed by Article 2 of the Code, general contract law continues to apply where the Code has not specifically modified such law. In other words, the law of sales is a specialized part of the general law of contracts, and the law of contracts continues to govern unless specifically displaced by the Code.

General contract law also continues to govern all contracts outside the scope of the Code. Transactions not within the scope of Article 2 include employment contracts, service contracts, insurance contracts, contracts involving real property, and contracts for the sale of intangibles such as stocks, bonds, patents, and copyrights. For an illustration of the relationship between the law of sales and the general law of contracts, see Figure 9-1. In determining whether a contract containing both a sale of goods and a service is a UCC contract or a general contract, the majority of states follow the predominant purpose test. This test holds that if the predominant purpose of the whole transaction is a sale of goods, then Article 2 applies to the entire transaction. If, on the other hand, the predominant purpose is the non-good or service portion, then Article 2 does not apply at all. A few states apply Article 2 to the goods part of a transaction and general contract law to the non-goods or service part of the transaction.

◆ SEE FIGURE 9-1 Law Governing Contracts

Although Article 2 governs sales, the drafters of the Article have invited the courts to extend Code principles to nonsale transactions in goods. To date, a number of courts have accepted this invitation and have applied Code provisions by analogy to other transactions in goods not expressly included within the Act, most frequently to leases and bailments. The Code has also greatly influenced the revision of the Restatement, Second, Contracts which, as previously discussed, has great effect upon all contracts.

Although lease transactions are governed by Article 2A of the Code, general contract law continues to apply where the Code has not specifically modified such law. In other words, the law of leases is a specialized part of the general law of contracts, and the law of contracts continues to govern unless specifically displaced by the Code.

CISG

The United Nations Convention on Contracts for the International Sale of Goods (CISG), which has been ratified by the United States and more than forty other countries, governs all contracts for the international sales of goods between parties located in different nations that have ratified the CISG. Because treaties are federal law, the CISG supersedes the UCC in any situation to which either could apply. The CISG includes provisions dealing with interpretation, trade usage, contract formation, obligations and remedies of sellers and buyers, and risk of loss. Parties to an international sales contract may, however, expressly exclude CISG governance from their contract. The CISG specifically excludes sales of (1) goods bought for personal, family, or household use; (2) ships or aircraft; and (3) electricity. In addition, it does not apply to contracts in which the primary obligation of the party furnishing the goods consists of supplying labor or services.

FUNDAMENTAL PRINCIPLES OF ARTICLE 2 AND ARTICLE 2A

The purpose of Article 2 is to modernize, clarify, simplify, and make uniform the law of sales. Furthermore, the Article is to be interpreted in accordance with these underlying principles and not according to some abstraction such as the passage of title. The Code

> is drawn to provide flexibility so that, since it is intended to be a semi-permanent piece of legislation, it will provide its own machinery for expansion of commercial practices. It is intended to make it possible for the law embodied in this Act to be developed by the courts in the light of unforeseen and new circumstances and practices. However, the proper construction of the Act requires that its interpretation and application be limited to its reason. Section 1–102, Comment 1.

This open-ended drafting includes the following fundamental concepts.

CISG

The CISG governs only the formation of the contract of sales and the rights and obligations of the seller and buyer arising from such contract. It does not cover the validity of the contract or any of its provisions. In addition, one of the purposes of the CISG is to promote uniformity of the law of sales.

Good Faith

All parties who enter into a contract or duty within the scope of the Code must perform their obligations in good faith. The Code defines **good faith** as "honesty in fact in the conduct or transaction concerned." Section 1–201(19). For a merchant (defined later), good faith also requires the observance of reasonable commercial standards of fair dealing in the trade. Section 2–103(1)(b); Section 2A–103(3). For instance, if the parties agree that the seller is to set the price term, the seller must establish the price in good faith.

CISG

The CISG is also designed to promote the observation of good faith in international trade.

Unconscionability

The court may scrutinize every contract of sale to determine whether in its commercial setting, purpose, and effect it is unconscionable. The court may refuse to enforce an unconscionable contract or any part of it found to be unconscionable or may limit its application to prevent an unconscionable result. Section 2–302. Though the Code itself does not define *unconscionable*, the *New Webster's Dictionary* (Deluxe Encyclopedic Edition) defines the term as "contrary to the dictates of conscience; unscrupulous or unprincipled; exceeding that which is reasonable or customary; inordinate, unjustifiable."

The Code denies or limits enforcement of an unconscionable contract for the sale of goods to promote fairness and decency and to correct harshness or oppression in contracts resulting from inequality in the bargaining positions of the parties.

The doctrine of unconscionability has been justified on the basis that it permits the courts to resolve issues of unfairness explicitly on that basis without recourse to formalistic rules or legal fictions. In policing contracts for fairness, the courts have again demonstrated their willingness to limit freedom of contract to protect the less advantaged from overreaching by dominant contracting parties. Accordingly, most cases concerning unconscionability have involved low-income consumers.

The doctrine of unconscionability has evolved through its application by the courts to include both procedural and substantive unconscionability. **Procedural unconscionability** involves scrutiny for the presence of "bargaining naughtiness." In other words, was the negotiation process fair? Or were there procedural irregularities such as burying important terms of the agreement in fine print or obscuring the true meaning of the contract with impenetrable legal jargon?

In checking for **substantive unconscionability**, the court examines the actual terms of the contract for oppressive or grossly unfair provisions such as an exorbitant price or an unfair exclusion or limitation of contractual remedies. An all-too-common example places a necessitous buyer in an unequal bargaining position with a seller who consequently obtains an exorbitant price for his product or service. In one case, a price of $749 ($920 on time payments) for a vacuum cleaner that cost the seller $140 was held unconscionable. In another case, the buyers, welfare recipients, purchased by time payment contract a home freezer unit for $900 plus time credit charges, credit life insurance, credit property insurance, and sales tax for a total price of $1,235. The maximum retail value of the freezer unit at the time of purchase was $300. The court held the contract unconscionable and reformed it by changing the price to the total payment ($620) the buyers had managed to make. *Jones v. Star Credit Corp.*, 59 Misc.2d 189, 298 N.Y.S.2d 264 (1969).

As to leases, Article 2A provides that a court faced with an unconscionable contract or clause may refuse to enforce either the entire contract or just the unconscionable clause, or may limit the application of the unconscionable clause to avoid an unconscionable result. This is similar to Article 2's treatment of unconscionable clauses in sales contracts. A lessee under a consumer lease, however, is provided with additional protection against unconscionability. In the case of a consumer lease, if a court as a matter of law finds that any part of the lease contract has been induced by unconscionable conduct, the court is expressly empowered to grant appropriate relief. Section 2A–108(2). The same is true when unconscionable conduct occurs in the collection of a claim arising from a consumer lease contract. The explicit availability of relief for consumers subjected to unconscionable conduct (procedural unconscionability)—in addition to a provision regarding unconscionable contracts (substantive unconscionability)—represents a departure from Article 2. An additional remedy that Article 2A provides for consumers is the award of attorneys' fees. If the court finds unconscionability with respect to a consumer lease, it shall award reasonable attorneys' fees to the lessee. Section 2A–108(4)(a).

Expansion of Commercial Practices

An underlying policy of the Code is "to permit the continued expansion of commercial practices through custom, usage and agreement of the parties." Section 1–102(2)(b). In particular, the Code emphasizes the course of dealings and the usage of trade in interpreting agreements.

A **course of dealing** is a sequence of previous conduct between the parties that may fairly be regarded as establishing a common basis of understanding for interpreting their expressions and agreement. Section 1–205(1). For example, Plaza, a sugar company, enters into a written agreement with Brown, a grower of sugar beets, by which Brown agrees to raise and deliver and Plaza agrees to purchase specified quantities of beets during the coming season. No price is fixed. The agreement is on a standard form used by Plaza for Brown and many other growers in prior years. Plaza's practice is to pay all growers uniformly according to a formula based on Plaza's established accounting system. Unless otherwise agreed, the established pricing pattern is part of the agreement between Plaza and Brown as a course of dealing.

A **usage of trade** is a practice or method of dealing regularly observed and followed in a place, vocation, or trade. Section 1–205(2). To illustrate: Tamara contracts to sell Seth one thousand feet of San Domingo mahogany. By usage of dealers in mahogany, known to Tamara and Seth, good mahogany of a certain density is known as San Domingo mahogany, though it does not come from San Domingo. Unless otherwise agreed, the usage is part of the contract.

CISG

The parties are bound by any usage or practices that they have agreed to or established between themselves. In addition, the parties are considered, unless otherwise agreed, to be bound by any usage of international trade that is widely known and regularly observed in the particular trade.

Sales by and between Merchants

The Code establishes separate rules that apply to transactions transpiring between merchants or involving a merchant as a party. A **merchant** is defined as a person who (1) is a dealer in the type of goods the transaction involves, (2) by his occupation holds himself out as having knowledge or skill peculiar to the goods or practices involved, or (3) employs an agent or broker whom he holds out as having such knowledge or skill. Section 2–104(1); Section 2A–103(3). These rules exact a higher standard of conduct from merchants because of their knowledge of trade and commerce and because merchants as a class generally set these standards for themselves. The most significant of these merchant rules are listed in Figure 7-2.

◆ SEE FIGURE 7-2 Selected Rules Applicable to Merchants

Liberal Administration of Remedies

Section 1–106 of the Code provides that its remedies shall be liberally administered to place the aggrieved party in a position as good as the one she would have occupied had the defaulting party fully performed. The Code states clearly, however, that remedies are limited to compensation and do not include consequential or punitive damages, unless specifically provided by the Code. Nevertheless, the Code provides that even in cases where it does not expressly provide a remedy for a right or obligation, the courts should provide an appropriate remedy.

Freedom of Contract

Most of the Code's provisions are not mandatory but permit the parties by agreement to vary or displace them altogether. The parties may not, however, disclaim by agreement the obligations of good faith, diligence, reasonableness, and care the Code prescribes, though they may by agreement determine the standards by which to measure the performance of these obligations, so long as such standards are not obviously unreasonable. Section 1–102(3). Through this approach, the Code not only maximizes freedom of contract but also permits the continued expansion of commercial practices through private agreement.

◆ Figure 7-2 Selected Rules Applicable to Merchants

Section of UCC	Chapter in Text Merchant Rules	Where Discussed
2-103(1)(b), 2-103(3)	Good faith	7
2-201	Confirmation of oral contracts	10, 7
2-205, 2A-205	Firm offers	6, 7
2-207(2)	Battle of the forms	6, 7

Validation and Preservation of Sales Contracts

One of the requirements of commercial law is the establishment of rules that determine when an agreement is valid. The Code approaches this requirement by minimizing formal requisites and attempting to preserve agreements whenever the parties manifest an intent to enter into a contract.

Formation of Sales and Lease Contracts

The Code's basic approach to validation is to recognize contracts whenever the parties manifest such an intent. This is so whether or not the parties can identify a precise moment at which the contract was formed. Section 2–204(2); Section 2A–204(2).

As already noted, the law of sales and leases is a subset of the general law of contracts and is governed by general contract law unless particular provisions of the Code displace the general law. Although the Code leaves most issues of contract formation to general contract law, it has modified the general law of contract formation in several significant respects. These modifications serve to modernize contract law, to relax the validation requirements of contract formation, and to promote fairness.

MANIFESTATION OF MUTUAL ASSENT

For a contract to exist, there must be an objective manifestation of mutual assent: an offer and an acceptance. This section examines the UCC rules that affect offers and acceptances.

Definiteness of an Offer

At common law, the terms of a contract were required to be definite and complete. The Code has rejected the strict approach of the common law by recognizing an agreement as valid, despite missing terms, if there is any reasonably certain basis for granting a remedy. Accordingly, the Code provides that even a contract from which one or more terms have been omitted need not fail for indefiniteness. Section 2–204(3); Section 2A–204(3). The Code provides standards by which the courts may ascertain and supply omitted essential terms, provided the parties intended to enter into a binding agreement. Nevertheless, the more terms the parties leave open, the less likely their intent to enter into a binding contract. Article 2A generally does not provide the same gap-filling provisions.

C I S G

An offer to contract is sufficiently definite if it indicates the goods and fixes or makes provision, expressly or implicitly, for determining price and quality.

Open Price The parties may enter into a contract for the sale of goods even though they have reached no agreement on the price (that is, left open the price term). Under the Code, the price is reasonable at the time for delivery where the agreement (1) says nothing as to price, (2) provides that the parties shall agree later as to the price and they fail to so agree, or (3) fixes the price in terms of some agreed market or other standard as set by a third person or agency, and the price is not so set. Section 2–305(1). An agreement that the price is to be fixed by the seller or buyer means that it must be fixed in good faith.

Open Delivery Unless otherwise agreed, the place of delivery is the seller's place of business. Moreover, in the absence of specific instructions, the delivery must be made within a reasonable time and in a single delivery. Section 2–308.

Open Quantity: Output and Requirement Contracts A buyer's agreement to purchase a seller's entire output for a stated period, or a seller's agreement to fulfill a buyer's need for certain goods used in her business operations, may appear to lack definiteness and mutuality of obligation. In neither case do the parties specify the exact quantity of goods, and the seller and the buyer may have some control over their respective output and requirements. Nonetheless, such agreements are enforceable by the application of an objective standard based upon the good faith of both parties, and the quantities may not be disproportionate to any stated estimate or the prior output or requirements. Section 2–306(1). For example, the seller cannot operate his factory twenty-four hours a day and insist that the buyer take all of the output when the seller operated the factory only eight hours a day at the time the agreement was made. Nor can the buyer unilaterally triple the size of her business and insist that the seller supply all of her requirements.

Other Open Terms The Code further provides rules, where the parties do not agree, as to the terms of payment, the duration of the contract, and the particulars of performance. Sections 2–310, 2–309, 2–307, 2–311.

Irrevocable Offers

An offeror generally may withdraw an offer at any time prior to its acceptance. To be effective, notice of revocation must reach the offeree before he has accepted the offer.

An **option** is a *contract* by which the offeror is bound to hold open an offer for a specified time. It must comply with all the requirements of a contract, including consideration. Option contracts apply to all types of contracts, including those for sales of goods.

The Code has made certain offers—called **firm offers**— irrevocable without any consideration being given for the promise to keep the offer open. The Code provides that a merchant who gives assurance in a signed writing that an offer will be held open is bound to keep the offer open for a maximum of three months. Section 2–205; Section 2A–205. The Code, therefore, makes a merchant's written promise not to revoke an offer for a stated time enforceable even though no consideration is given the merchant–offeror for that promise.

For example, Ben's Brewery approached Flora Flooring, Inc., to purchase tile for Ben's floor. Ben's employees would install the tile after it was delivered by Flora. On June 6, Flora sent Ben a written, signed offer to provide the tile

according to Ben's specifications for $26,000 and promised that "the offer will remain open until July 17." Flora is bound by her firm offer to keep the offer open until July 17. The result would differ, however, if Flora had merely stated that the "offer terminates on July 17" or that "the offer will terminate if not accepted on or before July 17." In both of these instances, there is no assurance to keep the offer open: because it is not a firm offer, Flora could revoke it at any time prior to Ben's acceptance.

Any firm offer on a form supplied by the offeree must be separately signed by the offeror.

CISG

An offer may not be revoked if it indicates that it is irrevocable; it need not be in writing.

Variant Acceptances

The realities of modern business practices have necessitated the modification by the Code of the common law's "**mirror image**" rule, by which the acceptance cannot vary or deviate from the terms of the offer. A vast number of business transactions use standardized business forms, resulting in what has been termed the **battle of the forms**. For example, a merchant buyer sends to the merchant seller on the buyer's order form a purchase order for 1,000 dozen cotton shirts at $60 per dozen with delivery by October 1 at the buyer's place of business. On the reverse side of this standard form are twenty-five numbered paragraphs containing provisions generally favorable to the buyer. When the seller receives the buyer's order, he sends to the buyer an unequivocal acceptance of the offer on his acceptance form. Although the seller agrees to the buyer's quantity, price, and delivery terms, on the back of the form the seller utilizes in sending his unequivocal acceptance to the buyer are thirty-two numbered paragraphs generally favorable to the seller and in significant conflict with the buyer's form. Under the common law's "mirror image" rule, no contract would exist, for the seller has not in fact accepted unequivocally all of the material terms of the buyer's offer.

By comparison, Section 2–207 of the Code addresses variant acceptances by providing:

(1) A definite and seasonable expression of acceptance or a written confirmation which is sent within a reasonable time operates as an acceptance even though it states terms additional to or different from those offered or agreed upon, unless acceptance is expressly made conditional on assent to the additional or different terms.

(2) The additional terms are to be construed as proposals for addition to the contract. Between merchants such terms become part of the contract unless:

(a) the offer expressly limits acceptance to the terms of the offer;

(b) they materially alter it; or

(c) notification of objection to them has already been given or is given within a reasonable time after notice of them is received.

(3) Conduct by both parties which recognizes the existence of a contract is sufficient to establish a contract for sale although the writings of the parties do not otherwise establish a contract. In such case the terms of the particular contract consist of those terms on which the writings of the parties agree, together with any supplementary terms incorporated under any other provisions of this Act.

Thus, the Code attempts to settle the battle of the forms by focusing upon the intent of the parties. If the offeree expressly makes his acceptance conditioned upon the offeror's assent to the additional or different terms, no contract is formed. If the offeree does not expressly make his acceptance conditional upon such assent, a contract is formed. The issue then becomes whether the offeree's different or additional terms should become part of the contract. If both offeror and offeree are merchants, **additional** terms (terms the offeree proposed for the contract for the first time) will become part of the contract, provided they do not materially alter the agreement and are not objected to either in the offer itself or within a reasonable time. If either of the parties is not a merchant, or if the additional terms materially alter the offer, then the terms are merely construed as proposals for addition to the contract. **Different** terms (terms that contradict terms of the offer) proposed by the offeree also will generally not become part of the contract unless specifically accepted by the offeror. The courts are divided over what terms are included when the terms conflict. The majority of courts hold that the terms cancel each other out and look to the Code to provide the missing terms; other courts hold that the offeror's terms govern. Some states follow a third alternative and apply the additional terms test to different terms.

Applying Section 2–207 to the example above: because both parties are merchants and the seller did not condition his acceptance upon the buyer's assent to the additional or different terms, (1) the contract will be formed without the *seller's different terms* unless the buyer specifically accepts them; (2) the contract will be formed without the *seller's additional terms* unless (a) the buyer specifically accepts or (b) the additional terms do not materially alter the offer and the buyer does not object to them; and (3) depending upon the jurisdiction, either (a) the conflicting (different) terms cancel each other out and the Code provides the missing terms or (b) the buyer's conflicting terms are included in the contract or (c) the additional terms test is applied.

CISG

A reply to an offer that contains additions, limitations, or other modifications is a counteroffer that rejects the original offer. Nevertheless, a purported acceptance that contains additional or different terms acts as an acceptance if the terms do not materially alter the contract unless the offeror objects to the change. Changes in price, payment, quality, quantity, place and time of delivery, terms of delivery, liability of the parties, and settlement of a dispute are always considered to be material alterations.

Finally, subsection 3 of 2–207 deals with those situations in which the writings do not form a contract but the conduct of the parties recognizes the existence of one. For instance, Ernest makes an offer to Gwen, who replies with a conditional acceptance. Although no contract has been formed, Gwen ships the ordered goods and Ernest accepts the goods. Subsection 3 provides that in this instance the contract consists of the written terms to which both parties agreed together with supplementary provisions of the Code.

◆ SEE FIGURE 7-3 Battle of the Forms

◊ SEE CASE 7-1

Manner of Acceptance

As with the common law, the offeror may specify the manner in which the offer must be accepted. If the offeror does not and the circumstances do not otherwise clearly indicate, an offer to make a contract invites acceptance in any manner and by any medium reasonable under the circumstances. Section 2–206(1)(a); Section 2A–206(1). The Code, therefore, allows flexibility of response and the ability to keep pace with new modes of communication.

An offer to buy goods for prompt or current shipment may be accepted either by a prompt promise to ship or by prompt shipment. Section 2–206(1)(b). Acceptance by performance requires notice within a reasonable time, or the offer may be treated as lapsed. Section 2–206(2); Section 2A–206(2).

Auctions

The Code provides that if an auction sale is advertised or announced in explicit terms to be **without reserve**, the auctioneer may not withdraw the article put up for sale unless no bid is made within a reasonable time. Unless the sale is advertised as being without reserve, the sale is **with reserve**, and the auctioneer may withdraw the goods at any time until he announces completion of the sale. Whether the sale is with or without reserve, a bidder may retract his bid at any time prior to acceptance by the auctioneer. Such retraction does not, however, revive any previous bid. Section 2–328.

◆FIGURE 7-3   Battle of the Forms

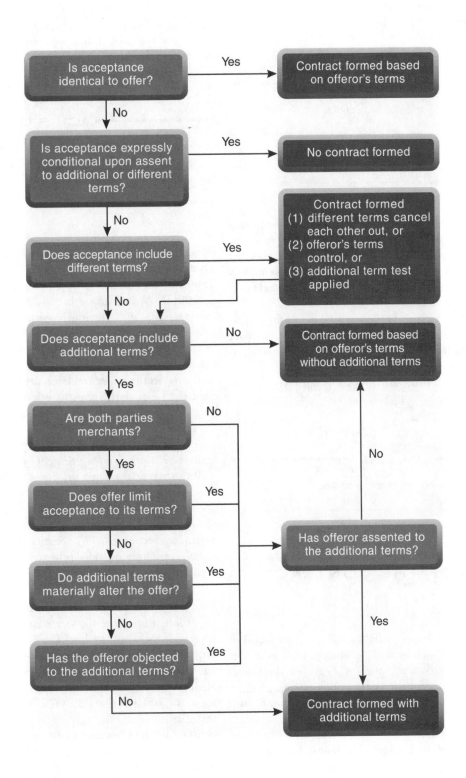

If the auctioneer knowingly receives a bid by or on behalf of the seller, and notice has not been given that the seller reserves the right to bid at the auction sale, the bidder to whom the goods are sold can either avoid the sale or take the goods at the price of the last good faith bid.

C I S G

The CISG does not apply to sales by auctions.

CONSIDERATION

The Code has abandoned the common law rule requiring that a modification of an existing contract be supported by consideration to be valid. The Code provides that a contract for the sale of goods can be effectively modified without new consideration, provided the modification is made in good faith. Section 2–209(1); Section 2A–208(1).

In addition, (1) any claim of right arising out of an alleged breach of contract can be discharged in whole or in part without consideration by a written waiver or renunciation signed and delivered by the aggrieved party, Section 1–107; and (2) as previously noted, a firm offer is not revocable for lack of consideration.

C I S G

Consideration is not needed to modify a contract.

FORM OF THE CONTRACT

Statute of Frauds

The original statute of frauds, which applied to contracts for the sale of goods, has been used as a prototype for the Article 2 statute of frauds provision. Section 2–201 of the Code provides that a contract for the sale of goods costing *$500 or more* is not enforceable unless there is some writing or record sufficient to evidence the existence of a contract between the parties ($1,000 or more for leases, Section 2A–201). Over 40 states have adopted the **Uniform Electronic Transactions Act (UETA)**, which gives full effect to contracts formed by electronic records and signatures. The Act applies to con-

tracts governed by Articles 2 and 2A. In addition, Congress in 2000 enacted the **Electronic Signatures in Global and National Commerce (E-Sign)**. The Act, which uses language very similar to that of UETA, makes electronic records and signatures valid and enforceable across the United States for many types of transactions in or affecting interstate or foreign commerce.

C I S G

A contract need not be evidenced by a writing, unless one of the parties has her place of business in a country that provides otherwise.

Modification of Contracts An agreement modifying a contract must be evidenced by a writing or record if the resulting contract is within the statute of frauds. Section 2–209(3) (Article 2A omits this provision). Conversely, if a contract that was previously within the statute of frauds is modified so as to no longer fall within it, the modification is enforceable even if it is oral. Thus, if the parties enter into an oral contract to sell for $450 a dining room table to be delivered to the buyer and later, prior to delivery, orally agree that the seller shall stain the table and that the buyer shall pay a price of $550, the modified contract is unenforceable. In contrast, if the parties have a written contract for the sale of 150 bushels of wheat at a price of $4.50 per bushel and later, upon oral agreement, decrease the quantity to 100 bushels at the same price per bushel, the agreement, as modified, is enforceable.

A signed agreement that requires modifications or rescissions to be in a signed writing cannot be otherwise modified or rescinded. Section 2–209(2); Section 2A–208(2). If this requirement is on a form provided by a merchant, the other party must separately sign it unless the other party is a merchant.

Written Compliance The statute of frauds compliance provisions under the Code are more liberal than the rules under general contract law. The Code requires merely some writing or record (1) sufficient to indicate that a contract has been made between the parties, (2) signed by the party against whom enforcement is sought or by her authorized agent or broker, that (3) includes a term specifying the quantity of goods the agreement involves. Whereas general contract law requires that a writing include all essential terms, even a writing or record that omits or incorrectly states a term agreed upon may be sufficient under the Code. This is consistent with other provisions of the Code stating that contracts may be enforced despite the omission of material terms. Nevertheless, the contract is enforceable only to the extent of the quantity set forth in the writing or record. Given proof that a contract was intended and a signed writing describing the goods, their quantity, and the names of the parties, under the Code the court can supply omitted terms such as price and particulars of performance. Many courts have concluded, however, that the Code does not require a clear and precise quantity term in a requirements or output contract. Moreover, several related documents may satisfy the writing or record requirement.

Between merchants, if within a reasonable time a writing in confirmation of the contract is received, the **written merchant confirmation**, if sufficient against the sender, is also sufficient against the recipient unless he gives written notice of his objection within ten days after receiving the confirmation. Section 2–201(2). (Article 2A does not have a comparable rule). This means that if these requirements have been met, the recipient of the writing or record is in the same position he would have assumed by signing it; and the confirmation, therefore, is enforceable against him. For example, Brown Co. and ATM Industries enter into an oral contract providing that ATM will deliver one thousand dozen shirts to Brown at $6 per shirt. The next day, Brown sends to ATM a letter signed by Brown's president confirming the agreement. The letter contains the quantity term but does not mention the price. Brown is bound by the contract when its authorized agent sends the letter, whereas ATM is bound by the oral contract ten days after receiving the letter, unless it objects in writing within that time. Therefore, it is essential that merchants examine their mail carefully and promptly to make certain that any written confirmations conform to their understanding of their outstanding contractual agreements. Where one or both of the parties is not a merchant, however, this rule does not apply.

Exceptions A contract that does not satisfy the writing requirement but is otherwise valid is enforceable in the following instances.

The Code permits an oral contract for the sale of goods to be enforced against a party who in his pleading, testimony, or otherwise in court **admits** that a contract was made, but limits enforcement to the quantity of goods so admitted. Section 2–201(3)(b); Section 2A–201(4)(b). This provision recognizes that the policy behind the statute of frauds does not apply when the party seeking to avoid the oral contract admits under oath the existence of the contract.

The Code also permits enforcement of an oral contract for goods **specially manufactured** for the buyer. Section 2–201(3)(a); Section 2A–201(4)(a). Nevertheless, if the goods, although manufactured on special order, are readily market-

able in the ordinary course of the seller's business, the contract is not enforceable unless in writing.

In most states, prior to the Code, delivery and acceptance of part of the goods or payment of part of the price and acceptance of the payment made the entire oral contract enforceable against the buyer who had received part delivery or against the seller who had received part payment. Under the Code such "partial performance" validates the contract only for the goods that have been **delivered and accepted** or for which **payment** has been **accepted.** Section 2–201(3)(c); Section 2A–201 (4)(c). To illustrate, Debra orally agrees to buy 1,000 watches from Brian for $15,000. Brian delivers 300 watches to Debra, who receives and accepts them. The oral contract is enforceable to the extent of 300 watches ($4,500)—those received and accepted—but is unenforceable to the extent of 700 watches ($10,500).

But what if part payment under an indivisible contract, such as one for the sale of an automobile, presents a choice between not enforcing the contract or enforcing it as a whole? Presently, there is a division of authority on this issue, although the better rule appears to be that such part payment and acceptance makes the entire contract enforceable.

Parol Evidence

Contractual terms that the parties set forth in a writing which they intend as a final expression of their agreement may not be contradicted by evidence of any prior agreement or of a contemporaneous agreement. Nevertheless, under the Code, the terms may be explained or supplemented by (1) course of dealing, usage of trade, or course of performance; and (2) evidence of consistent additional terms, unless the writing was intended as the complete and exclusive statement of the terms of the agreement. Section 2–202; Section 2A–202.

For a comparison of general contract law and the law governing sales and leases of goods, see Figure 7-4.

CISG

The CISG permits a court to consider all relevant circumstances of the agreement, including the negotiations, any course of performance between the parties, trade usages, and any subsequent conduct.

◆ **SEE FIGURE 7-4** Contract Law Compared with Law of Sales

◆ Figure 7-4 Contract Law Compared with Law of Sales

Section of UCC	Contract Law	Law of Sales/Leases
Definiteness	Contract must include all material terms.	Open terms permitted if parties intend to make a contract. Section 2-204; 2A-204.
Counteroffers	Acceptance must be a mirror image of offer. Counteroffer and conditional acceptance are rejections.	Battle of forms. Section 2-207. See Figure 7-3.
Modification of Contract	Consideration is required.	Consideration is not required. Section 2-209; 2A-208.
Irrevocable Offers	Options.	Options. Firm offers up to three months binding without consideration. Section 2-205; 2A-205.
Statute of Frauds	Writing must include all material terms.	Writing must include quantity term. Specially manufactured goods. Confirmation by merchants. Delivery or payment and acceptance. Admissions. Section 2-201; 2A-201 (except merchant confirmation).

CHAPTER SUMMARY

Nature of Sales and Leases

Definitions	**Goods** movable personal property **Sale** transfer of title to goods from seller to buyer for a price **Lease** a transfer of right to possession and use of goods in return for consideration • *Consumer Leases* leases by a merchant to an individual who leases for personal, family, or household purposes for no more than $25,000 • *Finance Leases* special type of lease transaction generally involving three parties: the lessor, the supplier, and the lessee **Governing Law** • *Sales Transactions* governed by Article 2 of the Code, but where general contract law has not been specifically modified by the Code, general contract law continues to apply • *Lease Transactions* governed by Article 2A of the Code, but where general contract law has not been specifically modified by the Code, general contract law continues to apply • *Transactions outside the Code* include employment contracts, service contracts, insurance contracts, contracts involving real property, and contracts for the sale of intangibles
Fundamental Principles of Article 2 and Article 2A	**Purpose** to modernize, clarify, simplify, and make uniform the law of sales and leases **Good Faith** the Code requires all sales and lease contracts to be performed in good faith, which means honesty in fact in the conduct or transaction concerned; in the case of a merchant, it also includes the observance of reasonable commercial standards **Unconscionability** a court may refuse to enforce an unconscionable contract or any part of a contract found to be unconscionable • *Procedural Unconscionability* unfairness of the bargaining process • *Substantive Unconscionability* oppressive or grossly unfair contractual provisions

Expansion of Commercial Practices
- *Course of Dealing* a sequence of previous conduct between the parties establishing a common basis for interpreting their agreement
- *Usage of Trade* a practice or method of dealing regularly observed and followed in a place, vocation, or trade

Sales by and between Merchants the Code establishes separate rules that apply to transactions between merchants or involving a merchant (a dealer in goods or a person who by his occupation holds himself out as having knowledge or skill peculiar to the goods or practice involved, or who employs an agent or broker whom he holds out as having such knowledge or skill)

Liberal Administration of Remedies

Freedom of Contract most provisions of the Code may be varied by agreement

Validation and Preservation of Sales Contract the Code reduces formal requisites to the bare minimum and attempts to preserve agreements whenever the parties manifest an intention to enter into a contract

Formation of Sales and Lease Contracts

Manifestation of Mutual Assent	**Definiteness of an Offer** the Code provides that a sales or lease contract does not fail for indefiniteness even though one or more terms may have been omitted; the Code provides standards by which missing essential terms may be supplied for sales of goods **Irrevocable Offers** • *Option* a contract to hold open an offer • *Firm Offer* a signed writing by a merchant to hold open an offer for the purchase or sale of goods for a maximum of three months **Variant Acceptances** the inclusion of different or additional terms in an acceptance is addressed by focusing on the intent of the parties **Manner of Acceptance** an acceptance can be made in any reasonable manner and is effective upon dispatch **Auction** auction sales are generally with reserve, permitting the auctioneer to withdraw the goods at any time prior to sale
Consideration	**Contractual Modifications** the Code provides that a contract for the sale or lease of goods may be modified without new consideration if the modification is made in good faith **Firm Offers** are not revocable for lack of consideration
Form of the Contract	**Statute of Frauds** sale of goods costing $500 or more (or lease of goods for $1,000 or more) must be evidenced by a signed writing to be enforceable • *Written Compliance* the Code requires some writing or writings sufficient to indicate that a contract has been made between the parties, signed by the party against whom enforcement is sought or by her authorized agent or broker, and including a term specifying the quantity of goods • *Alternative Methods of Compliance* written confirmation between merchants, admission, specially manufactured goods, and delivery or payment and acceptance **Parol Evidence** contractual terms that are set forth in a writing intended by the parties as a final expression of their agreement may not be contradicted by evidence of any prior agreement or of a contemporaneous oral agreement, but such terms may be explained or supplemented by course of dealing, usage of trade, course of performance, or consistent additional evidence

CASE

7-1

In the following case, which illustrates the 'battle of the forms,' the court attempts to determine whether a provision calling for arbitration of disputes is actually part of the parties' contract.

COMMERCE & INDUSTRY INSURANCE COMPANY
v. BAYER CORPORATION

Supreme Judicial Court of Massachusetts, 2001
433 Mass. 388, 742 N.E.2d 567, 44 U.C.C. Rep.Serv.2d 50
http://caselaw.lp.findlaw.com/scripts/getcase.pl?court=ma&vol=sjcslip/8358&invol=1

Greaney, J.
We granted the application for direct appellate review of the defendant, Bayer Corporation (Bayer), to determine the enforceability of an arbitration provision appearing in the plaintiff's, Malden Mills Industries, Inc. (Malden Mills), orders purchasing materials from Bayer. In a written decision, a judge in the Superior Court concluded that the provision was not enforceable. * * * We affirm the order.

The background of the case is as follows. Malden Mills manufactures internationally-known apparel fabrics and other textiles. On December 11, 1995, an explosion and fire destroyed several Malden Mills's buildings at its manufacturing facility. Subsequently, Malden Mills and its property insurers, the plaintiffs Commerce and Industry Insurance Company and Federal Insurance Company, commenced suit in the Superior Court against numerous defendants, including Bayer. In their complaint, the plaintiffs allege, insofar as relevant here, that the cause of the fire was the ignition, by static electrical discharge, of nylon tow (also known as bulk nylon fiber), which was sold by Bayer (but manufactured by a French business entity) to Malden Mills * * * .

Malden Mills initiated purchases of nylon tow from Bayer either by sending its standard form purchase order to Bayer, or by placing a telephone order to Bayer, followed by a standard form purchase order. Each of Malden Mills's purchase orders contained, on the reverse side, as one of its "terms and conditions," an arbitration provision stating:

> Any controversy arising out of or relating to this contract shall be settled by arbitration in the City of New York or Boston as [Malden Mills] shall determine in accordance with the Rules then obtaining of the American Arbitration Association or the General Arbitration Council of the Textile Industry, as [Malden Mills] shall determine.

Another "term and condition" appearing in paragraph one on the reverse side of each purchase order provides:

> This purchase order represents the entire agreement between both parties, not withstanding any Seller's order form, * * * , and this document cannot be modified except in writing and signed by an authorized representative of the buyer.

In response, Bayer transmitted Malden Mills's purchase orders to the manufacturer with instructions, in most instances, that the nylon tow was to be shipped directly to Malden Mills. Thereafter, Bayer prepared and sent Malden Mills an invoice. Each of the Bayer invoices contained the following language on its face, located at the bottom of the form in capital letters:

> TERMS AND CONDITIONS: NOTWITHSTANDING ANY CONTRARY OR INCONSISTENT CONDITIONS THAT MAY BE EMBODIED IN YOUR PURCHASE ORDER, YOUR ORDER IS ACCEPTED SUBJECT TO THE PRICES, TERMS AND CONDITIONS OF THE MUTUALLY EXECUTED CONTRACT BETWEEN US, OR, IF NO SUCH CONTRACT EXISTS, YOUR ORDER IS ACCEPTED SUBJECT TO OUR REGULAR SCHEDULED PRICE AND TERMS IN EFFECT AT TIME OF SHIPMENT AND SUBJECT TO THE TERMS AND CONDITIONS PRINTED ON THE REVERSE SIDE HEREOF.

The following "condition" appears in paragraph fourteen on the reverse side of each invoice:

> "This document is not an Expression of Acceptance or a Confirmation document as contemplated in Section 2–207 of the Uniform Commercial Code. The acceptance of any order entered by [Malden Mills] is expressly conditioned on [Malden Mills's] assent to any additional or conflicting terms contained herein.

Malden Mills usually remitted payment to Bayer within thirty days of receiving an invoice.

Based on the arbitration provision in Malden Mills's purchase orders, Bayer demanded that Malden Mills arbitrate its claims against Bayer. After Malden Mills refused, Bayer moved to compel arbitration and to stay the litigation against it. The judge denied Bayer's motion, concluding, under § 2–207 of * * * the Massachusetts enactment of the Uniform Commercial Code, that the parties' conduct, as opposed to their writings, established a contract. As to whether the arbitration provision was an enforceable term of the parties' contract, the judge concluded that subsection (3) of § 2–207 governed, and, pursuant thereto, the arbitration provision was not enforceable because the parties had not agreed in their writings to arbitrate. * * *

This case presents a dispute arising from what has been styled a typical "battle of the forms" sale, in which a buyer and a seller each attempt to consummate a commercial transaction through the exchange of self-serving preprinted forms that clash, and contradict each other, on both material and minor terms. [Citation.] Here, Malden Mills's form, a purchase order, contains an arbitration provision, and Bayer's form, a seller's invoice, is silent on how the parties will resolve any disputes. Oddly enough, the buyer, Malden Mills, the party proposing the arbitration provision, and its insurers, now seek to avoid an arbitral forum.

Section 2–207 was enacted with the expectation of creating an orderly mechanism to resolve commercial disputes resulting from a "battle of the forms." The section has been characterized as "an amphibious tank that was originally designed to fight in the swamps, but was sent to fight in the desert." [Citation.] Section 2–207 sets forth rules and principles concerning contract formation and the procedures for determining the terms of a contract. As to contract formation, under § 2-207, there are essentially three ways by which a contract may be formed. [Citation.] "First, if the parties exchange forms with divergent terms, yet the seller's invoice does not state that its acceptance is made 'expressly conditional' on the buyer's assent to any additional or different terms in the invoice, a contract is formed [under subsection (1) of § 2–207]." "Second, if the seller does make its acceptance 'expressly conditional' on the buyer's assent to any additional or divergent terms in the seller's invoice, the invoice is merely a counteroffer, and a contract is formed [under subsection (1) of § 2–207] only when the buyer expresses its affirmative acceptance of the seller's counteroffer." Third, "where for any reason the exchange of forms does not result in contract formation (e.g., the buyer 'expressly limits acceptance to the terms of [its offer]' under § 2–207(2)(a), or the buyer does not accept the seller's counteroffer under the second clause of § 2–207[1]), a contract nonetheless is formed [under subsection (3) of § 2–207] if their subsequent conduct—for instance, the seller ships and the buyer accepts the goods—demonstrates that the parties believed that a binding agreement had been formed."

Bayer correctly concedes that its contract with Malden Mills resulted from the parties' conduct, and, thus, was formed pursuant to subsection (3) of § 2–207. A contract never came into being under subsection (1) of § 2–207 because (1) paragraph fourteen on the reverse side of Bayer's invoices expressly conditioned acceptance on Malden Mills's assent to "additional or different" terms, and (2) Malden Mills never expressed "affirmative acceptance" of any of Bayer's invoices. In addition, the exchange of forms between Malden Mills and Bayer did not result in a contract because Malden Mills, by means of language in paragraph one of its purchase orders, expressly limited Bayer's acceptance to the terms of Malden Mills's offers. [Citation.]

Although Bayer acknowledges that its contract with Malden Mills was formed under subsection (3) of § 2–207, it nonetheless argues, * * * , that the terms of the contract are determined through an application of the principles in subsection (2) of § 2–207. Under this analysis, Bayer asserts that the arbitration provision became part of the parties' contract because it was not a "material alteration," and to include the provision would cause no "surprise or hardship" to the plaintiffs. This analysis is incorrect.

* * * Where a contract is formed by the parties' conduct (as opposed to writings), as is the case here, the terms of the contract are determined exclusively by subsection (3) of § 2–207. [Citation.]. Under subsection (3) of § 2–207, "the terms of the particular contract consist of those terms on which the writings of the parties agree, together with any supplementary terms incorporated under any other provisions of this chapter." § 2–207 (3). In this respect, one commentator has aptly referred to subsection (3) of § 2–207 as the "fall-back" rule. [Citation.] Under this rule, the Code accepts "common terms but rejects all the rest." While this approach "serves to leave many matters uncovered," terms may be filled by "recourse to usages of trade or course of dealing under [§] 1–205 or, perhaps, the gap filling provisions of [§§] 2–300s." [Citation.]

Contrary to Bayer's contentions, subsection (2) of § 2–207 is not applicable for several reasons. First, subsection (2) instructs on how to ascertain the terms of a contract when the contract is formed either by the parties' writings or by a party's written confirmation of an oral contract, situations not present here (the parties' contract was formed by their conduct). [Citation.] * * *

* * *

Thus, the judge correctly concluded, under subsection (3) of § 2–207, that the arbitration provision in Malden Mills's purchase orders did not become a term of the parties' contract. The arbitration provision was not common to both Malden Mills's purchase orders and Bayer's invoices. Bayer properly does not argue that any of the gap-filling provisions of [the UCC] apply. Because Bayer concedes that it never previously arbitrated a dispute with Malden Mills, we reject Bayer's claim that the parties' course of dealing requires us to enforce the arbitration provision.

* * *

Bayer may be right that the drafters of the Massachusetts version of the Code did not intend that § 2–207 should provide "an avenue for a party to strike the terms of its own purchase documents." Bayer, however, cannot ignore the fact that the use of its own boilerplate invoices contributed to the result that Bayer now finds problematic. The order denying the motion to compel arbitration and to stay litigation is affirmed.

QUESTIONS

1. Distinguish a sale and a lease from other kinds of transactions that affect goods.
2. Identify and discuss the fundamental principles of Article 2 and Article 2A.
3. Discuss the significant changes Article 2 and Article 2A have made in the need for an offer to include all material terms.
4. Distinguish between the common law's mirror image rule and the Uniform Commercial Code's (UCC's) provisions for dealing with variant acceptances.
5. Discuss (a) the UCC's approach to the requirement that certain contracts must be in writing and (b) the alternative methods of compliance.

PROBLEMS

1. Adams orders one thousand widgets at $5 per widget from International Widget to be delivered within sixty days. After the contract is consummated and signed, Adams requests that International deliver the widgets within thirty days rather than sixty days. International agrees. Is the contractual modification binding?

2. In question 1, what effect, if any, would the following telegram have?

> International Widget:
> In accordance with our agreement of this date you will deliver the 1,000 previously ordered widgets within thirty days. Thank you for your cooperation in this matter.
>   (signed) Adams

3. Browne & Assoc., a San Francisco company, orders from U.S. Electronics, a New York company, ten thousand electronic units. Browne & Assoc.'s order form provides that any dispute would be resolved by an arbitration panel located in San Francisco. U.S. Electronics executes and delivers to Browne & Assoc. its acknowledgment form, which accepts the order and contains the following provision: "All disputes will be resolved by the state courts of New York." A dispute arises concerning the workmanship of the parts, and Browne & Assoc. wishes the case to be arbitrated in San Francisco. What result?

4. Explain how the result in problem 3 might change if the U.S. Electronics form contained any of the following provisions:

   (a) "The seller's acceptance of the purchase order to which this acknowledgment responds is expressly made conditional on the buyer's assent to any or different terms contained in this acknowledgment."

   (b) "The seller's acceptance of the purchase order is subject to the terms and conditions on the face and reverse side hereof and which the buyer accepts by accepting the goods described herein."

   (c) "The seller's terms govern this agreement—this acknowledgment merely constitutes a counteroffer."

5. Reinfort executed a written contract with Bylinski to purchase an assorted collection of shoes for $3,000. A week before the agreed shipment date, Bylinski called Reinfort and said, "We cannot deliver at $3,000; unless you agree to pay $4,000, we will cancel the order." After considerable discussion, Reinfort agreed to pay $4,000 if Bylinski would ship as agreed in the contract. After the shoes had been delivered and accepted by Reinfort, Reinfort refused to pay $4,000 and insisted on paying only $3,000. Is the contractual modification binding? Explain.

6. On November 23, Acorn, a dress manufacturer, mailed to Bowman a written and signed offer to sell one thousand sundresses at $50 per dress. The offer stated that it would "remain open for ten days" and that it could "not be withdrawn prior to that date."

Two days later, Acorn, noting a sudden increase in the price of sundresses, changed his mind. Acorn therefore sent Bowman a letter revoking the offer. The letter was sent on November 25 and received by Bowman on November 28.

Bowman chose to disregard the letter of November 25; instead, she happily continued to watch the price of sundresses rise. On December 1, Bowman sent a letter accepting the original offer. The letter, however, was not received by Acorn until December 9, due to a delay in the mails.

Bowman has demanded delivery of the goods according to the terms of the offer of November 23, but Acorn has refused. Does a contract exist between Acorn and Bowman? Explain.

7. Henry and Wilma, an elderly immigrant couple, agreed to purchase from Brown a refrigerator with fair market value of $450 for twenty-five monthly installments of $60 per month. Henry and Wilma now wish to void the contract, asserting that they did not realize the exorbitant price they were paying. Result?

8. Courts Distributors needed two hundred compact refrigerators on a rush basis. It contacted Eastinghouse Corporation, a manufacturer of refrigerators. Eastinghouse said it would take some time to quote a price on an order of that size. Courts replied, "Send the refrigerators immediately and bill us later." The refrigerators were delivered three days later, and the invoice ten days after that. The invoice price was $140,000. Courts believes that the wholesale market price of the refrigerators is only $120,000. Do the parties have a contract? If so, what is the price? Explain.

9. While adjusting a television antenna beside his mobile home and underneath a high-voltage electric transmission wire, Prince received an electric shock resulting in personal injury. He claims the high-voltage electric current jumped from the transmission wire to the antenna. The wire, which carried some 7,200 volts of electricity, did not serve his mobile home but ran directly above it. Prince sued the Navarro County Electric Co-Op, the owner and operator of the wire, for breach of implied warranty of merchantability under the Uniform Commercial Code. He contends that the Code's implied warranty of merchantability extends to the container of a product—in this instance the wiring—and that the escape of the current shows that the wiring was unfit for its purpose of transporting electricity. The electric company argues that the electricity passing through the transmission wire was not being sold to Prince and that, therefore, there was no sale of goods to Prince. Is the contract covered by the UCC?

10. HMT, already in the business of marketing agricultural products, decided to try its hand at marketing potatoes for processing. Nine months before the potato harvest, HMT contracted to supply Bell Brand with 100,000 sacks of potatoes. At harvest time, Bell Brand would accept only 60,000 sacks. HMT sues for breach of contract. Bell Brand argues that custom and usage in marketing processing potatoes allows buyers to give *estimates* in contracts, not fixed quantities, because the contracts are established so far in advance. HMT responds that the quantity term in the contract was definite and unambiguous. Can custom and trade usage be used to interpret an unambiguous contract? Discuss.

11. Schreiner, a cotton farmer, agreed over the telephone to sell 150 bales of cotton to Loeb & Co. Schreiner had sold cotton to Loeb & Co. for the past five years. Written confirmation of the date, parties, price, and conditions was mailed to Schreiner, who did not respond to the confirmation in any way. Four months later, when the price of cotton had doubled, Loeb & Co. sought to enforce the contract. Is the contract enforceable?

12. American Sand & Gravel, Inc., agreed to sell sand to Clark at a special discount if 20,000 to 25,000 tons were ordered. The discount price was 45¢ per ton, compared with the normal price of 55¢ per ton. Two years later, Clark orders, and receives, 1,600 tons of sand from American Sand & Gravel. Clark refuses to pay more then 45¢ per ton. American Sand & Gravel sues for the remaining 10¢ per ton. Decision?

13. In September 1973, Auburn Plastics (defendant) submitted price quotations to CBS (plaintiff) for the manufacture of eight cavity molds to be used in making parts for CBS's toys. Each quotation specified that the offer would not be binding unless accepted within fifteen days. Furthermore, CBS would be subject to an additional 30 percent charge for engineering services upon delivery of the molds. In December 1973 and January 1974, CBS sent detailed purchase orders to Auburn Plastics for cavity molds. The purchase order forms stated that CBS reserved the right to remove the molds from Auburn Plastics without an additional or "withdrawal" charge. Auburn Plastics acknowledged the purchase order and stated that the sale would be subject to all conditions contained in the price quotation. CBS paid Auburn for the molds, and Auburn began to fabricate toy parts from the molds for CBS. Later, Auburn announced a price increase, and CBS demanded delivery of the molds. Auburn refused to deliver the molds unless CBS paid the additional charge for engineering services. CBS claimed that the contract did not provide for a withdrawal charge. Who will prevail? Why?

14. Terminal Grain Corporation brought an action against Glen Freeman, a farmer, to recover damages for breach of an oral contract to deliver grain. According to the company, Freeman orally agreed to two sales of wheat to Terminal Grain of 4,000 bushels each at $1.65 1/2 per bushel and $1.71 per bushel, respectively. Dwayne Maher, merchandising manager of Terminal Grain, sent two written confirmations of the agreements to Freeman, who never made any written objections to the confirmations. After the first transaction had occurred, the price of wheat rose to between $2.25 and $2.30 per bushel, and Freeman refused to deliver the remaining 4,000 bushels at the agreed-upon price. Freeman denies entering into any agreement to sell the second 4,000 bushels of wheat to Terminal Grain but admits that he received the two written confirmations sent by Maher. Decision?

15. Frank's Maintenance and Engineering, Inc., orally ordered steel tubing from C.A. Roberts Co. for use in the manufacture of motorcycle front fork tubes. Because these front fork tubes bear the bulk of the weight of a motorcycle, the steel used must be of high quality. Roberts Co. sent an acknowledgment with conditions of sale including one that limited consequential damages and restricted remedies available upon breach by requiring claims for defective equipment to be promptly made upon receipt. The conditions were located on the back of the acknowledgment. The legend "conditions of sale on reverse side" was stamped over so that on first appearance it read "No conditions of sale on reverse side." Roberts delivered the order in December 1975. The steel had no visible defects; however, when Frank's Maintenance began using the steel in its manufacture in the summer of 1976, it discovered that the steel was pitted and cracked beyond repair. Frank's Maintenance informed Roberts Co. of the defects, revoked its acceptance of the steel, and sued for breach of warranty of merchantability. Is the limitation of rights enforceable?

16. Dorton, as a representative for The Carpet Mart, purchased carpets from Collins & Aikman that were supposedly manufactured of 100 percent Kodel polyester fiber but were, in fact, made of cheaper and inferior fibers. Dorton then brought suit for compensatory and punitive damages against Collins & Aikman for its fraud, deceit, and misrepresentation in the sale of the carpets. Collins & Aikman moved for a stay pending arbitration, claiming that Dorton was bound to an arbitration agreement printed on the reverse side of Collins & Aikman's printed sales acknowledgment form. A provision printed on the face of the acknowledgment form stated that its acceptance was "subject to all of the terms and conditions on the face and reverse side thereof, including arbitration, all of which are accepted by buyer." Is the arbitration clause enforceable?

17. Defendant, Gray Communications, desired to build a television tower. After a number of negotiation sessions conducted by telephone between the Defendant and Plaintiff, Kline Iron, the parties allegedly reached an oral agreement under which the Plaintiff would build a tower for the Defendant for a total price of $1,485,368. A few days later, Plaintiff sent a written document, referred to as a proposal, for execution by Defendant. The Proposal indicated that it had been prepared for immediate acceptance by Defendant and that prior to formal acceptance by Defendant it could be modified or withdrawn without notice. A few days later, without having executed the Proposal, Defendant advised Plaintiff that a competitor had provided a lower bid for construction of the tower. Defendant requested that Plaintiff explain its higher bid price, which Plaintiff failed to do. Defendant then advised Plaintiff by letter that it would not be retained to construct the tower. Plaintiff then commenced suit alleging breach of an oral contract, asserting that the oral agreement was enforceable because the common law of contracts, not the UCC, governed the transaction and that under the common law a writing is not necessary to cover this type of transaction. Even if the transaction was subject to the UCC, Plaintiff alternatively argued, the contract was within the UCC "merchant's exception." Is the plaintiff correct in its assertions? Discuss.

18. Due to high gasoline prices, American Bakeries Company (ABC) considered converting its fleet of more than 3,000 vehicles to a much less expensive propane fuel system. After negotiations with Empire Gas Corporation (Empire), ABC signed a contract for approximately three thousand converter units, "more or less

depending upon requirements of Buyer," as well as agreeing to buy all propane to be used for four years from Empire. Without giving any reasons, however, ABC never ordered any converter units or propane from Empire, having apparently decided not to convert its vehicles. Empire brought suit against ABC for $3,254,963, representing lost profits on 2,242 converter units and the propane that would have been consumed during the contract period. Is ABC liable? Explain.

19. Emery Industries (Emery) contracted with Mechanicals, Inc. (Mechanicals), to install a pipe system to carry chemicals and fatty acids under high pressure and temperature. The system required stainless steel "stub ends" (used to connect pipe segments), which Mechanicals ordered from McJunkin Corporation (McJunkin). McJunkin in turn ordered the stub ends from the Alaskan Copper Companies, Inc. (Alaskan). McJunkin's purchase order required the seller to certify the goods and to relieve the buyer of liabilities that might arise from defective goods. After shipment of the goods to McJunkin, Alaskan sent written acknowledgment of the order, containing terms and conditions of sale different from those in McJunkin's purchase order. The acknowledgment provided a disclaimer of warranty and a requirement for inspection of the goods within ten days of receipt. The acknowledgment also contained a requirement that the buyer accept all of the seller's terms.

The stub ends were delivered to Mechanicals in several shipments over a five-month period. Each shipment included a document reciting terms the same as those on Alaskan's initial acknowledgment. Apparently, McJunkin never objected to any of the terms contained in any of Alaskan's documents.

After the stub ends were installed, they were found to be defective. Mechanicals had to remove and replace them, causing Emery to close its plant for several days. McJunkin filed a complaint alleging that Mechanicals had failed to pay $26,141.88 owed on account for the stub ends McJunkin supplied. Mechanicals filed an answer and counterclaim against McJunkin, alleging $93,586.13 in damages resulting from the replacement and repair of the defective stub ends. McJunkin filed a third-party complaint against Alaskan, alleging that Alaskan was liable for any damages Mechanicals incurred as a result of the defective stub ends. Discuss.

 Internet Exercise Compare the provisions governing the formation of sales contracts under the United Nations Convention on Contracts for the International Sale of Goods (Vienna, 1980) with the provisions of Article 2 of the Uniform Commercial Code.

Conduct Invalidating Assent

The preceding chapter considered one of the essential requirements of a contract, namely, the objective manifestation of mutual assent by each party to the other. In addition to requiring that the offer and acceptance be satisfied, the law demands that the agreement be voluntary and knowing. If these requirements are not met, then the agreement is either voidable or void. This chapter deals with situations in which the consent manifested by one of the parties to the contract is not effective because it was not knowingly and voluntarily given. These situations are considered under the headings of duress, undue influence, fraud, nonfraudulent misrepresentation, and mistake.

DURESS

A person should not be held to an agreement into which she has not entered voluntarily. Accordingly, the law will not enforce any contract induced by **duress**, which in general is any wrongful or unlawful act or threat that overcomes the free will of a party.

Physical Compulsion

There are two basic types of duress. The first occurs when one party compels another to manifest assent to a contract through actual **physical force**, such as pointing a gun at a person or taking a person's hand and compelling him to sign a written contract. This type of duress, while extremely rare, renders the agreement **void**. Restatement, Section 174(1).

Improper Threats

The second type of duress involves the use of improper threats or acts, *including economic and social coercion*, to compel a person to enter into a contract. The threat may be explicit or may be inferred from words or conduct; in either case, it must leave the victim with no reasonable alternative. This type of duress makes the contract **voidable** at the option of the coerced party. Restatement, Section 175(2). For example, if Lance, a landlord, induces Tamara, an infirm, bedridden tenant, to enter into a new lease on the same apartment at a greatly increased rent by wrongfully threatening to terminate Tamara's lease and evict her, Tamara can escape or *avoid* the new lease by reason of the duress exerted upon her.

With respect to the second and more common type of duress, the fact that the act or threat would not affect a person of average strength and intelligence is not determinative if it places the particular person in fear and induces him to perform an action against his will. The test is *subjective*, and the question is, did the threat actually induce assent on the part of the person claiming to be the victim of duress? Threats that would suffice to induce assent by one person may not suffice to induce assent by another. All circumstances must be considered, including the age, background, and relationship of the parties. Restatement, Section 175. Indeed, as comment c to this section of the Restatement states,

Persons of a weak or cowardly nature are the very ones that need protection; the courageous can usually protect themselves. Timid and inexperienced persons are particularly subject to threats, and it does not lie in the mouths of the unscrupulous to excuse their imposition on such persons on the ground of their victims' infirmities.

Ordinarily, the acts or threats constituting duress are themselves crimes or torts. But this is not true in all cases. The acts need not be criminal or tortious to be *wrongful*; they merely need to be contrary to public policy or morally reprehensible. For example, if the threat involves a breach of a contractual duty of good faith and fair dealing or the use of the civil process in bad faith, it is improper.

Moreover, the courts have generally held that contracts induced by threats of criminal prosecution are voidable, regardless of whether the coerced party had committed an unlawful act. Likewise, threatening the criminal prosecution of a near relative, such as a son or husband, is duress, regardless of the guilt or innocence of the relative.

To be distinguished from such threats of prosecution are threats to resort to ordinary civil remedies to recover a debt due from another. Threatening to bring a civil suit against an individual to recover a debt is not wrongful. What is prohibited is threatening to bring a civil suit when bringing such a suit would be abuse of process.

◆ See Case 8-1

UNDUE INFLUENCE

Undue influence is the unfair persuasion of a person by a party generally in a dominant position based upon a **confidential relationship**. The law very carefully scrutinizes contracts between those in a relationship of trust and confidence that is likely to permit one party to take unfair advantage of the other. Examples are the relationships of guardian-ward, trustee-beneficiary, principal-agent, spouses to each other, parent-child, attorney-client, physician-patient, and clergy-parishioner.

A transaction induced by unfair influence on the part of the dominant party is **voidable**. The ultimate question in undue influence cases is whether the dominant party induced the transaction by influencing a freely exercised and competent judgment or by dominating the mind or emotions of a submissive party. The weakness or dependence of the person persuaded is a strong indicator of the fairness or unfairness of the persuasion. For example, Ronald, a person without business experience, has for years relied in business matters on the advice of Nancy, who is experienced in business. Nancy, without making any false representations of fact, induces Ronald to enter into a contract with Nancy's confederate, George, that is disadvantageous to Ronald, as both Nancy and George know. The transaction is voidable on the grounds of undue influence.

Undue influence, as previously mentioned, generally arises in the context of relationships in which one person is in a position of dominance, or is likely to be. Where such a relationship exists at the time of the transaction, and it appears that the dominant party has gained at the other party's expense, the transaction is presumed to be voidable. For example, in a legally challenged contract between a guardian and his ward, the law presumes that advantage was taken by the guardian. It is, therefore, incumbent upon the guardian to rebut this presumption. Important factors in determining whether a contract is fair are (1) whether the dominant party made full disclosure of all relevant information known to him, (2) whether the consideration was adequate, and (3) whether the dependent party received competent and independent advice before completing the transaction. Without limitation, in every situation in which a confidential relationship exists, the dominant party is held to utmost good faith in his dealings with the other.

FRAUD

Another factor affecting the validity of consent given by a contracting party is fraud, which prevents assent from being knowingly given. There are two distinct types of fraud: fraud in the execution and fraud in the inducement.

Fraud in the Execution

Fraud in the execution, which is extremely rare, consists of a misrepresentation that deceives the defrauded person as to the very nature of the contract. Such fraud occurs when a person does not know, or does not have reasonable opportunity to know, the character or essence of a proposed contract because the other party misrepresents its character or essential terms. Fraud in the execution renders the transaction **void**.

For example, Abigail delivers a package to Boris, requests that Boris sign a receipt for it, holds out a simple printed form headed "Receipt," and indicates the line on which Boris is to sign. This line, which to Boris appears to be the bottom line of the receipt, is actually the signature line of a promissory note cleverly concealed underneath the receipt. Boris signs where directed without knowing that he is signing a note. This is fraud in the execution. The note is void and of no legal effect because Boris has not actually given his assent, even though his signature is genuine and appears to manifest his assent to the terms of the note. The nature of Abigail's fraud precluded consent to the signing of the note because it prevented Boris from reasonably knowing what he was signing.

Fraud in the Inducement

Fraud in the inducement, generally referred to as fraud or deceit, is an intentional misrepresentation of material fact by one party to the other, who consents to enter into a contract in justifiable reliance upon the misrepresentation. Fraud in the inducement renders the contract **voidable** by the defrauded party. For example, Ada, in offering to sell her dog to Ben, tells Ben that the dog won first prize in its class in a recent national dog show. In fact, the dog had not even been entered in the show. Nonetheless, Ada's statement induces Ben to accept the offer and pay a high price for the dog. A contract exists, but it is voidable by Ben because of Ada's fraud, which induced his assent.

The requisites for fraud in the inducement are:

1. a false representation
2. of a fact
3. that is material and
4. made with knowledge of its falsity and the intention to deceive (scienter) and
5. which representation is justifiably relied upon.

False Representation A basic element of fraud is a false representation or misrepresentation, that is, an assertion not in accord with the facts, made through positive statement or conduct that misleads. **Concealment** is an action intended or known to be likely to keep another from learning of a fact of which he would otherwise have learned. Active concealment is a form of misrepresentation that can form the basis for fraud, as where a seller puts heavy oil or grease in a car engine to conceal a knock. Truth may be suppressed by concealment as much as by misrepresentation.

Expressly denying knowledge of a fact which a party knows to exist is a misrepresentation if it leads the other party to believe that the facts do not exist or cannot be discovered. Moreover, a statement of misleading half-truth is considered the equivalent of a false representation.

As a general rule, **silence** or nondisclosure alone does *not* amount to fraud. A seller generally is not obligated to tell a purchaser everything he knows about the subject of a sale. Thus, it is not fraud when a buyer possesses advantageous information about the seller's property, of which he knows the seller to be ignorant, and does not disclose such information to the seller. Likewise, a buyer is under no duty to inform a seller of the greater value or other advantages of his property. Assume that Sid owns a farm which, as a farm, is worth $10,000. Brenda knows that there is oil under Sid's farm and knows that Sid is ignorant of this fact. Brenda, without disclosing this information to Sid, makes an offer to Sid to buy the farm for $10,000. Sid accepts the offer, and a contract is duly made. Sid, on later learning the facts, can do nothing about the matter, either at law or in equity. As one case puts it, "a purchaser is not bound by our laws to make the man he buys from as wise as himself."

Although nondisclosure usually does not constitute a misrepresentation, in certain situations it does. One such situation arises when (1) a person fails to disclose a fact known to him, (2) he knows that the disclosure of that fact would correct a mistake of the other party as to a basic assumption on which that party is making the contract, and (3) nondisclosure of the

fact amounts to a failure to act in a good faith and in accordance with reasonable standards of fair dealing. Restatement, Section 161. Accordingly, if the property at issue in the contract possesses a substantial latent (hidden) defect, one that the buyer would not discover by an ordinary examination, the seller may be obliged to reveal it. Suppose, for example, that Judith owns a valuable horse, which Judith knows is suffering from a disease only a competent veterinary surgeon might detect. Judith offers to sell this horse to Curt, but does not inform Curt about the condition of the horse. Curt makes a reasonable examination of the horse and, finding it in apparently normal condition, purchases it from Judith. Curt, on later discovering the disease in question, can have the sale set aside. Judith's silence, under the circumstances, was a misrepresentation.

There are other situations in which the law imposes a duty of disclosure. For example, one may have a duty of disclosure because of prior representations, innocently made before entering into the contract, which are later discovered to be untrue. Another instance in which silence may constitute fraud is a transaction involving a fiduciary. A **fiduciary** is a person in a confidential relationship who owes a duty of trust, loyalty, and confidence to another. For example, an agent owes a fiduciary duty to his principal, as does a trustee to the beneficiary of a trust and a partner to her copartners. A fiduciary may not deal at *arm's length* but rather owes a duty to make full disclosure of all relevant facts when entering into a transaction with the other party to the relationship. In contrast, in most everyday business or market transactions, the parties are said to deal at "arm's length," meaning that they deal with each other on equal terms.

Fact The basic element of fraud is the misrepresentation of a material fact. A **fact** is an event that actually took place or a thing that actually exists. Suppose that Dale induces Mike to purchase shares in a company unknown to Mike at a price of $100 per share by representing that she had paid $150 per share for them during the preceding year, when in fact she had paid only $50. This representation of a past event is a misrepresentation of fact.

Actionable fraud rarely can be based upon what is merely a statement of **opinion**. A representation is one of opinion if it expresses only the uncertain belief of the representer as to the existence of a fact or his judgment as to quality, value, authenticity, or other matters of judgment.

The line between fact and opinion is not an easy one to draw and in close cases presents an issue for the jury. The solution will often turn upon the superior knowledge of the person making the statement and the information available to the other party. Thus, if Dale said to Mike that the shares were "a good investment," she is merely stating her opinion, and in the usual case Mike ought to regard it as no more than that. Other common examples of opinion are statements of value, such as "This is the best car for the money in town" or "This deluxe model will give you twice the wear of a cheaper model." Such exaggerations and commendations of articles offered for sale are to be expected from dealers, who are merely puffing their wares with sales talk. If, however, the representer is a professional advising a client, the courts are more likely to regard as actionable an untrue statement of opinion. When the person expressing the opinion is one who holds himself out as having expert knowledge, the tendency is to grant relief to those who have sustained loss through reasonable reliance upon the expert evaluation.

Also to be distinguished from a representation of fact is a **prediction** of the future. Predictions, which are similar to opinions in that no one can know with certainty what will happen in the future, normally are not regarded as factual statements. Likewise, promissory statements ordinarily do not constitute a basis of fraud, as a breach of promise does not necessarily indicate that the promise was fraudulently made. A promise that the promisor, at the time of making, had no intention of keeping, however, is a misrepresentation of fact. Most courts take the position that a misrepresented state of mind "is as much a fact as the state of a person's digestion." *Edgington v. Fitzmaurice*, 29 Ch.D. 459 (1885). If a dealer promises, "I will service this machine free for the next year," but at the time has no intention of doing so, his conduct is actionable if the other elements of fraud are present.

Historically, courts held that representations of **law** were not statements of fact but rather of opinion. The present trend is to recognize that a statement of law may have either the effect of a statement of fact or a statement of opinion. Restatement, Torts, Section 545. For example, a statement of law asserting that a particular statute has been enacted or repealed has the effect of a statement of fact. On the other hand, a statement as to the legal consequences of a particular set of facts is a statement of opinion. Nonetheless, such a statement may imply that the facts known to the maker are consistent with the legal conclusion stated. For example, an assertion that a company has the legal right to do business in a state may include the assurance that the company has taken all the steps required to be duly qualified. Moreover, a statement by one who is learned in the law, such as a practicing attorney, may be considered a statement of fact.

❧ SEE CASE 8-2

Materiality   In addition to being a misrepresentation of fact, a misrepresentation also must be **material**. A misrepresentation is material if (1) it would be likely to induce a reasonable person to manifest his assent or (2) the maker knows that it would be likely to induce the recipient to do so. Restatement, Section 162. In the sale of a racehorse, whether a certain jockey rode the horse in its most recent race may not be material, but its running time for the race probably would be. The Restatement of Contracts provides that a contract justifiably induced by a misrepresentation is voidable if the misrepresentation is either fraudulent *or* material. Therefore, a fraudulent misrepresentation does not have to be material for the recipient to obtain rescission, but it must be material if she is to recover damages. Restatement, Section 164; Restatement, Torts, Section 538.

❧ SEE CASE 8-3

Knowledge of Falsity and Intention to Deceive   To establish fraud, the misrepresentation must have been known by the one making it to be false and must have been made with an intent to deceive. This element of fraud is known as **scienter**. Knowledge of falsity can consist of (a) actual knowledge, (b) lack of belief in the statement's truthfulness, or (c) reckless indifference as to its truthfulness.

Justifiable Reliance   A person is not entitled to relief unless he has justifiably relied upon the misrepresentation. If the misrepresentation in no way influenced the complaining party's decision, he must abide by the terms of the contract. He is not deceived if he does not rely. Justifiable reliance requires that the misrepresentation contribute substantially to the misled party's decision to enter into the contract. If the complaining party knew or it was obvious that the defendant's representation was untrue, but he still entered into the contract, he has not justifiably relied. Moreover, where the misrepresentation is fraudulent, the party who relies on it is entitled to relief even though he does not investigate the statement or is contributorily negligent in relying on it. Restatement, Torts, Sections 540, 545A. Not knowing or discovering the facts before making a contract does not constitute unjustified reliance unless it amounts to a failure to act in good faith and in accordance with reasonable standards of fair dealing. Restatement, Section 172. Thus, most courts will not allow a person who concocts a deliberate and elaborate scheme to defraud—one that the defrauded party should readily detect—to argue that the defrauded party did not justifiably rely upon the misrepresentation.

❧ SEE CASE 8-4

NONFRAUDULENT MISREPRESENTATION

Nonfraudulent misrepresentation is a material, false statement that induces another to rely justifiably but is made without *scienter*.

Negligent misrepresentation is a false representation that is made without due care in ascertaining its truthfulness. **Innocent misrepresentation** is a false representation made without knowledge of its falsity but with due care. To obtain relief for nonfraudulent misrepresentation, all of the other elements of fraud must be present *and* the misrepresentation must be material. The remedies that may be available for nonfraudulent misrepresentation are rescission and damages (see Chapter 5).

◆ SEE FIGURE 8-1 **Misrepresentation**

MISTAKE

A **mistake** is a belief that is not in accord with the facts. Where the mistaken facts relate to the basis of the parties' agreement, the law permits the adversely affected party to avoid or reform the contract under certain circumstances. But because permitting avoidance for mistake undermines the objective approach to mutual assent, the law has experienced considerable difficulty in specifying those circumstances that justify permitting the subjective matter of mistake to invalidate an otherwise objectively satisfactory agreement. As a result, establishing clear rules to govern the effect of mistake has proven elusive.

The Restatement and modern cases treat mistakes of law in existence at the time of making a contract no differently than mistakes of fact. For example, Susan contracts to sell a parcel of land to James with the mutual understanding that James will build an apartment house on the land. Both Susan and James believe that such a building is lawful. Unknown to them, however, the town in which the land is located had enacted an ordinance precluding such use of the land three days before they entered into the contract. This mistake of law, which the courts would treat as a mistake of fact, would lead to the consequences discussed below.

Mutual Mistake

Mutual mistake occurs when *both* parties are mistaken as to the same set of facts. If the mistake relates to a basic assumption on which the contract is made and has a material effect on the agreed exchange, then it is **voidable** by the adversely affected party unless he bears the risk of the mistake. Restatement, Section 152.

Usually, market conditions and the financial situation of the parties are not considered basic assumptions. Thus, if Gail contracts to purchase Pete's automobile under the belief that she can sell it at a profit to Jesse, she is not excused from liability if she is mistaken in this belief. Nor can she rescind the agreement simply because she was mistaken as to her estimate of what the automobile was worth. These are the ordinary risks of business, and courts do not undertake to relieve against them. But suppose that the parties contract upon the assumption that the automobile is a 1993 Cadillac with fifteen thousand miles of use, when in fact the engine is that of a cheaper model and has been run in excess of fifty thousand miles. Here, a court would likely allow a rescission because of mutual mistake of a material fact. The sale was voidable by the purchaser for mutual mistake. In a New Zealand case, the plaintiff purchased a "stud bull" at an auction. There were no express warranties as to "sex, condition, or otherwise." Actually, the bull was sterile. Rescission was allowed, the court observing that it was a "bull in name only."

◥ SEE CASE 8-5

Unilateral Mistake

Unilateral mistake occurs when only one of the parties is mistaken. Courts have been hesitant to grant relief for unilateral mistake even though it relates to a basic assumption on which the party entered into the contract and has a material effect on the agreed exchange. Nevertheless, relief will be granted where the nonmistaken party knows, or reasonably should know, that such a mistake has been made (palpable unilateral mistake) or

◆ FIGURE 8-1 **Misrepresentation**

	Fraudulent	Negligent	Innocent
False statement of fact	Yes	Yes	Yes
Materiality	Yes for damages No for rescission	Yes	Yes
Fault	Scienter (knowledge and intent)	Without due care	Without knowledge and due care
Reliance	Yes	Yes	Yes
Injury	Yes for damages No for rescission	Yes for damages No for rescission	Yes for damages No for rescission
Remedies	Damages Rescission	Damages Rescission	Damages Rescission

where the mistake was caused by the fault of the nonmistaken party. For example, suppose a building contractor makes a serious error in his computations and as a result submits a bid on a job that is one-half the amount it should be. If the other party knows that he made such an error, or reasonably should have known, she cannot, as a general rule, take advantage of the other's mistake by accepting the offer. In addition, many courts and the Restatement allow rescission where the effect of the unilateral mistake makes enforcement of the contract unconscionable. Section 153.

❖ SEE CASE 8-6

Assumption of Risk of Mistake

A party who has undertaken to bear the risk of a mistake will be unable to avoid the contract, even though the mistake (which may be either mutual or unilateral) would otherwise have permitted her to do so. This allocation of risk may occur by agreement of the parties. For instance, a ship at sea may be sold "lost or not lost." In such case the buyer is liable whether the ship was lost or not lost at the time the contract was made. There is no mistake; instead, there is a conscious allocation of risk.

Conscious ignorance may serve to allocate the risk of mistake when the parties recognize that they have limited knowledge of the facts. For example, the Supreme Court of Wisconsin refused to set aside the sale of a stone for which the purchaser paid one dollar, but which was subsequently discovered to be an uncut diamond valued at $700. The parties did not know at the time of sale what the stone was and knew they did not know. Each consciously assumed the risk that the value might be more or less than the selling price.

Effect of Fault upon Mistake

The Restatement provides that a mistaken party's fault in not knowing or discovering a fact before making a contract does not prevent him from avoiding the contract "unless his fault amounts to a failure to act in good faith and in accordance with reasonable standards of fair dealing." Restatement, Section 157. This rule does not, however, apply to a failure to read a contract. As a general proposition, a party is held to what she signs. Her signature authenticates the writing, and she cannot repudiate that which she has voluntarily approved. Generally, one who assents to a writing is presumed to know its contents and cannot escape being bound by its terms merely by contending that she did not read them; her assent is deemed to cover unknown as well as known terms. Restatement, Section 157, Comment b.

Mistake in Meaning of Terms

Somewhat related to mistakes of facts is the situation in which the parties misunderstand the meaning of one another's manifestations of mutual assent. A famous case involving this problem is *Raffles v. Wichelhaus*, 2 Hurlstone & Coltman 906 (1864), popularly known as the "*Peerless* Case." A contract of purchase was made for 125 bales of cotton to arrive on the *Peerless* from Bombay. It happened, however, that there were two ships by the name of *Peerless*, each sailing from Bombay, one in October and the other in December. The buyer had in mind the ship that sailed in October, while the seller reasonably believed the agreement referred to the *Peerless* sailing in December. Neither party was at fault, but both believed in good faith that a different ship was intended. The English court held that no contract existed. The Restatement, Section 20, is in accord.

There is no manifestation of mutual assent where the parties attach materially different meanings to their manifestations and neither party knows or has reason to know the meaning attached by the other. If blame can be ascribed to either party, however, that party will be held responsible. Thus, if the seller knew of two ships by the name of *Peerless* sailing from Bombay, then he would be at fault, and the contract would be for the ship sailing in October as the buyer expected. If neither party is to blame or both are to blame, there is no contract at all; that is, the agreement is void.

━━━━━━━━━   **CHAPTER SUMMARY**   ━━━━━━━━━

Duress

Definition wrongful or unlawful act or threat that overcomes the free will of a party
Physical Compulsion coercion involving physical force renders the agreement void
Improper Threats improper threats or acts, including economic and social coercion, render the contract voidable

Undue Influence

Definition taking unfair advantage of a person by reason of a dominant position based on a confidential relationship
Effect renders a contract voidable

Fraud	**Fraud in the Execution** a misrepresentation that deceives the other party as to the nature of a document evidencing the contract renders the agreement void

Fraud in the Inducement renders the agreement voidable if the following elements are present:

- *False Representation* positive statement or conduct that misleads
- *Fact* an event that occurred or thing that exists
- *Materiality* of substantial importance
- *Knowledge of Falsity and Intention to Deceive* called *scienter* and includes (a) actual knowledge, (b) lack of belief in statement's truthfulness, or (c) reckless indifference to its truthfulness
- *Justifiable Reliance* a defrauded party is reasonably influenced by the misrepresentation

Nonfraudulent Misrepresentation

Negligent Misrepresentation misrepresentation made without due care in ascertaining its truthfulness; renders agreement voidable

Innocent Misrepresentation misrepresentation made without knowledge of its falsity but with due care; renders contract voidable

Mistake

Definition an understanding that is not in accord with existing fact

Mutual Mistake both parties have a common but erroneous belief forming the basis of the contract; renders the contract voidable by either party

Unilateral Mistake courts are unlikely to grant relief unless the error is known or should be known by the nonmistaken party

Assumption of Risk a party may assume the risk of a mistake

Effect of Fault upon Mistake not a bar to avoidance unless the fault amounts to a failure to act in good faith

---

CASES

CASE 8-1

The following case demonstrates the type of circumstances a party must show to be entitled to rescission of a contract on the grounds of economic duress.

AUSTIN INSTRUMENT, INC. v. LORAL CORPORATION

Court of Appeals of New York, 1971
29 N.Y. 2d 124

FULD, Chief Judge. The defendant, Loral Corporation, seeks to recover payment for goods delivered under a contract which it had with plaintiff Austin Instrument, Inc., on the ground that the evidence establishes, as a matter of law, that it was forced to agree to an increase in price on the items in question under circumstances amounting to economic duress.

In July of 1965, Loral was awarded a $6,000,000 contract by the Navy for the production of radar sets. The contract contained a schedule of deliveries, a liquidated damages clause applying to late deliveries and a cancellation clause in case of default by Loral. The latter thereupon solicited bids for some 40 precision gear components needed to produce the radar sets,

and awarded Austin a subcontract to supply 23 such parts. That party commenced delivery in early 1966.

In May 1966, Loral was awarded a second Navy contract for the production of more radar sets and again went about soliciting bids. Austin bid on all 40 gear components but, on July 15, a representative from Loral informed Austin's president, Mr. Krauss, that his company would be awarded the subcontract only for those items on which it was low bidder. The Austin officer refused to accept an order for less than all 40 of the gear parts and on the next day he told Loral that Austin would cease deliveries of the parts due under the existing subcontract unless Loral consented to substantial increases in the prices provided for by that agreement — both retroactively for parts already delivered and prospectively on those not yet shipped — and placed with Austin the order for all 40 parts needed under Loral's second Navy contract. Shortly thereafter, Austin did, indeed, stop delivery. After contacting 10 manufacturers of precision gears and finding none who could produce the parts in time to meet its commitments to the Navy, Loral acceded to Austin's demands; in a letter dated July 22, Loral wrote to Austin that "We have feverishly surveyed other sources of supply and find that because of the prevailing military exigencies, were they to start from scratch as would have to be the case, they could not even remotely begin to deliver on time.... Accordingly, we are left with no choice or alternative but to meet your conditions."

Loral thereupon consented to the price increases insisted upon by Austin under the first subcontract and the latter was awarded a second subcontract making it the supplier of all 40 gear parts for Loral's second contract with the Navy. Although Austin was granted until September to resume deliveries, Loral did, in fact, receive parts in August and was able to produce the radar sets in time to meet its commitments to the Navy on both contracts. After Austin's last delivery under the second subcontract in July, 1967, Loral notified it of its intention to seek recovery of the price increases.

On September 15, 1967, Austin instituted this action against Loral to recover an amount in excess of $17,750 which was still due on the second subcontract. On the same day, Loral commenced an action against Austin claiming damages of some $22,250 — the aggregate of the price increases under the first subcontract — on the ground of economic duress. The two actions were consolidated and, following a trial, Austin was awarded the sum it requested and Loral's complaint against Austin was dismissed on the ground that it was not shown that "it could not have obtained the items in question from other sources in time to meet its commitment to the Navy under the first contract." A closely divided Appellate Division affirmed.... There was no material disagreement concerning the facts; as Justice STEUER stated in the course of his dissent below, "the facts are virtually undisputed, nor is there any serious question of law. The difficulty lies in the application of the law to these facts.".…

The applicable law is clear and, indeed, is not disputed by the parties. A contract is voidable on the ground of duress when it is established that the party making the claim was forced to agree to it by means of a wrongful threat precluding the exercise of his free will.... The existence of economic duress or business compulsion is demonstrated by proof that "immediate possession of needful goods is threatened"... or, more particularly, in cases such as the one before us, by proof that one party to a contract has threatened to breach the agreement by withholding goods unless the other party agrees to some further demand.... However, a mere threat by one party to breach the contract by not delivering the required items, though wrongful, does not in itself constitute economic duress. It must also appear that the threatened party could not obtain the goods from another source of supply and that the ordinary remedy of an action for breach of contract would not be adequate.

We find without any support in the record the conclusion reached by the courts below that Loral failed to establish that it was the victim of economic duress. On the contrary, the evidence makes out a classic case, as a matter of law, of such duress.

It must be remembered that Loral was producing a needed item of military hardware. Moreover, there is authority for Loral's position that nonperformance by a subcontractor is not an excuse for default in the main contract.... In light of all this, Loral's claim should not be held insufficiently supported because it did not request an extension from the Government.

Loral, as indicated above, also had the burden of demonstrating that it could not obtain the parts elsewhere within a reasonable time, and there can be no doubt that it met this burden. The 10 manufacturers whom Loral contacted comprised its entire list of "approved vendors" for precision gears, and none was able to commence delivery soon enough. As Loral was producing a highly sophisticated item of military machinery requiring parts made to the strictest engineering standards, it would be unreasonable to hold that Loral should have gone to other vendors, with whom it was either unfamiliar or dissatisfied, to procure the needed parts. As Justice STEUER noted in his dissent, Loral "contacted all the manufacturers whom it believed capable of making these parts," and this was all the law requires.

It is hardly necessary to add that Loral's normal legal remedy of accepting Austin's breach of the contract and then suing for damages would have been inadequate under the circumstances, as Loral would still have had to obtain the gears elsewhere with all the concomitant consequences mentioned above. In other words, Loral actually had no choice, when the prices were raised by Austin, except to take the gears at the "coerced" prices and then sue to get the excess back. Austin's final argument is that Loral, even if it did enter into the contract under duress, lost any rights it had to a refund of money by waiting until July, 1967, long after the termination date of the contract, to disaffirm it. It is true that one who would recover moneys allegedly paid under duress must act promptly to make his claim known.... In this case, Loral delayed making its demand for a refund until three days after Austin's last delivery on the second subcontract. Loral's reason — for waiting until that time — is that it feared another stoppage of deliveries which would again put it in an untenable situation. Considering Austin's conduct in the past, this was perfectly reasonable, as the possibility of an application by Austin of further business compulsion still existed until all of the parts were delivered.

In sum, the record before us demonstrates that Loral agreed to the price increases in consequence of the economic duress employed by Austin. Accordingly, the matter should be remanded to the trial court for a computation of its damages.

A statement of opinion generally may not be the basis of a claim for fraud. This case discusses when a statement of opinion may be regarded as a statement of fact and thus may be actionable as fraud.

VOKES v. ARTHUR MURRAY, INC.
Florida Court of Appeals, 1968
221 So.2d 906

Pierce, J.

[Audrey E. Vokes, plaintiff, appeals from a final order dismissing her complaint, for failure to state a cause of action.]

Defendant Arthur Murray, Inc., a corporation, authorizes the operation throughout the nation of dancing schools under the name of "Arthur Murray School of Dancing" through local franchised operators, one of whom was defendant J.P. Davenport whose dancing establishment was in Clearwater.

Plaintiff Mrs. Audrey E. Vokes, a widow of 51 years and without family, had a yen to be "an accomplished dancer" with the hopes of finding "new interest in life." So, on February 10, 1961, a dubious fate, with the assist of a motivated acquaintance, procured her to attend a "dance party" at Davenport's "School of Dancing" where she whiled away the pleasant hours, sometimes in a private room, absorbing his accomplished sales technique, during which her grace and poise were elaborated upon and her rosy future as "an excellent dancer" was painted for her in vivid and glowing colors. As an incident to this interlude, he sold her eight 1/2-hour dance lessons to be utilized within one calendar month therefrom, for the sum of $14.50 cash in hand paid, obviously a baited "come-on."

Thus she embarked upon an almost endless pursuit of the terpsichorean art during which, over a period of less than sixteen months, she was sold fourteen "dance courses" totalling in the aggregate 2,302 hours of dancing lessons for a total cash outlay of $31,090.45, all at Davenport's dance emporium.

* * *

These dance lesson contracts and the monetary consideration therefor of over $31,000 were procured from her by means and methods of Davenport and his associates which went beyond the unsavory, yet legally permissible, perimeter of "sales puffing" and intruded well into the forbidden area of undue influence, the suggestion of falsehood, the suppression of truth, and the free exercise of rational judgment, if what plaintiff alleged in her complaint was true. From the time of her first contact with the dancing school in February, 1961, she was influenced unwittingly by a constant and continuous barrage of flattery, false praise, excessive compliments, and panegyric encomiums, to such extent that it would be not only inequitable, but unconscionable, for a court exercising inherent chancery power to allow such contracts to stand.

She was incessantly subjected to overreaching blandishment and cajolery. She was assured she had "grace and poise;" that she was "rapidly improving and developing in her dancing skill;" that the additional lessons would "make her a beautiful dancer, capable of dancing with the most accomplished dancers;" that she was "rapidly progressing in the development of her dancing skill and gracefulness;" etc. She was given "dance aptitude tests" for the ostensible purpose of "determining" the number of remaining hours of instruction needed by her from time to time.

At one point she was sold 545 additional hours of dancing lessons to be entitled to the award of the "Bronze Medal" signifying that she had reached "the Bronze Standard," a supposed designation of dance achievement by students of Arthur Murray, Inc.

Later she was sold an additional 926 hours in order to gain the "Silver Medal," indicating she had reached "the Silver Standard," at a cost of $12,501.35.

At one point, while she still had to her credit about 900 unused hours of instructions, she was induced to purchase an additional 24 hours of lessons to participate in a trip to Miami at her own expense, where she would be "given the opportunity to dance with members of the Miami Studio."

She was induced at another point to purchase an additional 126 hours of lessons in order to be not only eligible for the Miami trip but also to become "a life member of the Arthur Murray Studio," carrying with it certain dubious emoluments, at a further cost of $1,752.30.

At another point, while she still had over 1,000 unused hours of instruction she was induced to buy 151 additional hours at a cost of $2,049.00 to be eligible for a "Student Trip to Trinidad," at her own expense as she later learned.

Also, when she still had more than 1,000 unused hours to her credit, she was prevailed upon to purchase an additional 347 hours at a cost of $4,235.74 to qualify her to receive a "Gold Medal" for achievement, indicating she had advanced to "the Gold Standard."

On another occasion, while she still had over 1,200 unused hours, she was induced to buy an additional 175 hours of instruction at a cost of $2,472.75, to be eligible "to take a trip to Mexico."

Finally, sandwiched in between other lesser sales promotions, she was influenced to buy an additional 481 hours of instruction at a cost of $6,523.81 in order to "be classified as a Gold Bar Member, the ultimate achievement of the dancing studio."

All the foregoing sales promotions, illustrative of the entire fourteen separate contracts, were procured by defendant Davenport and Arthur Murray, Inc., by false representations to her that she was improving in her dancing ability, that she had excellent potential, that she was responding to instructions in dancing grace, and that they were developing her into a beautiful dancer, whereas in truth and in fact she did not develop in her dancing ability, she had no "dance aptitude," and in fact had difficulty in "hearing the musical beat." The complaint alleged that such representations to her "were in fact false and known by the defendant to be false and contrary to the plaintiff's true ability, the truth of plaintiff's ability being fully known to the defendants, but withheld from the plaintiff for the sole and specific intent to deceive and defraud the plaintiff and to induce her in the purchasing of additional hours of dance lessons." It was averred that the lessons were sold to her "in total disregard to the true physical, rhythm, and mental ability of the plaintiff." In other words, while she first exulted that she was entering the "spring of her life," she finally was awakened to the fact there was "spring" neither in her life nor in her feet.

* * *

It is true that "generally a misrepresentation, to be actionable, must be one of fact rather than of opinion." [Citation.] But this rule has significant qualifications, applicable here.* * * As stated by Judge Allen of this court [citation]: "A statement of a party having* * *superior knowledge may be regarded as a statement of fact although it would be considered as opinion if the parties were dealing on equal terms."

It could be reasonably supposed here that defendants had "superior knowledge" as to whether plaintiff had "dance potential" and as to whether she was noticeably improving in the art of terpsichore. And it would be a reasonable inference from the undenied averments of the complaint that the flowery eulogiums heaped upon her by defendants as a prelude to her contracting for 1,944 additional hours of instruction in order to attain the rank of the Bronze Standard, thence to the bracket of the Silver Standard, thence to the class of the Gold Bar Standard, and finally to the crowning plateau of a Life Member of the Studio, proceeded as much or more from the urge to "ring the cash register" as from any honest or realistic appraisal of her dancing prowess or a factual representation of her progress.

Even in contractual situations where a party to a transaction owes no duty to disclose facts within his knowledge or to answer inquiries respecting such facts, the law is if he undertakes to do so he must disclose the *whole truth*. [Citations.] From the face of the complaint, it should have been reasonably apparent to defendants that her vast outlay of cash for the many hundreds of additional hours of instruction was not justified by her slow and awkward progress, which she would have been made well aware of if they had spoken the "whole truth."

* * *

Reversed.

CASE

8-3

In this case, a California court discusses whether the seller of a home must disclose to a buyer that the house was the site of a notorious crime.

REED v. KING
California Court of Appeals, 1983
145 Cal.App.3d 261, 193 Cal.Rprt. 130

Blease, J.
In the sale of a house, must the seller disclose it was the site of a multiple murder?

Dorris Reed purchased a house from Robert King. Neither King nor his real estate agents (the other named defendants) told Reed that a woman and her four children were murdered there 10 years earlier. However, it seems "truth will come to light; murder cannot be hid long." (Shakespeare, *Merchant of Venice*, act II, scene II.) Reed learned of the gruesome episode from a neighbor after the sale. She sues seeking rescission and damages. King and the real estate agent defendants successfully demurred to her first amended complaint for failure to state a cause of action. Reed appeals the ensuing judgment of dismissal. We will reverse the judgment.

* * *King and his real estate agent knew about the murders and knew the event materially affected the market value of the house when they listed it for sale. They represented to Reed the

premises were in good condition and fit for an "elderly lady" living alone. They did not disclose the fact of the murders. At some point King asked a neighbor not to inform Reed of that event. Nonetheless, after Reed moved in neighbors informed her no one was interested in purchasing the house because of the stigma. Reed paid $76,000, but the house is only worth $65,000 because of its past.

* * *

Does Reed's pleading state a cause of action? Concealed within this question is the nettlesome problem of the duty of disclosure of blemishes on real property which are not physical defects or legal impairments to use.

Reed seeks to state a cause of action sounding in contract, i.e., rescission, or in tort, i.e., deceit. In either event her allegations must reveal a fraud. [Citation.] "The elements of actual fraud, whether as the basis of the remedy in contract or tort, may be stated as follows: There must be (1) a *false representa-*

tion or concealment of a material fact (or, in some cases, an opinion) susceptible of knowledge, (2) made with *knowledge* of its falsity or without sufficient knowledge on the subject to warrant a representation, (3) with the *intent* to induce the person to whom it is made to act upon it; and such person must (4) act in *reliance* upon the representation (5) to his *damage*." (Original italics.) [Citation.]

The trial court perceived the defect in Reed's complaint to be a failure to allege concealment of a material fact.* * *

Concealment is a term of art which includes mere nondisclosure when a party has a duty to disclose. [Citation.] Rest.2d Contracts, "§ 161; Rest.2d Torts, "§ 551; Reed's complaint reveals only nondisclosure despite the allegation King asked a neighbor to hold his peace. There is no allegation the attempt at suppression was a cause in fact of Reed's ignorance. [Citations.] Accordingly, the critical question is: does the seller have a duty to disclose here? Resolution of this question depends on the materiality of the fact of the murders.

In general, a seller of real property has a duty to disclose: "where the seller knows of facts *materially* affecting the value or desirability of the property which are known or accessible only to him and also knows that such facts are not known to, or within the reach of the diligent attention and observation of the buyer, the seller is under a duty to disclose them to the buyer. [Citation.] This broad statement of duty has led one commentator to conclude: "The ancient maxim *caveat emptor* ('let the buyer beware') has little or no application to California real estate transactions." [Citation.]

Whether information "is of sufficient materiality to affect the value or desirability of the property* * *depends on the facts of the particular case." [Citation.] Materiality "is a question of law, and is part of the concept of right to rely or justifiable reliance." [Citation.]* * *Three considerations bear on this legal conclusion; the gravity of the harm inflicted by nondisclosure; the fairness of imposing a duty of discovery on the buyer as an alternative to compelling disclosure, and the impact on the stability of contracts if rescission is permitted.

Numerous cases have found nondisclosure of physical defects and legal impediments to use of real property are material. [Citation.] However, to our knowledge, no prior real estate sale case has faced an issue of nondisclosure of the kind presented here.

* * *

The murder of innocents is highly unusual in its potential for so disturbing buyers they may be unable to reside in a home where it has occurred. This fact may foreseeably deprive a buyer of the intended use of the purchase. Murder is not such a common occurrence that *buyers* should be charged with anticipating and discovering this disquieting possibility. Accordingly, the fact is not one for which a duty of inquiry and discovery can sensibly be imposed upon the buyer.

Reed alleges the fact of the murders has a quantifiable effect on the market value of the premises. We cannot say this allegation is inherently wrong and, in the pleading posture of the case, we assume it to be true. If information known or accessible only to the seller has a significant and measurable effect on market value and, as is alleged here, the seller is aware of this effect, we see no principled basis for making the duty to disclose turn upon the character of the information. Physical usefulness is not and never has been the sole criterion of valuation.* * *

Reputation and history can have a significant effect on the value of realty. "George Washington slept here" is worth something, however physically inconsequential that consideration may be. Ill repute or "bad will" conversely may depress the value of property.* * *

Whether Reed will be able to prove her allegation the decade-old multiple murder has a significant effect on market value we cannot determine. If she is able to do so by competent evidence she is entitled to a favorable ruling on the issues of materiality and duty to disclose. Her demonstration of objective tangible harm would still the concern that permitting her to go forward will open the floodgates to rescission on subjective and idiosyncratic grounds.

* * *

The judgment is reversed.

CASE
8-4

The following case deals with the question of whether a party has a claim for fraud based on an affirmative misrepresentation of a material fact, when the party has been put on notice of material facts that have not been documented, but nevertheless goes forward with the transaction.

RODAS v. MANITARAS
Appellate Division, New York (1st Dept.), 1990
159 A.D. 2d 341; 552 N.Y.S. 2d 618

MEMORANDUM.
Pursuant to a contract of sale dated November 6, 1987, plaintiffs purchased a restaurant business from defendant Oyster House, Inc. Plaintiffs later signed a lease agreement for the premises dated March 9, 1988 with defendant Manitaras.

Plaintiffs brought this action seeking rescission of the sale and lease agreements on the ground that defendants' false representations that the income of the business was $20,000 a week fraudulently induced them to enter into said agreements.

Paragraph 20 of the contract of sale contains a general merger clause and specifically recites that the business, its equipment, fixtures, chattels and furnishings are purchased in the exercise of plaintiffs' business judgment "and not upon any representations made by the seller, or by anyone acting in his behalf, as to the character, condition or quality of said chattels, fixtures, equipment and furnishings or as to the past, present or prospective income or profits of the said business, other than those contained in this agreement." While a general merger clause will not operate to bar parol evidence of fraud in the inducement where the parties expressly disclaim reliance on the representations alleged to be fraudulent, parol evidence as to those representations will not be admitted. Plaintiffs, however, allege that a specific disclaimer clause cannot bar the introduction of parol evidence of prior misrepresentations where the facts misrepresented were peculiarly within the knowledge of the defendant.

The defect in plaintiffs' reasoning lies not in the statement of the rule, but in their perception of its application. A classic example is provided by Tahini Invs. v Bobrowsky, in which the purchaser of land discovered 15 or more drums containing a hazardous material buried on the property. Although the contract contained specific language that the purchaser was not relying on representations as to the physical condition of the property, the court ruled that questions of fact were presented as to (1) whether the seller knew of the existence of the dumping site and (2) whether the purchaser, with reasonable diligence, could have ascertained the site's existence. The case illustrates that a party seeking to avoid a specific disclaimer clause must demonstrate that the facts alleged to have been fraudulently concealed could not be discovered through the exercise of reasonable diligence.

In the matter under review, by contrast, plaintiffs specifically requested examination of the records of the business and were refused. It is apparent that they were aware that the income of the business was a material fact in which they had received no documentation. In entering into the contract, with the assistance of counsel and without conducting an examination of the books and records, plaintiffs clearly assumed the risk that the documentation might not support the $20,000 weekly income that was represented to them.

Plaintiffs could have easily protected themselves by insisting on an examination of the books as a condition of closing. Alternatively, the contract could have included a condition subsequent that the sale would be rescinded if the actual sales experienced were significantly less than the represented figure. The standard which a party claiming fraud must meet in order to overcome a specific disclaimer clause is set forth in Danann Realty Corp. v Harris, relied upon by plaintiffs. It quotes Schumaker v Mather, which states that "if the facts represented are not matters peculiarly within the party's knowledge, and the other party has the means available to him of knowing, by the exercise of ordinary intelligence, the truth or the real quality of the subject of the representation, he must make use of those means, or he will not be heard to complain that he was induced to enter into the transaction by misrepresentations."

Where a party has no knowledge of a latent condition and no way of discovering the existence of that condition in the exercise of reasonable diligence then, as in Tahini Invs. v Bobrowsky, he may overcome a specific disclaimer clause and introduce parol evidence of fraudulent inducement. But where, as here, a party has been put on notice of the existence of material facts which have not been documented and he nevertheless proceeds with a transaction without securing the available documentation or inserting appropriate language in the agreement for his protection, he may truly be said to have willingly assumed the business risk that the facts may not be as represented. Succinctly put, a party will not be heard to complain that he has been defrauded when it is his own evident lack of due care which is responsible for his predicament.

CASE

8-5

In the following case, the court discusses the circumstances under which a party may be entitled to relief from a contract on the grounds of a unilateral mistake.

BALABAN-GORDON CO., INC. v. BRIGHTON SEW. DIST.

Appellate Division, New York (4th Dept.), 1973
41 A.D. 2d 246; 342 N.Y.S. 2d 435

SIMONS, Judge. This appeal questions the right of a contractor to withdraw its bid on a public construction contract because of a unilateral mistake in interpreting the engineers' specifications concerning equipment to be included in the bid price.

A bid is a binding offer to make a contract. It may be withdrawn in the case of unilateral mistake by the bidder where the mistake is known to the other party to the transaction and (1) the bid is of such consequence that enforcement would be unconscionable, (2) the mistake is material, (3) the mistake occurred despite the exercise of ordinary care by the bidder and (4) it is possible to place the other party in status quo....

In 1967 the appellant Brighton Sewer District No. 2 advertised for bids to construct two sewage treatment plants. Bids were received for the general construction, plumbing, heating and electrical work for each facility and bidders could bid each contract separately or in combination. Respondent Balaban-

Gordon Company, Inc. was the lowest bidder on the general construction contract for both plants. Its total bid for the work was $2,249,700, $530,300 below the second bidder. It also bid on the plumbing contract. It was the high bidder for that job, its bid being $376,230 higher than the low bid of $687,770. The respondent's representatives, upon learning of the difference in the bids, checked with the appellant's engineers and re-examined their worksheets. They determined that they had incorrectly interpreted the specifications and had included the cost of several pieces of mechanical equipment in the bid for the plumbing contract which should have been in the bid for the general construction. The trial court has found this mistake was due to the bidder's negligence. The respondent explained the error in detail at a conference with appellant's representatives and asked that its bid be withdrawn. The appellant insisted that the bid could not be withdrawn under General Municipal Law (§ 105) and demanded that respondent execute the contracts for general construction. When the respondent refused to do so, the appellant readvertised for bids and declared the respondent's bid bond forfeited. This action to rescind the bid and to cancel the bond followed. The trial court granted judgment for respondent, holding that it was entitled to rescind its mistaken bid notwithstanding its negligence.

If the bid may be rescinded, then the bid bond must be canceled because the municipality may not retain the proceeds either as a penalty or liquidated damages. If there is no legal obligation on the part of the contractor to fulfill its bid, it may not be held on the bid bond for its failure to do so....

It is apparent from the facts that there was a material mistake of serious consequence to the bidder from which it should be relieved if the appellant can be placed in status quo and if respondent's mistake is excusable. The mistake in computing the bid was "palpable," i.e., known to the other party because of the disparity in the bids and because of the prompt actual notice to appellant once the bids were opened and before the contract was awarded. Furthermore, the appellant's position has not been damaged. It could have awarded the contract to the second bidder. The election to rebid the job was its own and not required by any act of respondent. Appellant lost the bargain but that is not a compensable loss if the bid may be rescinded, because it was a bargain to which the appellant was never entitled. The case turns on whether this is the type of a mistake which justifies relief by rescission. Mistakes by definition reflect oversight or some lack of care and so the requirement that the mistake occur in the exercise of ordinary care may not be interpreted narrowly. The question is whether the mistake is of the variety considered excusable, and each case must be considered on its own facts....

The parties are in agreement that relief is available where the mistake is clerical or arithmetical.... In such a case, the mistaken bid does not express the true intention of the bidder. If he were to recompute the bid or if another person were to do so, the obvious error would be discovered and corrected. Its existence may be objectively determined. In those circumstances, there is said to be no meeting of the minds because the bid was one which the bidder never intended to make.

On the other hand, it is commonly recognized that a bidder will not be relieved from an error in a value judgment in estimating the requirements or costs necessary to fulfill a contract. Mistakes of this type are inherent business risks assumed by contractors in all bidding situations. If the specifics of the job were recalculated by the bidder, his bid would be the same, for these estimates do not involve oversights. They represent subjective judgments deliberately made with respect to the requirements of the job. Another person calculating the bid might or might not make the same "mistake," depending upon his mental evaluation of the work to be performed, but in any event, the minds of the bidder and the offeree meet because the bid is precisely what the bidder intends even though his judgment later proves faulty.

The appellant claims that the error must be considered one of these two types, either clerical and arithmetical, or an error of judgment, relief by rescission being available in the former case but not in the latter. Since the incorrect interpretation of the specifications was not clerical or arithmetical appellant claims that respondent should be held to the bid and liable for liquidated damages under its bid bond. Unfortunately, not all mistakes made by contractors are categorized so easily. Applying the reasoning of the two types of mistakes to the facts of this case illustrates the difficulty. If respondent's representatives were to recompute its bid, they doubtless would interpret the specifications the same way. In that sense, the bid accurately represented the contract respondent was willing to make and there was a meeting of the minds. Nevertheless, the error was objectively discoverable. Another contractor computing the bid would not, and in fact no others did, make the same mistake in interpretation and in that sense the bid did not represent the bid intended because respondent was working under a misapprehension with respect to the particulars called for by the specifications. Reasonable care probably dictated that respondent should have asked the engineers to clarify the meaning of the ambiguous specifications (at least one other bidder did so), but respondent's failure to investigate should not prevent it from obtaining relief.

The case fits squarely within the factual pattern of President & Council of Mount St. Mary's Coll. v. Aetna Cas. & Sur. Co. There, the court granted relief by rescission to a bidder who, because of an error in interpreting the specifications, failed to include the cost of certain equipment in his bid. Although the error was the result of negligence by the bidder in not asking the architect for an interpretation of the specifications, relief was granted because the bidder's negligence was not "culpable." Similar analyses of the degree of the bidder's mistake, i.e., whether the bidder is "more" or "less" negligent, have been made in other cases.... When an effort is made to apply these tests, they are found to be elusive to say the least. The decisive factual question is whether the mistake is one the courts will excuse. Then, if the mistake concerns a material matter in an executory contract under circumstances where relief to the bidder results in no damage to the municipality but enforcement results in serious harm to the bidder, rescission will be granted. Manifestly, rescission may be allowed more readily for a mistake made by a bidder which is objectively established and which does not evolve from an inherent risk of business. Even though the mistake is the product of negligence on the part of the bidder, relief should be granted because the assurance exists from the objective proof that the transaction is free from mischief. This satisfies a fundamental purpose of the public bidding statutes.

The error in this case did not pertain to an evaluation of risks or estimation of requirements or costs by the bidder and the effect of the mistake was verifiable in much the same way as a clerical error, the impossibility of performance or an arithmetical error. That being the case, it should be excused and rescission granted. In these days of multi-million dollar construction contracts, the public interest requires stability in bidding of public contracts under rules that protect against chicane and overreaching. Nevertheless, little is to be gained if a contractor is forced to perform a contract at an extravagant loss or the risk of possible bankruptcy. If a mistake has been made under circumstances justifying relief, the municipality should not be allowed to enforce the bargain. Its remedy to avoid loss is to award the contract to the next bidder or assume the responsibility of rebidding.

The judgment granting respondent rescission of its bid and canceling the bond should therefore be affirmed. Judgment unanimously affirmed, with costs.

CASE

8-6

The following case illustrates the standards for determining when a party may be granted rescission of a contract because of a mutual mistake.

LESHER v. STRID

Court of Appeals of Oregon, 2000
165 Or.App. 34, 996 P.2d 988
http://caselaw.findlaw.com/scripts/getcase.pl?court=OR&vol=A99602&invol=1

WOLLHEIM, J. Defendant appeals from a judgment of the trial court granting plaintiff's request for rescission of a contract for the sale of real property. As relevant to this appeal, plaintiffs Vernon and Janene Lesher, purchasers of an 18-acre parcel of property in Josephine County (the subject property), sought rescission of the contract under theories of a mutual mistake of fact or an innocent misrepresentation of fact regarding the existence of water rights appurtenant [belongs to] to the property. The trial court granted rescission on those grounds. . . . [W]e affirm.

In May 1995, plaintiffs agreed to purchase the subject property from defendant with the intention of using it to raise horses. In purchasing the subject property, they relied on their impression that at least four acres of the subject property had a right to irrigation from Slate Creek. The earnest money agreement to the contract provided:

Water Rights are being conveyed to Buyer at the close of escrow. . . . Seller will provide Buyer with a written explanation of the operation of the irrigation system, water right certificates, and inventory of irrigation equipment included in sale." (Bold in original.)

The earnest money agreement also provided:

"THE SUBJECT PROPERTY IS BEING SOLD 'AS IS' subject to the Buyer's approval of the tests and conditions as stated herein. Buyer declares that Buyer is not depending on any other statement of the Seller or licensees that is not incorporated by reference in this earnest money contract." (Bold in original.)

Before signing the earnest money agreement, defendants presented to plaintiffs, through their mutual realtor, a 1977 Water Resources Department water rights certificate and a map purporting to show an area of the subject property to be irrigated ("area to be irrigated" map). The 1977 water rights certificate . . . [showed that the property] carries a four-acre water right with a priority of 1892. * * *

Vernon Lesher testified that, at the time plaintiffs purchased the subject property, he believed that the subject property carried four acres of appurtenant water rights by virtue of the 1977 certificate and "area to be irrigated" map. Defendant's representative, Sally Doss, agreed that, at the time of the conveyance, Doss believed that a 1892 four-acre irrigation right was appurtenant to the subject property and that, if it was not, she was mistaken. Vernon testified that before buying the subject property, plaintiffs owned property with two irrigated acres. Vernon testified that plaintiffs intended to and, in fact, did sell the two-acre water right property and sought the subject property to expand their ability to raise horses. In particular, plaintiffs needed to have adequate acreage for pasturing the horses. Vernon testified that irrigation was necessary for creating pasture. He stated that, without a right to irrigate four acres, plaintiffs would not have purchased the property.

* * *

After purchasing the subject property and before establishing a pasture, plaintiffs learned that the property might not carry a four-acre water right. * * *

* * *

* * * [The trial court] found that both plaintiffs and defendant believed at the time of the sale that the right was appurtenant to the property and that the supply of adequate irrigated land was an essential part of the bargain for plaintiffs. In the alternative, the court found that defendant innocently misrepresented to plaintiffs that those rights existed appurtenant to the subject property. It found that plaintiffs reasonably relied on the representations and documents provided to plaintiffs pertaining to the water rights, and that plaintiffs' belief about the water rights was a material inducement to their purchase of the subject property. The trial court found that a mutual mistake of a material fact by plaintiffs and defendant "and/or" an innocent misrepresentation of fact by defendant merited rescission of the contract.

On appeal, defendant argues that plaintiffs are not entitled to rescission, because they have not proven by clear and convincing evidence that a mistake of fact occurred about the water rights. In the alternative, defendant argues that plaintiffs unjustifiably relied on defendant's representation about the water rights because defendant's representation was extrinsic to the contract and because plaintiffs were grossly negligent in relying on the 1977 certificate and the "area to be irrigated" map to conclude that four acres of irrigation water rights with an 1892 priority date were appurtenant to the subject property.

Grounds for rescission on the basis of a mutual mistake of fact or innocent misrepresentation must be proved by clear and convincing evidence. [Citations.] An innocent misrepresentation of fact renders a contract voidable by a party if the party's "manifestation of assent is induced by . . . a material misrepresentation by the other party upon which the recipient is justified in relying[.]" [Citations.] A mutual mistake of fact renders a contract voidable by the adversely affected party, "where the parties are mistaken as to the facts existing at the time of the contract, if the mistake is so fundamental that it frustrates the purpose of the contract," [citation], and where the adversely affected party does not bear the risk of the mistake, [citation]. A mistake "is a state of mind which is not in accord with the facts." [Citation].

Even though it appears that the trial court did not apply the clear and convincing standard, . . . , we find that plaintiffs' evidence meets that standard. Both defendant and plaintiffs testified that they believed that the four acres of water rights were appurtenant to the subject property. Defendant does not dispute that the 1977 water rights certificate and the "area to be irrigated" map are her representation about the water right.

* * *

Plaintiffs also established by clear and convincing evidence that the existence of the four-acre water right was material and essential to the contract. Vernon testified that the motivation for the purchase was to expand his ability to raise horses from property they already owned where they had a two-acre irrigation right and that the subject property's water right was essential to the contract. Certainly, a smaller water right would limit, not expand, plaintiffs' ability to raise horses. The mistake, therefore, goes to the very essence of the contract.

We next consider defendant's arguments that plaintiffs bore the risk of that mistake. The Restatement (Second) of Contracts § 154 explains that a party bears the risk of a mistake, in part, if the risk is allocated to the party by agreement of the parties, or if the risk is allocated to the party "by the court on the ground that it is reasonable in the circumstances to do so." We find nothing in the contract that would allocate to plaintiffs the risk of a mistake as to the existence of a fouracre water right.

Defendant argues in the alternative that plaintiffs' mistake of fact is the result of defendant's misrepresentation, on which plaintiffs could not reasonably rely. An "innocent misrepresentation may support a claim for rescission of a real estate agreement if the party who relied on the misrepresentations of another establishes a right to have done so." [Citations.]

Defendant argues that her representations about the fouracre water right were extrinsic to the contract and that the contract's "as is" clause expressly excluded reliance on such extrinsic representations. . . . The "as is" clause specifically contemplated reliance on any statements by the seller that were "incorporated by reference" in the earnest money agreement. The earnest money agreement specifically referred to the conveyance of water rights.

* * *

Plaintiffs have established that both a mutual mistake of fact and an innocent misrepresentation of fact entitle them to rescission of the deed of sale.

Affirmed.

QUESTIONS

1. Identify the types of duress and discuss the legal effect of each.
2. Identify the types of fraud and the elements that must be shown to establish the existence of each.
3. Discuss undue influence and identify some of the situations giving rise to a confidential relationship.

4. Identify and discuss the situations involving voidable mistakes.
5. Define the two types of nonfraudulent misrepresentation.

PROBLEMS

1. Smith owned five acres of land in Wilton, New York, on which were two springs of mineral water and machinery to bottle the mineral water. Smith sold the real property to Brown for $300,000, representing that the water was natural mineral water and could be bottled or sold as it flowed from the ground. Smith also represented to Brown that the daily natural flow of water from the two springs was 4,200 gallons. Brown entered into possession and purchased and installed modern machinery for the bottling and distribution of the mineral water. He soon discovered that the water was not natural mineral water, but fresh water to which certain chemicals had been added. He also discovered that the daily flow did not exceed 160 gallons. By the time he discovered these facts, Brown had expended $75,000 for the installation of new machinery.

(a) Did Smith commit fraud? Explain. *5 facts of fraud*

(b) What remedy or remedies, if any, are available to Brown? Explain.

2. On April 1, Santos, a dealer in mining stocks, sold to Burns, 10,000 shares of Alaska Uranium, Inc., at $5 per share, knowingly misrepresenting that Alaska Uranium, Inc. had proven uranium deposits in its Alaska properties. Burns paid Santos for the stock on April 1.

On April 15, on the advice of friends, Burns had the corporation investigated and found that it had never had any prospects of uranium, but that it had just discovered a copper vein on its property and was putting it into production. During the following February, Burns received and deposited a $100 check from Alaska Uranium, Inc. for its one cent per share dividend. One month later, Burns regretted his purchase.

(a) In an action by Burns against Santos to disaffirm the contract on the grounds of fraud, judgment for whom? Explain.

(b) In an action by Burns against Santos to recover damages based on fraud, judgment for whom? Explain.

(c) In an action by Burns against Alaska Uranium, Inc. to recover damages based on fraud, judgment for whom? Explain.

3. On February 13, Mario purchased an engagement ring from John, a jeweler, for $5,000, relying upon John's representation that the ring was set with a genuine diamond. The next morning, Mario had the ring appraised by a gemologist and learned to his amazement that the center stone was not a genuine diamond, but rather a zircon, a cheap imitation that looked like a diamond but was worth only $50, and that the entire value of the ring was $200. Nevertheless, the next day, Mario gave the engagement ring to Gina, his fiancée, on Valentine's Day, as he had promised. One month later, Gina terminated her engagement to Mario and returned the ring to him. The following day, Mario decided to rescind his contract with John and to sue John for damages.

(a) Does Mario have the right to rescind his contract with John? Explain.

(b) Does Mario have the right to recover damages, from John and if so, how would the damages be computed? Explain.

4. Harris owned a farm that was worth about $600 per acre. By false representations of fact, Harris induced Pringle to buy the farm at $1,500 per acre. Shortly after taking possession of the farm, Pringle discovered oil under the land. Harris, on learning this, sues to have the sale set aside on the ground that it was voidable because of fraud. Decision?

5. In February, Gardner, a schoolteacher with no experience in running a tavern, entered into a contract to purchase for $40,000 the Punjab Tavern from Meiling. The contract was contingent upon Gardner's obtaining a five-year lease for the tavern's premises and a liquor license from the state. Prior to the formation of the contract, Meiling had made no representations to Gardner concerning the gross income of the tavern. Approximately three months after the contract was signed, Gardner and Meiling met with an inspector from the Oregon Liquor Control Commission (OLCC) to discuss transfer of the liquor license. Meiling reported to the agent, in Gardner's presence, that the tavern's gross income figures for February, March, and April were $5,710, $4,918, and $5,009, respectively. The OLCC granted the required license, the transaction was closed, and Gardner took possession on June 10. After discovering that the tavern's income was very low, Gardner contacted Meiling's bookkeeping service and learned that the actual gross income for those three months had been approximately $1,400 to $2,000. Gardner then sued for rescission of the contract. Decision?

6. Columbia University brought suit against Jacobsen on two notes signed by him and his parents, representing the balance of tuition he owed the University. Jacobsen counter-claimed for money damages due to Columbia's deceit or fraudulent misrepresentation. Jacobsen argues that Columbia fraudulently misrepresented that it would teach wisdom, truth, character, enlightenment, and similar virtues and qualities. He specifically cites as support the Columbia motto: "in lumine tuo videbimus lumen" ("In your light we shall see light"); the inscription over the college chapel: "Wisdom dwelleth in the heart of him that hath understanding;" and various excerpts from its brochures, catalogues, and a convocation address made by the University's president. Jacobsen, a senior who was not graduated because of poor scholastic standing, claims that the University's failure to meet its

promises made through these quotations constituted fraudulent misrepresentation or deceit. Decision?

7. M Corporation, a well-known television manufacturer, had several odd lots of discontinued models, which it desired to clear out. M, the president, invited D, the owner of D Discount Chain, to come in and examine the different models and make M an offer for the entire lot. The sets were segregated from the regular inventory. Fifteen televisions that were not discontinued models were accidentally included in this segregated group by one of M's employees. D was unaware that M did not intend to include the fifteen televisions in the group. D made M an offer of $10,000 for the entire lot. Unaware of his employee's error, M accepted the offer. M would not have accepted D's offer if M had known the fifteen current models had been included. Upon learning of the error, M Corporation refused to perform and alleged mistake as a defense. D Discount Chain sued M Corporation for breach of contract. Judgment for whom? Explain.

8. Cynthia was bequeathed an oil painting by her childless aunt. Cynthia was not favorably disposed toward the painting because it reminded her that her aunt had left her entire estate (except the painting) to the Society for the Prevention of Cruelty to Animals. When Cynthia's best friend, Beatrice, admired the painting, Cynthia offered to sell it to her for $10. Beatrice accepted, paid the $10 and took the painting. The painting was clearly an original and bore the signature, "Ad Schreyer," but neither Cynthia nor Beatrice had ever heard of the painter.

Several weeks later, Beatrice informed Cynthia that she had inquired about the artist and had learned that the painting was worth $15,000. On hearing this, Cynthia tendered $10 to Beatrice and demanded the return of the painting. Beatrice refused and Cynthia brought suit against Beatrice to recover the painting.

(a) Judgment for whom? Explain.

(b) Would your answer to (a) be the same if Beatrice had heard Cynthia say that Ad Schreyer was an amateur American 20th century painter and that Beatrice knew that Ad Schreyer was in fact a well-known German 19th Century artist? Explain.

9. Jorge is the owner of a 20-story office building undergoing renovation. A flooring contractor, Mikhail, came to the building to measure the job in preparation for making an offer. Mikhail mistakenly failed to include one of the floors, and his offer was thus 5% lower than it otherwise would have been. Jorge, who did not know of Mikhail's error, accepted Mikhail's offer. When Mikhail's workers came to start the job, they noticed the error. Mikhail now wants to avoid the contract. Will he be successful? Explain.

10. Sally and Belinda are owners of contiguous proper ties in Chappaqua, New York. Sally is also the registered title owner of Lot # 2, a vacant lot measuring 125' by 125', which is situated ten (10) street blocks from their respective properties. Sally and Belinda are negotiating the sale of Lot #2 to Belinda.

Belinda tells Sally that she will purchase Lot #2 for $200,000, on an all-cash basis, closing to take place in two (2) months, if Sally can assure her that the lot is zoned for one-family residences only. Sally responds by telling Belinda that all lots in Chappaqua are zoned for one-family residences.

After the contract for sale has been executed and Belinda has made a 10% deposit, held in escrow by Sally's attorney, Belinda discovers that Sally was misinformed and that Lot #2 is not zoned for one-family residences, but is, instead, zoned for multiple-residence dwellings.

(a) Belinda seeks to rescind the contract for sale and to recover her 10% deposit. Sally insists that the closing take place. Judgment for whom?

(b) Would your answer to (a) be different if Sally in fact knew that Lot #2 was zoned for multiple dwelling use and did not answer Belinda's question as to the zoning of the lot?

11. Dorothy and John Huffschneider listed their house and lot for sale with C. B. Property. The asking price was $165,000, and the owners told C. B. that the size of the property was 6.8 acres. Dean Olson, a salesman for C. B., advertised the property in local newspapers as consisting of six acres. James and Jean Holcomb signed a contract to purchase the property through Olson after first inspecting the property with Olson and being assured by Olson that the property was at least 6.6 acres. The Holcombs never asked for or received a copy of the survey. In actuality, the lot was only 4.6 acres. The Holcombs now seek to rescind the contract. Decision?

12. Adler owes Panessi, a police captain, $500. Adler threatens that unless Panessi discharges him from the debt, Adler will disclose the fact that Panessi has on several occasions become highly intoxicated and has been seen in the company of certain disreputable persons. Panessi, induced by fear that such a disclosure would cost him his position or in any event lead to social disgrace, gives Adler a release, but subsequently sues to set it aside and recover on his claim. Decision?

13. Barnes accepted Clark's offer to sell to him a portion of Clark's coin collection. Clark forgot that his prized $20 gold piece, at the time of the offer and acceptance, was included in the portion that he offered to sell to Barnes. Clark did not intend to include the gold piece in the sale. Barnes, at the time of inspecting the offered portion of the collection and prior to accepting the offer, saw the gold piece. Is Barnes entitled to the $20 gold piece?

14. Anita and Barry were negotiating, and Anita's attorney prepared a long and carefully drawn contract, which was given to Barry for examination. Five days later and prior to its execution, Barry's eyes became so infected that it was impossible for him to read. Ten days thereafter and during the continuance of the illness, Anita called upon Barry and urged him to sign the contract, telling him that time was running out. Barry signed the contract despite the fact he was unable to read it. In a subsequent action by Anita, Barry claimed that the contract was not binding upon him because it was impossible for him to read and he did not know what it contained prior to his signing it. Should Barry be held to the contract?

15. (a) Johnson tells Davis that he paid $150,000 for his farm in 2001, and that he believes it is worth twice that at the present time. Relying upon these statements, Davis buys the farm from Johnson for $225,000. Johnson did pay $150,000 for the farm in 2001, but its value has increased only slightly, and it is presently not worth $300,000. On discovering this, Davis offers to reconvey the farm to Johnson and sues for the return of his $225,000. Result?

(b) Modify the facts in (a) by assuming that Johnson had paid $100,000 for the property in 2001. What result?

16. On February 2, Phillips induced Miller to purchase from her fifty shares of stock in the XYZ Corporation for $10,000, representing that the actual book value of each share was $200. A certificate for fifty shares was delivered to Miller. On February 16, Miller discovered that the book value on February 2 was only $50 per share. Will Miller be successful in a lawsuit against Phillips? Why?

17. Doris mistakenly accused Peter's son, Steven, of negligently burning down her barn. Peter believed that his son was guilty of the wrong

and that he, Peter, was personally liable for the damage, as Steven was only fifteen years old. Upon demand made by Doris, Peter paid Doris $2,500 for the damage to her barn. After making this payment, Peter learned that his son had not caused the burning of Doris's barn and was in no way responsible for its burning. Peter then sued Doris to recover the $2,500 he had paid her. Will he be successful?

18. Beginning in 1971, Treasure Salvors and the state of Florida entered into a series of four annual contracts governing the salvage of the *Nuestra Senora de Atocha*. The *Atocha* is a Spanish galleon that sank in 1622, carrying a treasure now worth well over $250 million. Both parties had contracted under the impression that the seabed on which the *Atocha* lay was land owned by Florida. Treasure Salvors agreed to relinquish 25 percent of the items recovered in return for the right to salvage on state lands. In accordance with these contracts, Treasure Salvors delivered to Florida its share of the salvaged artifacts. In 1975, the United States Supreme Court held that the part of the continental shelf on which the *Atocha* was resting had *never* been owned by Florida. Treasure Salvors then brought suit to rescind the contracts and to recover the artifacts it had delivered to the state of Florida. Should Treasure Salvors prevail?

19. Conrad Schaneman was a Russian immigrant who could neither read nor write the English language. In 1975 Conrad deeded (conveyed) a farm he owned to his eldest son, Laurence, for $23,500, which was the original purchase price of the property in 1945. The value of the farm in 1975 was between $145,000 and $160,000. At the time he executed the deed, Conrad was an eighty-two-year-old invalid, severely ill, and completely dependent on others for his personal needs. He weighed between 325 and 350 pounds, had difficulty breathing, could not walk more than fifteen feet, and needed a special jackhoist to get in and out of the bathtub. Conrad enjoyed a long-standing, confidential relationship with Laurence, who was his principal adviser and handled Conrad's business affairs. Laurence also obtained a power of attorney from Conrad and made himself a joint owner of Conrad's bank account and $20,000 certificate of deposit. Conrad brought this suit to cancel the deed, claiming it was the result of Laurence's undue influence. The district court found that the deed was executed as a result of undue influence, set aside the deed, and granted title to Conrad. Laurence appealed. Decision?

Internet Exercise Find information for businesses and consumers about avoiding and detecting fraud and scams (including online, credit card, and telemarketing).

Contractual Capacity

A binding promise or agreement requires that the parties to the agreement have contractual capacity. Everyone is regarded as having such capacity unless the law for reasons of public policy holds that the individual lacks such capacity. This essential ingredient of a contract will be discussed by considering those classes and conditions of persons who are legally limited in their capacity to contract: (1) minors, (2) incompetent persons, and (3) intoxicated persons.

MINORS

A **minor**, also called an infant, is a person who has not attained the age of legal majority. At common law, a minor was a person who was under twenty-one years of age. Today the age of majority has been changed in nearly all jurisdictions by statute, usually to age eighteen. Almost without exception, a minor's contract, whether executory or executed, is **voidable** at his or his guardian's option. Restatement, Section 14. Thus, the minor is in a favored position by having the option to disaffirm the contract or to enforce it. Even an "emancipated" minor, one who because of marriage or other reason is no longer subject to strict parental control, may avoid contractual liability in most jurisdictions. Consequently, businesspeople deal at their peril with minors and in situations of consequence generally require an adult to cosign or guarantee the performance of the contract. Nevertheless, most states recognize special categories of contracts that cannot be avoided (such as student loans or contracts for medical care) or that have a lower age for capacity (such as bank account, marriage, and insurance contracts).

Liability on Contracts

A minor's contract is not entirely void and of no legal effect; rather, it is *voidable* at the minor's option. The exercise of this power of avoidance, called a **disaffirmance**, ordinarily releases the minor from any liability on the contract. On the other hand, after the minor becomes of age, she may choose to adopt or **ratify** the contract, in which case she surrenders her power of avoidance and becomes bound.

Disaffirmance　As previously stated, a minor's contract is voidable at his or his guardian's option, conferring upon him a power to avoid liability. He, or in some jurisdictions his guardian, may, through words or conduct manifesting an intention not to abide by the contract, exercise the power to disaffirm.

In general, a minor's disaffirmance must come either during his minority or within a reasonable time after he reaches majority, as long as he has not already ratified the contract. In most states, defining a reasonable time depends upon such circumstances as the nature of the transaction, whether either party has caused the delay, and the extent to which either party has been injured by the delay. Some states, however, statutorily prescribe a time period, generally one year, in which the minor may disaffirm the contract.

A notable exception is that a sale of land by a minor cannot be disaffirmed until after he reaches his majority. But must he disaffirm immediately upon becoming an adult? In the case of a sale of land, there is a strong precedent that the minor may wait until the period of the statute of limitations has expired, if the sale involves no questions of fairness and equity.

Disaffirmance may be either *express* or *implied*. No particular form of words is essential, so long as they show an intention not to be bound. This intention also may be manifested by acts or by conduct. For example, a minor agrees to sell property to Alice and then sells that property to Brian. The sale to Brian would constitute a disaffirmance of the contract with Alice.

A troublesome yet important problem in this area, upon which the courts are not in agreement, pertains to the minor's duty upon disaffirmance. The majority hold that the minor must return any property he has received from the other party, provided he has it in his possession at the time of disaffirmance. Nothing more is required. If the minor disaffirms the purchase of an automobile and the vehicle has been wrecked, he need only return the wrecked vehicle. Other States require at least the payment of a reasonable amount for the use of the property or the amount of its depreciation while in the hands of the minor. A few States, either by statute or court ruling, recognize a duty upon the part of the minor to make *restitution*, that is, return an equivalent of what has been received in order to place the seller in approximately the same position she would have occupied had the sale not occurred.

Finally, can a minor disaffirm and recover property that his buyer has transferred to a good faith purchaser for value? Traditionally, the minor could avoid the contract and recover the property, despite the fact that the third person gave value for it and had no notice of the minority. Thus, in the case of the sale of real estate, a minor may rescind her deed of conveyance even against a good faith purchaser of the land who did not know of the minority. Regarding the sale of goods, however, this principle has been changed by Section 2–403 of the UCC, which provides that a person with voidable title (e.g., the person buying goods from a minor) has power to transfer valid title to a good faith purchaser for value. For example, a minor sells his car to an individual who resells it to a used car dealership, a good faith purchaser for value. The used car dealer would acquire legal title even though he bought the car from a seller who had only voidable title.

❧ SEE CASE 9-1

Ratification   A minor has the option of ratifying a contract after reaching the age of majority. Ratification makes the contract binding *ab initio* (from the beginning). That is, the result is the same as if the contract had been valid and binding from its inception. Ratification, once effected, is final and cannot be

withdrawn. Further, it must be in total, validating the entire contract. The minor can ratify the contract only as a whole, both as to burdens and benefits. He cannot, for example, ratify so as to retain the consideration he received and escape payment or other performance on his part, nor can he retain part of the contract and disaffirm the rest.

Ratification may be express, implied from conduct, or represent the failure to make a timely disaffirmance. Suppose that a minor makes a contract to buy property from an adult. The contract is voidable by the minor, and she can escape liability. But suppose that after reaching her majority, she promises to go through with the purchase. Because she has *expressly* ratified the contract she entered when she was a minor, her promise is binding, and the adult can recover for breach upon her failure to perform. In the absence of a statutory provision to the contrary, an express ratification may be oral.

Note that a minor has no power to ratify a contract while he remains a minor. A ratification cannot be based on words or conduct occurring while a minor is still underage, for his ratification at that time would be no more effective than his original contractual promise. The ratification must take place after the individual has acquired contractual capacity by attaining his majority.

Ratification, as previously stated, need not be express; it may be *implied* from the minor's conduct. Suppose that the minor, after attaining her majority, uses the property involved in the contract, undertakes to sell it to someone else, or performs some other act showing an intention to affirm the contract. She may not thereafter disaffirm the contract but is bound by it. Perhaps the most common form of implied ratification occurs when a minor, after attaining her majority, continues to use the property which she purchased as a minor. This use is obviously inconsistent with the nonexistence of the contract, and whether the contract is performed or still partly executory, it will amount to a ratification and prevent a disaffirmance by the minor. Simply keeping the goods for an unreasonable time after attaining majority also has been construed as a ratification. Although the courts are divided on the issue, payments by the minor upon reaching majority, either on principal or interest or on the purchase price of goods, have been held to amount to a ratification. Some courts require additional evidence of an intention to abide by the contract, such as an express promise to that effect or the actual use of the subject matter of the contract.

❧ SEE CASE 9-2

Liability for Necessaries

Contractual incapacity does not excuse a minor from an obligation to pay for necessaries, those things that suitably and reasonably supply his personal needs, such as food, shelter, medicine, and clothing. Even here, however, the minor is liable not for the agreed price but for the *reasonable* value of the items furnished. Recovery is based on quasi contract. Thus, if a clothier sells a minor a suit that the minor needs, the clothier can successfully sue the minor. The clothier's recovery is limited, however, to the reasonable value of the suit, even if this amount is much less than the agreed-upon selling price.

Defining "necessaries" is a difficult problem. In general, the States regard as **necessary** those things that the minor needs to maintain himself in his particular station in life. Items necessary for subsistence and health, such as food, lodging, clothing, medicine, and medical services, are obviously included. But other less essential items, such as textbooks, school instruction, and legal advice, may be included as well. Further, many States enlarge the concept of necessaries to include articles of property and services that a minor needs to earn the money required to provide the necessities of life for himself and his dependents. Nevertheless, many States limit necessaries to items that are not provided to the minor. Thus, if a minor's guardian provides her with an adequate wardrobe, a blouse the minor purchased would not be considered a necessity. In addition, a minor is *not* liable for anything on the ground that it is necessary unless it has been actually furnished to him and used or consumed by him. In other words, a minor may disaffirm his executory contracts for necessaries and refuse to accept the clothing, lodging, or other items or services.

Ordinarily, luxury items such as cameras, tape recorders, stereo equipment, television sets, and motorboats seldom qualify as necessaries. Whether automobiles and trucks are necessaries has caused considerable controversy, but some courts have recognized that under certain circumstances an automobile may be necessary when it is used by the minor for his business activities.

❖ See Case 9-3

Liability for Misrepresentation of Age

The States do not agree on whether a minor who has fraudulently misrepresented her age when entering into contract has the power to disaffirm. Suppose a contracting minor says that she is eighteen years of age (or twenty-one if that is the year of attaining majority) and actually looks that old or even older. By the prevailing view in this country, the minor may nevertheless disaffirm the contract. Some States, however, prohibit disaffirmance if a minor misrepresents her age and the adult party, in good faith, reasonably relied upon the misrepresentation. Other States not following the majority rule either (a) require the minor to restore the other party to the position she occupied before the making of the contract or (b) allow the defrauded party to recover damages against the minor in tort.

Liability for Tort Connected with Contract

It is well settled that minors are generally liable for their torts. There is, however, a legal doctrine providing that if a tort and a contract are so "interwoven" that the court must enforce the contract to enforce the tort action, the minor is not liable in tort. Thus, if a minor rents an automobile from an adult, he enters into a contractual relationship obliging him to exercise reasonable care and diligence to protect the property from injury. By negligently damaging the automobile, he breaches that contractual undertaking. But his contractual immunity protects him from an action by the adult based on the contract. Can the adult nonetheless recover damages on a tort theory? By the majority view, he cannot. For, it is reasoned, a tort recovery would, in effect, be an enforcement of the contract and would defeat the protection that contract law affords the minor.

A different result arises, however, when the minor departs from the terms of the agreement, as by using a rental automobile for an unauthorized purpose and in so doing negligently causing damage to the automobile. In that event, most courts would hold that the tort is independent, and the adult can collect from the minor. Such a situation would not involve the breach of a contractual duty, but rather the commission of a tort while performing an activity completely beyond the scope of the rental agreement.

INCOMPETENT PERSONS

This section discusses the contract status of incompetent persons who are under court-appointed guardianship and those who are not adjudicated incompetents.

Person under Guardianship

If a person is under guardianship by court order, her contracts are **void** and of no legal effect. Restatement, Section 13. A *guardian* is appointed by a court, generally under the terms of a statute, to control and preserve the property of a person (the *ward*) whose impaired capacity prevents her from managing her own property. Nevertheless, a party dealing with an individual under guardianship may be able to recover the fair value of any necessaries provided to the incompetent. Moreover, the contracts of the ward may be ratified by her guardian or by herself upon termination of the guardianship.

❖ See Case 9-4

Mental Illness or Defect

A contract is a consensual transaction; therefore, for a contract to be valid, it is necessary that the parties have a certain level of mental capacity. If a person lacks such capacity (is mentally incompetent), he may avoid liability under the agreement (because the contract is **voidable**).

Under the traditional, cognitive ability test, a person who is lacking in sufficient mental capacity to enter into a contract is one unable to comprehend the subject of the contract, its nature, and probable consequences. To avoid the contract, he need not be proved permanently incompetent; but his mental defect must be something more than a weakness of intellect or a lack of average intelligence. In short, a person is competent unless he is unable to understand the nature and effect of his act in entering a contract. Restatement, Section 15. In this situation, the incompetent may disaffirm the contract even if the other party did not know or had no reason to know of the incompetent's mental condition.

A second type of mental incompetence recognized by the Restatement and some States is a mental condition that impairs a person's ability to act in a reasonable manner. Section 15. In other words, the person understands what he is doing but cannot control his behavior in order to act in a reasonable and rational way. If the contract he enters is entirely executory or grossly unfair, it is voidable. If, however, the contract is executed, fair, and the competent party had no reason to suspect the incompetency of the other, the incompetent must restore the competent party to the *status quo* by returning the consideration he has received or its equivalent in money. If restoration to the *status quo* is impossible, avoidance will depend upon the equities of the situation.

Like minors and persons under guardianship, an incompetent person is liable for necessaries furnished him on the principle of quasi contract, the amount of recovery being the reasonable value of the goods or services. Moreover, an incompetent person may ratify or disaffirm his voidable contracts when he becomes competent or during a lucid period.

INTOXICATED PERSONS

A person may avoid any contract that he enters into if the other party has reason to know that, because of intoxication, he is unable either to understand the nature and consequences of his actions or to act in a reasonable manner. Restatement, Section 16. Such contracts are voidable, although they may be ratified when the intoxicated person regains his capacity. Slight intoxication will not destroy one's contractual capacity, but neither is it essential that one be so drunk as to be totally without reason or understanding.

The effect of intoxication on contractual capacity is similar to that accorded contracts that are voidable because of the second type of incompetency, although the courts are even more strict with contracts a party enters while intoxicated, given the idea that the condition is voluntary. Most courts, therefore, require that the intoxicated person on regaining his capacity must act promptly to disaffirm and must generally offer to restore the consideration received. Individuals who are taking prescribed medication or who are involuntarily intoxicated are treated the same as those who are incompetent under the cognitive ability test. As with incompetent persons, intoxicated persons are liable in quasi contract for necessaries furnished them during their incapacity.

Figure 9-1 illustrates the various types of contractual incapacities and the resulting effects.

◆ SEE FIGURE 9-1 Contractual Incapacity

◊ SEE CASE 9-4

◆ FIGURE 9-1 Contractual Incapacity

Incapacity	Effect	Incapacity	Effect
Minority	Voidable	**Guardianship for incompetency**	Void
Mental illness or defect	Voidable	**Intoxication**	Voidable

CHAPTER SUMMARY

Minors

Definition persons who are under the age of majority (usually 18 years)

Liability on Contracts a minor's contracts are voidable at the minor's option

- *Disaffirmance* avoidance of the contract; may be done during minority and for a reasonable time after reaching majority
- *Ratification* affirmation of the entire contract; may be done upon reaching majority

Liability for Necessaries a minor is liable for the reasonable value of necessary items (those that reasonably supply a person's needs)

Liability for Misrepresentation of Age prevailing view is that a minor may disaffirm the contract

Liability for Tort Connected with Contract if a tort and a contract are so intertwined that to enforce the tort the court must enforce the contract, the minor is not liable in tort

---

Incompetent and Intoxicated Persons

Person under Guardianship contracts made by a person placed under guardianship by court order are void

Mental Illness or Defect a contract entered into by a mentally incompetent person (one who is unable to understand the nature and consequences of his acts) is voidable

Intoxicated Persons a contract entered into by an intoxicated person (one who cannot understand the nature and consequence of her actions) is voidable

---

CASES

CASE
9-1

Generally, a contract made by a minor is voidable by the minor and the minor is entitled to the return of the consideration he gave to the other party. In this case, the Tennessee Supreme Court considers whether and under what circumstances the other party should be allowed to retain a reasonable compensation for the use of, depreciation of, or willful or negligent damage to the article purchased by the minor.

DODSON v. SHRADER
Supreme Court of Tennessee, 1992
824 S.W.2d 545

O'Brien, J.

This is an action to disaffirm the contract of a minor for the purchase of a pick-up truck and for a refund of the purchase price. The issue is whether the minor is entitled to a full refund of the money he paid or whether the seller is entitled to a setoff for the decrease in value of the pick-up truck while it was in the possession of the minor.

In early April of 1987, Joseph Eugene Dodson, then 16 years of age, purchased a used 1984 pick-up truck from Burns and Mary Shrader. The Shraders owned and operated Shrader's Auto Sales in Columbia, Tennessee. Dodson paid $4,900 in cash for the truck, using money he borrowed from his girlfriend's grandmother. At the time of the purchase there was no inquiry by the Shraders, and no misrepresentation by Mr. Dodson, concerning his minority. However, Mr. Shrader did testify that at the time he believed Mr. Dodson to be 18 or 19 years of age.

In December 1987, nine (9) months after the date of purchase, the truck began to develop mechanical problems. A mechanic diagnosed the problem as a burnt valve, but could not be certain without inspecting the valves inside the engine. Mr. Dodson did not want, or did not have the money, to effect these repairs. He continued to drive the truck despite the mechanical problems. One month later, in January, the truck's engine "blew up" and the truck became inoperable.

Mr. Dodson parked the vehicle in the front yard at his parents' home where he lived. He contacted the Shraders to rescind the purchase of the truck and requested a full refund. The Shraders refused to accept the tender of the truck or to give Mr. Dodson the refund requested.

Mr. Dodson then filed an action* * *seeking to rescind the contract and recover the amount paid for the truck.* * * Before the circuit court could hear the case, the truck, while parked in Dodson's front yard, was struck on the left front fender by a hit-and-run driver. At the time of the circuit court trial, according to Shrader, the truck was worth only $500 due to the damage to the engine and the left front fender.

The case was heard in the circuit court in November 1988. The trial judge, based on previous common-law decisions and, under the doctrine of *stare decisis* reluctantly granted the rescission. The Shraders were ordered, upon tender and delivery of the truck, to reimburse the $4,900 purchase price to Mr. Dodson. The Shraders appealed.

The Court of Appeals***affirmed;* * *

The earliest recorded case in this State, on the issue involved, appears to be in *Wheaton v. East*, [citation] (1833). In pronouncing the rule to apply governing infants' contracts, the court said: We do not perceive that any general rule, as to contracts which are void and voidable, can be stated with more precision than***this: "that when the court can pronounce the contract to be to the infant's prejudice, it is void, and when to his benefit, as for necessaries, it is good; and when the contract is of any uncertain nature, as to benefit or prejudice, it is voidable only, at the election of the infant."* * *

The law on the subject of the protection of infants' rights has been slow to evolve. However, in *Human v. Hartsell*, [citation] (1940) the Court of Appeals noted:

***the modern rule that contracts of infants are not void but only voidable and subject to be disaffirmed by the minor either before or after attaining majority appears to have been favored. Under this rule the efforts of early authorities to classify contracts as beneficial or harmful and determine whether they are void or only voidable upon the basis of such classification are abandoned in favor of permitting the infant himself when he has become of age to determine what contracts are and what are not to his interest and liking.* * *

As noted by the Court of Appeals, the rule in Tennessee, as modified, is in accord with the majority rule on the issue among our sister states. This rule is based upon the underlying purpose of the "infancy doctrine" which is to protect minors from their lack of judgment and "from squandering their wealth through improvident contracts with crafty adults who would take advantage of them in the marketplace." [Citation.]

There is, however, a modern trend among the states, either by judicial action or by statute, in the approach to the problem of balancing the rights of minors against those of innocent merchants. As a result, two (2) minority rules have developed which allow the other party to a contract with a minor to refund less than the full consideration paid in the event of rescission.

The first of these minority rules is called the "Benefit Rule." [Citations.] The rule holds that, upon rescission, recovery of the full purchase price is subject to a deduction for the minor's use of the merchandise. This rule recognizes that the traditional rule in regard to necessaries has been extended so far as to hold an infant bound by his contracts, where he failed to restore what he has received under them to the extent of the benefit actually derived by him from what he has received from the other party to the transaction. [Citations.]

The other minority rule holds that the minor's recovery of the full purchase price is subject to a deduction for the minor's "use" of the consideration he or she received under the contract, or for the "depreciation" or "deterioration" of the consideration in his or her possession. [Citations.]

***At a time when we see young persons between 18 and 21 years of age demanding and assuming more responsibilities in their daily lives; when we see such persons emancipated, married, and raising families; when we see such persons charged with the responsibility for committing crimes; when we see such persons being sued in tort claims for acts of negligence; when we see such persons subject to military service; when we see such persons engaged in business and acting in almost all other respects as an adult, it seems timely to re-examine the case law pertaining to contractual rights and responsibilities of infants to see if the law as pronounced and applied by the courts should be redefined.

* * *

We state the rule to be followed hereafter, in reference to a contract of a minor, to be where the minor has not been overreached in any way, and there has been no undue influence, and the contract is a fair and reasonable one, and the minor has actually paid money on the purchase price, and taken and used the article purchased, that he ought not to be permitted to recover the amount actually paid, without allowing the vendor of the goods reasonable compensation for the use of, depreciation, and willful or negligent damage to the article purchased, while in his hands. If there has been any fraud or imposition on the part of the seller or if the contract is unfair, or any unfair advantage has been taken of the minor inducing him to make the purchase, then the rule does not apply. Whether there has been such an overreaching on the part of the seller, and the fair market value of the property returned, would always, in any case, be a question for the trier of fact. This rule will fully and fairly protect the minor against injustice or imposition, and at the same time it will be fair to a business person who has dealt with such minor in good faith.

This rule is best adapted to modern conditions under which minors are permitted to, and do in fact, transact a great deal of business for themselves, long before they have reached the age of legal majority.* * *

* * *

We note that in this case, some nine (9) months after the date of purchase, the truck purchased by the plaintiff began to develop mechanical problems. Plaintiff was informed of the probable nature of the difficulty which apparently involved internal problems in the engine. He continued to drive the vehicle until the engine "blew up" and the truck became inoperable. Whether or not this involved gross negligence or intentional conduct on his part is a matter for determination at the trial level. It is not possible to determine from this record whether a counterclaim for tortious damage to the vehicle was asserted. After the first tender of the vehicle was made by plaintiff, and refused by the defendant, the truck was damaged by a hit-and-run driver while parked on plaintiff's property. The amount of that damage and the liability for that amount between the purchaser and the vendor, as well as the fair market value of the vehicle at the time of tender, is also an issue for the trier of fact.

The case is remanded to the trial court for further proceedings in accordance with this judgment.

The right to disaffirm a contract entered into while a minor will be lost if the minor ratifies the contract after reaching the age of majority. In the following case, the court determines whether the actions of NBA star Kobe Bryant constituted ratification of a contract he made when he was seventeen.

In re THE SCORE BOARD, INC.

United States District Court, D. New Jersey, 1999
238 B.R. 585
http://lawlibrary.rutgers.edu/fed/html/ca99-259-1.html

Irenas, J.

During the Spring of 1996, Appellant Kobe Bryant ("Bryant"), then a seventeen-year old star high school basketball player, declared his intention to forego college and enter the 1996 lottery draft of the National Basketball Association. On May 8, 1996, The Score Board Inc. ("Debtor"), then a New Jersey based company in the business of licensing, manufacturing and distributing sports and entertainment-related memorabilia, contacted Bryant's Agent, Arn Tellem ("Tellem" or "Agent") in anticipation of making a deal with Bryant.

* * *

In early July 1996, after the above [initial] negotiations, Debtor prepared and forwarded a signed written licensing agreement ("agreement") to Bryant. The agreement granted Debtor the right to produce licensed products, such as trading cards, with Bryant's image. Bryant was obligated to make two personal appearances on behalf of Debtor and provide between a minimum of 15,000 and a maximum of 32,500 autographs. Bryant was to receive a $2.00 stipend for each autograph, after the first 7,500. Under the agreement, Bryant could receive a maximum of $75,000 for the autographs.

In addition to being compensated for the autographs, Bryant was entitled to receive base compensation of $10,000. Moreover, Debtor agreed to pay Bryant $5,000, of the $10,000, within ten days following receipt of the fully executed agreement. Finally, Bryant was entitled to a $5,000 bonus if he returned the agreement within six weeks.

Bryant rejected the above agreement, and on July 11, 1996, while still a minor, Bryant made a counter-offer ("counter-offer"), signed it and returned it to Debtor. The counter-offer made several changes to Debtor's agreement, including the number of autographs. Bryant also changed the amount of prepaid autographs from 7,500 to 500.

Balser claimed that he signed the counter-offer and placed it into his files. The copy signed by Debtor was subsequently misplaced, however, and has never been produced by Debtor during these proceedings. Rather, Debtor has produced a copy signed only by Bryant.

On August 23, 1996, Bryant turned eighteen. Three days later, Bryant deposited a check for $10,000 into his account from Debtor.

On or about September 1, 1996, Bryant began performing his obligations under the agreement, including autograph signing sessions and public appearances. He subsequently performed his contractual duties for about a year and a half.

By late 1997, Bryant grew reluctant to sign any more autographs under the agreement and his Agent came to the conclusion that a fully executed contract did not exist. By this time, Tellem became concerned with Debtor's financial condition because it failed to make certain payments to several other players. Debtor claims that the true motivation for Bryant's reluctance stems from his perception that he was becoming a "star" player, and that his autograph was "worth" more than $2.00.

* * *

On March 17, 1998, Debtor sent Bryant a check for $1,130 as compensation for unpaid autographs. Bryant alleges that he was entitled to $10,130, not $1,130. The Bankruptcy Court found that Bryant was owed $10,130 and the check for $1,130 was based on a miscalculation.

On March 18, 1998, Debtor filed a voluntary Chapter 11 bankruptcy petition. On March 23, 1998, Tellem returned the $1,130 check upon learning of Debtor's financial trouble. Included with the check was a letter that questioned the validity of the agreement between Bryant and Debtor.

***On April 20, 1998, Tellem stated that no contract existed because the counter-offer was never signed by Debtor and there was never a meeting of the minds. Tellem added that the counter-offer expired and that Kobe Bryant withdrew from the counter-offer.

Subsequently, Debtor began to sell its assets, including numerous executory contracts with major athletes, including Bryant. Bryant argued that Debtor could not do this, because he believed that a contract never existed. In the alternative, if a contract was created, Bryant contended that it was voidable because it was entered into while he was a minor.

* * *

On December 21, 1998, the Honorable Gloria M. Burns ruled in her memorandum opinion that Debtor accepted Bryant's counter-offer and, therefore, a valid contract existed between Bryant and Debtor. In the alternative, the Bankruptcy Court held that even if Bryant's counter-offer was not signed by Debtor, the parties' subsequent conduct demonstrated their acceptance of the contractual obligation by performance, thereby creating an enforceable contract. Judge Burns denied Bryant's claims of mutual mistake, infancy and his motion for stay relief.

* * *

On February 2, 1999, the Bankruptcy Court entered its final orders: (1) granting Debtor's motion to assume its executory contract with Bryant and assign it to Oxxford; and (2) over-ruling Bryant's objection to the sale.

Bryant challenges the Bankruptcy Court's finding that he ratified the agreement upon attaining majority. Contracts made during minority are voidable at the minor's election within a reasonable time after the minor attains the age of majority. [Citations]

The right to disaffirm a contract is subject to the infant's con-duct which, upon reaching the age of majority, may amount to ratification. [Citation.] "Any conduct on the part of the former infant which evidences his decision that the transaction shall not be impeached is sufficient for this purpose." [Citation.]

On August 23, 1996, Bryant reached the age of majority,

approximately six weeks after the execution of the agreement. On August 26, 1996, Bryant deposited the $10,000 check sent to him from Debtor. Bryant also performed his contractual duties by signing autographs.

The Bankruptcy Court did not presume ratification from inaction as Bryant asserts. It is clear that Bryant ratified the contract from the facts, because Bryant consciously performed his contractual duties.

Bryant asserts that he acted at the insistence of his Agent, who believed that he was obligated to perform by contract. Yet, neither Bryant nor his Agent disputed the existence of a contract until the March 23, 1998, letter by Tellem. That Bryant may have relied on his Agent is irrelevant to this Court's inquiry and is proper evidence only in a suit against the Agent. To the contrary, by admitting that he acted because he was under the belief that a contract existed, Bryant confirms the existence of the contract. Moreover, it was Bryant who deposited the check, signed the autographs, and made personal appearances.

For the above reasons, Bryant's appeal of the Bankruptcy Court's orders finding that a valid and enforceable contract exists is denied.

CASE

9-3

This case discusses the standards for determining a minor's liability for "necessaries."

GASTONIA PERSONNEL CORP. v. ROGERS

Supreme Court of North Carolina, 1970
276 N.C. 279, 172 S.E.2d 19

BOBBITT, C.J.

[Rogers (defendant) was a nineteen-year-old (the age of major-ity being twenty-one) high school graduate pursuing a civil engineering degree when he learned that his wife was expecting a child. As a result he quit school and sought assistance from Gastonia Personnel Corporation (plaintiff) in finding a job. Rogers signed a contract with the employment agency providing that he would pay the agency a service charge if it obtained suit-able employment for him. The employment agency found him such a job, but Rogers refused to pay the service charge asserting that he was a minor when he signed the contract. Plaintiff sued to recover the agreed upon service charge from Rogers.]

Under the common law, persons, whether male or female, are classified and referred to as infants until they attain the age of twenty-one years. [Citations.]

"By the fifteenth century it seems to have been well settled that an infant's bargain was in general void at his election (that is, voidable), and also that he was liable for necessaries." [Citation.]

In accordance with this ancient rule of the common law, this Court has held an infant's contract, unless for "necessar-ies" or unless authorized by statute, is voidable by the infant,

at his election, and may be disaffirmed during infancy or upon attaining the age of twenty-one. [Citations.]

* * *

In general, our prior decisions are to the effect that the "necessaries" of an infant, his wife and child, include only such necessities of life as food, clothing, shelter, medical attention, etc. In our view, the concept of "necessities" should be enlarged to include such articles of property and such services as are reasonably necessary to enable the infant to earn the money required to provide the necessities of life for himself and those who are legally dependent upon him.

The evidence before us tends to show that defendant, when he contracted with plaintiff, was nineteen years of age, emanci-pated, married, a high school graduate, within "a quarter or 22 hours" of obtaining his degree in applied science, and capable of holding a job at a starting annual salary of $4,784.00. To hold, as a matter of law, that such a person cannot obligate himself to pay for services rendered him in obtaining employment suitable to his ability, education, and specialized training, enabling him to provide the necessities of life for himself, his wife and his expected child, would place him and others similarly situated under a serious economic handicap.

In the effort to protect "older minors" from improvident or unfair contracts, the law should not deny to them the opportunity and right to obligate themselves for articles of property or services which are reasonably necessary to enable them to provide for the proper support of themselves and their dependents. The minor should be held liable for the reasonable value of articles of property or services received pursuant to such contract.

To establish liability, plaintiff must satisfy the jury by the greater weight of the evidence that defendant's contract with plaintiff was an appropriate and reasonable means for defendant to obtain suitable employment. If this issue is answered in plaintiff's favor, plaintiff must then establish by the greater weight of the evidence the reasonable value of the services received by defendant pursuant to the contract. Thus, plaintiff's recovery, if any, cannot exceed the reasonable value of its services to defendant.

[Judgment for plaintiff awarding a new trial in accordance with legal principles stated in this opinion.]

CASE
9-4

This case deals with the enforceability of a contract that one party entered into while incapacitated through the use of alcohol.

FIRST STATE BANK OF SINAI v. HYLAND
Supreme Court of South Dakota, 1987
399 N.W.2d 894

Henderson, J.

Plaintiff-appellant First State Bank of Sinai (Bank) sued defendant-appellee Mervin Hyland (Mervin) seeking to hold him responsible for payment on a promissory note which he cosigned.* * *[T]he circuit court entered***judgment holding Mervin not liable for the note's payment. Bank appeals, advocating that the court erred when it ruled that

1. Mervin was incompetent to transact business when he signed the note;
2. Mervin's obligation to Bank was void; and
3. Mervin did not subsequently accept/ratify the obligation.

* * *

On March 10, 1981, Randy Hyland (Randy) and William Buck (Buck), acting for Bank, executed two promissory notes. One note was for $6,800 and the other note was for $3,000. Both notes became due on September 19, 1981.

The notes remained unpaid on their due date and Bank sent notice to Randy informing him of the delinquencies. On October 20, 1981, Randy came to the Bank and met with Buck. Buck explained to Randy that the notes were past due. Randy requested an extension. Buck agreed, but on the condition that Randy's father, Mervin, act as cosigner. One $9,800 promissory note dated October 20, 1981 (the two notes of $6,800 and $3,000 were combined) was created. Randy was given the note for the purpose of obtaining his father's signature. According to Randy, Mervin signed the note on October 20 or 21, 1981.

Mervin had transacted business with Bank since 1974. Previously, he executed approximately 60 promissory notes with Bank. Mervin was apparently a good customer and paid all of his notes on time. Buck testified that he knew Mervin drank, but that he was unaware of any alcohol-related problems.

Randy returned to the Bank about one week later. Mervin had properly signed the note. In Buck's presence, Randy signed the note, which had an April 20, 1982 due date.

On April 20, 1982, the note was unpaid. Buck notified Randy of the overdue note. On May 5, 1982, Randy appeared at the Bank. He brought a blank check signed by Mervin with which the interest on the note was to be paid. Randy filled in the check amount at the Bank for $899.18 (the amount of interest owing). Randy also requested that the note be extended. Buck agreed, but required Mervin's signature as a prerequisite to any extension. A two-month note for $9,800 with a due date of July 2, 1982, was prepared and given to Randy.

Randy did not secure his father's signature on the two-month note, and Mervin testified that he refused to sign that note. On June 22, 1982, Randy filed for bankruptcy which later resulted in the total discharge of his obligation on the note.

On July 14, 1982, Buck sent a letter to Randy and Mervin informing them of Bank's intention to look to Mervin for the note's payment. On December 19, 1982, Bank filed suit against Mervin, requesting $9,800 principal and interest at the rate of 17 percent until judgment was entered. Mervin answered on January 14, 1983. His defense hinged upon the assertion that he was incapacitated through the use of liquor when he signed the note. He claimed he had no recollection of the note, did not remember seeing it, discussing it with his son, or signing it.

Randy testified that when he brought the note home to his father, the latter was drunk and in bed. Mervin then rose from his bed, walked into the kitchen, and signed the note. Later, Randy returned to the Bank with the signed note.

The record reveals that Mervin was drinking heavily from late summer through early winter of 1981. During this period, Mervin's wife and son accepted responsibilities for managing the farm. Mervin's family testified that his bouts with liquor left him weak, unconcerned with regard to family and business matters, uncooperative, and uncommunicative. When Mervin was drinking, he spent most of his time at home, in bed.

Mervin's problems with alcohol have five times resulted in his involuntary commitment to hospitals. Two of those commitments occurred near the period of the October 1981 note. On September 10, 1981, Mervin was involuntarily committed to the Human Services Center at Yankton. He was released on September 19, 1981. On November 20, 1981, he was involuntarily committed to River Park at Pierre.

Between the periods of his commitments, September 19, 1981 until November 20, 1981, Mervin did transact some business himself.* * *

A trial was held on October 4, 1985. Mervin was found to be entirely without understanding (as a result of alcohol consumption) when he signed the October 20, 1981 promissory note. The court pointed to Mervin's lack of personal care and nonparticipation in family life and farming business as support for finding the contractual relationship between the parties void at its inception. It was further held that Bank had failed to show Mervin's subsequent ratification of the contract. Bank appeals.

* * *

Historically, the void contract concept has been applied to nullify agreements made by mental incompetents who have contracted***after a judicial determination of incapacity had been entered. [Citations.]* * *

Mervin had numerous and prolonged problems stemming from his inability to handle alcohol. However, he was not judicially declared incompetent during the note's signing.

* * *

Contractual obligations incurred by intoxicated persons may be voidable. [Citation.] Voidable contracts (contracts other than those entered into following a judicial determination of incapacity)***may be rescinded by the previously disabled party. [Citation.] However, disaffirmance must be prompt, upon the recovery of the intoxicated party's mental abilities, and upon his notice of the agreement, if he had forgotten it. [Citation.]* * *

A voidable contract may also be ratified by the party who had contracted while disabled. Upon ratification, the contract becomes a fully valid legal obligation. [Citation.] Ratification can either be express or implied by conduct. [Citations.] In addition, failure of a party to disaffirm a contract over a period of time may, by itself, ripen into a ratification, especially if rescission will result in prejudice to the other party. [Citations.]

Mervin received both verbal notice from Randy and written notice from Bank on or about April 27, 1982, that the note was overdue. On May 5, 1982, Mervin paid the interest owing with a check which Randy delivered to Bank. This by itself could amount to ratification through conduct. If Mervin wished to avoid the contract, he should have then exercised his right of rescission. We find it impossible to believe that Mervin paid almost $900 in interest without, in his own mind, accepting responsibility for the note. His assertion that paying interest on the note relieved his obligation is equally untenable in light of his numerous past experiences with promissory notes.

* * *

We conclude that Mervin's obligation to Bank is not void. ***Mervin's obligation on the note was voidable and his subsequent failure to disaffirm (lack of rescission) and his payment of interest (ratification) then transformed the voidable contract into one that is fully binding upon him.

We reverse and remand.

QUESTIONS

1. Define a necessary and explain how it affects the contracts of a minor.
2. How and when may a minor ratify a contract?
3. What is the liability of a minor who disaffirms a contract?
4. Distinguish between the legal capacity of a person under guardianship and a mentally incompetent person who is not under guardianship.
5. What is the rule governing an intoxicated person's capacity to enter into a contract?

PROBLEMS

1. Michael, a minor, operates a one-man automobile repair shop. Anderson, having heard of Michael's good work on other cars, takes her car to Michael's shop for a thorough engine overhaul. Michael, while overhauling Anderson's engine, carelessly fits an unsuitable piston ring on one of the pistons, with the result that Anderson's engine is seriously damaged. Michael offers to return the sum that Anderson paid him for his work, but refuses to make good the damage. Anderson sues Michael in tort for the damage to her engine. Decision?

2. (a) On March 20, Andy Small became seventeen years old, but he appeared to be at least twenty-one. On April 1, he moved into a room-

ing house in Chicago where he orally agreed to pay the landlady $300 a month for room and board, payable at the end of each month.

(b) On April 4, he went to Honest Hal's Carfeteria and signed a contract to buy a used car on credit with a small down payment. He made no representation as to his age, but Honest Hal represented the car to be in A-1 condition, which it subsequently turned out not to be.

(c) On April 7, Andy sold and conveyed to Adam Smith a parcel of real estate, which he owned.

On April 30, he refused to pay his landlady for his room and board for the month of April; he returned the car to Honest Hal and demanded a refund of his down payment; and he demanded that Adam Smith reconvey the land although the purchase price, which Andy received in cash, had been spent in riotous living. Decisions as to each claim?

3. Carol White ordered a $225 pair of contact lenses through an optometrist. White, an emancipated minor, paid $100 by check and agreed to pay the remaining $125 at a later time. The doctor ordered the lenses, incurring a debt of $100. After the lenses were ordered, White called to cancel her order and stopped payment on the $100 check. The lenses could be used by no one but White. The doctor sued White for the value of the lenses. Decision?

4. In May, Mike, a 17-year-old college student, was introduced to Dover, the operator of a summer camp, through Excel Employment Agency. Mike and Dover entered into a written agreement whereby Dover hired Mike as a camp counselor during the summer vacation period at a salary of $2,000 per month. Mike also agreed in writing to pay Excel Employment Agency a certain commission for their services. In June, Mike discovered that he had failed one of his final exams, and decided that, instead of working, he would attend college during the summer session. Mike disaffirmed both contracts.

(a) What rights, if any, do Dover and Excel Employment Agency have against Mike? Explain.

(b) Would your answer to (a) be the same if, when he entered into the contracts, Mike had fraudulently misrepresented his age as 18? Explain.

5. The father of a 17-year-old daughter, Alicia, sent his daughter away to college, and paid Alicia's expenses for board, clothing and tuition.

(a) Assume that Alicia decided to occupy her spare time, and accordingly contracted to take a two-year correspondence course in computer repair with Careers Correspondence School. After Alicia became 18, she continued to receive the course materials for 6 months, did the correspondence lessons, used the books sent to her, and made six monthly payments. Then she notified Careers Correspondence School that she disaffirmed any further obligation under the contract. In an action by Careers Correspondence School against Alicia to recover the balance due under the contract, judgment for whom? Explain.

(b) Assume that while Alicia was 17, her father suffered financial reverses and Alicia and her father agreed that thereafter Alicia was on her own. In order to return to college, Alicia borrowed $25,000 from the college's Student Aid Fund to cover her expenses for the next year. The loan was payable at the end of 3 years. When Alicia became 18, she immediately notified the college that she disaffirmed the loan agreement. May the college enforce the loan agreement against Alicia? Explain.

6. On his 17th birthday, Alex received a deed to Blackacre, a tract of farmland, as a gift from his uncle. Alex cut down a number of trees suitable for making railroad ties. Alex sold Blackacre to Bertha for $100,000 and the felled timber to Carmen for $3,000. He spent the money and, immediately after his 18th birthday, notified Bertha and Carmen that he disaffirmed the respective contracts. In the meantime, how ever, Bertha had sold Blackacre to Marvin and Carmen had sold the timber to Ned. Is Alex entitled to recover:

(a) Blackacre from Marvin? Explain.

(b) the timber from Ned? Explain.

7. Bob, who was 17 years old, bought a used sports car for $12,000 from Ace Motors on the installment plan. He had already paid $3,000 on the car when he disaffirmed the contract on his 18th birthday. He offered to return the car and demanded the return of the $3,000 he had paid. The car is now worth only $8,000. What are the rights of the parties? Explain.

8. Daniel, while under the influence of alcohol, agreed to sell his 1990 automobile to Belinda for $8,000. The next morning, when Belinda went to Daniel's house with the $8,000 in cash, Daniel stated that he did not remember the transaction but that "a deal is a deal." One week after completing the sale, Daniel decides that he wishes to avoid the contract. What result?

9. Jones, a minor, owned a 2003 automobile. She traded it to Stone for a 2004 car. Jones went on a three-week trip and found that the 2004 car was not as good as the 2003 car. She asked Stone to return the 2003 car but was told that it had been sold to Tate. Jones thereupon sued Tate for the return of the 2003 car. Is Jones entitled to regain ownership of the 2003 car? Explain.

 Internet Exercise Find and review information on (a) laws governing the employment of minors, (b) gifts to minors, and (c) the Uniform Guardianship and Protective Proceedings Act.

Contracts in Writing

An **oral** contract, that is, one not written, is in every way as enforceable as a written contract unless otherwise provided by statute. Although most contracts are not required to be in writing to be enforceable, it is highly desirable that significant contracts be written. Written contracts avoid the numerous problems that proving the terms of oral contracts inevitably involves. The process of setting down the contractual terms in a written document also tends to clarify the terms and to reveal problems the parties might not otherwise foresee. Moreover, the terms of a written contract do not change over time, while the parties' recollections of the terms might.

When the parties do reduce their agreement to a complete and final written expression, the law (under the parol evidence rule) honors this document by not allowing the parties to introduce any evidence in a lawsuit that would alter, modify, or vary the terms of the written contract. Nevertheless, the parties may differ as to the proper or intended meaning of language contained in the written agreement where such language is ambiguous or susceptible to different interpretations. To ascertain the proper meaning requires an interpretation, or construction, of the contract. The rules of construction permit the parties to introduce evidence to resolve ambiguity and to show the meaning of the language employed and the sense in which both parties used it.

This chapter will examine (1) the types of contracts that must be in writing to be enforceable, (2) the parol evidence rule, and (3) the rules of contractual interpretation.

Statute of Frauds

The statute of frauds requires that certain designated types of contracts be evidenced by a writing to be enforceable. The original statute became law in 1677, when the English Parliament adopted "An Act for Prevention of Frauds and Perjuries," commonly referred to as the statute of frauds. From the early days of U.S. history practically every State had and continues to have a statute of frauds patterned upon the original English statute.

The statute of frauds has no relation whatever to any kind of fraud practiced in the making of contracts. The common law rules relating to such fraud were discussed in Chapter 8. The purpose of the statute is to prevent perjured testimony in court from creating fraud in the proof of certain oral contracts, which purpose the statute accomplishes by requiring that certain contracts be evidenced by a signed writing. On the other hand, the statute does not prevent the performance of oral contracts if the parties are willing to perform. In brief, the statute relates only to the proof or evidence of a contract. It has nothing to do with the circumstances surrounding the making of a contract or with a contract's validity.

CONTRACTS WITHIN THE STATUTE OF FRAUDS

Many more types of contracts are *not* subject to the statute of frauds than are subject to it. Most oral contracts, as previously indicated, are as enforceable and valid as a written contract. If, however, a given contract is subject to the statute of frauds, the contract is said to be **within** the statute; to be enforceable, it must comply with the statute's requirements. All other types of contracts are said to be "not within" or "outside" the statute and need not comply with its requirements to be enforceable.

The following kinds of contracts are within the original English statute and remain within most state statutes; compliance requires a writing signed by the party to be charged (the party against whom the contract is to be enforced).

1. Promises to answer for the duty of another
2. Promises of an executor or administrator to answer personally for a duty of the decedent whose funds he is administering
3. Agreements upon consideration of marriage
4. Agreements for the transfer of an interest in land
5. Agreements not to be performed within one year

A sixth type of contract within the statute applied to contracts for the sale of goods. Section 2–201 of the UCC now governs the enforceability of contracts of this kind.

The various provisions of the statute of frauds apply independently. Accordingly, a contract for the sale of an interest in land may also be a contract in consideration of marriage, a contract not to be performed in one year, *and* a contract for the sale of goods.

In addition to those contracts specified in the original statute, most states require that other contracts be evidenced by a writing as well; for example, a contract to make a will, to authorize an agent to sell or purchase real estate, or to pay a commission to a real estate broker. Moreover, the UCC requires that a contract for the sale of securities, contracts creating certain types of security interests, and contracts for the sale of other personal property for more than $5,000 also be in writing.

Electronic Records

One significant impediment to e-commerce has been the questionable enforceability of contracts entered into through electronic means such as the Internet or e-mail because of the writing requirements under contract and sales law (statute of frauds). In response, over 40 States have adopted the **Uniform Electronic Transactions Act (UETA)**. UETA gives full effect to electronic contracts, encouraging their widespread use, and develops a uniform legal framework for their implementation. UETA protects electronic signatures and contracts from being denied enforcement because of the statute of frauds. Section 7 of UETA accomplishes this by providing:

1. A record or signature may not be denied legal effect or enforceability solely because it is in electronic form.
2. A contract may not be denied legal effect or enforceability solely because an electronic record was used in its formation.
3. If a law requires a record to be in writing, an electronic record satisfies the law.
4. If a law requires a signature, an electronic signature satisfies the law.

Section 14 of UETA further validates contracts formed by machines functioning as electronic agents for parties to a transaction: "A contract may be formed by the interaction of electronic agents of the parties, even if no individual was aware of or reviewed the electronic agents' actions or the resulting terms and agreements." The Act excludes from its coverage wills, codicils, and testamentary trusts as well as all Articles of the UCC except Articles 2 and 2A.

In addition, Congress in 2000 enacted the **Electronic Signatures in Global and National Commerce Act (E-Sign)**. The Act, which uses language very similar to that of UETA, makes electronic records and signatures valid and enforceable across the United States for many types of transactions in or affecting interstate or foreign commerce. E-Sign defines an electronic record as "a contract or other record created, generated, sent, communicated, received, or stored by electronic means." It defines an electronic signature as "an electronic sound, symbol, or process, attached to or logically associated with a contract or other record and executed or adopted by a person with the intent to sign the record." Like UETA, E-Sign ensures that Internet and e-mail agreements will not be unenforceable because of the statute of frauds by providing that:

1. a signature, contract, or other record relating to such transaction may not be denied legal effect, validity, or enforceability solely because it is in electronic form; and
2. a contract relating to such transaction may not be denied legal effect, validity, or enforceability solely because an electronic signature or electronic record was used in its formation.

Suretyship Provision

The **suretyship** provision applies to a contractual promise by a **surety** (*promisor*) to a **creditor** (*promisee*) to perform the duties or obligations of a third person (**principal debtor**) if the principal debtor does not perform. Thus, if a mother tells a merchant to extend $1,000 worth of credit to her son and says, "If he doesn't pay, I will," the promise must be in writing (or have a sufficient electronic record) to be enforceable. The factual situation can be reduced to the simple statement "If X doesn't pay, I will." The promise is said to be **collateral**, in that the promisor is not primarily liable. The mother does not promise to pay in any event; her promise is to pay only if the one primarily obligated, her son, defaults.

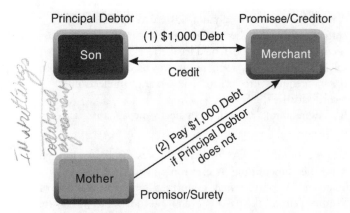

Principal Debtor — Son — (1) $1,000 Debt → Merchant — Promisee/Creditor; Credit; Mother — Promisor/Surety — (2) Pay $1,000 Debt if Principal Debtor does not

The rule applies only to cases involving three parties and two contracts. The primary contract, between the principal debtor and the creditor, creates the indebtedness. The collateral contract is made by the third person (surety) directly with the creditor, whereby the surety promises to pay the debt to the creditor in case the principal debtor fails to do so.

Original Promise   If the promisor makes an **original promise** by undertaking to become primarily liable, then the statute of frauds does not apply. For example, a father tells a merchant to deliver certain items to his daughter and says, "I will pay $400 for them." The father is not promising to answer for the debt of another; rather, he is making the debt his own. It is to the father, and the father alone, that the merchant extends credit; only from the father may the creditor seek payment. The statute of frauds does not apply, and the promise may be oral.

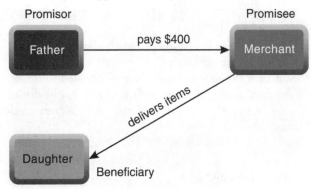

Promisor — Father — pays $400 → Promisee — Merchant; delivers items → Daughter — Beneficiary

◈ SEE CASE 10-1

Main Purpose Doctrine   The courts have developed an exception to the suretyship provision based on the purpose or object of the promisor, called the "main purpose doctrine" or "leading object rule." Where the object or purpose of the promisor is to obtain an economic benefit for himself, the promise is *not* within the statute. Restatement, Section 116. The expected benefit to the surety "must be such as to justify the conclusion that his main purpose in making the promise is to advance his own interest." Restatement, Section 116, Comment b. The fact

that the surety received consideration for his promise or that he might receive a slight and indirect advantage is insufficient to bring the promise within the main purpose doctrine.

Suppose that a supply company has refused to furnish materials upon the credit of a building contractor. Facing a possible slowdown in the construction of his building, the owner of the land promises the supplier that if he will extend credit to the contractor, the owner will pay if the contractor does not. Here, the primary purpose of the promisor is to serve his own economic interest, even though the performance of the promise would discharge the duty of another. The intent to benefit the contractor is at most incidental, and courts will uphold oral promises of this type.

Promise Made to Debtor   The suretyship provision has been interpreted not to include promises made to a debtor. For example, D owes a debt to C. S promises D that she will pay D's debt in return for valid consideration from D. Because S made the promise to the debtor (D), not the creditor, the promise may be oral. The promise is not a collateral promise to pay C if D fails to pay and thus is not a promise to discharge the obligation of another.

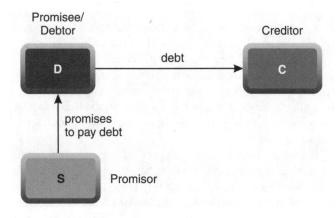

Promisee/Debtor — D — debt → Creditor — C; S — Promisor — promises to pay debt

Executor-Administrator Provision

The executor-administrator provision applies to the contractual promises of an executor of a decedent's will, or to those of the administrator of his estate if the decedent dies without a will, to answer personally for a duty of the decedent. An **executor** or **administrator** is a person appointed by a court to carry on, subject to order of court, the administration of the estate of a deceased person. If the will of a decedent nominates a certain person as executor, the court customarily appoints that person. If an executor or administrator promises to pay personally a debt of the decedent, the promise must be in writing—or in proper electronic form—to be enforceable. For example, Brian, who is Ann's son and executor of her will, recognizing that Ann's estate will not provide funds sufficient to pay all of her debts, orally promises Curtis, one of Ann's creditors, that he, Brian, will personally pay all of his mother's creditors in full in return for valid consideration from Curtis. Brian's oral promise is not enforceable. This provision does not apply to promises to pay debts of the deceased out of assets of the estate.

The executor-administrator provision is thus a specific application of the suretyship provision. Accordingly, the exceptions to the suretyship provision apply to this provision as well.

Marriage Provision

The notable feature of the marriage provision is that it does *not* apply to mutual promises to marry. The provision applies only if a promise to marry is made in consideration for some promise other than a reciprocal promise to marry. Restatement, Section 124. If, for example, Greg and Betsy each orally promise and agree to marry each other, their agreement is not within the statute and is a binding contract between them. If, however, Greg promises to convey title to a certain farm to Betsy if she accepts his proposal of marriage, their agreement would fall within the statute of frauds.

Land Contract Provision

The land contract provision covers promises to transfer "any interest in land," which includes any right, privilege, power, or immunity in real property. Restatement, Section 125. Thus, all promises to transfer, buy, or pay for an interest in land, including ownership interests, leases, mortgages, options, and easements, are within the provision.

❧ See GOL § 5-703(1)

The land contract provision does not include contracts to transfer an interest in personal property. It also does not cover short-term leases, which by statute in most states are those for one year or less; contracts to build a building on a piece of land; contracts to do work on the land; or contracts to insure a building on the land.

The courts may enforce an oral contract for the transfer of an interest in land if the party seeking enforcement has so changed his position in reasonable reliance upon the contract that injustice can be prevented only by enforcing the contract. Restatement, Section 129. In applying this **part performance** exception, many states require that the transferee have paid a portion or all of the purchase price *and* either have taken possession of the real estate or have started to make valuable improvements on the land. New York state requires all three elements in order for the part performance exception to be fulfilled. For example, Aaron orally agrees to sell land to Barbara for $30,000. With Aaron's consent, Barbara takes possession of the land, pays Aaron $10,000, builds a house on the land, and occupies it. Several years later, Aaron repudiates the contract. The courts will enforce the contract against Aaron. On the other hand, the courts will not enforce the promise unless equity so demands.

An oral promise by a purchaser is also enforceable if the seller fully performs by conveying the property to the purchaser. As previously indicated, however, payment of part or all of the price is not sufficient in itself to remove the contract from the scope of the statute.

❧ See Cases 10-2 and 10-3

One-Year Provision

The statute of frauds requires all contracts that *cannot* be fully performed within one year of their making to be in writing or in proper electronic form. Restatement, Section 130.

❧ See GOL § 5-701(A)(1)

The Possibility Test To determine whether a contract can be performed within a year, the courts ask whether it is *possible* to complete its performance within a year. The **possibility test** does not ask whether the agreement is likely to be performed within one year from the date it was formed; nor does it ask whether the parties think that performance will be within the year. The enforceability of the contract depends not on probabilities or on the actuality of subsequent events but on whether the terms of the contract make it possible for performance to occur within one year. For example, an oral contract between Alice and Bill for Alice to build a bridge, which should reasonably take three years, is enforceable if it is possible, although extremely unlikely and difficult, for Alice to perform the contract in one year. Similarly, if Alice agrees to employ Bill for life, this contract also is not within the statute of frauds. Given the possibility that Bill may die within the year (in which case the contract would be completely performed), the contract is therefore one that is *fully performable* within a year. Contracts of indefinite duration are likewise excluded from the provision. On the other hand, an oral contract to employ another person for thirteen months could not possibly be performed within a year and is unenforceable.

❧ See Case 10-4

Computation of Time The year runs from the time the agreement is made, not from the time when the performance

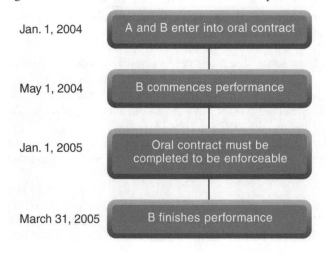

Jan. 1, 2004	A and B enter into oral contract
May 1, 2004	B commences performance
Jan. 1, 2005	Oral contract must be completed to be enforceable
March 31, 2005	B finishes performance

is to begin. For example, on January 1, 2004, A orally hires B to work for eleven months starting on May 1, 2004. That contract will be fully performed on March 31, 2005, which is more than one year after January 1, 2004, the date the contract was made. Consequently, it is *within* the statute of frauds and unenforceable as it is oral.

Similarly, a contract for a year's performance, which is to begin three days after the date on which the contract is made, is within the statute and, if oral, is unenforceable. If, however, the performance is to begin the following day or, under the terms of the agreement, could have begun the following day, the contract is not within the statute and need not be in writing, as the one year's performance would be completed on the anniversary date of the making of the contract. This rule appears to conflict with the rule regarding short term leases—would a contract for a one-year lease beginning one month from now have to be in writing? The answer is no. Leases for a year or less do not have to be in writing no matter how far in to the future the lease will actually begin.

Full Performance by One Party   Where one party to a contract has fully performed, most courts hold that the promise of the other party is enforceable, even though by its terms the performance of the contract was not possible within the period of a year. Restatement, Section 130. For example, Vince borrows $4,800 from Julie, orally promising to pay Julie $4,800 in three annual installments of $1,600. Vince's promise is enforceable, notwithstanding the one-year provision, because Julie has fully performed by making the loan.

Sales of Goods

The original statute of frauds, which applied to contracts for the sale of goods, has been used as a prototype for the UCC Article 2 statute of frauds provision. Section 2–201 of the UCC provides that a contract for the sale of goods for the price of **$500 or more** is not enforceable unless there is some writing or record sufficient to indicate that the parties have made a contract for sale. **Goods**, as previously indicated, are defined as movable personal property. Section 2–105(1). The definition expressly includes growing crops and unborn animals.

Admission   The Code permits an oral contract for the sale of goods to be enforced against a party who in his pleading, testimony, or otherwise in court admits that a contract was made, but limits enforcement to the quantity of goods so admitted. Section 2–201(3)(b). The language "otherwise in court" may include pretrial deposition and written interrogatories of the defendant. Some courts now apply this exception to other statute of frauds provisions.

Specially Manufactured Goods   The Code permits a seller to enforce an oral contract for goods specially manufactured for a buyer, but only if evidence indicates that the goods were made

for the buyer and the seller can show that he made a *substantial beginning* of their manufacture prior to receiving any notice of repudiation. Section 2–201(3)(a). If goods manufactured on special order are nonetheless readily marketable in the ordinary course of the seller's business, this exception does not apply.

For example, if Jim brings an action against Robin alleging breach of an oral contract under which Robin agreed to purchase from Jim three million balloons with Robin's trademark imprinted on them at a price of $30,000, the action is not subject to the defense of the statute of frauds unless Robin can show (1) that the balloons are suitable for sale to other buyers, which is highly improbable in view of the trademark, or (2) that Jim received notice of repudiation before he had made a substantial start on the production of the balloons or had otherwise substantially committed himself to procuring them.

❖ SEE CASE 10-5

Delivery or Payment and Acceptance   Prior to the Code, delivery and acceptance of part of the goods or payment of part of the price made the entire oral contract enforceable against the buyer who had received part delivery or against the seller who had received part payment. Under the Code, such "partial performance" validates the contract only for the goods that have been accepted or for which payment has been accepted. Section 2–201(3)(c). To illustrate, Johnson orally agrees to buy 1,000 watches from Barnes for $15,000. Barnes delivers 300 watches to Johnson, who receives and accepts the watches. The oral contract is enforceable to the extent of 300 watches ($4,500)—those received and accepted—but is unenforceable to the extent of 700 watches ($10,500).

But what if the contract, such as one for the sale of an automobile, is indivisible so that the making of part payment creates only a choice between not enforcing the contract or enforcing it as a whole? Presently, authority is divided on this issue, although the better rule appears to be that such part payment and acceptance makes the entire contract enforceable.

❖ SEE FIGURE 10-1   The Statute of Frauds

Modification or Rescission of Contracts within the Statute of Frauds

Oral contracts modifying previously existing contracts are unenforceable if the resulting contract is within the statute of frauds. The reverse is also true: an oral modification of a prior contract is enforceable if the new contract is not within the statute. Thus, examples of unenforceable oral contractual modifications include an oral promise to guarantee additional duties of another, an oral agreement to substitute different land for that described in the original contract, and an oral agreement to extend an employee's contract for six months to a total of two years. On the other hand, an oral agreement to modify an

◆ FIGURE 10-1 The Statute of Frauds

Contracts within the Statute of Frauds	Exceptions
Suretyship—a promise to answer for the duty of another	• Main purpose rule • Original promise • Promise made to debtor
Executor-Administrator—a promise to answer personally for debt of decedent	• Main purpose rule • Original promise • Promise made to debtor
Agreements made upon consideration of marriage	• Mutual promises to marry
Agreements for the transfer of an interest in land	• Part performance plus detrimental reliance • Seller conveys property
Agreements not to be performed within one year	• Full performance by one party • Possibility of performance within one year
Sale of goods for $500 or more	• Admission • Specially manufactured goods • Delivery or payment acceptance

employee's contract from two years to six months at a higher salary is not within the statute of frauds and is enforceable.

By extension, an oral rescission is effective and discharges all unperformed duties under the original contract. For example, Linda and Donald enter into a written contract of employment for a two-year term. Later they orally agree to rescind the contract. The oral agreement is effective, and the written contract is rescinded. Where, however, land has been transferred, an agreement to rescind the transaction constitutes a contract to retransfer the land and is within the statute of frauds.

Under the UCC, the decisive point is the contract price *after* the modification. Section 2–209(3). If the parties enter into an oral contract to sell for $450 a motorcycle to be delivered to the buyer and later, prior to delivery, orally agree that the seller shall paint the motorcycle and install new tires and that the buyer shall pay a price of $550, the modified contract is unenforceable. Conversely, if the parties have a written contract for the sale of 200 bushels of wheat at a price of $4 per bushel and later orally agree to decrease the quantity to 100 bushels at the same price per bushel, the agreement, as modified, is for a total price of $400 and thus is enforceable.

COMPLIANCE WITH THE STATUTE OF FRAUDS

Even though a contract is within the statute of frauds, a sufficient *writing*, *memorandum*, or *record* may justify its enforcement. The writing or record need not be in any specific form,

nor be an attempt by the parties to enter into a binding contract, nor represent their entire agreement: it need only comply with the requirements of the statute of frauds.

General Contracts Provisions

The English statute of frauds and most modern statutes of frauds require that the agreement be evidenced by a writing or record to be enforceable. The note or memorandum, which may be formal or informal, must:

1. specify the parties to the contract;
2. specify with reasonable certainty the subject matter and the essential terms of the unperformed promises; and
3. be signed by the party to be charged or by his agent.

The statute's purpose in requiring a writing or record is to ensure that the parties have entered into a contract. The writing or record, therefore, need not exist at the time of the litigation; showing that the memorandum once existed is sufficient.

The memorandum may be a receipt, a check, or a telegram. It may be such that the parties themselves view it as having no legal significance whatever, as, for example, a personal letter between the parties, an interdepartmental communication, an advertisement, or the record books of a business. The writing or record need not have been delivered to the party who seeks to take advantage of it, and it may even contain a repudiation of the oral agreement. For example, Adrian and Joseph enter into an oral agreement that Adrian will sell Blackacre to Joseph for $5,000. Adrian subsequently receives a better offer and sends

Joseph a signed letter, which begins by reciting all the material terms of the oral agreement. The letter concludes, "Since my agreement to sell Blackacre to you for $5,000 was oral, I am not bound by my promise. I have since received a better offer and will accept that one." Adrian's letter constitutes a sufficient memorandum for Joseph to enforce Adrian's promise to sell Blackacre. It should be recognized that because Joseph did not sign the memorandum, the writing does not bind him. Thus, a contract may be enforceable against only one of the parties.

The "signature" may be initials or may even be typewritten or printed, so long as the party intended it to authenticate the writing or record. Furthermore, the signature need not be at the bottom of the page or at the customary place for a signature. The memorandum may consist of *several* papers or documents, none of which would be sufficient by itself. The several memoranda, however, must together satisfy all of the requirements of a writing or record to comply with the statute of frauds and must clearly indicate that they relate to the same transaction. Restatement, Section 132. The latter requirement can be satisfied if (1) the writings are physically attached, (2) the writings refer to each other, or (3) an examination of the writings shows them to be in reference to each other.

◆ SEE CASE 10-6

Sale of Goods

The statute of frauds provision under Article 2 of the UCC is more liberal. For a sale of goods, Section 2–201 of the Code requires merely some writing or record:

1. sufficient to indicate that a contract has been made between the parties;
2. specifying the quantity of goods to be sold; and
3. signed by the party against whom enforcement is sought or by her authorized agent or broker.

The writing or record is sufficient even if it omits or incorrectly states an agreed-upon term; however, where the quantity term is misstated, the contract can be enforced only to the extent of the quantity stated in the writing or record.

As with general contracts, several related documents may satisfy the writing or record requirement. Moreover, the signature again may be by initials or even typewritten or printed, so long as the party intended thereby to authenticate the writing or record.

In addition, the Code provides relief to a merchant who, within a reasonable time after entering into the oral contract, confirms the contract for the sale of goods by a letter or signed writing to the other party if he too is a merchant. As between **merchants**, the **written confirmation**, if sufficient against the sender, is also sufficient against the recipient unless he gives written notice of his objection within ten days after receiving the confirmation. Section 2–201(2). This means that if these requirements have been met, the recipient of the writing or record is in the same position he would have assumed by signing it; and the

confirmation, therefore, is enforceable against him.

For example, Brown Co. and ATM Industries enter into an oral contract which provides that ATM will deliver twelve thousand shirts to Brown at $6 per shirt. Brown sends a letter to ATM acknowledging the agreement. The letter, containing the quantity term but not the price, is signed by Brown's president and is mailed to ATM's vice president for sales. Brown was bound by the contract once its authorized agent signs the letter; ATM cannot raise the defense of the statute of frauds if ATM does not object to the letter within ten days after receiving it. Therefore, it is extremely important for merchants to examine their mail carefully and promptly to make certain that any written confirmations conform to their understanding of their outstanding contractual agreements.

EFFECT OF COMPLIANCE

The English statute provided that "no action shall be brought" upon a contract to which the statute of frauds applied *and* which did not comply with its requirements. The Code, by comparison, states that the contract "is not enforceable by way of action or defense." Despite the difference in language the basic legal effect is the same: a contracting party has a defense to an action by the other party to enforce an oral contract that is within the statute and that does not comply with its requirements. In short, the oral contract is **unenforceable**.

For example, if Tia, a painter, and James, a homeowner, make an oral contract under which James is to give Tia a certain tract of land in return for her painting his house, the contract is unenforceable under the statute of frauds. It is a contract for the sale of an interest in land. Either party can repudiate and has a defense to an action by the other to enforce the contract.

Full Performance

After all the promises of an oral contract have been performed by all the parties, the statute of frauds no longer applies. Accordingly, neither party can have the contract set aside on the ground that it should have been in writing. The purpose of the statute is not to prohibit the performance of oral contracts but simply to exclude oral evidence of contracts within its provisions. Courts, in other words, will not "unscramble" a fully performed contract merely because it was not in writing or a proper record. In short, the statute applies to executory contracts only.

Restitution

A party to a contract that is unenforceable because of the statute of frauds may have, nonetheless, acted in reliance upon the contract. In such a case the party may recover in restitution the benefits he conferred upon the other in relying upon the unenforceable contract. Thus, if Wilton makes an oral contract to furnish services to Rochelle that are not to be performed within a year and Rochelle discharges Wilton after three months, Wilton may recover as restitution the value of the services he rendered during the three months. Most courts require, however, that the party seeking restitution not be in default.

Promissory Estoppel

A growing number of courts have used the doctrine of promissory estoppel to displace the requirement of a writing by enforcing oral contracts within the statute of frauds where the party seeking enforcement has reasonably and foreseeably relied upon a promise in such a way that injustice can be avoided only by enforcing the promise. Restatement, Section 139. This section is essentially identical to Section 90 of the Restatement, which, as discussed in Chapter 11, dispenses with the requirement of consideration, although the comments to Section 139 state that "the requirement of consideration is more easily displaced than the requirement of a writing." The remedy granted is limited, as justice requires, and depends upon such factors as the availability of other remedies; the foreseeability, reasonableness, and substantiality of the reliance; and the extent to which reliance corroborates evidence of the promise.

Parol Evidence Rule

A contract reduced to writing and signed by the parties is frequently the result of many conversations, conferences, proposals, counterproposals, letters, and memoranda and sometimes is the product of negotiations conducted, or partly conducted, by agents of the parties. Any given stage in the negotiations may have produced tentative agreements that were superseded (or regarded as such by one of the parties) by subsequent negotiations. Offers may have been made and withdrawn, either expressly or by implication, or forgotten in the give-and-take of negotiations. Ultimately, though, the parties prepare and sign a final draft of the written contract, which may or may not include all of the points that were discussed and agreed upon during the negotiations. By signing the agreement, however, the parties have declared it to be their contract; and the terms it contains represent the contract they have made. As a rule of substantive law, neither party is later permitted to show that the contract they made differs from the terms and provisions that appear in the written agreement. This rule, which also applies to wills and deeds, is called the parol evidence rule.

THE RULE

When a contract is expressed in a writing that is intended to be the complete and final expression of the rights and duties of the parties, parol evidence of *prior* oral or written negotia-

tions or agreements of the parties, or their *contemporaneous* oral agreements that vary or change the written contract, are not admissible. The word *parol* means literally "speech" or "words." The term **parol evidence** refers to any evidence, whether oral or in writing, which is outside the written contract and not incorporated into it either directly or by reference.

The parol evidence rule applies only to an *integrated* contract; that is, one contained in a certain writing or writings to which the parties have assented as the statement of the complete agreement or contract between them. When a contract is thus integrated, the courts will not permit parol evidence of any prior or contemporaneous agreement to vary, change, alter, or modify any of the terms or provisions of the written contract. Restatement, Section 213.

A writing may contain a **merger clause**, which states that the writing is intended to be the complete and final expression of the agreement between the parties. Most courts consider a merger clause to be conclusive proof of an integrated contract, while a few courts view a merger clause only as evidence of an integrated contract.

The reason for the parol evidence rule is that the parties, by reducing their entire agreement to writing, are regarded as having intended the writing that they signed to include the whole of their agreement. The terms and provisions contained in the writing are there because the parties intended them to be there. Conversely, any provision not in the writing is regarded as having been omitted because the parties intended that it should not be a part of their contract. In safeguarding the contract as made by the parties, the rule excluding evidence that would tend to change, alter, vary, or modify the terms of a written agreement applies to all integrated written contracts and deals with what terms are part of the contract. The rule differs from the statute of frauds, which governs what contracts must be evidenced by a writing to be enforceable.

❧ SEE CASE 10-7

SITUATIONS TO WHICH THE RULE DOES NOT APPLY

The parol evidence rule, in spite of its name, is neither an exclusionary rule of evidence nor a rule of construction or interpretation; rather, it is a rule of substantive law that defines the limits of a contract. Bearing this in mind, as well as the reason underlying the rule, it should be clear that the rule does **not** apply to any of the following:

1. A contract that is partly written and partly oral; that is, one in which the parties do not intend the writing to be their entire agreement.
2. A clerical or *typographical error* that obviously does not represent the agreement of the parties. Where, for example,

a written contract for the services of a skilled mining engineer provides that his rate of compensation is to be $7 per day, a court of equity would permit reformation (correction) of the contract to rectify the mistake upon a showing that both parties intended the rate to be $700 per day.

3. Evidence showing the lack of *contractual capacity* of one of the parties, such as proof of minority, intoxication, or mental incompetency. Such evidence would not tend to vary, change, or alter any of the terms of the written agreement, but rather would show that the written agreement was voidable or void.

4. A *defense* of fraud, misrepresentation, duress, undue influence, mistake, illegality, or unconscionability. Though evidence establishing any of these defenses would not purport to vary, change, or alter any of the terms of the written agreement, it would show such agreement to be voidable, void, or unenforceable.

5. A *condition precedent* to which the parties agreed orally at the time they executed the written agreement and to which they made the entire agreement subject. Again, such evidence does not tend to vary, alter, or change any of the terms of the agreement, but rather shows whether the entire written agreement, unchanged and unaltered, ever became effective. For example, if John signs a subscription agreement to buy stock in a corporation to be formed and delivers the agreement to Thompson with the mutual understanding that it is not to be binding unless the other persons financially responsible under it shall each agree to buy at least an equivalent amount of such stock, John is permitted to show by parol evidence this condition.

6. A *subsequent mutual rescission or modification* of the written contract. Parol evidence of a later agreement does not tend to show that the integrated writing did not represent the contract between the parties at the time it was made. Parties to an existing contract, whether written or oral, may agree to change the terms of their contract as they see fit, or to cancel it completely, if they so desire.

7. Parol evidence is admissible to explain *ambiguous* terms in the contract. To enforce a contract, it is necessary to understand its intended meaning. Nevertheless, such interpretation is not to alter, change, or vary the terms of the contract.

8. The rule does not prevent a party from proving the existence of a separate, distinct contract between the same parties.

SUPPLEMENTAL EVIDENCE

Although a written agreement may not be contradicted by evidence of a prior agreement or of a contemporaneous agreement, under the Restatement, Section 216, and the Code, Section 2–202, a written contract may be explained or supplemented by (1) course of dealing between the parties, (2) usage of trade, (3) course of performance, or (4) evidence of consistent additional terms, unless the parties intended the writing to be a complete and exclusive statement of their agreement.

A **course of dealing** is a sequence of previous conduct between the parties under an agreement that the court reasonably may regard as establishing a common basis of understanding for interpreting their expressions and other conduct.

A **usage of trade** is a practice or method of dealing, regularly observed and followed in a place, vocation, or trade.

Course of performance refers to the manner and extent to which the respective parties to a contract have accepted without objection successive tenders of performance by the other party.

The Restatement and the Code permit *supplemental consistent evidence* to be introduced into a court proceeding, but only if it does not contradict a term or terms of the original agreement and would probably not have been included in the original contract.

◆ **SEE FIGURE 10-2** Parol Evidence Rule

Interpretation of Contracts

Although the written words or language in which the parties embodied their agreement or contract may not be changed by parol evidence, the ascertainment (determination) of the meaning to be given the written language is outside the scope of the parol evidence rule. Though written words embody the terms of the contract, words are but symbols. If their meaning is unclear, the courts may clarify this meaning by applying rules of interpretation or construction and by using extrinsic (external) evidence, where necessary.

The Restatement, Section 200, defines **interpretation** as the ascertainment of the meaning of a promise or agreement or a term of the promise or agreement. Where the language in a contract is unambiguous, the courts will not accept extrinsic evidence tending to show a meaning different from that which the words clearly convey. Its function being to interpret and construe written contracts and documents, the court adopts rules of interpretation to apply a legal standard to the words contained in the agreement. The courts will attempt to interpret a contract in accordance with the intent of the parties. If the subjective intent of the parties fails to provide a clear interpretation, the courts will make an objective interpretation. Among the rules that aid interpretation are the following:

1. Words and other conduct are interpreted in the light of all the circumstances, and the principal purpose of the parties, if ascertainable, is given great weight.

2. A writing is interpreted as a whole, and all writings that are part of the same transaction are interpreted together.

◆ FIGURE 10-2 Parol Evidence Rule

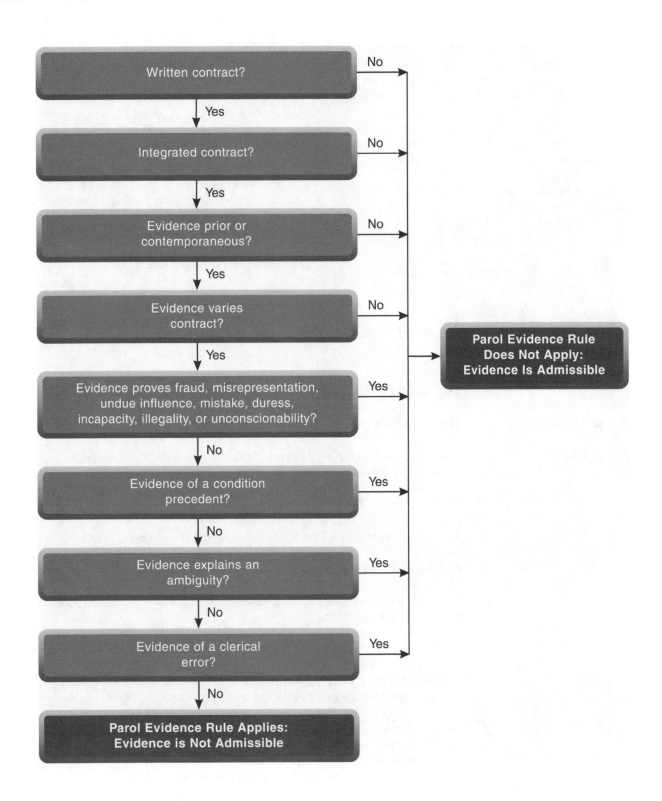

3. Unless a different intention is manifested, language that has a commonly accepted meaning is interpreted in accordance with that meaning.

4. Unless a different intention is manifested, technical terms and words of art are given their technical meanings.

5. Wherever reasonable, the manifestations of intention of the parties to a promise or agreement are interpreted as consistent with each other and with any relevant course of performance, course of dealing, or usage of trade.

6. An interpretation that gives a reasonable, lawful, and effective meaning to all the terms is preferred over an interpretation that leaves a part unreasonable, unlawful, or of no effect.

7. Specific terms and exact terms are given greater weight than general language.

8. Separately negotiated or added terms are given greater weight than standardized terms or other terms not separately negotiated.

9. Express terms, course of performance, course of dealing, and usage of trade are weighted in that order.

10. Where a term or promise has several possible meanings, it will be interpreted against the party who supplied the contract or the term. Restatement, Sections 201, 202, and 203.

11. Where written provisions are inconsistent with typed or printed provisions, the written provision is given preference. Likewise, typed provisions are given preferences to printed provisions.

12. If the amount payable is set forth in both figures and words and the amounts differ, the words control the figures.

It may be observed that, through the application of the parol evidence rule (where properly applicable) and the above rules of interpretation and construction, the law not only enforces a contract but, in so doing, exercises great care that the contract being enforced is the one the parties made and that the sense and meaning of the parties' intentions are carefully ascertained and given effect.

CHAPTER SUMMARY

Statute of Frauds

Contracts within the Statute of Frauds

Rule contracts within the statute of frauds must be evidenced by a writing to be enforceable

Electronic Records full effect is given to electronic contracts and signatures

Suretyship Provision applies to promises to pay the debts of others
- *Promise Must Be Collateral* promisor must be secondarily, not primarily, liable
- *Main Purpose Doctrine* if primary object is to provide an economic benefit to the surety, then the promise is not within the statute

Executor-Administrator Provision applies to promises to answer personally for duties of decedents

Marriage Provision applies to promises made in consideration of marriage but not to mutual promises to marry

Land Contract Provision applies to promises to transfer any rights, privileges, powers, or immunities in real property

One-Year Provision applies to contracts that cannot be performed within one year
- *The Possibility Test* the criterion is whether it is possible, not likely, for the agreement to be performed within one year
- *Computation of Time* the year runs from the time the agreement is made
- *Full Performance by One Party* makes the promise of the other party enforceable under majority view

Sales of Goods a contract for the sale of goods for the price of $500 or more must be evidenced by a writing or record to be enforceable
- *Admission* an admission in pleadings, testimony, or otherwise in court makes the contract enforceable for the quantity of goods admitted
- *Specially Manufactured Goods* an oral contract for specially manufactured goods is enforceable

- *Delivery or Payment and Acceptance* validates the contract only for the goods that have been accepted or for which payment has been accepted

Modification or Rescission of Contracts within the Statute of Frauds oral contracts modifying existing contracts are unenforceable if the resulting contract is within the statute of frauds

---

Methods of Compliance

General Contract Law the writing(s) or record must
- specify the parties to the contract
- specify the subject matter and essential terms
- be signed by the party to be charged or by her agent

Sale of Goods provides a general method of compliance for all parties and an additional one for merchants
- *Writing(s) or Record Must* (1) be sufficient to indicate that a contract has been made between the parties, (2) be signed by the party against whom enforcement is sought or by her authorized agent, and (3) specify the quantity of goods to be sold
- *Written Confirmation* between merchants, a written confirmation that is sufficient against the sender is also sufficient against the recipient unless the recipient gives written notice of his objection within ten days

---

Effect of Noncompliance

Oral Contract within Statute of Frauds is unenforceable

Full Performance statute does not apply to executed contracts

Restitution is available in quasi contract for benefits conferred in reliance on the oral contract

Promissory Estoppel oral contracts will be enforced where the party seeking enforcement has reasonably and justifiably relied on the promise and the court can avoid injustice only by enforcement

Parol Evidence Rule and Interpretation of Contracts

Parol Evidence Rule

Statement of Rule when parties express a contract in a writing that they intend to be the complete and final expression of their rights and duties, evidence of their prior oral or written negotiations or agreements of their contemporaneous oral agreements that vary or change the written contract are not admissible

Situations to Which the Rule Does Not Apply
- a contract that is not an integrated document
- correction of a typographical error
- showing that a contract was void or voidable
- showing whether a condition has in fact occurred
- showing a subsequent mutual rescission or modification of the contract

Supplemental Evidence may be admitted
- *Course of Dealing* previous conduct between the parties
- *Usage of Trade* practice engaged in by the trade or industry
- *Course of Performance* conduct between the parties concerning performance of the particular contract
- *Supplemental Consistent Evidence*

Interpretation of Contracts

Definition the ascertainment of the meaning of a promise or agreement or a term of the promise or agreement

Rules of Interpretation include these:

- all the circumstances are considered and the principal purpose of the parties is given great weight
- a writing is interpreted as a whole
- commonly accepted meanings are used unless the parties manifest a different intention
- wherever possible, the intentions of the parties are interpreted as consistent with each other and with course of performance, course of dealing, or usage of trade
- technical terms are given their technical meaning
- specific terms are given greater weight than general language
- separately negotiated terms are given greater weight than standardized terms or those not separately negotiated
- the order for interpretation is express terms, course of performance, course of dealing, and usage of trade
- where a term has several possible meanings, the term will be interpreted against the party who supplied the contract or term
- written provisions are given preference over typed or printed provisions, and typed provisions are given preference over printed provisions
- if an amount is set forth in both words and figures and they differ, words control figures

---

CASES

CASE
10-1

In the following case, the court determines whether an insurance company's oral promise to settle a claim against its insured is an original promise or is a suretyship promise that is unenforceable under the Statute of Frauds.

CARTER v. ALLSTATE INSURANCE COMPANY

Court of Appeals of Texas, Houston (1st Dist.), 1997
962 S.W.2d 268, review denied

Taft, J.

Appellants [plaintiffs], Jesse Carter and Jesse Thomas, had an auto accident with Allstate's insured.* * *

Appellants' car collided with Allstate's insured's car on November 5, 1993. Appellants hired attorney Joseph Onwuteaka to represent them in their claim for injuries from the automobile collision. On April 11, 1994, Mr. Onwuteaka sent a demand letter for settlement of appellants' claims to Allstate's adjustor, Gracie Weatherly. Mr. Onwuteaka claims Ms. Weatherly made, and he accepted, oral settlement agreements on behalf of appellants. When Allstate did not honor the agreements, appellants filed suit on May 30, 1995, for breach of contract.

Allstate filed for summary judgment based on [the] Statute of Frauds.* * *On October 5, 1995, the trial court granted summary judgment without stating a particular basis.

* * *

[T]he appellants contend the alleged oral agreement is not governed by the Statute of Frauds. Allstate claims the Statute of Frauds is applicable to the alleged agreement as "a promise by another person to answer for the debt, default, or miscarriage of another person." [Citation.] This provision of the Statute of Frauds is commonly referred to as the "suretyship provision." [Citation.]

One test for determining whether a promise to pay the debt of another is within or without the Statute of Frauds is whether the promisor is a surety, only secondarily liable, or has accepted primary responsibility for the debt. [Citations.] If the party is primarily liable, its promise to pay a debt is not required to be in writing by the Statute of Frauds. [Citation.] However, if the party is a surety, the promise to pay the debt of a third party is required to be in writing. [Citation.]

If Allstate were merely a surety, its obligation would have been to pay its insured's debt upon default by its insured. However, as an insurer, Allstate contracted with its insured to assume responsibility for the liability of its insured, at least to the limits of the insurance policy. By Allstate's oral promise to settle, it was settling not only its insured's potential liability but its own possible obligation to pay and its own duty to defend its insured. The oral promise to settle was an original undertaking, not a promise to answer for the debt of the insured. Therefore, the suretyship provision of the Statute of Frauds does not apply to Allstate's promise to settle. [Citation.]

We reverse the trial court's summary judgment and remand for further proceedings.

CASE 10-2

The Statute of Frauds may be satisfied by a written a note or memorandum of the contract that is signed by the party against whom enforcement of the contract is sought. The following case considers whether the buyer's deposit check, which the seller endorsed and deposited, is sufficient to satisfy the Statute of Frauds for a contract for the sale of real property.

H. ROTHVOSS & SONS, INC. v. ESTATE OF NEER

Supreme Court of New York, Appellate Division, New York (3rd Dept.), 1988
139 A.D.2d 37; 530 N.Y.S.2d 331

MERCURE, Judge. Plaintiff seeks specific performance and money damages resulting from the alleged breach of a contract for the sale of real property by S. Hollis Neer, defendants' decedent and predecessor in title, to plaintiff. The complaint alleges the terms of the purported contract, that "[a]s evidence of plaintiff's good faith and intentions to carry out the contract" plaintiff's officer executed and delivered to Neer a check in the amount of $500 dated July 24, 1984, which check was endorsed and deposited by Neer, and that Neer died on October 30, 1985, prior to completion of the contract of sale. Annexed to the complaint is a detailed and unsigned contract for the sale of real property.

Defendants moved to dismiss the complaint on grounds that it failed to state a cause of action and was barred by the Statute of Frauds. In opposition thereto, plaintiff submitted the affidavit of its vice-president, Henry F. Rothvoss, Jr., in which he stated that the terms of the oral contract of sale with Neer were embodied in the unexecuted contract, that the contract was prepared by Neer's attorney, and that, as evidence of his good faith and "to insure that the contract would be carried out," he handed the $500 check to Neer. The check, annexed to the affidavit, contains the purported endorsement of Neer. The memo portion thereof contains the words "land on Rt 22" and "down payment." There is no dispute that the land in question is located on State Route 22 in the Town of Ancram, Columbia County.

Supreme Court denied the motion, finding that the canceled check, endorsed and thereby subscribed by Neer, together with the unexecuted contract, satisfied the Statute of Frauds and the provision that a "contract for * * * the sale, of any real property, or an interest therein, is void unless the contract or some note or memorandum thereof, expressing the consideration, is in writing, subscribed by the party to be charged" (General Obligations Law § 5-703 [2]). Defendants appeal.

We reverse. The action is barred by the Statute of Frauds, and the motion to dismiss should have been granted on that basis. Although the requisite memorandum may be pieced together out of several writings, some signed and others unsigned, and parol evidence may be resorted to in aid thereof, it is essential that the separate writings sought to be so employed clearly refer to the same subject matter or transaction. Additionally, in such case the signed writing must establish a contractual relationship between the parties. Here, the

signed writing, the check, does not establish such a contractual relationship. Moreover, it does not contain even a general description of the land to be conveyed and fails to state the purchase price and other essential terms of sale, such as financing. In *Mulford v Borg-Warner Acceptance Corp.*, this court rejected the contention that an endorsed check could establish the necessary contractual relationship. We conclude that just as the check notation "(new lease)" was insufficient to establish a tenancy involving all the provisions of a proposed unsigned lease, including the term, the words "land on Rt 22" and "down payment" noted on the check herein are insufficient to establish an agreement involving all the terms of a proposed unsigned contract of sale including the purchase price, terms of payment and description of property to be conveyed. Further, although plaintiff is the drawer of the check, the purchasers under the formal written contract of sale are plaintiff and two other individuals, August F. Corsini and Laura M. Corsini, thereby creating uncertainty as to the identity of the parties to the purported contract. Additionally, the $500 actually paid is not reflected in and bears no relationship to the claimed contract, which provides for a $15,000 down payment upon execution.

Nor would treatment of the $500 as partial payment of thepurchase price remove the contract from the Statute of Frauds. "With respect to land contracts, part payment of the purchase price, or even full payment thereof, is not considered part performance of the contract, standing alone; such payment, to be sufficient, must be accompanied by other acts, such as possession, or possession and improvements." Clearly, the $500 check was nothing more than earnest money to show plaintiff's good intentions and was not intended to evidence a completed contract. Where, as here, the parties contemplate a formal, binding, written contract, which is never executed, there is no mutual assent and no contract.

Order reversed, on the law, with costs, motion granted and complaint dismissed.

CASE

10-3

The following case illustrates the type of circumstances that may constitute "part performance" sufficient to satisfy the real property provision of the New York Statute of Frauds.

SCHAFER v. ALBRO

Appellate Division, New York (4th Dept.), 1996
233 A.D.2d 900,649 N.Y.S.2d 260

Memorandum: Supreme Court properly denied that part of defendant's motion seeking partial summary judgment dismissing the cause of action alleging breach of a real estate contract between the parties. Although the alleged contract is not in writing or subscribed by plaintiffs (see, General Obligations Law § 5-703 [2]), plaintiffs allege in their verified complaint that they had possession of the property; made part payment of the purchase price to defendant and her husband; made extensive improvements to the property at a total cost of over $ 20,000; paid off the second mortgage in the amount of $25,733.76; and, from November 1, 1988 to February 1991, made the payments on the first mortgage. Plaintiffs have thereby raised an issue of fact whether they are entitled to specific performance of the contract based upon part performance (see, General Obligations Law § 5-703 [4] [Citations]).

* * *

CASE

10-4

This case illustrates that in determining whether a contract is within the one year provision of the Statute of Frauds, a key issue is whether, at the time the parties made the contract, it was possible that the contract could be fully performed within one year.

IACONO v. LYONS

Court of Appeals of Texas, 2000
962 S.W.2d 268, rehearing denied

O'Connor, J.

Mary Iacono, the plaintiff below and appellant here, appeals from a take-nothing summary judgment rendered in favor of Carolyn Lyons, the defendant below and appellee here. We reverse and remand.

Background

The plaintiff and defendant had been friends for almost 35 years. In late 1996, the defendant invited the plaintiff to join her on a trip to Las Vegas, Nevada. There is no dispute that the defendant paid all the expenses for the trip, including providing money for gambling.

The plaintiff contended she was invited to Las Vegas by the defendant because the defendant thought the plaintiff was lucky. Sometime before the trip, the plaintiff had a dream about winning on a Las Vegas slot machine. The plaintiff's dream convinced her to go to Las Vegas, and she accepted the defendant's offer to split "50-50" any gambling winnings.

In February 1997, the plaintiff and defendant went to Las Vegas. They started playing the slot machines at Caesar's Palace. The plaintiff contends that, after losing $47, the defendant wanted to leave to see a show. The plaintiff begged the defendant to stay, and the defendant agreed on the condition that she (the defendant) put the coins into the machines because doing so took the plaintiff too long. The plaintiff agreed, and took the defendant to a dollar slot machine that looked like the machine in her dream. The machine did not pay on the first try. The plaintiff then said, "Just one more time," and the defendant looked at the plaintiff and said, "This one's for you, Puddin."

The slot machine paid $1,908,064. The defendant refused to share the winnings with the plaintiff, and denied they had an agreement to split any winnings. The defendant told Caesar's Palace she was the sole winner and to pay her all the winnings.

The plaintiff sued the defendant for breach of contract. The defendant moved for summary judgment on the grounds that any oral agreement was unenforceable under the statute of frauds or was voidable for lack of consideration. The trial court rendered summary judgment in favor of the defendant.* * *

* * *

Consideration

The defendant asserted the agreement, if any, was unenforceable under the statute of frauds because it could not be performed within one year. There is no dispute that the winnings were to be paid over a period of 20 years.

* * *

[The one year provision of the statute of frauds] does not apply if the contract, from its terms, could possibly be performed within a year—however improbable performance within one year may be. [Citations.]

To determine the applicability of the statute of frauds with indefinite contracts, this Court may use any reasonably clear method of ascertaining the intended length of performance.

[Citation.] The method is used to determine the parties' intentions at the time of contracting. [Citation.] The fact that the entire performance within one year is not required, or expected, will not bring an agreement within the statute. [Citations.]

Assuming without deciding that the parties agreed to share their gambling winnings, such an agreement possibly could have been performed within one year. For example, if the plaintiff and defendant had won $200, they probably would have received all the money in one pay-out and could have split the winnings immediately.* * *

Therefore, the defendant was not entitled to summary judgment based on her affirmative defense of the statute of frauds.

* * *

We reverse the trial court's judgment and remand for further proceedings.

CASE

10-5

This case illustrates an application of the UCC's exception to the Statute of Frauds for "specially manufactured goods."

KALAS v. COOK

Appellate Court of Connecticut, 2002

70 Conn.App. 477, 800 A.2d 553, 47 U.C.C. Rep.Serv.2d 1307
http://www.jud.state.ct.us/external/supapp/Cases/AROap/70ap412.pdf

Peters, J.

Pursuant to a long-standing oral agreement, a print shop manufactured and delivered written materials designed by the buyer for the buyer's use and sale. After the buyer's death, the executor of her estate refused to pay for the last deliveries of these materials to the buyer. The principal issue in this appeal is whether the statute of frauds, as codified in the Uniform Commercial Code, [citation], bars enforcement of the oral agreement.* * *[W]e agree with the [trial] court's conclusion that, under the circumstances of this case, the seller is entitled to be paid.

The plaintiff, Barbara H. Kalas, owner of the print shop, filed a complaint against the defendant, Edward W. Cook, executor of the estate of the buyer, Adelma G. Simmons. The plaintiff alleged that the defendant, in breach of the obligations contained in an oral contract with Simmons for the sale of goods, had refused to pay for goods delivered to her. The defendant denied these allegations and interposed a number of special defenses, including a defense under the statute of frauds* * *.

The trial court held that the transaction between the plaintiff and the deceased was a sale of goods as that term is defined in [UCC] § 2–105. That determination has not been challenged on appeal. As a contract for the sale of goods, its enforcement was not precluded by the statute of frauds provision* * *. Accordingly, the court rendered a judgment in favor of the plaintiff in the amount of $24,599.38. The defendant has appealed.

The facts found by the trial court, which are currently uncontested, establish the background for the court's judgment. The plaintiff, doing business as Clinton Press of Tolland, operated a printing press and, for several decades, provided written materials, including books and pamphlets for Simmons. Simmons ordered these materials for use and sale at her farm, known as Caprilands Herb Farm (Caprilands). The defendant has not suggested that these materials could have been sold on the open market.

Due to limited space at Caprilands, the plaintiff and Simmons agreed that the written materials would remain stored at the plaintiff's print shop until Simmons decided that delivery was necessary. The materials were delivered either routinely, based on Simmons' ordinary need for materials, or upon her request for a special delivery. After each delivery, the plaintiff sent an invoice requesting payment by Simmons. These invoices were honored.

In 1991, the town of Tolland acquired the land on which the plaintiff resided. In early 1997, the plaintiff was notified that she would have to vacate the property by the end of that calendar year. Upon receiving that notice, the plaintiff decided to close her business. The plaintiff and Simmons agreed that the materials printed for Caprilands and stored at the plaintiff's print shop would be delivered on an accelerated basis.* * *

On December 3, 1997, after several months of deterioration of her physical health, Simmons died.* * *The plaintiff submitted a claim against the estate for $24,599.38 for unpaid deliveries to Caprilands. These deliveries took place from February 12, 1997 to December 11, 1997, with the last two deliveries occurring after Simmons' death.

* * *

On appeal, the defendant argues that the oral contract was invalid* * *because a writing was required by [UCC] § 2–201. This argument is unpersuasive* * *.

* * *

* * *Contracts for the sale of goods* * *are governed by § 2–201. [Citations.]

Under § 2–201, oral agreements for the sale of goods at a price of $500 or more are presumptively unenforceable. [Citations.] The applicable provisions in this case, however, are other subsections of § 2–201.

Under § 2–201 (3) (a), an oral contract for the sale of goods is enforceable if the goods in question are "specially manufactured." In determining whether the specially manufactured goods exception applies, courts generally apply a four part standard: "(1) the goods must be specially made for the buyer; (2) the goods must be unsuitable for sale to others in the ordinary course of the seller's business; (3) the seller must have substantially begun to have manufactured the goods or to have a commitment for their procurement; and (4) the manufacture or commitment must have been commenced under circumstances reasonably indicating that the goods are for the buyer and prior to the seller's receipt of notification of contractual repudiation." [Citation.] In applying this standard, "courts have traditionally looked to the goods themselves. The term 'specially manufactured,' therefore, refers to the nature of the particular goods in question and not to whether the goods were made in an unusual, as opposed to the regular, business operation or manufacturing process of the seller." [Citations.]

Printed material, particularly that, as in this case, names the buyer, has been deemed by both state and federal courts to fall within the exception set out for specially manufactured goods. [Citations.]

It is inherent in the court's findings that the printed materials in the present case were specially manufactured goods. The materials were printed specifically for Caprilands. The materials included brochures and labels with the Caprilands name, as well as books that were written and designed by Simmons. The plaintiff testified that the books were printed, as Simmons had requested, in a rustic style with typed inserts and hand-drawn pictures. Therefore, none of these materials was suitable for sale to others. It is undisputed that, at the time of breach of the alleged contract, goods printed for Simmons already had been produced.

We conclude that, in light of the nature of the goods at issue* * *this case falls within the exception for specially manufactured goods. To be enforceable, the agreement for their production was, therefore, not required to be in writing under § 2–201 (3) (a). Accordingly, we affirm the judgment of the court* * *. [Citations.]

CASE
10-6

The New York Statute of Frauds provides that the Statute of Frauds may be satisfied by a "note or memorandum" of the contract that is signed by the party against whom enforcement of the contract is sought. The following case answers several significant questions about what the note of memorandum must contain and whether it may be "pieced together" from several different documents.

CRABTREE V. ELIZABETH ARDEN SALES CORP.

Court of Appeals of New York, 1953
305 N.Y. 48

FULD, Judge. In September of 1947, Nate Crabtree entered into preliminary negotiations with Elizabeth Arden Sales Corporation, manufacturers and sellers of cosmetics, looking toward his employment as sales manager. Interviewed on September 26th, by Robert P. Johns, executive vice-president and general manager of the corporation, who had apprised him of the possible opening, Crabtree requested a three-year contract at $25,000 a year. Explaining that he would be giving up a secure well-paying job to take a position in an entirely new field of endeavor—which he believed would take him some years to master—he insisted upon an agreement for a definite term. And he repeated his desire for a contract for three years to Miss Elizabeth Arden, the corporation's president. When Miss Arden finally indicated that she was prepared to offer a two-year contract, based on an annual salary of $20,000 for the first six months, $25,000 for the second six months and $30,000 for the second year, plus expenses of $5,000 a year for each of those years, Crabtree replied that that offer was "interesting." Miss Arden thereupon had her personal secretary make this memorandum on a telephone order blank that happened to be at hand:

"EMPLOYMENT AGREEMENT WITH
NATE CRABTREE Date Sept 26-1947
At 681 - 5th Ave 6:PM
* * *

Begin $20,000.
6 months $25,000.
6 months $30,000.
$5,000. - per year
Expense money
2 years to make good

Arrangement with Mr. Crabtree
By Miss Arden
Present Miss Arden
Mr. John
Mr. Crabtree
Miss OLeary"

A few days later, Crabtree 'phoned Mr. Johns and telegraphed Miss Arden; he accepted the "invitation to join the Arden organization," and Miss Arden wired back her "welcome." When he reported for work, a "payroll change" card was made up and initialed by Mr. Johns, and then forwarded to the payroll department. Reciting that it was prepared on September 30, 1947, and was to be effective as of October 22d, it specified the names of the parties, Crabtree's "Job Classification" and, in addition, contained the notation that "This employee is to be paid as follows:

"First six months of employment $20,000. per annum Next six months of employment 25,000. per annum After one year of employment 30,000. per annum Approved by RPJ [initialed]"

After six months of employment, Crabtree received the scheduled increase from $20,000 to $25,000, but the further specified increase at the end of the year was not paid. Both Mr. Johns and the comptroller of the corporation, Mr. Carstens, told Crabtree that they would attempt to straighten out the matter with Miss Arden, and, with that in mind, the comptroller prepared another "payroll change" card, to which his signature is appended, noting that there was to be a "Salary increase" from $25,000 to $30,000 a year, "per contractual arrangements with Miss Arden." The latter, however, refused to approve the increase and, after further fruitless discussion, plaintiff left defendant's employ and commenced this action for breach of contract.

At the ensuing trial, defendant denied the existence of any agreement to employ plaintiff for two years, and further contended that, even if one had been made, the statute of frauds barred its enforcement. The trial court found against defendant on both issues and awarded plaintiff damages of about $14,000, and the Appellate Division, two justices dissenting, affirmed. Since the contract relied upon was not to be performed within a year, the primary question for decision is whether there was a memorandum of its terms, subscribed by defendant, to satisfy the statute of frauds....

Each of the two payroll cards—the one initialed by defendant's general manager, the other signed by its comptroller—unquestionably constitutes a memorandum under the statute. That they were not prepared or signed with the intention of evidencing the contract, or that they came into existence subsequent to its execution, is of no consequence...; it is enough, to meet the statute's demands, that they were signed with intent to authenticate the information contained therein and that such information does evidence the terms of the contract. Those two writings contain all of the essential terms of the contract—the parties to it, the position that plaintiff was to assume, the salary that he was to receive—except that relating to the duration of plaintiff's employment. Accordingly, we must consider whether that item, the length of the contract, may be supplied by reference to the earlier unsigned office memorandum, and, if so, whether its notation, "2 years to make good," sufficiently designates a period of employment.

The statute of frauds does not require the "memorandum to be in one document. It may be pieced together out of separate writings, connected with one another either expressly or by the internal evidence of subject matter and occasion." Where each

of the separate writings has been subscribed by the party to be charged, little if any difficulty is encountered. Where, however, some writings have been signed, and others have not—as in the case before us—there is basic disagreement as to what constitutes a sufficient connection permitting the unsigned papers to be considered as part of the statutory memorandum. The courts of some jurisdictions insist that there be a reference, of varying degrees of specificity, in the signed writing to that unsigned, and, if there is no such reference, they refuse to permit consideration of the latter in determining whether the memorandum satisfies the statute. That conclusion is based upon a construction of the statute which requires that the connection between the writings and defendant's acknowledgment of the one not subscribed, appear from examination of the papers alone, without the aid of parol evidence. The other position—which has gained increasing support over the years— is that a sufficient connection between the papers is established simply by a reference in them to the same subject matter or transaction. The statute is not pressed "to the extreme of a literal and rigid logic"... and oral testimony is admitted to show the connection between the documents and to establish the acquiescence, of the party to be charged, to the contents of the one unsigned.

The view last expressed impresses us as the more sound, and we now definitively adopt it, permitting the signed and unsigned writings to be read together, provided that they clearly refer to the same subject matter or transaction.

The language of the statute—"Every agreement... is void, unless... some note or memorandum thereof be in writing, and subscribed by the party to be charged," does not impose the requirement that the signed acknowledgment of the contract must appear from the writings alone, unaided by oral testimony. The danger of fraud and perjury, generally attendant upon the admission of parol evidence, is at a minimum in a case such as this. None of the terms of the contract are supplied by parol. All of them must be set out in the various writings presented to the court, and at least one writing, the one establishing a contractual relationship between the parties, must bear the signature of the party to be charged, while the unsigned document must on its face refer to the same transaction as that set forth in the one that was signed. Parol evidence to portray the circumstances surrounding the making of the memorandum—serves only to connect the separate documents and to show that there was assent, by the party to be charged, to the contents of the one unsigned. If that testimony does not convincingly connect the papers, or does not show assent to the unsigned paper, it is within the province of the judge to conclude, as a matter of law, that the statute has not been satisfied. True, the possibility still remains that, by fraud or perjury, an agreement never in fact made may occasionally be enforced under the subject matter or transaction test. It is better to run that risk, though, than to deny enforcement to all agreements, merely because the signed document made no specific mention of the unsigned writing. As the United States Supreme Court declared, in sanctioning the admission of parol evidence to establish the connection between the signed and unsigned writings. "There may be cases in which it would be a violation of reason and common sense to ignore a reference which derives its significance from such [parol] proof. If there is ground for any doubt in the matter, the general rule should be enforced. But where there is no ground for doubt, its enforcement would aid, instead of discouraging, fraud."...

Turning to the writings in the case before us—the unsigned office memo, the payroll change form initialed by the general manager Johns, and the paper signed by the comptroller Carstens—it is apparent, and most patently, that all three refer on their face to the same transaction. The parties, the position to be filled by plaintiff, the salary to be paid him, are all identically set forth; it is hardly possible that such detailed information could refer to another or a different agreement. Even more, the card signed by Carstens notes that it was prepared for the purpose of a "Salary increase per contractual arrangements with Miss Arden." That certainly constitutes a reference of sorts to a more comprehensive "arrangement," and parol is permissible to furnish the explanation.

The corroborative evidence of defendant's assent to the contents of the unsigned office memorandum is also convincing. Prepared by defendant's agent, Miss Arden's personal secretary, there is little likelihood that that paper was fraudulently manufactured or that defendant had not assented to its contents. Furthermore, the evidence as to the conduct of the parties at the time it was prepared persuasively demonstrates defendant's assent to its terms. Under such circumstances, the courts below were fully justified in finding that the three papers constituted the "memorandum" of their agreement within the meaning of the statute.

Nor can there be any doubt that the memorandum contains all of the essential terms of the contract. Only one term, the length of the employment, is in dispute. The September 26th office memorandum contains the notation, "2 years to make good". What purpose, other than to denote the length of the contract term, such a notation could have, is hard to imagine. Without it, the employment would be at will... and its inclusion may not be treated as meaningless or purposeless. Quite obviously, as the courts below decided, the phrase signifies that the parties agreed to a term, a certain and definite term, of two years, after which, if plaintiff did not "make good", he would

be subject to discharge. And examination of other parts of the memorandum supports that construction. Throughout the writings, a scale of wages, increasing plaintiff's salary periodically, is set out; that type of arrangement is hardly consistent with the hypothesis that the employment was meant to be at will. The most that may be argued from defendant's standpoint is that "2 years to make good", is a cryptic and ambiguous statement. But, in such a case, parol evidence is admissible to explain its meaning. Having in mind the relations of the parties, the course of the negotiations and plaintiff's insistence upon security of employment, the purpose of the phrase - or so the trier of the facts was warranted in finding - was to grant plaintiff the tenure he desired.secretary, there is little likelihood that that paper was fraudulently manufactured or that defendant had not assented to its contents. Furthermore, the evidence as to the conduct of the parties at the time it was prepared persuasively demonstrates defendant's assent to its terms. Under such circumstances, the courts below were fully justified in finding that the three papers constituted the "memorandum" of their agreement within the meaning of the statute.

Nor can there be any doubt that the memorandum contains all of the essential terms of the contract. Only one term, the length of the employment, is in dispute. The September 26th office memorandum contains the notation, "2 years to make good." What purpose, other than to denote the length of the contract term, such a notation could have, is hard to imagine. Without it, the employment would be at will... and its inclusion may not be treated as meaningless or purposeless. Quite obviously, as the courts below decided, the phrase signifies that the parties agreed to a term, a certain and definite term, of two years, after which, if plaintiff did not "make good", he would be subject to discharge. And examination of other parts of the memorandum supports that construction. Throughout the writings, a scale of wages, increasing plaintiff's salary periodically, is set out; that type of arrangement is hardly consistent with the hypothesis that the employment was meant to be at will. The most that may be argued from defendant's standpoint is that "2 years to make good", is a cryptic and ambiguous statement. But, in such a case, parol evidence is admissible to explain its meaning. Having in mind the relations of the parties, the course of the negotiations and plaintiff's insistence upon security of employment, the purpose of the phrase - or so the trier of the facts was warranted in finding - was to grant plaintiff the tenure he desired.

CASE

10-7

An Oregon court addresses the admissibility of evidence of an oral agreement between two parties to a disputed contract.

LEITZ v. THORSON

Court of Appeals of Oregon, 1992
113 Or.App. 557, 833 P.2d 343, review denied, 314 Or. 573, 840 P.2d 1295

Edmonds, J.

Defendant appeals from a judgment for breach of contract and fraud.* * *We affirm.

Plaintiffs leased commercial space from defendant to open a florist shop. After the lease was executed, plaintiffs learned that they could not place another freestanding sign along the highway to advertise the business, because the Deschutes County Code allows only one freestanding sign on the property. A freestanding sign advertising a business owned in part by defendant was already in place. Plaintiffs filed this action and alleged that defendant had breached the lease by failing to provide them with space in the complex for which a freestanding sign could be erected. Paragraph 16 of the lease provides, in part: "Tenant shall not erect or install any signs or advertising media or door lettering or placards visible from outside the leased premises with out [sic] the previous written consent of the Landlord."

During trial, plaintiffs sought to introduce evidence that, before the lease was executed, defendant told them that they could have a freestanding sign. Defendant objected to the testimony on the basis that proving the alleged oral agreement would violate the Parol Evidence Rule. [Citation.] The court admitted the testimony.

Defendant argues that the trial court erred by holding that the Parol Evidence Rule does not bar plaintiffs' testimony that defendant had orally agreed that they could have a freestanding sign.* * *The rule is a rule of integration. It prohibits oral evidence of those aspects of the bargain that the parties intended to memorialize in the writing. [Citation.] If the parties did not intend the writing to represent their entire agreement, the agreement is only partially integrated, and prior consistent additional terms not evidenced by the writing may still form part of the entire agreement. [Citation.] An oral agreement is not integrated in a contemporaneous writing if it is not inconsistent with the written agreement and is "such an agreement as might naturally be made as a separate agreement by parties situated as were parties to the written contract." [Citation.]

Our review is to determine whether the trial court's conclusion that the lease is not a fully integrated agreement is supported by the evidence. [Citation.] We start with a presumption that

the writing is intended to be a complete integration. [Citation.] The integration clause in this lease is an indication that the lease was intended to be a complete integration, but it is not conclusive. [Citation.] Oral admissions of a party may be probative of whether the agreement is integrated. [Citation.]

Defendant testified that the written form that he had used for the lease was not drafted to be used specifically for this property. Although the lease required attachment of exhibits, he admitted that no exhibits were attached to the lease. He conceded that he told plaintiffs that they could have a sign and that he did not require his written consent, despite the words in paragraph 16 of the lease. He admitted that, during the lease negotiations, the parties had discussed plaintiffs' renovations. He said that he did not require those plans to be in writing, even though the lease required his written consent before alterations, additions or installations on the premises. Defendant also testified: "Usually our detail comes later, after they've, you know, gotten their lease signed, and they're—they get it figured out, and they measure and come up with information on saying: well, this is what we're going to do."

There was evidence to support the trial court's conclusion that the parties did not intend the written lease to reflect their entire agreement, thereby overcoming the presumption of integration.

The next question is whether a separate oral agreement to allow a freestanding sign was inconsistent with the written lease. Although defendant admitted that he told plaintiffs they could have a sign, he disputes whether he told them that the sign could be "freestanding." No provision of the lease prohibits a freestanding sign. The disputed parol evidence was not inconsistent with the written agreement.

* * *

There is evidence to support the trial court's finding that the parties did not intend the written lease to be their complete agreement, that the oral agreement is not inconsistent with the written agreement and that the oral agreement would have been made naturally as a separate agreement. The trial court did not err.

Affirmed.

QUESTIONS

1. Identify and discuss the five types of general contracts covered by the statute of frauds and the contracts covered by the UCC statute of frauds' provisions.
2. Describe the writing that is required to satisfy the statute of frauds under general contract law and the UCC.
3. Identify and discuss the other methods of complying with the statute of frauds under general contract law and the UCC.
4. Explain the parol evidence rule and identify the situations to which the rule does not apply.
5. Discuss the rule that aids in the interpretation of a contract.

PROBLEMS

1. A, an adult college student, went to Brentwood Department store to buy clothes. He selected two new suits and a coat for $950 and asked to open up a charge account. The credit manager was willing to open account but was concerned about payment. A told the credit manager to call F, his father. On the telephone, F told the credit manager. "Go ahead, open the account for him. It will teach him to stand on his own feet if he has to pay his own bills. But don't worry, if A doesn't pay you, I will." The clothes were given to A and billed to A. A failed to pay. The store sues F who pleads the Statute of Frauds as a defense. Judgment for whom? Explain.

2. Assume in the previous question that the credit manager refused to open the account for A, that he called F on the telephone, and F said. "I have an account with your store, give A the clothes and charge them to my account." The clothes were given to A. Is F liable for payment if he pleads the Statute of Frauds as a defense? Explain.

3. B was the owner of Lot No. 1 on which he had built his home. S owned the adjoining Lots No. 2 and 3, which were undeveloped, along with Lot No. 4 on which S's home was located. B wished to acquire Lot No. 2 in order to protect his home site from crowding if Lot No. 2 should be sold to a stranger.

Meeting S on the street on January 2, B explained his wish to acquire Lot No. 2 and offered to buy it from S for $75,000 cash. S agreed and promised to deliver a deed to Lot No. 2 in 4 weeks. B paid S $1,000 as a deposit or down payment towards the purchase price of $75,000.

On February 1, S told B that he had changed his mind. B demands that S perform the contract. S contends that if there is any contract, it is unenforceable.

(a) Was there an offer and acceptance sufficient to constitute a contract between S and B? Explain.

(b) In an action by B against S for breach of contract, judgment for whom? Explain.

(c) Assume that on January 10, B sent to S his check for $1,000 bearing the notation "On account of purchase price of Lot No. 2" and that S cashed the check, but later refused to convey Lot No. 2. Would B's payment constitute sufficient part performance to enable B to enforce the contract against 5? Explain.

(d) If the contract is not enforceable, may B recover his $1,000? Explain.

(e) Assume that in addition to the payment, B, with S's knowledge and consent, entered on Lot No. 2 and had it cleared of brush on January 20 at a cost of $150, but S still refused to convey. Would B be entitled to obtain a decree of specific performance to compel S to deliver a deed to Lot. No. 2 to B upon paying to S the balance of $74,000? Explain.

(f) Would B be entitled to recover his $1,000 payment plus the $150 cost of clearing the land? Explain.

(g) Assume that on March 1. B instituted a suit for specific performance and that S denied he had agreed to sell. At the trial, the court decided that B was telling the truth. and ordered S to execute and deliver to B a deed to Lot. No. 2 upon B paying the balance of $74,000.

Is S entitled to have the decision reversed on appeal, if on the appeal S raises for the first time the defense that his agreement was not in a writing signed by the party to be charged? Explain.

4. Assume that in the preceding problem S had sent to B a receipt for the $1,000 reading as follows: "January 11. Received from B $1,000 on account of $75,000 purchase price of Lot No. 2 at 27 Y Street. Albans, NY Closing in 4 weeks. (Signed) S."

(a) Would B be entitled to a decree of specific performance against S? Explain.

(b) Assume that S is willing to perform, but that B refuses. Would S be entitled to damages against B? Explain.

5. On September 15, L agreed orally with T to lease a Store to T in Manhattan at $5,000 per month for one year starting the following January 1.

(a) Is the oral agreement enforceable? Explain.

Assume that the oral lease was for three years, that T moved in on January 1, and paid the monthly rent for six months, and that L then notified T to vacate.

(b) Is the oral agreement enforceable by T for the balance of the three-year term? Explain.

(c) Is the oral agreement enforceable by T for an additional six months? Explain.

6. Moriarity and Holmes enter into an oral contract by which Moriarity promises to sell and Holmes promises to buy Blackacre for $10,000. Moriarity repudiates the contract by writing a letter to Holmes in which she states accurately the terms of the bargain, but adds, "our agreement was oral. It, therefore, is not binding upon me, and I shall not carry it out. (signed) Moriarty." Thereafter, Holmes sues Moriarity for specific performance of the contract. Moriarity interposes the defense of the Statute of Frauds, arguing that the contract is within the Statute and, hence, unenforceable. Decision?

7. On December 15, L, a landlord, entered into an oral agreement with T to lease apartment 5W to T for one year starting on January 1, at a rental of $1,000 per month. On the same day L hired J as superintendent of the building for a period of one year starting January 1 at a salary of $3,000 per month. On December 20, L changed his mind and notified T and J that he would not rent to T or employ J.

(a) In an action by T against L, judgment for whom if L pleads the

Statute of Frauds as a defense? Explain.

(b) In an action by J against L. judgment for whom if L pleads the Statute of Frauds as a defense? Explain.

8. (a) On December 5, A entered into an oral agreement with C to perform certain advisory services for C for a fee of $15,000 per month. The services were to commence on the following February 15, and to end on December 15. Is the agreement enforceable? Explain.

(b) Also on December 5, A entered into an oral agreement with F for F to do some remodeling and rewiring of A's offices. The agreement provided that F was to be paid $20,000 and was to complete all work no later than the following February 15. Is the agreement enforceable? Explain.

9. B. wishing to start her own business, borrowed $15,000 from L. B orally agreed to repay the loan in two years. B refused to pay when the loan became due. L sued B for breach of contract. B asserts the oral contract is unenforceable according to the Statute of Frauds. Judgment for whom? Explain.

10. S and B entered into an oral agreement under which S agreed to sell to B 8 used air-conditioners at $200 each, delivery at B's place of business ten days later; payment C.O.D. B refused to complete the purchase.

(a) In a suit by S against B for damages, would S be entitled to judgment if B did not plead the Statute of Frauds as a defense? Explain.

Assume that in an action by S against B for damages, B pleaded the Statute of Frauds as a defense. Would S be entitled to judgment, if he can prove:

(b) that B made a down payment of $200? Explain.

(c) that B took 4 air-conditioners at the time the agreement was made? Explain.

11. During the examination of the financial statements of the W Watch Company, the following problem was discovered. On January 16, C, one of W's salesmen, called upon P, the vice president of purchasing for X Department Stores. He showed P the new line of plastic watches with large, bright-colored faces. P ordered 150 watches from $5 to $20 each at a total cost of $1,475.

Delivery was to be made not later than March 15. C wrote the orders in his order book as P orally indicated the quantity of each watch he desired. Neither party signed anything.

C promptly submitted the X Department Stores' order to the sales department of W Watch Company. The next day the order was recorded and a memorandum was sent to X Department Stores, in care of P. The memorandum described the transaction. indicated the number and prices of the watches purchased and was signed by S.A. Williams, vice president of marketing. However, the total price and delivery terms were erroneously omitted.

P received the memo on January 20. He read it and placed it in his goods-on-order file.

On February 20, the market for plastic watches collapsed. P promptly notified W Watch Company by phone that X Department Stores was not interested in the plastic watches and would refuse delivery. W Watch Company Store sued X Department Stores to recover damages for breach of contract. X Department Stores contends (1) there is no contract and (2) if there was a contract it is unenforceable under the Statute of Frauds. Will W Watch Company prevail in its action against X Department Stores? Explain.

12. On May 1, S and B, two college professors, entered into an oral contract under which S agreed to sell his computer to B for $1,300, with delivery and payment on May 15. On May 2, S sent B a signed letter confirming all the terms of their oral contract. B received S's letter on May 3 but never responded. On May 15, S tendered delivery of the computer to B, but B refused to accept or pay for it, stating that he had changed his mind and did not need S's computer. S sues B for breach of contract. B pleads the Statute of Frauds as a defense.

(a) Judgment for whom? Explain.

(b) If S and B were merchants who sold computers, judgment for whom? Explain.

13. Ames, Bell, Cain, and Dole each orally ordered color television sets from Marvel Electronics Company, which accepted the orders. Ames's set was to be specially designed and encased in an ebony cabinet. Bell, Cain, and Dole ordered standard sets described as "Alpha Omega Theatre." The price of Ames's set was $1,800, and the sets ordered by Bell, Cain, and Dole were $700 each. Bell paid the company seventy-five dollars to apply on his purchase; Ames, Cain, and Dole paid nothing.

The next day, Marvel sent Ames, Bell, Cain, and Dole written confirmations captioned "Purchase Memorandum," numbered 12345, 12346, 12347, and 12348, respectively, containing the essential terms of the oral agreements. Each memorandum was sent in duplicate with the request that one copy be signed and returned to the company. None of the four purchasers returned a signed copy.

Ames promptly sent the company a repudiation of the oral contract, which it received before beginning manufacture of the set for Ames or making commitments to carry out the contract.

Cain sent the company a letter reading in part, "Referring to your Contract No. 12347, please be advised I have canceled this contract. Yours truly, (Signed) Cain."

The four television sets were duly tendered by Marvel to Ames, Bell, Cain, and Dole, all of whom refused to accept delivery. Marvel brings four separate actions against Ames, Bell, Cain, and Dole for breach of contract. Decide each claim.

14. Yokel, a grower of soybeans, had sold soybeans to Campbell Grain and Seed Company and other grain companies in the past. Campbell entered into an oral contract with Yokel to purchase soybeans from him. Promptly after entering into the oral contract, Campbell signed and mailed to Yokel a written confirmation of the oral agreement. Yokel received the written confirmation but neither signed it nor objected to its content. Campbell now brings this action against Yokel for breach of contract upon Yokel's failure to deliver the soybeans. The trial court ruled in favor of the defendant, Yokel, on the ground that the defendant is not a "merchant" within the meaning of the Code. Decision?

15. Grant leased an apartment to Epstein for the term May 1, 1990 to April 30, 1991 at $550 a month "payable in advance on the first day of each and every month of said term." At the time the lease was signed, Epstein told Grant that he received his salary on the tenth of the month and that he would be unable to pay the rent before that date each month. Grant replied that would be satisfactory. On June 2, due to Epstein's not having paid the June rent, Grant sued Epstein for such rent. At the trial, Epstein offered to prove the oral agreement as to the date of payment each month. Decision?

16. Amos orally agrees to hire Elizabeth for an eight-month trial period. Elizabeth performs the job magnificently, and after several weeks Amos orally offers Elizabeth a six-month extension at a salary increase of 20 percent. Elizabeth accepts the offer. At the end of the eight-month trial period, Amos discharges Elizabeth, who brings suit against Amos for breach of contract. Is Amos liable? Why?

17. Green was the owner of a large department store. On Wednesday, January 26, he talked to Smith and said, "I will hire you as sales manager in my store for one year at a salary of $28,000; you are to begin work next Monday." Smith accepted and started work on Monday, January 31. At the end of three months, Green discharged Smith. On May 15, Smith brings an action against Green to recover the unpaid portion of the $28,000 salary. Is Smith's employment contract enforceable?

18. Clay orally promises Trent to sell him five crops of potatoes to be grown on Blackacre, a farm in Minnesota, and Trent promises to pay a stated price for them on delivery. Is the contract enforceable?

19. Dean was hired on February 12 as a sales manager of the Co-op Dairy for a minimum period of one year with the dairy agreeing to pay his moving expenses. By February 26, Dean had signed a lease, moved his family from Oklahoma to Arizona, and reported for work. After he worked for a few days, he was fired. Dean then brought this action against the dairy for his salary for the year, less what he was paid. The dairy argues that the statute of frauds bars enforcement of the oral contract because the contract was not to be performed within one year. Is the dairy correct in its assertion?

20. Alice solicited an offer from Robett Manufacturing Company to manufacture certain clothing that Alice intended to supply to the government. Alice contends that in a telephone conversation Robett made an oral offer that she immediately accepted. She then received the following letter from Robett, which, she claims, confirmed their agreement:

> Confirming our telephone conversation, we are pleased to offer the 3,500 shirts at $4.00 each and the trousers at $3.80 each with delivery approximately ninety days after receipt of order. We will try to cut this to sixty days if at all possible.
>
> This, of course, as quoted f.o.b. Atlanta and the order will not be subject to cancellation, domestic pack only.
>
> Thanking you for the opportunity to offer these garments, we are
>
> Very truly yours,
> ROBETT MANUFACTURING CO., INC.

Is the agreement enforceable?

21. When Mr. McClam died, he left the family farm, heavily mortgaged, to his wife and children. To save the farm from foreclosure, Mrs. McClam planned to use insurance proceeds and her savings to pay off the debts. She was unwilling to do so, however, unless she had full ownership of the property. Mrs. McClam wrote her daughter, stating that the daughter should deed over her interest in the family farm to her mother and promising that all the children would inherit the farm equally upon their mother's death. The letter further explained that if foreclosure occurred, each child would receive very little, but if they complied with their mother's plan, each would eventually receive a valuable property interest upon her death. Finally, the letter stated that all the other children had agreed to this plan. Consequently, the daughter also agreed. Years later, Mrs. McClam tries to convey the farm to her son Donald. The daughter challenges, arguing that the mother is contractually bound to convey the land equally to all of the children. Donald says this was an oral agreement to sell land and is unenforceable. The daughter argues that the letter satisfies the statute of frauds, making the contract enforceable. Who gets the farm? Explain.

26. On July 5, 1994, Richard Price signed a written employment contract as a new salesman with the Mercury Supply Company. The contract was of indefinite duration and could be terminated by either party for any reason upon fifteen days' notice. Between 1994 and 2002, Price was promoted several times. In 1999, Price was made vice president of sales. In September 2002, however, Price was told that his performance was not satisfactory and that if he did not improve he would be fired. In February 2005, Price received notice of termination. Price claims that in 1999 he entered into a valid oral employment contract with Mercury Supply Company wherein he was made vice president of sales for life or until he should retire. Is the alleged oral contract barred by the one-year provision of the statute of frauds?

http: **Internet Exercise** Search the Internet for information on why it is advantageous to have a written contract.

Consideration

Consideration is the primary—but not the only—basis for the enforcement of promises in our legal system. Consideration is the inducement to make a promise enforceable. The doctrine of consideration ensures that promises are enforced only where the parties have exchanged something of value in the eye of the law. Gratuitous (gift) promises, accordingly, are legally enforceable only under certain circumstances, which are discussed later in the chapter.

Consideration, or that which is exchanged for a promise, is present only when the parties intend an exchange. The consideration exchanged for the promise may be an act, a forbearance to act, or a promise to do either of these. In like manner, Section 71 of the Restatement defines consideration for a promise as (a) an act other than a promise, (b) a forbearance, (c) the creation, modification, or destruction of a legal relation, or (d) a return promise if any of these are bargained for and given in exchange for the promise.

Thus, consideration comprises two basic elements: (1) legal sufficiency (something of value) and (2) bargained-for exchange. Both must be present to satisfy the requirement of consideration. The consideration may be given to the promisor or to some other person; likewise, it may be given by the promisee or by some other person.

LEGAL SUFFICIENCY

To be legally sufficient, the consideration exchanged for the promise must be either a legal detriment to the promisee *or* a legal benefit to the promisor. In other words, in return for the promise the promisee must give up something of legal value or the promisor must receive something of legal value.

Legal detriment means (1) doing (or undertaking to do) that which the promisee was under no prior legal obligation to do or (2) refraining from doing (or the undertaking to refrain from doing) that which he was previously under no legal obligation to refrain from doing. On the other hand, **legal benefit** means the obtaining by the promisor of that which he had no prior legal right to obtain. Most, if not all, cases involving legal detriment to the promisee also will involve a legal benefit to the promisor. Nonetheless, the presence of **either** is sufficient.

❧ See Case 11-1

Adequacy

Legal sufficiency has nothing to do with adequacy of consideration. Restatement, Section 79. The subject matter that the parties agree to exchange does not need to have the same or equal value; rather, the law will regard consideration as adequate if the parties have freely agreed to the exchange. The requirement of legally sufficient consideration is, therefore, not at all concerned with whether the bargain was good or bad, or whether one party received disproportionately more or less than what he gave or promised in exchange. Such facts, however, may be relevant to the availability of certain defenses (such as fraud, duress, or undue influence) or certain remedies (such as specific performance). The requirement of legally sufficient consideration is simply (1) that the parties have agreed to an exchange and (2) that, with respect to each party, the subject matter exchanged, or promised in exchange, either imposed a legal detriment upon the promisee or conferred a legal benefit upon the promisor. If the purported consideration is clearly without value, however, such that the transaction is a sham, many courts would hold that consideration is lacking.

Unilateral Contracts

In a unilateral contract, a promise is exchanged for a completed act or a forbearance to act. Because only one promise exists, only one party, the **offeror**, makes a promise and is therefore the **promisor** while the other party, the **offeree**, is the person receiving the promise and thus is the **promisee**. For example, A promises to pay B $2,000 if B paints A's house. B paints A's house.

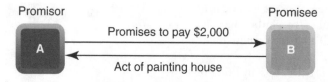

For A's promise to be binding, it must be supported by consideration consisting of either a legal detriment to B, the promisee (offeree), or a legal benefit to A, the promisor (offeror). B's having painted the house is a legal detriment to B, the promisee, because she was under no prior legal duty to paint A's house. Also, B's painting A's house is a legal benefit to A, the promisor, because A had no prior legal right to have his house painted by B.

A unilateral contract may also consist of a promise exchanged for a forbearance. To illustrate, A negligently injures B, for which B may recover damages in a tort action. A promises to pay B $5,000 if B forbears from bringing suit. B accepts by not filing suit.

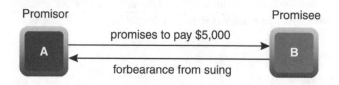

A's promise to pay B $5,000 is binding because it is supported by consideration: B, the promisee (offeree), has incurred a legal detriment by refraining from bringing suit, which he was under no prior legal obligation to refrain from doing. A, the promisor

(offeror), has received a legal benefit because she had no prior legal right to B's forbearance from bringing suit.

Bilateral Contracts

In a bilateral contract, the parties exchange promises. Thus, each party is *both* a promisor and a promisee. For example, if A (the offeror) promises (offers) to purchase an automobile from B (the offeree) for $15,000 and B promises to sell the automobile to A for $15,000 (accepts the offer), the following relationship exists:

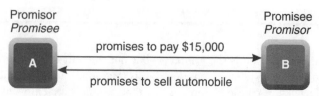

A's promise (the offer) to pay B $15,000 is binding and therefore enforceable by B, if that promise is supported by legal consideration from B (offeree), which may consist of either a legal detriment to B, the promisee, or a legal benefit to A, the promisor. B's promise to sell A the automobile is a legal detriment to B because he was under no prior legal duty to sell the automobile to A. Moreover, B's promise is also a legal benefit to A because A had no prior legal right to that automobile. Consequently, A's promise to pay $15,000 to B is supported by consideration and is enforceable.

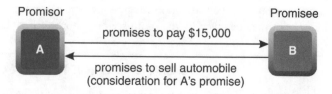

For **B's promise** (the acceptance) to sell the automobile to A to be binding, it likewise must be supported by consideration from A (offeror), which may be either a legal detriment to A, the promisee, or a legal benefit to B, the promisor. A's promise to pay B $15,000 is a legal detriment to A because he was under no prior legal duty to pay $15,000 to B. At the same time, A's promise is also a legal benefit to B because B had no prior legal right to the $15,000. Thus, B's promise to sell the automobile is supported by consideration and is enforceable.

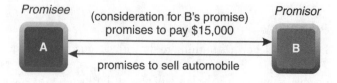

To summarize, for A's promise to B to be binding, B must support the promise with legally sufficient consideration, which requires that the promise A receives in exchange from B provide either a legal benefit to A (the promisor) or a legal detriment to B (the promisee). A, in turn, must support B's return promise with consideration for that promise to be binding on B.

Thus, in a bilateral contract each promise is the consideration for the other, a relationship that has been referred to as **mutuality of obligation**. A general consequence of mutuality of obligation is that each promisor in a bilateral contract must be bound, or neither is bound.

◆ SEE CASE 11-3

◆ SEE FIGURE 11-1 **Consideration in Unilateral and Bilateral Contracts**

Illusory Promises

Words of promise that make the performance of the purported promisor entirely optional constitute no promise at all. Consequently, they cannot serve as consideration. In this section, such illusory promises will be distinguished from promises that impose obligations of performance upon the promisor and thus can be legally sufficient consideration.

An **illusory promise** is a statement that is in the form of a promise but imposes no obligation upon the maker of the statement. An illusory promise is not consideration for a return promise. Thus, a statement committing the promisor to purchase such quantity of goods as she may "desire," "want," or "wish to buy" is an illusory promise because its performance is entirely optional. For example, if Ames, Inc., agrees to sell to Barnes Co. as many barrels of oil as Barnes shall choose at $40 per barrel, there would be no consideration: Barnes may wish or desire to buy none of the oil, yet in buying none it would fulfill its promise. An agreement containing such a promise as that made by Barnes, although accepted by both parties, does not create a contract because the promise is illusory—performance by Barnes is entirely optional, and the offer places no constraint upon its freedom. Barnes is not bound to do anything, nor can

Ames reasonably expect to receive any performance. Thus, Barnes, by its promise, suffers no legal detriment and confers no legal benefit. Consequently, Barnes's promise does not provide legally sufficient consideration for Ames's promise; thus, Ames's promise is not binding upon Ames.

Many courts have transformed otherwise illusory promises into actual promises by implying an obligation of good faith or fair dealing. Under this approach, courts have held to be nonillusory a promise "to spend such time as he personally sees fit in developing" a business and a clause "specifying that leases 'satisfactory' to plaintiff must be secured before he would be bound to perform."

Output and Requirements Contracts A seller's agreement to sell her entire production to a particular purchaser is called an **output contract**. It affords the seller an ensured market for her product. Conversely, a **requirements contract**, or a purchaser's agreement to buy from a particular seller all the materials of a particular kind he needs, ensures the buyer of a ready source of inventory or supplies. These contracts may or may not be accompanied by an estimate of the quantity to be sold or to be purchased. Nevertheless, these promises are not illusory. The buyer under a requirements contract does not promise to buy as much as she desires to buy but, rather, to buy as much as she *needs*. Similarly, under an output contract the seller promises to sell to the buyer the seller's entire production, not merely as much as the seller desires.

Furthermore, the Code, Section 2–306(1), imposes a good faith limitation upon the quantity to be sold or purchased under an output or requirements contract. Thus, a contract of this type involves such actual output or requirements as may occur in good faith, except that no quantity unreasonably disproportionate to any stated estimate or, in the absence of a stated estimate, to any normal prior output or requirements may be tendered or demanded. Therefore, after contracting to sell to Adler, Inc., its entire output, Benevito Company cannot increase its production from one eight-hour shift per day to three eight-hour shifts per day.

◆ FIGURE 11-1 **Consideration in Unilateral and Bilateral Contracts**

Type of Contract	Offer	Acceptance	Consideration
Unilateral	Promise by A	Performance of requested act or forbearance by B	*Promise* by A → ← *Performance* of requested act or forbearance by B
Bilateral	Promise by A	Return promise by B to perform requested act or forbearance	*Promise* by A → ← Return *promise* by B to perform requested act or forbearance

Exclusive Dealing Contracts   Where a manufacturer of goods grants an exclusive right to a distributor to sell its products in a designated territory, unless otherwise agreed, the manufacturer is under an implied obligation to use its best efforts to supply the goods, and the distributor must use his best efforts to promote their sale. UCC Section 2–306(2). The obligations that arise upon acceptance of an **exclusive dealing agreement** are sufficient consideration to bind both parties to the contract.

Conditional Promises   A conditional promise is a promise the performance of which depends upon the happening or nonhappening of an event not certain to occur (the condition). A conditional promise is sufficient consideration *unless* the promisor knows at the time of making the promise that the condition cannot occur. Restatement, Section 76.

Thus, if Debbie offers to pay John $8,000 for John's automobile, provided that Debbie receives such amount as an inheritance from the estate of her deceased uncle, and John accepts the offer, the duty of Debbie to pay $8,000 to John is *conditioned* upon her receiving $8,000 from her deceased uncle's estate. The consideration moving from John to Debbie is the promise to transfer title to the automobile. The consideration moving from Debbie to John is the promise of $8,000 subject to the condition.

Preexisting Obligation

The law does not regard the performance of, or the promise to perform, a preexisting legal duty, public or private, as either a legal detriment to the party under the prior legal obligation or a benefit to the other party. A **public duty** does not arise out of a contract; rather, it is imposed upon members of society by force of the common law or by statute. As illustrated in the law of torts, public duty includes the duty not to commit an assault, battery, false imprisonment, or defamation. The criminal law also imposes numerous public duties. Thus, if Cleon promises to pay Spike, the village ruffian, $100 not to abuse him physically, Cleon's promise is unenforceable because both tort and criminal law impose on Spike a preexisting public obligation to refrain from so acting.

By virtue of their public office, public officials, such as the mayor of a city, members of a city council, police officers, and firefighters, are under a preexisting obligation to perform their duties.

The performance of, or the promise to perform, a **preexisting contractual duty**, a duty the terms of which are neither doubtful nor the subject of honest dispute, is also legally insufficient consideration because the doing of what one is legally bound to do is neither a detriment to the promisee nor a benefit to the promisor. For example, Leigh and Associates employs Jason for one year at a salary of $2,000 per month and at the end of six months promises Jason that, in addition to the salary, it will pay him $3,000 if he remains on the job for the remainder of the period originally agreed upon. Leigh's promise is not binding because Jason's promise does not constitute legally sufficient consideration. If Jason's duties were changed in nature or amount, however, Leigh's promise would be binding because Jason's new duties are a legal detriment.

◆ SEE CASE 11-3

Modification of a Preexisting Contract   A modification of a contract occurs when the parties to the contract mutually agree to change one or more of its terms. Under the common law, a modification of an existing contract must be supported by mutual consideration to be enforceable. In other words, the modification must be supported by some new consideration beyond that which is already owing (thus, there must be a separate and distinct modification contract). For example, Fred and Jodie agree that Fred shall put in a gravel driveway for Jodie at a cost of $2,000. Subsequently, Jodie agrees to pay an additional $1,000 if Fred will blacktop the driveway. Because Fred was not bound by the original contract to provide blacktopping, he would incur a legal detriment in doing so and is therefore entitled to the additional $1,000.

The Code has modified the common law rule for contract modification by providing that the parties can effectively modify a contract for the sale of goods without new consideration, though the Comments to this section make the modification subject to the requirement of good faith. Moreover, the Restatement has moved toward this position by providing that a modification of an executory contract is binding if it is fair and equitable in light of surrounding facts that the parties did not anticipate when the contract was made. Restatement, Section 89. A few States have followed the Code's rule by statutorily providing that the parties need provide no new consideration when modifying any contract. These states vary, however, as to whether the modification must be in writing and whether the original contract must be executory. In New York, for example, General Obligations Law § 5-1103 provides that a promise to modify a contract will be enforceable if the promise is made in a signed writing, even if there is no consideration for that promise. The rule does not require that the contract be fully executory.

Substituted Contracts   A substituted contract results when the parties to a contract mutually agree to rescind their original contract and enter into a new one. This situation involves separate contracts: the original contract, the agreement of rescission, and the substitute contract. Substituted contracts are perfectly valid, allowing the parties effectively to discharge the original contract and to impose obligations under the new one. The rescission is binding in that each party, by giving up his rights under the original contract, has provided consideration to the other, as long as each party still has rights under the original contract. Where the rescission and new agreement are simultaneous, the effect is the same as a contractual modification. The Restatement takes the position that the substitute contract is *not* binding unless it is fair and equitable in view of circumstances the parties did not anticipate when they made the original contract. Section 89, Comment b.

Settlement of a Liquidated Debt

A **liquidated debt** is an obligation the existence or amount of which is undisputed. Under the common law, the partial payment of a sum of money in consideration of a promise to discharge a fully matured, undisputed debt is legally *insufficient* to support the promise of discharge. To illustrate, assume that Pamela owes Julie $100, and in consideration of Pamela's paying Julie $50, Julie agrees to discharge the debt. In a subsequent suit by Julie against Pamela to recover the remaining $50, at common law Julie is entitled to judgment for $50 on the ground that Julie's promise of discharge is not binding because Pamela's payment of $50 was no legal detriment to the promisee, Pamela, as she was under a *preexisting legal obligation* to pay that much and more. Consequently, the consideration for Julie's promise of discharge was legally insufficient, and Julie is not bound on her promise. If, however, Julie had accepted from Pamela any new or different consideration, such as the sum of $40 and a fountain pen worth $10 or less, or even the fountain pen with no payment of money, in full satisfaction of the $100 debt, the consideration moving from Pamela would be legally sufficient inasmuch as Pamela was under no legal obligation to give a fountain pen to Julie. In this example, consideration would also exist if Julie had agreed to accept $50 *before* the debt became due, in full satisfaction of the debt. Pamela was under no legal obligation to pay any of the debt before its due date. Consequently, Pamela's early payment would represent a legal detriment to Pamela as well as a legal benefit to Julie. The law is not concerned with the amount of the discount, as that is simply a question of adequacy for the courts to decide. Likewise, Pamela's payment of a lesser amount on the due date at an agreed-upon different place of payment would be legally sufficient consideration. The Restatement requires that the new consideration "differs from what was required by the duty in a way which reflects more than a pretense of bargain." Section 73. Under New York law, General Obligations Law § 5-1103 may be used to enforce a promise to settle a liquidated debt in exchange for partial payment. Under GOL § 5-1103, the promise or agreement to discharge a debt is binding, even without consideration, if the promise or agreement is in writing and signed by the creditor. A signature endorsing a check offered in full payment of a liquidated debt is not sufficient to meet the requirements of this rule. There must be a separate signed writing to satisfy GOL § 5-1103.

Settlement of an Unliquidated Debt

An **unliquidated debt** is an obligation disputed as to either its existence or its amount. A promise to settle a validly disputed claim in exchange for an agreed payment or other performance is supported by consideration. Where the dispute is based upon contentions which are nonmeritorious or not made in good faith, however,

the debtor's surrender of such a claim is no legal detriment to the claimant. The Restatement adopts a different position by providing that the settlement of a claim that proves invalid is consideration if at the time of the settlement (1) the claimant honestly believed that the claim was valid or (2) the claim was in fact doubtful because of uncertainty as to the facts or the law. Section 74.

For example, where a person has requested professional services from an accountant or a lawyer and the parties reached no agreement with respect to the amount of the fee to be charged, the accountant or lawyer is entitled to receive from her client a reasonable fee for the services rendered. As no definite amount has been agreed upon, the client's obligation is uncertain; nevertheless, his legal obligation is to pay the reasonable worth of the services performed. When the accountant or lawyer sends the client a bill for services rendered, even though the amount stated in the bill is an estimate of the reasonable value of the services, the debt does not become undisputed until and unless the client agrees to pay the amount of the bill. If the client honestly disputes the amount that is owing and tenders in full settlement an amount less than the bill, acceptance of the lesser amount by the creditor discharges the debt. Thus, if Ted sends to Betty, an accountant, a check for $120 in payment of his debt to Betty for services rendered, which services Ted considered worthless but for which Betty billed Ted $600, Betty's acceptance of the check releases Ted from any further liability. Ted has given up his right to dispute the billing further, while Betty has forfeited her right to further collection. Thus, there is mutuality of consideration. An agreement to pay a certain amount to settle an unliquidated debt and the subsequent payment of that amount can be viewed as an accord and satisfaction. This concept is discussed in Chapter 12.

❧ SEE CASE 11-2

Under the common law rules, if a debtor sent a check that clearly indicated that it was offered in full satisfaction of an unliquidated debt, the creditor's acceptance of the check resulted in an accord and satisfaction (see Chapter 12) that discharged the debt. Thus even if the creditor endorsed the check with language indicating that he did not intend to accept the check as full payment, the debtor had no further liability.

However, in Horn Waterproofing Corp. v. Bushwick Iron & Steel Corp. (Case 11-5), New York's highest court concluded that UCC § 1-207 has changed the common law rules. In the Court's view, UCC § 1-207 permits a creditor to expressly reserve his rights by writing words such as "under protest" or "without prejudice" on the check. If the creditor does so, he avoids entering into an accord and satisfaction, the unliquidated debt is not discharged and the creditor may seek to recover the remaining amounts he claims the debtor owes.

Another question in Horn Waterproofing was whether UCC § 1-207 allows a creditor to reserve his rights on a full satisfaction check when the underlying transaction from which the unliquidated debt arose is not one that is covered by any of the articles of the UCC, such as the contract for services in that case. The court concluded that UCC §1-207 did apply, as long as the payment of the unliquidated debt was by check, because checks themselves, as negotiable instruments, are covered Article 3 of the UCC.

❦ SEE CASES 11-5, 11-6, 11-7, 11-8

BARGAINED-FOR EXCHANGE

The central idea behind consideration is that the parties have intentionally entered into a bargained exchange with one another and have given to each other something in exchange for a promise or performance. "A performance or return promise is bargained for if it is sought by the promisor in exchange for his promise and is given by the promisee in exchange for that promise." Restatement, Section 71. Thus, a promise to give someone a birthday present is without consideration, as the promisor received nothing in exchange for his promise of a present.

Past Consideration

Consideration is the inducement for a promise or performance. The element of bargained-for exchange is absent where a promise is given for a past transaction. Therefore, unbargained-for past events are not consideration, despite their designation as "past consideration." A promise made on account of something that the promisee has already done is not enforceable. For example, Noel gives emergency care to Tim's adult son while the son is ill. Tim subsequently promises to pay Noel for her services, but his promise is not binding because there is no bargained-for exchange. As with certain other promises for which consideration is lacking, New York law will allow enforcement of a promise based on past consideration if the promise is made in a signed writing. Under General Obligations Law § 5-1105, the writing must describe the past consideration and the past consideration must "be a valid consideration but for the time when it was given or performed." In the above example, Tim's promise would be enforceable if he were to write a note to Noel saying "I promise to pay you for the emergency care that you rendered to my son. (Signed) Tim."

Third Parties

Consideration to support a promise may be given to a person other than the promisor if the promisor bargains for that exchange. For example, A promises to pay B $15 if B delivers a specified book to C.

A's promise is binding because B incurred a legal detriment by delivering the book to C, as B was under no prior legal obligation to do so, and A had no prior legal right to have the book given to C. A and B have bargained for A to pay B $15 in return for B's delivering to C the book. A's promise to pay $15 is also consideration for B's promise to give the book to C.

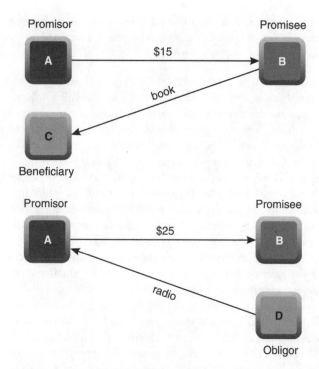

Conversely, consideration may be given by some person other than the promisee. For example, A promises to pay B $25 in return for D's promise to give A a radio.

A's promise to pay $25 to B is consideration for D's promise to give A a radio and vice versa.

CONTRACTS WITHOUT CONSIDERATION

Certain transactions are enforceable even though they are not supported by consideration. Such transactions include (1) promises to perform prior unenforceable obligations, (2) promises which induce detrimental reliance (promissory estoppel), (3) promises made under seal, and (4) promises made enforceable by statute.

Promises to Perform Prior Unenforceable Obligations

In certain circumstances the courts will enforce new promises to perform an obligation that originally was not enforceable or has become unenforceable by operation of law. These situations include promises to pay debts barred by the statute of limitations, debts discharged in bankruptcy, and voidable obligations. In addition, as previously indicated, some courts will enforce promises to pay moral obligations.

Promise to Pay Debt Barred by the Statute of Limitations

Every state has a statute of limitations, which provides that legal actions must be initiated within a prescribed period after the right to bring the action arose. Actions not commenced within the specified time period, which varies among the states and also with the nature of the legal action, will be dismissed.

An exception to the past consideration rule extends to promises to pay all or part of a contractual or quasi-contractual debt barred by the statute of limitations. The new promise is binding according to its terms without consideration for a second statutory period. Any recovery under the new promise is limited to the terms contained in the new promise. Most states require that new promises falling under this rule, except those indicated by part payment, be in writing to be enforceable.

Promise to Pay Debt Discharged in Bankruptcy Another exception to the requirement that consideration be given in exchange for a promise to make it binding is a promise to pay a debt that has been discharged in bankruptcy. Restatement, Section 83. The Bankruptcy Act, however, imposes a number of requirements before a promise to pay a debt discharged in bankruptcy may be enforced.

Voidable Promises Another promise that is enforceable without new consideration is a new promise to perform a voidable obligation that has not previously been avoided. Restatement, Section 85. The power of avoidance may be based on lack of capacity, fraud, misrepresentation, duress, undue influence, or mistake. For instance, a promise to perform an antecedent obligation made by a minor upon reaching the age of majority is enforceable without new consideration. To be enforceable, the promise itself must not be voidable. For example, if the new promise is made without knowledge of the original fraud or by a minor before reaching the age of majority, then the new promise is not enforceable.

Moral Obligation Under the common law, a promise made to satisfy a preexisting moral obligation is made for past consideration and therefore is unenforceable for lack of consideration. Instances involving such obligations include promises to pay for board and lodging previously furnished to a needy relative of the promisor, promises to pay debts owed by a relative, and an employer's promises to pay a completely disabled former employee a sum of money in addition to an award the employee has received under a workers' compensation statute. Although in many cases the moral obligation may be strong by reason of the particular facts and circumstances, no liability generally attaches to the promise.

The Restatement and a minority of states give considerable recognition to moral obligations as consideration. The Restatement provides that a promise made for "a benefit previously received by the promisor from the promisee is binding to the extent necessary to prevent injustice." Section 86. For instance, Tim's subsequent promise to Noel to reimburse her for the expenses she incurred in rendering emergency services to Tim's son is binding even though it is not supported by new consideration.

The Restatement also provides for enforcement of a moral obligation when a person promises to pay for a mistakenly conferred benefit. For example, Pam hires Elizabeth to pave her driveway, and Elizabeth mistakenly paves Chuck's driveway next door. Chuck subsequently promises to pay Pam $1,000 for the benefit conferred. Under the Restatement, Chuck's promise to pay the $1,000 is binding.

Promissory Estoppel

As discussed in Chapter 4, in certain circumstances where detrimental reliance has occurred, the courts will enforce noncontractual promises under the doctrine of promissory estoppel. When applicable, the doctrine makes gratuitous promises enforceable to the extent necessary to avoid injustice. The doctrine applies when a promise that the promisor reasonably should expect to induce detrimental reliance does induce such action or forbearance.

Promissory estoppel does not mean that every gratuitous promise is binding simply because it is followed by a change of position on the part of the promisee. To create liability, the promisee must make the change of position in justifiable reliance on the promise. For example, Smith promises to Barclay not to foreclose on a mortgage Smith holds on Barclay's factory for a period of six months. In justifiable reliance on Smith's promise, Barclay expends $900,000 on expanding the factory. Smith's promise not to foreclose is binding on Smith under the doctrine of promissory estoppel.

The most common application of the doctrine of promissory estoppel is to charitable subscriptions. Numerous churches, memorials, college buildings, hospitals, and other structures used for religious, educational, and charitable purposes have been built with the assistance of contributions fulfilling pledges or promises to contribute to particular worthwhile causes. Although the pledgor regards herself as making a gift for a charitable purpose and gift promises generally are not enforceable, the courts tend to enforce charitable subscription promises. Numerous reasons and theories have been advanced in support of liability: the most accepted argues that the subscription has induced a change of position by the promisee (the church, school, or charitable organization) in reliance on the promise. The Restatement, moreover, has relaxed the reliance requirement for charitable subscriptions so that actual reliance need not be shown; the probability of reliance is sufficient.

◆ SEE CASE 11-4

Promises Made Under Seal

Under the common law, when a person desired to bind himself by bond, deed, or solemn promise, he executed his promise under seal. He did not have to sign the document, his delivery of a document to which he had affixed his seal being sufficient. No consideration for his promise was necessary. In some States the courts still hold a promise under seal to be binding without consideration.

Nevertheless, most States have abolished by statute the distinction between contracts under seal and written unsealed contracts. In these States, the seal is no longer recognized as a substitute for consideration. The Code has also adopted this position, specifically eliminating the use of seals in contracts for the sale of goods.

Promises Made Enforceable by Statute

Some gratuitous promises that would otherwise be unenforceable have been made binding by statute. Most significant among these are (1) contract modifications, (2) renunciations, and (3) irrevocable offers.

Contract Modifications   As mentioned previously, the Uniform Commercial Code has abandoned the common law rule requiring that a modification of an existing contract be supported by consideration to be valid. The Code provides

that a contract for the sale of goods can be effectively modified without new consideration, provided the modification is made in good faith. Section 2–209.

Renunciation   Under the Code, Section 1–107, any claim or right arising out of an alleged breach of contract can be discharged in whole or in part without consideration by a written waiver or renunciation signed and delivered by the aggrieved party.

Irrevocable Offers   Under the Code, a *firm offer*, a written offer signed by a merchant offeror promising to keep open an offer to buy or sell goods, is not revocable for lack of consideration during the time stated, not to exceed three months, or if no time is stated, for a reasonable time. Section 2–205.

CHAPTER SUMMARY

Consideration

Definition the inducement to enter into a contract
Elements legal sufficiency and bargained-for exchange

Legal Sufficiency

Definition consists of either a benefit to the promisor or a detriment to the promisee
- *Legal Benefit* obtaining something to which one had no prior legal right
- *Legal Detriment* doing an act one is not legally obligated to do or not doing an act that one has a legal right to do

Adequacy not required where the parties have freely agreed to the exchange
Illusory Promise promise that imposes no obligation on the promisor; the following promises are *not* illusory:
- *Output Contract* agreement to sell all of one's production to a single buyer
- *Requirements Contract* agreement to buy all of one's needs from a single producer
- *Exclusive Dealing Contract* grant to a franchisee or licensee by a manufacturer of the sole right to sell goods in a defined market
- *Conditional Promise* one where the obligations are contingent upon the occurrence of a stated event

Preexisting Public Obligations public duties such as those imposed by tort or criminal law are neither a legal detriment nor a legal benefit
Preexisting Contractual Obligation performance of a preexisting contractual duty is not consideration
- *Modification of a Preexisting Contract* under the common law a modification of a preexisting contract must be supported by mutual consideration; under the Code a contract can be modified without new consideration
- *Substituted Contracts* the parties agree to rescind their original contract and to enter into a new one; rescission and new contract are supported by consideration
- *Settlement of an Undisputed Debt* payment of a lesser sum of money to discharge an undisputed debt (one whose existence or amount is not contested) does not constitute legally sufficient consideration
- *Settlement of a Disputed Debt* payment of a lesser sum of money to discharge a disputed debt (one whose existence or amount is contested) is legally sufficient consideration

Bargained-For Exchange	**Definition** a mutually agreed-upon exchange
	Past Consideration an act done before the contract is made is not consideration

Contracts without Consideration

Promises to Perform Prior Unenforceable Obligations

- *Promise to Pay Debt Barred by the Statute of Limitations* a new promise by the debtor to pay the debt renews the running of the statute for a second statutory period
- *Promise to Pay Debt Discharged in Bankruptcy* may be enforceable without consideration
- *Voidable Promises* a new promise to perform a voidable obligation that has not been previously avoided is enforceable
- *Moral Obligation* a promise made to satisfy a preexisting moral obligation is generally unenforceable for lack of consideration

Promissory Estoppel doctrine that prohibits a party from denying her promise when the promisee takes action or forbearance to his detriment reasonably based upon the promise

Promises under Seal where still recognized, the seal acts as a substitute for consideration

Promises Made Enforceable by Statute some gratuitous promises have been made enforceable by statute; the Code makes enforceable (1) contract modifications, (2) renunciations, and (3) firm offers

---

━━━━━ C A S E S ━━━━━

CASE

11-1

The common law rule requires that consideration be given by each party to the other in order for the contract to be binding. This leading case addresses the question of whether consideration is given when a party incurs a legal detriment by giving up a legal right if the other party receives no benefit.

HAMER v. SIDWAY
Court of Appeals of New York, 1891
124 N.Y. 538

PARKER, Judge. The question which provoked the most discussion by counsel on this appeal, and which lies at the foundation of plaintiff's asserted right of recovery, is whether by virtue of a contract defendant's testator William E. Story became indebted to his nephew William E. Story, 2d, on his twenty-first birthday in the sum of five thousand dollars. The trial court found as a fact that "on the 20th day of March, 1869, William E. Story agreed to and with William E. Story, 2d, that if he would refrain from drinking liquor, using tobacco, swearing, and playing cards or billiards for money until he should become 21 years of age then he, the said William E. Story, would at that time pay him, the said William E. Story, 2d, the sum of $5,000 for such refraining, to which the said William E. Story, 2d, agreed," and that he "in all things fully performed his part of said agreement."

The defendant contends that the contract was without consideration to support it, and, therefore, invalid. He asserts that the promisee by refraining from the use of liquor and tobacco was not harmed but benefited; that that which he did was best for him to do independently of his uncle's promise, and insists that it follows that unless the promisor was benefited, the contract was without consideration. A contention, which if well

founded, would seem to leave open for controversy in many cases whether that which the promisee did or omitted to do was, in fact, of such benefit to him as to leave no consideration to support the enforcement of the promisor's agreement. Such a rule could not be tolerated, and is without foundation in the law. The Exchequer Chamber, in 1875, defined consideration as follows: "A valuable consideration in the sense of the law may consist either in some right, interest, profit or benefit accruing to the one party, or some forbearance, detriment, loss or responsibility given, suffered or undertaken by the other." Courts "will not ask whether the thing which forms the consideration does in fact benefit the promisee or a third party, or is of any substantial value to anyone. It is enough that something is promised, done, forborne or suffered by the party to whom the promise is made as consideration for the promise made to him."

"In general a waiver of any legal right at the request of another party is a sufficient consideration for a promise."

"Any damage, or suspension, or forbearance of a right will be sufficient to sustain a promise."

Pollock, in his work on contracts, page 166, after citing the definition given by the Exchequer Chamber already quoted, says: "The second branch of this judicial description is really the most important one. Consideration means not so much that one party is profiting as that the other abandons some legal right in the present or limits his legal freedom of action in the future as an inducement for the promise of the first."

Now, applying this rule to the facts before us, the promisee used tobacco, occasionally drank liquor, and he had a legal right to do so. That right he abandoned for a period of years upon the strength of the promise of the testator that for such forbearance he would give him $5,000. We need not speculate on the effort which may have been required to give up the use of those stimulants. It is sufficient that he restricted his lawful freedom of action within certain prescribed limits upon the faith of his uncle's agreement, and now having fully performed the conditions imposed, it is of no moment whether such performance actually proved a benefit to the promisor, and the court will not inquire into it, but were it a proper subject of inquiry, we see nothing in this record that would permit a determination that the uncle was not benefited in a legal sense.

The cases cited by the defendant on this question are not in point.

CASE
11-2

Often good faith disputes arise between a creditor and debtor as to whether any money is owed or how much money is owed. In such cases, a debtor may tender a check to the creditor for a smaller amount and may write words such as "paid in full" on the check or indicate such facts in a letter. May the creditor cash the check and still sue to collect the balance he claims is due? The following case illustrates the common law rules as to whether a debt is unliquidated and whether an accord and satisfaction discharging the debt has occurred.

SCHNELL v. PERLMON
Court of Appeals of New York, 1924
238 N.Y. 362

CRANE, Judge. This action is brought to recover an alleged balance due for goods, wares and merchandise sold by the plaintiffs to the defendant. Defendant pleaded an accord and satisfaction. The trial court directed a verdict for the plaintiffs for the full amount claimed, and the judgment entered thereon has been unanimously affirmed by the Appellate Division. That court, however, granted leave to appeal to this court, certifying that in its opinion there is a question of law involved which ought to be reviewed by us.

The question of law referred to arises through the payment by the defendant of an amount less than the agreed price in full payment and satisfaction of the claimed debt. As in all like cases the result depends very much upon the facts of each case, it is, therefore, necessary at the outset to state fully the transaction between these parties. The plaintiffs, trading under the firm name of H. Schnell & Co., sold to Sol Perlmon, the defendant, trading under the firm name of Detroit Celery & Produce Co., ten cars of Spanish onions, pursuant to the terms of a written contract dated November 14, 1921. These ten carloads were to consist of 2,500 crates to be shipped by the Michigan Central Railroad from New York to Detroit; all goods sold F. O. B. New York, delivery to the common carrier being delivery to the purchaser. When the onions arrived in Detroit some of them were found to be in a defective condition due to decay consisting of fusarean rot, slimy soft rot, and a bacteria heart rot involving the greater portion of the onions. The defendant had the onions inspected by the Food Products Inspector of the United States Department of Agriculture, who gave five separate certificates certifying to this condition of the onions examined by him and stating that the decay amounted in some of the containers from ten per cent to thirty-five per cent, in others from fifteen to twenty-five per cent of the contents. The percentage varied in these certificates, running as high, however, as fifty per cent and as low as three per cent. The defendant notified the plaintiffs by letter regarding this condition, and sent them copies of the government official's report. On December 13, 1921, the defendant sent to the plaintiffs five checks in payment of five of the cars shipped and deducted a total of $425 for a percentage of the decay as covered by the government reports. Accompanying these checks was a letter in which an explanation of the deduction was made in the following words: "These deductions are made to cover the percentage of decay on each car. We mailed you, some time ago, the inspection reports covering each of these cars in order that you might satisfy yourself that we are making only reasonable deductions." Each of the checks was marked in full payment of the car number for which payment was remitted.

On December 16th the plaintiffs acknowledged receipt of checks totaling $4,575, which they stated they had placed to the credit of the defendant, but insisted that there was still a balance due of $425 for which they demanded payment. In other words, they accepted the checks but rejected the proposed deduction.

On February 11, 1922, the defendant, who was still indebted to the plaintiffs for five cars, sent to them a check for $2,000 and a promissory note for $2,328.70 with interest payable in thirty days. On the back of this note there was this notation: "Payment in full of balance owing you on the following cars of Onions:" (giving numbers of cars). A letter also accompanied this note showing the reasons for the deductions mentioned therein, reading as follows:

"We have already advised you the percentage of decay on cars NYC-138745 and NYC-138762 and have deducted off the first car Two Hundred and Eight Dollars ($208.00), representing twenty per cent of the invoice which the Government inspection shows as running from ten to thirty-five per cent decay and an average of fifteen to twenty-five per cent. You know that decay of this particular kind Slimy Soft Rot, hurts the sale of the entire shipment as the onions that are sound lose in value after being sorted over as they are never so bright and clean as when shipment is sound.

Car NYC-138762 also shows the same kind of decay and we have deducted fifteen per cent from the invoice and this in no way represents what we should have deducted as the bad onions affected the sale and condition of the others."

The plaintiffs replied to this letter crediting these amounts on the account of the defendant and demanding all the balance due, $801.29, the amount sued for in this action....

The facts, briefly stated, therefore, are: The plaintiffs sold to the defendant onions for an agreed price. The shipment in part was rotten and decayed. The defendant notified the plaintiffs of the fact sending to them the government reports made by the Food Products Inspector. The defendant paid for the goods which were in good condition, deducting $801.29 for those which he claimed to have been decayed. The payment was made by checks and notes and accompanying letters notifying the plaintiffs that if accepted by them they would be in full payment of the amount due, and the balance, $801.29, the amount of the deduction, would thus be paid by agreement or by accord and satisfaction (to use the legal terms). The claim put forth by the defendant for deduction was apparently made in good faith, and in view of the government reports seems to be reasonable and fair. The percentage of the deduction made by the defendant was not as large as the percentage of decay reported by the government reports sent to the plaintiffs and might be less than the amount which the defendant could have recovered if he had sued the plaintiffs for damages or upon their warranty. Under these circumstances, was the trial judge justified in holding as a matter of law that there had been no accord and satisfaction and that the plaintiffs were entitled to the balance claimed?

The general rule is that a liquidated claim, that is, a claim which is not disputed, but admitted to be due, cannot be discharged by any payment of a less amount. In Jackson v. Volkening we find the following language used: "The rule of law is well established, undoubtedly, that where a liquidated sum is due, the payment of part only, although accepted in satisfaction, is not, for want of consideration, a discharge of the entire indebtedness, but this rule is not looked upon with favor and is confined strictly to cases falling within it." In Fuller v. Kemp it was said: "Where the demand is liquidated, and the liability of the debtor is not in good faith disputed, a different rule has been applied. In such cases the acceptance of a less sum than is the creditor's due, will not of itself discharge

the debt, even if a receipt in full is given." And in Simons v. Supreme Council American Legion of Honor the point was stated in these words: "Now it is the settled law of this state that if a debt or claim be disputed or contingent at the time of payment, the payment, when accepted, of a part of the whole debt is a good satisfaction and it matters not that there was no solid foundation for the dispute." And in Eames Vacuum Brake Co. v. Prosser this court said: "It is only in cases where a dispute has arisen between the parties as to the amount due and a check is tendered on one side in full satisfaction of the matter in controversy that the other party will be deemed to have acquiesced in the amount offered by an acceptance and a retention of the check." The term "liquidated," therefore, when used in connection with the subject of accord and satisfaction has reference to a claim which the debtor does not dispute; a claim which he admits to be due but attempts to satisfy by the payment of a smaller amount. Thus in Nassoiy v. Tomlinson this court said: "A demand is not liquidated, even if it appears that something is due, unless it appears how much is due; and when it is admitted that one of two specific sums is due, but there is a genuine dispute as to which is the proper amount, the demand is regarded as unliquidated, within the meaning of that term as applied to the subject of accord and satisfaction."

In this case before us, the full amount claimed by the plaintiffs was not admittedly due. The fact that the contract called for a stated amount or an amount which could be easily figured according to deliveries did not make the claim liquidated within this meaning of the law as applied to accord and satisfaction. The term "liquidated" has an entirely different meaning in this connection than it has when used to determine whether or not interest is payable upon a recovery. The amount claimed by the plaintiffs and specified in the contract was repudiated by the defendant. He denied that he owed the money. He disputed the plaintiffs' demand. The contract had not been fulfilled and completed. Deliveries had not been made as called for. The goods were rotten and decayed, and not as warranted. For the purpose of this subject, to my mind, it makes no difference whether the defendant had a claim for breach of warranty or whether he had a right to reject or claimed a right to reject the imperfect goods. The fact still exists that he insisted with the plaintiffs that he should not be obliged to pay for articles he had not purchased. It is a statement inconsistent with the fact to say that the plaintiffs' claim was liquidated in the sense that it was admitted and acknowledged to be due by the defendant. He disputed it at every step, and sent to the plaintiffs written evidence to justify the honesty and good faith of his statements. Thus there was a difference between these parties over the amount due on this contract. If the plaintiffs had sued the defendant for the full amount, the latter could have defended. There was some evidence at least to indicate that the onions were rotten at the heart when delivered to the railroad. Thus, there never had been a complete delivery and the defendant might have defended, or if there had been acceptance and no rejection within a reasonable time, then the defendant having given notice, could have coun-terclaimed on his warranty. However we look at it there was relief at law in some form for the defendant. He was not obliged to pay for rotten onions.

Thus within all the cases the claim of the plaintiffs was not liquidated within the meaning of that term as used in this connection. It was a disputed claim. The plaintiffs knew it was disputed. They knew also that the checks and notes which they received and cashed were received in full payment of their disputed claim. They could not under these circumstances keep the money and reject the conditions attached to payment. Having accepted payment the conditions attached and the balance of $801.29 has been satisfied.

Therefore, the judgments below must be reversed and judgment directed for the defendant dismissing the complaint....

CASE

11-3

Can the employees of a bank that had been robbed and various law enforcement officers claim a reward for helping to apprehend and convict the three bank robbers?

DENNEY v. REPPERT

Court of Appeals of Kentucky, 1968

432 S. W.2d 647

Myre, Special Commissoner

The sole question presented in this case is which of several claimants is entitled to an award for information leading to the apprehension and conviction of certain bank robbers.

* * *

On June 12th or 13th, 1963, three armed men entered the First State Bank, Eubank, Kentucky, and with a display of arms and threats robbed the bank of over $30,000. Later in the day they were apprehended by State Policemen Garret Godby, Johnny Simms, and Tilford Reppert, placed under arrest, and the entire loot was recovered. Later all of the prisoners were convicted and Garret Godby, Johnny Simms, and Tilford Reppert appeared as witnesses at the trial.

The First State Bank of Eubank was a member of the Kentucky Bankers Association which provided and advertised a reward of $500.00 for the arrest and conviction of each bank robber. Hence the outstanding reward for the three bank robbers was $1,500.00. Many became claimants for the reward and the Kentucky State Bankers Association, being unable to determine the merits of the claims for the reward, asked the circuit court to determine the merits of the various claims and to adjudge who was entitled to receive the reward or share in it. All of the claimants were made defendants in the action.

At the time of the robbery the claimants Murrell Denney, Joyce Buis, Rebecca McCollum, and Jewell Snyder were employees of the First State Bank of Eubank and came out of the grueling situation with great credit and glory. Each one of them deserves approbation and an accolade. They were vigilant in disclosing to the public and the peace officers the details of the crime, and in describing the culprits, and giving all the information that they possessed that would be useful in capturing the robbers. Undoubtedly, they performed a great service. It is in the evidence that the claimant Murrell Denney was conspicuous and energetic in his efforts to make known the robbery, to acquaint the officers as to the personal appearance of the criminals, and to give other pertinent facts.

The first question for determination is whether the employees of the robbed bank are eligible to receive or share in the reward. The great weight of authority answers in the negative.* * *

> To the general rule that, when a reward is offered to the general public for the performance of some specified act, such reward may be claimed by any person who performs such act, is the exception of agents, employees, and public officials who are acting within the scope of their employment or official duties.* * *

* * *

At the time of the robbery the claimants Murrell Denney, Joyce Buis, Rebecca McCollum, and Jewell Snyder were employees of the First State Bank of Eubank. They were under duty to protect and conserve the resources and moneys of the bank, and safeguard every interest of the institution furnishing them employment. Each of these employees exhibited great courage and cool bravery, in a time of stress and danger. The community and the county have recompensed them in commendation, admiration, and high praise, and the world looks on them as heroes. But in making known the robbery and assisting in acquainting the public and the officers with details of the crime and with identification of the robbers, they performed a duty to the bank and the public, for which they cannot claim a reward.

The claims of Corbin Reynolds, Julia Reynolds, Alvie Reynolds, and Gene Reynolds also must fail. According to their statements they gave valuable information to the arresting officers. However, they did not follow the procedure as set forth in the offer of reward in that they never filed a claim with the Kentucky Bankers Association. It is well established that a claimant of a reward must comply with the terms and conditions of the offer of reward. [Citation.]

State Policemen Garret Godby, Johnny Simms, and Tilford Reppert made the arrest of the bank robbers and captured the stolen money. All participated in the prosecution. At the time of the arrest, it was the duty of the state policemen to apprehend the criminals. Under the law they cannot claim or share in the reward and they are interposing no claim to it.

This leaves the defendant, Tilford Reppert the sole eligible claimant. The record shows that at the time of the arrest he was a deputy sheriff in Rockcastle County, but the arrest and recovery of the stolen money took place in Pulaski County. He was out of his jurisdiction, and was thus under no legal duty to make the arrest, and is thus eligible to claim and receive the reward. In *Kentucky Bankers Ass'n et al. v. Cassady* [citation], it was said:

> It is***well established that a public officer with the authority of the law to make an arrest may accept an offer of reward or compensation for acts or services performed outside of his bailiwick or not within the scope of his official duties.* * *

* * *

It is manifest from the record that Tilford Reppert is the only claimant qualified and eligible to receive the reward. Therefore, it is the judgment of the circuit court that he is entitled to receive payment of the $1,500.00 reward now deposited with the clerk of this court.

The judgment is affirmed.

CASE

11-4

Here, a court addresses whether an employee's decision to remain in a job constitutes consideration for the purposes of enforcing an alleged promise by the employer.

DILORENZO v. VALVE AND PRIMER CORPORATION

Appellate Court of Illinois, First District, Fifth Division, 2004
807 N.E.2d 673, 283 Ill.Dec. 68
http://www.state.il.us/court/Opinions/AppellateCourt/2003/1stDistrict/June/Html/1012803.htm

Reid, J.

Background

DiLorenzo was an officer, director and shareholder of 100 shares of stock of Valve & Primer. M. Chris Dickson was the chief executive officer and majority shareholder of Valve & Primer. DiLorenzo was employed by Valve & Primer for approximately 40 years prior to the events that led to this lawsuit.

According to DiLorenzo, on or about May 12, 1987, he informed Valve & Primer that he wanted incentives in any future employment agreements. DiLorenzo claims that, through Dickson, Valve & Primer offered him a 10-year stock option that would allow DiLorenzo to purchase an additional 300 shares at the fixed price of $250 per share. Dickson and the board of directors allegedly favorably voted on the agreement at a meeting held on June 8, 1987. DiLorenzo claims he received a copy of the minutes of that meeting. DiLorenzo also claims that in reliance on the minutes of the special board meeting, which were never altered or revoked by the board of directors during the time he remained employed by Valve & Primer, he stayed in his job for over nine additional years. According to DiLorenzo, while he was working for Valve & Primer, in reliance upon the minutes of the special board meeting, when he was approached by other companies with employment opportunities he did not follow up on any of these recruitment offers.

Valve & Primer claims the 1987 employment agreement between it and DiLorenzo did not contain a stock purchase agreement. The only purported proof of the agreement is an unsigned copy of board meeting minutes of which DiLorenzo had the only copy. Valve & Primer claimed the purported minutes were inconsistent in subject matter and format from other corporate minutes it produces in the ordinary course of business.

In January 1996, DiLorenzo entered into a semi-retirement agreement with Valve & Primer. Valve & Primer claims he attempted to tender his remaining 100 shares pursuant to a stock redemption agreement. According to Valve & Primer, DiLorenzo demanded $4,000 per share for the remaining 100 shares. It claims DiLorenzo admitted he came up with the proposed share value himself and that no one of any expertise valued the stock. DiLorenzo responded that he had corporate accountants review financial statements before valuing the company's shares. Valve & Primer declined to purchase the shares at DiLorenzo's price. This resulted in a dispute between DiLorenzo and Valve & Primer through Dickson. Shortly thereafter, Valve & Primer fired DiLorenzo. After the termination, DiLorenzo claims he attempted to exercise the purported stock purchase agreement.

In addition to DiLorenzo, George Christofidis, another longtime employee, attempted to exercise the stock option.***In the alternative, DiLorenzo argued before the trial court that, even if the purported agreement was not found to be valid, it should be enforced along promissory estoppel grounds.

* * *

Analysis

DiLorenzo argues on appeal that the trial court misapplied the law in finding there was insufficient consideration to support the stock option agreement. He argues that substantial continued employment is sufficient consideration for agreements entered into in the employment setting. DiLorenzo argues that he has provided consideration for the stock option. It was as an incentive for continued employment. He also argues that, even if there was an initial lack of consideration, performance may ameliorate an initial lack of consideration, if the performance was clearly invited. He claims his continued employment for nine years in reliance on the agreement satisfied the condition of the performance being invited. Here he claims Valve & Primer benefitted both from the pre-1987 employment and the post-1987 work. DiLorenzo argues that he was not promising to do something he was already obligated to do, which he concedes would not be valid consideration.

Valve & Primer responds that the trial court correctly granted it summary judgment because DiLorenzo failed to show any consideration to support the alleged stock option. Valve & Primer, without admitting that the board meeting minutes are genuine, argues that they indicate that the alleged stock option was given to "reward" him for his long service to the company. Valve & Primer's position is that, if the alleged consideration for a promise has been conferred prior to the promise upon which the alleged agreement is based, then no contract is formed. Valve & Primer also argues that the argument that the option was based, at least in part, on his claimed continued employment must fail because it relies on something DiLorenzo was already obligated to do. According to Valve & Primer, because DiLorenzo contends that the stock option vested immediately, only past performance could serve as consideration. As the trial court noted, that is insufficient consideration.* * *

In reply, DiLorenzo contends that there is sufficient consideration to support the stock option. He argues that whether the 1987 corporate minutes are authentic is not an issue on appeal. Since the trial court took the minutes as true, the appellate court should do likewise. * * *

The purported minutes of the June 8, 1987, special meeting contain the following relevant language:

> That in order to *retain and reward* such dedication George Christofidis be given an option to purchase additional shares not to exceed 300; and that Ralph DiLorenzo be given an option to purchase additional shares not to exceed 300. Said option to be exercised within 10 years from below date at the price of $250.00 per share. Each share was to be restricted wherein the share must first be offered to Valve and Primer Corporation to be paid by Valve and Primer Corporation and held as Treasury Stock. Valve and Primer Corporation would be given 45 days to consummate the purchase. In the event that Valve and Primer Corporation did not choose to purchase, said stock would be offered to the existing shareholders on a pro rate basis also to be purchased within 45 days. And in the event the shareholders did not purchase said shares, the shares could be sold to any interested person or persons. Purchase price of shares would be based upon the book value pursuant to a certified audit of the worth of the Corporation at the time of sale.

We begin by addressing whether there was consideration for the stock options. "A stock option is the right to buy a share or shares of stock at a specified price or within a specified period."

[Citation.] In order to evaluate the nature and scope of the stock options issued to DiLorenzo, we must assume, for purposes of this portion of our discussion, that DiLorenzo's corporate minutes are valid.

"A contract, to be valid, must contain offer, acceptance, and consideration; to be enforceable, the agreement must also be sufficiently definite so that its terms are reasonably certain and able to be determined." [Citation.] "A contract is sufficiently definite and certain to be enforceable if the court is able from its terms and provisions to ascertain what the parties intended, under proper rules of construction and applicable principles of equity." [Citation.] "A contract may be enforced even though some contract terms may be missing or left to be agreed upon, but if essential terms are so uncertain that there is no basis for deciding whether the agreement has been kept or broken, there is no contract." [Citation.] A bonus promised to induce an employee to continue his employment is supported by adequate consideration if the employee is not already bound by contract to continue. [Citation.] Because we are assuming the validity of the document issuing the stock options, we now turn to whether the underlying option is supported by valid consideration so as to make it a proper contract.

"Consideration is defined as the bargained-for exchange of promises or performances and may consist of a promise, an act or a forbearance." [Citation.]

> The general principles applicable to option contracts have been long established. An option contract has two elements, an offer to do something, or to forbear, which does not become a contract until accepted; and an agreement to leave the offer open for a specified time [citation], or for a reasonable time [citation]. An option contract must be supported by sufficient consideration; and if not, it is merely an offer which may be withdrawn at any time prior to a tender of compliance. [Citation.] If a consideration of 'one dollar' or some other consideration is stated but which has, in fact, not been paid, the document is merely an offer which may be withdrawn at any time prior to a tender of compliance. The document will amount only to a continuing offer which may be withdrawn by the offeror at any time before acceptance. [Citation.] The consideration to support an option consists of 'some right, interest, profit or benefit accruing to one party, or some forbearance, detriment, loss or responsibility given, suffered or undertaken by the other' [citation]; or otherwise stated, 'Any act or promise which is of benefit to one party or disadvantage to the other* * *. [Citation.]

"The preexisting duty rule provides that where a party does what it is already legally obligated to do, there is no consideration because there has been no detriment." [Citation.]

Focusing on the lack of a detriment to the employee, the trial court found no valid consideration. Based upon our view of the discussion in [citation], the trial court was correct in concluding that the option contract is merely an offer which may be withdrawn at any time prior to a tender of compliance. DiLorenzo could have exercised the option the moment it was purportedly made, then immediately quit, thereby giving nothing to the employer. Though the exercise of the option would require the transfer of money for the stock, the option itself carries with it no detriment to DiLorenzo. Therefore, there was no consideration for the option.

* * *

We next address DiLorenzo's claim that he is entitled to the value of the shares of stock based upon the theory of promissory estoppel. DiLorenzo argues that the trial court misapplied the law in finding that there was insufficient reliance to support a claim for promissory estoppel. He claims that, once the trial court decided there was insufficient consideration to support the option contract, promissory estoppel should have been applied by the court to enforce the agreement as a matter of equity. DiLorenzo argues that he detrimentally relied upon Valve & Primer's promise in that he worked at Valve & Primer for an additional period in excess of nine years in reliance on the stock option agreement.* * *

Valve & Primer responds that the trial court was correct in finding insufficient reliance to support the promissory estoppel claim. Valve & Primer argues that the DiLorenzo could not satisfy the detrimental reliance prong of the promissory estoppel elements. Though DiLorenzo claimed he did not act upon offers of employment he claims were made by other companies during the course of his employment with Valve & Primer, he presented to the trial court nothing but his own testimony in support of his claim. Valve & Primer argues that, since DiLorenzo essentially is claiming his stock option vested immediately, he cannot contend that he detrimentally relied upon the purported agreement in the corporate minutes by turning down those other opportunities.***For purposes of promissory estoppel, if DiLorenzo's allegations are taken as true, and the purported option vested immediately, it required nothing of him in order to be exercised other than the payment of $250 per share.

"Promissory estoppel arises when (1) an unambiguous promise was made, (2) the defendant relied on the promise, (3) the defendant's reliance on the promise was reasonable, and (4) the defendant suffered a detriment." [Citation.] Whether detrimental reliance has occurred is determined according to the specific facts of each case. [Citation.]

While we would accept that, under certain circumstances, it may be possible for a relinquishment of a job offer to constitute consideration sufficient to support a contract, this is not such a case. There is nothing in the language of the corporate minutes or any other source to be found in this record to suggest that Valve & Primer conditioned the alleged stock option on DiLorenzo's promise to remain in his employment. While the corporate minutes say the alleged grant of the stock option was intended to "retain and reward," it contains no mechanism making the retention mandatory. Since the corporate minutes lack a mandatory obligation on which DiLorenzo could have reasonably detrimentally relied, and he could have elected to buy the shares of stock immediately, DiLorenzo's decision to remain on the job for the additional period of over nine years must be viewed as a voluntary act. Under those circumstances, promissory estoppel would not apply. It was, therefore, not an abuse of discretion to grant Valve & Primer's motion for summary judgment on that issue.

* * *

Affirmed.

CASE

11-5

The following case explains how and why the Uniform Commercial Code has changed common law rules regarding accord and satisfaction in New York. The changes allow a creditor who complies with UCC § 1-207 to cash a debtor's "full satisfaction" check but avoid an accord and satisfaction and reserve its rights against the debtor for the balance the creditor claims is due.

HORN WATERPROOFING CORP. v. BUSHWICK IRON & STEEL CO.
Court of Appeals of New York, 1985 66 N.Y. 2d 321

JASEN, Judge. This appeal presents an issue of first impression: whether the common-law doctrine of accord and satisfaction has been superseded by operation of Uniform Commercial Code § 1-207 in situations involving the tender of a negotiable instrument as full payment of a disputed claim.

The relevant facts are uncomplicated. The parties entered into an oral agreement whereby plaintiff was to repair the leaking roof on defendant's building. After two days work, plaintiff concluded that a new roof was needed and submitted a bill for work already done. Defendant disputed the amount

charged and plaintiff revised the bill downward from $1,241 to $1,080. Defendant remained unsatisfied with the charges and sent plaintiff a check for only $500. The check bore the following notation affixed on the reverse side: "This check is accepted in full payment, settlement, satisfaction, release and discharge of any and all claims and/or demands of whatsoever kind and nature." Directly thereunder, plaintiff printed the words "Under Protest," indorsed the check with its stamp, and deposited the $500 into its account.

Plaintiff then commenced this action in Civil Court seeking

$580 as the balance due on its revised bill. Defendant moved for summary judgment on the ground that plaintiff's acceptance and negotiation of the check constituted an accord and satisfaction. The motion was denied and the Appellate Term affirmed. The court held that the Uniform Commercial Code (the Code) was applicable to the type of commercial transaction in which the parties were involved and that, under the provisions of § 1-207, plaintiff was entitled to reserve its right to demand the balance due.

On appeal by leave of the Appellate Term, the Appellate Division reversed, granted defendant's motion, and dismissed the complaint. The majority of that court held that the parties' agreement, being a contract for the performance of services, fell outside the scope of the Code. It was, therefore, concluded that the common law applied and that the doctrine of accord and satisfaction precluded plaintiff's recovery. In dissent, Justice Weinstein argued that application of the common-law doctrine to the facts of this case is inequitable and needlessly constricts the modernizing effect of the Code. We now reverse and hold that, under § 1-207 of the Code, a creditor may preserve his right to the balance of a disputed claim, by explicit reservation in his indorsement of a check tendered by the debtor as full payment.

The effect of Code § 1-207 upon the common-law doctrine of accord and satisfaction has been much debated. Indeed, the courts that have addressed the issue in this state have rendered conflicting decisions, and our sister state courts are likewise divided. In our view, applying § 1-207 to a "full payment" check situation, to permit a creditor to reserve his rights and, thereby, preclude an accord and satisfaction, more nearly comports with the content and context of the statutory provision and with the legislative history and underlying purposes of the Code as well, and is a fairer policy in debtor-creditor transactions.

It has long been the general rule in this state that "if a debt or claim be disputed or contingent at the time of payment, the payment, when accepted, of a part of the whole debt is a good satisfaction and it matters not that there was no solid foundation for the dispute. The test in such cases is, Was the dispute honest or fraudulent? If honest, it affords the basis for an accord between the parties, which the law favors, the execution of which is the satisfaction."

The theory underlying this common-law rule of accord and satisfaction is that the parties have thus entered into a new contract displacing all or part of their original one. Although the creditor might have been confronted with an "embarrassing… choice" upon the debtor's presentment to him of partial payment, such as in the case of a "full payment" or "conditional" check, nevertheless, the rule of accord and satisfaction has generally been accepted as a legitimate and expeditious means of settling contract disputes. As this court stated more than 70 years ago: "The law wisely favors settlements, and where there is a real and genuine contest between the parties and a settlement is had without fraud or misrepresentation for an amount determined upon as a compromise between the conflicting claims such settlement should be upheld, although such amount is materially less than the amount claimed by the person to whom it is paid."

Still, where the creditor is presented with partial payment as satisfaction in full, but, nevertheless, wishes to preserve his claim to the balance left unpaid, it cannot be gainsaid that conflicting considerations of policy and fairness are implicated. This is particularly so in the case of a full payment check. On the one hand, the debtor, as the master of his offer, has reason to expect that his offer will either be accepted or his check returned. At the same time, however, the creditor has good cause to believe that he is fully entitled to retain the partial payment that is rightfully his and presently in his possession, without having to forfeit entitlement to whatever else is his due.

In dismissing these latter considerations with specific regard to the applicability of Code § 1-207 to a check tendered as "full payment," one commentary argued that: "Besides operating as an unnecessary destruction of a valuable common law doctrine, the expansive interpretation of U.C.C. § 1-207 conflicts with another basic principle of the Uniform Commercial Code, the duty of good faith imposed by § 1-203, certainly the more fundamental concept…. It is unfair to the party who writes the check thinking that he will be spending his money only if the whole dispute will be over, to allow the other party, knowing of that reasonable expectation, to weasel around the deal by putting his own markings on the other person's checks. There is no reason why § 1-207 should be interpreted as being an exception to the basic duty of good faith, when it is possible to interpret the two sections consistently. The academic writers who support this result offer no analysis, to the current knowledge of this treatise, which would justify licensing the recipient of the check to so deceive the drawer."

However, an entirely different conclusion is reached in another commentary which explains that:

"Offering a check for less than the contract amount, but 'in full settlement' inflicts an exquisite form of commercial torture on the payee. If the offer is reasonable it creates a marvelous anxiety in some recipients: 'Shall I risk the loss of $9,000 for the additional $1,000 that the bloke really owes me?'" In general the law has authorized such drawer behavior by regarding such a check as an offer of accord and satisfaction which the payee accepts if he cashes the check. Traditionally the payee could write all manner of disclaimers over his indorsement without avail; by cashing the check he was held to have accepted the offer on the drawer's terms. Even if he scratched out the drawer's notation or indorsed it under protest he was deemed to have accepted subject to the conditions under which the drawer offered it.

* * * *

"However, we believe… that 1-207 authorizes the payee to indorse under protest and accept the amount of the check without entering an accord and satisfaction or otherwise forsaking his claim to any additional sum allegedly due him."

We concur with the latter view. Indeed, the common-law doctrine of accord and satisfaction creates a cruel dilemma for the good-faith creditor in possession of a full payment check. Under that rule, the creditor would have no other choice but to surrender the partial payment or forfeit his right to the remainder. We are persuaded, however, that the common law was changed with the adoption of § 1-207 pursuant to which a fairer rule now prevails.

§ 1-207 provides: "A party who with explicit reservation of rights performs or promises performance or assents to performance in a manner demanded or offered by the other party does not thereby prejudice the rights reserved. Such words as 'without prejudice', 'under protest' or the like are sufficient." The plain language of the provision, "without much stretching", would seem applicable to a full payment check. A fortiori, if liberally construed, as the Code's provisions are explicitly intended to be, it seems clear that the reach of § 1-207 is sufficiently extensive to alter the doctrine of accord and satisfaction by permitting a creditor to reserve his rights though accepting the debtor's check.

The Comment prepared by the National Conference of Commissioners on Uniform State Laws and the American Law Institute is fairly subject to a variety of interpretations as to the purpose of § 1-207. It simply does not, however, specifically address the law of accord and satisfaction and how it might have been altered. By contrast, the Report of the State of New York Commission on Uniform State Laws quite clearly took the position that the common-law doctrine would be changed. With specific reference to § 1-207, the report stated:

"This section permits a party involved in a Code-covered transaction to accept whatever he can get by way of payment, performance, etc., without losing his rights to demand the remainder of the goods, to set-off a failure of quality, or to sue for the balance of the payment, so long as he explicitly reserves his rights.

"In *Nassoiy v. Tomlinson*, the debtor paid no more than the exact amount he claimed was due. The court held that the conditional payment was payment of an unliquidated claim if any part was disputed, and that the acceptance of the payment discharged the entire debt. The Code rule would permit, in Code-covered transactions, the acceptance of a part performance or payment tendered in full settlement without requiring the acceptor to gamble with his legal right to demand the balance of the performance or payment." (Report of Comm. on Uniform State Laws to Legislature, at 19-20 [1961].)

This interpretive analysis, which was submitted to the Legislature together with the Commission's recommendation for enactment of the Code, unmistakably addresses the common-law doctrine and notes that the section permits a reservation of rights upon acceptance of partial payment where an accord and satisfaction might otherwise have resulted. Particularly significant is the reference to *Nassoiy v Tomlinson*, a seminal decision in this state applying the doctrine of accord and satisfaction under facts involving a full payment check. This commentary

clearly apprised the Legislature that § 1-207 would change the rule upheld in that case. Moreover, it is notable that the analysis explicitly speaks of the acceptance of part "payment tendered in full settlement." The section was clearly not deemed restricted to situations involving the acceptance of goods or such other "performance" in part.

This view derives further support from the very context of § 1-207 within the Code. The provision is set forth in the introductory article 1, among the general provisions of the Code dealing with such matters as its title, underlying purposes, general definitions, and principles of interpretation. Presumably, § 1-207, as with other provisions in the introductory article, is to apply to any commercial transaction within the reach of one of the substantive articles — i.e., to any "Code-covered" transaction, as denominated in the New York Annotations. There is simply no language in § 1-207 expressing or intimating a more restrictive intention to limit its application to specific kinds of transactions particular to one of the articles, or sections, of the Code such as the purchase and acceptance of goods (art 2), investment securities (art 8) or chattel paper (art 9). Rather, the nonlimiting language of § 1-207 and its placement in the Code with the other generally applicable provisions of article 1 is persuasive that the section is, indeed, applicable to all commercial transactions fairly considered to be "Code-covered."

Hence, the payment of a contract debt by check or other commercial paper and its acceptance by the creditor fall within the reach of § 1-207. Whether the underlying contract between the parties be for the purchase of goods, chattel paper or personal services, the use of a negotiable instrument for the purpose of payment or attempted satisfaction of a contract debt is explicitly and specifically regulated by the provisions of article 3 and, therefore, undeniably a Code-covered transaction. Consequently, a debtor's tender of a full payment check is an article 3 transaction which is governed by § 1-207, regardless of the nature of the contract underlying the parties' commercial relationship.

Indeed, Dean Rosenthal, who otherwise contended that § 1-207 was not originally intended by the drafters to alter the doctrine of accord and satisfaction by full payment checks, observed that:

Article three ('Commercial Paper'), however, is a special case. Does the fact that a check is used as the device to effect a settlement in itself bring the transaction within the Code (and therefore make § 1-207 arguably applicable) even if the underlying transaction was one not otherwise covered by the Code? Article three contains no scope provision analogous to the 'transactions in goods' language in [article 2].

* * * *

"[I]t seems fairly clear that if such a check is tendered in settlement, the transaction must be regarded as being within article three, and if § 1-207 is otherwise relevant its application cannot be avoided by showing either that article one was not meant to be applied to non-Code transactions or that the underlying obligation did not arise out of one of the other substantive articles of the Code." (Rosenthal, *Discord and Dissatisfaction: § 1-207 of the Uniform Commercial Code*, 78 Colum L Rev 48, 70.)

Finally, . . . such a reading of § 1-207 would seem to promote the underlying policies and purposes of the Code. . . . By construing the section to permit a reservation of rights whenever a negotiable instrument is used to make payment on an existing debt, regardless of the nature of the underlying obligation between the parties, the commercial law of negotiable instruments is rendered more simple, clear and uniform. Moreover, the policy embodied in § 1-207, to favor a preservation of rights despite acceptance of partial satisfaction of the underlying obligation, is thus extended to reach all commercial transactions in which the Code is implicated by reason of payment by an article 3 instrument. As a consequence, such a reading of § 1-207 serves to liberalize, or "de-technicalize", that important branch of commercial law governing the full payment check.

Application of the foregoing to the facts of this case is evident. Defendant presented a "full payment" check for $500 in satisfaction of a debt in the amount of $1,080. Plaintiff indorsed the check below its notation, "Under Protest", thereby indicating its intent to preserve all rights to the $580 balance. Such an explicit reservation of rights, falling squarely within § 1-207 as we construe that provision today, was an effective means of precluding an accord and satisfaction or any other prejudice to the rights thus reserved. Regardless of whether the underlying transaction between the parties was a contract for the performance of services rather than for the sale of goods, defendant's tender of a check to plaintiff brought the attempted full payment or satisfaction of the underlying obligation within the scope of article 3, thereby rendering it a "Code-covered" transaction to which the provisions of § 1-207 are applicable.

Accordingly, the order of the Appellate Division should be reversed, with costs, and defendant's motion to dismiss denied.

CASE
11-6

The following case interprets what is required under UCC § 1-207 for a creditor to make an "explicit reservation" of rights to avoid an accord and satisfaction when cashing a "full satisfaction" check.

SULLIVAN v. CONANT VALLEY ASSOCIATES
Supreme Court of New York, (Westchester County), 1990
148 Misc. 2d 483; 560 N.Y.S. 2d 617

DONOVAN, Judge. Plaintiff... has sued the two first-named defendants in contract for a balance of moneys allegedly due him for performing plumbing work and providing certain materials improving defendants' property.

By motion, the main defendants... seek summary judgment dismissing the complaint upon ground of payment or accord and satisfaction....

The central issue presented is whether plaintiff's scratching out of "complete and final payment" verbiage placed by defendants at the top of the endorsement blocks, followed by his depositing of the checks for collection, sufficiently reserved his rights so as to permit the subsequent suit here for the higher claimed amount. The court concedes that a close and novel question of law is presented.

The rule at common law is that acceptance and cashing of a final check even with explicit words of reservation of rights by the payee as to further claims constitute in all events an accord and satisfaction. This rule was, however, substantially changed upon the passage of Uniform Commercial Code § 1-207 which allows for such reservation by the payee. That section reads in full as follows: "A party who with explicit reservation of rights performs or promises performance or assents to performance in a manner demanded or offered by the other party does not thereby prejudice the rights reserved. Such words as 'without

prejudice', 'under protest' or the like are sufficient."

While much case law has construed the section, it has primarily dealt with the types of transactions and situations covered by the provision. Research by the court has not disclosed any precedent examining what verbiage short of the type indicated in the statute would still be "explicit". The common thread, however, running between both the near cases examined and the statute itself is the necessity for "explicit" verbiage reserving further rights despite endorsement and cashing (see, "Horn Waterproofing Corp."). Here, in addition to the defendants' "full payment" conditions appearing over the endorsement blocks on the checks themselves, letters accompanying the checks from the defendants indicated the existence of the dispute and tender of the checks as a "complete amount and final payment" and "should you elect not to accept this final payment then all documents and backcharges are withdrawn".

On strength of general case authority, the statute itself which must be narrowly interpreted since in derogation of the common law and under the particular facts here, the court must conclude that standing alone, mere scratching out of final payment conditions on a check followed by endorsement and cashing is not the explicit and unambiguous reservation of rights required; further added words clearly bespeaking reservation are necessary.

Each of the following two cases deals with a claim by a debtor that a creditor's acceptance of a "full satisfaction" check resulted in an accord and satisfaction that discharged the debtor's liquidated debt.

CENTURY 21 KAATERSKILL REALTY v. GRASSO
Appellate Division, New York (3rd Dept.), 1986
124 A.D.2d 316; 508 N.Y.S.2d 99

MIKOLL, Judge. Appeal from an order of the Supreme Court at Special Term (Williams, J.), entered August 8, 1985 in Sullivan County, which denied defendants' motion to dismiss the complaint.

Plaintiff sued defendants seeking judgment in the sum of $2,200 claimed to be the balance due and owing for a real estate broker's commission for the sale of real property belonging to defendant Michele Grasso (hereinafter Grasso).

Defendants moved to dismiss the complaint on the grounds of discharge and failure to state a cause of action.

Plaintiff was retained to sell land owned by Grasso, who agreed pursuant to a written contract to pay brokerage fees of 10% of the purchase price. The property was sold for $82,000 and title was transferred on May 11, 1984. Plaintiff demanded payment of $8,200. Grasso's attorney sent plaintiff a check for $6,000 which bore the legend:

In full accord and satisfaction for any real estate commission claimed by Centruy 21 against Michele Grasso.

The check was indorsed by Rubin J. Katz, an officer of plaintiff, and deposited in plaintiff's account. Defendants contend that the $2,200 sought in plaintiff's complaint was discharged by plaintiff's acceptance without protest of the check tendered on Grasso's behalf in full satisfaction of the debt owed. Special Term held that defendants were not entitled to a dismissal of the complaint based on an accord and satisfaction in that the submissions failed to evidence the existence of a dispute which would make viable the accord and satisfaction defense.

Defendants contend that plaintiff's failure to protest the partial payment as to conform to UCC 1-207 entitles defendants to a dismissal of the complaint. . . . We concur with Special Term's interpretation that UCC 1-207 is not implicated absent a pending dispute as to delivery, acceptance or payment. Defendants never disputed the amount owed before the check was sent to plaintiff. Accord and satisfaction pursuant to UCC 1-207 pertains only to a method of procedure where one party is claiming as of right something which the other feels is unwarranted.

Order affirmed, with costs.

KING METAL PRODUCTS, INC. v. WORKMEN'S COMPENSATION BD.
Appellate Division, New York (2d Dept.), 1963
20 A.D.2d 565, 245 N.Y.S.2d 882

MEMORANDUM.

In our opinion, respondent's retention and deposit of a check in the sum of $250, drawn by petitioner's attorney to its order and bearing legends on the face and back thereof indicating that it was in full satisfaction and settlement of the judgment, did not constitute an accord and satisfaction. On the record presented,

the general rule applies that a liquidated and undisputed claim cannot be discharged by the payment of a lesser amount.

We are also of the opinion that the endorsement of the check did not constitute an agreement which was enforceable under section [5-1103 of the General Obligations Law].

QUESTIONS

1. Define consideration and what is meant by legal sufficiency.
2. Discuss illusory promises, output contracts, requirements contracts, exclusive dealing contracts, and conditional contracts.
3. Explain whether preexisting public and contractual obligations satisfy the legal requirement of consideration.

4. Explain the concept of bargained-for exchange. Is this element present with past consideration or third-party beneficiaries? Explain.
5. Identify and discuss those contracts that are enforceable even though they are not supported by consideration.

PROBLEMS

1. The chairman of the board of directors of X Corp. wrote a signed letter to P, the president, who is 60 years old and planned to retire at the end of the year. "The corporation will pay you a pension of $60,000 a year for life if you retire as planned, and agree not to take another job in this industry." P replied, "I promise to do as you wish." Two years later, X Corp. stopped the pension payments. P sues X Corp. for the current installment.

(a) May he recover? Explain.

(b) Instead of the above letter, assume that at P's retirement dinner, the chairman of the board of directors of X Corp., in his speech, said "In view of the fact that you have been faithful to X Corp. for 30 years and have resisted efforts of our competitors to hire you away from us, the corporation promises to pay you a pension of $60,000 a year for life." P stood up and said, "I accept your pension promise with gratitude." Is X Corp.'s promise enforceable by P and if not, what would be necessary to make it enforceable? Explain.

2. Alfalfa, a novice rock climber, decided to go on a very difficult climb. Half way up, he found himself in trouble. Darla, a more experienced climber, at great peril to herself, rescued Alfalfa from almost certain serious injury, if not death. Alfalfa was so grateful for what Darla had done that he promised to send her a check for $1,000. Alfalfa failed to send the check and Darla sues him for breach of contract. Judgment for whom? Explain.

3. D owed C $50,000 on a contract for the purchase of 200 air-conditioners on credit, the terms of payment stating "Payment due 60 days after delivery." Delivery was made on January 2. On March 10, D met C and told him, "I'm sorry I missed out on paying you what I owe you. Collections have been slow. If you give me until May 1, I'll pay you what I owe plus interest at 9%." C said, "O.K. I'll give you until May 1." On March 15, C changed his mind and sued D for $50,000. D's contends that the debt is not due until May 1. Is D's contention valid? Explain.

4. B borrowed $1,000 from L at 5% interest and gave L a promissory note for $1,050 payable in one year. The year having elapsed, B tendered a check for $900 with these words written on the back above the space where L would endorse it: "I (L) hereby accept the face amount of this check in complete satisfaction of the debt owed by B." L cashed the check and now seeks to recover the balance from B. Is the entire debt discharged? Explain.

5. S shipped 10 refrigerators to B pursuant to a sales contract under which title to the goods and risk of loss would pass to B upon delivery to X Railroad. The agreed price was $5,000. When the refrigerators were delivered to B, he found they were damaged. An estimate for repairing them showed it would cost up to $1,000, and an expert opinion was to the effect that they were defective when shipped. B put in a claim to S, which S rejected. B then wrote to S, "I don't like to get into a dispute of this nature. I am enclosing my check for $4,000 in full payment of the shipment." S did not reply, but he cashed the check and then sued B for the $1,000 balance. May he recover? Explain.

6. In the previous problem, assume that there was no damage to the refrigerators and no dispute, but that B did not pay. One month after payment was due, B wrote to S, "I'll pay you $4,000 if you will accept it in full payment." S wrote back, "Since I have despaired of getting any more out of you, I'll take the $4,000 in full payment. (signed) S." B paid the $4,000 and later, S sued B for the $1,000 balance. May he recover? Explain.

7. Ann owed $500 to Barry for services Barry rendered to Ann. The debt was due June 30, 1991. In March 1992, the debt was still unpaid. Barry was in urgent need of ready cash and told Ann that if she would pay $150 of the debt at once, Barry would release her from the balance. Ann paid $150 and stated to Barry that all claims had been paid in full.

(a) In August 1992, Barry demanded the unpaid balance and subsequently sued Ann for $350. Decision?

(b) Would your answer be the same if Barry had given Ann a signed receipt stating that all claims had been paid in full?

8. Eva and Maria entered into a written contract pursuant to which Eva was to render decorating services for Maria for a total price of $75,000. After the services had been performed, a good faith dispute arose between Eva and Maria over whether all of the services had been properly performed. Eva claimed that the full amount was due, but Maria argued that only $50,000 worth of services had been performed. After several weeks of argument, Maria sent a check for $60,000 to Eva on which Maria had written "payment in full for decorating services."

(a) Eva endorsed the check, without making any further notations on it, deposited it and sued Maria for the remaining $15,000 she claims is due. Judgment for whom? Explain.

(b) Instead of the facts in (a) assume that Eva wrote "under protest" on the check when she endorsed it and, after depositing it, sues Maria for $15,000. What result? Explain.

(c) Instead of the facts in (a) and (b), assume that Eva and Maria had a telephone conversation in which Eva agreed to take $60,000 in full satisfaction of Maria's obligation under the contract. Maria then sent the check, with a letter referencing the telephone conversation. Eva wrote "under protest" on the check, endorsed and deposited it, and then sued Maria for $15,000. What result? Explain.

9. Alan purchased shoes from Barbara on open account. Barbara sent Alan a bill for $10,000. Alan wrote back that 200 pairs of the shoes were defective and offered to pay $6,000 and to give Barbara his promissory note for $1,000. Barbara telephoned Alan and accepted the offer. Alan sent his check for $6,000 and his note, in accordance with the agreement. Barbara cashed the check, collected on the note, and one month later sued Alan for $3,000. Decision? Explain.

10. D owed C $10,000 under a valid loan agreement. Payment was due on September 1. D informed C that he was unable to pay on September 1.

(a) Assume that on September 5, C orally agreed to accept $8,000 plus the transfer of D's stamp collection (which C admired) as payment in full, if D would do so by September 10. D did pay the $8,000 and transferred the stamp collection to C on September 8. The stamp collection had a market value of $1,000. On September 15, C sued D for the $1,000 balance C claims is due. How much, if anything, will C recover from D? Explain.

(b) Instead of the assumption in (a), assume that on September 5, C orally agreed to accept $9,000 in full payment of D's debt if D paid before September 10. Thereupon, D paid C $9,000 on September 8. On September 15, C sued D for $1,000. How much, if anything, will C recover from D? Explain.

(c) Would your answer to (b) be different if C agreed in a signed writing to accept $9,000 in full payment of D's debt? Explain.

11. George owed Keith $800 on a personal loan. Neither the amount of the debt nor George's liability to pay the $800 was disputed. Keith had also rendered services as a carpenter to George without any agreement as to the price to be paid. When the work was completed, an honest and reasonable difference of opinion developed between George and Keith with respect to the value of Keith's services. Upon receiving from Keith a bill of $600 for the carpentry services, George mailed in a properly stamped and addressed envelope his check for $800 to Keith. In an accompanying letter, George stated that the enclosed check was in full settlement of both claims. Keith endorsed and cashed the check. Thereafter, Keith unsuccessfully sought to collect from George an alleged unpaid balance of $600. Keith then sued George for $600. Decision?

12. C, a building contractor, entered into a written agreement with O, the owner of 27 Y Street, to build for O a new wing on his house for $50,000. After the work was one-half done, C complained about the rising cost of materials and stopped work. O said to C: "If you go ahead and finish the job, I'll pay you a bonus of $5,000." C agreed and finished the job. C then demanded payment of $55,000, but O refused to pay more than $50,000.

(a) How much may C collect from O? Explain.

(b) Assume that C wrote on the bottom of the written contract, "The agreed price for the above work is $55,000" and said to O: "I'll go ahead if you sign that," which O did. How much may C collect from O? Explain.

13. Armand was hired to work as the chef for the restaurant at Scallop's seaside resort for 3 months during the summer, under a written contract that provided that Armand would receive compensation of $50,000. During the first month, the guests were wildly enthusiastic about the quality of the food and Scallop's reservations for the resort and restaurant doubled. Noticing this, Armand felt he was entitled to share in Scallop's increased profits. During a conversation, Scallop promised to pay Armand a $20,000 bonus at the end of the summer if he continued to work under his contract. At the end of the three months, Scallop paid Armand $50,000 and refused to pay the $20,000 bonus he had promised. Armand sued Scallop for breach of contract. Judgment for whom? Explain.

14. Taylor assaulted his wife, who then took refuge in Ms. Harrington's house. The next day, Mr. Taylor entered the house and began another assault on his wife, who knocked him down and, while he was lying on the floor, attempted to cut his head open or decapitate him with an axe. Harrington intervened to stop the bloodshed, and the axe, as it was descending, fell upon her hand, mutilating it badly, but sparing Taylor his life. Afterwards, Taylor orally promised to compensate Harrington for her injury He paid a small sum but nothing more. Harrington sued to enforce Taylor's promise. Decision?

15. (a) Judy orally promises her daughter, Liza, that she will give her a tract of land for her home. Liza, as intended by Judy, gives up her homestead and takes possession of the land. Liza lives there for six months and starts construction of a home. Is Judy bound to convey the real estate?

(b) Ralph, knowing that his son, Ed, desires to purchase a tract of land, promises to give him the $25,000 he needs for the purchase. Ed, relying on this promise, buys an option on the tract of land. Can Ralph rescind his promise?

16. Anna Feinberg began working for the Pfeiffer Company in 1950 at age 17. By 1987 she had attained the position of bookkeeper, office manager, and assistant treasurer. In appreciation for her skill, dedication, and long years of service, the Pfeiffer Board of Directors resolved to increase Feinberg's monthly salary to $1,400 and to create for her a retirement plan. The plan allowed that Feinberg would be given the privilege of retiring from active duty at any time she chose and that she would receive retirement pay of $700 per month, although the Board expressed the hope that Feinberg would continue to serve the company for many years. Feinberg, however, chose to retire two years later, in 1989. The Pfeiffer Company paid Feinberg her retirement pay until 1996. The company discontinued payments, alleging that no contract had been made by the Board of Directors as there had been no consideration paid by Feinberg, and that the resolution was merely a promise to make a gift. Feinberg sued. Is the promise supported by consideration? Is the promise enforceable? Explain.

http: **Internet Exercise** Find several contracts and determine what consideration is given by the parties.

Performance, Breach, and Discharge

The subject of discharge of contracts concerns the termination of contractual duties. In earlier chapters we have seen how parties may become bound to a contract. It is also important to know how a person may become unbound from a contract. For although contractual promises are made for a purpose, and the parties reasonably expect this purpose to be fulfilled by performance, performance of a contractual duty is only one method of discharge.

Whatever causes a binding promise to cease to be binding constitutes a discharge of the contract. In general, there are four kinds of discharge: (1) performance by the parties, (2) material breach by one or both of the parties, (3) agreement of the parties, and (4) operation of law. Moreover, many contractual promises are not absolute promises to perform but rather are conditional; that is, they are dependent upon the happening or nonhappening of a specific event. After a discussion of conditions, the four kinds of discharge will be covered.

CONDITIONS

A **condition** is an event whose happening or nonhappening affects a duty of performance under a contract. Some conditions must be satisfied before any duty to perform arises; others terminate the duty to perform; still others either limit or modify the duty to perform. A promisor inserts conditions into a contract for her protection and benefit. Furthermore, the more conditions to which a promise is subject, the less content the promise has. For example, a promise to pay $8,000, provided that such sum is realized from the sale of an automobile, provided the automobile is sold within sixty days, and provided that the automobile, which has been stolen, can be found, is clearly different from, and worth considerably less than, an unconditional promise by the same promisor to pay $8,000.

A fundamental difference exists between the breach or nonperformance of a contractual promise and the failure or nonhappening of a condition. A breach of contract subjects the promisor to liability. It may or may not, depending upon its materiality, excuse nonperformance by the nonbreaching party of his duty under the contract. The happening or nonhappening of a condition, on the other hand, either prevents a party from acquiring a right to performance by the other party or deprives him of such a right, but subjects neither party to any liability.

Conditions may be classified by *how* they are imposed: express conditions, implied-in-fact conditions, or implied-in-law conditions (also called constructive conditions). They also may be classified by *when* they affect a duty of performance: conditions concurrent, conditions precedent, or conditions subsequent. These two ways of classifying conditions are not mutually exclusive; for example, a condition may be constructive and concurrent or express and precedent.

Express Condition

An **express condition** is explicitly set forth in language. No particular form of words is necessary to create an express condition, so long as the event to which the performance of the promise is made subject is clearly expressed. An express condition is usually preceded by such words as "provided that," "on condition that," "if," "while," "after," "upon," or "as soon as."

The basic rule applied to express conditions is that they must be fully and literally performed before the conditional duty to perform arises. Where application of the full and literal performance test would result in a forfeiture, however, the courts usually apply to the completed portion of the condition a *substantial satisfaction* test, as discussed later in this chapter under the section titled "Substantial Performance."

Satisfaction of a Contracting Party   The parties to a contract may agree that performance by one of them will be to the **satisfaction** of the other, who will not be obligated to pay for such performance unless he is satisfied. This is an express condition to the duty to pay for the performance. Assume that tailor Melissa contracts to make a suit of clothes to Brent's satisfaction, and that Brent promises to pay Melissa $350 for the suit if he is satisfied with it when completed. Melissa completes the suit using materials ordered by Brent. Though the suit fits Brent beautifully, he tells Melissa that he is not satisfied with it and refuses to accept or pay for it. If Brent's dissatisfaction is honest and in good faith, even if it is unreasonable, Melissa is not entitled to recover $350 or any amount from Brent by reason of the nonhappening of the express condition. Where satisfaction relates to a matter of personal taste, opinion, or judgment, the law applies the **subjective satisfaction** standard: if the promisor in good faith is dissatisfied, the condition has not occurred.

If the contract does not clearly indicate that satisfaction is subjective, or if the performance contracted for relates to mechanical fitness or utility, the law assumes an **objective satisfaction** standard. For example, the objective standard would apply to the sale of a building or standard goods, such as steel, coal, or grain. In such cases, the question would not be whether the promisor was actually satisfied with the performance by the other party but whether, as a reasonable person, he ought to be satisfied.

◆ SEE CASE 12-1

Satisfaction of a Third Party   A contract may condition the duty to accept and pay for the performance of the other party upon the approval of a third party. For example, building contracts commonly provide that before the owner is required to pay, the builder shall furnish a certificate of the architect stating that the building has been constructed according to the plans and specifications. For although the owner is paying for the building, not for the certificate, he must have both the building and the certificate before he is obligated to pay. The duty of payment was made expressly conditional upon the presentation of the certificate.

Implied-in-Fact Conditions

Implied-in-fact conditions are similar to express conditions, in that they must fully and literally occur and in that the parties understand them to be part of the agreement. They differ in that they are not stated in express language; rather, they are necessarily inferred from the terms of the contract, the nature of the transaction, or the conduct of the parties. Thus, if Fernando, for $750, contracts to paint Peggy's house any color Peggy desires, it is necessarily implied in fact that Peggy will inform Fernando of the desired color before Fernando begins to paint. The notification of choice of color is an implied-in-fact condition, an operative event that must occur before Fernando is subject to the duty of painting the house.

Implied-in-Law Conditions

An **implied-in-law condition**, or a **constructive condition**, is imposed by law to accomplish a just and fair result. It differs from an express condition and an implied-in-fact condition in two ways: (1) it is not contained in the language of the contract or necessarily inferred from the contract, and (2) it need only be substantially performed. For example, Melinda contracts to sell a certain tract of land to Kelly for $18,000, but the contract is silent as to the time of delivery of the deed and payment of the price. The law will imply that the respective performances are not independent of one another; consequently, the courts will treat the promises as mutually dependent and will therefore hold that a delivery or tender of the deed by Melinda to Kelly is a condition to Kelly's duty to pay the price. Conversely, Melinda's duty to deliver the deed to Kelly is conditioned upon the payment or tender of $18,000 by Kelly to Melinda. If the contract specifies a sale on credit, however, giving Kelly thirty days after delivery of the deed within which to pay the price, these conditions are not implied by law because the parties have expressly agreed to make their respective duties of performance independent of each other.

Concurrent Conditions

Concurrent conditions occur when the mutual duties of performances are to take place simultaneously. As indicated in the previous section, in the absence of an agreement to the contrary, the law assumes that the respective performances under a contract are concurrent conditions.

Conditions Precedent

A **condition precedent** is an event that must occur before performance under a contract is due. For instance, if Gail is to deliver shoes to Mike on June 1, with Mike's duty to pay for the shoes on July 15, Gail's delivery of the shoes is a condition precedent to Mike's performance. Similarly, if Seymour promises to buy Edna's land for $50,000, provided Seymour can obtain financing in the amount of $40,000 at 10 percent interest or less for thirty years within sixty days of signing the contract, Seymour's obtaining the specified financing is a condition precedent to his duty. If the condition is satisfied, Seymour is bound to perform; if it is not, he is not so bound. Seymour, however, is under an implied-in-law duty to use his best efforts to obtain financing under these terms.

Conditions Subsequent

A **condition subsequent** is an event that terminates an existing duty. For example, where goods are sold under terms of "sale or return," the buyer has the right to return the goods to the seller within a stated period but is under an immediate duty to pay the price unless she and the seller have agreed upon credit. A return of the goods, which operates as a condition subsequent, terminates the duty to pay the price. Conditions subsequent occur very infrequently in contract law, while conditions precedent are quite common.

DISCHARGE BY PERFORMANCE

Discharge by performance is undoubtedly the most frequent method of discharging a contractual duty. If a promisor exactly performs his duty under the contract, he is no longer subject to that duty.

Every contract imposes upon each party a duty of good faith and fair dealing in its performance and its enforcement. Restatement, Section 205. As discussed in Chapter 7, the UCC imposes a comparable duty. Section 1–203.

Tender is an offer by one party—who is ready, willing, and able to perform—to the other party to perform his obligation according to the terms of the contract. Under a bilateral contract, the refusal or rejection of a tender of performance may be treated as a repudiation that excuses or discharges the tendering party from further duty of performance under the contract. For example, on the due date of contractual performance, George arrives at Thelma's house prepared to do plumbing work under their contract. Thelma, however, refuses to allow George to enter the premises. George is therefore discharged from performing the contract and has a legal claim against Thelma for material breach.

If a debtor owes money on several accounts and tenders to his creditor less than the total amounts due, the debtor has the right to designate the account or debt to which the payment is to be applied, and the creditor must accept this direction. If the debtor does not direct the application of the payment, the creditor may apply it to any account owing to him by the debtor or distribute it among several such accounts.

DISCHARGE BY BREACH

Breach of contract is the unexcused failure of a party to perform her promise. While breach of contract always gives rise to a cause of action for damages by the aggrieved (injured) party, it may have a more important effect: an uncured (uncorrected) *material* breach by one party operates as an excuse for nonperformance by the other party and discharges the aggrieved party from any further duty under the contract. If, on the other hand, the breach is not material, the aggrieved party is not discharged from the contract, although she may recover money damages. Under the Code, *any* deviation discharges the aggrieved party.

Material Breach

An unjustified failure to perform *substantially* the obligations promised in a contract constitutes a **material breach**. The key is whether, despite the breach, the aggrieved party obtained substantially what he bargained for or whether the breach significantly impaired his rights under the contract. A material breach discharges the aggrieved party from his duty of performance. For instance, Esta orders a custom-made, tailored suit from Stuart to be made of wool; but Stuart instead makes the suit of cotton. Assuming that the labor component of this contract predominates and thus the contract is not considered a sale of goods, Stuart has materially breached the contract. Consequently, Esta not only is discharged from her duty to pay for the suit but may also recover money damages from Stuart due to his breach.

Although there are no clear-cut rules as to what constitutes a material breach, the Restatement, Section 241, lists a number of relevant factors:

In determining whether a failure to render or to offer performance is material, the following circumstances are significant:

(a) the extent to which the injured party will be deprived of the benefit which he reasonably expected;

(b) the extent to which the injured party can be adequately compensated for the part of that benefit of which he will be deprived;

(c) the extent to which the party failing to perform or to offer to perform will suffer forfeiture;

(d) the likelihood that the party failing to perform or to offer to perform will cure his failure, taking account of all the circumstances including any reasonable assurances;

(e) the extent to which the behavior of the party failing to perform or to offer to perform comports with standards of good faith and fair dealing.

An *intentional* breach of contract is generally held to be material. Moreover, a failure to perform a promise promptly is a material breach if "**time is of the essence,**" that is, if the parties have clearly indicated that a failure to perform by the stated time is material; otherwise, the aggrieved party may recover damages only for the loss caused by the delay. Finally, the parties to a contract may, within limits, specify what breaches are to be considered material.

◆ SEE CASES 12-2 AND 12-3

Prevention of Performance   One party's substantial interference with or **prevention of performance** by the other generally constitutes a material breach that discharges the other party to the contract. For instance, Craig prevents an architect from giving Maud a certificate that is a condition to Craig's liability to pay Maud a certain sum of money. Craig may not then use Maud's failure to produce a certificate as an excuse for his nonpayment. Likewise, if Harold has contracted to grow a certain crop for Rafael, and Rafael plows the field and destroys the seedlings after Harold has planted the seed, his interference with Harold's performance discharges Harold from his duty under the contract. It does not, however, discharge Rafael from his duty under the contract.

Perfect Tender Rule   The Code greatly alters the common law doctrine of material breach by adopting what is known as the **perfect tender rule**. This rule essentially provides that *any* deviation from the promised performance in a sales contract under the Code constitutes a material breach of the contract and discharges the aggrieved party from his duty of performance. Thus, if a seller of camera accessories delivers to a buyer ninety-nine of the hundred ordered pieces, or ninety-nine correct accessories and one incorrect accessory, the buyer may rightfully reject the improper delivery.

Substantial Performance

If a party substantially, but not completely, performs her obligations under a contract, the common law generally will allow her to obtain the other party's performance, less any damages caused by the partial performance. Thus, in the specially ordered suit illustration discussed in the previous section, if Stuart, the tailor, used the correct fabric but improperly used black buttons instead of blue, Stuart would be permitted to collect from Esta the contract price of the suit less the damage, if any, caused to Esta by the substitution of the wrongly colored buttons. The doctrine of substantial performance assumes particular importance in the construction industry in cases where a structure is built on the aggrieved party's land. Consider the following: Kent Construction Co. builds a $300,000 house for Martha but deviates from the specifications, causing Martha $10,000 in damages. If this breach were considered material, then Martha would not have to pay for the house that is now on her land. This would clearly constitute an unjust forfeiture on Kent's part. Therefore, because Kent's performance is substantial, the courts would probably not deem the breach material. As a result, Kent would be able to collect $290,000 from Martha.

Anticipatory Repudiation

A breach of contract, as previously discussed, is a failure to perform the terms of a contract. Although it is logically and physically impossible to fail to perform a duty before the date on which that performance is due, a party nonetheless may announce before the due date that she will not perform, or she may commit an act that makes her unable to perform. Either act repudiates the contract, which notifies the other party that a breach is imminent. Such repudiation before the performance date fixed by the contract is called an **anticipatory repudiation**. The courts, as shown in the leading case of *Hochster v. De La Tour*, view it as a breach that discharges the nonrepudiating party's duty to perform and permits her to bring suit immediately. Nonetheless, the nonbreaching party may wait until the time the performance is due, to see if the repudiator will retract his repudiation and perform his contractual duties. If the repudiator does perform, then there is a discharge by performance; if he does not perform, there is a material breach.

❖ SEE CASE 12-4

Material Alteration of Written Contract

An unauthorized alteration or change of any of the material terms or provisions of a written contract or document is a discharge of the entire contract. To be a discharge, the alteration must be material and fraudulent and must be the act of a party to the contract or someone acting on his behalf. An alteration is material if it would vary any party's legal relations with the maker of the alteration or would adversely affect that party's legal relations with a third person. Restatement, Section 286. An unauthorized change in the terms of a written contract by a person who is not a party to the contract does not discharge the contract.

DISCHARGE BY AGREEMENT OF THE PARTIES

The parties to a contract may by agreement discharge each other from performance under the contract. They may do this by rescission, substituted contract, accord and satisfaction, or novation.

Mutual Rescission

A **mutual rescission** is an agreement between the parties to terminate their respective duties under the contract. Literally a contract to end a contract, it must contain all the essentials of a contract. In rescinding an executory, bilateral contract, each party furnishes consideration in giving up his rights under the contract in exchange for the other party's relinquishment of his rights under the contract. Where one party has already fully performed, a mutual rescission may not be binding at common law because of lack of consideration.

Substituted Contract

A **substituted contract** is a new contract accepted by both parties in satisfaction of their duties under the original contract.

Restatement, Section 279. A substituted contract immediately discharges the original duty and imposes new obligations. For example, the Restatement, Section 279, gives the following illustration:

> A and B make a contract under which A promises to build on a designated spot a building, for which B promises to pay $100,000. Later, before this contract is performed, A and B make a new contract under which A is to build on the same spot a different building, for which B is to pay $200,000. The new contract is a substituted contract and the duties of A and B under the original contract are discharged.

Accord and Satisfaction

An **accord** is a contract by which an obligee promises to accept a stated performance in satisfaction of the obligor's existing contractual duty. Restatement, Section 281. The performance of the accord is called a **satisfaction**, and it discharges the original duty. Thus, if Ted owes Alan $500 and the parties agree that Ted shall paint Alan's house in satisfaction of the debt, the agreement is an accord. The debt, however, is not discharged until Ted performs the accord by painting Alan's house.

◈ SEE CASE 12-2

Novation

A **novation** is a substituted contract that involves an agreement among *three* parties to substitute a new promisee for the existing promisee, or to replace the existing promisor with a new one. Restatement, Section 280. A novation discharges the old obligation by creating a new contract in which there is either a new promisee or a new promisor. Thus, if B owes A $500, and A, B, and C agree that C will pay the debt and B will be discharged, the novation is the substitution of the new promisor C for B. Alternatively, if the three parties agree that B will pay $500 to D instead of to A, the novation is the substitution of a new promisee (D for A). In each instance, the debt B owes to A is discharged.

DISCHARGE BY OPERATION OF LAW

This chapter has considered various ways by which contractual duties may be discharged. In all of these cases, the discharge resulted from the action of one or both of the parties to the contract. This section examines discharge brought about by the operation of law.

Impossibility

"Contract liability is strict liability…[and an] obligor is therefore liable for in damages breach of contract even if he is without fault and even if circumstances have made the contract more burdensome or less desirable than he had anticipated." Restatement, Introductory Note to Chapter 11. Historically, the common law excused a party from contractual duties for **objective impossibility**; that is, where no one could render the performance. If, by comparison, a particular contracting party is unable to perform because, for instance, of financial inability or lack of competence, this **subjective impossibility** does not excuse the promisor from liability for breach of contract. For example, the Christys entered into a written contract to purchase an apartment house from Pilkinton for $30,000. Pilkinton tendered a deed to the property and demanded payment of the unpaid balance of $29,000 due on the purchase price. Because of a decline in their used car business, the Christys, who did not possess and could not borrow the unpaid balance, asserted that it was impossible for them to perform their contract. The court held for Pilkinton, identifying a distinction between objective impossibility, which amounts to saying, "the thing cannot be done," and subjective impossibility—"I cannot do it." The latter, which is illustrated by a promisor's financial inability to pay, does not discharge the contractual duty. *Christy v. Pilkinton*, 224 Ark. 407, 273 S.W.2d 533 (1954).

The **death** or **incapacity** of a person who has contracted to render *personal services* discharges his contractual duty due to objective impossibility. Restatement, Section 262. For example, a singer unable to perform a contractual engagement because of a severe cold is excused from performance, as is a pianist or violinist who is unable to perform because of a hand injury.

Destruction of Subject Matter Destruction of the subject matter or of the agreed-upon means of performance of a contract, without the fault of the promisor, is also excusable impossibility. "Subject matter" here means specific subject matter. Suppose that Alice contracts to sell to Gary five office chairs at an agreed price. Alice has 100 of these chairs in stock, out of which she expects to deliver five to Gary. Before she can do so, fire destroys the entire 100 chairs. Though not at fault, Alice is not excused from performance. This was not a contract for the sale of specific goods; consequently, Alice could perform the contract by delivering to Gary any five chairs of the kind and grade specified in the contract, assuming that more such chairs are available from the manufacturer. Her failure to do so will render her liable to Gary for breach of contract. Suppose, now, that Alice and Gary make a contract for Alice to manufacture these five chairs in her factory but that prior to their manufacture, fire destroys the factory. Again, Alice is not at fault. Although the chairs are available from other manufacturers, the destruction of the factory discharges Alice's duty to deliver the chairs. Suppose further that Alice and Gary enter into a contract under which Alice is to sell to Gary the particular desk that she uses in her private office. This desk, and no other, is the specific subject matter of the contract. If, before the sale is completed, this desk is destroyed by fire without Alice's fault, it is then impossible for Alice to perform. The contract is therefore discharged.

Subsequent Illegality If the performance of a contract which was legal when formed becomes illegal or impractical by reason of a subsequently enacted law, the duty of performance is discharged. Restatement, Section 264. For example, Jill contracts to sell and deliver to Fred ten cases of a certain whiskey each month for one year. A subsequent prohibition law makes the manufacture, transportation, or sale of intoxicating liquor unlawful. The contractual duties that Jill has yet to perform are discharged.

Frustration of Purpose Where, after a contract is made, a party's principal purpose is substantially frustrated without his fault by the occurrence of an event the nonoccurrence of which was a basic assumption on which the contract was made, his remaining duties to render performance are discharged, unless the party has assumed the risk. Restatement, Second 265. This rule developed from the so-called coronation cases. When, upon the death of his mother, Queen Victoria, Edward VII became King of England, impressive coronation ceremonies were planned, including a procession along a designated route through certain streets in London. Owners and lessees of buildings along the route made contracts to permit the use of rooms with a view on the date scheduled for the procession. The King, however, became ill, and the procession did not take place. The purpose for using the rooms having failed, the rooms

were not used. Numerous suits were filed, some by landowners seeking to hold the would-be viewers liable on their promises, and some by the would-be viewers seeking to recover money they paid in advance for the rooms. The principle involved was novel, but from these cases evolved the **frustration of purpose doctrine**, under which a contract is discharged if supervening circumstances make impossible the fulfillment of the purpose that both parties had in mind, unless one of the parties has contractually assumed that risk.

Commercial Impracticability The Restatement, Section 261, and the Code, Section 2–615, have relaxed the traditional test of objective impossibility by providing that performance need not be actually or literally impossible, but that commercial impracticability will excuse nonperformance. This does not mean mere hardship or an unexpectedly increased cost of performance. A party will be discharged from performing his duty only when a supervening event not caused by his fault makes his performance impracticable. Moreover, the nonoccurrence of the subsequent event must have been a "basic assumption" both parties made when entering into the contract, neither party having assumed the risk that the event would occur. Commercial impracticability could include "a severe shortage of raw materials or of supplies due to a contingency such as war, embargo, local crop failure, unforeseen shutdown of major sources of supply or the

◆ FIGURE 12-1 Discharge of Contracts

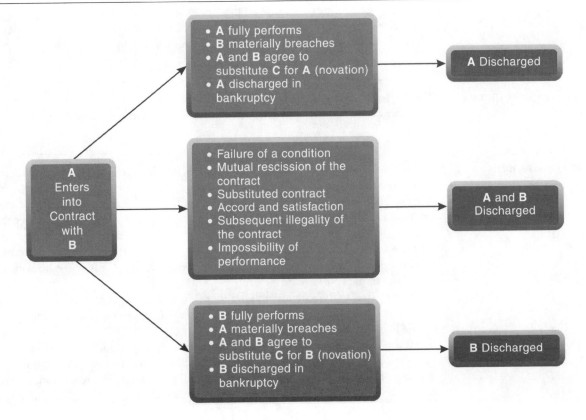

like, which either causes a marked increase in cost or altogether prevents the seller from securing supplies necessary to his performance...." UCC Section 2–615, Comment 4.

◆ SEE CASE 12-5

Bankruptcy

Bankruptcy is a discharge of a contractual duty by operation of law available to a debtor who, by compliance with the requirements of the Bankruptcy Code, obtains an order of discharge by the bankruptcy court. It is applicable only to obligations that the Code provides are dischargeable in bankruptcy.

Statute of Limitations

At common law a plaintiff was not subject to any time limitation within which to bring an action. Now, however, all States have statutes providing such a limitation. The majority of courts hold that the running of the period of the statute of limitations does not operate to discharge the obligation, but only to bar the creditor's right to bring an action.

◆ SEE FIGURE 12-1 Discharge of Contracts

CHAPTER SUMMARY

Conditions

Definition of a Condition an event whose happening or nonhappening affects a duty of performance

Express Condition contingency explicitly set forth in language
- *Satisfaction* express condition making performance contingent upon one party's approval of the other's performance
- *Subjective Satisfaction* approval based upon a party's honestly held opinion
- *Objective Satisfaction* approval based upon whether a reasonable person would be satisfied

Implied-in-Fact Conditions contingency understood by the parties to be part of the agreement, though not expressed

Implied-in-Law Conditions contingency not contained in the language of the contract but imposed by law; also called a constructive condition

Concurrent Conditions conditions that are to take place at the same time

Conditions Precedent an event that must or must not occur before performance is due

Conditions Subsequent an event that terminates a duty of performance

---

Discharge by Performance

Discharge termination of a contractual duty

Performance fulfillment of a contractual obligation resulting in a discharge

---

Discharge by Breach

Definition of Breach a wrongful failure to perform the terms of a contract that gives rise to a right to damages by the injured party

Material Breach nonperformance that significantly impairs the injured party's rights under the contract and discharges the injured party from any further duty under the contract
- *Prevention of Performance* one party's substantial interference with or prevention of performance by the other; constitutes a material breach and discharges the other party to the contract
- *Perfect Tender Rule* standard under the UCC that a seller's performance under a sales contract must strictly comply with contractual duties and that any deviation discharges the injured party

Substantial Performance performance that is incomplete but that does not defeat the purpose of the contract; does not discharge the injured party but entitles him to damages

Anticipatory Repudiation an inability or refusal to perform, before performance is due, that is treated as a breach, allowing the nonrepudiating party to bring suit immediately

Material Alteration a material and fraudulent alteration of a written contract by a party to the contract; discharges the entire contract

---

Discharge by Agreement of the Parties

Mutual Rescission an agreement between the parties to terminate their respective duties under the contract

Substituted Contract a new contract accepted by both parties in satisfaction of the parties' duties under the original contract

Accord and Satisfaction substituted duty under a contract (accord) and the discharge of the prior contractual obligation by performance of the new duty (satisfaction)

Novation a substituted contract involving a new third-party promisor or promisee

---

Discharge by Operation of Law **Impossibility** performance of contract cannot be done

- *Subjective Impossibility* the promisor—but not all promisors—cannot perform; does not discharge the promisor
- *Objective Impossibility* no promisor is able to perform; generally discharges the promisor
- *Destruction of Subject Matter* will discharge contract if it occurs without the promisor's fault
- *Subsequent Illegality* if performance becomes illegal or impractical as a result of a change in the law, the duty of performance is discharged
- *Frustration of Purpose* principal purpose of a contract cannot be fulfilled because of a subsequent event
- *Commercial Impracticability* where performance can be accomplished only under unforeseen and unjust hardship, the contract is discharged under the Code and the Restatement

Bankruptcy discharge available to a debtor who obtains an order of discharge by the bankruptcy court

Statute of Limitations after the statute of limitations has run, the debt is not discharged, but the creditor cannot maintain an action against the debtor

---

CASES

The following case involves an employment contract pursuant to which the employee must perform to the employer's satisfaction. The court discusses how satisfaction must be defined or measured.

CASE

12-1

APPELGATE v. MACFADDEN NEWSPAPER CORP.

Appellate Division, New York (1st Dept.), 1925
214 A.D.221, 212 N.Y.S. 67

MERRELL, Judge. The action was brought to recover the sum of $12,000 damages alleged to have been sustained by the plaintiff by reason of his wrongful discharge by the defendant from its employ. The contract between the parties whereby the plaintiff was employed by the defendant was in writing. The defendant is a newspaper publishing corporation and employed the plaintiff "as Editor of the Saturday feature section and to have charge of the Rotogravure section" of the defendant's newspaper. The contract, a copy of which is annexed to the complaint, recites that "Whereas, Mr. Appelgate is an editor possessing unique and original ability," and the employer desired to secure his exclusive services, the said Appelgate desiring to secure and accept employment with the defendant, "First. The Employer does hereby employ the Employee to render his services as Editor of the Saturday feature section and to have charge of the Rotogravure Section of the newspaper to be published by the MacFadden Newspaper Publishing Corporation exclusively...." It is further provided "that the Employee will work for and devote his entire time, skill, attention and energy to the Employer exclusively," and that "it being conceded by the Employee that his services are special, unique and extraordinary." In the 4th paragraph of the contract it is provided: "Fourth. The Employee shall faithfully execute to the satisfaction of the Employer all instructions in respect to his duties given by his Employer."

The plaintiff alleges that the contract in question was entered into between the parties on July 28, 1924, and that pursuant thereto and on or about August 4, 1924, the plaintiff entered upon his duties as editor of the Saturday feature section and took charge of the rotogravure section of the newspaper published by the defendant, and continued to perform such duties until on or about November 7, 1924, and duly performed all the terms and conditions on the part of the plaintiff to be performed under the said agreement; that on or about said last-mentioned date the defendant wrongfully and without just cause therefor discharged the plaintiff to plaintiff's damage in the sum of $12,000.

A perusal of the contract discloses that the parties regarded the services of the plaintiff for which the defendant contracted as of the character commonly known as unique. The contract itself recites that "Mr. Appelgate is an editor possessing unique and original ability." Plaintiff was hired as "Editor of the Saturday feature section and to have charge of the Rotogravure Section" of the defendant's newspaper. There can be no doubt that the parties understood that the plaintiff was to render services involving "art, taste, fancy and judgment."

In a contract for services involving fancy, taste and judgment, the question whether the fancy, taste or judgment of the employer is arbitrary or unreasonable does not arise, the question being whether the claimed dissatisfaction was feigned or genuine.

In *Crawford v. Mail & Express Publishing Co.* the plaintiff was employed as an editor to write at least two columns a week on the progress of the world or other appropriate subjects for publication in The Mail and Express, and in his contract with the defendant agreed that his services would be satisfactory to the defendant, and that in case they were not he should receive one week's notice. In discussing the absence of limitation upon the exercise by the employer of its judgment as to what was satisfactory to it, the Court of Appeals said "But, on the part of the publishers of The Mail & Express, it is very clear that they did not intend to be bound for a period longer than his

services proved satisfactory, and that they expressly reserved the right to discharge him upon a week's notice. It is also apparent from a reading of the contract that the employment was not intended to be that of an ordinary servant to perform work, labor and services of an ordinary business or of a commercial nature. He was not called upon to perform the work of an ordinary reporter, writing up the general news of the day, but contracted to prepare articles on the progress of the world or other appropriate subjects in the line of the policy of the paper for the purpose, as expressed, of promoting the general interests of the paper, of aiding in its circulation and the obtaining of advertisements, by improving the quality of its contents. The evident design was that the articles should be interesting and attractive, involving art, taste, fancy and judgment. There is no provision in the contract in any manner limiting the publishers in the exercise of their judgment as to what is satisfactory, but if his services are unsatisfactory for any reason they are given the right to terminate the employment upon a week's notice, at any time they so elect."

In Diamond v. Mendelsohn the contract required the employee to "perform the duties of foreman competently and energetically to the best of his abilities and complete satisfaction of his employers." Mr. Justice CLARKE of this court, now its presiding justice, in writing in that case said: "There is no doubt that under the terms of this written contract it lay within the power of the defendants to discharge the plaintiff because he did not perform his duties to their complete satisfaction and that it would not be proper to submit to a jury the question whether they ought to have been satisfied."

It, therefore, seems very clear to me that the only question to be determined upon the trial was as to whether the dissatisfaction pleaded by the defendant as ground for the discharge of the plaintiff was real or feigned. If the dissatisfaction was a mere whim of the employer, then, of course, it was not justified in terminating the contract, but if, in fact, the defendant was dissatisfied with the special and unique services rendered by the plaintiff as editor, then the defendant was justified in discharging him. The contract with the plaintiff clearly involved personal taste, fancy and judgment, and when the employer became dissatisfied with the services of the character specified which its employee was to render, it had the right to discharge him and was not called upon to give reasons therefor.

The order appealed from should be reversed.

ASSOCIATED BUILDERS, INC. v. WILLIAM M. COGGINS et al.

Supreme Judicial Court of Maine, 1999
1999 ME 12, 722 A.2d 1278
http://caselaw.lp.findlaw.com/scripts/getcase.pl?court=me&vol=99me12as&invol=1

Dana, J.

Associated Builders, Inc. appeals from a grant of a summary judgment entered in the Superior Court***in favor of the defendants William M. Coggins and Benjamin W. Coggins, d/b/a Ben & Bill's Chocolate Emporium. Associated contends that the court erred when it held that despite a late payment by the Cogginses, an accord and satisfaction relieved the Cogginses of a contractual liability. The Cogginses argue that the three-day delay in payment was not a material breach of the accord and, even if the breach was material, Associated waived its right to enforce the forfeiture. We agree with the Cogginses and affirm the judgment.

Associated provided labor and materials to the Cogginses to complete a structure on Main Street in Bar Harbor. After a dispute arose regarding compensation, Associated and the Cogginses executed an agreement stating that there existed an outstanding balance of $70,005.54 and setting forth the following terms of repayment:

> It is agreed that, two payments will be made by [the Cogginses] to [Associated] as follows: Twenty Five Thousand Dollars ($25,000.00) on or before June 1, 1996 and Twenty Five Thousand Dollars ($25,000.00) on or before June 1, 1997. No interest will be charged or paid providing payments are made as agreed. If the payments are not made as agreed then interest shall accrue at 10% [ ] per annum figured from the date of default. There will be no prepayment penalties applied. It is further agreed that Associated Builders will forfeit the balance of Twenty Thousand and Five Dollars and Fifty Four Cents ($20,005.54) providing the above payments are made as agreed.

The Cogginses made their first payment in accordance with the agreement. The second payment, however, was delivered three days late on June 4, 1997. Claiming a breach of the contract, Associated filed a complaint demanding the balance of $20,005.54, plus interest and cost. The Cogginses answered the complaint raising the affirmative defense of an accord and satisfaction and waiver. Both parties moved for a summary judgment. The court granted the Cogginses' motion and Associated appealed.

* * *

"An accord 'is a contract under which an obligee promises to accept a substituted performance in future satisfaction of the obligor's duty.'" [Citation.] Settlement of a disputed claim is sufficient consideration for an accord and satisfaction. [Citation.] Here, the court correctly found the June 15, 1995 agreement to be an accord.

Satisfaction is the execution or performance of the accord. See RESTATEMENT (SECOND) OF CONTRACTS § 281(1) (1981). If the obligor breaches the accord, the obligee may enforce either the original duty or any duty pursuant to the accord. [Citations.] The obligor's breach of the accord, however, must be material. [Citations.] The question before the court, therefore, was whether the Cogginses' late payment constituted a material breach of the accord. The court found that it was not.

We apply traditional contract principles to determine if a party has committed a material breach. [Citation.] A material breach "is a nonperformance of a duty that is so material and important as to justify the injured party in regarding the whole transaction as at an end." [Citation]; see RESTATEMENT (SECOND) OF CONTRACTS § 241 (1981). [Court's footnote: The Restatement lists five factors as significant in determining if a failure to render performance is material: (a) the extent to which the injured party will be deprived of the benefit which he reasonably expected; (b) the extent to which the injured party can be adequately compensated for the part of the benefit of which he will be deprived; (c) the extent to which the party failing to perform***will suffer forfeiture; (d) the likelihood that the party failing to perform***will cure his failure***; (e) the extent to which the behavior of the party failing to perform or to offer to perform comports with standards of good faith and fair dealing.]

"Time of performance is merely one element in determining whether a defective or incomplete or belated performance is substantial [performance]." [Citation.] Applying these principles, courts have found that a slight delay of payment that causes no detriment or prejudice to the obligee is not a material breach. [Citations.]

We discern no error in the Superior Court's finding that the Cogginses' payment to Associated after a three-day delay was not a material breach and, therefore, satisfied the June 15, 1995 accord. [Citation.] By receiving the second and final payment of $25,000, Associated was not deprived of the benefit that it reasonably expected. See RESTATEMENT (SECOND) OF CONTRACTS § 241(a) (1981). Moreover, Associated has not alleged any prejudice from this three-day delay. [Citations.] Further, the Cogginses' late payment was not made in bad faith. [Citations.] Finally, neither the purpose of the June 15, 1995 accord nor the language of the accord suggests that time was of the essence. [Citation.] Because the late payment was not a material breach of the June 15, 1995 accord, the Cogginses have complied with the June 15, 1995 agreement relieving them of further liability to Associated.

* * *

Judgment affirmed.

CASE

12-3

This case distinguishes between material and trivial breaches of contract and discusses the appropriate measure of damage for each kind of breach.

JACOB & YOUNG v. KENT
Court of Appeals of New York, 1921
230 N.Y. 239

CARDOZO, Judge. The plaintiff built a country residence for the defendant at a cost of upwards of $77,000, and now sues to recover a balance of $3,483.46, remaining unpaid. The work of construction ceased in June, 1914, and the defendant then began to occupy the dwelling. There was no complaint of defective performance until March, 1915. One of the specifications for the plumbing work provides that "all wrought iron pipe must be well galvanized, lap welded pipe of the grade known as 'standard pipe' of Reading manufacture." The defendant learned in March, 1915, that some of the pipe, instead of being made in Reading, was the product of other factories. The plaintiff was accordingly directed by the architect to do the work anew. The plumbing was then encased within the walls except in a few places where it had to be exposed. Obedience to the order meant more than the substitution of other pipe. It meant the demolition at great expense of substantial parts of the completed structure. The plaintiff left the work untouched, and asked for a certificate that the final payment was due. Refusal of the certificate was followed by this suit.

The evidence sustains a finding that the omission of the prescribed brand of pipe was neither fraudulent nor willful. It was the result of the oversight and inattention of the plaintiff's subcontractor. Reading pipe is distinguished from Cohoes pipe and other brands only by the name of the manufacturer stamped upon it at intervals of between six and seven feet. Even the defendant's architect, though he inspected the pipe upon arrival, failed to notice the discrepancy. The plaintiff tried to show that the brands installed, though made by other manufacturers, were the same in quality, in appearance, in market value and in cost as the brand stated in the contract — that they were, indeed, the same thing, though manufactured in another place. The evidence was excluded, and a verdict directed for the defendant. The Appellate Division reversed, and granted a new trial.

We think the evidence, if admitted, would have supplied some basis for the inference that the defect was insignificant in its relation to the project. The courts never say that one who makes a contract fills the measure of his duty by less than full performance. They do say, however, that an omission, both trivial and innocent, will sometimes be atoned for by allowance

of the resulting damage, and will not always be the breach of a condition to be followed by a forfeiture. The decisions in this state commit us to the liberal view, which is making its way, nowadays, in jurisdictions slow to welcome it. Where the line is to be drawn between the important and the trivial cannot be settled by a formula. "In the nature of the case precise boundaries are impossible" (2 Williston on Contracts, sec. 841). The same omission may take on one aspect or another according to its setting. Substitution of equivalents may not have the same significance in fields of art on the one side and in those of mere utility on the other. Nowhere will change be tolerated, however, if it is so dominant or pervasive as in any real or substantial measure to frustrate the purpose of the contract. There is no general license to install whatever, in the builder's judgment, may be regarded as "just as good." The question is one of degree, to be answered, if there is doubt, by the triers of the facts and, if the inferences are certain, by the judges of the law. We must weigh the purpose to be served, the desire to be gratified, the excuse for deviation from the letter, the cruelty of enforced adherence. Then only can we tell whether literal fulfillment is to be implied by law as a condition. This is not to say that the parties are not free by apt and certain words to effectuate a purpose that performance of every term shall be a condition of recovery. That question is not here. This is merely to say that the law will be slow to impute the purpose, in the silence of the parties, where the significance of the default is grievously out of proportion to the oppression of the forfeiture. The willful transgressor must accept the penalty of his transgression. For him there is no occasion to mitigate the rigor of implied conditions. The transgressor whose default is unintentional and trivial may hope for mercy if he will offer atonement for his wrong.

In the circumstances of this case, we think the measure of the allowance is not the cost of replacement, which would be great, but the difference in value, which would be either nominal or nothing. Some of the exposed sections might perhaps have been replaced at moderate expense. The defendant did not limit his demand to them, but treated the plumbing as a unit to be corrected from cellar to roof. In point of fact, the plaintiff never reached the stage at which evidence of the extent of the allowance became necessary. The trial court had excluded evidence that the defect was unsubstantial, and in view of that ruling there was no occasion for the plaintiff to go farther with an offer of proof. We think, however, that the offer, if it had been made, would not of necessity have been defective because directed to difference in value. It is true that in most cases the cost of replacement is the measure. The owner is entitled to the money which will permit him to complete, unless the cost of completion is grossly and unfairly out of proportion to the good to be attained. When that is true, the measure is the difference in value. Specifications call, let us say, for a foundation built of granite quarried in Vermont. On the completion of the building, the owner learns that through the blunder of a subcontractor part of the foundation has been built of granite of the same quality quarried in New Hampshire. The measure of allowance is not the cost of reconstruction. "There may be omissions of that which could not afterwards be supplied exactly as called for by the contract without taking down the building to its foundations, and at the same time the omission may not affect the value of the building for use or otherwise, except so slightly as to be hardly appreciable." The rule that gives a remedy in cases of substantial performance with compensation for defects of trivial or inappreciable importance, has been developed by the courts as an instrument of justice. The measure of the allowance must be shaped to the same end.

CASE 12-4

This is an historical case that concerns the options available to the aggrieved party when there has been an anticipatory breach of the contract (anticipatory repudiation).

HOCHSTER v. DE LA TOUR
Queen's Bench of England, 1853
2 Ellis and Blackburn Reports 678

Lord Campbell, C. J.

[On April 12, 1852, Hochster contracted with De La Tour to serve as a guide for De La Tour on his three-month trip to Europe, beginning on June 1 at an agreed-upon salary. On May 11, De La Tour notified Hochster that he would not need Hochster's services. He also refused to pay Hochster any compensation. Hochster brings this action to recover damages for breach of contract.]

On this motion***the question arises, Whether, if there be an agreement between A. and B., whereby B. engages to employ A. on and from a future day for a given period of time, to travel with him into a foreign country as a [guide], and to start with him in that capacity on that day, A. being to receive a monthly salary during the continuance of such service, B. may, before the day, refuse to perform the agreement and break and renounce it, so as to entitle A. before the day to commence an action against B. to recover damages for breach of the agreement; A. having been ready and willing to perform it, till it was broken and renounced by B.

* * *

If the plaintiff has no remedy for breach of the contract unless he treats the contract as in force, and acts upon it down to the 1st June, 1852, it follows that, till then, he must enter into no employment which will interfere with his promise "to start with the defendant on such travels on the day and year" and that he must then be properly equipped in all respects as a [guide] for a three months' tour on the continent of Europe. But it is surely much more rational, and more for the benefit of both parties, that, after the renunciation of the agreement by the defendant, the plaintiff should be at liberty to consider himself absolved from any future performance of it, retaining his right to sue for any damage he has suffered from the breach of it. Thus, instead of remaining idle and laying out money in preparations which must be useless, he is at liberty to seek service under another employer, which would go in mitigation of the damages to which he would otherwise be entitled for a breach of the contract. It seems strange that the defendant after renouncing the contract, and absolutely declaring that he will never act under it, should be permitted to object that faith is given to his assertion, and that an opportunity is not left to him of changing his mind.* * *

***The man who wrongfully renounces a contract into which he has deliberately entered cannot justly complain if he is immediately sued for a compensation in damage by the man whom he has injured: and it seems reasonable to allow an option to the injured party, either to sue immediately, or to wait till the time when the act was to be done, still holding it as prospectively binding for the exercise of this option, which may be advantageous to the innocent party, and cannot be prejudicial to the wrongdoer.

Judgment for plaintiff.

This case involves the doctrine of impossibility of performance of a contract.

NORTHERN CORP. v.
CHUGACH ELECTRICAL ASSOCIATION
Supreme Court of Alaska, 1974
518 P.2d 76

Boochever, J.

[Northern Corporation entered into a contract with Chugach in August 1966 to repair and upgrade the upstream face of Cooper Lake Dam in Alaska. The contract required Northern to obtain rock from a quarry site at the opposite end of the lake and to transport the rock to the dam during the winter across the ice on the lake. In December 1966, Northern cleared the road on the ice to permit deeper freezing, but thereafter water overflowed on the ice, preventing the use of the road. Northern complained of the unsafe condition of the lake ice, but Chugach insisted on performance. In March 1967, one of Northern's loaded trucks broke through the ice and sank. Northern continued to encounter difficulties and ceased operations with the approval of Chugach. On January 8, 1968, Chugach notified Northern that it would be in default unless all rock was hauled by April 1. After two more trucks broke through the ice, causing the deaths of the drivers, Northern ceased operations and notified Chugach that it would make no more attempts to haul across the lake. Northern advised Chugach it considered the contract terminated for impossibility of performance and commenced suit to recover the cost incurred in attempting to complete the contract.]

* * *

The focal question is whether the***contract was impossible of performance. The September 27, 1966 directive specified that the rock was to be transported "across Cooper Lake to the dam site when such lake is frozen to a sufficient depth to permit heavy vehicle traffic thereon," and*** specified that the hauling to the dam site would be done during the winter of 1966–67. It is therefore clear that the parties contemplated that the rock would be transported across the frozen lake by truck. Northern's repeated efforts to perform the contract by this method during the winter of 1966–67 and subsequently in February 1968, culminating in the tragic loss of life, abundantly support the trial court's findings that the contract was impossible of performance by this method.

Chugach contends, however, that Northern was nevertheless bound to perform, and that it could have used means other than hauling by truck across the ice to transport the rock. The answer to Chugach's contention is that***the parties contemplated that the rock would be hauled by truck once the ice froze to a sufficient depth to support the weight of the vehicles. The specification of this particular method of performance

presupposed the existence of ice frozen to the requisite depth. Since this expectation of the parties was never fulfilled, and since the provisions relating to the means of performance was clearly material, Northern's duty to perform was discharged by reason of impossibility.

There is an additional reason for our holding that Northern's duty to perform was discharged because of impossibility. It is true that in order for a defendant to prevail under the original common law doctrine of impossibility, he had to show that no one else could have performed the contract. However, this harsh rule has gradually been eroded, and the Restatement of Contracts has departed from the early common law rule by recognizing the principle of "commercial impracticability." Under this doctrine, a party is discharged from his contract obligations, even if it is technically possible to perform them, if the costs of performance would be so disproportionate to that reasonably contemplated by the parties as to make the contract totally impractical in a commercial sense.***Removed from the strictures of the common law, "impossibility" in its modern context has become a coat of many colors, including among its hues the point argued here—namely, impossibility predicated upon "commercial impracticability." This concept—which finds expression both in case law***and in other authorities***is grounded upon the assumption that in legal contemplation something is impracticable when it can only be done at an excessive and unreasonable cost. As stated in *Transatlantic Financing Corp. v. United States* [citation]

> ***The doctrine ultimately represents the ever-shifting line, drawn by courts hopefully responsive to commercial practices and mores, at which the community's interest in having contracts enforced according to their terms is outweighed by the commercial senselessness of requiring performance.* * *

* * *

In the case before us the detailed opinion of the trial court clearly indicates that the appropriate standard was followed. There is ample evidence to support its findings that "[t]he ice haul method of transporting riprap ultimately selected was within the contemplation of the parties and was part of the basis of the agreement which ultimately resulted in amendment No. 1 in October 1966," and that that method was not commercially feasible within the financial parameters of the contract. We affirm the court's conclusion that the contract was impossible of performance.

QUESTIONS

1. Identify and distinguish among the various types of conditions.
2. Distinguish between full performance and tender of performance.
3. Explain the difference between material breach and substantial performance. Explain how the UCC perfect tender rule differs.
4. Distinguish among a mutual rescission, substituted contract, accord and satisfaction, and novation.
5. Identify and discuss the ways discharge may be brought about by operation of law.

PROBLEMS

1. A-1 Roofing Co. entered into a written contract with Jaffe to put a new roof on the latter's residence for $1,800, using a specified type of roofing, and to complete the job without unreasonable delay. A-1 undertook the work within a week thereafter, but when all the roofing material was at the site and the labor 50 percent completed, the premises were totally destroyed by fire caused by lightning. A-1 submitted a bill to Jaffe for $1,200 for materials furnished and labor performed up to the time of the destruction of the premises. Jaffe refused to pay the bill, and A-1 sued Jaffe. Decision?

2. By contract dated January 5, Rebecca agreed to sell to Nancy, and Nancy agreed to buy from Rebecca, a certain parcel of land then zoned commercial. The specific intent of Nancy, which was known to Rebecca, was to erect a storage plant on the land; and the contract stated that the agreement was conditioned upon Nancy's ability to construct such a plant upon the land. The closing date for the transaction was set for April 1. On February 15, the City Council rezoned the land from commercial to residential, which precluded the erection of the storage plant. As the closing date drew near, Nancy made it known to Rebecca that she did not intend to go through with the purchase because the land could no longer be used as intended. On April 1, Rebecca tendered the deed to Nancy, who refused to pay Rebecca the agreed purchase price. Rebecca brought an action against Nancy for breach of their contract. Decision?

3. By contract dated May 1, Rob agreed to sell to Nancy, and Nancy agreed to buy from Rob, a certain house located at 10 Melbourne Road. At the time she signed the contact, Nancy transferred to Rob a deposit equal to 10% of the purchase price. The contract stated that closing and transfer of the property would occur on or before July 15. Nancy's finances were such that she needed to obtain a loan to pay the full purchase price for the house. Pursuant to the terms of the contract, Nancy was to obtain financing for the house in an amount of $180,000. The contract stated that Nancy was to apply for such financing in good faith within 7 days of the signing of the contract. It further stated that if Nancy could not obtain $180,000 in financing from a bank, savings bank, or savings and loan association, then Nancy could cancel the contract and recover her deposit.

(a) On May 5, Nancy applied for the $180,000 loan in good faith, but on July 1, the bank notified her that she would only be allowed a loan of $50,000. Rob demands that Nancy close on the purchase and sale of the house on July 15 and Nancy sues Rob for return of her deposit. Judgment for whom? Explain.

(b) Assume instead that Nancy waits until July 1 to apply for a bank loan, and when she applies, she does not give complete or accurate information to the bank about her income or assets. On July 10, the bank denies Nancy's application for a loan. On July 15, Rob demands that Nancy close on the purchase and sale of the house and she demands return of her deposit. Rob sues Nancy for breach of contract. Judgment for whom?

4. The Perfection Produce Company entered into a written contract with Hiram Hodges for the purchase of 300 tons of potatoes to be grown on Hodge's farm in Maine at a stipulated price per ton. Although the land would ordinarily produce 1,000 tons and the planting and cultivation were properly done, Hodges was able to deliver only 100 tons because of a partial crop failure owing to an unprecedented drought. Hodges sued the produce company to recover an unpaid balance of the agreed price for 100 tons of potatoes. The produce company, by an appropriate counterclaim against Hodges, sought damages for his failure to deliver the additional 200 tons. Decision?

5. On November 23, Sylvia agreed to sell to Barnett her Pontiac automobile for $7,000, delivery and payment to be made on December 1. On November 26, Barnett informed Sylvia that he wished to rescind the contract and would pay Sylvia $350 if Sylvia agreed. She agreed and took the $350 cash. On December 1, Barnett tendered to Sylvia $6,650 and demanded that she deliver the automobile. Sylvia refused and Barnett initiated a lawsuit. Decision?

6. Webster, Inc. dealt in automobile accessories at wholesale. Although he manufactured a few items in his own factory, among them windshield wipers, Webster purchased most of his supplies from a large number of other manufacturers. In January, Webster entered into a written contract to sell Hunter 2,000 windshield wipers for $4,900, delivery to be made June 1. In April, Webster's factory burned to the ground, and Webster failed to make delivery on June 1. Hunter, forced to buy windshield wipers elsewhere at a higher price, brings an action against Webster for breach of contract. Decision?

7. Erwick Construction Company contracted to build a house for Charles. The specifications called for the use of Karlene Pipe for all plumbing. Erwick, however, got a better price on Boynton Pipe and substituted the equally good Boynton Pipe for Karlene Pipe. Upon inspection, Charles discovered the change, and he now refuses to make the final payment. The contract price was for $200,000, and the final payment is $20,000. Erwick now brings suit seeking the $20,000. Decision?

8. By written contract Ames agreed to build a house on Bowen's lot for $65,000, commencing within ninety days of the date of the contract. Prior to the date for beginning construction, Ames informed Bowen that he was repudiating the contract and would not perform. Bowen refused to accept the repudiation and demanded fulfillment of the contract. Eighty days after the date of the contract, Bowen entered into a new contract with Curd for $62,000. The next day, without knowledge or notice of Bowen's contract with Curd, Ames began construction. Bowen ordered Ames from the premises and refused to allow him to continue. Ames sued Bowen for damages. Decision?

9. Jacobs, owner of a farm, entered into a contract with Earl Walker in which Walker agreed to paint the buildings on the farm. Walker purchased the paint from Jones. Before the work was completed,

Jacobs ordered Walker to stop because she was dissatisfied with the results. Jones and Walker made offers to complete the job, but Jacobs declined to permit Walker to fulfill his contract. Jones and Walker bring an action against Jacobs for breach of contract. Decision?

10. Dacor, a famous interior decorator and music lover, ordered a custom made, state of the art, big screen entertainment center from High Tech Manufacturing. Dacor maintained a lavish apartment that he used as a showcase to impress his wealthy clientele. In making the contract, Dacor insisted that the center meet his personal approval, and the contract guaranteed personal satisfaction. Skilled craftsman worked for months on the center and even competitors of High Tech considered it one of the finest products ever produced. Dacor, however, was not satisfied. He did not like the finish and he did not find the picture and sound quality to be as outstanding as he wished. He therefore refused to accept the entertainment center unless it was refinished and substantial improvements were made in the picture and sound quality. High Tech, stating that the entertainment center was the best that could be made, refused to make the changes and sued Dacor for breach of contract. Judgment for whom? Explain.

11. Nissan Corp., wishing to dispose of its surplus warehouse, offered it for sale for $500,000 cash. Belle informed Nissan that she would pay the price asked. A contract of sale was executed by the parties and Belle paid 10% of the price as a down payment to Nissan. The closing was set for 4 weeks later, at which time Belle was to pay the balance by certified check and Nissan was to deliver the deed. The contract provided that Nissan Corp. would retain the down payment as liquidated damages if Belle defaulted. When the time for the closing arrived, Belle told Nissan Corp that her arrangements to borrow the balance of the purchase price had not been completed and she requested an additional two weeks to complete the arrangements, Nissan Corp. refused and stated that it was cancelling the contract and retaining the down payment.

(a) Did Belle's failure to pay on time constitute a material breach of the contract? Explain.

(b) If Belle raises the money in two weeks, is she entitled to a decree of specific performance of the contract against Nissan Corp.? Explain.

(c) Assume that Nissan Corp. granted Belle an additional 6 weeks to raise the money, but notified her that it would grant no further extensions and that Belle agreed. At the end of 6 weeks, Belle had still been unable to raise the money, and Nissan Corp. notified her that it was cancelling the contract. A month later, Nissan Corp. sold the warehouse to Chin for $550,000. Is Belle now entitled to recover her $50,000 down payment? Explain.

Assume that when Belle originally negotiated for the purchase, Nissan Corp. had little confidence in Belle's ability to raise the money. Accordingly, the parties agreed to a clause in the contract stating, "Time is of the essence in this contract."

At the closing Nissan Corp was unable to tender clear title to Belle

because the day before the State Tax Department had notified Nissan that an unpaid franchise tax constituted a lien on the warehouse. Nissan Corp. requested a delay of 3 days to pay the tax and satisfy the lien. Belle, who had reconsidered her bargain, refused any extension, tendered her certified check for the balance, and demanded that Nissan deliver clear title. When Nissan Corp. was unable to comply, Belle said she was cancelling the contract.

(d) Is Belle entitled to the return of her down payment? Explain.

(e) Is Nissan Corp. liable in damages to Belle for Belle's cost of conducting a title search? Explain.

12. Saul, a cotton merchant, had 50 bales of cotton in his warehouse. Brown, a prospective buyer, inspected the bales in the warehouse, and entered into a signed written contract with Saul to buy the bales at a price of $1,000 per bale. Delivery was to be made by Saul to Brown's factory in two weeks. Two days before the delivery date, Saul's warehouse and the cotton that Brown had inspected were destroyed by fire caused by lightning. Brown demanded that Saul deliver another 50 bales of similar grade cotton. Upon Saul's refusal, Brown sued Saul for breach of contract. Judgment for whom? Explain.

13. Schlosser entered into an agreement to purchase a cooperative apartment from Flynn Company. The written agreement contained the following provision:

> This entire agreement is conditioned on Purchaser's being approved for occupancy by the board of directors of the Cooperative. In the event approval of the Purchaser shall be denied, this agreement shall thereafter be of no further force or effect.

When Schlosser unilaterally revoked her "offer," Flynn sued for breach of contract. Schlosser claims the approval provision was a condition precedent to the existence of a binding contract and, thus, she was free to revoke. Decision?

14. Barta entered into a written contract to buy the K&K Pharmacy, located in the local shopping center. Included in the contract was a provision stating that "this Agreement shall be contingent upon Buyer's ability to obtain a new lease from Landlord for the premises presently occupied by Seller. In the event Buyer is unable to obtain a lease satisfactory to Buyer, this Agreement shall be null and void." Barta planned to sell "high traffic" grocery items such as bread, milk, and coffee to attract customers to his drugstore. A grocery store in the local shopping center, however, held the exclusive right to sell grocery items. Barta, therefore, could not obtain a leasing agreement meeting his approval. Barta refused to close the sale. In a suit by K&K Pharmacy against Barta for breach of contract, who will prevail? Explain.

Internet Exercise Compare the provisions governing performance and breach of contract contained in the Principles of European Contract Law with the provisions of the U.S. common law.

Third Parties to Contracts

Whereas prior chapters considered contractual situations essentially involving only two parties, this chapter deals with the rights or duties of third parties, namely, persons who are not parties to the contract but who have a right to, or an obligation for, its performance. These rights and duties arise either by (1) an assignment of the rights of a party to the contract, (2) a delegation of the duties of a party to the contract, or (3) the express terms of a contract entered into for the benefit of a third person. In an assignment or delegation, the third party's rights or duties arise after the contract is made, whereas in the third situation the third-party beneficiary's rights arise at the time the contract was formed. We will consider these three situations in that order.

ASSIGNMENT OF RIGHTS

Every contract creates both rights and duties. A person who owes a duty under a contract is an **obligor**, while a person to whom a contractual duty is owed is an **obligee**. For instance, Ann promises to sell to Bart an automobile for which Bart promises to pay $10,000 in monthly installments over the next three years. Ann's right under the contract is to receive payment from Bart, whereas Ann's duty is to deliver the automobile. Bart's right is to receive the automobile; his duty is to pay for it.

Bargain

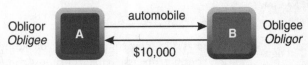

An **assignment of rights** is the voluntary transfer to a third party of the rights arising from the contract. In the above example, if Ann were to transfer her right under the contract (the installment payments due from Bart) to Clark for $8,500 in cash, this would constitute a valid assignment of rights. In this case, Ann would be the **assignor**, Clark would be the **assignee**, and Bart would be the **obligor**.

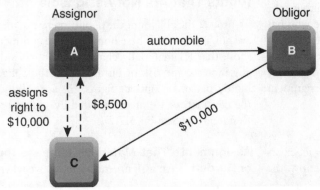

An effective assignment terminates the assignor's right to receive performance by the obligor. After an assignment, only the assignee has a right to the obligor's performance.

On the other hand, if Ann and Doris agree that Doris should deliver the automobile to Bart, this would constitute a delegation, not an assignment, of duties between Ann and Doris. A **delegation of duties** is a transfer to a third party of a contractual obligation. In this instance, Ann would be the **delegator**, Doris would be the **delegatee**, and Bart would be the **obligee**. Delegations of duties are discussed later in this chapter.

Law Governing Assignments

The law governing assignments arises principally from the common law of contracts, Article 2 of the UCC, and Article 9 of the UCC. Article 2 applies to assignments of rights under a contract for the sale of goods. Article 9 covers all assignments made to secure the performance of an obligation *and* all assignments involving rights to payment for goods sold or leased or for services rendered.

Requirements of an Assignment

The Restatement defines an assignment of a right as a "manifestation of the assignor's intention to transfer it by virtue of which the assignor's right to performance by the obligor is extinguished in whole or in part and the assignee acquires a right to such performance." Section 317(1). No special form or particular words are necessary to create an assignment. Any words that fairly indicate an intention to make the assignee the owner of the right are sufficient. For instance, Eve delivers to Harold a writing addressed to Mary stating, "Pay Harold for his own use $1,000 out of the amount you owe me." This writing is a legally sufficient assignment. Restatement, Section 325, Illustration 1.

Unless otherwise provided by statute, an assignment may be oral. The UCC imposes a writing requirement on all assignments beyond $5,000. Section 1–206. In addition, Article 9 requires certain assignments to be in writing.

Consideration is not required for an effective assignment. Consequently, gratuitous assignments are valid and enforceable. By giving value for the assignment, the assignee manifests his assent to the assignment as part of the bargained-for exchange. On the other hand, when the assignment is gratuitous, the assignee's assent is not always required. Any assignee who has not assented to an assignment may, however, disclaim the assignment within a reasonable time after learning of its existence and terms. Restatement, Section 327. No particular formality is required for the disclaimer, which renders the assignment inoperative from the beginning.

Revocability of Assignments When the assignee gives consideration in exchange for an assignment, a contract exists between the assignor and the assignee. Consequently, the assignor may not revoke the assignment without the assignee's assent. A gratuitous assignment, in contrast, is revocable by the assignor and is terminated by her death, incapacity, or subsequent assignment of the right, unless she has made an effective delivery of the assignment to the assignee by transferring a deed or other document evidencing the right, such as a stock certificate or savings passbook. Delivery may also consist of physically delivering a signed, written assignment of the contract right.

A gratuitous assignment is also rendered irrevocable if, prior to the attempted revocation, the donee-assignee receives payment of the claim from the obligor, obtains a judgment against the obligor, or obtains a new contract with the obligor. For example, Nancy owes Howard $50,000. Howard signs a written statement granting Paul a gratuitous assignment of his rights from Nancy but dies prior to delivering to Paul the signed, written assignment of the contract right. The assignment is terminated and therefore ineffective. On the other hand, had Howard delivered the signed, written assignment to Paul before he died, the assignment would have been effective and irrevocable.

Partial Assignments A partial assignment is a transfer of a portion of the contractual rights to one or more assignees. Although partial assignments were not enforceable at early common law, such assignments now are permitted and are enforceable. The obligor, however, may require all the parties entitled to the promised performance to litigate the matter in one action, thus ensuring that all parties are present and thereby avoiding the undue hardship of multiple lawsuits. For example, Jack owes Richard $2,500. Richard assigns $1,000 to Mildred. Neither Richard nor Mildred can maintain an action against Jack if Jack objects, unless the other is joined in the lawsuit against Jack.

Rights That Are Assignable

As a general rule, most contract rights, including rights under an option contract, are assignable. The most common contractual right that may be assigned is the right to the payment of money, such as an account receivable or interest due or to be paid. The right to property other than money, such as goods or land, is also frequently assignable.

Rights That Are Not Assignable

To protect the obligor or the public interest, some contract rights are not assignable. These nonassignable contract rights include those that (1) materially change the obligor's duty or materially increase the risk or burden upon the obligor, (2) transfer highly personal contract rights, (3) are validly prohibited by the contract, or (4) are prohibited by statute or public policy. Restatement, Section 317(2).

Assignments That Materially Increase the Duty, Risk, or Burden An assignment is ineffective where performance by the obligor to the assignee would differ materially from her performance to the assignor; that is, where the assignment would significantly change the nature or extent of the obligor's duty. Thus, an automobile liability insurance policy issued to Alex is not assignable by Alex to Betty. The risk assumed by the insurance company was liability for Alex's negligent operation of the automobile. Liability for operation of the same automobile by Betty would be a risk entirely different from the one that the insurance company had assumed. Similarly, Alex would not be allowed to assign to Cynthia, the owner of a twenty-five-room mansion, his contractual right to have Betty paint his small, two-bedroom house. Clearly, such an assignment would materially increase Betty's duty of performance. By comparison, the right to receive monthly payments under a contract may be assigned; for mailing the check to the assignee costs no more than mailing it to the assignor. Moreover, if a contract explicitly provides that it may be assigned, then rights under it are assignable even if the assignment would change the duty, risk, or burden of performance on the obligor. Restatement, Section 323(1).

Assignments of Personal Rights Where the rights under a contract are highly personal, in that they are limited to the person of the obligee, such rights are not assignable. An extreme example of such a contract is an agreement of two persons to marry one another. The prospective groom obviously cannot transfer to some third party the prospective bride's promise to marry him. A more typical example of a contract involving personal rights would be a contract between a teacher and a school. The teacher could not assign to another teacher her right to a faculty position. Similarly, a student who is awarded a scholarship cannot assign his right to some other person.

❖ See Case 13-1

Express Prohibition against Assignment Contract terms prohibiting assignment of rights under the contract are strictly construed. Moreover, most courts interpret a general prohibition against assignments as a mere promise not to assign. As a consequence, the prohibition, if violated, gives the obligor a right to damages for breach of the terms forbidding assignment but does *not* render the assignment ineffective.

Section 322(1) of the Restatement provides that, unless circumstances indicate the contrary, a contract term prohibiting assignment of the contract bars only the delegation to the assignee (delegatee) of the assignor's (delegator's) duty of performance, not the assignment of rights. Thus, Abe and Bill contract for the sale of land by Bill to Abe for $30,000 and provide in their contract that Abe may not assign his rights under it. Abe pays Bill $30,000 and thereby fully performs his obligations under the contract. Abe then assigns his rights to Cheryl, who is entitled to receive the land from Bill (the obligor) despite the contractual prohibition of assignment.

UCC Section 2–210(2) provides that a right to damages for breach of the whole contract or a right arising out of the assignor's due performance of his entire obligation can be assigned despite a contractual provision to the contrary. UCC Section 2–210(3) provides that, unless circumstances indicate the contrary, a contract term prohibiting assignment of the contract bars only the delegation to the assignee (delegatee) of the assignor's (delegator's) duty of performance, not the assignment of rights. UCC Section 9–318(4) makes ineffective any term in a contract prohibiting the assignment of any right to payment for goods sold or leased or for services rendered.

❖ See Case 13-2

Assignments Prohibited by Law Various federal and state statutes, as well as public policy, prohibit or regulate the assignment of certain types of contract rights. For instance, assignments of future wages are subject to statutes, some of which prohibit such assignments altogether while others require them to be in writing and subject to certain restrictions. Moreover, an assignment that violates public policy will be unenforceable even in the absence of a prohibiting statute.

Rights of the Assignee

Obtains Rights of Assignor The general rule is that an assignee **stands in the shoes** of the assignor. He acquires the rights of the assignor, but no new or additional rights, and takes the assigned rights with all of the defenses, defects, and infirmities to which they would be subject, were the assignor to bring an action against the obligor. Thus, in an action brought by the assignee against the obligor, the obligor may plead fraud, duress, undue influence, failure of consideration, breach of contract, or any other defense against the assignor arising out of the original contract. The obligor also may assert rights of setoff or counterclaim arising against the assignor out of entirely separate matters, provided they arose prior to his receiving notice of the assignment.

The Code permits the buyer under a contract of sale to agree as part of the contract that he will not assert against an assignee any claim or defense that the buyer may have against the seller if the assignee takes the assignment for value and in good faith. UCC Section 9–206. Such a provision in an agreement renders the seller's rights more marketable. The Federal Trade Commission, however, has invalidated such waiver of defense provisions in consumer credit transactions. Most states also have statutes protecting buyers in consumer transactions by prohibiting waiver of defenses.

Notice To be valid, notice of an assignment does not have to be given to the obligor. Nonetheless, giving such notice is advisable because an assignee will lose his rights against an obligor who pays the assignor without notice of the assignment: to compel an obligor to pay a claim a second time, when she was not notified that a new party was entitled to payment would be unfair. For example, Donald owes Gary $1,000 due on September 1. Gary assigns the debt to Paula on August 1, but neither he nor Paula informs Donald. On September 1, Donald pays Gary. Donald is fully discharged from his obligation, whereas Gary is liable for $1,000 to Paula. On the other hand, if Paula had given notice of the assignment to Donald before September 1 and Donald had paid Gary nevertheless, Paula would then have the right to recover the $1,000 from either Donald or Gary.

Furthermore, notice cuts off any defenses based on subsequent agreements between the obligor and assignor. Moreover, as already indicated, notice precludes subsequent setoffs and counterclaims of the obligor that arise out of entirely separate matters.

Implied Warranties of Assignor

An **implied warranty** is an obligation imposed by law upon the transfer of property or contract rights. In the absence of an express intention to the contrary, an assignor who receives value makes the following implied warranties to the assignee with respect to the assigned right:

1. that he will do nothing to defeat or impair the assignment;
2. that the assigned right actually exists and is subject to no limitations or defenses other than those stated or apparent at the time of the assignment;
3. that any writing evidencing the right delivered to the assignee or exhibited to him as an inducement to accept the assignment is genuine and what it purports to be; and
4. that the assignor has no knowledge of any fact that would impair the value of the assignment.

Thus, Eric has a right against Julia and assigns it for value to Gwen. Later, Eric gives Julia a release. Gwen may recover damages from Eric for breach of the first implied warranty.

Express Warranties of Assignor

An **express warranty** is an explicitly made contractual promise regarding property or contract rights transferred. The assignor is further bound by any express warranties he makes to the assignee with respect to the right assigned. The assignor does not, however, guarantee that the obligor will pay the assigned debt or otherwise perform, unless such a guarantee is explicitly stated.

Successive Assignments of the Same Right

The owner of a right could conceivably make successive assignments of the same claim to different persons. Assume that B owes A $1,000. On June 1, A for value assigns the debt to C. Thereafter, on June 15, A assigns it to D, who in good faith gives value and has no knowledge of the prior assignment by A to C. If the assignment is subject to Article 9, then that article's priority

rules will control. Otherwise, the priority is determined by the common law. The majority rule in the United States is that the **first assignee in point of time** (here, C) prevails over subsequent assignees. By comparison, in England and in a minority of the states, the first assignee to notify the obligor prevails.

The Restatement adopts a third view: a prior assignee is entitled to the assigned right and its proceeds to the exclusion of a subsequent assignee, *except* where the prior assignment is revocable or voidable by the assignor or where the subsequent assignee in good faith and without knowledge of the prior assignment gives value and obtains one of the following: (1) payment or satisfaction of the obligor's duty, (2) a judgment against the obligor, (3) a new contract with the obligor, or (4) possession of a writing of a type customarily accepted as a symbol or evidence of the right assigned. Restatement, Section 342.

DELEGATION OF DUTIES

As indicated earlier, contractual duties are *not* assignable, but their performance generally may be *delegated* to a third person. A **delegation of duties** is a transfer of a contractual obligation to a third party. For example, A promises to sell B a new automobile, for which B promises to pay $10,000 by monthly installments over the next three years. If A and D agree that D should deliver the automobile to B, this would not constitute an assignment but would be a delegation of duties between A and D. In this instance, A would be the **delegator**, D would be the **delegatee**, and B would be the **obligee**.

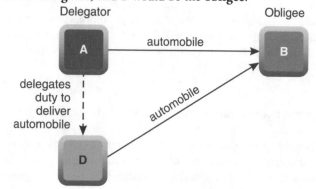

A delegation of duty does not extinguish the delegator's obligation to perform, because A remains liable to B. When the delegatee accepts, or assumes, the delegated duty, both the delegator and delegatee are held liable to the obligee for performance of the contractual duty.

Delegable Duties

Although contractual duties generally are delegable, a delegation will not be permitted if:

1. the nature of the duties is personal in that the obligee has a substantial interest in having the delegator perform the contract;

2. the performance is expressly made nondelegable; or

3. the delegation is prohibited by statute or public policy.

Restatement, Section 318 and UCC Section 2–210. The courts will examine a delegation more closely than an assignment because a delegation compels the nondelegating party to the contract (the obligee) to receive performance from a party with whom she has not dealt.

For example, a schoolteacher may not delegate her performance to another teacher, even if the substitute is equally competent; for this is a contract that is personal in nature. In the frequently quoted words of an English case: "You have a right to the benefit you contemplate from the character, credit and substance of the person with whom you contract." On the other hand, under a contract in which performance involves no peculiar or special skill and in which no personal trust or confidence is involved, the party may delegate the performance of his duty. For example, the duty to pay money, to deliver fungible goods such as corn, or to mow a lawn is usually delegable.

◆ See Case 13-3

Duties of the Parties

Even when permitted, a delegation of a duty to a third person still leaves the delegator bound to perform. If the delegator desires to be discharged of the duty, she is allowed to enter into an agreement by which she obtains the consent of the obligee to substitute a third person (the delegatee) in her place. This is a **novation**, whereby the delegator is discharged and the third party becomes directly bound upon his promise to the obligee.

Though a delegation authorizes a third party to perform a duty for the delegator, a delegatee becomes liable for performance only if he assents to perform the delegated duties. Thus, if Frank owes a duty to Grace, and Frank delegates that duty to Henry, Henry is not obligated to either Frank or Grace to perform the duty unless Henry agrees to do so. Nevertheless, if Henry promises either Frank (the delegator) or Grace (the obligee) that he will perform Frank's duty, Henry is said to have **assumed the delegated duty** and becomes liable to both Frank and Grace for nonperformance. Accordingly, when duties are both delegated and assumed, both the delegator and the delegatee are liable to the obligee for proper performance of the original contractual duty. The delegatee's promise to perform creates contract rights in the obligee who may bring an action against the delegatee as a third party beneficiary of the contract between the delegator and the delegatee. (Third-party contracts are discussed later in this chapter.)

The question of whether a delegatee has assumed delegated duties frequently arises in the following ambiguous situation: Marty and Carol agree to an assignment of Marty's contract with Bob. The Code clearly resolves this ambiguity by providing that, unless the language or circumstances indicate the contrary, an assignment of "the contract," or of "all my rights under the contract," or an assignment in similar general terms is an assignment of rights *and* a delegation of performance of the assignor's duties; its acceptance by the assignee constitutes a promise by her to perform those duties. Section 2–210(4). The Restatement, Section 328, has also adopted this position. For example, Cooper Oil Co. has a contract to deliver oil to Halsey. Cooper Oil Co. delivers to Lowell Oil Co. a writing assigning to Lowell Oil Co. "all Cooper Oil Co.'s rights under the contract." Lowell Oil Co. is under a duty to Halsey to deliver the oil called for by the contract, and Cooper Oil Co. is liable to Halsey if Lowell Oil Co. does not perform. It should also be recalled that the Restatement and the Code provide that a clause prohibiting an assignment of "the contract" is to be construed as barring only the delegation to the assignee (delegatee) of the assignor's (delegator's) performance, unless the circumstances indicate the contrary.

THIRD-PARTY BENEFICIARY CONTRACTS

A contract in which a party (the **promisor**) promises to render a certain performance not to the other party (the **promisee**) but to a third person (the **beneficiary**) is called a third-party beneficiary contract. The third person is not a party to the contract but is merely a beneficiary of it. Such contracts may be divided into two types: (1) intended beneficiary and (2) incidental beneficiary. An **intended beneficiary** is intended by the two parties to the contract (the promisor and promisee) to receive a benefit from the performance of their agreement. Accordingly, the courts generally permit intended beneficiaries to enforce third-party contracts. For example, Abbott promises Baldwin to deliver an automobile to Carson if Baldwin promises to pay $10,000. Carson is the intended beneficiary.

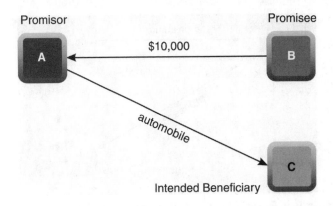

In an **incidental beneficiary** contract, the third party is not intended to receive a benefit under the contract. Accordingly, courts do not enforce the third party's right to the benefits of the contract. For example, Abbott promises to purchase and deliver to Baldwin an automobile for $10,000. In all probability, Abbott would acquire the automobile from Davis. Davis would be an incidental beneficiary and would have no enforceable rights against either Abbott or Baldwin.

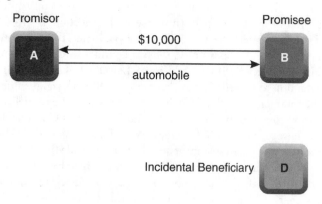

Promisor

Promisee

$10,000

automobile

Incidental Beneficiary D

Intended Beneficiary

Unless otherwise agreed between the promisor and promisee, a beneficiary of a promise is an intended beneficiary if the parties intended this to be the result of their agreement. Restatement, Section 302. There are two types of intended beneficiaries: (1) donee beneficiaries and (2) creditor beneficiaries.

Donee Beneficiary A third party is an intended donee beneficiary if the promisee's purpose in bargaining for and obtaining the agreement with the promisor is to make a gift of the promised performance to the beneficiary. The ordinary life insurance policy illustrates this type of contract. The insured (the promisee) makes a contract with an insurance company (the promisor) that promises, in consideration of premiums paid to it by the insured, to pay upon the death of the insured a stated sum of money to the named beneficiary, who is an intended donee beneficiary.

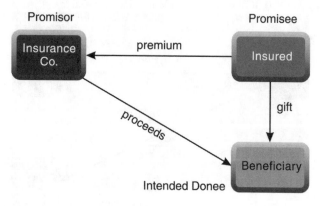

Promisor

Promisee

Insurance Co.

premium

Insured

proceeds

gift

Beneficiary

Intended Donee

Creditor Beneficiary A third person is also an intended beneficiary if the promisee intends the performance of the promise to satisfy a legal duty he owes to the beneficiary, who is a creditor of the promisee. The contract involves consideration moving from the promisee to the promisor in exchange for the promisor's engaging to pay a debt or to discharge an obligation the promisee owes to the third person.

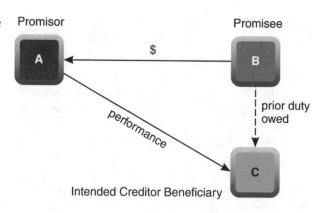

Promisor

Promisee

A

$

B

performance

prior duty owed

C

Intended Creditor Beneficiary

To illustrate, in a contract for the sale by Wesley of his business to Susan, Susan promises Wesley that she will pay all of his outstanding business debts, as listed in the contract. Here, Wesley's creditors are creditor beneficiaries. Similarly, in the classic *Lawrence v. Fox,* 20 N.Y. 268 (1859), Holly loaned Fox $300 in consideration for Fox's promise to pay that sum to Lawrence, a creditor of Holly. Fox failed to pay Lawrence, who sued Fox for the $300. The court held for Lawrence, who was permitted to recover as a third-party creditor beneficiary to the contract between Holly and Fox.

Rights of Intended Beneficiary An intended *donee* beneficiary may enforce the contract only against the promisor. He cannot maintain an action against the promisee, as the promisee was under no legal obligation to him. An intended *creditor* beneficiary, however, may enforce the contract against either or both parties. If Willard owes Lola $500, and Julie contracts with Willard to pay this debt to Lola, Willard is not thereby relieved of his liability to Lola. If Julie breaks the contract, Lola, as a creditor beneficiary, may sue her. In addition, Lola may sue Willard as her debtor. If Lola should obtain judgments against both Julie and Willard, she is, of course, entitled to collect only one judgment. If Lola recovers against Willard, Willard has a right of reimbursement from Julie, the promisor. Restatement, Section 310.

Vesting of Rights A contract for the benefit of an intended beneficiary confers upon that beneficiary rights that she may enforce. Until these rights **vest** (take effect), however, the promisor and promisee may, by later agreement, vary or completely discharge them. The states vary considerably as to when vesting occurs. Some hold that vesting takes place immediately upon the making of the contract. In others, vesting occurs when the third party learns of the contract and assents to it. In another group of states, vesting requires the third party to change his position in reliance upon the promise made for his benefit. The Restatement has adopted the following position: If the contract between the promisor and promisee provides that they may not vary its terms without the consent of the beneficiary, such a provision is effective. Otherwise, the parties to the contract may rescind or vary the contract unless the intended beneficiary (1) has brought an action upon the promise, (2) has changed her position in reliance upon it, or (3) has assented to the promise at the request of the promisor or promisee. Restatement, Section 311.

On the other hand, the promisor and promisee may provide that the benefits will *never* vest. For example, Mildred purchases an insurance policy on her own life, naming her husband as beneficiary. Her policy, as such policies commonly do, reserves to Mildred the right to change the beneficiary or even to cancel the policy entirely.

Defenses Against Beneficiary   In an action by the intended beneficiary of a third-party contract to enforce the promise, the promisor may assert any defense that would be available to her if the action had been brought by the promisee. The rights of the third party are based upon the promisor's contract with the promisee. Thus, the promisor may assert the absence of mutual assent or consideration, lack of capacity, fraud, mistake, and the like against the intended beneficiary. Once an intended beneficiary's rights have vested, however, the promisor may not assert the defense of contractual modification or rescission.

Incidental Beneficiary

An incidental third-party beneficiary is a person whom the parties to a contract did not intend to benefit but who nevertheless would derive some benefit from its performance. For instance, a contract to raze an old, unsightly building and replace it with a costly, modern house would benefit the owner of the adjoining property by increasing his property's value. He would have no rights under the contract, however, as the benefit to him would be unintended and incidental.

A third person who may benefit incidentally from the performance of a contract to which he is not a party has no rights under the contract. Neither the promisee nor the promisor intended that the third person benefit. Assume that for a stated consideration George promises Kathy that he will purchase and deliver to Kathy a brand-new Sony television of the latest model. Kathy performs. George does not. As an incidental beneficiary, Cosmos Appliances, Inc., the local exclusive Sony dealer, has no rights under the contract, although performance by George would produce a sale from which Cosmos would benefit.

❧ See Case 13-4

CHAPTER SUMMARY

Assignment of Rights

Definition of Assignment voluntary transfer to a third party of the rights arising from a contract so that the assignor's right to performance is extinguished
- *Assignor* party making an assignment
- *Assignee* party to whom contract rights are assigned
- *Obligor* party owing a duty to the assignor under the original contract
- *Obligee* party to whom a duty of performance is owed under a contract

Requirements of an Assignment include intent but not consideration
- *Revocability of Assignment* when the assignee gives consideration the assignor may not revoke the assignment without the assignee's consent
- *Partial Assignment* transfer of a portion of contractual rights to one or more assignees

Assignability most contract rights are assignable, except
- assignments that materially increase the duty, risk, or burden upon the obligor
- assignments of personal rights
- assignments expressly forbidden by the contract
- assignments prohibited by law

Rights of Assignee the assignee stands in the shoes of the assignor
- *Defenses of Obligor* may be asserted against the assignee
- *Notice* is not required but is advisable

Implied Warranty obligation imposed by law upon the assignor of a contract right

Express Warranty explicitly made contractual promise regarding contract rights transferred

Successive Assignments the majority rule is that the first assignee in point of time prevails over later assignees; minority rule is that the first assignee to notify the obligor prevails

---

Delegation of Duties

Definition of Delegation transfer to a third party of a contractual obligation
- *Delegator* party delegating his duty to a third party
- *Delegatee* third party to whom the delegator's duty is delegated

- *Obligee* party to whom a duty of performance is owed by the delegator and delagatee
Delegability most contract duties may be delegated, *except*
- duties that are personal
- duties that are expressly nondelegable
- duties whose delegation is prohibited by statute or public policy
Duties of Parties
- *Delegation* delegator is still bound to perform original obligation
- *Novation* contract, to which the obligee is a party, substituting a new promisor for an existing promisor, who is consequently no longer liable on the original contract and is not liable as a delegator

---

Third-Party Beneficiary Contracts

Definition a contract in which one party promises to render a performance to a third person (the beneficiary)

Intended Beneficiaries third parties intended by the two contracting parties to receive a benefit from their contract
- *Donee Beneficiary* a third party intended to receive a benefit from the contract as a gift
- *Creditor Beneficiary* a third person intended to receive a benefit from the agreement to satisfy a legal duty owed to her
- *Rights of Intended Beneficiaries* an intended donee beneficiary may enforce the contract against the promisor; an intended creditor beneficiary may enforce the contract against either or both the promisor and the promisee
- *Vesting of Rights* if the beneficiary's rights vest, the promisor and promisee may not thereafter vary or discharge these vested rights
- *Defenses Against Beneficiary* in an action by the intended beneficiary of a third-party contract to enforce the promise, the promisor may assert any defense that would be available to her if the action had been brought by the promisee

Incidental Beneficiary third party whom the two parties to the contract have no intention of benefiting by their contract and who acquires no rights under the contract

---

CASES

The assignment of contractual rights may be barred explicitly by the terms of the contract or implicitly by reason of the personal relationships between the contracting parties as, for example, when their "personalities" are material to the bargain. The following case deals with both of these issues in determining whether golf club memberships may be assigned in a bankruptcy proceeding.

REISER v. DAYTON COUNTRY CLUB COMPANY
United States Court of Appeals, Sixth Circuit, 1992
972 F.2d 689

Joiner, J.

In this case we are asked to review an order barring a trustee in bankruptcy under Chapter 7 from assuming and assigning a golf membership in a country club as an executory contract, pursuant to section 365 of the Bankruptcy Code. [Citation.]

The Dayton Country Club is an organization, in the form of a corporation, consisting of several hundred individuals who have joined together for recreation and entertainment. Its shares of stock may be held only by the members of the club and may not be accumulated in any substantial amount by one member.

The club offers social events, dining facilities, tennis courts, a swimming pool, and a golf course. It became apparent over a period of time that each of these diverse programs could be enjoyed to full advantage by a different number of members. For example, since there was only one 18-hole golf course available, and because of the nature of the game, the maximum number of members eligible to play golf needed to be limited in order to make the playing of the game enjoyable to those playing. There was no need to so limit the number of members who could use the tennis courts, the pool, the restaurants, or who could enjoy the social events of the club.

The club developed within its membership a special membership category for those who had full golfing privileges. This category was limited to 375 members. Detailed rules, procedures, and practices were developed to ensure the fair selection of golfing members. These rules, procedures, and practices define how this additional privilege is allocated, how the number of members is maintained at 375, how vacancies occur, how they are filled, and what additional fees are charged.

The record reflects that members of the club are entitled to play, eat, and socialize in all activities of the club except golf. If, in addition to these activities, a member desires to play golf, he or she asks to become a golfing member in one of several golf membership categories. When he or she makes this request, an additional substantial fee is paid to the club and the individual is placed on a waiting list. At the time the record was made in this case, there were about 70 persons on that list. When a vacancy occurs because of a failure to pay dues or a resignation, the first person on the waiting list is given the option to become a golfing member by paying an additional substantial fee. Upon becoming a golfing member, the monthly dues also increase substantially. If the person at the top of the waiting list declines the membership, then that person is placed at the bottom of the list and the next person on the list is given the opportunity to become a golfing member. There is no provision for any person to assign or sell the golf membership to any other person or for any person to become a golfing member in any other way except in two intimate and personal situations dealt with in discrete ways. When the death of a golfing member occurs, a spouse (who had been enjoying the hospitality of the club) may take the deceased member's place. If a divorce occurs, the member may designate his or her spouse as the golfing member. The club also has a program to encourage the younger generation of member families to become golfing members. Golfing members are permitted also to invite guests. Through its membership committee, the club makes the rules and establishes the procedures to describe whom among its larger membership list may be golfing members.

The nature of the golf membership within the overall club membership is the heart of this case. We are not dealing with the right to be a member of the club and there is nothing in this case relating to laws and social policies against discrimination. The issues in this case relate solely to the rights, duties, and privileges of the club and its members arising from the club's effort to provide golfing privileges to some but not all of its members, and the effect of the bankruptcy laws upon that effort.

This matter involves appeals from separate orders entered in the bankruptcies of debtors Magness and Redman, both of whom were golfing members of the Dayton Country Club. The trustee in bankruptcy sought to assume and assign, through sale, the rights under these memberships to (1) members on the waiting list, (2) other club members, or (3) the general public, provided that the purchaser first obtains membership in the Dayton Country Club. In other words, the trustee seeks to increase the value of the bankruptcy estate by taking value for and assigning to others a relationship between the bankrupt and the club. The assignment would be to the detriment of other club members who had paid for and acquired the right to become golfing members in due course. The question is whether the trustee has the right to make the assignment.

The arrangement between the members of the club, including Magness and Redman, and the Dayton Country Club, is a complex one involving rights, privileges, and duties, all of which are bound up in what is loosely called the contract for "full golf membership." At the least, this contract involves (1) an executed portion, the achievement of "full golf membership," and the payment of the nonrefundable fee the club charges for that membership in accordance with the rules, procedures, and practices prescribed by the club; (2) the rights of other club members to apply for golf membership as set out in the rules, procedures, and practices of the club; (3) the rights of those in the club who have applied for and have been accepted and have made substantial payments for full golf membership; (4) the obligation of the members to pay monthly dues; and (5) the obligation of the club to provide recreational facilities called for in its charter and bylaws. In other words, this contract between the debtors and the club and others is neither a simple contract to buy and sell a product or a service nor is it a lease.

Not only is it appropriate to cast these complex relationships in terms of both executed and executory contracts, it is not inappropriate to think of these contracts as creating a type of property interest. The full golf membership and the rights that come from that relationship with the club can be described as a property right of that member, the parameters of which are defined by the rules, procedures, and practices of the club. These rules, procedures, and practices, and therefore the extent of the members' property interest, do not extend to any right on the members' part to pass on the membership to others, except in the two situations described above (death or divorce). The persons on the waiting list also can be described as having a type of property interest in the relationship described in their contracts with the club. Theirs is a lesser interest than that of the full golfing members, but a real one nonetheless. They have paid the club for the right to be considered in the numbered order on the list to become full golfing members as vacancies occur. They, like the full golfing members, have a status defined by the various rules, procedures, and practices pertaining to filling the membership roster.

The bankruptcy courts found, and the district court affirmed, that the full golf memberships are executory contracts under § 365 of the Bankruptcy Code. [Citation.] Section 365(f)(1) of the Bankruptcy Code provides that executory contracts may be assigned notwithstanding non-assignment provisions in the contract or the law.* * *

Section 365(c)(1) contains an exception to section 365(f)'s bar to enforcement of non-assignment provisions:

(c) The trustee may not assume or assign any executory contract or unexpired lease of the debtor, whether or not such contract or lease prohibits or restricts assignment of rights or delegation of duties, if—

(1)(A) applicable law excuses a party, other than the debtor, to such contract or lease from accepting performance from or rendering performance to an entity other than the debtor or the debtor in possession, whether or not such contract or lease prohibits or restricts assignment of rights or delegation of duties; and (B) such party does not consent to such assumption or assignment.* * *[Citation.]

The bankruptcy courts found that the trustee was barred from assigning the full golf memberships by Ohio law under § 365(c). The courts concluded that the club's rules were, in effect, anti-assignment provisions, and that Ohio law excused the club from accepting performance by others. The court thus gave effect to the provisions.* * *

The trustee appealed these rulings to the district court.* * *

The district court affirmed the order barring assignment of Magness' full golf membership on the basis of the bankruptcy court's reasoning, and observed as well that the case did not involve "the legal equivalent of a long-term commercial lease" but rather "a non-commercial dispute over the possession of a valuable membership in a recreational and social club."

The trustee then appealed to this court.* * *We conclude that the decision of the district court was correct.* * *We now affirm.

* * *

As stated earlier in this opinion, the contracts involve complex issues and multiple parties: the members of the club, in having an orderly procedure for the selection of full golfing members; the club itself, in demonstrating to all who would become members that there is a predictable and orderly method of filling vacancies in the golfing roster; and more particularly, persons on the waiting list who have deposited substantial sums of money based on an expectation and a developed procedure that in due course they, in turn, would become full golfing members.

If the trustee is permitted to assume and assign the full golf membership, the club would be required to breach its agreement with the persons on the waiting list, each of whom has contractual rights with the club. It would require the club to accept performance from and render performance to a person other than the debtor.* * *

* * *

The contracts creating the complex relationships among the parties and others are not in any way commercial. They create personal relationships among individuals who play golf, who are waiting to play golf, who eat together, swim and play together. They are personal contracts and Ohio law does not permit the assignment of personal contracts. [Citation.]

So-called personal contracts, or contracts in which the personality of one of the parties is material, are not assignable. Whether the personality of one or both parties is material depends on the intention of the parties, as shown by the language which they have used, and upon the nature of the contract.

The claim that the assignment will be made only to those who are already members of the club is not relevant. "Nor would the fact that a particular person it attempted to designate [assign] was personally unexceptionable affect the nature of the contract." [Citation.]

Therefore, we believe that the trustee's motion to assign the full golf membership should be denied. We reach this conclusion because the arrangements for filling vacancies proscribe assignment, the club did not consent to the assignment and sale, and applicable law excuses the club from accepting performance from or rendering performance to a person other than the debtor.

CASE
13-2

The following case concerns the rule of construction that a contract provision barring assignment of the contract has the effect of prohibiting the assignment of substantive rights and duties, but does not bar the assignment of "administrative" rights, such as the right to receive payments due. The case also illustrates the liability of an obligor who, with notice of an assignment of the obligee/assignor's right to payment, ignores the assignment and pays the assignor.

ALDANA v. COLONIAL PALMS PLAZA, INC.
District Court of Appeal of Florida, Third District, 1991
591 So.2d 953

Per Curiam
The appellant, Robert Aldana, appeals an adverse summary judgment in favor of appellee, Colonial Palms Plaza, Inc. and an order awarding Colonial Palms Plaza, Inc. attorney's fees pursuant to the offer of judgment rule. We reverse.

Colonial Palms Plaza, Inc. [Landlord], entered into a lease agreement with Abby's Cakes On Dixie, Inc. [Tenant] for commercial space in a shopping center. The lease included a provision in which Landlord agreed to pay Tenant a construction allowance of up to $11,250 after Tenant satisfactorily completed certain improvements to the rented premises.

Prior to the completion of the improvements, Tenant

assigned its right to receive the first $8,000 of the construction allowance to Robert Aldana [Assignee]. In return, Assignee loaned Tenant $8,000 to finance the construction. Assignee recorded the assignment and sent notice to the assignment by certified mail to Landlord.

When Tenant completed the improvements to the rented premises, Landlord ignored the assignment and paid Tenant the construction allowance. Assignee sued Landlord for the money due pursuant to the assignment. The trial court granted Landlord's motion for summary judgment. The trial court also awarded Landlord attorney's fees pursuant to the offer of judgment rule, [citation], and costs pursuant to [citation].

Landlord relies on an anti-assignment clause in the lease agreement to argue that the assignment was void and unenforceable. The clause states in part:

> TENANT agrees not to assign, mortgage, pledge, or encumber this Lease, in whole or in part, or to sublet the whole or any part of the DEMISED PREMISES, or to permit the use of the whole or any part of the DEMISED PREMISES by any licensee or concessionaire, without first obtaining the prior, specific written consent of LANDLORD at LANDLORD'S sole discretion. * * *Any such assignment, encumbrance or subletting without such consent shall be void and shall at LANDLORD'S option constitute a default.

* * *

Assignee argues* * *that under ordinary contract principles, the lease provision at issue here does not prevent the assignment of the right to receive contractual payments. We agree.

So far as pertinent here, the lease provides that "TENANT agrees not to assign* * *this Lease, in whole or in part. * * *" Tenant did not assign the lease, but instead assigned a right to receive the construction allowance.

The law in this area is summarized in Restatement (Second) of Contracts, § 322(1), as follows:

> Unless the circumstances indicate the contrary, a contract term prohibiting assignment of "the contract" bars only the delegation to an assignee of the performance by the assignor of a duty or condition.

As a rule of construction, in other words, a prohibition against assignment of the contract (or in this case, the lease) will prevent assignment of contractual duties, but does not prevent assignment of the right to receive payments due—unless the circumstances indicate the contrary. [Citations.]

Landlord was given notice of the assignment. Delivery of the notice of the assignment to the debtor fixes accountability of the debtor to the assignee. [Citation.] Therefore, Landlord was bound by the assignment. [Citation.] The trial court improperly granted final summary judgment in favor of Landlord and the judgment must be reversed. Consequently, the trial court's award of attorney's fees and costs to Landlord must also be reversed. The cause is remanded for further proceedings consistent herewith.

Reversed and remanded.

CASE 13-3

This case deals with the question of whether, in the absence of a provision to the contrary, a promisor may delegate contractual duties if: (1) they are not of a personal or unique nature and (2) the quality of the delegatee's performance is materially the same as that bargained for between the promisor/delegator and the promisee.

MACKE COMPANY v. PIZZA OF GAITHERSBURG, INC.

Court of Appeals of Maryland, 1970
259 Md. 479, 270 A.2d 645

Singley, J.

The appellees and defendants below, Pizza of Gaithersburg, Inc.; Pizzeria, Inc.; The Pizza Pie Corp., Inc.; and Pizza Oven, Inc., four corporations under the common ownership of Sidney Ansell, Thomas S. Sherwood, and Eugene Early and the same individuals as partners or proprietors (the Pizza Shops) operated at six locations in Montgomery and Prince George's Counties. The appellees had arranged to have installed in each of their locations cold drink vending machines owned by Virginia Coffee Service, Inc., and on 30 December 1966, this arrangement was formalized at five of the locations, by contracts for terms of one year, automatically renewable for a like term in the absence of 30 days' written notice. A similar contract for

the sixth location, operated by Pizza of Gaithersburg, Inc., was entered into on 25 July 1967.

On 30 December 1967, Virginia's assets were purchased by The Macke Company (Macke) and the six contracts were assigned to Macke by Virginia. In January, 1968, the Pizza Shops attempted to terminate the five contracts having the December anniversary date, and in February, the contract which had the July anniversary date.

Macke brought suit in the Circuit Court for Montgomery County against each of the Pizza Shops for damages for breach of contract. From judgments for the defendants, Macke has appealed.

* * *

In the absence of a contrary provision—and there was none here—rights and duties under an executory bilateral contract may be assigned and delegated, subject to the exception that duties under a contract to provide personal services may never be delegated, nor rights be assigned under a contract where *delectus personae* [choice of person] was an ingredient of the bargain. [Citations.] *Crane Ice Cream Co. v. Terminal Freezing & Heating Co.*, [citation], held that the right of an individual to purchase ice under a contract which by its terms reflected a knowledge of the individual's needs and reliance on his credit and responsibility could not be assigned to the corporation which purchased his business. In [citation], our predecessors held that an advertising agency could not delegate its duties under a contract which had been entered into by an advertiser who had relied on the agency's skill, judgment and taste.

The six machines were placed on the appellees' premises under a printed "Agreement-Contract" which identified the "customer," gave its place of business, described the vending machine, and* * *.

We cannot regard the agreements as contracts for personal services. They were either a license or concession granted Virginia by the appellees, or a lease of a portion of the appellees' premises, with Virginia agreeing to pay a percentage of gross sales as a license or concession fee or as rent, [citations], and were assignable by Virginia unless they imposed on Virginia duties of a personal or unique character which could not be delegated, [citation].

The appellees earnestly argue that they had dealt with Macke before and had chosen Virginia because they preferred the way it conducted its business. Specifically, they say that service was more personalized, since the president of Virginia kept the machines in working order, that commissions were paid in cash, and that Virginia permitted them to keep keys to the machines so that minor adjustments could be made when needed. Even if we assume all this to be true, the agreements with Virginia

were silent as to the details of the working arrangements and contained only a provision requiring Virginia to "install* * *the above listed equipment and* * *maintain the equipment in good operating order and stocked with merchandise." We think the Supreme Court of California put the problem of personal service in proper focus a century ago when it upheld the assignment of a contract to grade a San Francisco street:

> All painters do not paint portraits like Sir Joshua Reynolds, nor landscapes like Claude Lorraine, nor do all writers write dramas like Shakespeare or fiction like Dickens. Rare genius and extraordinary skill are not transferable, and contracts for their employment are therefore personal, and cannot be assigned. But rare genius and extraordinary skill are not indispensable to the workmanlike digging down of a sand hill or the filling up of a depression to a given level, or the construction of brick sewers with manholes and covers, and contracts for such work are not personal, and may be assigned. [Citation.]

* * *Moreover, the difference between the service the Pizza Shops happened to be getting from Virginia and what they expected to get from Macke did not mount up to such a material change in the performance of obligations under the agreements as would justify the appellees' refusal to recognize the assignment, [citation].

* * *

* * *Modern authorities* * *hold that, absent provision to the contrary, a duty may be delegated, as distinguished from a right which can be assigned, and that the promisee cannot rescind, if the quality of the performance remains materially the same.* * *

As we see it, the delegation of duty by Virginia to Macke was entirely permissible under the terms of the agreements.

* * *

[Judgment reversed.]

CASE
13-4

This case discusses the factors to be considered in determining whether a third party is an "incidental beneficiary," who is without any rights under the contract or is an "intended third party beneficiary," who may enforce the contractual promises.

SCOTT v. MAMARI CORPORATION

Court of Appeals of Georgia, 2000
242 Ga.App. 455, 530 S.E.2d 208
http://www.appeals.courts.state.ga.us/appeals/opinions/index.cgi

POPE, J.
Robert Lewis Scott, Jr. d/b/a Scott Construction reconstructed a dam located on a real estate development but was not fully paid for his services. Apparently unable to recover from the developer with whom he contracted, Scott filed claims against two of the development's creditors and claimed that he was a

third-party beneficiary to certain financing agreements related to the development. The trial court granted the creditors' motion for summary judgment, and Scott appeals. Because we find that Scott was neither a third-party beneficiary of these agreements nor entitled to equitable relief against the creditors, we affirm. * * *

In 1995, Mountain Lakes Resort, Inc. (the "Resort") solicited several bids for the dam restoration and eventually accepted Scott's bid to perform the work. The Resort applied for a line of credit for the project from its primary lender, First National Bank of Gainesville, now known as Regions Bank (the "Bank"), and it requested $200,000 based in part on Scott's bid of $111,992 plus approximately $55,200 for required engineering fees. The Bank issued a line of credit in the amount of $175,000, and the Resort signed a promissory note for this amount. Scott began work and was paid on two of three invoices he submitted. The Bank made the payments payable jointly to Scott and the Resort.

The cost of the project grew larger because of unforeseen developments, and the Resort sought an additional $63,879.24 from the Bank. The amount was based in part on Scott's estimated cost to complete the project. The Bank agreed to extend the line of credit by the requested amount. There is a promissory note associated with the extension in the record dated January 10, 1996, and identified as "Note No. 2500," but it is not signed by the Resort. Shortly after Scott submitted his third invoice for the final payment, certain other Resort creditors filed an involuntary bankruptcy petition naming the Resort as the debtor.

On February 16, 1996, the Bank assigned all its rights, title and interest as a creditor for the development, including the loans related to the dam project, to the Mamari Corporation. But the Bank agreed that it would remain responsible for funding the $63,879.24 line of credit. Paragraph 8 of the Mamari agreement provides:

> Bank's Commitment to Fund Draw Note: The Bank has committed to advance up to $63,879.24 to [the Resort] under that certain draw note no. 2500 from [the Resort] to the Bank dated January 10, 1996. The Bank hereby assures MAMARI that it will honor that commitment unless prevented from doing so by statute, court order or other rule of law.

Scott was not a party to this agreement. On July 1, 1997, apparently after the bankruptcy was resolved, the Resort made a request to the Bank for a draw in the full amount of the second note. The request was supported in part by the final invoice from Scott, but also by other contractors' invoices. The request stated that the contractors had been paid for their work, and it requested that payment be made directly to the Resort. In December 1997, promissory note no. 9001 was signed by the Resort in the amount of $63,879.24. The Bank disbursed a check in that amount payable to the Resort, but the Resort never paid Scott on his third invoice. Scott brought suit against Mamari and the Bank for payment of the final invoice, claiming to be a third-party beneficiary of both the promissory note between the Resort and the Bank and paragraph 8 of the Mamari agreement.

Scott contends the trial court erred in determining that he was not a third-party beneficiary to the two agreements. Intent to create a third-party beneficiary must be shown in the contract: "In order for a third party to have standing to enforce a contract . . . it must clearly appear from the contract that it was intended for his benefit. The mere fact that he would benefit from performance of the agreement is not alone sufficient." [Citation.] "Unless such an intention is shown on the face of the contract, defendant is under no duty and consequently plaintiff acquires no right as the third party beneficiary." [Citation.] A contract is intended to benefit a third party when the promisor engages to the promisee to render some performance to a third person. [Citation.]

As for the promissory notes, not one of the various notes is signed by the Bank, which, according to Scott, was bound to make loan disbursements to him. Rather, the notes are promises by the Resort to repay the Bank. They do not even purport to contain any promises by the Bank to do anything for the Resort, let alone Scott. There is no indication of any intent to benefit Scott in any of the notes, which is what Scott claimed. The only indication of intent is found in the original note, and it says that the purpose of the loan was to "provide for unbudgeted expenses." Further, the fact that the Resort used Scott's estimated cost to complete as a basis for the amount it sought in the loan extension did not create a third-party obligation for the Bank to issue the loan proceeds to Scott. It is commonplace to base a loan request on anticipated need. This fact alone does not create an obligation on the lender to disburse the loan to the party to whom the borrower intends to pay with the borrowed funds.

Scott contends that the fact that the first two loan disbursements were made jointly payable to him is evidence that the Bank intended that the loan agreement would benefit him. But, again, there is no indication of an intent to benefit Scott on the face of any note or loan agreement. Joint payments could have been made for any one of a number of reasons.

Finally, the fact that everyone knew that the loan was for the dam project does not mean that the contractors who were going to perform the work were intended beneficiaries of the loan agreement.

As for the Mamari agreement, Scott focuses on paragraph 8. It is true that, "Notwithstanding the ultimate purpose of [an] agreement, individual contract provisions may be intended to benefit a stranger to the contract, thus creating a third-party beneficiary." [Citation.] But Scott is not mentioned in the Mamari agreement by name or otherwise. There is no limitation in the agreement on how the Resort could use the loan proceeds. The funds were not earmarked for use only by Scott. There is no promise in the agreement that the Bank would disburse the loan proceeds to Scott or jointly to Scott and the Resort. Thus, there is nothing in the agreement that "clearly indicates" the contract was intended to benefit Scott. [Citation.]

Rather, paragraph 8 of the Mamari agreement merely represents an agreement between Mamari and the Bank as to who would fund the loan which had already been entered into. Simply agreeing who would satisfy the obligation did not create a third-party beneficiary where none previously existed.

Scott was only an incidental beneficiary to the various loans and the Mamari agreement. The trial court correctly held that Scott was not a third-party beneficiary.

* * * Judgment affirmed.

QUESTIONS

1. Distinguish between an assignment of rights and a delegation of duties.
2. Identify
   (a) the requirements of an assignment of contract rights and
   (b) those rights that are not assignable.
3. Identify those situations in which a delegation of duties is not permitted.
4. Distinguish between an intended beneficiary and an incidental beneficiary.
5. Explain when the rights of an intended beneficiary vest.

PROBLEMS

1. On December 1, Euphonia, a famous singer, contracted with Boito to sing at Boito's theatre on December 31 for a fee of $25,000 to be paid immediately after the performance.

(a) Euphonia, for value received, assigns this fee to Carter.

(b) Euphonia, for value received, assigns this contract to sing to Dumont, an equally famous singer.

(c) Boito sells his theatre to Edmund and assigns his contract with Euphonia to Edmund.

State the effect of each of these assignments.

2. Georgia purchased an option on Blackacre from Pamela for $1,000. The option contract contained a provision by which Georgia promised not to assign the option contract without Pamela's permission. Georgia, without Pamela's permission, assigns the contract to Michael. Michael seeks to exercise the option, and Pamela refuses to sell Blackacre to him. Decision?

3. Julia contracts to sell to Hayden, an ice cream manufacturer, the amount of ice Hayden may need in his business for the ensuing three years to the extent of not more than 250 tons a week at a stated price per ton. Hayden makes a corresponding promise to Julia to buy such an amount of ice. Hayden sells his ice cream plant to Clark and assigns to Clark all Hayden's rights under the contract with Julia. Upon learning of the sale, Julia refuses to furnish ice to Clark. Clark sues Julia for damages. Decision?

4. Brown enters into a written contract with Ideal Insurance Company under which, in consideration of her payment of the premiums, the insurance company promises to pay XYZ College the face amount of the policy, $100,000, on Brown's death. Brown pays the premiums until her death. Thereafter, XYZ College makes demand for the $100,000, which the insurance company refuses to pay upon the ground that XYZ College was not a party to the contract. Decision?

5. Rebecca owes Lewis $2,500 due on November 1. On August 15, Lewis assigns this right for value received to Julia, who gives notice on September 10 of the assignment to Rebecca. On August 25, Lewis assigns the same right to Wayne, who in good faith gives value and has

no prior knowledge of the assignment by Lewis to Julia. Wayne gives Rebecca notice of the assignment on August 30. What are the rights and obligations of Rebecca, Lewis, Julia, and Wayne?

6. Salvador, who owned a retail shoe store, decided to sell the business. The assets of the business consisted of a one story building worth $100,000, merchandise worth $50,000, accounts receivable of $10,000, fixtures worth $30,000 and goodwill estimated at $50,000. He owed various wholesalers a total of $20,000 for shoes bought by him on credit.

Salvador offered to sell all of these assets to Byron for $220,000 cash, provided that Byron would also agree to assume payment of the $20,000 owed for merchandise. Byron agreed, and a written contract was executed by both parties. Upon payment of $220,000 by Byron, Salvador signed a deed and bill of sale for all the assets listed.

Charles, who is one of the wholesalers, to whom Salvador owed $5,000, demanded that Salvador pay the $5,000 owed. Salvador informed him that Byron was to pay. Charles sued Salvador and Byron for payment.

(a) Byron defended on the ground that he had made no contract with Charles. Is the defense valid? Explain.

(b) Salvador defended on the ground that Byron had agreed to pay. Is the defense valid? Explain.

(c) Assume that the court entered judgment against Salvador and Byron for $5,000 as a joint liability. If Salvador paid $2,500 and Byron paid $2,500, has either any claim against the other? Explain.

(d) Would your answer to (a) be the same if Byron had paid $240,000 for the assets but had not agreed to pay the $20,000 owed to Salvador's creditors. Explain.

7. In the previous question, assume that Salvador wished to make a present to his wife, Wilma, of one half of the sales value of the business, and that Byron agreed to pay for the business in two installments. Accordingly, the contract between Salvador and Byron provided that Byron would "pay $110,000 to Salvador upon taking over

the store, and $110,000 to Wilma two years later." Wilma was not one of the parties to the contract. Two years have elapsed and Byron has not paid Wilma.

(a) Does Wilma have a cause of action against Byron for the $110,000 promised to her? Explain.

(b) Would the one year Statute of Frauds be a defense to Byron if the agreement between Salvador and Byron were oral? Explain.

8. In question 7, assume that Salvador, on closing the con tract with Byron, signed a document reading as follows: "May 1. For value received, I hereby transfer to Byron all of my right, title and interest in and to the following accounts receiv able owed to me: (1) From Darren, $5,000 due June 1; (2) From Ellen, $2,000 presently due, and (3) From Fatima, $3,000 due July 1."

(a) If Darren paid Salvador $5,000 on June 3, without knowledge of the assignment, what are Byron's rights against Darren and Salvador?

(b) If Byron immediately notified Ellen of the assignment, and then Ellen paid Salvador the $2,000, what are Byron's rights against Ellen and Salvador? Explain.

(c) If Byron notified Ellen of the assignment, but Ellen did not pay because she was insolvent, what are Byron's rights against Salvador?

(d) Assume that Byron notified Fatima of the assignment on June 15 and Fatima failed to pay on the due date. Byron then sued Fatima for $3,000, and Fatima interposed as a defense the fact that the goods sold to her by Salvador (the transaction from which her debt to Salvador arose) were defective, and worth only $1,000. What are Byron's rights against Fatima and Salvador?

(e) Assume that in (d), Fatima instead interposed as a defense the fact that she had paid the $3,000 on June 10 to Xavier, to whom Salvador had assigned the same debt on June 1. What are Byron's rights against Fatima, Xavier and Salvador? Explain

(f) In (c) and (d) above, what steps could Byron have taken to ensure the collectibility of the debts? Explain.

9. Tom sold goods to Gerard on 30 days credit for $10,000. The next day, Tom assigned this account receivable to Lou, who promptly notified Gerard in writing of the assignment. One week after receiving notice of the assignment from Lou, Gerard discovered that $2,000 of Tom's goods were defective and were worth only $500. Gerard promptly reported this information to Tom and Lou. Tom acknowledged that the defective goods were his fault but said that he could do nothing about it because he had already assigned the account receivable to Lou. Lou informed Gerard that he should pursue his claim with Tom, but should pay Lou the $10,000 due.

(a) What rights, if any, does Lou have against Gerard to recover the $10,000? Explain.

(b) Assume Lou agrees to accept $8,500 from Gerard, after deducting $1,500 for defective goods What rights, if any, does Lou have against Tom? Explain.

10. Ed owned a company that cleaned swimming pools. He charged his customers $100 per month and billed them every two months. At the beginning of September, Ed had not yet collected for the months of July and August from his customer, Suzy, whose pool he had cleaned during that period.

On September 5, Ed spoke with Larry, who was selling a used mountain bike. Larry said that he would sell the bike to Ed for $250.

Ed accepted this offer, gave Larry $50 and a signed writing assigning to Larry the debt owed by Suzy.

The next day, Larry attempted to collect the $200 from Suzy. She refused to pay, telling Larry that she was not prepared to pay anything because Ed had been adding the wrong chemicals to the water, causing her to suffer a severe skin rash. She only discovered the cause, she said, after seeing a doctor in mid-August. Larry sues both Suzy and Ed for $200.

(a) How much if anything, may Larry recover from Suzy?

(b) How much, if anything, may Larry recover from Ed?

11. Abbott enters into a written signed contract with Costello to sell Costello 3,000 reels of comedy films for $60,000. Without the knowledge or consent of Costello, Abbott assigns his right to receive Costello's payment to Edgar, a creditor of Abbott.

Edgar gives notice of the assignment to Costello and demands payment of $60,000. Costello, however, contends that he has no obligation to pay Edgar because: (1) Costello never consented to the assignment and (2) in any event, 2,000 of the film reels are totally defective and, therefore, Costello only owes $20,000.

Assume that Costello's claim of defective reels is proven and that Edgar did not know of the defects at the time the assignment was made. What rights, if any, does Edgar have:

(a) against Costello? Explain.

(b) against Abbott? Explain.

12. On January 10, Simpson sold her business to Bart for $250,000 under an executed contract that provided that Bart would pay Simpson's indebtedness to Homer, which was due on February 10.

On February 10, Simpson refused Homer's demand for payment, explaining that Bart has agreed to pay Homer and that Homer should look to Bart for payment.

The next day, Homer demanded payment from Bart, who refused to pay upon the grounds that: (1) Bart had no contract with Homer requiring Bart to pay Homer and (2) Homer cannot enforce the contract between Simpson and Bart because Homer gave no consideration.

(a) In an action by Homer against Bart, judgment for whom? Explain.

(b) In an action by Homer against Simpson, judgment for whom? Explain.

13. Grant and Debbie enter into a contract binding Grant personally to do some delicate cabinetwork. Grant assigns his rights and delegates performance of his duties to Clarence.

(a) On being informed of this, Debbie agrees with Clarence, in consideration of Clarence's promise to do the work, that Debbie will accept Clarence's work, if properly done, instead of the performance promised by Grant. Later, without cause, Debbie refuses to allow Clarence to proceed with the work, though Clarence is ready to do so, and makes demand on Grant that Grant perform. Grant refuses. Can Clarence recover damages from Debbie? Can Debbie recover from Grant?

(b) Instead, assume that Debbie refuses to permit Clarence to do the work, employs another carpenter, and brings an action against Grant, claiming as damages the difference between the contract price and the cost to employ the other carpenter. Explain whether Debbie will prevail.

14. Lisa hired Jay in the spring, as she had for many years, to set out in beds the flowers Lisa had grown in her greenhouses during the winter. The work was to be done in Lisa's absence for $300. Jay became ill the day after Lisa departed and requested his friend, Curtis, to set out the flowers, promising to pay Curtis $250 when Jay received his payment. Curtis agreed. Upon completion of the planting, an agent of Lisa's, who had authority to dispense the money, paid Jay, and Jay paid Curtis. Within two days it became obvious that the planting was a disaster. Everything set out by Curtis had died of water rot because he had operated Lisa's automatic watering system improperly.

May Lisa recover damages from Curtis? May she recover damages from Jay? If so, does Jay have an action against Curtis?

15. Caleb, operator of a window-washing business, dictated a letter to his secretary addressed to Apartments, Inc., stating, "I will wash the windows of your apartment buildings at $4.10 per window to be paid upon completion of the work." The secretary typed the letter, signed Caleb's name, and mailed it to Apartments, Inc. Apartments, Inc., replied, "Accept your offer."

Caleb wrote back, "I will wash them during the week commencing July 10 and direct you to pay the money you will owe me to my son, Bernie. I am giving it to him as a wedding present." Caleb sent a signed copy of the letter to Bernie.

Caleb washed the windows during the time stated and demanded payment to him of $8,200 (2,000 windows at $4.10 each), informing Apartments, Inc., that he had changed his mind about having the money paid to Bernie.

What are the rights of the parties?

Internet Exercise Find a sample of one of the following: (a) an assignment of a contract, (b) a delegation of a contractual duty, or (c) a third-party beneficiary contract.

Illegal Bargains

An essential requirement of a binding promise or agreement is legality of objective. When the formation or performance of an agreement is criminal, tortious, or otherwise contrary to public policy, the agreement is illegal and **unenforceable** (as opposed to being void). The law does not provide a remedy for the breach of an unenforceable agreement and thus "leaves the parties where it finds them." It is preferable to use the term *illegal bargain* or *illegal agreement* rather than *illegal contract*, because the word *contract*, by definition, denotes a legal and enforceable agreement. The illegal bargain is made unenforceable (1) to discourage such undesirable conduct and (2) to preclude the inappropriate use of the judicial process in carrying out such socially undesirable bargains.

The Restatement avoids defining the term *illegal bargain*, instead focusing upon whether public policy should bar enforcement of the agreement. By relying upon the concept of public policy, the Restatement provides the courts with greater flexibility in determining the enforceability of questioned agreements by weighing the strength of legally recognized policies against the effect that declaring a particular bargain to be against public policy would have on the contracting parties and on the public.

This chapter will discuss (1) agreements in violation of a statute, (2) agreements contrary to public policy, and (3) the effect of illegality upon agreements.

VIOLATIONS OF STATUTES

The courts will not enforce an agreement declared illegal by statute. For example, wagering or gambling contracts are specifically declared unenforceable in most states. In addition, an agreement to violate a statute prohibiting crimes, such as murder, robbery, embezzlement, forgery, and price fixing, is unenforceable. Likewise, an agreement that is induced by criminal conduct will not be enforced. For example, if Alice enters into an agreement with Brent Co. through the bribing of Brent Co.'s purchasing agent, the agreement would be unenforceable.

Licensing Statutes *For the final*

Every jurisdiction has laws requiring a license for those who engage in certain trades, professions, or businesses. Common examples are licensing statutes which apply to lawyers, doctors, dentists, accountants, brokers, plumbers, and contractors. Some licensing statutes mandate schooling and/or examination, while others require only financial responsibility and/or good moral character. Whether or not a person may recover for services rendered if he has failed to comply with a licensing requirement depends upon the terms or type of licensing statute. This rule pertains only to the rights of the unlicensed party to enforce the obligations of the other party.

final exam

The statute itself may expressly provide that an unlicensed person engaged in a business or profession for which a license is required shall not recover for services rendered. Absent such statutory provision, the courts commonly distinguish between those statutes or ordinances that are **regulatory** in character and those that are enacted merely to raise **revenue** through the issuance of licenses. If the statute is regulatory, a person cannot recover for professional services unless he has the required license, as long as the public policy behind the regulatory purpose clearly outweighs the person's interest in being paid for his services. Restatement, Section 181. Some courts have gone further by balancing the penalty the unlicensed party suffers against the benefit the other party receives. In contrast, if the law is for revenue purposes only, agreements for such services are enforceable.

A regulatory license, including those issued under statutes prescribing standards for those wishing to practice law or medicine, is a measure designed to protect the public against unqualified persons. A revenue license, on the other hand, does not seek to protect against incompetent or unqualified practitioners but simply to furnish revenue. An example is a statute requiring a license of plumbers but not establishing standards of competence for those who seek to follow the trade. The courts regard such legislation as a taxing measure lacking any expression of legislative intent to preclude unlicensed plumbers from enforcing their business contracts.

◈ See Case 14-1

Gambling Statutes *final exam*

In a wager the parties stipulate that one shall win and the other lose depending upon the outcome of an event in which their sole "interest" arises from the possibility of such gain or loss. All states have legislation pertaining to gambling or wagering, and U.S. courts generally refuse to recognize the enforceability of a gambling agreement. Thus, if Arnold makes a bet with Bernice on the outcome of a ball game, the agreement is unenforceable by either party. Some states, however, now permit certain kinds of regulated gambling. Wagering conducted by governmental agencies, principally state-operated lotteries, has come to constitute an increasingly important source of public revenues.

To be distinguished from wagers are ordinary insurance contracts in which the insured, having an "insurable interest," pays a certain sum of money or premium in exchange for an insurance company's promise to pay a larger amount upon the occurrence of some event, such as a fire, which causes loss to the insured. Here, the agreement compensates for loss under an existing risk; it does not create an entirely new risk. In a wager, the parties contemplate gain through mere chance, whereas in an insurance contract they seek to distribute possible loss. Furthermore, most games at fast-food restaurants and grocery store drawings have been upheld because the participants need not make a purchase to be eligible for the prize.

Usury Statutes *NY is 16%*

A **usury statute** is a law establishing a maximum rate of permissible interest for which a lender and borrower of money may contract. Though, historically, every state had a usury law, a recent trend has been to limit or relax usury statutes. The maximum rates permitted vary greatly from state to state and among types of transactions. These statutes typically are general in their application, although certain specified types of transactions are exempted. For example, numerous states impose no limit on the rate of interest that may be charged on loans to corporations. Furthermore, some states permit the parties to contract for any rate of interest on loans made to individual proprietorships or partnerships for the purpose of carrying on a business.

In addition to the exceptions accorded certain designated types of borrowers, a number of states have exempted specific lenders. For example, the majority of the states have enacted installment loan laws, which permit eligible lenders a return on installment loans that is higher than the applicable general interest statute would permit. These specific lender usury statutes, which have all but eliminated general usury statutes, vary greatly but generally have included small consumer loans, corporate loans, loans by small lenders, real estate mortgages, and numerous other transactions.

For a transaction to be usurious, courts usually require evidence of the following factors: (a) a loan or forbearance (b) of money (c) which is repayable absolutely and in all events (d) for which an interest charge is exacted in excess of the interest rate allowed by law. Transactions that are really loans may not be clothed with the trappings of a sale for the purpose of avoiding the usury laws.

The legal effect to be given a usurious loan varies from state to state. In a few states, New York, for example, the lender forfeits both principal and interest. In some jurisdictions, the lender can recover the principal but forfeits all interest. In other states, only that portion of interest exceeding the permitted maximum is forfeited. In several states, the amount forfeited is a multiple (double or treble) of the interest charged. Disposition of usurious interest already paid also varies. Some states do not allow any recovery of usurious interest paid; others allow recovery of such interest or a multiple of it.

◈ See GOL § 5-511

Sunday Statutes

In the absence of a statutory prohibition, the common law does not prohibit entering into contracts on Sunday. Some states, however, have legislation, referred to as **Blue Laws**, modifying this common law rule and prohibiting certain types of commercial activity on Sunday. Even in a state which prohibits contracts on Sunday, a court nonetheless will enforce a subsequent weekday ratification of a loan made on Sunday or a promise to pay for goods sold and delivered on Sunday. In addition, Blue Laws usually do not apply to activities of "necessity" and "charity."

VIOLATIONS OF PUBLIC POLICY

The reach of a statute may extend beyond its language. Sometimes, the courts, by analogy, use the statute and the policy it seeks to serve as a guide in determining the private contract rights of one harmed by a violation of the statute. In addition, the courts must frequently articulate the "public policy" of the state without significant help from statutory sources. This judicially declared public policy is very broad in scope, it often being said that agreements having "a tendency to be injurious to the public or the public good" are contrary to public policy. Thus, the term *public policy* eludes precise definition. Contracts raising questions of public policy include agreements that (1) restrain trade, (2) exempt or exculpate a party from liability for his own tortious conduct, (3) are unconscionable, (4) involve tortious conduct, (5) tend to obstruct the administration of justice, (6) tend to corrupt public officials or impair the legislative process, or (7) impair family relationships. This section will focus on the first four of these types of agreements.

Common Law Restraint of Trade

A **restraint of trade** is any contract or agreement that eliminates or tends to eliminate competition or otherwise obstructs trade or commerce. One type of restraint is a **covenant not to compete**, which is an agreement to refrain from entering into a competing trade, profession, or business.

An agreement to refrain from a particular trade, profession, or business is enforceable if (1) the purpose of the restraint is to protect a property interest of the promisee and (2) the restraint is no more extensive than is reasonably necessary to protect that interest. Restraints typically arise in two situations: the sale of a business and employment contracts.

Sale of a Business

As part of an agreement to sell a business, the seller frequently promises not to compete in that particular type of business in a *defined area* for a stated *time*. To protect the business's goodwill (an asset that the buyer has purchased), the buyer must be allowed to enforce such a covenant (promise) by the seller not to compete with the purchaser within reasonable limitations. Most litigation on this subject has involved the requirement that the restraint be no greater than is reasonably necessary. Whether the restraint is reasonable or not depends on the geographic area it covers, the time period for which it is to be effective, and the hardship it imposes on the promisor and the public.

For example, the promise of a person selling a service station business in Detroit not to enter the service station business in Michigan for the next twenty-five years is unreasonable, both as to area and time. The business interest to be protected would not include the entire state, so it is not necessary to the protection of the purchaser that the seller be prevented from engaging in the service station business in the entire state or perhaps, for that matter, in the entire city of Detroit. Limiting the area to the neighborhood in which the station is located or to a radius of a few miles would probably be adequate.

The same type of inquiry must be made about time limitations. In the sale of a service station, a twenty-five-year ban on competition from the seller would be unreasonable; a one-year ban probably would not. The court, in determining what is reasonable under particular circumstances, must consider each case on its own facts.

Employment Contracts

Salespeople, management personnel, and other employees frequently are required to sign employment contracts prohibiting them from competing with their employers during their time of employment and for some additional stated period after termination. The same is also frequently true among corporations or partnerships involving professionals, such as accountants, lawyers, investment brokers, stockbrokers, or doctors. Although the courts readily enforce a covenant not to compete during the period of employment, the promise not to compete after termination is subjected to an even stricter test of reasonableness than that applied to noncompetition promises included in a contract for the sale of a business. One reason for this is that the employer is in a stronger bargaining position than the employee.

A court order enjoining a former employee from competing in a described territory for a stated time is the usual method by which an employer seeks to enforce the employee's promise not to compete. Before granting such injunctions, the courts insist that the employer demonstrate that the restriction is *necessary* to protect his legitimate interests, such as trade secrets or customer lists. Because issuing the injunction may place the employee out of work, the courts must carefully balance the public policy favoring the employer's right to protect his business interests against the public policy favoring full opportunity for individuals to gain employment.

Thus, one court has held unreasonable a covenant in a contract requiring a travel agency employee, after termination of her employment, to refrain from engaging in a like business in any capacity in either of two named towns or within a sixty-mile radius of those towns for two years. There was no indication that the employee had enough influence over customers to cause them to move their business to her new agency, nor was it shown that any trade secrets were involved. *United Travel Service, Inc. v. Weber,* 108 Ill.App.2d 353, 247 N.E.2d 801 (1969). Instead of refusing to enforce an unreasonable covenant, some courts, considering the action justifiable under the circumstances of the case, will reform the agreement to make it reasonable and enforceable.

Due to the rapid evolution of business practices in the Internet industry, it has been argued that non-compete agreements for Internet company employees need their own rules. For instance, a period of time that is reasonable for a conventional company might be unreasonable for an Internet company.

◆ See Case 14-2

Exculpatory Clauses

Some contracts contain an exculpatory clause that excuses one party from liability for her own tortious conduct. The courts generally agree that exculpatory clauses relieving a person from tort liability for harm caused intentionally or recklessly are unenforceable as violating public policy. On the other hand, exculpatory clauses that excuse a party from liability for harm caused by negligent conduct are scrutinized carefully by the courts, which often require that the clause be conspicuously placed in the contract and clearly written. Accordingly, an exculpatory clause on the reverse side of a parking lot claim check, which attempts to relieve the parking lot operator of liability for negligently damaging the customer's automobile, will generally be held unenforceable as against public policy. Indeed, some states, New York among them, have adopted laws explicitly prohibiting garages or parking lots from fully exempting themselves from liability for their own negligence. See GOL 5-325.

The Restatement provides that exculpatory clauses excusing negligent conduct are unenforceable on grounds of public policy if they exempt (1) an employer from liability to an employee, (2) a public service business (such as a common carrier) from liability to a customer, or (3) a person from liability to a party who is a member of a protected class. Restatement, Section 195. For example, a railroad company will not be permitted to avoid liability for the negligent operation or maintenance of its trains.

A similar rule applies to a contractual provision unreasonably exempting a party from the legal consequences of a misrepresentation. Restatement, Section 196. Such a term is unenforceable on the grounds of public policy with respect to both fraudulent and nonfraudulent misrepresentations.

Further, where the superior bargaining position of one party has enabled him to impose upon the other party such a provision, the courts are inclined to nullify the provision. Such a situation may arise in residential leases exempting a landlord from liability for his negligence. Moreover, an exculpatory clause may be unenforceable for unconscionability.

◆ See Cases 14-3 and 14-4

Unconscionable Contracts

The court may scrutinize every contract of sale to determine whether it is, in its commercial setting, purpose, and effect, **unconscionable**. The court may refuse to enforce an unconscionable contract in its entirety or any part it finds to be unconscionable. Section 2–302 of the UCC provides:

If the court as a matter of law finds the contract or any clause of the contract to have been unconscionable at the time it was made the court may refuse to enforce the contract, or it may enforce the remainder of the contract without the unconscionable clause, or it may so limit the application of any unconscionable clause as to avoid any unconscionable result.

Similarly, Section 208 of the Restatement parallels this provision and provides:

If a contract or term thereof is unconscionable at the time the contract is made a court may refuse to enforce the contract, or may enforce the remainder of the contract without the unconscionable term, or may so limit the application of any unconscionable term as to avoid any unconscionable result.

Neither the Code nor the Restatement defines the word *unconscionable*; however, the *New Webster's Dictionary* (Deluxe Encyclopedic Edition) defines the term as "contrary to the dictates of conscience; unscrupulous or unprincipled; exceeding that which is reasonable or customary; inordinate, unjustifiable."

The doctrine of unconscionability has been justified on the basis that it permits the courts to resolve issues of unfairness explicitly as regards that unfairness without recourse to formalistic rules or legal fictions. In policing contracts for fairness, the courts have again demonstrated their willingness to limit freedom of contract to protect the less advantaged from overreaching by dominant contracting parties. The doctrine of unconscionability has evolved through its application by the courts to include both procedural and substantive unconscionability.

Procedural unconscionability involves scrutiny for the presence of "bargaining naughtiness." In other words, was the negotiation process fair, or were there procedural irregularities, such as burying important terms of the agreement in fine print or obscuring the true meaning of the contract with impenetrable legal jargon?

Substantive unconscionability, which involves the actual terms of the contract, consists of oppressive or grossly unfair provisions, such as an exorbitant price or an unfair exclusion or limitation of contractual remedies. An all-too-common example is that involving a necessitous buyer in an unequal bargaining position with a seller, who consequently obtains an exorbitant price for his product or service. In one case, a court held unconscionable a price of $749 ($920 on time) for a vacuum cleaner that cost the seller $140. In another case the buyers, welfare recipients, purchased by time payment contract a home freezer unit for $900 which, when added to time credit charges, credit life insurance, credit property insurance, and sales tax, amounted to $1,235. The purchase resulted from a visit to the buyer's home by a salesman representing Your Shop At Home Service, Inc.; the maximum retail value of the freezer unit at time of purchase was $300. The court held the contract unconscionable and reformed it by reducing the price to the total payment ($620) the buyers had managed to make.

Some courts hold that in order for a contract to be unenforceable both substantive and procedural unconscionability must be present. Nevertheless, they need not exist to the same degree; the more oppressive one is, the less evidence of the other is required.

Closely akin to the concept of unconscionability is the doctrine of contracts of adhesion. A standard-form contract prepared by one party, an **adhesion contract** generally involves the preparer's offering the other party the contract on a "take-it-or-leave-it" basis. Such contracts are not automatically unenforceable but are subject to greater scrutiny for procedural or substantive unconscionability.

❧ See Case 14-5

Tortious Conduct

"A promise to commit a tort or to induce the commission of a tort is unenforceable on grounds of public policy." Restatement, Section 192. The courts will not permit contract law to violate the law of torts. Any agreement attempting to do so is considered contrary to public policy. For example, Andrew and Barlow Co. enter into an agreement under which Andrew promises Barlow that in return for $5,000 he will disparage the product of Barlow Co.'s competitor Cosmo, Inc., in order to provide Barlow Co. with a competitive advantage. Andrew's promise is to commit the tort of disparagement and is unenforceable as contrary to public policy.

EFFECT OF ILLEGALITY

As a general rule, illegal contracts are unenforceable. In a few instances, however, one of the parties may be permitted to enforce all or part of the contract; whereas, under other circumstances, the courts will allow one party to recover in restitution for his performance of the illegal contract.

General Rule: Unenforceability

In most cases when an agreement is illegal, neither party can successfully sue the other for breach or recover for any performance rendered. Whichever party is plaintiff is immaterial to the courts. As is frequently said in these cases, the court will leave the parties where it finds them.

Exceptions

The courts recognize several exceptions to the general rule regarding the effect of illegality on a contract and may, after considering the circumstances surrounding a particular contract, grant relief to one of the parties, though not to the other. The following sections will consider these exceptions.

Party Withdrawing before Performance   A party to an illegal agreement may, prior to performance, withdraw from the transaction and recover whatever she has contributed, if the party has not engaged in serious misconduct. Restatement, Section 199. A common example is recovery of money left with a stakeholder pursuant to a wager before it is paid over to the winner.

Party Protected by Statute   Sometimes an agreement is illegal because it violates a statute designed to protect persons in the position of one of the parties. For example, state "Blue Sky Laws" prohibiting the sale of unregistered securities are designed primarily for the protection of investors. In such cases, even though there is an unlawful agreement, the statute usually expressly gives the purchaser the right to rescind the sale and recover the money paid.

Party Not Equally at Fault   Where one of the parties is less at fault than the other, he will be allowed to recover payments made or property transferred. Restatement, Section 198. For example, this exception would apply where one party induces the other to enter into an illegal bargain through fraud, duress, or undue influence.

Excusable Ignorance   An agreement that appears on its face to be entirely permissible may, nevertheless, be illegal by reason of facts and circumstances of which one of the parties is completely unaware. For example, a man and woman make mutual promises to marry, but unknown to the woman, the man is already married. This is an agreement to commit the crime of bigamy, and the marriage, if entered into, is void. In such case the courts permit the party who is ignorant of the illegality to maintain a lawsuit against the other party for damages.

A party may also be excused for ignorance of relatively minor legislation. Restatement, Section 180. For instance, Jones and Old South Building Co. enter into a contract to build a factory that contains specifications in violation of the town's building ordinance. Jones did not know of the violation and had no reason to know. Old South's promise to build would not be rendered unenforceable on grounds of public policy, and Jones would have a claim against Old South for damages for breach of contract.

Partial Illegality   A contract may be partly unlawful and partly lawful. The courts view such a contract in one of two ways. First, the partial illegality may be held to taint the entire contract with illegality, so that it is wholly unenforceable. Second, it may be possible to separate the illegal from the legal part, in which case the court will hold the illegal part unenforceable but will enforce the legal part. For example, if a contract contains an illegal covenant not to compete, the covenant will not be enforced, though the rest of the contract may be.

CHAPTER SUMMARY

Violations of Statutes

General Rule the courts will not enforce agreements declared illegal by statute

Licensing Statutes require formal authorization to engage in certain trades, professions, or businesses

- *Regulatory License* licensing statute that is intended to protect the public against unqualified persons; an unlicensed person may not recover for services she has performed
- *Revenue License* licensing statute that seeks to raise money; an unlicensed person may recover for services he has performed

Gambling Statutes prohibit wagers, which are agreements that one party will win and the other lose depending upon the outcome of an event in which their only interest is the gain or loss

Usury Statutes establish a maximum rate of interest

Sunday Statutes prohibition of certain types of commercial activity on Sunday (also called Blue Laws)

Violations of Public Policy

Common Law Restraint of Trade unreasonable restraints of trade are not enforceable

- *Sale of a Business* the promise by the seller of a business not to compete in that particular business in a reasonable geographic area for a reasonable period of time is enforceable
- *Employment Contracts* an employment contract prohibiting an employee from competing with his employer for a reasonable period following termination is enforceable provided the restriction is necessary to protect legitimate interests of the employer

Exculpatory Clauses the courts generally disapprove of contractual provisions excusing a party from liability for her own tortious conduct

Unconscionable Contracts unfair or unduly harsh agreements are not enforceable

- *Procedural Unconscionability* unfair or irregular bargaining
- *Substantive Unconscionability* oppressive or grossly unfair contractual terms

Tortious Conduct an agreement that requires a person to commit a tort is unenforceable

Corrupting Public Officials agreements that corrupt public officials are not enforceable

Effect of Illegality

Unenforceability neither party may recover under an illegal agreement where both parties are *in pari delicto* (in equal fault)

Exceptions permit one party to recover payments

- *Party Withdrawing before Performance*
- *Party Protected by Statute*
- *Party Not Equally at Fault*
- *Excusable Ignorance*
- *Partial Illegality*

CASES

Licensing statutes can present courts with difficult questions when a party to a contract is technically unlicensed to perform the service contracted for but nonetheless performs that service as promised. In this case, a California appeals court considers whether to compel payment for work done by a contractor who reasonably should have known that its license had lapsed.

PACIFIC CUSTOM POOLS, INC. v. TURNER CONSTRUCTION COMPANY

Court of Appeal, Second District, Division 4, California, 2000
79 Cal.App.4th 1254, 94 Cal.Rptr.2d 756
http://www.courtinfo.ca.gov/opinions/archive/B122853.DOC

Berle J.

On this* * *appeal, Pacific Custom Pools, Inc., challenges the trial court's granting of summary judgment based on the failure of Pacific Custom Pools to substantially comply with the contractor's licensing requirements,* * *. We hold that the trial court properly granted summary judgment* * *.

Factual Background and Procedural History

Universal City Studios, Inc. ("Universal") entered into a general contract with Turner Construction Company ("Turner") for the construction of the Jurassic Park ride (the "project") at the theme park in Universal City, California. In turn, Turner entered into a subcontract ("the Agreement") on the project with Pacific Custom Pools, Inc. ("PCP"), pursuant to which PCP agreed to furnish and install all water treatment work for the project for the contract price of $959,131. PCP further subcontracted its work to Harrington Industrial Plastics, Inc. ("Harrington") and Pacific Engineered Projects ("PEP") for those companies to provide materials and supplies on the project. PCP performed work on the project from April 1995 until June 1996 for which it was paid $897,719. During the period of October 12, 1995 to March 14, 1996, PCP's contractor's license was under suspension, and although the license had also expired as of January 31, 1996, it was not renewed until May 5, 1996.

[PCP brought suit against Universal and Turner, the defendants, for the remainder of the contract price. The trial court granted the defendants' motion for summary judgment on the basis that PCP had not been licensed in California and thus could not bring suit. PCP appealed.]

* * *

Doctrine of Substantial Compliance with Licensing Requirements

Section 7031, subdivision (a) provides that a contractor may not maintain an action for the recovery of compensation for the performance of work requiring a license unless it was "a duly licensed contractor at all times during the performance of that" work. In *Hydrotech Systems, Ltd. v. Oasis Waterpark* (1991) [citation] the [California] Supreme Court set forth the social policy underpinning section 7031:

The purpose of the licensing law is to protect the public from incompetence and dishonesty in those who provide building and construction services. [Citation.] The licensing requirements provide minimal assurance that all persons offering such services in California have the requisite skill and character, understand applicable local laws and codes, and know the rudiments of administering a contracting business. [Citation.]

Section 7031 advances this purpose by withholding judicial aid from those who seek compensation for unlicensed contract work. The obvious statutory intent is to discourage persons who have failed to comply with the licensing law from offering or providing their unlicensed services for pay.

"Because of the strength and clarity of this policy, it is well settled that section 7031 applies despite injustice to the unlicensed contractor. 'Section 7031 represents a legislative determination that the importance of deterring unlicensed persons from engaging in the contracting business outweighs any harshness between the parties, and that such deterrence can best be realized by denying violators the right to maintain any action for compensation in the courts of this state. [Citation.]'* * *"

Through a series of cases beginning in 1966, the courts attempted to alleviate the severity of the application of section 7031 by allowing recovery to a contractor who has substantially complied with the licensing statutory scheme. [Citations.]

In reaction to this development in the law, the Legislature amended section 7031 in 1989 to add a subsection (d) which provided that the substantial compliance doctrine shall not apply to that statute. [Citations.] In 1991, the Legislature further amended section 7031 to provide an exception to the prohibition of the substantial compliance doctrine where noncompliance with licensure requirements was the result of inadvertent clerical error or other error or delay not caused by the negligence of the licensee. [Citation.]

* * *

An unlicensed contractor may thus avoid the consequences of the prohibition against the substantial compliance doctrine under section 7031, subd. (d) if the contractor proves that it had been licensed before performing work, acted reasonably in trying to maintain a license and did not know or reasonably should not have known that it was not licensed. The parties concur that PCP was licensed before commencing work on the project. However, the parties dispute whether PCP acted reasonably and in good faith to maintain its license, and whether PCP knew or should have reasonably known that it was not licensed.

* * *

In* * *the case at bar: (a) PCP was aware in November 1995 that its license was suspended for failure to file a judgment bond and that the deadline date for license renewal was January 31, 1996; (b) PCP knew shortly after February 23, 1996 that a renewal application sent in February 1996 was untimely; and

(c) that PCP was advised on April 22, 1996 that its license had not been renewed because PCP's filing fee check had been dishonored. These facts do not suggest that PCP acted reasonably or in good faith to maintain licensure or that PCP did not know or reasonably should not have known that it was not duly licensed, to support a claim of substantial compliance within the meaning of section 7031.

* * *

The summary judgment is affirmed * * *.

CASE
14-2

Employment agreements may contain provisions prohibiting the employee from working for competing companies for a specified period of time after the employee leaves her current employer. However, such prohibitions must be limited in scope and duration and must be reasonable and necessary to protect the legitimate interests of the employer. The following case involves an attempt by an internet company to prevent its former employee from taking a job with an enterprise that it viewed as its competition.

EARTHWEB, INC. v. SCHLACK

United States District Court for the Southern District of New York, 1999
71 F. Supp.2d 299 aff'd, Docket No. 99-9302 (2d Circuit Court of Appeals, 2000)
http://www.nysd.uscourts.gov/courtweb/pdf/D02NYSC/99-06890.PDF

Pauley III, J.

Findings of Fact and Conclusions of Law

Background

EarthWeb, which was founded in 1994, provides online products and services to business professionals in the information technology ("IT") industry. IT professionals are individuals who manage and run computer systems, develop software and perform related tasks for the companies that employ them.

EarthWeb employs approximately 230 individuals in offices located in New York City and around the country. Its stock is publicly traded. EarthWeb operates through a family of websites offering IT professionals information, products and services to use for facilitating tasks and solving technology problems in a business setting. Some of EarthWeb's websites are free to the user, while others require a subscription fee. EarthWeb's websites contain,* * *, (1) articles on subjects tailored to IT professionals that discuss and examine the implementation of technology in the corporate environment; (2) lists of articles, training materials, periodicals, books and downloads organized and indexed by subject matter; (3) compilations and aggregations of technical news; (4) a reference library of full-text versions of technical books; and (5) an online forum of discussion groups.

EarthWeb obtains this content primarily through licensing agreements with third parties. Advertising is EarthWeb's primary source of revenue. In 1998, the company generated approximately $3.3 million in revenue.

Schlack has worked in the publishing industry for the

past 16 years. Prior to joining EarthWeb, Schlack had been employed as senior editor and/or editor-in-chief of several print magazines, such as BYTE and Web Builder.

Schlack began his employment with EarthWeb in its New York City office on October 19, 1998, and he remained with the company until his resignation on September 22, 1999. His title at EarthWeb was Vice President, Worldwide Content, and as the name suggests, Schlack was responsible for the content of all of EarthWeb's websites.* * *

* * *

On September 22, 1999, Schlack tendered to EarthWeb senior vice president William F. Gollan his letter of resignation. Upon inquiry by Gollan, Schlack revealed that he had accepted a position with ITworld.com, a subsidiary of IDG. According to EarthWeb, IDG is the world's leading provider of IT print-based information. The company generates over $1 billion in annual revenues and publishes more than 280 monthly periodicals. The position IDG offered Schlack is based in Massachusetts and would provide him a significant increase in compensation.

Schlack's Employment with EarthWeb

EarthWeb describes Schlack as one of its most important officers, while Schlack claims that EarthWeb has inflated the nature of his duties and responsibilities. Schlack also argues that the position waiting for him at IDG is so different that he would have no occasion to divulge any trade secrets belonging to EarthWeb.* * *

Strategic Content Planning EarthWeb claims that Schlack's primary job responsibilities involved making all significant strategic decisions relating to content. The company also asserts that Schlack either authored or supervised the creation of the content plans for a number of EarthWeb websites within the last year. Thus, Schlack was involved in deciding what content EarthWeb licensed and how that content would be structured on its websites in order to reach specific types of IT professionals. Schlack was also involved in determining whether the users of a particular EarthWeb website should pay for access to the site, and if so, what the appropriate price should be. As a result, Schlack knows the specific target audience for each website, how EarthWeb aggregated content on those websites to reach the targeted audience, and how EarthWeb may intend to improve the content and delivery of particular websites.

Schlack* * *also contends that whatever he knows about EarthWeb's strategic planning is likely to become obsolete rather quickly because the company's websites are constantly changing.

Licensing Agreements and Acquisitions During his employment, Schlack was involved in negotiating at least two licensing agreements with third parties, and he was generally aware of the terms and conditions of other such agreements. Schlack also knows of companies whose content EarthWeb is interested in licensing. As vice president for content, Schlack often played a key role in determining whether particular content should be licensed, and if so, what the terms of the deal would be. With respect to acquisitions, Schlack analyzed and evaluated websites and companies that EarthWeb later acquired. Schlack also knows of at least four companies that EarthWeb continues to view as desirable acquisitions.

* * *

Advertising Schlack was also involved, albeit less directly, with EarthWeb's marketing and sales efforts. Schlack describes his role as "explaining EarthWeb's editorial focus and how [it] might relate to the advertiser's customer."* * *

Technical Knowledge Schlack's job responsibilities required him to be familiar with the software and hardware infrastructure that supports EarthWeb's websites. Thus, Schlack has general knowledge of how EarthWeb customized and deployed the products of outside vendors and consultants in order to fit EarthWeb's programming needs. Schlack also gained an understanding of the technical problems that EarthWeb successfully tackled in order to make its websites operate efficiently.

However, Schlack had no access to EarthWeb's source codes or configuration files, so his knowledge of EarthWeb's proprietary software and infrastructure is necessarily limited. In addition, EarthWeb plans to revamp its software infrastructure in the near future, so any knowledge Schlack has may soon become obsolete.

* * *

Schlack's Prospective Position with ITworld.com

At the moment, ITworld.com does not exist; the website is scheduled to be launched in January 2000. According to its president and CEO, William Reinstein, ITworld.com will consolidate four online publications of IDG—Computerworld, Network World, InfoWorld and CIO—and three additional wholly-owned websites. When operational, ITworld.com will be a single website for IT professionals that contains news, product information and editorial opinions written primarily by an internal staff of more than 275 journalists.

Thus, in contrast to EarthWeb's emphasis on obtaining the products and services of third parties through acquisitions and licensing agreements and then making those materials readily accessible on its websites, ITworld.com will rely on original content for over 70% of its website's material. Content such as product reviews and technical research will be created in-house by ITworld.com's staff.

Schlack contends that ITworld.com will also be distinguishable from EarthWeb in the type of audience it targets. While both EarthWeb and ITworld.com are intended to appeal to IT professionals, Schlack argues that the products and services offered by EarthWeb are aimed at programmers and technicians, while ITworld.com will focus on upper level executives, such as technology managers and chief information officers. EarthWeb disputes this assertion, and claims that it offers "a wide range of technology-related content" tailored to,* * *, IT managers and chief information officers.* * *

Given the dynamics of the Internet, such comparisons may be ephemeral. This underscores the difficulty in assessing the characteristics of ITworld.com, an embryonic business entity that will compete in a nascent industry which is evolving and re-inventing itself with breathtaking speed.* * *

* * *

Discussion

* * *

The Non-Compete Provision

* * *

Even if the terms of EarthWeb's restrictive covenant reached Schlack's prospective employment at ITworld.com, EarthWeb would still have to establish that the restraint is reasonable and necessary to protect its legitimate interests. In New York, non-compete covenants will be enforced only if reasonably limited in scope and duration, and only "to the extent necessary (1) to prevent an employee's solicitation or disclosure of trade secrets, (2) to prevent an employee's release of confidential information regarding the employer's customers, or (3) in those cases where the employee's services to the employer are deemed special or unique." [Citations.]

The policy underlying this strict approach rests on notions of employee mobility and free enterprise. "Once the term of an employment agreement has expired, the general public policy favoring robust and uninhibited competition should not give way merely because a particular employer wishes to insulate himself from competition." [Citation.] "Important, too, are the powerful considerations of public policy which militate against sanctioning the loss of a man's livelihood." [Citation.] On the other hand, "the employer is entitled to protection from unfair or illegal conduct that causes economic injury." [Citations.]

Applying these principles here, EarthWeb's restrictive covenant would fail to pass muster even if Schlack's position at ITworld.com fell within the provision's relatively narrow parameters.

1. Duration As a threshold matter, this Court finds that the one-year duration of EarthWeb's restrictive covenant is too long given the dynamic nature of this industry, its lack of geographical borders, and Schlack's former cutting-edge position with EarthWeb where his success depended on keeping abreast of daily changes in content on the Internet. By comparison, the court in *DoubleClick* enjoined the defendants for only a six-month period. The *DoubleClick* court observed that "given the speed with which the Internet advertising industry apparently changes, defendants' knowledge of DoubleClick's operation will likely lose value to such a degree that the purpose of a preliminary injunction will have evaporated before the year is up." [Citation.] Similar considerations predominate here, making a one-year restrictive covenant unreasonably long.* * *

2. Unique and Extraordinary Services Contrary to EarthWeb's contention, Schlack's services are not "unique and extraordinary." Such characteristics have traditionally been associated with "various categories of employment where the services are dependent on an employee's special talents; such categories include musicians, professional athletes, actors and the like." [Citations.] However, in order to justify a enforcement of a restrictive covenant,

> more must* * *be shown to establish such a quality than that the employee excels at his work or that his performance is of high value to his employer. It must also appear that his services are of such character as to make his replacement impossible or that the loss of such services would cause the employer irreparable injury.

[Citations.] EarthWeb has not shown that the nature of Schlack's services are unique or that he cultivated the type of special client relationships that the Second Circuit found worthy of protection in [citation].

* * *

Conclusion

For all these reasons, plaintiff's motion for a preliminary injunction is denied, and the temporary restraining order entered by this Court on September 28, 1999 and thereafter extended on October 12, 1999 is dissolved.

CASE
14-3

Unless prohibited by statute, courts may enforce contracts in which parties agree to waive claims arising from another party's negligence. The following case illustrates how the courts view such exculpatory clauses in general and what tests must be met before a court will enforce an exculpatory clause and deny recovery to an injured party. Not surprisingly, these issues have arisen in the context of recreational parachute jumping.

GROSS v. SWEET
Court of Appeals of New York, 1979
49 N.Y.2d 102

FUCHSBERG, Judge. We hold that, in the circumstances of this case, a release signed by the plaintiff as a precondition for his enrollment in defendant's parachute jumping course does not bar him from suing for personal injuries he allegedly incurred as a result of defendant's negligence.

Plaintiff Bruce Gross, wishing to learn how to parachute, enrolled in the Stormville Parachute Center Training School, a facility owned and operated by the defendant William Sweet for the purpose of offering instruction in the sport. The ensuing events are essentially undisputed. As a prerequisite for admission into the course, Gross had to pay a fee and sign a form entitled "Responsibility Release." He was then given the standard introductory lesson, which consisted of approximately one hour of on-land training, including oral instruction as well as several jumps off a two and a half foot table. Plaintiff then was equipped

with a parachute and flown to an altitude of 2,800 feet for his first practice jump. Upon coming in contact with the ground on his descent, plaintiff suffered serious personal injuries.

The suit is grounded on negligence, breach of warranty and gross negligence. In the main, plaintiff claims that defendant failed to provide adequate training and safe equipment, violated certain rules and procedures promulgated by the Federal Aviation Administration governing the conduct of parachute jumping schools and failed to warn him sufficiently of the attendant dangers.

Defendant pleaded the release plaintiff had signed and moved for summary judgment, contending that the terms of the release exculpated the defendant from any liability. Plaintiff, in turn, cross-moved to strike this affirmative defense contending, primarily, that the terms of the release did not specifically bar a suit for personal injuries negligently caused by the defendant. He also urged that, as a matter of policy, the release should not be enforceable as between a student and his teacher, a relationship in which one of the parties holds himself out as qualified and responsible to provide training in a skill and the other party relies on this expertise, particularly in the context of an activity in which the degree of training necessary for safe participation is much greater than might be apparent to a novice. Alternatively, plaintiff argues that the release in any event does not excuse defendant's violation of the Federal Aviation Administration's regulations governing parachute jumping schools and student parachutists, one of which allegedly required that a medical certificate be furnished as a prerequisite to enrollment in a parachute jumping course. Defendant's failure to request one, plaintiff asserts, bore critically on his situation because, despite his having informed defendant that several years earlier an orthopedic pin had been inserted in his leg, he was accepted as a student though, as the school must have known, landing in a parachute puts special stress on one's legs.

However, Special Term granted defendant's motion, denied plaintiff's cross motion and dismissed the complaint. On plaintiff's appeal from that order, a divided Appellate Division reversed, reinstated the complaint and granted plaintiff's motion to dismiss the affirmative defense. The appeal is now before us on a certified question: "Was the order of this Court, which reinstated the complaint and granted plaintiff's motion to dismiss the affirmative defense of release, correct as a matter of law?" Our answer is that it was.

We begin with the proposition, too well settled to invoke any dispute, that the law frowns upon contracts intended to exculpate a party from the consequences of his own negligence and though, with certain exceptions, they are enforceable, such agreements are subject to close judicial scrutiny…. To the extent that agreements purport to grant exemption for liability for willful or grossly negligent acts they have been viewed as wholly void…. And so, here, so much of plaintiff's complaint as contains allegations that defendant was grossly negligent, may not be barred by the release in any event. But we need not explore further this possibility for we conclude the complaint in its entirety withstands the exculpatory agreement.

Nor need we consider plaintiff's request that we ignore the release on the grounds that the special relationship of the parties and the public interest involved forbids its enforcement. While we have, for example, had occasion to invalidate such provisions when they were contained in the contract between a passenger and a common carrier… or in a contract between a customer and a public utility under a duty to furnish telephone service… or when imposed by an employer as a condition of employment… the circumstances here do not fit within any of these relationships. And, though we note that a recent statute renders void agreements purporting to exempt from liability for negligence those engaged in a variety of businesses that serve the public (e.g., landlords (General Obligations Law, § 5-321);

caterers (§ 5-322); building service or maintenance contractors (§ 5-323); those who maintain garages or parking garages (§ 5-325); or pools, gymnasiums or places of public amusement or recreation (§ 5-326)), defendant's occupation does not fall within any of these classes either. We also decline, at this point, plaintiff's invitation that we proceed further to consider what effect, if any, the alleged contravention of federal regulations may have on the relationship of the parties or the public interest involved. Such questions need not be reached in view of our holding that the wording of the exculpatory agreement does not preclude plaintiff's suit for negligence.

As the cases make clear, the law's reluctance to enforce exculpatory provisions of this nature has resulted in the development of an exacting standard by which courts measure their validity. So, it has been repeatedly emphasized that unless the intention of the parties is expressed in unmistakable language, an exculpatory clause will not be deemed to insulate a party from liability for his own negligent acts…. Put another way, it must appear plainly and precisely that the "limitation of liability extends to negligence or other fault of the party attempting to shed his ordinary responsibility"….

Not only does this stringent standard require that the drafter of such an agreement make its terms unambiguous, but it mandates that the terms be understandable as well. Thus, a provision that would exempt its drafter from any liability occasioned by his fault should not compel resort to a magnifying glass and lexicon…. Of course, this does not imply that only simple or monosyllabic language can be used in such clauses. Rather, what the law demands is that such provisions be clear and coherent….

By and large, if such is the intention of the parties, the fairest course is to provide explicitly that claims based on negligence are included…. That does not mean that the word "negligence" must be employed for courts to give effect to an exculpatory agreement; however, words conveying a similar import must appear….

We are, of course, cognizant of the fact that the general rule of strict judicial construction has been somewhat liberalized in its application to exoneration clauses in indemnification agreements, which are usually "negotiated at arm's length between… sophisticated business entities" and which can be viewed as merely "allocating the risk of liability to third parties between themselves, essentially through the employment of insurance". In such cases, the law, reflecting the economic realities, will recognize an agreement to relieve one party from the consequences of his negligence on the strength of a broadly worded clause framed in less precise language than would normally be required, though even then it must evince the "unmistakable intent of the parties."

The case before us today obviously does not fit within this exception to the strict legal standard generally employed by the courts of this state under which exculpatory provisions drawn in broad and sweeping language have not been given effect. For example, agreements to release from "any and all responsibility or liability of any nature whatsoever for any loss of property or personal injury occurring on this trip"… or to "waive claim for any loss to personal property, or for any personal injury while a member of (a) club"… have not barred claims based on negligence…. Moreover, in Boll v Sharp & Dohme… we held not sufficiently unambiguous a release form in which a blood donor was required to agree that defendants were not "in any way responsible for any consequences… resulting from the giving of such blood or from any of the tests, examinations or procedures incident thereto", and further "release(d) and discharge(d) (defendants) from all claims and demands whatsoever against them or any of them by reason of any matter relative or incident to such donation of blood"…. The donor was thus allowed to sue in negligence for injuries he sustained when, on the completion of the blood donation, he fainted and fell to the floor.

With all this as background, the language of the "Responsibility Release" in the case before us, must be viewed as no more explicit than that in Boll. In its entirety, it reads:

"I, the undersigned, hereby, and by these covenants, do waive any and all claims that I, my heirs, and/or assignees may have against Nathaniel Sweet, the Stormville Parachute Center, the Jumpmaster and the Pilot who shall operate the aircraft when used for the purpose of parachute jumping for any personal injuries or property damage that I may sustain or which may arise out of my learning, practicing or actually jumping from an aircraft. I also assume full responsibility for any damage that I may do or cause while participating in this sport."

Assuming that this language alerted the plaintiff to the dangers inherent in parachute jumping and that he entered into the sport with apprehension of the risks, it does not follow that he was aware of, much less intended to accept, any enhanced exposure to injury occasioned by the carelessness of the very persons on which he depended for his safety. Specifically, the release nowhere expresses any intention to exempt the defendant from liability for injury or property damages which may result from his failure to use due care either in his training methods or in his furnishing safe equipment. Thus, whether on a running reading or a careful analysis, the agreement could most reasonably be taken merely as driving home the fact that the defendant was not to bear any responsibility for injuries that ordinarily and inevitably would occur, without any fault of the defendant, to those who participate in such a physically demanding sport.

In short, instead of specifying to prospective students that they would have to abide any consequences attributable to the instructor's own carelessness, the defendant seems to have preferred the use of opaque terminology rather than suffer the possibility of lower enrollment. But, while, with exceptions not pertinent to this case, the law grudgingly accepts the proposition that men may contract away their liability for negligently caused injuries, they may do so only on the condition that their intention be expressed clearly and in "unequivocal terms."

Accordingly, the certified question is answered in the affirmative, and the order of the Appellate Division reversing the grant of summary judgment, reinstating the complaint and dismissing the defense based on the release should be affirmed.

CASE 14-4

Courts are reluctant to enforce contracts exculpating professionals from acts of negligence. In the following case, a New York court addressed the enforceability of a contract that attempted to release dentists from liability for malpractice.

DEVITO v. N.Y.U. COLLEGE OF DENTISTRY
Supreme Court of New York (N.Y. Co.), 1989
145 Misc. 2d 144, 544 N.Y.S.2d 109

PREMINGER, Judge. Defendants move for summary judgment dismissing this dental malpractice action on the ground that a release executed by plaintiff precludes the action.

Defendant New York University College of Dentistry (NYU) operates a dental clinic where, in exchange for reduced fees, patients agree to be treated by students working under faculty supervision. Plaintiff was treated at the clinic for approximately one year beginning in December 1982 by various students including defendants Wisun and Chiha.

Prior to any treatment plaintiff executed a release which reads, in relevant part: "In consideration of the reduced rates given to me by New York University, I hereby release and agree to save harmless New York University, its doctors, and students, from any and all liability arising out of, or in connection with, any injuries or damages which I may sustain while on its premises, or as a result of any treatment in its infirmaries."

Defendants contend that this release bars plaintiff's claims against them for malpractice. Plaintiff argues that the release was not intended to relieve defendants from responsibility for their negligent acts, and that to give the release such effect would be against public policy.

The very release involved here has been examined by several New York courts with disparate results. * * *

… [t]his court will reexamine the legal principles governing the validity and effect of contracts which attempt to release a doctor or hospital from liability to a patient.

In general, the law frowns upon contracts which seek to exculpate persons from their own negligence, and to the extent such contracts bar suits against willful or gross negligence, they are void. However, where, as here, the claim sought to be foreclosed is one grounded in ordinary negligence, the contract may generally be enforced, but only after being subjected to intense judicial scrutiny on a variety of issues.

The threshold consideration is whether the parties have a special relationship which would make enforcement of an exculpatory clause between them against the public interest. This occurs where the party seeking exculpation is in a business or profession which is either publicly regulated or providing an essential service to members of the public. Examples include common carriers and their passengers; public utilities and their customers; employers who impose the clause as a condition of employment and a host of statutorily created prohibited persons, such as landlords, caterers, and those who maintain parking lots, gymnasiums, and other public places. (See, GOL § 5-321 et seq.)

In these relationships, the consumer's need for the service creates an inequality in bargaining strength which enables the purveyor to insist upon a release, generally on its own prepared form, as a condition to providing the service. As in any adhesion contract a true and voluntary meeting of the minds on the terms of the agreement is unlikely. * * *

The courts of this state have not conclusively determined whether it would be against the public interest to allow physicians to insulate themselves from liability for negligence. However, other jurisdictions have held that the physician-patient relationship precludes the enforcement of such exculpatory agreements.

Thus, in Olson v Molzen the Supreme Court of Tennessee declared that the "general rule [that] a party may contract against his or her own negligence... do[es] not afford a satisfactory solution in a case involving a professional person operating in an area of public interest and pursuing a profession subject to licensure by the state. The rules that govern tradesmen in the marketplace are of little relevancy in dealing with professional persons who hold themselves out as experts and whose practice is regulated by the state." To the same effect are Meiman v Rehabilitation Center (Kentucky), Tunkl v Regents of Univ. of Cal. and Smith v Hospital Auth. (Georgia).

Assuming that the status of the parties withstands scrutiny, it next becomes necessary to examine the actual wording of the agreement. One must determine whether its terms are so clear, explicit and unambiguous that it appears certain that the limitation of liability is intended to cover negligent, as well as ordinary, acts of the party seeking to shed responsibility....

Although the word "negligent" need not actually be used, the Court of Appeals has indicated that such would be the "fairest course." In those instances where releases from liability which do not contain the word "negligence" have been construed to include negligent behavior, the words used have referred to the concept of fault in specific and unambiguous terms.

All-encompassing or open-ended phrases such as "any and all claims" or "any and all responsibility or liability of any nature whatsoever" and "all claims and demands whatsoever" are considered insufficient to indicate an intention to waive injury occasioned by fault.

Even if a clause is found to be clear and unambiguous, it must be examined further to determine whether it would be understandable to a layman, which, while not requiring "only... monosyllabic language," does compel that the language used be "clear and coherent."

The NYU release cannot survive the close scrutiny mandated by the concepts discussed above. It fails, in all particulars, to meet the established standards. Even if the status of the parties is removed from consideration, the contract cannot be construed to include exemption from negligent acts. There is no reference, either explicitly or implicitly, by "words... [of] similar import" to the concept of negligence or fault. No layman perusing this release would find it immediately understandable that the signatory had contracted to accept not only injuries that might ordinarily and inevitably occur, but also any and all consequences of defendants' carelessness.

Although the law grudgingly accepts the proposition that men may contract away their liability for negligently caused injuries it may not do so here. The circumstances of this case and the wording of the release militate against such a result. The parties' status is, at the very least, suspect, the contract is ambiguous, and the language used is far from instantly coherent to a layman.

For all of the foregoing reasons, defendants' motion for summary judgment is denied. Although no cross motion was brought by plaintiff the court searches the record (CPLR 3212 [b]) and awards summary judgment dismissing defendants' affirmative defense based on the release.

The following court discusses the factors a court considers in determining whether a contract is unconscionable and, therefore, unenforceable.

WILLIAMS v. WALKER-THOMAS FURNITURE CO.

Court of Appeals, District of Columbia, 1965
350 F.2d 445

WRIGHT, C.J.

Appellee, Walker-Thomas Furniture Company, operates a retail furniture store in the District of Columbia. During the period from 1957 to 1962 each appellant in these cases purchased a number of household items from Walker-Thomas, for which payment was to be made in installments. The terms of each purchase were contained in a printed form contract which set forth the value of the purchased item and purported to lease the item to appellant for a stipulated monthly rent payment. The contract then provided, in substance, that title would remain in Walker-Thomas until the total of all the monthly payments made equaled the stated value of the item, at which time appellants could take title. In the event of a default in the payment of any monthly installment, Walker-Thomas could repossess the item.

The contract further provided that "the amount of each periodical installment payment to be made by [purchaser] to the Company under this present lease shall be inclusive of and not in addition to the amount of each installment payment to be made by [purchaser] under such prior leases, bills, or accounts; and all payments now and hereafter made by [purchaser] shall be credited pro rata on all outstanding leases, bills, and accounts due the Company by [purchaser] at the time each such payment is made." (Emphasis added.) The effect of this rather obscure provision was to keep a balance due on every item purchased until the balance due on all items, whenever purchased, was liquidated. As a result, the debt incurred at the time of purchase of each item was secured by the right to repossess all the items previously purchased by the same purchaser, and each new item purchased automatically became subject to a security interest arising out of the previous dealings.

On May 12, 1962, appellant Thorne purchased an item described as a Daveno, three tables, and two lamps, having total stated value of $391.10. Shortly thereafter, he defaulted on his monthly payments and appellee sought to replevy all the items purchased since the first transaction in 1958. Similarly, on April 7, 1962, appellant Williams bought a stereo set of stated value of $514.95. She too defaulted shortly thereafter, and appellee sought to replevy all the items purchased since December 1957. The Court of General Sessions granted judgment for appellee. The District of Columbia Court of Appeals affirmed, and we granted appellants' motion for leave to appeal to this court.

Appellants' principal contention, rejected by both the trial and the appellate courts . . . , is that these contracts, or at least some of them, are unconscionable and, hence, not enforceable.

* * *

Unconscionability has generally been recognized to include an absence of meaningful choice on the part of one of the parties together with contract terms which are unreasonably favorable to the other party. Whether a meaningful choice is present in a particular case can only be determined by consideration of all the circumstances surrounding the transaction. In many cases the meaningfulness of the choice is negated by a gross inequality of bargaining power. The manner in which the contract was entered is also relevant to this consideration. Did each party to the contract, considering his obvious education or lack of it, have a reasonable opportunity to understand the terms of the contract, or were the important terms hidden in a maze of fine print and minimized by deceptive sales practices? Ordinarily, one who signs an agreement without full knowledge of its terms might be held to assume the risk that he has entered a one-sided bargain. But when a party of little bargaining power, and hence little real choice, signs a commercially unreasonable contract with little or no knowledge of its terms, it is hardly likely that his consent, or even an objective manifestation of his consent, was ever given to all the terms. In such a case the usual rule that the terms of the agreement are not to be questioned should be abandoned and the court should consider whether the terms of the contract are so unfair that enforcement should be withheld.

In determining reasonableness or fairness, the primary concern must be with the terms of the contract considered in light of the circumstances existing when the contract was made. The test is not simple, nor can it be mechanically applied. The terms are to be considered "in the light of the general commercial background and the commercial needs of the particular trade or case." Corbin suggests the test as being whether the terms are "so extreme as to appear unconscionable according to the mores and business practices of the time and place." [Citation.] We think this formulation correctly states the test to be applied in those cases where no meaningful choice was exercised upon entering the contract.

Because the trial court and the appellate court did not feel that enforcement could be refused, no findings were made on the possible unconscionability of the contracts in these cases.

Since the record is not sufficient for our deciding the issue as a matter of law, the cases must be remanded to the trial court for further proceedings.

Reversed and remanded.

QUESTIONS

1. Identify and explain the types of contracts that may violate a statute, and distinguish between the two types of licensing statutes.
2. Describe when a covenant not to compete will be enforced, and discuss the two situations in which these types of covenants most frequently arise.
3. Explain when exculpatory agreements, agreements involving the

commission of a tort, and agreements inv[...]
will be held to be illegal.
4. Distinguish between procedural and substantive unconscionability.
5. Explain the usual effects of illegality and the major exceptions to this rule.

PROBLEMS

1. Anthony promises to pay McCarthy $10,000 if McCarthy reveals to the public that Washington is a Communist. Washington is not a Communist and never has been. McCarthy successfully persuades the media to report that Washington is a Communist and now seeks to recover the $10,000 from Anthony, who refuses to pay. McCarthy initiates a lawsuit against Anthony. What result?

2. On July 5, 1992, Barbara and Kitty entered into a bet on the outcome of the 1992 presidential election. On January 28, 1993, Barbara, who bet on the winner, approached Kitty, seeking to collect the $3,000 Kitty had wagered. Kitty paid Barbara the wager but now seeks to recover the funds from Barbara. Result?

3. Carl, a salesman for Smith, comes to Benson's home and sells him a complete set of "gourmet cooking utensils" that are worth approximately $300. Benson, an eighty-year-old man living alone in a one-room efficiency apartment, signs a contract to buy the utensils for $1,450, plus a credit charge of $145, and to make payment in ten equal monthly installments Three weeks after Carl leaves with the signed contract,

Benson decides he cannot afford the cooking utensils and has no use for them. What can Benson do? Explain.

4. Consider the same facts as in problem 3 , but assume that the price was $350. Benson, nevertheless, wishes to avoid the contract based on the allegation that Carl befriended and tricked him into the purchase. Decision?

5. Carolyn Murphy, a welfare recipient with four minor children, responded to an advertisement that offered the opportunity to purchase televisions without a deposit or credit history. She entered into a rent-to-own contract for a twenty-five-inch console color television set that required seventy-eight weekly payments of $16 (a total of $1,248. which was two and one-half times the retail value of the set). Under the contract, the renter could terminate the agreement by returning the television and forfeiting any payments already made. After Murphy had paid $436 on the television, she read a newspaper article criticizing the lease plan. She stopped payment and sued the television company. The television company has attempted to take possession of the set. Decision?

6. Tovar applied for the position of resident physician in Paxton Community Memorial Hospital. The hospital examined his background and licensing and assured him that he was qualified for the position. Relying upon the hospital's promise of permanent employment, Tovar resigned from his job and began work at the hospital. He was discharged two weeks later, however, because he did not hold a license to practice medicine in Illinois as required by state law. He had taken the examination but had never passed it. Tovar claims that the hospital promised him a position of permanent employment

and that by discharging him it breached their employment contract. Decision?

7. Albert Bennett, an amateur cyclist, participated in a bicycle race conducted by the United States Cycling Federation. During the race, Bennett was hit by an automobile. He claims that employees of the Federation improperly allowed the car onto the course. The Federation claims that it cannot be held liable to Bennett because Bennett signed a release exculpating the Federation from responsibility for any personal injury resulting from his participation in the race. Decision?

8. Ad and Bookem, an accounting firm operating nationally over a long period of years, with branch offices in all major cities and coverage of all major industrial areas in the United States, acquired the entire practice and goodwill of Sub and Div. another accounting firm operating nationally, with branch offices in all major cities. The price was to be paid in ten annual installments. The agreement contained a provision that provided that the five major partners of Sub and Div, both individually and as members of the accounting firm, were not to engage in practice anywhere in the United States for three years.

(a) Is the provision enforceable? Explain.

(b) Assuming the provision is enforceable, what remedies does Ad and Bookem have against any of the partners who breach the contract provision? Explain.

9. On February 1, Brad purchased the assets of Smalls, a small management-consulting firm based in Manhattan. Under their written agreement, Brad agreed to pay $80,000 a year for five years. The agreement required Smalls to transfer all of his assets and goodwill to Brad. Further, the agreement required Smalls not to compete with Brad for a period of five years within Manhattan, where the majority of Small's clients were located. Other clients of Smalls were located throughout New York state. Three months later, on May 1, Brad learned that Smalls had opened a management consulting firm three blocks from where Smalls' office had been located on February 1. What rights, if any, does Brad have against Smalls?

10. Dr. Livingston was the only oral dental surgeon in the village of Briarcliff Manor, New York, which has a population of 10,000. The nearest oral dental surgeon to Briarcliff Manor was 15 miles away. Dr. Livingston, who intended to retire that year, learned that Dr. Stanley, a recently licensed oral dental surgeon, intended to open her dental office in Briarcliff Manor within the next two months. Dr. Livingston persuaded Dr Stanley to execute a contract with Dr. Livingston. which provided that Dr. Livingston would pay Dr Stanley $25,000 if she would not open her dental office in Briarcliff Manor during the next six months. Seven months later, Dr. Livingston retired and Dr. Stanley

...mediately thereafter opened her dental office in Briarcliff Manor. When Dr. Livingston refused to pay Dr. Stanley $25,000, she sued him for breach of contract. Judgment for whom? Explain.

11. OmniHealth, a national biotechnology firm, executed a three-year written employment contract with Edgar, who was to be in charge of the research and development division responsible for developing new drugs, at an annual salary of $350,000. At that time, OmniHealth was working on several different highly experimental drugs, trying to bring them to market. OmniHealth was anxious to protect its trade secrets and Edgar agreed in his employment contract that he would not work for any of OmniHealth's competitors anywhere in the United States for a period of one year after his employment terminated. At the end of the second year of Edgar's employment, Edgar resigned and promptly went to work for Technology, Inc. Technology, Inc. had known of Edgar's con tract with OmniHealth, but persuaded Edgar to breach that contract and to become an employee of Technology, Inc.

(a) What rights, if any, does OmniHealth have against Edgar? Explain.

(b) What rights, if any, does OmniHealth have against Technology, Inc.? Explain.

12. Johnson and Wilson were the principal shareholders in XYZ Corporation, located in the city of Jonesville, Wisconsin. This corporation was engaged in the business of manufacturing paper novelties, which were sold over a wide area in the Midwest. The corporation was also in the business of binding books. Johnson purchased Wilson's shares of the XYZ Corporation and, in consideration thereof, Wilson agreed that for a period of two years he would not (a) manufacture or sell in Wisconsin any paper novelties of any kind that would compete with those sold by the XYZ Corporation or (b) engage in the book-binding business in the city of Jonesville. Discuss the validity and effect, if any, of this agreement.

13. Charles Leigh, engaged in the industrial laundry business in Central City, employed Tim Close, previously employed in the home laundry business, as a route salesman on July 1, 1984. Leigh rents linens and industrial uniforms to commercial customers; the soiled linens and uniforms are picked up at regular intervals by route drivers and replaced with clean ones. Every employee is assigned a list of customers. The contract of employment stated that in consideration of being employed, upon termination of his employment, Close would not "directly or indirectly engage in the linen supply business or any competitive business within Central City, Illinois, for a period of one year from the date when his employment under this contract ceases." On May 10 of the following year, Leigh terminated Close's employment for valid reasons. Thereafter, Close accepted employment with Ajax Linen Service, a direct competitor of Leigh in Central City. He commenced soliciting former customers whom he had called on for Leigh and obtained some of them as customers for Ajax. Leigh brings an action to enforce the provisions of the contract. Decision?

For problems 14 to 16, assume that the legal rate of interest in New York is 16%.

14. For each of the following transactions, explain whether the transaction is usurious and how much, if any thing, the lender may recover.

(a) Jack lends Bobby $1,000 and Bobby signs a promissory note for $1,160, payable in one year.

(b) Jack lends Bobby $1,000 and Bobby signs a promissory note for $1,160, payable in three months.

(c) Barry agrees to sell Lisa his valuable oil painting for $50,000 and to buy it back from her in three months for $75,000.

15. Devin had been down on his luck for years. Unable to pay his bills, Devin approached his best friend Craig for a loan. On January 1, 2000, Craig and Devin agreed in a signed writing that Craig would lend Devin $10,000. The terms of the loan agreement called for Devin to repay the loan, along with $3,250 in interest, on January 1, 2002.

On December 31, 2001, Devin called Craig and advised that he would not repay the above loan.

(a) In an action by Craig against Devin for money damages, judgment for whom?

(b) In an action by Craig against Devin for equitable relief, judgment for whom?

16. Caleb and Dexter entered into a loan agreement on February 1, 2001. The agreement called for Caleb to lend Dexter $5,000, and in return Dexter was to pay off the loan in monthly installments of $900 for a period of six (6) months. In addition, the agreement also called for Dexter to pay Caleb a monthly $3.00 service fee on the loan. In fact, this fee did not relate to any services performed by Caleb either in connection with the loan, or in connection with the processing of Dexter's loan repayment checks.

After making the first two monthly installment payments, Dexter made no further payments to Caleb.

In an action by Caleb against Dexter, judgment for whom?

17. Johnson and Wilson were the principal shareholders in XYZ Corporation, located in the city of Jonesville, Wisconsin. This corporation was engaged in the business of manufacturing paper novelties, which were sold over a wide area in the Midwest. The corporation was also in the business of binding books. Johnson purchased Wilson's shares of the XYZ Corporation and, in consideration thereof, Wilson agreed that for a period of two years he would not (a) manufacture or sell in Wisconsin any paper novelties of any kind that would compete with those sold by the XYZ Corporation or (b) engage in the book-binding business in the city of Jonesville. Discuss the validity and effect, if any, of this agreement.

10. Adrian rents a bicycle from Barbara. The bicycle rental contract Adrian signed provides that Barbara is not liable for any injury to the renter caused by any defect in the bicycle or the negligence of Barbara. Injured when she is involved in an accident due to Barbara's improper maintenance of the bicycle, Adrian sues Barbara for her damages. Will Barbara be protected from liability by the provision in their contract?

18. In 1964 Michelle Marvin and actor Lee Marvin began living together, holding themselves out to the general public as man and wife without actually being married. The two orally agreed that while they lived together they would share equally any and all property and earnings accumulated as a result of their individual and combined efforts. In addition, Michelle promised to render her services as "companion, homemaker, housekeeper and cook" to Lee. Shortly thereafter, she gave up her lucrative career as an entertainer in order to devote her full time to being Lee's companion, homemaker, housekeeper, and cook. In return he agreed to provide for all of her financial support and needs for the rest of her life. In 1970, Lee compelled Michelle to leave his household but continued to provide for her support. In late 1971, however, he refused to provide further support. Michelle sued to recover support payments and half of their accumulated property. Lee contends that their agreement is so closely related to the supposed "immoral" character of their relationship that its enforcement would violate public policy. The trial court granted Lee's motion for judgment on the pleadings. Decision?

19. Richard Brobston was hired by Insulation Corporation of America (ICA) in 1982. Initially, he was hired as a territory sales manager but was promoted to national account manager in 1986 and to general manager in 1990. In 1992, ICA was planning to acquire computer-assisted design (CAD) technology to upgrade its product line. Prior to acquiring this technology, ICA required that Brobston and certain other employees sign employment contracts that contained restrictive covenants or be terminated. These restrictive covenants provided that in the event of Brobston's termination for any reason, Brobston would not reveal any of ICA's trade secrets or sales information and would not enter into direct competition with ICA within three hundred miles of Allentown, Pennsylvania, for a period of two years from the date of termination. The purported consideration for Brobston's agreement was a $2,000 increase in his base salary and proprietary information concerning the CAD system, customers, and pricing.

Brobston signed the proffered employment contract. In October 1992, Brobston became vice president of special products, which included responsibility for sales of the CAD system products as well as other products. Over the course of the next year, Brobston failed in several respects to properly perform his employment duties and on August 13, 1993, ICA terminated Brobston's employment. In December 1993, Brobston was hired by a competitor of ICA who was aware of ICA's restrictive covenants. Can ICA enforce the employment agreement by enjoining Brobston from disclosing proprietary information about ICA and by restraining him from competing with ICA? If so, for what duration and over what geographic area?

 Internet Exercise Find and review information on lotteries, including which states have them and how the proceeds are used.

Employment Law

Though in general the common law governs the relationship between employer and employee in terms of tort and contract duties (rules that are part of the law of agency), this common law has been supplemented—and in some instances replaced—by statutory enactments, principally at the federal level. In fact, government regulation now affects the balance and working relationship between employers and employees in three areas. First, the general framework in which management and labor negotiate the terms of employment is regulated by federal statutes designed to promote both labor–management harmony and the welfare of society at large. Second, federal law prohibits employment discrimination based upon race, sex, religion, age, disability, or national origin. Finally, Congress, in response to the changing nature of American industry and the tremendous number of industrial accidents, has mandated that employers provide their employees with a safe and healthy work environment. Moreover, all of the states have adopted workers' compensation acts to provide compensation to employees injured during the course of employment.

This chapter will focus upon two categories of government regulation of the employment relationship: (1) employment discrimination law, and (2) employee protection.

EMPLOYMENT DISCRIMINATION LAW

A number of federal statutes prohibit discrimination in employment on the basis of race, sex, religion, national origin, age, and disability. The cornerstone of federal employment discrimination law is Title VII of the 1964 Civil Rights Act, but other statutes and regulations also are significant, including two recently enacted discrimination laws: the Civil Rights Act of 1991 and the Americans with Disabilities Act of 1990. In addition, most states have enacted similar laws prohibiting discrimination based on race, sex, religion, national origin, and disability. The Civil Rights Act of 1991 extended the coverage of both Title VII and the Americans with Disabilities Act to include United States citizens working for U.S.-owned or controlled companies in foreign countries.

Equal Pay Act

The **Equal Pay Act** prohibits an employer from discriminating between employees on the basis of sex by paying unequal wages for the same work. The Act forbids an employer from paying wages at a rate less than the rate at which he pays wages to employees of the opposite sex for equal work at the same establishment. Most courts define *equal work* to mean "substantially equal" rather than identical. The burden of proof is on the claimant to make a *prima facie* showing that the employer pays unequal wages for work requiring equal skill, effort, and responsibility under similar working conditions. Once the employee has demonstrated that the employer pays members of the opposite sex unequal wages for equal work, the burden shifts to the employer to prove that the pay differential is based on:

1. a seniority system,
2. a merit system,
3. a system that measures earnings by quantity or quality of production, or
4. any factor except sex.

Remedies include the recovery of back pay, an award of liquidated damages (an additional amount equal to back pay), and enjoining the employer from further unlawful conduct. Although the Department of Labor is the federal agency designated by the statute to interpret and enforce the Act, these functions were transferred to the Equal Employment Opportunity Commission in 1979.

Civil Rights Act of 1964

Title VII of the **Civil Rights Act of 1964** prohibits **employment discrimination** on the basis of race, color, sex, religion, or national origin in hiring, firing, compensating, promoting, training, and other employment-related processes. The definition of *religion* includes all aspects of religious observance and practice, and the statute provides that an employer must make reasonable efforts to accommodate an employee's religious belief. The Act applies to employers engaged in an industry affecting commerce and having fifteen or more employees. The Act also covers federal, state and local governments, as well as labor organizations with fifteen or more members.

http: **Civil Rights Act of 1964:** http://assembler.law.cornell.edu/ uscode/html/uscode42/usc_sec_42_00002000---a000- notes.html

When Congress passed the **Pregnancy Discrimination Act of 1978**, it extended the benefits of Title VII to pregnant women. Under the Act, an employer cannot refuse to hire a pregnant woman, fire her, or force her to take maternity leave unless the employer can establish a *bona fide* occupational qualification defense (discussed later in this chapter). The Act, which protects the job reinstatement rights of women returning from maternity leave, requires employers to treat pregnancy like any other temporary disability.

The enforcement agency for Title VII is the Equal **Employment Opportunity Commission (EEOC)**. The EEOC is empowered (1) to file legal actions in its own name or to intervene in actions filed by third parties; (2) to attempt to resolve alleged violations through informal means prior to bringing suit; (3) to investigate all charges of discrimination; and (4) to issue guidelines and regulations concerning enforcement policy.

http: **Equal Employment Opportunity Commission:** http:// www.eeoc.gov/

❖ SEE CASE 15-1

SEE FIGURE 15-1   **Charges Filed in 2003 with the EEOC**

Proving Discrimination Each of the following constitutes discriminatory conduct prohibited by the Act:

1. **Disparate Treatment.** An individual shows that an employer used a prohibited criterion in making an employment decision by treating some people less favorably than others. Liability is based on proving that the employer's decision was motivated by the protected characteristic or trait. *Raytheon Co. v. Hernandez*, 537 U.S. 1187 (2003). The Supreme Court held in *McDonnell Douglas Corp. v. Green*, 411 U.S. 792 (1973), that a *prima facie* case of discrimination would be shown if the plaintiff (a) is within a protected class, (b) applied for an open position, (c) was qualified for the position, (d) was denied the job, and (e) the employer continued to try to fill the position from a pool of applicants with the complainant's qualifications or gave it to someone with similar qualifications from

◆ FIGURE 15-1   Charges Filed in 2003 with the EEOC

Category	Number of Charges
Race	28,526
Sex	24,362
National Origin	8,450
Religion	2,532
Retaliation	22,690
Age	19,124
Disability	15,377
Equal Pay	1,167

Source: The U.S. Equal Employment Opportunity Commission, March 8, 2004, http://www.eeoc.gov/stats/charges.html

a different class. Once the plaintiff establishes a *prima facie* case, the burden of proof shifts to the defendant to "articulate legitimate and nondiscriminatory reasons for the plaintiff's rejection." If the defendant so rebuts, the plaintiff then has the opportunity to demonstrate that the employer's stated reason was merely a pretext.

If the employer's decision was based on a "mixed motive" (the employer used both lawful and unlawful reasons in making its decision) the courts employ a shifting burden of proof standard. First, the plaintiff must prove by a preponderance of the evidence that the employer used the protected characteristic as a motivating factor. The defendant, however, can limit the remedies available to the plaintiff by proving by a preponderance of the evidence that the defendant would have made the same decision even without the forbidden motivating factor. If the defendant sustains its burden of proof, under the Civil Rights Act of 1991 the remedies are limited to declaratory relief, certain types of injunctive relief, and attorney's fees and costs.

2. **Present Effects of Past Discrimination.** An employer engages in conduct that on its face is "neutral," that is, nondiscriminatory, but that actually perpetuates past discriminatory practices. For example, it has been held illegal for a union that had previously limited its membership to whites to adopt a requirement that new members be related to or recommended by existing members. *Local 53 of International Association of Heat and Frost Insulators and Asbestos Workers v. Vogler*, 407 F.2d 1047 (5th Cir. 1969).

3. **Disparate Impact.** An employer adopts "neutral" rules that adversely affect a protected class and that are not justified as being necessary to the business. *Raytheon Co. v. Hernandez*, 537 U.S. 1187 (2003). Despite the employee's proof of disparate impact, the employer may prevail if it can demonstrate that the challenged practice is "job related for the position in question and consistent with business necessity." *Wards Cove Packing Co. v. Antonio*, 490 U.S. 642, 109 S.Ct. 2115 (1989). Thus, all requirements that might have a disparate impact upon women, such as height and weight requirements, must be shown to be job related. Nevertheless, under the **Civil Rights Act of 1991**, even if the employer can demonstrate the business necessity of the questioned practice, the complainant will still prevail if she shows that a nondiscriminatory alternative practice exists.

❧ SEE CASE 15-1

Defenses The Act provides several basic defenses: (1) a *bona fide* seniority or merit system; (2) a professionally developed ability test; (3) a compensation system based on performance results, and (4) a *bona fide* occupational qualification (BFOQ). The BFOQ defense does not apply to discrimination based on race. A fifth defense, business necessity, is available in a dispa-

rate impact case. In addition, a defendant can reduce damages in a "mixed motive" case by showing that it would have discharged the plaintiff for legal reasons.

❧ SEE CASE 15-2

Remedies Remedies for violation of the Act include enjoining the employer from engaging in the unlawful behavior, appropriate affirmative action, and reinstatement of employees to their rightful place (which may include promotion) and award of back pay from a date not more than two years prior to the filing of the charge with the EEOC. First employed by Executive Order, as discussed below, **affirmative action** generally means the active recruitment of minority applicants, although courts also have used the remedy to impose numerical hiring ratios (quotas) and hiring goals based on race and sex. In 1985, the EEOC defined affirmative action in employment as "actions appropriate to overcome the effects of past or present practices, policies, or other barriers to equal employment opportunity."

Prior to 1991, only victims of *racial* discrimination could recover compensatory and punitive damages from the courts. Today, however, under the Civil Rights Act of 1991, *all* victims of *intentional* discrimination—whether based on race, sex, religion, national origin, or disability—can recover compensatory and punitive damages, except in cases involving disparate impact. In cases not involving race, the Act limits the amount of recoverable damages according to the number of persons the defendant employs. Companies with 15 to 100 employees are required to pay no more than $50,000; companies with 101 to 200 employees, no more than $100,000; those with 201 to 500 employees, no more than $200,000; and those with 501 or more employees, no more than $300,000. Either party may demand a jury trial. Victims of racial discrimination are still entitled to recover unlimited compensatory and punitive damages.

Reverse Discrimination A major controversy has arisen over the use of reverse discrimination in achieving affirmative action. In this context, **reverse discrimination** refers to affirmative action that directs an employer to remedy the underrepresentation of a given race or sex in a traditionally segregated job by considering an individual's race or gender when hiring or promoting. An example would be an employer who discriminates against white males to increase the proportion of females or members of a racial minority in a company's workforce. This question was presented in *United Steelworkers of America v. Weber*, 443 U.S. 193 (1979). In *Weber*, the employer and union were implementing a collectively bargained affirmative action plan that granted preference to blacks even though the employer had engaged in no proven racial discrimination. There was, however, a conspicuous racial imbalance in the employer's skilled labor force. The Supreme Court upheld the affirmative action plan against a challenge under Title VII, even though the plan favored black employees with less seniority than white employees. The Court held,

> We need not today define in detail the line of demarcation between permissible and impermissible affirmative action plans [under Title VII]. It suffices to hold that the challenged Kaiser-USWA affirmative action plan falls on the permissible side of the line. The purposes of the plan mirror those of the statute. Both were designed to break down old patterns of racial segregation and hierarchy. Both were structured to "open employment opportunities for Negroes in occupations which have been traditionally closed to them." [Citation.]
>
> At the same time, the plan does not unnecessarily trammel the interests of the white employees. The plan does not require the discharge of white workers and their replacement with new black hires. [Citation.] Nor does the plan create an absolute bar to the advancement of white employees; half of those trained in the program will be white. Moreover, the plan is a temporary measure; it is not intended to maintain racial balance, but simply to eliminate a manifest racial imbalance.

Due to the absence of state action, challenges to affirmative action plans adopted by private employers—those that are not governmental units at the local, state, or federal level—are tested under Title VII of the Civil Rights Act of 1964, not under the Equal Protection Clause of the U.S. Constitution.

In *Johnson v. Transportation Agency*, 480 U.S. 616 (1987), also an action under Title VII, the Supreme Court upheld the employer's right to promote a female employee rather than a white male employee who had scored higher on a qualifying examination:

> In making our decision, we find that the employment decision was justified by the existence of a "manifest imbalance" that reflected underrepresentation of women in "traditionally segregated job categories." The Agency's [employer's] Plan did not authorize such blind hiring but expressly directed that numerous factors be taken into account in making employment decisions. Furthermore, the Plan did not trammel male employees' rights or create a bar to their advancement as it set aside no positions for women. Substantial evidence shows that the Agency has sought to take a moderate, gradual approach to eliminating the imbalance in its work force, one which establishes realistic guidance for employment decisions. Given this fact, as well as the Agency's express commitment to "attain" a balanced work force, there is ample assurance that the Agency does not seek to use its Plan to "maintain" a permanent racial and sexual balance. Thus, we do not find the Agency in violation of Title VII.

When a state or local government adopts an affirmative action plan that is challenged as constituting illegal reverse discrimination, the plan is subject to strict scrutiny under the **Equal Protection Clause** of the Fourteenth Amendment. Under the strict scrutiny test, the subject classification must (1) be justified by a compelling governmental interest and (2) be the least intrusive means available. With regard to racial discrimination, the U.S. Supreme Court, in 1995, placed significant constraints upon the ability of governments to create programs favoring minorities over whites: benign and invidious discrimination are both held to the standard under which the government must show a compelling interest that is as narrowly tailored as feasible. Following this decision, the EEOC issued a statement which provided that "affirmative action is lawful only when it is designed to respond to a demonstrated and serious imbalance in the work force, is flexible, time-limited, applies only to qualified workers, and respects the rights of non-minorities and men."

Sexual Harassment In 1980, the EEOC issued a definition of sexual harassment:

> Unwelcome sexual advances, requests for sexual favors, and other verbal or physical conduct of a sexual nature constitute sexual harassment when
> (1) submission to such conduct is made either explicitly or implicitly a term or condition of an individual's employment,
> (2) submission to or rejection of such conduct by an individual is used as the basis for employment decisions affecting such individual, or
> (3) such conduct has the purpose or effect of reasonably interfering with an individual's work performance or creating an intimidating, hostile or offensive working environment.

The courts, including the Supreme Court, have held that sexual harassment may constitute illegal sexual discrimination in violation of Title VII. Moreover, an employer will be held liable for sexual harassment committed by one of its employees if it does not take reasonable action when it knows or should have known of the harassment. When the employee engaging in sexual harassment is an agent of the employer or holds a supervisory position over the victim, the employer may be liable without knowledge or reason to know.

In 1998, the U.S. Supreme Court held that sex discrimination consisting of same-sex harassment is actionable under Title VII.

◆ SEE CASE 15-3

Comparable Worth Industrial statistics indicate that women earn approximately two-thirds as much as men do. Studies have suggested that between one-third and one-half of this disparity in earnings results from sexual discrimination. Other probable causes for the gap include (1) the differing educational backgrounds and job skills of males and females, (2) the tendency for females to be employed in lower-paying occupations, and (3) the idea that females are more likely to interrupt their careers to raise families.

Because the Equal Pay Act requires equal pay for equal work only, it does not apply to different jobs even if they are comparable. Thus, that statute provides no remedy for women who have been systematically undervalued and underpaid in "traditional" occupations, such as secretary, teacher, or nurse. As a result, women have sought redress under Title VII by arguing that the failure to pay comparable worth is discrimination on the basis of sex. The concept of **comparable worth** provides that employers should measure the relative values of different jobs through a job evaluation rating system that is free of any potential sex bias. Theoretically, the consistent application of objective criteria (including factors such as skill, effort, working conditions, responsibility, and mental demands) across job categories will ensure fair payment for all employees. For example, if under such a system the jobs of truck driver and nurse were evaluated at the same level, then workers in both jobs would receive the same pay.

In 1981, the Supreme Court held that a claim of discriminatory undercompensation based on sex may be brought under Title VII, even where the plaintiffs (women, in the 1981 case) were performing jobs different from those of their opposite-sex counterparts. As the Court noted, however, the case involved a situation in which the defendant intentionally discriminated in wages; and the defendant, not the courts, had compared the jobs in terms of value. *County of Washington v. Gunther,* 452 U.S. 161 (1981). The Court also held that the four defenses available under the Equal Pay Act would apply to a Title VII claim. Since *Gunther,* the concept of comparable worth has met with limited success in the courts. Nonetheless, a number of states have adopted legislation requiring public and private employers to pay equally for comparable work.

Executive Order

In 1965, President Johnson issued an executive order that prohibits discrimination by federal contractors on the basis of race, color, sex, religion, or national origin in employment on any work the contractor performs during the period of the federal contract. Federal contractors are also required to implement affirmative action in recruiting. The Secretary of Labor, **Office of Federal Contract Compliance Programs (OFCCP)**, enforces compliance with the program.

The program applies to all contractors (and all of their subcontractors in excess of $10,000) who enter into a federal contract to be performed in the United States. Compliance with the affirmative action requirement differs for construction and nonconstruction contractors. All **nonconstruction** contractors with fifty or more employees or with contracts for more than $50,000 must have a written affirmative action plan to be in compliance. The plan must include a workforce analysis; planned corrective action, if necessary, with specific goals and timetables; and procedures for auditing and reporting. The Director of the OFCCP periodically issues goals and timetables for each segment of the construction industry for each region of the country. As a condition precedent to bidding on a federal contract, a contractor must agree to make a good faith effort to achieve current published goals.

Age Discrimination in Employment Act of 1967

The **Age Discrimination in Employment Act (ADEA)** prohibits discrimination in hiring, firing, compensating, or other employment-related processes on the basis of age when the employee or applicant is over forty years old. The Act applies to private employers having twenty or more employees and to all governmental units regardless of size. The Act also prohibits the mandatory retirement of most employees, no matter what their age, though it provides employers a limited exception regarding *bona fide* executives and high policymaking employees. In 2004 the United States Supreme Court held that the ADEA does not prevent an employer from favoring an older employee over a younger employee.

The major statutory defenses include (1) a *bona fide* occupational qualification; (2) a *bona fide* seniority system; and (3) any other reasonable action, including the voluntary retirement of an individual. Remedies include back pay, injunctive relief, affirmative action, and liquidated damages equal to the amount of the award for "willful" violations. Furthermore, an ADEA claimant is entitled to a jury trial.

http: **Age Discrimination in Employment Act of 1967:** http://www4.law.cornell.edu/uscode/29/621.html

Disability Law

The **Rehabilitation Act of 1973** attempts to assist the handicapped in obtaining rehabilitation training, access to public facilities, and employment. The Act requires federal contractors and federal agencies to take affirmative action to hire qualified handicapped persons. It also prohibits discrimination on the basis of handicap in federal programs and programs receiving federal financial assistance.

A **handicapped person** is defined as an individual who (1) has a physical or mental impairment that substantially affects one or more of her major life activities; (2) has a history of major life activity impairment; *or* (3) is regarded as having such an impairment. Major life activities include such functions as caring for oneself, seeing, speaking, or walking. Alcohol and drug abuses are not considered handicapping conditions for the purposes of this statute.

http: **Rehabilitation Act of 1967:** http://www4.law.cornell.edu/uscode/29/701.html

The **Americans with Disabilities Act (ADA) of 1990** forbids an employer from discriminating against any person with a disability with regard to "hiring or discharge..., employee compensation, advancement, job training and other terms, conditions and privileges of employment." In addition, businesses must make special accommodations, such as installing wheelchair-accessible bathrooms, for handicapped workers and customers unless the cost is unduly burdensome. An employer may use qualification standards, tests, or selection criteria that screen out handicapped workers if these measures are job related and consistent with business necessity *and* if no reasonable accommodation is possible. The ADA took effect on July 26, 1992, for employers with twenty-five or more employees and on July 26, 1994, for employers with fifteen or more employees. Remedies for violation of the ADA are those generally allowed under Title VII and include injunctive relief, reinstatement, back pay, and, for intentional discrimination, compensatory and punitive damages (capped according to company size by the Civil Rights Act of 1991).

http: **Americans with Disabilities Act:** http://www.usdoj.gov/crt/ada/statute.html

In addition, the **Vietnam Veterans Readjustment Act of 1974** requires firms having $10,000 or more in federal contracts to take affirmative action regarding handicapped veterans and Vietnam era veterans.

◆ SEE FIGURE 15-3   **Federal Employment Discrimination Laws**

◈ SEE CASE 15-4

EMPLOYEE PROTECTION

Employees are accorded a number of job-related protections. These include a limited right not to be unfairly dismissed, a right to a safe and healthy workplace, compensation for injuries sustained in the workplace, and some financial security upon retirement or loss of employment. This section discusses (1) employee termination at will, (2) occupational safety and health, (3) employee privacy, (4) workers' compensation, (5) Social Security and unemployment insurance, (6) the Fair Labor Standards Act, (7) employee notice of termination or layoff, and (8) family and health leave.

Employee Termination at Will

Under the common law, a contract of employment is terminable at will by either party unless the employment is for other than a definite term or the employee is represented by a labor union. Accordingly, under the common law, employers may "dismiss their employees at will for good cause, for no cause or even for cause morally wrong, without being thereby guilty of legal wrong." In recent years, however, the courts have delineated a growing number of judicial exceptions to the rule, based on implied contract, tort, and public policy. A number of federal and state statutes enacted in the last sixty years further limit the rule, which also may be restricted by contractual agreement between employer and employee. In particular, most collective bargaining agreements negotiated through union representatives contain a provision prohibiting dismissal "without cause."

Statutory Limitations In 1934, as previously discussed, Congress enacted the National Labor Relations Act, which provided employees with the right to unionize free of intimidation or coercion from their employers, including freedom from dismissal for engaging in union activities. Since the enactment of the NLRA, additional federal legislation, such as ADEA, ADA, ERISA, and Fair Labor Standards Act has limited the employer's right to discharge. These statutes fall into three categories: (1) those protecting certain employees from discriminatory discharge; (2) those protecting certain employees in their exercise of statutory rights; and (3) those protecting certain employees from discharge without cause.

At the state level, statutes protect workers from discriminatory discharge for filing workers' compensation claims. Also, many state statutes parallel federal legislation. Some states have adopted statutes similar to the NLRA, and many states prohibit discrimination in employment on the basis of factors such as race, creed, nationality, sex, or age. In addition, some states have statutes prohibiting employers from discharging employees or taking other punitive actions in order to influence voting or, in some states, political activity.

Judicial Limitations Judicial limitations on the employment-at-will doctrine have been based on contract law, tort law, and public policy. Cases founded in contract theory have relied on arguments contending, among other things, (1) that the dismissal was improper because the employee had detrimentally relied on the employer's promise of work for a reasonable time; (2) that the employment was not at will because of implied-in-fact promises of employment for a specific duration, which meant that the employer could not terminate the employee without just cause; (3) that the employment contract implied or provided expressly that the employee would not be dismissed so long as he satisfactorily performed his work; (4) that the employer had assured the employee that he would not be dismissed except for cause; or (5) that, upon entering into the employment contract, the employee gave consideration over and above the performance of services to support a promise of job security.

Some courts have circumvented the common law at-will doctrine under implied contract theories by finding that employment contracts contain an implied promise to deal in good faith, including a duty on the part of the employer to terminate only in good faith. These cases provide a remedy for an employee whose discharge was motivated by bad faith, malice, or retaliation.

Courts have also created exceptions to the employment-at-will doctrine by imposing tort obligations on employers, particularly the torts of intentional infliction of emotional distress and of interference with employment relations.

A majority of states now consider a discharge as wrongful if it violates a statutory or other established public policy. In general, this public policy exception renders a discharge wrongful if it involves a dismissal for (1) refusing to violate a statute, (2)

◆ Figure 43-3   Federal Employment Discrimination Laws

	Protected Characteristics	Prohibited Conduct	Defenses	Remedies
Equal Pay Act	Sex	Wages	Seniority Merit Quality or quantity measures Any factor other than sex	Back pay Injunction Liquidated damages Attorneys' fees
Title VII of Civil Rights Act	Race Color Sex Religion National origin	Terms, conditions, or privileges of employment	Seniority Ability test BFOQ (except for race) Business necessity (disparate impact only)	Back pay Injunction Reinstatement Compensatory and punitive damages for intentional discrimination • unlimited for race • limited for all others Attorneys' fees
Age Discrimination in Employment Act	Age	Terms, conditions, or privileges of employment	Seniority BFOQ Any other reasonable act	Back Pay Injunction Reinstatement Liquidated damages for willful violation Attorneys' fees
Americans with Disabilities Act	Disability	Terms, conditions, or privileges of employment	Undue hardship Job-related criteria and business necessity Risk to public health and safety	Back pay Injunction Reinstatement Compensatory and punitive damages for intentional discrimination (limited) Attorneys' fees

exercising a statutory right, (3) performing a statutory obligation, or (4) reporting an alleged violation of a statute that is of public interest ("whistle-blowing").

New York Law Unlike courts in a number of states, New York's highest court has refused to create judicial limitations on the employment-at-will doctrine under either tort theories or implied contract theories. (See Case 16-5.) Thus in New York, an employee at will is only protected from discharge if the reason for her termination violates a statute or constitutional provision.

In addition to antidiscrimination statutes, New York has statutes that protect employees against retaliation for activities such as serving on jury duty, pursuing Workers Compensation claims and engaging in legal activities off the job. However, New York's "whistleblower" statute for private employees, Labor Law § 740, provides very limited protection for an employee who is terminated for disclosing, objecting to or refusing to engage in an activity, practice or policy of the employer that the employee believes to be illegal. Under that statute, the employee is only protected if the challenged activity presented *a substantial and specific danger to the public health and safety* and also constitutes an *actual violation* of a law, rule or regulation. Whistleblower protection for public employees is broader. Civil Service Law 75-b. New York Labor Law 201(d). New York Labor Law 741.

◊ See Case 15-5

Employee Privacy

Over the last decade, employee privacy has become a major issue. The fundamental right to privacy is a product of common law protection, discussed in Chapter 16. Thus, employee protection from unwanted searches, electronic monitoring and other forms of surveillance, and disclosure of confidential records is safeguarded by the tort of invasion of privacy, which actually consists of four different torts: (1) unreasonable intrusion into the seclusion of another; (2) unreasonable public disclosure of private facts; (3) unreasonable publicity that places another in a false light; and (4) appropriation of a person's name or likeness. In addition, the federal government and some states have legislatively supplemented the common law in certain areas.

Drug and Alcohol Testing Although no federal legislation deals comprehensively with drug and alcohol tests, legislation in a number of states either prohibits such tests altogether or prescribes certain scientific and procedural standards for conducting them. In the absence of a state statute, *private* sector employees have little or no protection from such tests. The NLRB has held, however, that drug and alcohol testing in a union setting is a mandatory subject of collective bargaining.

In 1989, the U.S. Supreme Court ruled that the employer of a *public* sector employee whose position involved public health or safety or national security could subject the employee to a drug or alcohol test without either first obtaining a search warrant or having reasonable grounds to believe the individual had engaged in any wrongdoing. Based on Supreme Court and lower court decisions, it appears that a government employer may use (1) random or universal testing where the public health or safety or national security is involved and (2) selective drug testing where there is sufficient cause to believe an employee has a drug problem.

Lie Detector Tests The **Federal Employee Polygraph Protection Act of 1988** prohibits private employers from requiring employees or prospective employees to undergo a lie detector test, inquiring about the results of such a test, or using the results of such a test or the refusal to be thus tested as grounds for an adverse employment decision. The Act exempts government employers and, in certain situations, Energy Department contractors or persons providing consulting services for federal intelligence agencies. In addition, security firms and manufacturers of controlled substances may use a polygraph to test prospective employees. Moreover, an employer, as part of an ongoing investigation of economic loss or injury to its business, may utilize a polygraph test. Nevertheless, the use of the test must meet the following requirements: (1) it must be designed to investigate a specific incident or activity, not to document a chronic problem; (2) the employee to be tested must have had access to the property that is the subject of the investigation; and (3) the employer must have reason to suspect the particular employee.

Employees and prospective employees tested under any of these exemptions cannot be terminated, disciplined, or denied employment solely as a result of the test. The Act further provides that those subjected to a polygraph test (1) cannot be asked intrusive or degrading questions regarding topics such as their religious beliefs, opinions as to racial matters, political views, or sexual preferences or behaviors; (2) must be given the right to review all questions before the test and to terminate the test at any time; and (3) must receive a complete copy of the test results.

Workers' Compensation

At common law, the basis of most actions by an injured employee against his employer was the employer's failure to use reasonable care under the circumstances to ensure the employee's safety. In such an action, however, the employer could make use of several well-established defenses, including the fellow servant rule, contributory negligence on the part of the employee, and the doctrine of assumption of risk by the employee. By establishing any of these defenses, the employer was not liable to the injured employee.

The **fellow servant rule** relieved an employer from liability for injuries an employee sustained through the negligence of a fellow employee. Under the common law defense of **contributory negligence**, if an employer established that an employee's negligence contributed to the injury he sustained in the course of his employment, in many jurisdictions the employee could not recover damages from the employer. Additionally, at common law, an employer was not liable to an employee for harm or injury caused by the unsafe condition of the premises if the employee, with knowledge of the facts and an understanding of the risks involved, voluntarily entered into or continued in the employment. This was regarded as a **voluntary assumption of risk** by the employee.

To provide speedier and more certain relief to injured employees, all states have adopted statutes providing for workers' compensation. (Several states, however, exempt specified employers from such statutes.) Workers' compensation statutes create commissions or boards that determine whether an injured employee is entitled to receive compensation and, if so, how much. The basis of recovery under workers' compensation is strict liability: the employee does not have to prove that the employer was negligent. The common law defenses discussed previously are not available to employers in proceedings under these statutes. Such defenses are abolished. The only requirement is that the employee be injured and that the injury arises out of and in the course of his employment. The amounts recoverable are fixed by statute for each type of injury and are lower than the amounts a court or jury would probably award in an action at common law. The courts, therefore, do not have jurisdiction over such cases, except to review decisions of the board or commission; even then, the courts may determine only whether such decisions are in accordance with the statute. If a third party causes the injury, however, the employee may bring a tort action against that third party.

Early workers' compensation laws did not provide coverage for occupational disease, and most courts held that occupational injury did not include disease. Today, virtually all states provide general compensation coverage for occupational diseases, although the coverage varies greatly from state to state.

> **http:** **U.S. Department of Labor: Employment Standards Administration Office of Workers' Compensation Programs:** http://www.dol.gov/esa/owcp_org.htm

Social Security and Unemployment Insurance

Social Security was enacted in 1935 in an attempt to provide limited retirement and death benefits to certain employees. Since then, the benefits have increased greatly; the federal Social Security system, which has expanded to cover almost all employees, now contains four major benefit programs: (1) Old-Age and Survivors Insurance (OASI) (providing retirement and survivor benefits), (2) Disability Insurance (DI), (3) Hospitalization Insurance (Medicare), and (4) Supplemental Security Income (SSI).

The system is financed by contributions (taxes) paid by employers, employees, and self-employed individuals. Employees and employers pay matching contributions. These contributions are calculated by multiplying the Social Security tax (a fixed percentage) times the employee's wages up to a specified maximum. Both the base tax rate and the maximum dollar amount are subject to change by Congress. It is the employer's responsibility to withhold the employee's contribution and to forward the full amount of the tax to the Internal Revenue Service. Contributions made by the employee are not tax deductible by the employee, while those made by the employer are tax deductible.

> **http:** **Social Security Administration:** http://www.ssa.gov/

The federal **unemployment insurance** system was initially created by Title IX of the Social Security Act of 1935. Subsequently, Title IX was supplemented by the federal Unemployment Tax Act and by numerous other federal statutes. This complex system depends upon cooperation between state and federal entities. Federal law provides the general guidelines, standards, and requirements for the program, while the states administer the program through their employment laws. The system is funded by employer taxes: federal taxes generally pay the administrative costs of the program, and state contributions pay for the actual benefits.

Under the federal Unemployment Tax Act, unemployment compensation is provided to workers who have lost their jobs, usually through no fault of their own. The Act is meant to help workers who are temporarily out of work and who need to support themselves while they search for jobs. Unemployed workers usually receive weekly payments in an amount based on each state's particular formula. Employees who voluntarily quit without good cause, who have been dismissed for misconduct, or who fail to look for or who refuse suitable work are not eligible for unemployment benefits.

Fair Labor Standards Act

The **Fair Labor Standards Act (FLSA)** regulates the employment of child labor outside of agriculture. The Act prohibits the employment of anyone under fourteen years of age in all nonfarm work except newspaper delivery and acting. Fourteen- and fifteen-year-olds may work for a limited number of hours outside of school hours, under specific conditions, in certain nonhazardous occupations. Sixteen- and seventeen-year-olds may work in any nonhazardous job, while persons eighteen years old or older may work in any job, whether it is hazardous or not. The Secretary of Labor determines which occupations are considered hazardous.

In addition, the FLSA imposes wage and hour requirements upon covered employers. With certain exceptions, the Act provides for a minimum hourly wage and overtime pay of time-and-a-half for hours worked in excess of forty hours per week; those workers exempted from both the FLSA's minimum wage and overtime provisions include professionals, managers, and outside salespersons.

> **http:** **Fair Labor Standards Act:** http://www4.law.cornell.edu/ uscode/29/201.html

Worker Adjustment and Retraining Notification Act

The **Worker Adjustment and Retraining Notification Act (WARN)** requires an employer to provide sixty days' advance notice of a plant closing or mass layoff. A "plant closing" is defined as the permanent or temporary shutting down of a single site or units within a site if the shutdown results in fifty or more employees losing employment during any thirty-day period. A "mass layoff" is defined as a loss of employment during a thirty-day period either for 500 employees or for at least one-third of the employees at a given site, if that one-third equals or exceeds fifty employees. WARN requires that notification be given to specified state and local officials as well as to the affected employees or their union representatives. The Act, which reduces the notification period with regard to failing companies and emergency situations, applies to employers with a total of 100 or more employees who in the aggregate work at least 2,000 hours per week, not including overtime.

> **http:** **Worker Adjustment and Retraining Notification Act:** http://www4.law.cornell.edu/uscode/29/2101.html

Family and Medical Leave Act of 1993

The **Family and Medical Leave Act of 1993** requires employers with fifty or more employees and governments at the federal, state, and local levels to grant employees up to twelve weeks of leave during any twelve-month period for the birth of a child; adopting or gaining foster care of a child; or the care of a spouse, child, or parent who suffers from a serious health condition. A "serious health condition" is defined as an "illness, injury, impairment or physical or mental condition" that involves inpatient medical care at a hospital, hospice, or residential care facility or continuing medical treatment by a health care provider. Employees are eligible for such leave if they have been employed by their present employer for at least twelve months and have worked at least 1,250 hours for their employer during the twelve months preceding the leave request. The requested leave may be paid, unpaid, or a combination of both.

http:	**Family and Medical Leave Act of 1993:**
	http://www4.law.cornell.edu/uscode/29/2601.html

CHAPTER SUMMARY

Labor Law

Purpose to provide the general framework in which management and labor negotiate terms of employment

Norris–La Guardia Act established as United States policy the full freedom of labor to form labor unions without employer interference and withdrew from the federal courts the power to issue injunctions in nonviolent labor disputes (any controversy concerning terms or conditions of employment or union representation)

National Labor Relations Act
- *Right to Unionize* declares it a federally protected right of employees to unionize and to bargain collectively
- *Prohibits Unfair Employer Practices* the Act identifies five unfair labor practices by an employer
- *National Labor Relations Board (NLRB)* created to administer these rights

Labor-Management Relations Act
- *Prohibits Unfair Union Practices* the Act identifies seven unfair labor practices by a union
- *Prohibits Closed Shops* which are agreements that mandate that employers can hire only union members
- *Allows Union Shops* an employer can hire nonunion members, but the employee must join the union

Labor-Management Reporting and Disclosure Act aimed at eliminating corruption in labor unions

---

Employment Discrimination Law

Equal Pay Act prohibits an employer from discriminating between employees on the basis of gender by paying unequal wages for the same work

Civil Rights Act of 1964 prohibits employment discrimination on the basis of race, color, gender, religion, or national origin
- *Pregnancy Discrimination Act of 1978* extends the benefits of the Civil Rights Act to pregnant women
- *Equal Employment Opportunity Commission (EEOC)* enforcement agency for the Act
- *Affirmative Action* the active recruitment of a designated group of applicants
- *Discrimination* prohibited by the Act; includes (1) using proscribed criteria to produce disparate treatment, (2) engaging in nondiscriminatory conduct that perpetuates past discrimination, and (3) adopting neutral roles that have a disparate impact
- *Reverse Discrimination* affirmative action that directs an employer to consider an individual's race or gender when hiring or promoting for the purpose of remedying underrepresentation of that race or gender in traditionally segregated jobs

- *Defenses* four defenses are provided by the Act (1) a *bona fide* seniority or merit system, (2) a professionally developed ability test, (3) a compensation system based on performance results, and (4) a *bona fide* occupational qualification
- *Remedies* remedies for violation of the Act include injunctions, affirmative action, reinstatement, back pay, and compensatory and punitive damages
- *Sexual Harassment* an illegal form of sexual discrimination that includes unwelcome sexual advances, requests for sexual favors, and other verbal or physical conduct of a sexual nature
- *Comparable Worth* equal pay for jobs that are of equal value to the employer

Executive Order prohibits discrimination by federal contractors on the basis of race, color, gender, religion, or national origin on any work the contractors perform during the period of the federal contract

Age Discrimination in Employment Act of 1967 prohibits discrimination on the basis of age in hiring, firing, or compensating

Disability Law several federal acts, including the Americans with Disabilities Act, provide assistance to the disabled in obtaining rehabilitation training, access to public facilities, and employment

---

Employee Protection

Employee Termination at Will under the common law, a contract of employment for other than a definite term is terminable at will by either party
- *Statutory Limitations* have been enacted by the federal government and some states
- *Judicial Limitations* based on contract law, tort law, or public policy
- *Limitations Imposed by Union Contract*

Occupational Safety and Health Act enacted to assure workers of a safe and healthful work environment

Employee Privacy
- *Drug and Alcohol Testing* some states either prohibit such tests or prescribe certain scientific and procedural safeguards
- *Lie Detector Tests* federal statute prohibits private employers from requiring employees or prospective employees to take such tests

Workers' Compensation compensation awarded to an employee who is injured in the course of his employment

Social Security measures by which the government provides economic assistance to disabled or retired employees and their dependents

Unemployment Compensation compensation awarded to workers who have lost their jobs and cannot find other employment

Fair Labor Standards Act regulates the employment of child labor outside of agriculture

Worker Adjustment and Retraining Notification Act federal statute that requires an employer to provide sixty days' advance notice of a plant closing or mass layoff

Family and Medical Leave Act of 1993 requires some employers to grant employees leave for serious health conditions or certain other events

Blackmun, J.

CASES

Johnson Controls excluded females who are capable of bearing children from certain jobs in its plant because of concern for the health of the fetuses the women might conceive. In the following case, the court considers whether such a policy constitutes impermissible discrimination on the basis of gender and whether gender is a bona fide occupational qualification in those circumstances.

INTERNATIONAL UNION, UNITED AUTOMOBILE, AEROSPACE AND AGRICULTURAL IMPLEMENT WORKERS OF AMERICA, UAW v. JOHNSON CONTROLS, INC.

Supreme Court of the United States, 1991
499 U.S. 187, 111 S.Ct. 1196, 113 L.Ed.2d 158
http://supct.law.cornell.edu/supct/html/89-1215.ZS.html

In this case we are concerned with an employer's gender-based fetal-protection policy. May an employer exclude a fertile female employee from certain jobs because of its concern for the health of the fetus the woman might conceive?

Respondent Johnson Controls, Inc., manufactures batteries. In the manufacturing process, the element lead is a primary ingredient. Occupational exposure to lead entails health risks, including the risk of harm to any fetus carried by a female employee.

Before the Civil Rights Act of 1964, [citation], became law, Johnson Controls did not employ any woman in a battery-manufacturing job. In June 1977, however, it announced its first official policy concerning its employment of women in lead-exposure work:

[P]rotection of the health of the unborn child is the immediate and direct responsibility of the prospective parents. While the medical profession and the company can support them in the exercise of this responsibility, it cannot assume it for them without simultaneously infringing their rights as persons.

* * *

* * *Since not all women who can become mothers wish to become mothers (or will become mothers), it would appear to be illegal discrimination to treat all who are capable of pregnancy as though they will become pregnant.

Consistent with that view, Johnson Controls "stopped short of excluding women capable of bearing children from lead exposure," but emphasized that a woman who expected to have a child should not choose a job in which she would have such exposure. The company also required a woman who wished to be considered for employment to sign a statement that she had been advised of the risk of having a child while she was exposed to lead. The statement informed the woman that although there was evidence "that women exposed to lead have a higher rate of abortion," this evidence was "not as clear * * *as the relationship between cigarette smoking and cancer," but that it was, "medically speaking, just good sense not to run that risk if you want children and do not want to expose the unborn child to risk, however small * * *."

Five years later, in 1982, Johnson Controls shifted from a policy of warning to a policy of exclusion. Between 1979 and 1983, eight employees became pregnant while maintaining blood lead levels in excess of 30 micrograms per deciliter. This appeared to be the critical level noted by the Occupational Health and Safety Administration (OSHA) for a worker who was planning to have a family. The company responded by announcing a broad exclusion of women from jobs that exposed them to lead:

* * *[I]t is [Johnson Controls'] policy that women who are pregnant or who are capable of bearing children will not be placed into jobs involving lead exposure or which could expose them to lead through the exercise of job bidding, bumping, transfer or promotion rights.

* * *

In April 1984, petitioners filed in the United States District Court for the Eastern District of Wisconsin a class action challenging Johnson Controls' fetal-protection policy as sex discrimination that violated Title VII of the Civil Rights Act of 1964. Among the individual plaintiffs were petitioners Mary Craig, who had chosen to be sterilized in order to avoid losing her job, Elsie Nason, a 50-year-old divorcee, who had suffered a loss in compensation when she was transferred out of a job where she was exposed to lead, and Donald Penney, who had been denied a request for a leave of absence for the purpose of lowering his lead level because he intended to become a father. * * *

The District Court granted summary judgment for defendant-respondent Johnson Controls. Applying a three-part business necessity defense * * *Court concluded that while "there is a disagreement among the experts regarding the effect of lead on the fetus," the hazard to the fetus through exposure to lead was established by "a considerable body of opinion"; * * *and that petitioners had "failed to establish that there is an acceptable alternative policy which would protect the fetus." The court stated that, in view of this disposition of the business necessity defense, it did not "have to undertake a bona fide occupational qualification's (BFOQ) analysis."

The Court of Appeals for the Seventh Circuit, sitting en banc, affirmed the summary judgment by a 7-to-4 vote. The majority held that the proper standard for evaluating the fetal-protection policy was the defense of business necessity; that Johnson Controls was entitled to summary judgment under that defense; and that even if the proper standard was a BFOQ, Johnson Controls still was entitled to summary judgment.

* * *

The bias in Johnson Controls' policy is obvious. Fertile men, but not fertile women, are given a choice as to whether they wish to risk their reproductive health for a particular job. [T]he Civil Rights Act of 1964, [citation], prohibits sex-based classifications in terms and conditions of employment, in hiring and discharging decisions, and in other employment decisions that adversely affect an employee's status. Respondent's fetal-protection policy explicitly discriminates against women on the basis of their sex. The policy excludes women with childbearing capacity from lead-exposed jobs and so creates a facial classification based on gender.

* * *

We concluded above that Johnson Controls' policy is not neutral because it does not apply to the reproductive capacity of the company's male employees in the same way as it applies to that of the females. Moreover, the absence of a malevolent motive does not convert a facially discriminatory policy into a neutral policy with a discriminatory effect. Whether an employment practice involves disparate treatment through explicit facial discrimination does not depend on why the employer discriminates but rather on the explicit terms of the discrimination. * * *

In sum, Johnson Controls' policy "does not pass the simple test of whether the evidence shows 'treatment of a person in a manner which but for that person's sex would be different.'" [Citation.] We hold that Johnson Controls' fetal-protection policy is sex discrimination forbidden under Title VII unless respondent can establish that sex is a "bona fide occupational qualification."

Under Title VII, an employer may discriminate on the basis of "religion, sex, or national origin in those certain instances where religion, sex, or national origin is a bona fide occupational qualification reasonably necessary to the normal operation of that particular business or enterprise." * * *

The BFOQ defense is written narrowly, and this Court has read it narrowly. [Citations.]

* * *

The wording of the BFOQ defense contains several terms of restriction that indicate that the exception reaches only special situations. The statute thus limits the situations in which discrimination is permissible to "certain instances" where sex discrimination is "reasonably necessary" to the "normal operation" of the "particular" business. Each one of these terms—certain, normal, particular—prevents the use of general subjective standards and favors an objective, verifiable requirement. But the most telling term is "occupational;" this indicates that these objective, verifiable requirements must concern job-related skills and aptitudes.

* * *

Our case law, therefore, makes clear that the safety exception is limited to instances in which sex or pregnancy actually interferes with the employee's ability to perform the job. This approach is consistent with the language of the BFOQ provision itself, for it suggests that permissible distinctions based on sex must relate to ability to perform the duties of the job. Johnson Controls suggests, however, that we expand the exception to allow fetal-protection policies that mandate particular standards for pregnant or fertile women. We decline to do so. Such an expansion contradicts not only the language of the BFOQ and the narrowness of its exception but the plain language and history of the Pregnancy Discrimination Act.

The PDA's amendment to Title VII contains a BFOQ standard of its own: unless pregnant employees differ from others "in their ability or inability to work," they must be "treated the same" as other employees "for all employment-related purposes."

* * *

We conclude that the language of both the BFOQ provision and the PDA which amended it, as well as the legislative history and the case law, prohibit an employer from discriminating against a woman because of her capacity to become pregnant unless her reproductive potential prevents her from performing the duties of her job. * * *

We have no difficulty concluding that Johnson Controls cannot establish a BFOQ. Fertile women, as far as appears in the record, participate in the manufacture of batteries as efficiently as anyone else. Johnson Controls' professed moral and ethical concerns about the welfare of the next generation do not suffice to establish a BFOQ of female sterility. Decisions about the welfare of future children must be left to the parents who conceive, bear, support, and raise them rather than to the employers who hire those parents. Congress has mandated this choice through Title VII, as amended by the Pregnancy Discrimination Act.

* * *

Johnson Controls argues that it must exclude all fertile women because it is impossible to tell which women will become pregnant while working with lead. This argument is somewhat academic in light of our conclusion that the company may not exclude fertile women at all; it perhaps is worth noting, however, that Johnson Controls has shown no "factual basis for believing that all or substantially all women would be unable to perform safely and efficiently the duties of the job involved." [Citation.] Even on this sparse record, it is apparent that Johnson Controls is concerned about only a small minority of women. Of the eight pregnancies reported among the female employees, it has not been shown that any of the babies have birth defects or other abnormalities. The record does not reveal the birth rate for Johnson Controls' female workers but national statistics show that approximately nine percent of all fertile women become pregnant each year. The birthrate drops to two percent for blue collar workers over age 30. [Citation.] Johnson Controls' fear of prenatal injury, no matter how sincere, does not begin to show that substantially all of its fertile women employees are incapable of doing their jobs.

A word about tort liability and the increased cost of fertile women in the workplace is perhaps necessary. One of the dissenting judges in this case expressed concern about an employer's tort liability and concluded that liability for a potential injury to a fetus is a social cost that Title VII does not require a company to ignore. It is correct to say that Title VII does not prevent the employer from having a conscience. The statute, however, does prevent sex-specific fetal-protection policies. These two aspects of Title VII do not conflict.

* * *

If state tort law furthers discrimination in the workplace and prevents employers from hiring women who are capable of manufacturing the product as efficiently as men, then it will impede the accomplishment of Congress' goals in enacting Title VII. Because Johnson Controls has not argued that it faces any costs from tort liability, not to mention crippling ones, the preemption question is not before us. We therefore say no more than that the concurrence's speculation [about potential tort liability] appears unfounded as well as premature.

The tort-liability argument reduces to two equally unper-

suasive propositions. First, Johnson Controls attempts to solve the problem of reproductive health hazards by resorting to an exclusionary policy. Title VII plainly forbids illegal sex discrimination as a method of diverting attention from an employer's obligation to police the workplace. Second, the spectre of an award of damages reflects a fear that hiring fertile women will cost more. The extra cost of employing members of one sex, however, does not provide an affirmative Title VII defense for a discriminatory refusal to hire members of that gender. [Citation.] Indeed, in passing the PDA, Congress considered at length the considerable cost of providing equal treatment of pregnancy and related conditions, but made the "decision to forbid special treatment of pregnancy despite the social costs associated therewith." [Citations.]

We, of course, are not presented with, nor do we decide, a case in which costs would be so prohibitive as to threaten the survival of the employer's business. We merely reiterate our prior holdings that the incremental cost of hiring women cannot justify discriminating against them.

* * *

The judgment of the Court of Appeals is reversed and the case is remanded for further proceedings consistent with this opinion.

Thomas, J.

CASE

15-2

This opinion from the Supreme Court of the United States interprets the requirements for bringing a claim of unlawful employment discrimination under Title VII as amended in 1991.

DESERT PALACE, INC. v. COSTA
Supreme Court of the United States, 2003
539 U.S. 90, 123 S.Ct. 2148, 156 L.Ed.2d 84
http://www.supremecourtus.gov/opinions/02pdf/02-679.pdf

The question before us in this case is whether a plaintiff must present direct evidence of discrimination in order to obtain a mixed-motive instruction under Title VII of the Civil Rights Act of 1964, as amended by the Civil Rights Act of 1991 (1991 Act). We hold that direct evidence is not required.

I

A

Since 1964, Title VII has made it an "unlawful employment practice for an employer * * *to discriminate against any individual * * *, *because* of such individual's race, color, religion, sex, or national origin." [Citation.] In *Price Waterhouse v. Hopkins*, [citation], the Court considered whether an employment decision is made "because of" sex in a "mixed-motive" case, i.e., where both legitimate and illegitimate reasons motivated the

decision. The Court concluded that, under [Title VII], an employer could "avoid a finding of liability * * *by proving that it would have made the same decision even if it had not allowed gender to play such a role." [Citation.] The Court was divided, however, over the predicate question of when the burden of proof may be shifted to an employer to prove the affirmative defense.

Justice Brennan, writing for a plurality of four Justices, would have held that "when a plaintiff * * *proves that her gender played a motivating part in an employment decision, the defendant may avoid a finding of liability only by proving by a preponderance of the evidence that it would have made the same decision even if it had not taken the plaintiff's gender into account." [Citation.] * * *

* * *

Two years after *Price Waterhouse*, Congress passed the 1991 Act "in large part [as] a response to a series of decisions of this Court interpreting the Civil Rights Acts of 1866 and 1964." [Citation.] In particular, §107 of the 1991 Act, which is at issue in this case, "respond[ed]" to Price Waterhouse by "setting forth standards applicable in 'mixed motive' cases" in two new statutory provisions. [Citation.] The first establishes an alternative for proving that an "unlawful employment practice" has occurred:

> Except as otherwise provided in this subchapter, an unlawful employment practice is established when the complaining party demonstrates that race, color, religion, sex, or national origin was a motivating factor for any employment practice, even though other factors also motivated the practice. [Citation.]

The second provides that, with respect to "a claim in which an individual proves a violation under [Title VII]," the employer has a limited affirmative defense that does not absolve it of liability, but restricts the remedies available to a plaintiff. The available remedies include only declaratory relief, certain types of injunctive relief, and attorney's fees and costs. [Citation.] In order to avail itself of the affirmative defense, the employer must "demonstrat[e] that [it] would have taken the same action in the absence of the impermissible motivating factor." [Citation.]

Since the passage of the 1991 Act, the Courts of Appeals have divided over whether a plaintiff must prove by direct evidence that an impermissible consideration was a "motivating factor" in an adverse employment action. * * * , a number of courts have held that direct evidence is required to establish liability * * * . [Citations.] In the decision below, however, the Ninth Circuit concluded otherwise. [Citation.]

B

Petitioner Desert Palace, Inc., dba Caesar's Palace Hotel & Casino of Las Vegas, Nevada, employed respondent Catharina Costa as a warehouse worker and heavy equipment operator. Respondent was the only woman in this job and in her local Teamsters bargaining unit.

Respondent experienced a number of problems with management and her co-workers that led to an escalating series of disciplinary sanctions, including informal rebukes, a denial of privileges, and suspension. Petitioner finally terminated respondent after she was involved in a physical altercation in a warehouse elevator with fellow Teamsters member Herbert Gerber. Petitioner disciplined both employees because the facts surrounding the incident were in dispute, but Gerber, who had a clean disciplinary record, received only a 5-day suspension.

Respondent subsequently filed this lawsuit against petitioner in the United States District Court for the District of Nevada, asserting claims of sex discrimination and sexual harassment under Title VII. The District Court dismissed the sexual harassment claim, but allowed the claim for sex discrimination to go to the jury. At trial, respondent presented evidence that (1) she was singled out for "intense 'stalking" by one of her supervisors, (2) she received harsher discipline than men for the same conduct, (3) she was treated less favorably than men in the assignment of overtime, and (4) supervisors repeatedly "stack[ed]" her disciplinary record and "frequently used or tolerated" sex-based slurs against her. [Citation.]

Based on this evidence, the District Court denied petitioner's motion for judgment as a matter of law, and submitted the case to the jury with instructions, two of which are relevant here. First, without objection from petitioner, the District Court instructed the jury that "[t]he plaintiff has the burden of proving * * *by a preponderance of the evidence" that she "suffered adverse work conditions" and that her sex "was a motivating factor in any such work conditions imposed upon her." [Citation.]

Second, the District Court gave the jury the following mixed-motive instruction:

> You have heard evidence that the defendant's treatment of the plaintiff was motivated by the plaintiff's sex and also by other lawful reasons. If you find that the plaintiff's sex was a motivating factor in the defendant's treatment of the plaintiff, the plaintiff is entitled to your verdict, even if you find that the defendant's conduct was also motivated by a lawful reason.
>
> However, if you find that the defendant's treatment of the plaintiff was motivated by both gender and lawful reasons, you must decide whether the plaintiff is entitled to damages. The plaintiff is entitled to damages unless the defendant proves by a preponderance of the evidence that the defendant would have treated plaintiff similarly even if the plaintiff's gender had played no role in the employment decision.

Petitioner unsuccessfully objected to this instruction, claiming that respondent had failed to adduce "direct evidence" that sex was a motivating factor in her dismissal or in any of the other adverse employment actions taken against her. The jury rendered a verdict for respondent, awarding backpay, compensatory damages, and punitive damages. The District Court denied petitioner's renewed motion for judgment as a matter of law.

The Court of Appeals initially vacated and remanded, holding that the District Court had erred in giving the mixed-motive instruction because respondent had failed to present "substantial evidence of conduct or statements by the employer directly reflecting discriminatory animus." [Citation.] In addition, the panel concluded that petitioner was entitled to judgment as a matter of law on the termination claim because the evidence was insufficient to prove that respondent was "terminated because she was a woman." [Citation.]

The Court of Appeals reinstated the District Court's judgment after rehearing the case en banc. [Citation.] The en banc court * * *concluded that * * *references to "direct evidence" had been "wholly abrogated" by the 1991 Act. [Citation.] * * *Accordingly, the court concluded that a "plaintiff * * *may establish a violation through a preponderance of evidence (whether direct or circumstantial) that a protected characteristic played "a motivating factor." [Citation.] Based on that standard, the Court of Appeals held that respondent's evidence was sufficient to warrant a mixed-motive instruction and that a reasonable jury could have found that respondent's sex was a "motivating factor in her treatment." [Citation.] * * *

We granted certiorari. [Citation.]

II

This case provides us with the first opportunity to consider the effects of the 1991 Act on jury instructions in mixed-motive cases. Specifically, we must decide whether a plaintiff must present direct evidence of discrimination in order to obtain a mixed-motive instruction under [Title VII]. * * *

Our precedents make clear that the starting point for our analysis is the statutory text. [Citation.] And where, as here, the words of the statute are unambiguous, the "judicial inquiry is complete." [Citation.] [Title VII] unambiguously states that a plaintiff need only "demonstrat[e]" that an employer used a forbidden consideration with respect to "any employment practice." On its face, the statute does not mention, much less require, that a plaintiff make a heightened showing through direct evidence. * * *

Moreover, Congress explicitly defined the term "demonstrates" in the 1991 Act, leaving little doubt that no special evidentiary showing is required. Title VII defines the term "demonstrates" as to "mee[t] the burdens of production and persuasion." [Citation.] If Congress intended the term "demonstrates" to require that the "burdens of production and persuasion" be met by direct evidence or some other heightened showing, it could have made that intent clear by including language to that effect * * *. Its failure to do so is significant, for Congress has been unequivocal when imposing heightened proof requirements in other circumstances, * * *. [Citation.]

In addition, Title VII's silence with respect to the type of evidence required in mixed-motive cases also suggests that we should not depart from the "[c]onventional rul[e] of civil litigation [that] generally appl[ies] in Title VII cases." [Citation.] * * *We have often acknowledged the utility of circumstantial evidence in discrimination cases. * * *

* * *

For the reasons stated above, we agree with the Court of Appeals that no heightened showing is required * * *.

* * *

In order to obtain an instruction under [Title VII], a plaintiff need only present sufficient evidence for a reasonable jury to conclude, by a preponderance of the evidence, that "race, color, religion, sex, or national origin was a motivating factor for any employment practice." Because direct evidence of discrimination is not required in mixed-motive cases, the Court of Appeals correctly concluded that the District Court did not abuse its discretion in giving a mixed-motive instruction to the jury. Accordingly, the judgment of the Court of Appeals is affirmed.

CASE

15-3

Sexual harassment that is so severe and pervasive that it creates an abusive working environment is a violation of Title VII. In the following case, the United States Supreme Court establishes the circumstances under which an employer may be held liable for the acts of a supervisory employee which create a hostile work environment for subordinate employees.

FARAGHER v. CITY OF BOCA RATON

Supreme Court of the United States, 1998
524 U.S. 775, 118 S.Ct. 2275, 141 L.Ed.2d 662
http://supct.law.cornell.edu/supct/html/97-282.ZS.html

Souter, J.

This case calls for identification of the circumstances under which an employer may be held liable under Title VII of the Civil Rights Act of 1964, [citation], for the acts of a supervisory employee whose sexual harassment of subordinates has created a hostile work environment amounting to employment discrimination. We hold that an employer is vicariously liable for actionable discrimination caused by a supervisor, but subject to an affirmative defense looking to the reasonableness of the employer's conduct as well as that of a plaintiff victim.

I

Between 1985 and 1990, while attending college, petitioner

Beth Ann Faragher worked part time and during the summers as an ocean lifeguard for the Marine Safety Section of the Parks and Recreation Department of respondent, the City of Boca Raton, Florida (City). During this period, Faragher's immediate supervisors were Bill Terry, David Silverman, and Robert Gordon. In June 1990, Faragher resigned.

* * *

In February 1986, the City adopted a sexual harassment policy, which it stated in a memorandum from the City Manager addressed to all employees. [Citation.] In May 1990, the City revised the policy and reissued a statement of it. Although the

City may actually have circulated the memos and statements to some employees, it completely failed to disseminate its policy among employees of the Marine Safety Section, with the result that Terry, Silverman, Gordon, and many lifeguards were unaware of it. [Citation.]

From time to time over the course of Faragher's tenure at the Marine Safety Section, between 4 and 6 of the 40 to 50 lifeguards were women. During that 5-year period, Terry repeatedly touched the bodies of female employees without invitation, [citation], would put his arm around Faragher, with his hand on her buttocks, [citation], and once made contact with another female lifeguard in a motion of sexual simulation, [citation]. He made crudely demeaning references to women generally, and once commented disparagingly on Faragher's shape, [citation]. During a job interview with a woman he hired as a lifeguard, Terry said that the female lifeguards had sex with their male counterparts and asked whether she would do the same. [Citation.]

Silverman behaved in similar ways. He once tackled Faragher and remarked that, but for a physical characteristic he found unattractive, he would readily have had sexual relations with her. [Citation.] Another time, he pantomimed an act of oral sex. [Citation.] Within ear-shot of the female lifeguards, Silverman made frequent, vulgar references to women and sexual matters, commented on the bodies of female lifeguards and beachgoers, and at least twice told female lifeguards that he would like to engage in sex with them. [Citation.]

Faragher did not complain to higher management about Terry or Silverman. Although she spoke of their behavior to Gordon, she did not regard these discussions as formal complaints to a supervisor but as conversations with a person she held in high esteem. [Citation.] Other female lifeguards had similarly informal talks with Gordon, but because Gordon did not feel that it was his place to do so, he did not report these complaints to Terry, his own supervisor, or to any other city official. [Citation.] Gordon responded to the complaints of one lifeguard by saying that "the City just [doesn't] care." [Citation.]

In April 1990, however, two months before Faragher's resignation, Nancy Ewanchew, a former lifeguard, wrote to Richard Bender, the City's Personnel Director, complaining that Terry and Silverman had harassed her and other female lifeguards. Following investigation of this complaint, the City found that Terry and Silverman had behaved improperly, reprimanded them, and required them to choose between a suspension without pay or the forfeiture of annual leave. [Citation.]

On the basis of these findings, the District Court concluded that the conduct of Terry and Silverman was discriminatory harassment sufficiently serious to alter the conditions of Faragher's employment and constitute an abusive working environment. [Citation.] The District Court then ruled that there were three justifications for holding the City liable for the harassment of its supervisory employees. First, the court noted

that the harassment was pervasive enough to support an inference that the City had "knowledge, or constructive knowledge" of it. [Citation.] Next, it ruled that the City was liable under traditional agency principles because Terry and Silverman were acting as its agents when they committed the harassing acts. [Citation.] Finally, the court observed that Gordon's knowledge of the harassment, combined with his inaction, "provides a further basis for imputing liability on [sic] the City." [Citation.] The District Court then awarded Faragher one dollar in nominal damages on her Title VII claim. [Citation.]

A panel of the Court of Appeals for the Eleventh Circuit reversed the judgment against the City. [Citation.] Although the panel had "no trouble concluding that Terry's and Silverman's conduct * * *was severe and pervasive enough to create an objectively abusive work environment," [citation], it overturned the District Court's conclusion that the City was liable. The panel ruled that Terry and Silverman were not acting within the scope of their employment when they engaged in the harassment, that they were not aided in their actions by the agency relationship, [citation], and that the City had no constructive knowledge of the harassment by virtue of its pervasiveness or Gordon's actual knowledge, [citation].

In a 7-to-5 decision, the full Court of Appeals, sitting en banc, adopted the panel's conclusion. [Citation.]

* * *

II

A

Thus, in *Meritor* we held that sexual harassment so "severe or pervasive" as to "alter the conditions of [the victim's] employment and create an abusive working environment" violates Title VII. [Citation.]

In thus holding that environmental claims are covered by the statute, we drew upon earlier cases recognizing liability for discriminatory harassment based on race and national origin, [citations], just as we have also followed the lead of such cases in attempting to define the severity of the offensive conditions necessary to constitute actionable sex discrimination under the statute. [Citations.]

So, in *Harris*, we explained that in order to be actionable under the statute, a sexually objectionable environment must be both objectively and subjectively offensive, one that a reasonable person would find hostile or abusive, and one that the victim in fact did perceive to be so. [Citation.] We directed courts to determine whether an environment is sufficiently hostile or abusive by "looking at all the circumstances," including the "frequency of the discriminatory conduct; its severity; whether it is physically threatening or humiliating, or a mere offensive utterance; and whether it unreasonably interferes with an employee's work performance." [Citation.] Most recently, we explained that Title VII does not prohibit "genuine but innocuous differences in the ways men and women routinely interact with members of the same sex and of the opposite sex." *Oncale*, [citation]. A recurring "point in these opinions is that 'simple teasing,' [citation]," offhand comments, and isolated incidents (unless extremely serious) will not amount to discriminatory changes in the "terms and conditions of employment."

These standards for judging hostility are sufficiently demanding to ensure that Title VII does not become a "general civility code." [Citation.] Properly applied, they will filter out complaints attacking "the ordinary tribulations of the workplace, such as the sporadic use of abusive language, gender-related jokes, and occasional teasing." [Citations.]

While indicating the substantive contours of the hostile environments forbidden by Title VII, our cases have established few definite rules for determining when an employer will be liable for a discriminatory environment that is otherwise actionably abusive. * * *There have, for example, been myriad cases in which District Courts and Courts of Appeals have held employers liable on account of actual knowledge by the employer, or high-echelon officials of an employer organization, of sufficiently harassing action by subordinates, which the employer or its informed officers have done nothing to stop. * * *

Nor was it exceptional that standards for binding the employer were not in issue in *Harris*. In that case of discrimination by hostile environment, the individual charged with creating the abusive atmosphere was the president of the corporate employer, [citation], who was indisputably within that class of an employer organization's officials who may be treated as the organization's proxy. [Citations.]

Finally, there is nothing remarkable in the fact that claims against employers for discriminatory employment actions with tangible results, like hiring, firing, promotion, compensation, and work assignment, have resulted in employer liability once the discrimination was shown. [Citations.]

* * *

The soundness of the results in these cases (and their continuing vitality), in light of basic agency principles, was confirmed by this Court's only discussion to date of standards of employer liability, in *Meritor,* which involved a claim of discrimination by a supervisor's sexual harassment of a subordinate over an extended period. In affirming the Court of Appeals's holding that a hostile atmosphere resulting from sex discrimination is actionable under Title VII, we also anticipated proceedings on remand by holding agency principles relevant in assigning employer liability and by rejecting three *per se* rules of liability or immunity. * * *

We then proceeded to reject two limitations on employer liability, while establishing the rule that some limitation was intended. We held that neither the existence of a company grievance procedure nor the absence of actual notice of the harassment on the part of upper management would be dispositive of such a claim; while either might be relevant to the liability, neither would result automatically in employer immunity.

* * *

B

The Court of Appeals identified, and rejected, three possible grounds drawn from agency law for holding the City vicariously liable for the hostile environment created by the supervisors.

* * *

We therefore agree with Faragher that in implementing Title VII it makes sense to hold an employer vicariously liable for some tortious conduct of a supervisor made possible by abuse of his supervisory authority, and that the aided-by-agency-relation principle embodied in § 219(2)(d) of the Restatement provides an appropriate starting point for determining liability for the kind of harassment presented here.

* * *

There is certainly some authority for requiring active or affirmative, as distinct from passive or implicit, misuse of supervisory authority before liability may be imputed.

* * *

In order to accommodate the principle of vicarious liability for harm caused by misuse of supervisory authority, as well as Title VII's equally basic policies of encouraging forethought by employers and saving action by objecting employees, we adopt the following holding in this case and in *Burlington Industries, Inc. v. Ellerth*, [citation], also decided today. An employer is subject to vicarious liability to a victimized employee for an actionable hostile environment created by a supervisor with immediate (or successively higher) authority over the employee. When no tangible employment action is taken, a defending employer may raise an affirmative defense to liability or damages, subject to proof by a preponderance of the evidence, see [citation]. The defense comprises two necessary elements: (a) that the employer exercised reasonable care to prevent and correct promptly any sexually harassing behavior, and (b) that the plaintiff employee unreasonably failed to take advantage of any preventive or corrective opportunities provided by the employer or to avoid harm otherwise. While proof that an employer had promulgated an antiharassment policy with complaint procedure is not necessary in every instance as a matter of law, the need for a stated policy suitable to the employment circumstances may appropriately be addressed in any case when litigating the first element of the defense. And while proof that an employee failed to fulfill the corresponding obligation of reasonable care to avoid harm is not limited to showing an unreasonable failure to use any complaint procedure provided by the employer, a demonstration of such failure will normally suffice to satisfy the employer's burden under the second element of the defense. No affirmative defense is available, however, when the supervisor's harassment culminates in a tangible employment action, such as discharge, demotion, or undesirable reassignment. [Citation.]

Applying these rules here, we believe that the judgment of the Court of Appeals must be reversed. The District Court

* * *

found that the degree of hostility in the work environment rose to the actionable level and was attributable to Silverman and Terry. It is undisputed that these supervisors "were granted virtually unchecked authority" over their subordinates, "directly controll[ing] and supervis[ing] all aspects of [Faragher's] day-to-day activities." [Citation.] It is also clear that Faragher and her colleagues were "completely isolated from the City's higher management." [Citation.] The City did not seek review of these findings.

While the City would have an opportunity to raise an affirmative defense if there were any serious prospect of its presenting one, it appears from the record that any such avenue is closed. The District Court found that the City had entirely failed to disseminate its policy against sexual harassment among the beach employees and that its officials made no attempt to keep track of the conduct of supervisors like Terry and Silverman. The record also makes clear that the City's policy did not include any assurance that the harassing supervisors could be bypassed in registering complaints. Under such circumstances, we hold as a matter of law that the City could not be found to have exercised reasonable care to prevent the supervisors' harassing conduct. Unlike the employer of a small workforce, who might expect that sufficient care to prevent tortious behavior could

be exercised informally, those responsible for city operations could not reasonably have thought that precautions against hostile environments in any one of many departments in far-flung locations could be effective without communicating some formal policy against harassment, with a sensible complaint procedure.

III

The Court of Appeals also rejected the possibility that it could hold the City liable for the reason that it knew of the harassment vicariously through the knowledge of its supervisors. We have no occasion to consider whether this was error, however. We are satisfied that liability on the ground of vicarious knowledge could not be determined without further factfinding on remand, whereas the reversal necessary on the theory of supervisory harassment renders any remand for consideration of imputed knowledge entirely unjustifiable (as would be any consideration of negligence as an alternative to a theory of vicarious liability here).

IV

The judgment of the Court of Appeals for the Eleventh Circuit is reversed, and the case is remanded for reinstatement of the judgment of the District Court.

CASE
15-4

The Americans with Disabilities Act prohibits employers from discriminating against any "qualified individual with a disability." In this case, the United States Supreme Court identifies the standards for determining whether an individual is disabled

TOYOTA MOTOR MANUFACTURING, KENTUCKY, INC. v. WILLIAMS
Supreme Court of the United States, 2002
534 U.S. 184, 122 S.Ct. 681
http://laws.findlaw.com/us/000/00-1089.html

O'Connor, J.

Under the Americans with Disabilities Act of 1990 (ADA or Act), [citation], a physical impairment that "substantially limits one or more * * * *major life activities" is a "disability." [Citation.] Respondent, claiming to be disabled because of her carpal tunnel syndrome and other related impairments, sued petitioner, her former employer, for failing to provide her with a reasonable accommodation as required by the ADA. [Citation.] The District Court granted summary judgment to petitioner, finding that respondent's impairments did not substantially limit any of her major life activities. The Court of Appeals for the Sixth Circuit reversed, finding that the impairments substantially limited respondent in the major life activity of performing manual tasks, and therefore granting partial summary judgment to respondent on the issue of whether she was disabled under the ADA. We con-

clude that the Court of Appeals did not apply the proper standard in making this determination because it analyzed only a limited class of manual tasks and failed to ask whether respondent's impairments prevented or restricted her from performing tasks that are of central importance to most people's daily lives.

I

Respondent began working at petitioner's automobile manufacturing plant in Georgetown, Kentucky, in August 1990. She was soon placed on an engine fabrication assembly line, where her duties included work with pneumatic tools. Use of these tools eventually caused pain in respondent's hands, wrists, and arms. She sought treatment at petitioner's in-house medical service, where she was diagnosed with bilateral carpal tunnel syndrome and bilateral tendinitis. Respondent consulted a personal physician who placed her on permanent work restrictions that precluded her from lifting more than 20 pounds or from "frequently lifting or carrying of objects weighing up to 10 pounds," engaging in "constant repetitive * * *flexion or extension of [her] wrists or elbows," performing "overhead work," or using "vibratory or pneumatic tools." [Citation.]

In light of these restrictions, for the next two years petitioner assigned respondent to various modified duty jobs. Nonetheless, respondent missed some work for medical leave, and eventually filed a claim under the Kentucky Workers' Compensation Act. [Citation.] The parties settled this claim, and respondent returned to work. She was unsatisfied by petitioner's efforts to accommodate her work restrictions, however, and responded by bringing an action in the United States District Court for the Eastern District of Kentucky alleging that petitioner had violated the ADA by refusing to accommodate her disability. That suit was also settled, and as part of the settlement, respondent returned to work in December 1993.

Upon her return, petitioner placed respondent on a team in Quality Control Inspection Operations (QCIO). QCIO is responsible for four tasks: (1) "assembly paint;" (2) "paint second inspection;" (3) "shell body audit;" and (4) "ED surface repair." [Citation.] Respondent was initially placed on a team that performed only the first two of these tasks, and for a couple of years, she rotated on a weekly basis between them. In assembly paint, respondent visually inspected painted cars moving slowly down a conveyor. She scanned for scratches, dents, chips, or any other flaws that may have occurred during the assembly or painting process, at a rate of one car every 54 seconds. When respondent began working in assembly paint, inspection team members were required to open and shut the doors, trunk, and/or hood of each passing car. Sometime during respondent's tenure, however, the position was modified to include only visual inspection with few or no manual tasks. Paint second inspection required team members to use their hands to wipe each painted car with a glove as it moved along a conveyor. The parties agree that respondent was physically capable of performing both of these jobs and that her performance was satisfactory.

During the fall of 1996, petitioner announced that it wanted QCIO employees to be able to rotate through all four of the QCIO processes. Respondent therefore received training for the shell body audit job, in which team members apply a highlight oil to the hood, fender, doors, rear quarter panel, and trunk of passing cars at a rate of approximately one car per minute. The highlight oil has the viscosity of salad oil, and employees spread it on cars with a sponge attached to a block of wood. After they wipe each car with the oil, the employees visually inspect it for flaws. Wiping the cars required respondent to hold her hands and arms up around shoulder height for several hours at a time.

A short while after the shell body audit job was added to respondent's rotations, she began to experience pain in her neck and shoulders. Respondent again sought care at petitioner's in-house medical service, where she was diagnosed with myotendinitis bilateral periscapular, an inflammation of the muscles

and tendons around both of her shoulder blades; myotendinitis and myositis bilateral forearms with nerve compression causing median nerve irritation; and thoracic outlet compression, a condition that causes pain in the nerves that lead to the upper extremities. Respondent requested that petitioner accommodate her medical conditions by allowing her to return to doing only her original two jobs in QCIO, which respondent claimed she could still perform without difficulty.

The parties disagree about what happened next. According to respondent, petitioner refused her request and forced her to continue working in the shell body audit job, which caused her even greater physical injury. According to petitioner, respondent simply began missing work on a regular basis. Regardless, it is clear that on December 6, 1996, the last day respondent worked at petitioner's plant, she was placed under a no-work-of-any-kind restriction by her treating physicians. On January 27, 1997, respondent received a letter from petitioner that terminated her employment, citing her poor attendance record.

Respondent * * *filed suit against petitioner in the United States District Court for the Eastern District of Kentucky.* * *

Respondent based her claim that she was "disabled" under the ADA on the ground that her physical impairments substantially limited her in (1) manual tasks; (2) housework; (3) gardening; (4) playing with her children; (5) lifting; and (6) working, all of which, she argued, constituted major life activities under the Act. Respondent also argued, in the alternative, that she was disabled under the ADA because she had a record of a substantially limiting impairment and because she was regarded as having such an impairment. [Citation.]

* * *

We granted certiorari, [citation], to consider the proper standard for assessing whether an individual is substantially limited in performing manual tasks.* * *

II

The ADA requires covered entities, including private employers, to provide "reasonable accommodations to the known physical or mental limitations of an otherwise qualified individual with a disability who is an applicant or employee, unless such covered entity can demonstrate that the accommodation would impose an undue hardship." [Citation.] The Act defines a "qualified individual with a disability" as "an individual with a disability who, with or without reasonable accommodation, can perform the essential functions of the employment position that such individual holds or desires." [Citation.] In turn, a "disability" is:

(A) a physical or mental impairment that substantially limits one or more of the major life activities of such individual;

(B) a record of such an impairment; or

(C) being regarded as having such an impairment. § 12102(2).

There are two potential sources of guidance for interpreting the terms of this definition—the regulations interpreting the Rehabilitation Act of 1973, [citation], and the EEOC regulations interpreting the ADA. Congress drew the ADA's definition of disability almost verbatim from the definition of "handicapped individual" in the Rehabilitation Act and Congress' repetition of a well-established term generally implies that Congress intended the term to be construed in accordance with pre-existing regulatory interpretations * * * .

* * *

To qualify as disabled, a claimant must further show that the limitation on the major life activity is "substantial." [Citation.] Unlike "physical impairment" and "major life activities," the HEW regulations do not define the term "substantially limits." See Nondiscrimination on the Basis of Handicap in Programs and Activities Receiving or Benefiting from Federal Financial Assistance, citation (stating the Department of Health, Education, and Welfare's position that a definition of "substantially limits" was not possible at that time). The EEOC, therefore, has created its own definition for purposes of the ADA. According to the EEOC regulations, "substantially limited" means "unable to perform a major life activity that the average person in the general population can perform;" or "significantly restricted as to the condition, manner or duration under which an individual can perform a particular major life activity as compared to the condition, manner, or duration under which the average person in the general population can perform that same major life activity" [Citation.] In determining whether an individual is substantially limited in a major life activity, the regulations instruct that the following factors should be considered: "the nature and severity of the impairment; the duration or expected duration of the impairment; and the permanent or long-term impact, or the expected permanent or long-term impact of or resulting from the impairment." [Citation.]

III

The question presented by this case is whether the Sixth Circuit properly determined that respondent was disabled under * * *the ADA's disability definition at the time that she sought an accommodation from petitioner. [Citation.] The parties do not dispute that respondent's medical conditions, which include carpal tunnel syndrome, myotendinitis, and thoracic outlet compression, amount to physical impairments. The relevant question, therefore, is whether the Sixth Circuit correctly analyzed whether these impairments substantially limited respondent in the major life activity of performing manual tasks. Answering this requires us to address an issue about which the EEOC regulations are silent: what a plaintiff must demonstrate to establish a substantial limitation in the specific major life activity of performing manual tasks.

Our consideration of this issue is guided first and foremost by the words of the disability definition itself. "Substantially" in the phrase "substantially limits" suggests "considerable" or

"to a large degree." [Citations.] The word "substantial" thus clearly precludes impairments that interfere in only a minor way with the performance of manual tasks from qualifying as disabilities. [Citation.]

"Major" in the phrase "major life activities" means important. [Citation.] "Major life activities" thus refers to those activities that are of central importance to daily life. In order for performing manual tasks to fit into this category—a category that includes such basic abilities as walking, seeing, and hearing—the manual tasks in question must be central to daily life. If each of the tasks included in the major life activity of performing manual tasks does not independently qualify as a major life activity, then together they must do so.

That these terms need to be interpreted strictly to create a demanding standard for qualifying as disabled is confirmed by the first section of the ADA, which lays out the legislative findings and purposes that motivate the Act. [Citation.] When it enacted the ADA in 1990, Congress found that "some 43,000,000 Americans have one or more physical or mental disabilities." [Citation.] If Congress intended everyone with a physical impairment that precluded the performance of some isolated, unimportant, or particularly difficult manual task to qualify as disabled, the number of disabled Americans would surely have been much higher. [Citation.]

We therefore hold that to be substantially limited in performing manual tasks, an individual must have an impairment that prevents or severely restricts the individual from doing activities that are of central importance to most people's daily lives. The impairment's impact must also be permanent or long-term. [Citation.]

It is insufficient for individuals attempting to prove disability status under this test to merely submit evidence of a medical diagnosis of an impairment. Instead, the ADA requires those "claiming the Act's protection * * *to prove a disability by offering evidence that the extent of the limitation [caused by their impairment] in terms of their own experience * * *is substantial." [Citation.] That the Act defines "disability" "with respect to an individual," [citation], makes clear that Congress intended the existence of a disability to be determined in such a case-by-case manner. [Citations.]

An individualized assessment of the effect of an impairment is particularly necessary when the impairment is one whose symptoms vary widely from person to person. Carpal tunnel syndrome, one of respondent's impairments, is just such a condition. While cases of severe carpal tunnel syndrome are characterized by muscle atrophy and extreme sensory deficits, mild cases generally do not have either of these effects and create only intermittent symptoms of numbness and tingling. [Citation.] Studies have further shown that, even without surgical treatment, one quarter of carpal tunnel cases resolve in one month, but that in 22 percent of cases, symptoms last for eight years or longer. [Citation.] * * *Given these large potential differences in the severity and duration of the effects of carpal tunnel syndrome, an individual's carpal tunnel syndrome diagnosis, on its own, does not indicate whether the individual has a disability within the meaning of the ADA.

IV

The Court of Appeals' analysis of respondent's claimed disability suggested that in order to prove a substantial limitation in the major life activity of performing manual tasks, a "plaintiff must show that her manual disability involves a 'class' of manual activities," and that those activities "affect the ability to perform tasks at work." Both of these ideas lack support.

* * *

While the Court of Appeals in this case addressed the different major life activity of performing manual tasks, its analysis circumvented [citation] by focusing on respondent's inability to perform manual tasks associated only with her job. This was error. When addressing the major life activity of performing manual tasks, the central inquiry must be whether the claimant is unable to perform the variety of tasks central to most people's daily lives, not whether the claimant is unable to perform the tasks associated with her specific job. Otherwise, * * *restriction[s] on claims of disability based on a substantial limitation in working will be rendered meaningless because an inability to perform a specific job always can be recast as an inability to perform a "class" of tasks associated with that specific job.

There is also no support in the Act, our previous opinions, or the regulations for the Court of Appeals' idea that the question of whether an impairment constitutes a disability is to be answered only by analyzing the effect of the impairment in the workplace. * * *

Even more critically, the manual tasks unique to any particular job are not necessarily important parts of most people's lives. As a result, occupation-specific tasks may have only limited relevance to the manual task inquiry. In this case, "repetitive work with hands and arms extended at or above shoulder levels for extended periods of time," the manual task on which

the Court of Appeals relied, is not an important part of most people's daily lives. The court, therefore, should not have considered respondent's inability to do such manual work in her specialized assembly line job as sufficient proof that she was substantially limited in performing manual tasks.

At the same time, the Court of Appeals appears to have disregarded the very type of evidence that it should have focused upon. It treated as irrelevant "the fact that [respondent] can * * *tend to her personal hygiene [and] carry out personal or household chores." Yet household chores, bathing, and brushing one's teeth are among the types of manual tasks of central importance to people's daily lives, and should have been part of the assessment of whether respondent was substantially limited in performing manual tasks.

The District Court noted that at the time respondent sought an accommodation from petitioner, she admitted that she was able to do the manual tasks required by her original two jobs in QCIO. In addition, according to respondent's deposition testimony, even after her condition worsened, she could still brush her teeth, wash her face, bathe, tend her flower garden, fix breakfast, do laundry, and pick up around the house. The record also indicates that her medical conditions caused her to avoid sweeping, to quit dancing, to occasionally seek help dressing, and to reduce how often she plays with her children, gardens, and drives long distances. But these changes in her life did not amount to such severe restrictions in the activities that are of central importance to most people's daily lives that they establish a manual-task disability as a matter of law. On this record, it was therefore inappropriate for the Court of Appeals to grant partial summary judgment to respondent on the issue whether she was substantially limited in performing manual tasks, and its decision to do so must be reversed.

* * *

Accordingly, we reverse the Court of Appeals' judgment granting partial summary judgment to respondent and remand the case for further proceedings consistent with this opinion.

CASE

15-5

Courts in a number of states have allowed at-will employees to bring claims for "wrongful discharge" under tort or contract theories. In the following case, the New York Court of Appeals considers—and rejects—a plaintiff's arguments that New York should recognize such causes of action.

MURPHY v. AMERICAN HOME PRODUCTS CORPORATION
Court of Appeals of New York, 1983
58 N.Y. 2d 293, 461 N.Y.S. 2d 232. 448 N.E. 2d 86

Jones, J.

This court has not and does not now recognize a cause of action in tort for abusive or wrongful discharge of an employee; such recognition must await action of the Legislature. Nor does the complaint here state a cause of action for intentional infliction of

emotional distress, for prima facie tort, or for breach of contract. These causes of action were, therefore, properly dismissed. . . .

Plaintiff, Joseph Murphy, was first employed by defendant, American Home Products Corp., in 1957. He thereafter served in various accounting positions, eventually attaining the office of assistant treasurer, but he never had a formal contract of employment. On April 18, 1980, when he was 59 years old, he was discharged.

Plaintiff claims that he was fired for two reasons: because of his disclosure to top management of alleged accounting improprieties on the part of corporate personnel and because of his age. As to the first ground, plaintiff asserts that his firing was in retaliation for his revelation to officers and directors of defendant corporation that he had uncovered at least $50 million in illegal account manipulations of secret pension reserves which improperly inflated the company's growth in income and allowed high-ranking officers to reap unwarranted bonuses from a management incentive plan, as well as in retaliation for his own refusal to engage in the alleged accounting improprieties. He contends that the company's internal regulations required him to make the disclosure that he did. He also alleges that his termination was carried out in a humiliating manner.

* * *

The complaint set up four causes of action. As his first cause of action, plaintiff alleged that his discharge "was wrongful, malicious and in bad faith" and that defendant was bound "not to dismiss its employees for reasons that are contrary to public policy". In his second cause of action, plaintiff claimed that his dismissal "was intended to and did cause plaintiff severe mental and emotional distress thereby damaging plaintiff". His third claim was based on an allegation that the manner of his termination "was deliberately and viciously insulting, was designed to and did embarrass and humiliate plaintiff and was intended to and did cause plaintiff severe mental and emotional distress thereby damaging plaintiff". In his fourth cause of action, plaintiff asserted that, although his employment contract was of indefinite duration, the law imposes in every employment contract "the requirement that an employer shall deal with each employee fairly and in good faith". On that predicate he alleged that defendant's conduct in stalling his advancement and ultimately firing him for his disclosures "breached the terms of its contract requiring good faith and fair dealing toward plaintiff and damaged plaintiff thereby". Plaintiff demanded compensatory and punitive damages.

[D]efendant moved on July 27, 1981 to dismiss the complaint on the grounds that it failed to state a cause of action and that the fourth cause of action was barred by the Statute of Frauds. Defendant contended that plaintiff was an at-will employee subject to discharge at any time, that New York does not recognize a tort action for abusive or wrongful discharge, and that the prima facie tort and intentional infliction of emotional distress claims were unavailable and insufficient.

On October 16, 1981, plaintiff served an amended complaint with his opposing papers on the motion. The amended complaint, among other things, added a fifth cause of action, alleging that plaintiff was denied advancement due to his age which constituted "illegal employment discrimination on the basis of age in violation of New York Executive Law § 296. "

Special Term denied defendant's motion to dismiss the wrongful discharge tort claim but granted the motion as to the causes of action for breach of contract, prima facie tort, intentional infliction of emotional distress, and age discrimination. Although the court noted that New York had not yet adopted the doctrine of abusive discharge, it declined to put plaintiff out of court before he had had opportunity by means of disclosure procedures to elicit evidence which might put his claim on firmer footing. Special Term held the cause of action for breach of contract barred by the Statute of Frauds. As to the second and third causes of action the court ruled that plaintiff's allegations as to the manner of his dismissal were not sufficient to support causes of action for intentional infliction of emotional distress or for prima facie tort. . . .

On cross appeals, the Appellate Division, modified, to the extent of granting the motion to dismiss the first cause of action, and otherwise affirmed the order of Special Term. The court noted that it does not appear that New York recognizes a cause of action for abusive discharge and that, in any event, plaintiff had failed to show the type of violation of penal law or public policy that has been held sufficient in other jurisdictions to support a cause of action for abusive discharge. According to the appellate court, plaintiff's charge that the corporation's records were not kept in accordance with generally accepted accounting principles appeared to involve a dispute over a matter of judgment as to the proper accounting treatment to be given the terms involved and not a dispute over false book entries. As to the other causes of action, the court ruled that Special Term had properly dismissed them either for failure to state a cause of action [and] failure to comply with the Statute of Frauds or, regarding the age discrimination claim, failure to assert it within the statutory time period . . . We modify the order of the Appellate Division from which plaintiff appeals by reinstating the fifth cause of action for age discrimination and otherwise affirm. *[The age discrimination claim was reinstated because the court below had applied the wrong statute of limitations.]*

With respect to his first cause of action, plaintiff urges that the time has come when the courts of New York should recognize the tort of abusive or wrongful discharge of an at-will employee. To do so would alter our long- settled rule that where an employment is for an indefinite term it is presumed to be a hiring at will which may be freely terminated by either party at any time for any reason or even for no reason. . . . Plaintiff argues that a trend has emerged in the courts of other States to temper what is perceived as the unfairness of the traditional rule by allowing a cause of action in tort to redress abusive discharges. He accurately points out that this tort has elsewhere been recognized to hold employers liable for dismissal of employees in retaliation for employee conduct that is protected by public policy. Thus, the abusive discharge doctrine has been applied to impose liability on employers where employees have been discharged for disclosing illegal activities on the part of their employers . . . , where employees have been terminated due to their service on jury duty . . . , and where employees have been dismissed because they have filed workers' compensation . . . . Plaintiff would have this court adopt this emerging view. We decline his invitation, being of the opinion that such a significant change in our law is best left to the Legislature.

Those jurisdictions that have modified the traditional at-will rule appear to have been motivated by conclusions that the freedom of contract underpinnings of the rule have become outdated, that individual employees in the modern work force do not have the bargaining power to negotiate security for the jobs on which they have grown to rely, and that the rule yields harsh results for those employees who do not enjoy the benefits of express contractual limitations on the power of dismissal. Whether these conclusions are supportable or whether for other compelling reasons employers should, as a matter of policy, be held liable to at-will employees discharged in circumstances for which no liability has existed at common law, are issues better left to resolution at the hands of the Legislature. In addition to the fundamental question whether such liability should be recognized in New York, of no less practical importance is the definition of its configuration if it is to be recognized.

Both of these aspects of the issue, involving perception and declaration of relevant public policy (the underlying determinative consideration with respect to tort liability in general, . . . are best and more appropriately explored and resolved by the legislative branch of our government. The Legislature has infinitely greater resources and procedural means to discern the public will, to examine the variety of pertinent considerations, to elicit the views of the various segments of the community that would be directly affected and in any event critically interested, and to investigate and anticipate the impact of imposition of such liability. Standards should doubtless be established applicable to the multifarious types of employment and the various circumstances of discharge. If the rule of nonliability for termination of at-will employment is to be tempered, it should be accomplished through a principled statutory scheme, adopted after opportunity for public ventilation, rather than in consequence of judicial resolution of the partisan arguments of individual adversarial litigants.

Additionally, if the rights and obligations under a relationship forged, perhaps some time ago, between employer and employee in reliance on existing legal principles are to be significantly altered, a fitting accommodation of the competing interests to be affected may well dictate that any change should be given prospective effect only, or at least so the Legislature might conclude.

For all the reasons stated, we conclude that recognition in New York State of tort liability for what has become known as abusive or wrongful discharge should await legislative action.

Plaintiff's second cause of action is framed in terms of a claim for intentional infliction of emotional distress. To survive a motion to dismiss, plaintiff's allegations must satisfy the rule set out in Restatement of Torts, Second, which we adopted in *Fischer v Maloney* . . ., that: "One who by extreme and outrageous conduct intentionally or recklessly causes severe emotional distress to another is subject to liability for such emotional distress" (§ 46, subd [1]). Comment d to that section notes that: "Liability has been found only where the conduct has been so outrageous in character, and so extreme in degree, as to go beyond all possible bounds of decency, and to be regarded as atrocious, and utterly intolerable in a civilized community". The facts alleged by plaintiff regarding the manner of his termination fall far short of this strict standard. Further, in light of our holding above that there is now no cause of action in tort in New York for abusive or wrongful discharge of an at-will employee, plaintiff should not be allowed to evade that conclusion or to subvert the traditional at-will contract rule by casting his cause of action in terms of a tort of intentional infliction of emotional distress . . . .

Plaintiff's third cause of action was also properly dismissed. If considered, as plaintiff would have us, as intended to allege a prima facie tort it is deficient inasmuch as there is no allegation that his, discharge was without economic or social justification . . . . Moreover, we held in *James v Board of Educ.* . . ., which also involved the exercise of an unrestricted right to discharge an employee, that: "Plaintiff cannot, by the device of an allegation that the sole reason for the termination of his employment by these public officials acting within the ambit of their authority was to harm him without justification (a contention which could be advanced with respect to almost any such termination), bootstrap himself around a motion addressed to the pleadings". Nor does the conclusory allegation of malice by plaintiff here supply the deficiency. As with the intentional infliction of emotional distress claim, this cause of action cannot be allowed in circumvention of the unavailability of a tort claim for wrongful discharge or the contract rule against liability for discharge of an at-will employee.

Plaintiff's fourth cause of action is for breach of contract. Although he concedes in his complaint that his employment contract was of indefinite duration (inferentially recognizing that, were there no more, under traditional principles his employer might have discharged him at any time), he asserts that in all employment contracts the law implies an obligation on the part of the employer to deal with his employees fairly and in good faith and that a discharge in violation of that implied obligation exposes the employer to liability for breach of contract. Seeking then to apply this proposition to the present case, plaintiff argues in substance that he was required by the terms of his employment to disclose accounting improprieties and that defendant's discharge of him for having done so constituted a failure by the employer to act in good faith and thus a breach of the contract of employment.

No New York case upholding any such broad proposition is cited to us by plaintiff (or identified by our dissenting colleague), and we know of none. New York does recognize that in appropriate circumstances an obligation of good faith and fair dealing on the part of a party to a contract may be implied and, if implied will be enforced . . . . In such instances the implied obligation is in aid and furtherance of other terms of the agreement of the parties. No obligation can be implied, however, which would be inconsistent with other terms of the contractual relationship. Thus, in the case now before us, plaintiff's employment was at will, a relationship in which the law accords the employer an unfettered right to terminate the employment at any time. In the context of such an employment it would be incongruous to say that an inference may be drawn that the employer impliedly agreed to a provision which would be destructive of his right of termination. The parties may by express agreement limit or restrict the employer's right of discharge, but to imply such a limitation from the existence of an unrestricted right would be internally inconsistent. In sum, under New York law as it now stands, absent a constitutionally impermissible purpose, a statutory proscription, or an express limitation in the individual contract of employment, an employer's right at any time to terminate an employment at will remains unimpaired.

* * *

Accordingly, the fourth cause of action should have been dismissed for failure to state a cause of action. *[The Court notes that the courts below appear to have erred in dismissing this cause of action under the Statute of Frauds because the contract of employment was not one which, by its terms, could not have been performed within one year.]*

* * *

For the reasons stated, the order of the Appellate Division should be modified, with costs, to reinstate plaintiff's fifth cause of action for age discrimination.

* * *

QUESTIONS

1. List and briefly discuss the major labor law statutes.
2. List and describe the major laws prohibiting employment discrimination.
3. Discuss the defenses available to an employer under the various laws prohibiting discrimination in employment.
4. Discuss the doctrine of employment at will and the laws protecting employee privacy.

5. Discuss (a) the Occupational Safety and Health Administration (OSHA) and the Occupational Safety and Health Act, (b) workers' compensation, (c) unemployment compensation, (d) social security, (e) the Fair Labor Standards Act, (f) the Worker Adjustment and Retraining Notification Act, and (g) the Family and Medical Leave Act.

PROBLEMS

1. Janet, a twenty-year-old woman, applied for a position driving a truck for Federal Trucking, Inc. Janet, who is 5'4" tall and weighs 135 lbs., was denied the job because the company requires that all employees be at least 5'6" tall and weigh at least 150 lbs. Federal justifies this requirement on the basis that its drivers frequently are forced to move heavy loads when making pickups and deliveries. Janet brings a cause of action. Decision?

2. Tom, Dick and Jane are employed by Atlantic Motors, a large chain of used car lots with several hundred employees. None of them was hired for a definite period of time and each has an excellent record of sales. On April 15, all of them were fired.

(a) Tom, who is 50, was told by his manager that he was being fired so that the company could "make room for some young faces on the sales force."

(b) Dick, who is 49, was fired because, on April 15, he had become frustrated with a prospective customer who was arguing about prices and had punched the customer in the nose.

(c) Jane was fired because she repeatedly refused invitations from Al, the sole owner of Atlantic, to spend weekends with him at his beach house. Al had warned Jane that she would be fired if she continued to reject his advances. Discuss, separately, whether Tom, Dick or Jane has any claim against Atlantic Motors.

3. Dave, a 60-year-old man, and Annie, a 35-year-old woman, both apply for the job of office manager at Berker & MacKelly, a large New York City law firm. Dave is not offered the job because he has no experience working as an office manager and a number of more qualified applicants applied for the position. Annie is told that while she is very qualified, the firm prefers to hire men for this particular position. Annie is, however, offered a job as a legal assistant by Berker & MacKelly with a salary and benefits identical to that of office manager. Both Dave and Annie sue Berker & MacKelly, claiming that the firm engaged in illegal discrimination. Judgment for whom? Discuss each case separately.

4. Andy, a 62-year-old man employed as a computer programmer by IBC Computer Company, is fired because of his age. Sally, a 50-year-old woman is hired to replace him. Andy sues IBC under the Age Discrimination in Employment Act (ADEA) for illegal discrimination. IBC responds that it did not discriminate against Andy based on his age, since Sally is also covered by ADEA. Judgment for whom?

5. N.I.S. promoted John, a 42-year-old employee, to a foreman's position while passing over James, a 58-year-old employee. N.I.S. told James he was too old for the job and that the company preferred to have a younger man in the position. James brings a cause of action. Decision?

6. Anthony was employed as a forklift operator for Blackburn Construction Company. While on the job, Anthony carelessly and in

direct violation of Blackburn's procedure manually operated the forklift and caused himself severe injury. Blackburn denies liability based on Anthony's (a) gross negligence, (b) disobedience of the procedural manual, and (c) written waiver of liability. Anthony now brings a cause of action. Decision?

7. Johnson, president of the First National Bank of A, believes that it is appropriate to employ only female tellers. Hence, First National refuses to employ Ken Baker as a teller but does offer him a maintenance position at the same salary. Baker brings a cause of action against First National Bank. Decision?

8. Worth H. Percivil, a mechanical engineer, was first employed by General Motors in 1947 and remained in their employment until he was discharged in 1973. At the time his employment was terminated, Percivil was head of GM's Mechanical Development Department. Percivil sued GM for wrongful discharge. He contends that he was discharged as a result of: (a) a conspiracy among his fellow executives to force him out of his employment because of his age; and (b) because he had legitimately complained about certain deceptive practices of GM; he had refused to give the government false information though urged to do so by his superiors; and he had, on the contrary, undertaken to correct certain alleged misrepresentations made to the government. General Motors claims that Percivil's employment was terminable at the will of GM for any reason and with or without cause, provided that the discharge was not prohibited by statute.

Explain separately for (a) and (b) whether Percivil has a claim against GM if he proves that the asserted reasons were the motive for his termination.

9. Burdine, a female, was hired by the Texas Department of Community Affairs as a clerk in the Public Service Careers Division (PSC). The PSC provides training and employment opportunities for unskilled workers. At the time she was hired, Burdine already had several years' experience in employment training. She was soon promoted, and later, when her supervisor resigned, she performed additional duties that usually had been assigned to the supervisor. Burdine applied for the position of supervisor, but the position remained unfilled for six months until a male employee from another division was brought in to fill it.

Burdine alleges discrimination violating Title VII of the 1964 Civil Rights Act. The defendant, Texas Department of Community Affairs, responds that nondiscriminatory evaluation criteria were used to choose the new supervisor. In order to comply with Title VII, must the Texas Department of Community Affairs hire Burdine as supervisor if she and the male candidate are equally qualified? Explain.

10. Hazelwood School District, located in Sleepy Hollow Township, is being sued by several teachers who applied for teaching positions within the school district but were rejected. The plaintiffs, who are all African American, produce the following evidence:

(a) 1.8 percent of the Hazelwood School District's teachers are African American, whereas 15.4 percent of the teachers in Sleepy Hollow Township are African American; and

(b) the hiring decisions by Hazelwood School District are based solely on subjective criteria.

Will the plaintiffs prevail? Explain.

11. Burdine, a female, was hired by the Texas Department of Community Affairs as a clerk in the Public Service Careers Division (PSC). The PSC provides training and employment opportunities for unskilled workers. At the time she was hired, Burdine already

had several years' experience in employment training. She was soon promoted, and later, when her supervisor resigned, she performed additional duties that usually had been assigned to the supervisor. Burdine applied for the position of supervisor, but the position remained unfilled for six months until a male employee from another division was brought in to fill it. Burdine alleges discrimination violating Title VII of the 1964 Civil Rights Act. The defendant, Texas Department of Community Affairs, responds that nondiscriminatory evaluation criteria were used to choose the new supervisor. To comply with Title VII, must the Texas Department of Community Affairs hire Burdine as supervisor if she and the male candidate are equally qualified? Explain.

12. Ms. Wise was fired from her job at the Mead Corporation after she was involved in a fight with a coworker. On four other unrelated occasions, fights occurred between male coworkers. Only one of the males was fired, but this was after his second fight, in which he seriously injured another employee. There is no dispute that Ms. Wise was qualified and performed her duties adequately. Ms. Wise successfully establishes a *prima facie* case of discrimination; however, defendant Mead Corporation meets its burden to "articulate legitimate and nondiscriminatory reasons" for firing Ms. Wise. Can she prevail? Explain.

13. During the years prior to the passage of the Civil Rights Act of 1964, Duke Power openly discriminated against African Americans by allowing them to work only in the labor department of the plant's five departments. The highest paying job in the labor department paid less than the lowest paying jobs in the other four "operating" departments in which only whites were employed. In 1955, the company began requiring a high school education for initial assignment to any department except labor. However, when Duke Power stopped restricting African Americans to the labor department in 1965, it made completion of high school a prerequisite to transfer from labor to any other department. White employees hired before the high school education requirement was adopted continued to perform satisfactorily and to achieve promotions in the "operating" departments.

In 1965, the company also began requiring new employees in the departments other than labor to register satisfactory scores on two professionally prepared aptitude tests, in addition to having a high school education. In September 1965, Duke Power began to permit employees to qualify for transfer to another department from labor by passing two tests, neither of which was directed or intended to measure the ability to learn to perform a particular job or category of jobs. Griggs brought suit against Duke Power, claiming that the high school education and testing requirements were discriminatory and therefore prohibited by the Civil Rights Act of 1964. Is Griggs correct? Why?

14. Plaintiff, Beth Lyons, a staff attorney for the Legal Aid Society (Legal Aid) brought suit against her employer, alleging that Legal Aid violated the Americans with Disabilities Act (ADA) and the Rehabilitation Act by failing to provide her with a parking space near her office. Plaintiff worked for defendant in its lower Manhattan office.

Lyon's disability was the result of being struck and nearly killed by an automobile. From the date of the accident (September 1987) until June 1993, Lyons was on disability leave from Legal Aid; she underwent multiple reconstructive surgeries and received "constant" physical therapy. Since the accident, Lyons has been able to walk only by using walking devices, including walkers, canes, and crutches. Since returning to work Lyons has performed her job duties successfully. Nevertheless, her condition severely limits her ability to walk long distances either at one time or during the course of a day.

Before returning to work, Lyons asked Legal Aid to accommodate her disability by providing her a parking space near her office and the courts in which she would practice. She stated that this would be necessary because she is unable to take public transportation from her home in New Jersey to the Legal Aid office in Manhattan because such "commuting would require her to walk distances, climb stairs, and on occasion to remain standing for extended periods of time," thereby "overtax[ing] her limited physical capabilities." Lyons's physician advised Legal Aid by letter that such a parking space was "necessary to enable [Lyons] to return to work." Legal Aid informed Lyons that it would not pay for a parking space for her. Accordingly, Lyons has spent $300 to $520 a month, representing 15 percent to

26 percent of her monthly net salary, for a parking space adjacent to her office building. Are the accommodations requested by Lyons unreasonable? Why?

 Internet Exercise Find the Occupational Safety and Health Administration's home page and (a) explore "what's new," (b) determine what OSHA is doing about workplace violence and injury, (c) examine the Occupational Injury and Illness Incidence rates, and (d) review the latest news releases.

Intentional Torts

All forms of civil liability are either (1) voluntarily assumed, as by contract, or (2) involuntarily assumed, as imposed by law. Tort liability is of the second type. Tort law gives persons redress from civil wrongs or injuries to their person, property, and economic interests. Examples include assault and battery, automobile accidents, professional malpractice, and products liability. The law of torts has three principal objectives: (1) to compensate persons who sustain harm or loss resulting from another's conduct, (2) to place the cost of that compensation only on those parties who should bear it, and (3) to prevent future harms and losses. The law of torts therefore reallocates losses caused by human misconduct. In general, a tort is committed when:

1. a duty owed by one person to another
2. is breached and
3. proximately causes
4. injury or damage to the owner of a legally protected interest.

Each person is legally responsible for the damages his tortious conduct proximately causes. Moreover, businesses that conduct their business activities through employees are also liable for the torts their employees commit in the course of employment. The tort liability of employers makes the study of tort law essential to business managers.

Injuries may be inflicted intentionally, negligently, or without fault (strict liability). This chapter will discuss intentional torts; the following chapter will cover negligence and strict liability.

The same conduct may, and often does, constitute both a crime and a tort. An example would be an assault and battery committed by Johnson against West. For the commission of this crime, the state may take appropriate action against Johnson. In addition, however, Johnson has violated West's right to be secure in his person and so has committed a tort against West, who may, regardless of the criminal action by the state against Johnson, bring a civil action against Johnson for damages. On the other hand, an act may be criminal without being tortious, and, by the same token, an act may be a tort but not a crime.

In a tort action, the injured party sues to recover *compensation* for the injury sustained as a result of the defendant's wrongful conduct. The primary purpose of tort law, unlike criminal law, is to compensate the injured party, not to punish the wrongdoer. In certain cases, however, courts may award **punitive** or exemplary damages, which are damages over and above the amount necessary to compensate the plaintiff. Where the defendant's tortious conduct has been intentional and outrageous, exhibiting "malice" or a fraudulent or evil motive, most courts permit a jury to award punitive damages. The allowance of punitive damages is designed to deter others from similar conduct by punishing and making an example of the defendant.

◆ SEE CASE 16-1

Tort law is primarily common law. The Restatement of Torts provides an orderly presentation of this law. From 1934 to 1939, The American Law Institute adopted and promulgated the first Restatement. Since then, the Restatement has served as a vital force in shaping the law of torts. Between 1965 and 1978, the institute adopted and promulgated a revised edition of the Restatement of Torts, which supersedes the First Restatement. This text will refer to the revised Restatement simply as the Restatement.

State legislatures and, to a lesser extent, courts have actively assessed the need for **tort reform**. In general, tort reform has focused on limiting liability by restricting damages or narrowing claims. The majority of states have enacted at least one piece of legislation that falls into the broad category of tort reform, but these states have enacted different changes or different combinations of changes affecting specific aspects of tort law. Approaches to tort reform that have been taken at the state level include:

1. Laws that address specific types of claims; for example, limits on medical malpractice awards or on the liability of providers of alcohol.
2. Laws abolishing joint and several liability or limiting the application of this rule. Where joint and several liability is abolished, each one of the several defendants is liable only for his share of the plaintiff's damages.
3. Laws adding defenses to certain types of tort actions.
4. Laws capping noneconomic damages—so-called pain and suffering awards.
5. Laws to abolish or limit punitive damages, or to raise the standard of proof beyond the preponderance of the evidence.
6. Laws aimed at attorneys' fees; for example, laws that directly regulate contingent fees.

INTENT

Intent, as used in tort law, does not require a hostile or evil motive; rather, the term denotes either that the actor desires to cause the consequences of his act *or* that he believes that those consequences are substantially certain to result from it. Restatement, Section 8A.

The following examples illustrate the definition of intent: (1) If A fires a gun in the middle of the Mojave Desert, he intends to fire the gun; but when the bullet hits B, who is in the desert without A's knowledge, A does not intend that result. (2) A throws a bomb into B's office to kill B. A knows that C is in B's office and that the bomb is substantially certain to injure C, although A has no desire to harm C. A, nonetheless, is liable to C for any injury caused C. A's intent to injure B is *transferred* to C.

Infants (persons who have not reached the age of majority) are held liable for their intentional torts. The infant's age and knowledge, however, are critical in determining whether the infant had sufficient intelligence to form the requisite intent. Incompetents, like infants, are generally held liable for their intentional torts.

A number of established and specifically named torts protect an individual from various intentional interferences with his person, dignity, property, and economic interests. Because the law of torts is dynamic, new forms of relief continue to develop. To guide the courts in determining when they should impose liability for intentionally inflicted harm that does not fall within the requirements of an established tort, Section 870 of the Restatement provides a general catchall intentional tort:

> One who intentionally causes injury to another is subject to liability to the other for that injury, if his conduct is generally culpable and not justifiable under the circumstances. This liability may be imposed although the actor's conduct does not come within a traditional category of tort liability.

This section also provides a unifying principle both for long-established torts and for those that have developed more recently.

◆ SEE FIGURE 16-1 Intent

HARM TO THE PERSON

The law provides protection against intentional harm to the person. The primary interests protected by these torts are freedom from bodily contact (by the tort of battery), freedom from apprehension (assault), freedom from confinement (false imprisonment), and freedom from mental distress (infliction of emotional distress). Generally, intentional torts to the person entitle the injured party to recover damages for bodily harm, emotional distress, loss or impairment of earning capacity, reasonable medical expenses, and harm the tortious conduct caused to property or business.

Battery

Battery is an intentional infliction of harmful or offensive bodily contact. It may consist of contact causing serious injury, such as a gunshot wound or a blow to the head with a club. Or it may involve contact causing little or no physical injury, such as knocking a hat off of a person's head or flicking a glove in another's face. Bodily contact is offensive if it would offend a reasonable person's sense of dignity, even if the defendant intended the conduct only as a joke or a compliment. Restatement, Section 19. For instance, kissing another without permission would constitute a battery. Bodily contact may be accomplished by the use of objects, such as Arthur's throwing a rock at Bea with the intention of hitting her. If the rock hits Bea or any

◆ Figure 16-1   Intent

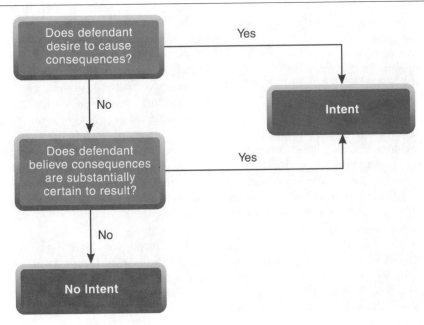

other person, Arthur has committed a battery. Nonetheless, in a densely populated society one cannot expect complete freedom from personal contact with others. Accordingly, neither casually bumping into another in a congested area nor gently tapping that other on the shoulder to get her attention would constitute a battery.

Assault

Assault is intentional conduct by one person directed at another which places the other in apprehension of imminent (immediate) bodily harm or offensive contact. It is usually committed immediately preceding a battery, but if the intended battery fails, the assault remains. Assault is principally a mental rather than a physical intrusion. Accordingly, damages for assault may include compensation for fright and humiliation. The person in danger of immediate bodily harm must have *knowledge* of the danger and be apprehensive of its imminent threat to his safety. For example, if Joan aims a loaded gun at Kelly's back but Pat subdues her before Kelly becomes aware of the danger, Joan has not committed an assault upon Kelly.

Historically, it has been said that words alone do not constitute an assault. Nonetheless, spoken words must be taken in context, and if as taken cause apprehension, these spoken words will constitute an assault. On the other hand, words sometimes will negate an apparent threat so that there is no assault. This does not mean that a defendant can avoid liability for an assault by making his threat conditional. The threat "If you do not give

me your book, I will break your arm" constitutes an assault.

False Imprisonment

The tort of **false imprisonment**, or false arrest, is the intentional confining of a person against her will within fixed boundaries if the person is conscious of the confinement or is harmed by it. Merely obstructing a person's freedom of movement is not false imprisonment so long as a reasonable alternative exit is available. False imprisonment may be brought about by physical force, by the threat of physical force (both express and implied), by physical barriers, or by force directed against the plaintiff's property. For instance, an individual who remains in a store after his wallet is confiscated or who remains on a train after the conductor refuses to allow her suitcase to be removed are both examples of false imprisonment through the use of force against personal property. Damages for false imprisonment may include compensation for loss of time, physical discomfort, inconvenience, physical illness, and mental suffering.

Merchants occasionally encounter potential liability for false imprisonment when they seek to question a suspected shoplifter. A merchant who detains an innocent person may face a lawsuit for false imprisonment. Nonetheless, most states have statutes protecting the merchant, provided she detains the suspect upon probable cause, in a reasonable manner, and for not more than a reasonable time.

◣ See Case 16-2

Infliction of Emotional Distress

One of the more recently recognized torts is that of intentional *or reckless* infliction of emotional distress. The Restatement, Section 46, states the rule as follows:

> One who by extreme and outrageous conduct intentionally or recklessly causes severe emotional distress to another is subject to liability for such emotional distress, and if bodily harm to the other results from it, for such bodily harm.

Recklessness is conduct that evidences a conscious disregard of or an indifference to the consequences of the act committed. Under this tort, the courts impose liability for conduct exceeding all bounds usually tolerated by society when such conduct intentionally or recklessly causes serious mental distress. Many courts allow recovery even in the absence of physical injury. This cause of action does not protect a person from abusive language or rudeness, but rather from atrocious, intolerable conduct beyond all bounds of decency. Examples of this tort would include leading to a person's home, when he is present, a noisy demonstrating mob yelling threats to lynch him unless he leaves town, or placing a rattlesnake in another's bed as a practical joke. Other examples would include sexual harassment on the job and outrageous, prolonged bullying tactics employed by creditors or collection agencies attempting to collect a debt or by insurance adjusters trying to force a settlement of an insurance claim.

HARM TO THE RIGHT OF DIGNITY

The law also protects a person against intentional harm to his right of dignity. This protection includes a person's reputation, privacy, and right to freedom from unjustifiable litigation.

Defamation

The tort of defamation is a false communication that injures a person's reputation by disgracing him and diminishing the respect in which he is held. An example would be the publication of a false statement that a person had committed a crime or had a loathsome disease. In *Beckman v. Dunn*, 276 Pa.Super. 527, 419 A.2d 583 (1980), the court stated,

> A communication is defamatory if it tends to harm the reputation of another so as to lower him in the estimation of the community or deter third persons from associating or dealing with him, and necessarily involves the idea of disgrace.

Elements of Defamation The elements of a defamation action are (1) a false and defamatory statement concerning another, (2) an unprivileged publication (communication) to a third party, (3) depending on the status of the defendant, negligence or recklessness on her part in knowing or failing to ascertain the falsity of the statement, and (4) in some cases, proof of special harm caused by the publication. Restatement,

Section 558. The burden of proof is on the plaintiff to prove the falsity of the defamatory statement.

If a defamatory communication is handwritten, typewritten, printed, pictorial, or in another medium with like communicative power, such as a television or radio broadcast, it is designated **libel.** If it is spoken or oral, it is designated **slander.** Restatement, Sections 568 and 568A. In either case, it must be communicated to a person or persons other than the one who is defamed, a process referred to as *publication.* If Maurice hands or mails to Pierre a defamatory letter he has written about Pierre's character, this is not a publication, as it is intended only for Pierre.

Any living person, as well as corporations, partnerships, and unincorporated associations, may be defamed. Restatement, Sections 561 and 562. Unless a statute provides otherwise, no action may be brought for defamation of a deceased person. Restatement, Section 560.

A significant trend affecting business has been the bringing of defamation suits against former employers by discharged employees. It has been reported that such suits comprise approximately one-third of all defamation lawsuits.

❖ See Case 16-3

Defenses to Defamation Truth and privilege are defenses to defamation. Generally, **truth** is a complete defense without regard to the purpose or intent of the words. **Privilege** is immunity from tort liability granted when the defendant's conduct furthers a societal interest of greater importance than the injury inflicted upon the plaintiff. Three types of **privileges** apply to defamation: absolute, conditional, and constitutional.

Absolute privilege protects the defendant regardless of his motive or intent. This type of privilege, which has been confined to those few situations where public policy clearly favors complete freedom of speech, includes (1) statements made by participants in a judicial proceeding regarding that proceeding; (2) statements made by members of Congress on the floor of Congress; (3) statements made by certain executive branch officers in the discharge of their governmental duties; and (4) statements regarding a third party made between spouses when they are alone.

Qualified or **conditional privilege** depends upon proper use of the privilege. A person has conditional privilege to publish defamatory matter to protect his own legitimate interests or, in some cases, the interests of another. Conditional privilege also extends to many communications in which the publisher and the recipient have a common interest, such as in letters of reference. A publisher who acts in an excessive manner, without probable cause, or for an improper purpose forfeits conditional privilege.

The First Amendment to the U.S. Constitution guarantees freedom of speech and freedom of the press. The U.S. Supreme Court has applied these rights to the law of defamation by extending a form of **constitutional privilege** to defamatory and false statements regarding public officials or public figures so long as it is done without malice. Restatement, Section 580A. For these purposes, *malice* is not ill will but clear and convincing proof of the publisher's knowledge of falsity or reckless disregard of the truth. Thus, under constitutional privilege the public official or public figure must prove that the defendant published the defamatory and false comment with knowledge or in reckless disregard of the comment's falsity and its defamatory character. In a defamation suit brought by a private person (one who is neither a public official nor a public figure) the plaintiff must prove that the defendant published the defamatory and false comment with malice *or* negligence.

Congress enacted legislation granting immunity to Internet service providers (ISPs) from liability for defamation when publishing information originating from a third party.

◆ See Case 16-4

Invasion of Privacy

The invasion of a person's right to privacy actually consists of four distinct torts: (1) appropriation of a person's name or likeness; (2) unreasonable intrusion upon the seclusion of another; (3) unreasonable public disclosure of private facts; or (4) unreasonable publicity which places another in a false light in the public eye. Restatement, Section 652A.

It is entirely possible and not uncommon for a person to invade another's right of privacy in a manner entailing two or more of these related torts. For example, Cindy forces her way into Ozzie's hospital room, takes a photograph of Ozzie, and publishes it to promote Cindy's cure for Ozzie's illness along with false statements about Ozzie that a reasonable person would consider highly objectionable. Ozzie would be entitled to recover on any or all of the four torts comprising invasion of privacy.

◆ See Figure 16-2 Privacy

Appropriation Appropriation is the unauthorized use of the plaintiff's name or likeness for the defendant's benefit, as, for example, in promoting or advertising a product or service. Restatement, Section 652C. The tort of appropriation,

also known as the **right of publicity**, seeks to protect the individual's right to the exclusive use of his identity. In the earlier example, Cindy's use of Ozzie's photograph to promote Cindy's business constitutes the tort of appropriation.

◆ See Case 16-5

Intrusion Intrusion is the unreasonable and highly offensive interference with the solitude or seclusion of another. Restatement, Section 652B. Such unreasonable interference would include improper entry into another's dwelling, unauthorized eavesdropping upon another's private conversations, and unauthorized examination of another's private papers and records. The intrusion must be offensive or objectionable to a reasonable person and must involve matters which are private. Thus, there is no liability if the defendant examines public records or observes the plaintiff in a public place. This form of invasion of privacy is committed once the intrusion occurs, as publicity is not required.

Public Disclosure of Private Facts Under the tort of public disclosure of private facts, the courts impose liability for publicity given to private information about another if the matter made public would be highly offensive and objectionable to a reasonable person. Like intrusion, this tort applies only to private, not public, information regarding an individual; unlike intrusion, it requires publicity. Under the Restatement, the publicity required differs in degree from the "publication" required under the law of defamation. This tort requires that private facts be communicated to the public at large or that they become public knowledge, whereas publication of a defamatory statement need only be made to a single third party. Section 652D, Comment a. Some courts, however, have allowed recovery where the disclosure was made to only one person. Thus, under the Restatement approach, Kathy, a creditor of Gary, will not invade Gary's privacy by writing a letter to Gary's employer to inform the employer of Gary's failure to pay a debt, but Kathy would be liable if she posted in the window of her store a statement that Gary will not pay the debt he owes to her. Also, unlike defamation, this tort applies to truthful private

◆ **Figure 16-2**   Privacy

	Appropriation	Intrusion	Public Disclosure	False Light
Publicity	Yes	No	Yes	Yes
Private facts	No	Yes	Yes	No
Offensiveness	No	Yes	Yes	Yes
Falsity	No	No	No	Yes

information if the matter published would be offensive and objectionable to a reasonable person of ordinary sensibilities.

False Light The tort of false light imposes liability for publicity that places another in a false light that is highly offensive if the defendant *knew* or acted in *reckless disregard* of the fact that the matter publicized was false. Restatement, Section 652E. For example, Linda includes Keith's name and photograph in a public "rogues' gallery" of convicted criminals. Because Keith has never been convicted of any crime, Linda is liable to him for placing him in a false light. Other examples include publicly and falsely attributing to a person an opinion, statement, or written work, as well as the unauthorized use of a person's name on a petition or on a complaint in a lawsuit.

Like defamation, the matter must be untrue; unlike defamation, it must be "publicized," not merely "published." Restatement, Section 652D, Comment a. Although the matter must be objectionable to a reasonable person, it need not be defamatory. In many instances, the same facts will give rise to actions both for defamation and for false light.

Defenses The defenses of absolute, conditional, and constitutional privilege apply to publication of any matter that is an invasion of privacy to the same extent that such defenses apply to defamation.

Misuse of Legal Procedure

Three torts comprise the misuse of legal procedure: malicious prosecution, wrongful civil proceedings, and abuse of process. Each protects an individual from being subjected to unjustifiable litigation. Malicious prosecution and wrongful civil proceedings impose liability for damages caused by improperly brought proceedings, including harm to reputation, credit, or standing; emotional distress; and the expenses incurred in defending against the wrongfully brought lawsuit. Abuse of process is a tort consisting of the use of a legal proceeding (criminal or civil) to accomplish a purpose for which the proceeding is not designed. Abuse of process applies even when there is probable cause or when the plaintiff or prosecution succeeds in the litigation.

HARM TO PROPERTY

The law also provides protection against invasions of a person's interests in property. Intentional harm to property includes the torts of (1) trespass to real property, (2) nuisance, (3) trespass to personal property, and (4) conversion.

Real Property

Real property is land and anything attached to it, such as buildings, trees, and minerals. The law protects the possessor's rights to the exclusive use and quiet enjoyment of the land. Accordingly, damages for harm to land include compensation for the resulting diminution in the value of the land, the loss of use of the land, and the discomfort caused to the possessor of the land. Restatement, Section 929.

Trespass Section 158 of the Restatement provides:

> One is subject to liability to another for trespass, irrespective of whether he thereby causes harm to any legally protected interest of the other, if he intentionally
>   (a) enters land in the possession of the other, or causes a thing or a third person to do so, or
>   (b) remains on the land, or
>   (c) fails to remove from the land a thing which he is under a duty to remove.

It is no defense that the intruder acted under the mistaken belief of law or fact that he was not trespassing. If the intruder intended to be upon the particular property, his reasonable belief that he owned the land or had permission to enter upon the land is irrelevant. Restatement, Section 164. An intruder is not liable if his own actions do not cause his presence on the land of another. For example, if Carol throws Ralph onto Tim's land, Ralph is not liable to Tim for trespass, although Carol is.

A trespass may be committed on, beneath, or above the surface of the land, although the law regards the upper air, above a prescribed minimum altitude for flight, as a public highway. Therefore, no aerial trespass occurs unless the aircraft enters into the lower reaches of the airspace and substantially interferes with the landowner's use and enjoyment. Restatement, Section 159.

Nuisance A nuisance is a nontrespassory invasion of another's interest in the private use and enjoyment of land. Restatement, Section 821D. In contrast to trespass, nuisance does not require interference with another's right to exclusive possession of land, but rather imposes liability for significant and unreasonable harm to another's use or enjoyment of land. Examples of nuisances include the emission of unpleasant odors, smoke, dust, or gas, as well as the pollution of a stream, pond, or underground water supply. In one case, a computer's serious disturbance of a television retailer's signal reception was considered a nuisance.

Personal Property

Personal property, or chattel, is any type of property other than an interest in land. The law protects a number of interests in the possession of personal property, including an interest in the property's physical condition and usability, an interest in the retention of possession, and an interest in its availability for future use.

Trespass Trespass to personal property consists of the intentional dispossession or unauthorized use of the personal property of another. Though the interference with the right to exclusive use and possession may be direct or indirect, liability is limited to instances in which the trespasser (1) dispossesses the other of the property; (2) substantially impairs the condition, quality, or value of the property; (3) deprives the possessor of the use of the property for a substantial time; or (4) causes harm to the possessor or to some person or thing in which the possessor has a legally protected interest. Restatement, Section 218. For example, Albert parks his car in front of his house. Ronald pushes Albert's car around the corner. Albert subsequently looks for his car but cannot find it for several hours. Ronald is liable to Albert for trespass.

Conversion Conversion is an intentional exercise of dominion or control over another's personal property which so seriously interferes with the other's right of control as to justly require the payment of full value for the property. Restatement, Section 222A. Thus, all conversions are trespasses, but not all trespasses are conversions.

Conversion may consist of the intentional destruction of personal property or the use of property in an unauthorized manner. For example, Ken entrusts an automobile to Barbara, a dealer, for sale. After she drives the car 8,000 miles on her own business, Barbara is liable to Ken for conversion. On the other hand, in the example in which Ronald pushed Albert's car around the corner, Ronald would *not* be liable to Albert for conversion. Moreover, a person who buys stolen property is liable to the rightful owner for conversion even if the buyer acquires the property in good faith and without knowledge that it was stolen. Restatement, Section 229.

HARM TO ECONOMIC INTERESTS

Economic interests comprise a fourth set of interests the law protects against intentional interference. Economic or pecuniary interests include a person's existing and prospective contractual relations, a person's business reputation, a person's name and likeness (previously discussed under the section titled "Appropriation"), and a person's freedom from deception. Business torts—those torts that protect a person's economic interests—are discussed in this section under the following headings: (1) interference with contractual relations, (2) disparagement, and (3) fraudulent misrepresentation.

Interference with Contractual Relations

To conduct business it is necessary to establish trade relations with employees, suppliers, and customers. Though these relations may or may not be contractual, those that are, or are capable of being established by contract, receive legal protection against interference. Section 766 of the Restatement provides:

One who intentionally and improperly interferes with the performance of a contract (except a contract to marry) between another and a third person by inducing or otherwise causing the third person not to perform the contract, is subject to liability to the other for the pecuniary loss resulting to the other from the failure of the third person to perform the contract.

The law imposes similar liability for intentional and improper interference with another's prospective contractual relation, such as a lease renewal or financing for construction. Restatement, Section 766B.

In either case, the rule requires that a person act with the purpose or motive of interfering with another's contract or with the knowledge that such interference is substantially certain to occur as a natural consequence of her actions. The interference may be by threats or by prevention through the use of physical force. Frequently, interference is accomplished through inducement, such as the offer of a better contract. For instance, Edgar may offer Doris, an employee of Frank, a yearly salary of $5,000 per year more than the contractual arrangement between Doris and Frank. If Edgar is aware that a contract exists between Doris and Frank and of the fact that his offer to Doris will interfere with that contract, then Edgar is liable to Frank for intentional interference with contractual relations.

To be distinguished is the situation where the contract may be terminated at will or where the contractual relation is only prospective. In these cases, competition is a proper basis for interference; for if one party is pursuing a contractual relation, others also are free to pursue a similar arrangement. For example, Amos and Brenda are competing distributors of transistors. Amos induces Carter, a prospective customer of Brenda, to buy transistors from Amos instead of Brenda. Amos has no liability to Brenda because his interference with Brenda's prospective contract with Carter is justified on the basis of competition, so long as Amos does not use predatory means such as physical violence, fraud, civil suits, or criminal prosecution to persuade Carter to deal with him.

Damages for interference with contractual relations include the pecuniary loss of the benefits of the contract, consequential losses caused by the interference, and emotional distress or actual harm to reputation. Restatement, Section 774A. In one case, Pennzoil had orally entered into a contract to merge with Getty Oil. Before the merger was consummated, however, Texaco induced Getty to merge with Texaco instead. Pennzoil sued Texaco for tortious interference with the merger contract and was awarded $7.53 billion in compensatory damages and $3 billion in punitive damages. *Texaco, Inc. v. Pennzoil, Co.,* 729 S.W.2d 768 (1987).

Disparagement

The tort of **disparagement** or injurious falsehood imposes liability upon a person who publishes a false statement that results in harm to another's interests which have pecuniary value, if the publisher knows that the statement is false or acts in reckless disregard of its truth or falsity. This tort most commonly involves false statements that the publisher intends to cast doubt upon the title or quality of another's property or products. Thus, Adam, while contemplating the purchase of merchandise that belongs to Barry, reads a newspaper advertisement in which Carol falsely asserts she owns the merchandise. Carol has disparaged Barry's property in the goods. Similarly, Marlene, knowing her statement to be false, tells Lionel that Matthew, an importer of wood, does not deal in mahogany. As a result, Lionel, who had intended to buy mahogany from Matthew, buys it elsewhere. Marlene is liable to Matthew for disparagement.

Absolute, conditional, and constitutional privileges apply to the same extent to the tort of disparagement as they do to defamation. In addition, a competitor has conditional privilege to compare her products favorably with those of a rival, even though she does not believe that her products are superior. No privilege applies, however, if the comparison contains false assertions of specific unfavorable facts about the competitor's property. For example, a manufacturer who advertises that his goods are the best in the market, even though he knows that a competitor's product is better, is not liable for disparagement. If he goes further, however, by falsely stating that his product is better because his competitor uses shoddy materials, then his disparagement would no longer be privileged, and he would be liable to his competitor for disparagement.

The pecuniary loss an injured person may recover is that which directly and immediately results from impairment of the marketability of the property disparaged. The injured party also may recover damages for expenses necessary to counteract the false publication, including litigation expenses, the cost of notifying customers, and the cost of publishing denials. Thus, Ursula publishes in a magazine an untrue statement that cranberries grown during the current season in a particular area are unwholesome. Shortly thereafter, the business of Victor, a jobber who has contracted to buy the entire output of cranberries grown in this area, falls off by 50 percent. If no other facts account for this decrease in his business, Victor is entitled to recover the amount of his loss from Ursula, plus the expenses necessary to counteract the misinformation published.

Fraudulent Misrepresentation

With respect to intentional, or fraudulent, misrepresentation, Section 525 of the Restatement provides:

> One who fraudulently makes a misrepresentation of fact, opinion, intention, or law for the purpose of inducing another to act or to refrain from action in reliance upon it, is subject to liability to the other in deceit for pecuniary loss caused to him by his justifiable reliance upon the misrepresentation.

For example, Smith represents to Jones that a tract of land in Texas is located in an area where oil drilling had recently commenced. Smith makes this statement knowing it to be false. In reliance upon the statement, Jones purchases the land from Smith, who is liable to Jones for fraudulent misrepresentation. Although fraudulent misrepresentation is a tort action, it is closely connected with contractual negotiations; the effects of such misrepresentation on assent to a contract are discussed in Chapter 18.

◆ **SEE FIGURE 16-3** Intentional Torts

DEFENSES TO INTENTIONAL TORTS

Even though the defendant has intentionally invaded the interests of the plaintiff, the defendant will not be liable if such conduct was privileged. A defendant's conduct is privileged if it furthers an interest of such social importance that the law confers immunity from tort liability for the damage the conduct causes to others. Examples of privilege include self-defense, defense of property, and defense of others. In addition, the plaintiff's consent to the defendant's conduct is a defense to intentional torts.

Consent

If one consents to conduct resulting in damage or harm to his own person, dignity, property, or economic interests, no liability will generally attach to the intentional infliction of injury. **Consent**, which signifies that one is willing for an act to occur, negates the wrongfulness of the act. A person may manifest consent expressly or impliedly, by words or by conduct.

Consent must be given by an individual with capacity to do so. Consent given by a minor, mental incompetent, or intoxicated individual is invalid if he is not capable of appreciating the nature, extent, or probable consequences of the conduct to which he has consented. Consent is not effective if given under duress, by which one constrains another's will by compelling that other to give consent unwillingly.

Privilege

A person who would otherwise be liable for a tort is *not* liable if he acts pursuant to and within the limits of a privilege. Restatement, Section 890. Conditional privileges, as discussed in the section on defamation, depend upon proper use of the privilege. Absolute privilege, on the other hand, protects the defendant regardless of his purpose. Examples of absolute privilege include untrue, defamatory statements made by participants during the course of judicial proceedings, by legislators, by certain governmental executives, and between spouses. Absolute immunity also protects a public prosecutor from civil liability for malicious prosecution.

FIGURE 16-3   Intentional Torts

Interest Protected	Tort
Person Freedom from contact Freedom from apprehension Freedom of movement Freedom from distress	Battery Assault False imprisonment Infliction of emotional distress
Dignity Reputation Privacy Freedom from wrongful legal actions	Defamation Appropriation Intrusion Public disclosure of private facts False light Misuse of legal procedure
Property Real Personal	Trespass Nuisance Trespass Conversion
Economic Contracts Goodwill Freedom from deception	Interference with contractual rights Disparagement Fraudulent misrepresentation

One conditional privilege—self-defense—entitles an individual to injure another's person without the other's consent. The law created the privilege of **self-defense** to enable an individual to protect himself against tortious interference. By virtue of this privilege an individual may inflict or impose what would otherwise constitute battery, assault, or false imprisonment.

Section 63 of the Restatement provides:

> An actor is privileged to use reasonable force, not intended or likely to cause death or serious bodily harm, to defend himself against unprivileged harmful or offensive contact or other bodily

harm which he reasonably believes that another is about to inflict intentionally upon him.

The privilege of self-defense exists whether or not the danger actually exists, provided that the defendant reasonably believed self-defense was necessary. The reasonableness of the defendant's actions is based upon what a person of average courage would have thought under the circumstances. A possessor of property is also permitted to use reasonable force, not intended or likely to cause death or serious bodily harm, to protect his real and personal property.

CHAPTER SUMMARY

Harm to the Person

Battery intentional infliction of harmful or offensive bodily contact

Assault intentional infliction of apprehension of immediate bodily harm or offensive contact

False Imprisonment intentional confining of a person against her will

Infliction of Emotional Distress extreme and outrageous conduct intentionally or recklessly causing severe emotional distress

Harm to the Right of Dignity

Defamation false communication that injures a person's reputation
- *Libel* written or electronically transmitted defamation
- *Slander* spoken defamation
- *Defenses* truth, absolute privilege, conditional privilege, and constitutional privilege are defenses to a defamation action

Invasion of Privacy
- *Appropriation* unauthorized use of a person's identity
- *Intrusion* unreasonable and offensive interference with the seclusion of another
- *Public Disclosure of Private Facts* offensive publicity of private information
- *False Light* offensive and false publicity about another

Misuse of Legal Procedure torts that protect an individual from unjustifiable litigation

Harm to Property

Real Property land and anything attached to it
- *Trespass* wrongfully entering on land of another
- *Nuisance* a nontrespassory interference with another's use and enjoyment of land

Personal Property any property other than land
- *Trespass* an intentional taking or use of another's personal property
- *Conversion* intentional exercise of control over another's personal property

Harm to Economic Interests

Interference with Contractual Relations intentionally causing one of the parties to a contract not to perform

Disparagement publication of false statements about another's property or products

Fraudulent Misrepresentation a false statement, made with knowledge of its falsity, intended to induce another to act

Defenses to Intentional Torts

Consent a person may not recover for injury to which he willingly and knowingly consents

Self-Defense a person may take appropriate action to prevent harm to himself where time does not allow resort to the law

---

C A S E S

CASE
16-1

This case, decided by the Supreme Court of the United States, illustrates courts' approach to reviewing awards of substantial punitive damages. In this case, the jury had awarded the plaintiff $145 million in punitive damages for the misconduct of his automobile insurance company.

STATE FARM MUTUAL AUTOMOBILE INSURANCE v. CAMPBELL

Supreme Court of the United States, 2003
538 U.S. 408, 123 S.Ct. 1513, 155 L.Ed.2d 585
http://laws.findlaw.com/us/000/01-1289.html

Kennedy, J.

We address once again the measure of punishment, by means of punitive damages, a state may impose upon a defendant in a civil case. The question is whether, in the circumstances we shall recount, an award of $145 million in punitive damages, where full compensatory damages are $1 million, is excessive and in violation of the Due Process Clause of the Fourteenth Amendment to the Constitution of the United States.

I

In 1981, Curtis Campbell was driving with his wife, Inez Preece Campbell, in Cache County, Utah. He decided to pass six vans traveling ahead of them on a two-lane highway. Todd Ospital was driving a small car approaching from the opposite direction. To avoid a head-on collision with Campbell, who by then was driving on the wrong side of the highway and toward oncoming traffic, Ospital swerved onto the shoulder, lost control of his automobile, and collided with a vehicle driven by Robert G. Slusher. Ospital was killed, and Slusher was rendered permanently disabled. The Campbells escaped unscathed.

* * *

* * * "a consensus was reached early on by the investigators and witnesses that Mr. Campbell's unsafe pass had indeed caused the crash." [Citation.] Campbell's insurance company, petitioner State Farm Mutual Automobile Insurance Company (State Farm), nonetheless decided to contest liability and declined offers by Slusher and Ospital's estate to settle the claims for the policy limit of $50,000 ($25,000 per claimant). State Farm also ignored the advice of one of its own investigators and took the case to trial, assuring the Campbells that "their assets were safe, that they had no liability for the accident, that [State Farm] would represent their interests, and that they did not need to procure separate counsel." [Citation.] To the contrary, a jury determined that Campbell was 100 percent at fault, and a judgment was returned for $185,849, far more than the amount offered in settlement.

At first State Farm refused to cover the $135,849 in excess liability. Its counsel made this clear to the Campbells: "You may want to put for sale signs on your property to get things moving." [Citation.] Nor was State Farm willing to post a * * * bond to allow Campbell to appeal the judgment against him. Campbell obtained his own counsel to appeal the verdict. * * *

In 1989, the Utah Supreme Court denied Campbell's appeal in the wrongful death and tort actions. [Citation.] State Farm then paid the entire judgment, including the amounts in excess of the policy limits. The Campbells nonetheless filed a complaint against State Farm alleging bad faith, fraud, and intentional infliction of emotional distress. The trial court initially granted State Farm's motion for summary judgment because State Farm had paid the excess verdict, but that ruling was reversed on appeal. [Citation.] On remand State Farm moved* * * to exclude evidence of alleged conduct that occurred in unrelated cases outside of Utah, but the trial court denied the motion. * * * the jury determined that State Farm's decision not to settle was unreasonable because there was a substantial likelihood of an excess verdict.

* * *

* * *The jury awarded the Campbells $2.6 million in compensatory damages and $145 million in punitive damages, which the trial court reduced to $1 million and $25 million respectively. Both parties appealed.

The Utah Supreme Court * * * reinstated the $145 million punitive damages award. * * * We granted certiorari. [Citation.]

II

We recognized in [citation], that in our judicial system compensatory and punitive damages, although usually awarded at the same time by the same decisionmaker, serve different purposes. [Citation.] Compensatory damages "are intended to redress the concrete loss that the plaintiff has suffered by reason of the defendant's wrongful conduct." [Citation.] By contrast, punitive damages serve a broader function; they are aimed at deterrence and retribution. [Citations.]

* * * The Due Process Clause of the Fourteenth Amendment prohibits the imposition of grossly excessive or arbitrary punishments on a tortfeasor. [Citations.] * * * To the extent an award is grossly excessive, it furthers no legitimate purpose and constitutes an arbitrary deprivation of property. [Citation.]

Although these awards serve the same purposes as criminal penalties, defendants subjected to punitive damages in civil cases have not been accorded the protections applicable in a criminal proceeding. This increases our concerns over the imprecise manner in which punitive damages systems are administered. We have admonished that "punitive damages pose an acute danger of arbitrary deprivation of property. Jury instructions typically leave the jury with wide discretion in choosing amounts, and the presentation of evidence of a defendant's net worth creates the potential that juries will use their verdicts to express biases against big businesses, particularly those without strong local presences." * * * Our concerns are heightened when the decisionmaker is presented, as we shall discuss, with evidence that has little bearing as to the amount of punitive damages that should be awarded. Vague instructions, or those that merely inform the jury to avoid "passion or prejudice,"[citation], do little to aid the decisionmaker in its task of assigning appropriate weight to evidence that is relevant and evidence that is tangential or only inflammatory.

In light of these concerns, in [*BMW of North America, Inc. v.*] *Gore,* [citation], we instructed courts reviewing punitive damages to consider three guideposts: (1) the degree of reprehensibility of the defendant's misconduct; (2) the disparity between the actual or potential harm suffered by the plaintiff and the punitive damages award; and (3) the difference between the punitive damages awarded by the jury and the civil penalties authorized or imposed in comparable cases. [Citation.] We reiterated the importance of these three guideposts in [citation] and mandated appellate courts to conduct *de novo* review of a trial court's application of them to the jury's award. [Citation.] Exacting appellate review ensures that an award of punitive damages is based upon an "'application of law, rather than a decisionmaker's caprice.'" [Citation.]

III

Under the principles outlined in *BMW of North America, Inc. v.*

Gore, this case is neither close nor difficult. It was error to reinstate the jury's $145 million punitive damages award. * * *

A

"The most important indicium of the reasonableness of a punitive damages award is the degree of reprehensibility of the defendant's conduct." [Citation.] We have instructed courts to determine the reprehensibility of a defendant by considering whether: the harm caused was physical as opposed to economic; the tortious conduct evinced an indifference to or a reckless disregard of the health or safety of others; the target of the conduct had financial vulnerability; the conduct involved repeated actions or was an isolated incident; and the harm was the result of intentional malice, trickery, or deceit, or mere accident. [Citation.] The existence of any one of these factors weighing in favor of a plaintiff may not be sufficient to sustain a punitive damages award; and the absence of all of them renders any award suspect. It should be presumed a plaintiff has been made whole for his injuries by compensatory damages, so punitive damages should only be awarded if the defendant's culpability, after having paid compensatory damages, is so reprehensible as to warrant the imposition of further sanctions to achieve punishment or deterrence. [Citation.]

Applying these factors in the instant case, we must acknowledge that State Farm's handling of the claims against the Campbells merits no praise. The trial court found that State Farm's employees altered the company's records to make Campbell appear less culpable. State Farm disregarded the overwhelming likelihood of liability and the near-certain probability that, by taking the case to trial, a judgment in excess of the policy limits would be awarded. State Farm amplified the harm by at first assuring the Campbells their assets would be safe from any verdict and by later telling them, postjudgment, to put a for-sale sign on their house. While we do not suggest there was error in awarding punitive damages based upon State Farm's conduct toward the Campbells, a more modest punishment for this reprehensible conduct could have satisfied the state's legitimate objectives, and the Utah courts should have gone no further.

This case, instead, was used as a platform to expose, and punish, the perceived deficiencies of State Farm's operations throughout the country. The Utah Supreme Court's opinion makes explicit that State Farm was being condemned for its nationwide policies rather than for the conduct direct toward the Campbells. * * *

* * *

A state cannot punish a defendant for conduct that may have been lawful where it occurred. [Citations.] * * * Nor, as a general rule, does a state have a legitimate concern in imposing punitive damages to punish a defendant for unlawful acts committed outside of the state's jurisdiction. * * *

For a more fundamental reason, however, the Utah courts erred in relying upon this and other evidence: The courts awarded punitive damages to punish and deter conduct that bore no relation to the Campbells' harm. A defendant's dissimilar acts, independent from the acts upon which liability was premised, may not serve as the basis for punitive damages. A defendant should be punished for the conduct that harmed the plaintiff, not for being an unsavory individual or business. Due process does not permit courts, in the calculation of punitive damages, to adjudicate the merits of other parties' hypothetical claims against a defendant under the guise of the reprehensibility analysis, but we have no doubt the Utah Supreme Court did that here. * * * Punishment on these bases creates the possibility of multiple punitive damages awards for the same conduct.* * *

* * *

B

Turning to the second *Gore* guidepost, we have been reluctant to identify concrete constitutional limits on the ratio between harm, or potential harm, to the plaintiff and the punitive damages award. [Citation.] We decline again to impose a bright-line ratio which a punitive damages award cannot exceed. Our jurisprudence and the principles it has now established demonstrate, however, that, in practice, few awards exceeding a single-digit ratio between punitive and compensatory damages, to a significant degree, will satisfy due process. In [citation], in upholding a punitive damages award, we concluded that an award of more than four times the amount of compensatory damages might be close to the line of constitutional impropriety. [Citation.] We cited that 4-to-1 ratio again in *Gore*. [Citation.] The Court further referenced a long legislative history, dating back over 700 years and going forward to today, providing for sanctions of double, treble, or quadruple damages to deter and punish. [Citation.] While these ratios are not binding, they are instructive. They demonstrate what should be obvious: Single-digit multipliers are more likely to comport with due process, while still achieving the state's goals of deterrence and retribution, than awards with ratios in range of 500 to 1, [citation], or, in this case, of 145 to 1.

* * * The precise award in any case, of course, must be based upon the facts and circumstances of the defendant's conduct and the harm to the plaintiff.

In sum, courts must ensure that the measure of punishment is both reasonable and proportionate to the amount of harm to the plaintiff and to the general damages recovered. In the context of this case, we have no doubt that there is a presumption against an award that has a 145-to-1 ratio. The compensatory award in this case was substantial; the Campbells were awarded $1 million for a year and a half of emotional distress. This was complete compensation. The harm arose from a transaction in the economic realm, not from some physical assault or trauma; there were no physical injuries; and State Farm paid the excess verdict before the complaint was filed, so the Campbells suffered only minor economic injuries for the 18-month period in which State Farm refused to resolve the claim against them. The compensatory damages for the injury suffered here, moreover, likely were based on a component which was duplicated in the punitive award. Much of the distress was caused by the outrage and humiliation the Campbells suffered at the actions of their insurer; and it is a major role of punitive damages to condemn such conduct. Compensatory damages, however, already contain this punitive element. [Citation.]

* * *

C

The third guidepost in *Gore* is the disparity between the punitive damages award and the "civil penalties authorized or imposed in comparable cases." * * * Punitive damages are not a substitute for the criminal process, and the remote possibility of a criminal sanction does not automatically sustain a punitive damages award.

* * * The most relevant civil sanction under Utah state law for the wrong done to the Campbells appears to be a $10,000 fine for an act of fraud, [citation], an amount dwarfed by the $145 million punitive damages award. The Supreme Court of Utah speculated about the loss of State Farm's business license, the disgorgement of profits, and possible imprisonment, but here again its references were to the broad fraudulent scheme drawn from evidence of out-of-state and dissimilar conduct. This analysis was insufficient to justify the award.

IV

An application of the *Gore* guideposts to the facts of this case, especially in light of the substantial compensatory damages awarded (a portion of which contained a punitive element), likely would justify a punitive damages award at or near the amount of compensatory damages. The punitive award of $145 million, therefore, was neither reasonable nor proportionate to the wrong committed, and it was an irrational and arbitrary deprivation of the property of the defendant. * * *

The judgment of the Utah Supreme Court is reversed, and the case is remanded for proceedings not inconsistent with this opinion.

It is so ordered.

CASE
16-2

In this case the court determines whether two girls who were briefly stopped by a store employee while they were shopping have a valid claim for false imprisonment.

VAUGHN v. WAL-MART STORES, INC.
Court of Appeal of Louisiana, Fifth Circuit, 1999
734 So.2d 156

Grisbaum, J.
On July 31, 1994, Amanda Vaughn and Jason Vaughn accompanied their mother, Emma Simpson Vaughn, to a Wal-Mart store located in Jefferson Parish. Amanda's friend, Kimberly Dickerson, was also with them. Once they entered the store, Mrs. Vaughn and Jason went into separate areas of the store. The two girls remained together in the front of the store and went to an area near the cash registers where they sold baseball cards, cigarettes, and stamp albums. After selecting a stamp album to purchase, Kimberly took the album to the register farthest from the store exit. While she was at the register, Kimberly also selected a pack of gum. Once Kimberly paid for her two items, they were placed in a bag and she was given her change. Kimberly testified that she did not immediately put the change in her wallet while she was at the register. Instead, Kimberly walked back into the merchandise area where Amanda had remained. Kimberly was in the merchandise area, away from the registers, when she placed her change in her purse. Kimberly proceeded to place her hand in the Wal-Mart bag to retrieve the gum she had just purchased.

At this time, Ms. Clara Lynn Neal, a customer service man-ager, was coming out the garden center when she saw the two girls standing at the register. Ms. Neal testified that she observed Kimberly's hand coming out of her Wal-Mart bag. According to Ms. Neal, because the two girls were in a somewhat secluded area of the store, Ms. Neal walked passed the two girls twice to observe them before she walked over to them.

Ms. Neal testified that she asked Kimberly if she could see her bag and her receipt and that Kimberly voluntarily gave her the bag. Plaintiffs alleged that Ms. Neal "detained the girls, snatched Kimberly's bag from her, searched the bag, discovered a receipt, tied the bag, and then personally escorted the girls to an area near the front door away from the registers. * * *" However, Kimberly's testimony stated that "[Ms. Neal] said she was going to have to check my bag because she doesn't know if I'm stealing something. So I didn't say anything. I didn't really give it to her because I was shocked. So she took it, and she was like searching through it."

Once Ms. Neal checked the purchases with the receipt, the girls were told to go to the front of the store and wait for their party. The girls were never told that they could not leave the store and the girls were not detained by anyone else. According to all parties, from the time Ms. Neal walked up to the girls, verified the purchases, and returned the bag to Kimberly, the entire incident only lasted about one minute.

While the girls were waiting at the front of the store, Jason was asked by his mother to inform the girls that she was ready to go. Jason approached the girls, and they responded that they could not leave. When Jason reported to his mother that the girls stated they could not leave the area, Mrs. Vaughn then went to the front of the store to investigate.

According to Mrs. Vaughn's testimony, the girls had informed her that they had been stopped by Ms. Neal and accused of stealing. Before Mrs. Vaughn took the children home, she explained to a store manager what had occurred. Mrs. Vaughn returned to the store with Sandra Dickerson, Kimberly's mother, to make further inquiries. Mrs. Vaughn, Mrs. Dickerson, Ms. Neal and the manager then went into an office to discuss the incident. Mrs. Vaughn testified that, at this meeting, Ms. Neal informed her she searched Kimberly because Kimberly had her hand in her bag and looked suspicious. Although Mrs. Vaughn also claims that Ms. Neal stated that she thought Jason was a "look-out" person, this claim was refuted later by Ms. Neal.

Plaintiffs, Woodrow Wilson, on behalf of his minor children, Amanda Vaughn and Jason Vaughn, and Whitney Dickerson, on behalf of his minor daughter, Kimberly Dickerson, filed suit against the defendant, Wal-Mart, to recover damages for wrongful detention. The trial court awarded the amount of $500.00 in damages to each child, plus court costs. The defendant appeals this judgment.

Under normal circumstances, private citizens have no authority to detain individuals for petty theft,* * *. However, [Louisiana law] gives quasi-police powers to merchants and their agents to protect against shoplifting and gives them immunity from liability for malicious prosecution when the detainer has reasonable cause to believe that a theft of goods has occurred on their premises. [Citation.]

* * *

Therefore, the test for false imprisonment claims is a plaintiff must prove either (1) unreasonable force was used, or (2) no reasonable cause existed for the belief that the suspect had committed a theft of goods, or (3) the detention lasted more than 60 minutes, unless it was reasonable under the circumstances that the suspect be detained longer. [Citation.]

First, we determine that Jason Vaughn's claim is without merit. The element of detention is an essential component of the tort of false imprisonment. [Citation.] Here, Jason was not even present at the time of the alleged incident. Jason subsequently was not stopped nor spoken to by Ms. Neal nor any other personnel. There is no evidence to support his claim that he was ever detained. * * *

Next, we also find Amanda Vaughn's claim is without merit. Although Amanda was with Kimberly when they were both approached by Ms. Neal, there is no evidence Ms. Neal even

spoke with Amanda individually, except to tell her and Kimberly to "go to the front of the store and stay there." Ms. Neal stated that the girls were given the option to go to the front of the store and wait for their party or to check their bag at the service desk. Importantly, Amanda testified that, at no time, did Ms. Neal ever ask her any questions. Consequently, we find that appellee, Amanda Vaughn, has also failed to demonstrate she was detained by appellant's employee. * * *

Finally, we address Kimberly Dickerson's claim that she was wrongfully detained by Ms. Neal. It is undisputed that no unreasonable force was used or that the detention lasted more than 60 minutes. Rather, the evidence establishes Kimberly was only stopped by Ms. Neal and handed her bag to Ms. Neal. Once Ms. Neal verified the purchases with the receipt, the two girls were told to go to the front of the store and to wait for their party.

The test of liability is not based upon the store patron's actual guilt or innocence, but rather on the reasonableness of the store employee's action under all the circumstances. [Citation.] Therefore, we must determine whether, under all of the circumstances, Ms. Neal acted reasonably in detaining Kimberly.

The trial court must decide whether reasonable cause existed to believe that the suspect committed a theft of goods. [Citation.] * * *

* * *Our jurisprudence recognizes that

[t]he purpose of [Louisiana law] is to provide merchants with authority to detain and question persons suspected of shoplifting without subjecting them to suits by those detained persons on the basis of false imprisonment when the merchant has reasonable cause to believe a theft of goods has occurred.

[Citation.] Furthermore, the statute provides immunity only to those merchants who have conducted a reasonable post detention inquiry of a person. [Citation.]

* * *

* * * we are compelled here to find the trial court was manifestly erroneous in failing to find that appellant had reasonable cause to detain Kimberly for questioning, * * *. [O]nce Ms. Neal confirmed that a theft had not taken place, the girls had the option of going to the front of the store and waiting for their party or checking the bag at the customer service desk. At no time was Kimberly told that she could not leave the store. Again, we note the detention did not involve unreasonable force given that none of the girls were touched or threatened in anyway. Furthermore, according to all parties, the detention lasted approximately one minute, well below the proscribed period of time. Considering the facts and circumstances presented, we find the actions of appellant's employee were reasonable.

* * *

For the reasons assigned, the trial court's judgment is hereby reversed.

This case examines the standards for determining when derogatory speech constitutes defamation.

CASE
16-3

FRANK B. HALL & CO., INC. v. BUCK

Court of Appeals of Texas, Fourteenth District, 1984

678 S.W.2d 612, cert. denied, *472 U.S. 1009, 105 S.Ct. 2704, 86 L.Ed.2d 720 (1985)*

Junell, J.

Larry W. Buck (Buck or appellee) sued his former employer, Frank B. Hall & Co. (Hall or appellant), for damages for defamation of character,* * *. By unanimous verdict, a jury found damages for* * *defamation of character and exemplary damages. The court entered judgment for appellee for $1,905,000.00 in damages, plus interest, attorney's fees and costs of court. For the reasons set forth below we affirm.

Appellee, an established salesman in the insurance business, was approached in the spring of 1976 by a representative of Hall with a prospective job offer. Appellee was then an executive vice-president of the insurance firm of Alexander & Alexander, and in the previous year he generated approximately $550,000.00 in commissions for the firm. He was the top producer in Alexander's Houston office and was ranked nationally among the top five salesmen for Alexander. After several meetings, Buck accepted Hall's offer of employment and began working for Hall on June 1, 1976. Hall agreed to pay Buck an annual salary of $80,000.00 plus additional compensation equal to seven and one-half percent of net retained commissions for each year to a maximum commission of $600,000.00, plus fringe benefits. The agreement was to be for a three year period. Several Alexander employees followed Buck to Hall's office. During the next several months Buck generated substantial commission income for Hall and succeeded in bringing several major accounts to the firm.

In October, 1976, Mendel Kaliff, then president of Frank B. Hall & Co. of Texas, held a meeting with Buck and Lester Eckert, Hall's office manager and a former Alexander employee. Kaliff informed Buck his salary was being reduced to $65,000.00 and that Hall was eliminating Buck's incentive and profit sharing benefits. Kaliff told Buck these measures were being taken because of Buck's failure to produce sufficient income for Hall. However, Kaliff added that if Buck could generate $400,000.00 net commission income by June 1, 1977, his salary and benefits would be reinstated retroactively.

On March 31, 1977, at another impromptu meeting, Kaliff and Eckert abruptly fired Buck and instructed him not to return to Hall's offices. Buck sought employment with several other insurance firms, but his efforts were fruitless. Distraught at having lost his job and being unable to find suitable employment in the insurance business, Buck hired an investigator, Lloyd Barber, in an attempt to discover Hall's true reasons for firing him. This suit is based upon statements made by Hall employees to Lloyd Barber and to Charles Burton, a prospective employer, and upon a note written by Virginia Hilley, a Hall employee.

Appellant brings eighty points of error, which will be grouped in thirteen categories.

* * *

Lloyd Barber contacted Mendel Kaliff, Lester Eckert and Virginia Hilley and told them that he was an investigator, Buck was being considered for a position of trust and responsibility, and Barber was seeking information about Buck's employment with Frank B. Hall & Co. Barber testified that he had interviewed Kaliff, Eckert and Hilley on separate occasions in September and October of 1977, and had tape-recorded the conversations. Appellee introduced into evidence Barber's properly authenticated investigative reports, which were based on these taped interviews. The report shows Kaliff remarked several times that Buck was untrustworthy, and not always entirely truthful; he said Buck was disruptive, paranoid, hostile and was guilty of padding his expense account. Kaliff said he had locked Buck out of his office and had not trusted him to return. He charged that Buck had promised things he could not deliver. Eckert told Barber that Buck was horrible in a business sense, irrational, ruthless, and disliked by office personnel. He described Buck as a "classical sociopath," who would verbally abuse and embarrass Hall employees. Eckert said Buck had stolen files and records from Alexander & Alexander. He called Buck "a zero," "a Jekyll and Hyde person" who was "lacking in compucture (sic) or scruples."

Virginia Hilley told Barber that Buck could have been charged with theft for materials he brought with him to Hall from Alexander & Alexander.

Any act wherein the defamatory matter is intentionally or negligently communicated to a third person is a publication. In the case of slander, the act is usually the speaking of the words. Restatement (Second) Torts § 577 comment a (1977). There is ample support in the record to show that these individuals intentionally communicated disparaging remarks to a third person. The jury was instructed that "Publication means to communicate defamatory words to some third person in such a way that he understands the words to be defamatory. A statement is not published if it was authorized, invited or procured by Buck and if Buck knew in advance the contents of the invited communication." In response to special issues, the jury found that the slanderous statements were made and published to Barber.

Hall argues that Buck could and should have expected Hall's employees to give their opinion of Buck when requested to do so. Hall is correct in stating that a plaintiff may not recover for a publication to which he has consented, or which he has authorized, procured or invited, [citation]; and it may be true that Buck could assume that Hall's employees would give their opinion when asked to do so. However, there is nothing in the record to indicate that Buck knew Hall's employees would defame him when Barber made the inquiries. The accusations made by Kaliff, Eckert and Hilley were not mere expressions of opinion but were false and derogatory statements of fact.

* * *

A defamer cannot escape liability by showing that, although he desired to defame the plaintiff, he did not desire to defame him to the person to whom he in fact intentionally published the defamatory communication. The publication is complete although the publisher is mistaken as to the identity of the person to whom the publication is made. Restatement (Second) of Torts § 577 comment 1 (1977). Likewise, communication to an agent of the person defamed is a publication, unless the communication is invited by the person defamed or his agent. Restatement § 577 comment e. We have already determined that the evidence is sufficient to show that Buck did not know what Kaliff, Eckert or Hilley would say and that he did not procure the defamatory statements to create a lawsuit. Thus, the fact that Barber may have been acting at Buck's request is not fatal to Buck's cause of action. There is absolutely no proof that Barber induced Kaliff, Eckert or Hilley to make any of the defamatory comments.

* * *

When an ambiguity exists, a fact issue is presented. The court, by submission of proper fact issues, should let the jury render its verdict on whether the statements were fairly susceptible to the construction placed thereon by the plaintiff. [Citation.] Here, the jury found (1) Eckert made a statement calculated to convey that Buck had been terminated because of serious misconduct; (2) the statement was slanderous or libelous; (3) the statement was made with malice; (4) the statement was published; and (5) damage directly resulted from the statement. The jury also found the statements were not substantially true. The jury thus determined that these statements, which were capable of a defamatory meaning, were understood as such by Burton.

* * *

We hold that the evidence supports the award of actual damages and the amount awarded is not manifestly unjust. Furthermore, in responding to the issue on exemplary damages, the jury was instructed that exemplary damages must be based on a finding that Hall "acted with ill will, bad intent, malice or gross disregard to the rights of Buck." Although there is no fixed ratio between exemplary and actual damages, exemplary damages must be reasonably apportioned to the actual damages sustained. [Citation.] Because of the actual damages [$605,000] and the abundant evidence of malice, we hold that the award of punitive damages [$1,300,000] was not unreasonable. * * * The judgment of the trial court is affirmed.

CASE
16-4

This case addressed the possible liability of an internet service provider for defamatory postings carried on one of its proprietary bulletin boards.

ZERAN v. AMERICA ONLINE, INC.
United States Court of Appeals, Fourth Circuit, 1997
971 F.3d 327
http://laws.findlaw.com/4th/971523p.html

Wilkinson, J.
"The Internet is an international network of interconnected computers," currently used by approximately 40 million people worldwide. Reno v. ACLU, [citation]. One of the many means by which individuals access the Internet is through an interactive computer service. These services offer not only a connection to the Internet as a whole, but also allow their subscribers to access information communicated and stored only on each computer service's individual proprietary network. Id. AOL is just such an interactive computer service. Much of the information transmitted over its network originates with the company's millions of subscribers. They may transmit information privately via electronic mail, or they may communicate publicly by posting messages on AOL bulletin boards, where the messages may be read by any AOL subscriber.

* * * On April 25, 1995, an unidentified person posted a message on an AOL bulletin board advertising "Naughty Oklahoma T-Shirts." The posting described the sale of shirts featuring offensive and tasteless slogans related to the April 19, 1995, bombing of the Alfred P. Murrah Federal Building in Oklahoma City. Those interested in purchasing the shirts were instructed to call "Ken" at Zeran's home phone number in Seattle, Washington. As a result of this anonymously perpetrated prank, Zeran received a high volume of calls, comprised primarily of angry and derogatory messages, but also including death threats. Zeran could not change his phone number because he relied on its availability to the public in running his business out of his home. Later that day, Zeran called AOL and informed a company representative of his predicament. The employee assured Zeran that the posting would be removed from AOL's bulletin board but explained that as a matter of policy AOL would not post a retraction. The parties dispute the date that AOL removed this original posting from its bulletin board.

On April 26, the next day, an unknown person posted another message advertising additional shirts with new tasteless slogans related to the Oklahoma City bombing. Again, interested buyers were told to call Zeran's phone number, to ask for "Ken," and to "please call back if busy" due to high demand. The angry, threatening phone calls intensified. Over the next four days, an unidentified party continued to post messages on AOL's bulletin board, advertising additional items including bumper stickers and key chains with still more offensive slogans. During this time period, Zeran called AOL repeatedly and was told by company representatives that the individual account from which the messages were posted would soon be closed. Zeran also reported his case to Seattle FBI agents. By April 30, Zeran was receiving an abusive phone call approximately every two minutes.

Meanwhile, an announcer for Oklahoma City radio station KRXO received a copy of the first AOL posting. On May 1, the announcer related the message's contents on the air, attributed them to "Ken" at Zeran's phone number, and urged the listening audience to call the number. After this radio broadcast, Zeran was inundated with death threats and other violent calls from Oklahoma City residents. Over the next few days, Zeran talked to both KRXO and AOL representatives. He also spoke to his local police, who subsequently surveilled his home to protect his safety. By May 14, after an Oklahoma City newspaper published a story exposing the shirt advertisements as a hoax and after KRXO made an on-air apology, the number of calls to Zeran's residence finally subsided to fifteen per day.

Zeran first filed suit on January 4, 1996, against radio station KRXO in the United States District Court for the Western District of Oklahoma. On April 23, 1996, he filed this separate suit against AOL in the same court. Zeran did not bring any action against the party who posted the offensive messages * * *. AOL answered Zeran's complaint and interposed § 230 [of the Communications Decency Act of 1996 ("CDA")] as an affirmative defense. AOL then moved for judgment on the pleadings pursuant to [citation.] The district court granted AOL's motion, and Zeran filed this appeal.

The relevant portion of § 230 states: "No provider or user of an interactive computer service shall be treated as the publisher or speaker of any information provided by another information content provider." [Citation.] By its plain language, § 230 creates a federal immunity to any cause of action that would make service providers liable for information originating with a third-party user of the service. Specifically, § 230 precludes courts from entertaining claims that would place a computer service provider in a publisher's role. Thus, lawsuits seeking to hold a service provider liable for its exercise of a publisher's traditional editorial functions—such as deciding whether to publish, withdraw, postpone, or alter content—are barred.

Zeran argues, however, that the § 230 immunity eliminates only publisher liability, leaving distributor liability intact. Publishers can be held liable for defamatory statements contained in their works even absent proof that they had specific knowledge of the statement's inclusion. [Citation.] According to Zeran, interactive computer service providers like AOL are normally considered instead to be distributors, like traditional news vendors or book sellers. Distributors cannot be held liable for defamatory statements contained in the materials they distribute unless it is proven at a minimum that they have actual knowledge of the defamatory statements upon which liability is predicated. [Citation.] Zeran contends that he provided AOL with sufficient notice of the defamatory statements appearing on the company's bulletin board. This notice is significant, says Zeran, because AOL could be held liable as a distributor only if it acquired knowledge of the defamatory statements' existence.

Because of the difference between these two forms of liability, Zeran contends that the term "distributor" carries a legally distinct meaning from the term "publisher." Accordingly, he asserts that Congress' use of only the term "publisher" in § 230 indicates a purpose to immunize service providers only from publisher liability. He argues that distributors are left unprotected by § 230 and, therefore, his suit should be permitted to proceed against AOL. We disagree. Assuming arguendo that Zeran has satisfied the requirements for imposition of distributor liability, this theory of liability is merely a subset, or a species, of publisher liability, and is therefore also foreclosed by § 230.

* * *

Zeran simply attaches too much importance to the presence of the distinct notice element in distributor liability. The simple fact of notice surely cannot transform one from an original publisher to a distributor in the eyes of the law. To the contrary, once a computer service provider receives notice of a potentially defamatory posting, it is thrust into the role of a traditional publisher. The computer service provider must decide whether to publish, edit, or withdraw the posting. In this respect, Zeran seeks to impose liability on AOL for assuming the * * * role for which § 230 specifically proscribes liability—the publisher role.

* * * If computer service providers were subject to distributor liability, they would face potential liability each time they receive notice of a potentially defamatory statement—from any party, concerning any message. Each notification would require a careful yet rapid investigation of the circumstances surrounding the posted information, a legal judgment concerning the information's defamatory character, and an on-the-spot editorial decision whether to risk liability by allowing the continued publication of that information. Although this might be feasible for the traditional print publisher, the sheer number of postings on interactive computer services would create an impossible burden in the Internet context. [Citation.] Because service providers would be subject to liability only for the publication of information, and not for its removal, they would have a natural incentive simply to remove messages upon notification,

whether the contents were defamatory or not. [Citation.] Thus * * * liability upon notice has a chilling effect on the freedom of Internet speech.

Similarly, notice-based liability would deter service providers from regulating the dissemination of offensive material over their own services. Any efforts by a service provider to investigate and screen material posted on its service would only lead to notice of potentially defamatory material more frequently and thereby create a stronger basis for liability. Instead of subjecting themselves to further possible lawsuits, service providers would likely eschew any attempts at self-regulation.

* * * Section 230 represents the approach of Congress to a problem of national and international dimension. The Supreme Court underscored this point in ACLU v. Reno [see Chapter 4], finding that the Internet allows "tens of millions of people to communicate with one another * * * and to access vast amounts of information from around the world. [It] is 'a unique and wholly new medium of worldwide human communication.'" [Citation.] Application of the canon invoked by Zeran here would significantly lessen Congress' power, derived from the Commerce Clause, to act in a field whose international character

is apparent. While Congress allowed for the enforcement of "any state law that is consistent with [§ 230]," [citation], it is equally plain that Congress' desire to promote unfettered speech on the Internet must supersede conflicting common law causes of action. Section 230(d)(3) continues: "No cause of action may be brought and no liability may be imposed under any state or local law that is inconsistent with this section." With respect to federal-state preemption, the Court has advised: "When Congress has 'unmistakably * * * ordained,' that its enactments alone are to regulate a part of commerce, state laws regulating that aspect of commerce must fall. The result is compelled whether Congress' command is explicitly stated in the statute's language or implicitly contained in its structure and purpose." [Citation.] Here, Congress' command is explicitly stated. Its exercise of its commerce power is clear and counteracts the caution counseled by the interpretive canon favoring retention of common law principles.

For the foregoing reasons, we affirm the judgment of the district court.

AFFIRMED

CASE 16-5

The following case examines the common law right of publicity and whether a plaintiff's identity can be appropriated in a case where neither the plaintiff's name or likeness was used by the defendant.

WHITE v. SAMSUNG ELECTRONICS AMERICA, INC.

United States Court of Appeals, Ninth Circuit, 1992
971 F.2d 1395, cert. denied,
508 U.S. 951, 113 S.Ct. 2443, 124 L.Ed.2d 660 (1993).

Goodwin, J.

This case involves a promotional "fame and fortune" dispute. In running a particular advertisement without Vanna White's permission, defendants Samsung Electronics America, Inc. (Samsung) and David Deutsch Associates, Inc. (Deutsch) attempted to capitalize on White's fame to enhance their fortune. White sued, alleging infringement of various intellectual property rights, but the district court granted summary judgment in favor of the defendants. We affirm in part, reverse in part, and remand.

Plaintiff Vanna White is the hostess of "Wheel of Fortune," one of the most popular game shows in television history. An estimated forty million people watch the program daily. Capitalizing on the fame which her participation in the show has bestowed on her, White markets her identity to various advertisers.

The dispute in this case arose out of a series of advertisements prepared for Samsung by Deutsch. The series ran in at least half a dozen publications with widespread, and in some cases national, circulation. Each of the advertisements in the series followed the same theme. Each depicted a current item

from popular culture and a Samsung electronic product. Each was set in the twenty-first century and conveyed the message that the Samsung product would still be in use by that time. By hypothesizing outrageous future outcomes for the cultural items, the ads created humorous effects. For example, one lampooned current popular notions of an unhealthy diet by depicting a raw steak with the caption: "Revealed to be health food, 2010 A.D." Another depicted irreverent "news"-show host Morton Downey Jr. in front of an American flag with the caption: "Presidential candidate. 2008 A.D."

The advertisement which prompted the current dispute was for Samsung videocassette recorders (VCRs). The ad depicted a robot, dressed in a wig, gown, and jewelry which Deutsch consciously selected to resemble White's hair and dress. The robot was posed next to a game board which is instantly recognizable as the Wheel of Fortune game show set, in a stance for which White is famous. The caption of the ad read: "Longest running game show. 2012 A.D." Defendants referred to the ad as the "Vanna White" ad. Unlike the other celebrities used in the campaign, White neither consented to the ads nor was she paid.

Following the circulation of the robot ad, White sued Samsung and Deutsch in federal district court under: * * *the California common law right of publicity; * * *. The district court granted summary judgment against White on each of her claims. White now appeals.

* * *

White * * * argues that the district court erred in granting summary judgment to defendants on White's common law right of publicity claim. In *Eastwood v. Superior Court*, [citation], the California court of appeal stated that the common law right of publicity cause of action "may be pleaded by alleging (1) the defendant's use of the plaintiff's identity; (2) the appropriation of plaintiff's name or likeness to defendant's advantage, commercially or otherwise; (3) lack of consent, and (4) resulting injury." [Citation.] The district court dismissed White's claim for failure to satisfy *Eastwood's* second prong, reasoning that defendants had not appropriated White's "name or likeness" with their robot ad. We agree that the robot ad did not make use of White's name or likeness. However, the common law right of publicity is not so confined.

The *Eastwood* court did not hold that the right of publicity cause of action could be pleaded only by alleging an appropriation of name or likeness. *Eastwood* involved an unauthorized use of photographs of Clint Eastwood and of his name. Accordingly, the *Eastwood* court had no occasion to consider the extent beyond the use of name or likeness to which the right of publicity reaches. That court held only that the right of publicity cause of action "may be" pleaded by alleging, *inter alia*, appropriation of name or likeness, not that the action may be pleaded only in those terms.

The "name or likeness" formulation referred to in *Eastwood* originated not as an element of the right of publicity cause of action, but as a description of the types of cases in which the cause of action had been recognized. The source of this formulation is Prosser, *Privacy*, 48 Cal.L.Rev. 383, 401–07 (1960), one of the earliest and most enduring articulations of the common law right of publicity cause of action. In looking at the case law to that point, Prosser recognized that right of publicity cases involved one of two basic factual scenarios: name appropriation, and picture or other likeness appropriation. [Citation.]

Even though Prosser focused on appropriations of name or likeness in discussing the right of publicity, he noted that "[i]t is not impossible that there might be appropriation of the plaintiff's identity, as by impersonation, without use of either his name or his likeness, and that this would be an invasion of his right of privacy." [Citation.] At the time Prosser wrote, he noted however, that "[n]o such case appears to have arisen." [Citation.]

Since Prosser's early formulation, the case law has borne out his insight that the right of publicity is not limited to the appropriation of name or likeness. In *Motschenbacher v. R.J. Reynolds Tobacco Co.*, [citation], the defendant had used a photograph of the plaintiff's race car in a television commercial. Although the plaintiff appeared driving the car in the photograph, his features were not visible. Even though the defendant had not appropriated the plaintiff's name or likeness, this court held that plaintiff's California right of publicity claim should reach the jury.

In *Midler*, this court held that, even though the defendants had not used Midler's name or likeness, Midler had stated a claim for violation of her California common law right of publicity because "the defendants* * *for their own profit in selling their product did appropriate part of her identity" by using a Midler sound-alike. [Citation.]

In *Carson v. Here's Johnny Portable Toilets, Inc.*, [citation], the defendant had marketed portable toilets under the brand name "Here's Johnny"—Johnny Carson's signature "Tonight Show" introduction—without Carson's permission. The district court had dismissed Carson's Michigan common law right of publicity claim because the defendants had not used Carson's "name or likeness." [Citation.] In reversing the district court, the sixth circuit found "the district court's conception of the right of publicity* * *too narrow" and held that the right was implicated because the defendant had appropriated Carson's identity by using, *inter alia*, the phrase "Here's Johnny." [Citation.]

These cases teach not only that the common law right of publicity reaches means of appropriation other than name or likeness, but that the specific means of appropriation are relevant only for determining whether the defendant has in fact appropriated the plaintiff's identity. The right of publicity does not require that appropriations of identity be accomplished through particular means to be actionable. It is noteworthy that the *Midler* and *Carson* defendants not only avoided using the plaintiff's name or likeness, but they also avoided appropriating the celebrity's voice, signature, and photograph. The photograph in *Motschenbacher* did include the plaintiff, but because the plaintiff was not visible the driver could have been an actor or dummy and the analysis in the case would have been the same.

Although the defendants in these cases avoided the most obvious means of appropriating the plaintiffs' identities, each of their actions directly implicated the commercial interests which the right of publicity is designed to protect. As the *Carson* court explained,

> [t]he right of publicity has developed to protect the commercial interest of celebrities in their identities. The theory of the right is that a celebrity's identity can be valuable in the promotion of products, and the celebrity has an interest that may be protected from the unauthorized commercial exploitation of that identity. * * * If the celebrity's identity is commercially exploited, there has been an invasion of his right whether or not his "name or likeness" is used.

[Citation.] It is not important how the defendant has appropriated the plaintiff's identity, but whether the defendant has done so. *Motschenbacher*, *Midler*, and *Carson* teach the impossibility of treating the right of publicity as guarding only against a laundry list of specific means of appropriating identity. A rule which says that the right of publicity can be infringed only through the use of nine different methods of appropriating identity merely challenges the clever advertising strategist to come up with the tenth.

Indeed, if we treated the means of appropriation as dispositive in our analysis of the right of publicity, we would not only weaken the right but effectively eviscerate it. The right would fail to protect those plaintiffs most in need of its protection. Advertisers use celebrities to promote their products. The more popular the celebrity, the greater the number of people who recognize her, and the greater the visibility for the product. The identities of the most popular celebrities are not only the most attractive for advertisers, but also the easiest to evoke without resorting to obvious means such as name, likeness, or voice.

Consider a hypothetical advertisement which depicts a mechanical robot with male features, an African-American complexion, and a bald head. The robot is wearing black hightop Air Jordan basketball sneakers, and a red basketball uniform with black trim, baggy shorts, and the number 23 (though not revealing "Bulls" or "Jordan" lettering). The ad depicts the robot dunking a basketball one-handed, stiff-armed, legs extended like open scissors, and tongue hanging out. Now envision that this ad is run on television during professional basketball games. Considered individually, the robot's physical attributes, its dress, and its stance tell us little. Taken together, they lead to the only conclusion that any sports viewer who has registered

a discernible pulse in the past five years would reach: the ad is about Michael Jordan.

Viewed separately, the individual aspects of the advertisement in the present case say little. Viewed together, they leave little doubt about the celebrity the ad is meant to depict. The female-shaped robot is wearing a long gown, blond wig, and large jewelry. Vanna White dresses exactly like this at times, but so do many other women. The robot is in the process of turning a block letter on a game-board. Vanna White dresses like this while turning letters on a game-board but perhaps similarly attired Scrabble-playing women do this as well. The robot is standing on what looks to be the Wheel of Fortune game show set. Vanna White dresses like this, turns letters, and does this on the Wheel of Fortune game show. She is the only one. Indeed, defendants themselves referred to their ad as the "Vanna White" ad. We are not surprised.

Television and other media create marketable celebrity identity value. Considerable energy and ingenuity are expended by those who have achieved celebrity value to exploit it for profit. The law protects the celebrity's sole right to exploit this value whether the celebrity has achieved her fame out of rare ability, dumb luck, or a combination thereof. We decline Samsung and Deutsch's invitation to permit the evisceration of the common law right of publicity through means as facile as those in this case. Because White has alleged facts showing that Samsung and Deutsch had appropriated her identity, the district court erred by rejecting, on summary judgment, White's common law right of publicity claim.

QUESTIONS

1. Identify and define the torts that protect against intentional harm to personal rights.
2. Explain the application of the various privileges to defamation suits and how they are affected by whether the plaintiff is (a) a public figure, (b) a public official, or (c) a private person.
3. Distinguish the four torts comprising invasion of privacy.
4. Identify and describe the torts that protect against harm to property.
5. Distinguish by example among interference with contractual relations, disparagement, and fraudulent misrepresentation.

PROBLEMS

1. The Penguin intentionally hits Batman with his umbrella. Batman, stunned by the blow, falls backwards, knocking Robin down. Robin's leg is broken in the fall, and he cries out, "Holy broken bat bones! My leg is broken." Who, if anyone, is liable to Robin? Why?
2. CEO was convinced by his employee, M. Ploy, that a coworker, A. Cused, had been stealing money from the company. At lunch that day in the company cafeteria, CEO discharges Cused from her employment, accuses her of stealing from the company, searches through her purse over her objections, and finally forcibly escorts her to his office to await the arrival of the police, which he has his secretary summon. Cused is indicted for embezzlement but subsequently is acquitted upon establishing her innocence. What rights, if any, does Cused have against CEO?

3. Ralph kisses Edith while she is asleep but does not waken or harm her. Edith sues Ralph for battery. Has a battery been committed?
4. Claude, a creditor seeking to collect a debt, calls on Dianne and demands payment in a rude and insolent manner. When Dianne says that she cannot pay, Claude calls Dianne a deadbeat and says that he will never trust her again. Is Claude liable to Dianne? If so, for what tort?
5. Lana, a ten-year-old child, is run over by a car negligently driven by Mitchel. Lana, at the time of the accident, was acting reasonably and without negligence. Clark, a newspaper reporter, photographs Lana while she is lying in the street in great pain. Two years later, Perry, the publisher of a newspaper, prints Clark's picture of Lana in his newspaper as a lead to an article concerning the negligence of

children. The caption under the picture reads: "They ask to be killed." Lana, who has recovered from the accident, brings suit against Clark and Perry. What result?

6. In 1963 the Saturday Evening Post featured an article entitled "The Story of a College Football Fix," characterized in the subtitle as " A Shocking Report of How Wally Butts and Bear Bryant Rigged a Game Last Fall." Butts was athletic director of the University of Georgia, and Bryant was head coach of the University of Alabama. The article was based on a claim by one George Burnett that he had accidentally overheard a long-distance telephone conversation between Butts and Bryant in the course of which Butts divulged information on plays Georgia would use in the upcoming game against Alabama. The writer assigned to the story by the Post was not a football expert, did not interview either Butts or Bryant, and did not personally see the notes Burnett had made of the telephone conversation. Butts admitted that he had a long-distance telephone conversation with Bryant but denied that any advance information on prospective football plays was given. Has Butts been defamed by the Post?

7. Joan, a patient confined in a hospital, has a rare disease that is of great interest to the public. Carol, a television reporter, requests Joan to consent to an interview. Joan refuses, but Carol, nonetheless, enters Joan's room over her objection and photographs her. Joan brings a suit against Carol. Is Carol liable? If so, for what tort?

8. Owner has a place on his land where he piles trash. The pile has been there for three months. John, a neighbor of Owner and without Owner's consent or knowledge, throws trash onto the trashpile. Owner learns that John has done this and sues him. What tort, if any, has John committed?

9. Chris leaves her car parked in front of a store. There are no signs that say Chris cannot park there. The store owner, however, needs the car moved to enable a delivery truck to unload. He releases the brake and pushes Chris's car three or four feet, doing no harm to the car. Chris returns and sees that her car has been moved and is very angry. She threatens to sue the store owner for trespass to her personal property. Can she recover?

10. Carr borrowed John's brand new car for the purpose of going to the store. He told John he would be right back. Carr then decided, however, to go to the beach while he had the car. Can John recover from Carr the value of the automobile? If so, for what tort?

11. Marcia Samms, a respectable married woman, claimed that David Eccles had repeatedly and persistently called her at various hours, including late at night, from May to December, soliciting her to have illicit sexual relations with him. She also claimed that on one occasion Eccles came over to her residence to again solicit sex and indecently exposed himself to her. Mrs. Samms had never encouraged Eccles but had continuously repulsed his "insulting, indecent, and obscene" proposals. She brought suit against Eccles, claiming she suffered great anxiety and fear for her personal safety and severe emotional distress, demanding actual and punitive damages. Can she recover? If so, for what tort?

12. National Bond and Investment Company sent two of its employees to repossess Whithorn's car after he failed to complete the payments. The two repossessors located Whithorn while he was driving his car. They followed him and hailed him down to make the repossession. Whithorn refused to abandon his car and demanded evidence of their authority. The two repossessors became impatient and called a wrecker. They ordered the driver of the wrecker to hook Whithorn's car and move it down the street while Whithorn was still inside the vehicle. Whithorn started the car and tried to escape, but the wrecker lifted the car off the road and progressed seventy-five to one hundred feet until Whithorn managed to stall the wrecker. Has National Bond committed the tort of false imprisonment?

13. In March 1975 William Proxmire, a United States senator from Wisconsin, initiated the "Golden Fleece of the Month Award" to publicize what he believed to be wasteful government spending. The second of these awards was given to the federal agencies that had for seven years funded Dr. Hutchinson's research on stress levels in animals. The award was made in a speech Proxmire gave in the Senate; the text was also incorporated into an advance press release that was sent to 275 members of the national news media. Proxmire also referred to the research in two subsequent newsletters sent to 100,000 constituents and during a television interview. Hutchinson then brought this action alleging defamation resulting in personal and economic injury. Assuming that Hutchinson proved that the statements were false and defamatory, would he prevail?

14. Capune was attempting a trip from New York to Florida on an eighteen-foot-long paddleboard. The trip was being covered by various media to gain publicity for Capune and certain products he endorsed. By water, Capune approached a pier owned by Robbins, who had posted signs prohibiting surfing and swimming around the pier. Capune was unaware of these notices and attempted to continue his journey by passing under the pier. Robbins ran up yelling and threw two bottles at Capune. Capune was frightened and tried to maneuver his paddleboard to go around the pier. Robbins then threw a third bottle that hit Capune in the head. Capune had to be helped out of the water and taken to the hospital. He suffered a physical wound which required twenty-four sutures and, as a result, had to discontinue his trip. Capune brought suit in tort against Robbins. Is Robbins liable? If so, for which tort or torts?

15. Ralph Nader, who has been a critic of General Motors for several years, claims that when General Motors learned that Nader was about to publish a book entitled Unsafe at Any Speed, criticizing one of its automobiles, it decided to conduct a campaign of intimidation against him. Specifically, Nader claims that GMC (1) conducted a series of interviews with Nader's acquaintances, questioning them about his political, social, racial, and religious views; (2) kept him under surveillance in public places for an unreasonable length of time; (3) caused him to be accosted by women for the purpose of entrapping him into illicit relationships; (4) made threatening, harassing, and obnoxious telephone calls to him; (5) tapped his telephone and eavesdropped by means of mechanical and electronic equipment on his private conversations with others; and (6) conducted a "continuing" and harassing investigation of him. Nader brought suit against GMC for invasion of privacy. Which, if any, of the alleged actions would constitute invasion of privacy?

16. Bill Kinsey was charged with murdering his wife while working for the Peace Corps in Tanzania. After waiting six months in jail he was acquitted at a trial that attracted wide publicity. Five years later, while a graduate student at Stanford University, Kinsey had a brief affair with Mary Macur. He abruptly ended the affair by telling Macur he would no longer be seeing her because another woman, Sally Allen, was coming from England to live with him. A few months later, Kinsey and Allen moved to Africa and were subsequently married. Soon after Bill ended their affair, Macur began a letter writing campaign designed to expose Bill and his mistreatment of her. Macur sent several letters to both Bill and Sally Kinsey, their former spouses, their parents, their neighbors, their parents' neighbors, members of Bill's dissertation committee, other faculty, and the president of Stanford University. The letters contained statements accusing Bill of murdering his first wife, spending six months in jail for the crime, being a rapist, and other questionable behavior. The Kinseys brought an action for invasion of privacy, seeking damages and a permanent injunction. Will the Kinseys prevail? If so, for what tort?

17. The Brineys (defendants) owned a large farm on which was located an abandoned farmhouse. For a ten-year period the house had been the subject of several trespassings and housebreakings. In an attempt to stop the intrusions, Briney boarded up the windows and doors and posted "no trespassing" signs. After one break-in, however, Briney set a spring gun in a bedroom. It was placed over the bedroom window so that the gun could not be seen from outside, and no warning of its presence was posted. The gun was set to hit an intruder in the legs. Briney loaded the gun with a live shell, but he claimed that he did not intend to injure anyone.

Katko (plaintiff) and a friend, McDonough, had broken into the abandoned farmhouse on an earlier occasion to steal old bottles and fruit jars for their antique collection. They returned for a second time after the spring gun had been set, and Katko was seriously wounded in the leg when the gun discharged as he entered the bedroom. He then brought this action for damages. Decision?

18. Plaintiff, John W. Carson, was the host and star of "The Tonight Show," a well-known television program broadcast by the National Broadcasting Company. Carson also appears as an entertainer in nightclubs and theaters around the country. From the time he began hosting "The Tonight Show" in 1962, he had been introduced on the show each night with the phrase "Here's Johnny." The phrase "Here's Johnny" is still generally associated with Carson by a substantial segment of the television viewing public. In 1967, to earn additional income, Carson began authorizing use of this phrase by outside business ventures.

Defendant, Here's Johnny Portable Toilets, Inc., is a Michigan corporation engaged in the business of renting and selling "Here's Johnny" portable toilets. Defendant's founder was aware at the time he formed the corporation that "Here's Johnny" was the introductory slogan for Carson on "The Tonight Show." He indicated that he coupled the phrase with a second one, "The World's Foremost Commodian," to make "a good play on a phrase." Carson brought suit for invasion of privacy. Should Carson recover? If so, for which tort?

19. Susan Jungclaus Peterson was a twenty-one-year-old student at Moorhead State University who had lived most of her life on her family farm in Minnesota. Though Susan was a dean's list student during her first year, her academic performance declined after she became deeply involved in an international religious cult organization known locally as The Way of Minnesota, Inc. The cult demanded an enormous psychological and monetary commitment from Susan. Near the end of her junior year, her parents became alarmed by the changes in Susan's physical and mental well-being and concluded that she had been "reduced to a condition of psychological bondage by The Way." They sought help from Kathy Mills, a self-styled "deprogrammer" of minds brainwashed by cults.

On May 24, 1976, Norman Jungclaus, Susan's father, picked up Susan at Moorhead State. Instead of returning home, they went to the residence of Veronica Morgel, where Kathy Mills attempted to deprogram Susan. For the first few days of her stay, Susan was unwilling to discuss her involvement. She lay curled in a fetal position in her bedroom, plugging her ears and hysterically screaming and crying while her father pleaded with her to listen. By the third day, however, Susan's demeanor changed completely. She became friendly and vivacious and communicated with her father. Susan also went roller skating and played softball at a nearby park over the following weekend. She spent the next week in Columbus, Ohio, with a former cult member who had shared her experiences of the previous week. While in Columbus, she spoke daily by telephone with her fiancé, a member of The Way, who begged her to return to the cult. Susan expressed the desire to get her fiancé out of the organization, but a meeting between them could not be arranged outside the presence of other members of The Way. Her parents attempted to persuade Susan to sign an agreement releasing them from liability for their actions, but Susan refused. After nearly sixteen days of "deprogramming" Susan left the Morgel residence and returned to her fiancé and The Way. Upon the direction of The Way ministry, she brought this action against her parents for false imprisonment. Will Susan prevail? Explain.

20. Debra Agis was a waitress in a restaurant owned by the Howard Johnson Company. On May 23, 1975, Roger Dionne, manager of the restaurant, called a meeting of all waitresses at which he informed them that "there was some stealing going on." Dionne also stated that the identity of the party or parties responsible was not known and that he would begin firing all waitresses in alphabetical order until the guilty party or parties were detected. He then fired Debra Agis, who allegedly "became greatly upset, began to cry, sustained emotional distress, mental anguish, and loss of wages and earnings." Mrs. Agis brought this complaint against the Howard Johnson Company and Roger Dionne, alleging that the defendants acted recklessly and outrageously, intending to cause emotional distress and anguish. The defendants argued that damages for emotional distress are not recoverable unless physical injury occurs as a result of the distress. Will Agis be successful on her complaint?

| http: | **Internet Exercise** Find information about punitive damages and review the proposed Model Punitive Damages Act. |

Negligence and Strict Liability

Whereas intentional torts deal with conduct that has a substantial certainty of causing harm, negligence involves conduct that creates an unreasonable risk of harm. The basis of liability for negligence is the failure to exercise reasonable care, under given circumstances, for the safety of another person or his property, which failure proximately causes injury to such person or damage to his property, or both. Thus, if the driver of an automobile intentionally runs down a person, she has committed the intentional tort of battery. If, on the other hand, the driver hits and injures a person while driving without reasonable regard for the safety of others, she is negligent.

Strict liability is not based upon the negligence or intent of the defendant but rather upon the nature of the activity in which he is engaging. Under this doctrine, defendants who engage in certain activities, such as keeping animals or maintaining abnormally dangerous conditions, are held liable for the injuries they cause, even if they have exercised the utmost care. The law imposes this liability to effect a just reallocation of loss, given that the defendant engaged in the activity for his own benefit and is in a better position to manage, by insurance or otherwise, the risk inherent in the activity.

Negligence

The Restatement defines negligence as "conduct which falls below the standard established by law for the protection of others against unreasonable risk of harm." Restatement, Section 282. The standard established by law is the conduct of a reasonable person acting prudently and with due care under the circumstances. The general rule is that a person is under a duty to all others at all times to exercise reasonable care for the safety of the others' person and property. This rule is subject to certain exceptions, however, which are discussed next.

Except when strict liability applies, a person is not liable for injury caused to another by an unavoidable accident—an unintended occurrence that the exercise of reasonable care could not have prevented. Thus, no liability results from the loss of control of an automobile because the driver suddenly and unforeseeably suffers a heart attack, stroke, or fainting spell. If, however, the driver had warning of the imminent heart attack or other infirmity, it would be negligent for him to drive at all.

An action for negligence consists of three elements, each of which the plaintiff must prove:

1. **Breach of duty of care:** that a legal duty required the defendant to conform to the standard of conduct established for the protection of others, and that the defendant failed to conform to that standard;

2. **Proximate cause:** that the defendant's failure to conform to the required standard of conduct proximately caused the injury and harm the plaintiff sustained; and
3. **Injury:** that the injury and harm is of a type protected against negligent interference, or conduct.

BREACH OF DUTY OF CARE

Negligence consists of conduct that creates an unreasonable risk of harm. In determining whether a given risk of harm was unreasonable, the law considers the following factors: (1) the probability that the harm will occur, (2) the gravity or seriousness of the resulting harm, (3) the social utility of the conduct creating the risk, and (4) the cost of taking precautions that would have reduced the risk. Thus, the standard of conduct, which is the basis for the law of negligence, is usually determined by a cost-benefit analysis.

Reasonable Person Standard

The duty of care imposed by law is measured by the degree of carefulness that a reasonable person would exercise in a given situation. The reasonable person is a fictitious individual who is always careful and prudent and never negligent. What the judge or jury determines a reasonable person would have done in light of the facts disclosed by the evidence in a particular case sets the standard of conduct for that case. The reasonable person standard is thus external and *objective*, as described by Justice Holmes:

> If, for instance, a man is born hasty and awkward, is always hurting himself or his neighbors, no doubt his congenital defects will be allowed for in the courts of Heaven, but his slips are no less troublesome to his neighbors than if they sprang from guilty neglect. His neighbors accordingly require him, at his peril, to come up to their standard, and the courts which they establish decline to take his personal equation into account. Holmes, *The Common Law.*

Children The standard of conduct to which a child must conform to avoid being negligent is that of a reasonable person of like age, intelligence, and experience under like circumstances. Restatement, Section 283A. For example, Alice, a five-year-old girl, was walking with her father on the crowded sidewalk along Main Street when he told her that he was going to take her to Disney World for her birthday next week. Upon hearing the news, Alice became so excited that she began to jump up and down and run around. During this fit of exuberance, Alice accidentally ran into and knocked down an elderly woman who was passing by. Alice's liability, if any, would be determined by whether a reasonable five-year-old person of like age, intelligence, and experience under like circumstances would have the capacity and judgment to understand the increased risk her enthusiastic display of joy caused to others.

The law applies an individualized test because children do not possess the judgment, intelligence, knowledge, and experience of adults. Moreover, children as a general rule do not engage in activities entailing high risk to others, and their conduct normally does not involve a potential for harm as great as that of adult conduct. A child who engages in an adult activity, however, such as flying an airplane or driving a boat or car, is held in about half the states to the standard of care applicable to adults. Finally, some states modify this individualized test by holding that under a minimum age, most commonly the age of seven, a child is incapable of committing a negligent act.

Physical Disability If a person is ill or otherwise physically disabled, the standard of conduct to which he must conform to avoid being negligent is that of a reasonable person having a like disability. Thus, a blind man must act as a reasonable man who is blind, and a woman with multiple sclerosis must act as a reasonable woman with multiple sclerosis.

Mental Deficiency The law does not allow for the insanity, voluntary intoxication, or other mental deficiency (in terms, for example, of intelligence, judgment, memory, or emotional stability) of the defendant in a negligence case; rather, the defendant is held to the standard of conduct of a reasonable person who is *not* insane, intoxicated, or mentally deficient, even though the defendant is, in fact, incapable of conforming to the standard. Thus, an adult with the mental acumen of a six-year-old will be held liable for his negligent conduct if he fails to act as carefully as a reasonable adult of normal intelligence. In this case the law may demand more of the individual than his mental limitations permit him to accomplish.

Superior Skill or Knowledge Persons who are qualified and who practice a profession or trade that calls for special skill and expertise are required to exercise that care and skill which members in good standing of their profession or trade normally possess. This standard applies to such professionals as physicians, surgeons, dentists, attorneys, pharmacists, architects, accountants, and engineers and to those who perform skilled trades, such as airline pilots, electricians, carpenters, and plumbers. A member of a profession or skilled trade who possesses greater skill than that common to the profession or trade is required to exercise that skill.

Emergencies An emergency is a sudden and unexpected event that calls for immediate action and permits no time for deliberation. In determining whether a defendant's conduct is reasonable, the law takes into consideration the fact that he was at the time confronted with a sudden emergency. Restatement, Section 296. The standard is still that of a reasonable person under the circumstances—the emergency is simply part of the circumstances. If, however, the defendant's own negligent or tortious conduct created the emergency, he is liable for the consequences of this conduct even if he acted reasonably in the resulting emergency situation.

Violation of Statute The reasonable person standard of conduct may be established by legislation. Restatement, Section

285. Some statutes expressly impose civil liability upon violators. Absent such a provision, courts may adopt the requirements of the statute as the standard of conduct if the statute is intended to protect a class of persons, which includes the plaintiff, against the particular hazard and kind of harm that resulted.

If the statute is found to be applicable, the majority of the courts hold that an unexcused violation is **negligence** *per se*; that is, the violation conclusively constitutes negligent conduct. In a minority of states, the violation is considered merely to be evidence of negligence. In either event, the plaintiff must also prove legal causation and injury.

For example, a statute enacted to protect employees from injuries requires that all factory elevators be equipped with specified safety devices. Arthur, an employee in Freya's factory, and Carlos, a business visitor to the factory, are injured when the elevator falls because the safety devices have not been installed. The court may adopt the statute as a standard of conduct as to Arthur and hold Freya negligent *per se* to Arthur, but not as to Carlos, because Arthur, not Carlos, is within the class of persons the statute is intended to protect. Carlos would have to establish that a reasonable person in the position of Freya under the circumstances would have installed the safety device.

On the other hand, compliance with a legislative enactment or administrative regulation does not prevent a finding of negligence if a reasonable person would have taken additional precautions. Restatement, Section 288C. For instance, driving at the speed limit may not constitute due care when traffic or road conditions require a lower speed. Legislative or administrative rules normally establish *minimum* standards.

◆ SEE FIGURE 17-1 Negligence and Negligence *Per Se*

◊ SEE CASE 17-1

Duty to Act

Except in special circumstances, no one is required to aid another in peril. As Prosser has stated, "The law has persistently refused to recognize the moral obligation of common decency and common humanity, to come to the aid of another human being who is in danger, even though the outcome is to cost him his life." For example, Toni, an adult standing at the edge of a steep cliff, observes a baby carriage with a crying infant in it slowly rolling toward the edge and certain doom. Toni could easily prevent the baby's fall at no risk to her own

◆ FIGURE 17-1   Negligence and Negligence *Per Se*

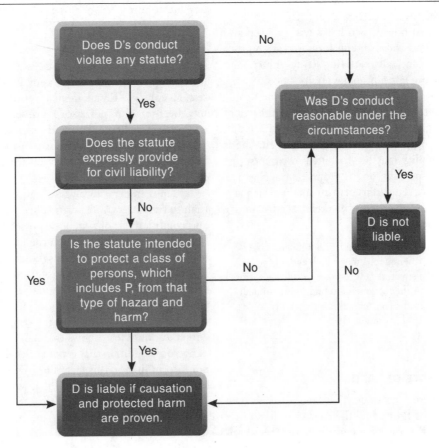

safety. Nonetheless, Toni does nothing, and the baby falls to his death. Toni is under no legal duty to act and, therefore, incurs no liability for failing to do so.

Section 314 of the Restatement reflects this position: "The fact that the actor realizes or should realize that action on his part is necessary for another's aid or protection does not of itself impose upon him a duty to take such action." Nonetheless, special relations between the parties may impose a duty upon the defendant to aid or protect the other. Thus, if in the example above, Toni were the baby's mother or baby-sitter, Toni would be under a duty to act and would therefore be liable for not taking action. The special relations giving rise to the duty to aid or protect another include common carrier-passenger, innkeeper–guest, employer–employee, store owner-customer, and parent–child. Restatement, Sections 314A and 314B.

The law also imposes a duty of affirmative action upon those whose conduct, whether tortious or innocent, has injured another and left him helpless and in danger of further harm. For example, Dale drives her car into Bob, rendering him unconscious. Dale leaves Bob lying in the middle of the road, where he is run over by a second car driven by Chen. Dale is liable to Bob for the additional injuries inflicted by Chen. Moreover, a person voluntarily coming to the assistance of another in need of aid incurs a duty to exercise care. In such an instance, the actor is liable if his failure to exercise reasonable care increases the risk of harm, causes harm, or leaves the other in a worse position. For example, Ann finds Ben drunk and stumbling along a dark sidewalk. Ann leads Ben halfway up a steep and unguarded stairway, where she abandons him. Ben attempts to climb the stairs but trips and falls, suffering serious injury. Ann is liable to Ben for having left him in a worse position.

A parent is not liable for the torts of his minor child simply because of the parental relationship. Where, however, the parent authorizes, encourages, or participates in the tort of his child, or ratifies it by knowingly participating in its benefits, he is liable. So, also, tort liability may be attributed to parents, just as it may be to all other persons, on the grounds of negligence, as where a parent places a dangerous instrumentality, such as a gun or knife, in the hands of a child, who thereby causes injury to another. For example,

> A is informed that his six-year-old child is shooting at a target in the street with a .22 rifle, in a manner which endangers the safety of those using the street. A fails to take the rifle away from the child, or to take any other action. The child unintentionally shoots B, a pedestrian, in the leg. A is subject to liability to B. Restatement, Section 316, Illustration 1.

◆ SEE CASE 17-1

Duties of Possessors of Land

The right of possessors of land to use that land for their own benefit and enjoyment is limited by their duty to do so in a reasonable manner; that is, by the use of their land, they can- not cause unreasonable risks of harm to others. Liability for breach of this obligation may arise from conduct in any of the three areas of torts discussed in this and the preceding chapter: intentional harm, negligence, or strict liability. Most of these cases fall within the classification of negligence.

In conducting activities on her land, the possessor of land is required to exercise reasonable care to protect others who are not on her property. For example, a property owner who constructs a factory on her premises must take reasonable care that it is not unreasonably dangerous to people off the site.

The duty of a possessor of land to persons who come upon the land depends on whether those persons are trespassers, licensees, or invitees. A few states have abandoned these distinctions, however, and simply apply ordinary negligence principles of foreseeable risk and reasonable care.

Duty to Trespassers A trespasser is a person who enters or remains on the land of another without permission or privilege to do so. The lawful possessor of the land is not liable to adult trespassers for her failure to maintain the land in a reasonably safe condition. Nonetheless, trespassers are not criminals, and the lawful possessor is not free to inflict intentional injury on them. Moreover, most courts hold that upon discovering the presence of trespassers on her land, the lawful possessor is required to exercise reasonable care for their safety in carrying on her activities and to warn the trespassers of potentially highly dangerous conditions that the trespassers are not likely to discover.

Duty to Licensees A licensee is a person who is privileged to enter or remain upon land only by virtue of the lawful possessor's consent. Restatement, Section 330. Licensees include members of the possessor's household, social guests, and salespersons calling at private homes. A licensee will become a trespasser, however, if he enters a portion of the land to which he is not invited or remains upon the land after his invitation has expired.

The possessor, who owes a higher duty of care to licensees than to trespassers, must warn a licensee of dangerous activities and conditions (1) of which the possessor has knowledge or has reason to know and (2) which the licensee does not and is not likely to discover. A licensee who is not warned may recover if the activity or dangerous condition resulted from the possessor's failure to exercise reasonable care to protect him from the danger. Restatement, Section 342. To illustrate: Jose invites a friend, Julia, to his place in the country at eight o'clock on a winter evening. Jose knows that a bridge in his driveway is in a dangerous condition that is not noticeable in the dark. Jose does not inform Julia of this fact. The bridge gives way under Julia's car, causing serious harm to Julia. Jose is liable to Julia.

Some states have extended to licensees the same protection traditionally accorded invitees. A number of states have included social guests in the invitee category.

Duty to Invitees An invitee is either a public invitee or a business visitor. Restatement, Section 332. A **public invitee** is a person invited to enter or remain on land as a member of the public for a purpose for which the land is held open to the public. Such invitees include those who use public parks, beaches, or swimming pools, as well as those who use governmental facilities, such as a post office or office of the Recorder of Deeds, where business with the public is transacted openly. A **business visitor** is a person invited to enter or remain on the premises for a purpose directly or indirectly concerning business dealings with the possessor of the land, such as one who enters a store or a tradesperson who enters a residence to make repairs.

With respect to the condition of the premises, the possessor of land is under a duty to exercise reasonable care to protect invitees against dangerous conditions they are unlikely to discover. This liability extends not only to those conditions of which the possessor knows but also to those she would discover by the exercise of reasonable care. Restatement, Section 343. For example, at the front of Tilson's supermarket is a large, glass front door that is well lit and plainly visible. Johnson, a customer, nonetheless mistakes the glass for an open doorway and walks into it, injuring himself. Tilson is not liable to Johnson. If, on the other hand, the glass was difficult to see and a person might foreseeably mistake the glass for an open doorway, then Tilson would be liable to Johnson if Johnson crashed into the glass while exercising reasonable care.

◆ SEE FIGURE 17-2 Duties of Possessors of Land

◈ SEE CASE 17-2

Res Ipsa Loquitur

A rule has developed that permits the jury to infer both negligent conduct and causation from the mere occurrence of certain types of events. This rule, called *res ipsa loquitur,* meaning "the thing speaks for itself," applies when the event is of a kind that ordinarily would not occur in the absence of negligence and the evidence sufficiently eliminates other possible causes. Section 328D of the Restatement provides as follows:

> (1) It may be inferred that harm suffered by the plaintiff is caused by negligence of the defendant when
> (a) the event is of a kind which ordinarily does not occur in the absence of negligence;
> (b) other responsible causes, including the conduct of the plaintiff and third persons, are sufficiently eliminated by the evidence; and
> (c) the indicated negligence is within the scope of the defendant's duty to the plaintiff.

For example, Abrams rents a room in Brown's motel. During the night a large piece of plaster falls from the ceiling and injures Abrams. In the absence of other evidence, the jury may infer that the harm resulted from Brown's negligence in permitting the plaster to become defective. Brown is permitted, however, to introduce evidence to contradict the inference of negligence.

PROXIMATE CAUSE

Liability for the negligent conduct of a defendant requires not only that the conduct in fact caused injury to the plaintiff, but also that it was the proximate cause of the injury. Most simply expressed, proximate cause consists of the judicial limitations imposed upon a person's liability for the consequences of his or her negligence. As a matter of social policy, legal responsibility has not been permitted to follow all the consequences of a negligent act. Responsibility has been limited—to a greater extent than with intentional torts—to those persons and results that are closely connected with the negligent conduct. Moreover,

◆ FIGURE 17-2 Duties of Possessors of Land

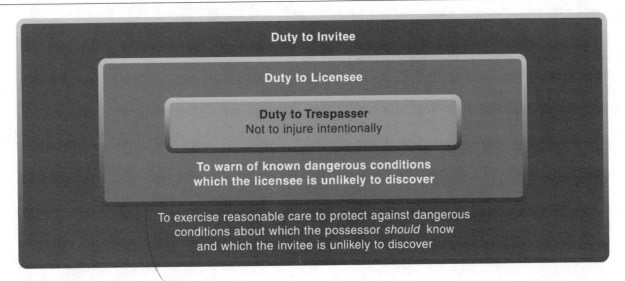

in strict liability cases the courts impose a narrower rule of proximate cause than they do in negligence cases.

Causation in Fact

To support a finding that the defendant's negligence was the proximate cause of the plaintiff's injury, it is first necessary that the defendant's conduct was the cause in fact (that is, the *actual cause*) of the injury. A widely applied test for causation in fact is the **but for rule**: A person's conduct is a cause of an event if the event would not have occurred *but for* the person's negligent conduct. Under this test, an act or omission to act is *not* a cause of an event if that event would have occurred regardless of the act or omission. For instance, Arnold fails to erect a barrier around an excavation. Doyle is driving a truck when its accelerator becomes stuck, and he and the truck plummet into the excavation. Arnold's negligence is not a cause in fact of Doyle's death if the runaway truck would have crashed through the barrier that Arnold could have erected. Similarly, the failure to install a proper fire escape on a hotel is not the cause in fact of the death of a person who is suffocated by smoke while sleeping in bed during a hotel fire.

The but for rule, however, is not useful where two or more forces, each of which is sufficient to bring about the harm in question, are active. For example, Wilson and Hart negligently set fires that combine to destroy Kennedy's property. Either fire would have destroyed the property. Under the but for rule, either Wilson or Hart, or both, could argue that the fire caused by the other would have destroyed the property and that he, therefore, is not liable. The **substantial factor** test addresses this problem by stating that negligent conduct is a legal cause of harm to another if the conduct is a substantial factor in bringing about the harm. Restatement, Section 431. Under this test the conduct of both Wilson and Hart would be found to be a cause in fact of the destruction of Kennedy's property.

Limitations on Causation in Fact

As a matter of policy, the law imposes limitations on the causal connection between the defendant's negligence and the plaintiff's injury. Two of the principal factors that are taken into consideration in determining such limitations are (1) unforeseeable consequences and (2) superseding cause.

Unforeseeable Consequences Determining the liability of a negligent defendant for unforeseeable consequences has proved to be troublesome and controversial. The Restate-ment and a majority of the courts have adopted the following position:

1. If the actor's conduct is a substantial factor in bringing about harm to another, the fact that the actor neither foresaw nor should have foreseen the extent of the harm or the manner in which it occurred does not prevent him from being liable.

2. The actor's conduct may be held not to be a legal cause of harm to another where after the event and looking back from the harm to the actor's negligent conduct, it appears to the court highly extraordinary that it should have brought about the harm. Section 435.

Even if the defendant's negligent conduct is a cause in fact of harm to the plaintiff, the conduct is not a proximate cause unless the defendant reasonably could have anticipated injuring the plaintiff or a class of persons to which the plaintiff belongs. Restatement, Section 281, Comment c. Proximate cause involves recognizing the risk of harm to the plaintiff individually or to a class of persons of which the plaintiff is a member.

For example, Albert, while negligently driving an automobile, collides with a car carrying dynamite. Albert is unaware of the contents of the other car and has no reason to know about them. The collision causes the dynamite to explode, shattering glass in a building a block away. The shattered glass injures Betsy, who is inside the building. The explosion also injures Calvin, who is walking on the sidewalk near the collision. Albert would be liable to Calvin because Albert should have realized that his negligent driving might result in a collision that would endanger pedestrians nearby, and the fact that the actual harm resulted in an unforeseeable manner does not affect his liability. Betsy, however, was beyond the zone of danger, and Albert, accordingly, is not liable to Betsy. Albert's negligent driving is not deemed to be the "proximate cause" of Betsy's injury because, looking from the harm back to Albert's negligence, it appears highly extraordinary that Albert's conduct should have brought about the harm to Betsy.

◆ SEE FIGURE 17-3 Proximate Cause

◆ SEE CASE 17-3

Intervening and Superseding Causes An intervening cause is an event or act that occurs after the defendant's negligent conduct and, together with the defendant's negligence, causes the plaintiff's harm. If the intervening cause is deemed a superseding cause, then it relieves the defendant of liability for harm to the plaintiff caused in fact by both the defendant's negligence and the intervening event or act. For example, Adams negligently leaves in a public sidewalk an excavation without a fence or warning lights, into which Bogues falls at night. Darkness is an intervening, but not a superseding, cause of harm to Bogues because it is a normal consequence of the situation caused by Adams's negligence. Therefore, Adams is liable to Bogues. In contrast, if Adams negligently leaves an excavation in a public sidewalk into which Carson intentionally hurls Bogues, Adams is not liable to Bogues because Carson's conduct is a superseding cause that relieves Adams of liability.

◆ FIGURE 17-3   Proximate Cause

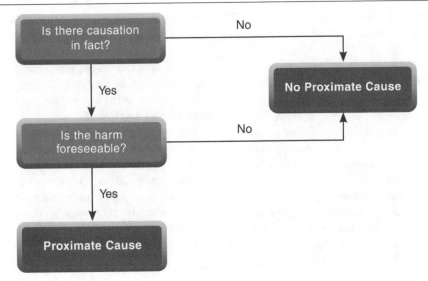

An intervening cause that is a foreseeable or normal consequence of the defendant's negligence is not a superseding cause. Thus, a person who negligently places another in imminent danger is liable for the injury sustained by a third-party rescuer who attempts to aid the imperiled victim. The same is true of attempts by the endangered person to escape the peril, as, for example, when a person swerves off the road to avoid a head-on collision with an automobile driven negligently on the wrong side of the road. It is commonly held that a negligent defendant is liable for the results of necessary medical treatment of the injured party, even if the treatment itself is negligent.

INJURY

The plaintiff must prove that the defendant's negligent conduct proximately caused harm to a legally protected interest. Certain interests receive little or no protection against such conduct, while others receive full protection. The courts determine the extent of protection for a particular interest as a matter of law on the basis of social policy and expediency. For example, negligent conduct that is the proximate cause of harmful contact with the person of another is actionable. Thus, if Bob negligently runs into Julie, a pedestrian, who is carefully crossing the street, Bob is liable for physical injuries Julie sustains as a result of the collision. On the other hand, if Bob's careless conduct causes only offensive contact with Julie's person, Bob is not liable because Julie did not sustain harm to a legally protected interest.

The courts traditionally have been reluctant to allow recovery for negligently inflicted emotional distress. Nevertheless, this view has changed gradually during this century, and the majority of courts now hold a person liable for negligently causing emotional distress if bodily harm—such as a heart attack—

results from the distress. Restatement, Section 436. In the great majority of states, a defendant is not liable for negligent conduct resulting solely in emotional disturbance. Restatement, Section 436A. A few courts, however, have recently allowed recovery of damages for negligently inflicted emotional distress even in the absence of resultant physical harm.

Most courts do not award damages for mental distress suffered by those who have witnessed injury to a closely related person caused by the negligence of another. A number of courts, however, recently have done so.

DEFENSES TO NEGLIGENCE

A plaintiff who has established by the preponderance of the evidence all the required elements of a negligence action may, nevertheless, be denied recovery if the defendant proves a valid defense. As a general rule, any defense to an intentional tort is also available in an action in negligence. In addition, contributory negligence, comparative negligence, and assumption of risk are three defenses available in negligence cases that are not defenses to intentional torts.

Contributory Negligence

The Restatement, Section 463, defines contributory negligence as "conduct on the part of the plaintiff which falls below the standard to which he should conform for his own protection, and which is a legally contributing cause co-operating with the negligence of the defendant in bringing about the plaintiff's harm." In those few states where it is still recognized, the contributory negligence of the plaintiff, whether slight or extensive, prevents him from recovering *any* damages from the defendant.

Notwithstanding the contributory negligence of the plaintiff, if the defendant had a **last clear chance** to avoid injury to the plaintiff but did not avail himself of such chance, the plaintiff's contributory negligence does not bar his recovery of damages. Restatement, Section 479.

Comparative Negligence

The harshness of the contributory negligence doctrine has caused all but a few states to reject its all-or-nothing rule and to substitute the doctrine of comparative negligence, which is also called comparative fault or comparative responsibility. (In states adopting comparative negligence, the doctrine of last clear chance has also been abandoned.) Approximately a dozen states have judicially or legislatively adopted "pure" comparative negligence systems. Under **pure comparative negligence**, the law apportions damages between the parties in proportion to the degree of fault or negligence found against them. For instance, Matthew negligently drives his automobile into Nancy, who is crossing against the light. Nancy sustains damages in the amount of $10,000 and sues Matthew. If the trier of fact determines that Matthew's negligence contributed 70 percent to Nancy's injury and that Nancy's contributory negligence contributed 30 percent to her injury, then Nancy would recover $7,000.

Most states have adopted the doctrine of "modified" comparative negligence. Under **modified comparative negligence** the plaintiff recovers as in pure comparative negligence unless her contributory negligence was "as great as" or "greater than" that of the defendant, in which case the plaintiff recovers nothing. Thus, in the example above, if the trier of fact determined that Matthew's negligence contributed 40 percent to Nancy's injury and Nancy's contributory negligence contributed 60 percent, then Nancy would recover nothing from Matthew.

Assumption of Risk

A plaintiff who has *voluntarily* and *knowingly* assumed the risk of harm arising from the negligent or reckless conduct of the defendant cannot recover from such harm. Restatement, Section 496A. In **express** assumption of the risk, the plaintiff expressly agrees to assume the risk of harm from the defendant's conduct. Usually, but not always, such an agreement is by contract. Courts usually construe these exculpatory contracts strictly and will hold that the plaintiff has assumed the risk only if the terms of the agreement are clear and unequivocal. Moreover, some contracts for assumption of risk are considered unenforceable as a matter of public policy. See Chapter 14.

In **implied** assumption of the risk, the plaintiff voluntarily proceeds to encounter a known danger. Thus, a spectator entering a baseball park may be regarded as consenting that the players may proceed with the game without taking precautions to protect him from being hit by the ball. Most states have abolished or modified the defense of implied assumption of risk. Some have abandoned it entirely while others have merged implied assumption of risk into their comparative negligence systems.

The American Law Institute recently adopted The Third Restatement of Torts: Apportionment Liability. Reflecting this general trend, the new Restatement has abandoned the doctrine of implied voluntary assumption of risk: it is no longer a defense that the plaintiff was aware of a risk and voluntarily confronted it. But if a plaintiff's conduct in the face of a known risk is unreasonable, it might constitute contributory negligence, thereby reducing the plaintiff's recovery under comparative negligence. The new Restatement limits the defense of assumption of risk to express assumption of risk, which consists of a contract between the plaintiff and another person to absolve the other person from liability for future harm. Section 2. Contractual assumption of risk may occur by written agreement, express oral agreement, or conduct that creates an implied-in-fact contract, as determined by the applicable rules of contract law. Some contractual assumptions of risk, however, are not enforceable under other areas of substantive law or as against public policy.

◆ **SEE FIGURE 17-4** Defenses to a Negligence Action

◈ **SEE CASE 17-4**

Strict Liability

In some instances, people may be held liable for injuries they have caused even though they have not acted intentionally or negligently. Such liability is called strict liability, absolute liability, or liability without fault. The law has determined that because certain types of otherwise socially desirable activities pose sufficiently high risks of harm regardless of how carefully they are conducted, those who perform these activities should bear the cost of any harm they cause. The doctrine of strict liability is not predicated upon any particular fault of the defendant, but rather upon the nature of the activity in which he is engaging.

ACTIVITIES GIVING RISE TO STRICT LIABILITY

The following activities giving rise to strict liability will be discussed in this section: (1) activities that are, in themselves, abnormally dangerous, (2) the keeping of animals, and (3) selling defective, unreasonably dangerous products. In addition, strict liability is imposed upon other activities. All states have enacted workers' compensation statutes that make employers liable to employees for injuries arising out of the course of employment. Because the law imposes this liability without regard to the employer's negligence, it is a form of strict liability. Moreover, the liability imposed upon an employer for torts that employees commit in the scope of their employment is a type

◆ FIGURE 17-4   Defenses to a Negligence Action

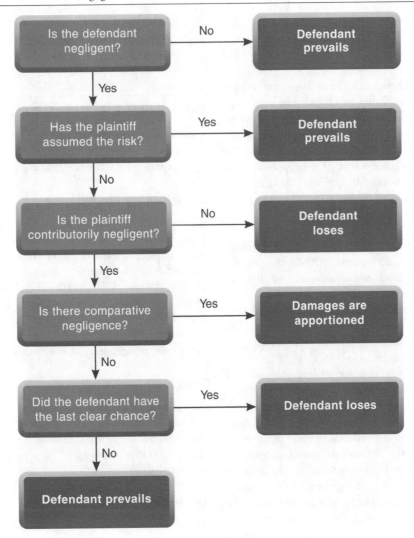

of strict liability. Additional instances of strict liability include carriers and innkeepers, innocent misrepresentation (Chapter 8), and some violations of the securities laws.

Abnormally Dangerous Activities

The law imposes strict liability for harm resulting from extraordinary, unusual, abnormal, or exceptional activities, as determined in light of the place, time, and manner in which the activity was conducted. An **abnormally dangerous activity** is one that (1) necessarily involves a high risk of serious harm to the person and/or chattels of others, which risk the exercise of reasonable care cannot eliminate, *and* (2) is not a matter of common usage. Activities to which the rule has been applied include collecting water in such quantity and location as to

make it dangerous; storing explosives or flammable liquids in large quantities; blasting or pile driving; crop dusting; drilling for or refining oil in populated areas; and emitting noxious gases or fumes into a settled community. On the other hand, courts have refused to apply the rule where the activity is a "natural" use of the land, such as drilling for oil in the oil fields of Texas, collecting water in a stock watering tank, or transmitting gas through a gas pipe or electricity through electric wiring.

◆ SEE CASE 17-5

Keeping of Animals

Strict liability for harm caused by animals existed at common law and continues today with some modification. As a general rule, those who possess animals for their own purposes do so at their peril and must protect against the harm those animals may cause to people and property.

Trespassing Animals Keepers of animals are generally held strictly liable for any damage their animals cause by trespassing on the property of another. There are three exceptions to this rule: (1) keepers of cats and dogs are liable only for negligence, except where a statute or ordinance has imposed strict liability; (2) keepers of animals are not strictly liable if those animals stray from a highway on which they are being lawfully driven, although the owner may be liable for negligence if he fails to properly control them; and (3) keepers of farm animals, typically cattle, in some western states are not strictly liable for harm caused by their trespassing animals that are allowed to graze freely.

Nontrespassing Animals Keepers of wild animals are strictly liable for harm caused by such animals, whether they are trespassing or not. **Wild animals** are defined as those that, in the particular region in which they are kept, are known to be likely to inflict serious damage and cannot be considered safe, no matter how domesticated they become. Animals included in this category are bears, lions, elephants, monkeys, tigers, wolves, zebras, deer, and raccoons.

Domestic animals are those that are traditionally devoted to the service of humankind and that as a class are considered safe. Examples of domestic animals are dogs, cats, horses, cattle, and sheep. Keepers of domestic animals are liable if they knew, or should have known, of an animal's dangerous propensity. Restatement, Section 509. The animal's dangerous propensity must be the cause of the harm. For example, merely because he knows that a dog has a propensity to fight with other dogs, a keeper is not liable when the dog bites a human. On the other hand, a person whose 150-pound sheepdog has a propensity to jump enthusiastically on visitors would be liable for any damage caused by the dog's playfulness.

Products Liability

A recent and important trend in the law is the imposition of a limited form of strict liability upon manufacturers and merchants who sell goods in a *defective condition* unreasonably dangerous to the user or consumer. Restatement, Section 402A. Such liability, imposed regardless of the seller's due care, applies to all merchant sellers. Nearly all states have adopted some version of strict products liability.

DEFENSES TO STRICT LIABILITY

This section will discuss the availability in a strict liability action of the following defenses: (1) contributory negligence, (2) comparative negligence, and (3) assumption of risk.

Contributory Negligence

Because the strict liability of one who carries on an abnormally dangerous activity, keeps animals, or sells products is not based on his negligence, the ordinary contributory negligence of the plaintiff is not a defense to such liability. In imposing strict liability, the law places on the defendant the full responsibility for preventing harm. For example, Adrian negligently fails to observe a sign on a highway warning of a blasting operation conducted by Benjamin. As a result, Adrian is injured by these operations; nonetheless, he may recover from Benjamin.

Comparative Negligence

Despite the rationale that disallows contributory negligence as a defense to strict liability, some states apply the doctrine of comparative negligence to some types of strict liability. Moreover, most states apply comparative negligence to strict products liability cases.

Assumption of Risk

Voluntary assumption of risk is a defense to an action based upon strict liability. If the owner of an automobile knowingly and voluntarily parks the vehicle in a blasting zone, he may not recover for harm to his automobile. The assumption of risk, however, must be voluntary. For example, the possessor of land located near a blasting operation is not required to move away; she may, in fact, recover for harm she suffers because of the operation.

CHAPTER SUMMARY

Negligence

Breach of Duty of Care	**Definition of Negligence** conduct that falls below the standard established by law for the protection of others against unreasonable risk of harm **Reasonable Person Standard** degree of care that a reasonable person would exercise in a given situation • *Children* must conform to conduct of a reasonable person of like age, intelligence, and experience

- *Physical Disability* a disabled person's conduct must conform to that of a reasonable person under like disability
- *Mental Deficiency* a mentally deficient person is held to the reasonable person standard
- *Superior Skill or Knowledge* professionals must exercise the same care and skill normally possessed by members of their professions
- *Emergencies* the reasonable person standard applies, but the emergency is considered part of the circumstances
- *Violation of Statute* if the statute applies, the violation is negligence *per se*

Duty to Act except in special circumstances, no one is required to aid another in peril

Duties of Possessors of Land

- *Duty to Trespassers* not to injure intentionally
- *Duty to Licensees* to warn of known dangerous conditions licensees are unlikely to discover for themselves
- *Duty to Invitees* to exercise reasonable care to protect invitees against dangerous conditions possessor should know of but invitees are unlikely to discover

Res Ipsa Loquitur permits the jury to infer both negligent conduct and causation

---

Proximate Cause

Causation in Fact the defendant's conduct was the actual cause of, or a substantial factor in causing, the injury

Limitations on Causation in Fact

- *Unforeseeable Consequences* no liability if defendant could not reasonably have anticipated injuring the plaintiff or a class of persons to which the plaintiff belongs
- *Superseding Cause* an intervening act that relieves the defendant of liability

---

Injury

Harm to Legally Protected Interest courts determine which interests are protected from negligent interference

Burden of Proof plaintiff must prove that defendant's negligent conduct caused harm to a legally protected interest

---

Defenses to Negligence

Contributory Negligence failure of a plaintiff to exercise reasonable care for his own protection, which in a few states prevents the plaintiff from recovering anything

Comparative Negligence damages are divided between the parties in proportion to their degree of negligence; applies in almost all states

Assumption of Risk plaintiff's express consent to encounter a known danger, some states still apply implied assumption of the risk

Strict Liability

Activities Giving Rise to Strict Liability

Definition of Strict Liability liability for nonintentional and nonnegligent conduct

Abnormally Dangerous Activities involve a high degree of serious harm and are not matters of common usage

Keeping of Animals strict liability is imposed for wild animals and usually for trespassing domestic animals

Products Liability imposed upon manufacturers and merchants who sell goods in a defective condition unreasonably dangerous to the user or consumer

Defenses to Strict Liability

Contributory Negligence is not a defense to strict liability
Comparative Negligence most states apply this doctrine to products liability cases
Assumption of Risk is a defense to an action based upon strict liability

---

CASES

CASE 17-1

In any negligence case, the plaintiff must prove duty and breach, proximate causation and damages. This case considers the question of whether a bartender had a duty to allow a person to use the establishment's telephone to call for aid of another.

SOLDANO v. O'DANIELS
California Court of Appeal, Fifth District, 1983
141 Cal.App.3d 443, 190 Cal.Rptr. 310

Andreen, J.

Does a business establishment incur liability for wrongful death if it denies use of its telephone to a good samaritan who explains an emergency situation occurring without and wishes to call the police?

This appeal follows a judgment of dismissal of the second cause of action of a complaint for wrongful death upon a motion for summary judgment. The motion was supported only by a declaration of defense counsel. Both briefs on appeal adopt the defense averments:

> This action arises out of a shooting death occurring on August 9, 1977. Plaintiff's father [Darrell Soldano] was shot and killed by one Rudolph Villanueva on that date at defendant's Happy Jack's Saloon. This defendant owns and operates the Circle Inn which is an eating establishment located across the street from Happy Jack's. Plaintiff's second cause of action against this defendant is one for negligence.

Plaintiff alleges that on the date of the shooting, a patron of Happy Jack's Saloon came into the Circle Inn and informed a Circle Inn employee that a man had been threatened at Happy Jack's. He requested the employee either call the police or allow him to use the Circle Inn phone to call the police. That employee allegedly refused to call the police and allegedly refused to allow the patron to use the phone to make his own call. Plaintiff alleges that the actions of the Circle Inn employee were a breach of the legal duty that the Circle Inn owed to the decedent.

We were advised at oral argument that the employee was the defendant's bartender. The state of the record is unsatisfactory in that it does not disclose the physical location of the telephone—whether on the bar, in a private office behind a closed door or elsewhere. The only factual matter before the trial court was a verified statement of the defense attorney which set forth those facts quoted above. Following normal rules applicable to motions for summary judgment, we strictly construe the defense affidavit. [Citation.] Accordingly, we assume the telephone was not in a private office but in a position where it could be used by a patron without inconvenience to the defendant or his guests. We also assume the call was a local one and would not result in expense to defendant.

There is a distinction, well rooted in the common law, between action and nonaction. [Citation.] It has found its way into the prestigious Restatement Second of Torts (hereafter cited as "Restatement"), which provides in section 314:

> The fact that the actor realizes or should realize that action on his part is necessary for another's aid or protection does not of itself impose upon him a duty to take such action.

* * *

As noted in [citation], the courts have increased the instances in which affirmative duties are imposed not by direct rejection of the common law rule, but by expanding the list of special relationships which will justify departure from that rule. * * *

* * *

Section 314A of the Restatement lists other special relationships which create a duty to render aid, such as that of a common carrier to its passengers, an innkeeper to his guest, possessors of land who hold it open to the public, or one who has a custodial relationship to another. A duty may be created by an undertaking to give assistance. [Citation.]

Here there was no special relationship between the defendant and the deceased. It would be stretching the concept beyond recognition to assert there was a relationship between the defendant and the patron from Happy Jack's Saloon who wished to summon aid. But this does not end the matter.

It is time to re-examine the common law rule of nonliability for nonfeasance in the special circumstances of the instant case.

* * *

We turn now to the concept of duty in a tort case. The [California] Supreme Court has identified certain factors to be considered in determining whether a duty is owed to third persons. These factors include:

> the foreseeability of harm to the plaintiff, the degree of certainty that the plaintiff suffered injury, the closeness of the connection between the defendant's conduct and the injury suffered, the moral blame attached to the defendant's conduct, the policy of preventing future harm, the extent of the burden to the defendant and consequences to the community of imposing a duty to exercise care with resulting liability for breach, and the availability, cost, and prevalence of insurance for the risk involved. [Citation.]

We examine those factors in reference to this case. (1) The harm to the decedent was abundantly foreseeable; it was imminent. The employee was expressly told that a man had been threatened. The employee was a bartender. As such he knew it is foreseeable that some people who drink alcohol in the milieu of a bar setting are prone to violence. (2) The certainty of decedent's injury is undisputed. (3) There is arguably a close connection between the employee's conduct and the injury: the patron wanted to use the phone to summon the police to intervene. The employee's refusal to allow the use of the phone prevented this anticipated intervention. If permitted to go to trial, the plaintiff may be able to show that the probable response time of the police would have been shorter than the time between the prohibited telephone call and the fatal shot. (4) The employee's conduct displayed a disregard for human life that can be characterized as morally wrong: he was callously indifferent to the possibility that Darrell Soldano would die as the result of his refusal to allow a person to use the telephone. Under the circumstances before us the bartender's burden was minimal and exposed him to no risk: all he had to do was allow the use of the telephone. It would have cost him or his employer nothing. It could have

saved a life. (5) Finding a duty in these circumstances would promote a policy of preventing future harm. A citizen would not be required to summon the police but would be required, in circumstances such as those before us, not to impede another who has chosen to summon aid. (6) We have no information on the question of the availability, cost, and prevalence of insurance for the risk, but note that the liability which is sought to be imposed here is that of employee negligence, which is covered by many insurance policies. (7) The extent of the burden on the defendant was minimal, as noted.

* * *

We acknowledge that defendant contracted for the use of his telephone, and its use is a species of property. But if it exists in a public place as defined above, there is no privacy or ownership interest in it such that the owner should be permitted to interfere with a good faith attempt to use it by a third person to come to the aid of another.

* * *

We conclude that the bartender owed a duty to the plaintiff's decedent to permit the patron from Happy Jack's to place a call to the police or to place the call himself.

It bears emphasizing that the duty in this case does not require that one must go to the aid of another. That is not the issue here. The employee was not the good samaritan intent on aiding another. The patron was.

* * *

We conclude there are sufficient justiciable issues to permit the case to go to trial and therefore reverse.

The duty one owes to another person is often specific to the circumstances of a particular case. In this case, the duty a restaurant owner owes to a business visitor, such as a customer, is examined.

CASE 17-2

LOVE v. HARDEE'S FOOD SYSTEMS, INC.

Court of Appeals of Missouri, Eastern District, Division Two, 2000
16 S.W.3d 739 http://caselaw.lp.findlaw.com/scripts/
getcase.pl?court=mo&vol=/appeals/052000/&invol=5050200_2000

Crane, J.

At about 3:15 P.M. on November 15, 1995, plaintiff, Jason Love, and his mother, Billye Ann Love, went to the Hardee's Restaurant in Arnold, Missouri, which is owned by defendant, Hardee's Food Systems, Inc. There were no other customers in the restaurant between 3:00 P.M. and 4:00 P.M., but two or three workmen were in the back doing construction. The workmen reported that they did not use the restroom and did not see anyone use the restroom. After eating his lunch, plain-

tiff, who was wearing rubber-soled boot shoes, went to use the restroom. He opened the restroom door, took one step in, and, upon taking his second step, slipped on water on the restroom floor. Plaintiff fell backwards, hit his head, and felt a shooting pain down his right leg. He found himself lying in an area of dirty water, which soaked his clothes. There were no barricades, warning cones, or anything else that would either restrict access to the bathroom or warn of the danger.

Plaintiff crawled up to the sink to pull himself up and made his way back to the table and told his mother that his back and leg were "hurting pretty bad." His mother reported the fall to another employee. Plaintiff's mother went back to the men's restroom and looked at the water on the floor. She observed that the water was dirty. The restaurant supervisor came out and interviewed plaintiff and viewed the water in the restroom. * * *The supervisor then filled out an accident report form, which reported that the accident occurred at 3:50 P.M. The supervisor testified that the water appeared to have come from someone shaking his hands after washing them. The supervisor told plaintiff he could not recall the last time the restroom had been checked. Plaintiff was taken to a hospital emergency room. As a result of his injuries, plaintiff underwent two back surgeries, missed substantial time from work, and suffered from continuing pain and limitations on his physical activities.

Defendant had a policy requiring that the restroom was to be checked and cleaned every hour by a maintenance man. The maintenance man was scheduled to work until 3:00 P.M., but normally left at 1:00 P.M. The supervisor could not recall whether the maintenance man left at 1:00 P.M. or 3:00 P.M. on November 15. The time clock activity report would show when the maintenance man clocked out, but defendant was unable to produce the time clock report for November 15.

It was also a store policy that whenever employees cleaned the tables, they would check the restroom. The restrooms were used by customers and employees. If an employee had to use the restroom, then that employee was also supposed to check the restroom. The restaurant supervisor did not ask if any employees had been in the restroom, or if they had checked it in the hour prior to the accident, and did not know if the restroom was actually inspected or cleaned at 3:00 P.M.

The restaurant had shift inspection checklists on which the manager would report on the cleanliness of the restrooms and whether the floors were clean and dry. However, the checklists for November 15 were thrown away.* * *

Plaintiff subsequently filed the underlying lawsuit against defendant to recover damages for negligence. The jury returned a verdict in plaintiff's favor in the amount of $125,000. * * *

* * *[Defendant] argues that plaintiff failed to make a submissible case of negligence because plaintiff failed to prove that defendant had actual or constructive notice of the water on the restroom floor in that there was no evidence showing the source of the water or the length of time the water had been on the floor.

* * *

In order to have made a submissible case, plaintiff had to show that defendant knew or, by using ordinary care, could have known of the dangerous condition and failed to use ordinary care to remove it, barricade it, or warn of it, and plaintiff sustained damage as a direct result of such failure. [Citation.]

"In order to establish constructive notice, the condition must have existed for a sufficient length of time or the facts must be such that the defendant should have reasonably known of its presence." [Citation.] [Prior] cases* * *placed great emphasis on the length of time the dangerous condition had been present and held that times of 20 or 30 minutes, absent proof of other circumstances, were insufficient to establish constructive notice as a matter of law. [Citations.]

* * *

Defendant's liability is predicated on the foreseeability of the risk and the reasonableness of the care taken, which is a question of fact to be determined by the totality of the circumstances, including the nature of the restaurant's business and the method of its operation. [Citations.]

In this case the accident took place in the restaurant's restroom which is provided for the use of employees and customers. The cause of the accident was water, which is provided in the restroom. The restaurant owner could reasonably foresee that anyone using the restroom, customers or employees, would use the tap water provided in the restroom and could spill, drop, or splash water on the floor. Accordingly, the restaurant owner was under a duty to use due care to guard against danger from water on the floor.

There was substantial evidence to support submissibility. First, there was evidence from which the jury could infer that the water came from the use of the restroom. It was on the floor of the restroom and the supervisor testified it appeared that someone had shaken water from his hands on the floor.

Next, there was evidence from which the jury could infer that, if the water was caused by a non-employee, the water was on the floor for at least 50 minutes, or longer, because there was evidence that no other customers were in the store to use the restroom after 3:00 P.M. and the workmen on the site advised that they had not used the restroom.

In addition, plaintiff adduced evidence from which the jury could have found that defendants' employees had the opportunity to observe the hazard. The restroom was to be used by the employees and was supposed to be checked by them when they used it; employees cleaning tables were supposed to check the restroom when they cleaned the tables; and a maintenance man was supposed to check and clean the restroom every hour.

There was evidence from which the jury could have inferred that the maintenance man charged with cleaning the restroom every hour did not clean the restroom at 3:00 P.M. as scheduled on the day of the accident. There was testimony that the maintenance man usually left at 1:00 P.M. The supervisor could not recall what time the maintenance man left that day and defendant was unable to produce the time clock reports for that day which would have shown when the maintenance man clocked out. This could have created a span of 2 hours and 50 minutes during which there was no employee working at the restaurant whose primary responsibility was to clean the restroom. [Citation.]

There was also evidence from which the jury could have

inferred that the restroom was not inspected by any employee who had the responsibility to inspect it during that same time period. The supervisor testified that he could not recall the last time the restroom had been checked and did not ask any employees if they had been in the restroom or had checked it in the hour before the accident. * * *

* * *

The judgment of the trial court is affirmed.

CASE

17-3

In addition to showing that the tortfeasor engaged in neglect conduct (duty and breach), the victim of negligence must show that the breach was the proximate cause of harm to him. This case examines the issue of proximate cause in the context of an unforeseeable victim.

PALSGRAF v. LONG ISLAND RAILROAD CO.

Court of Appeals of New York, 1928
248 N.Y. 339, 162 N.E. 99

Cardozo, C. J.

Plaintiff was standing on a platform of defendant's railroad after buying a ticket to go to Rockaway Beach. A train stopped at the station, bound for another place. Two men ran forward to catch it. One of the men reached the platform of the car without mishap, though the train was already moving. The other man, carrying a package, jumped aboard the car, but seemed unsteady as if about to fall. A guard on the car, who had held the door open, reached forward to help him in, and another guard on the platform pushed him from behind. In this act, the package was dislodged, and fell upon the rails. It was a package of small size, about fifteen inches long, and was covered by a newspaper. In fact it contained fireworks, but there was nothing in its appearance to give notice of its contents. The fireworks when they fell exploded. The shock of the explosion threw down some scales at the other end of the platform many feet away. The scales struck the plaintiff, causing injuries for which she sues.

The conduct of the defendant's guard, if a wrong in its relation to the holder of the package, was not a wrong in its relation to the plaintiff, standing far away. Relatively to her it was not negligence at all. Nothing in the situation gave notice that the falling package had in it the potency of peril to persons thus removed. Negligence is not actionable unless it involves the invasion of a legally protected interest, the violation of a right. "Proof of negligence in the air, so to speak, will not do." [Citations.] "Negligence is the absence of care, according to the circumstances." [Citations.]

* * *

If no hazard was apparent to the eye of ordinary vigilance, an act innocent and harmless, at least to outward seeming, with reference to her, did not take to itself the quality of a tort because it happened to be a wrong, though apparently not one involving the risk of bodily insecurity, with reference to someone else. "In every instance, before negligence can be predicated of a given act, back of the act must be sought and found a duty to the individual complaining, the observance of which would have averted or avoided the injury." [Citations.]

* * *

A different conclusion will involve us, and swiftly too, in a maze of contradictions. A guard stumbles over a package which has been left upon a platform. It seems to be a bundle of newspapers. It turns out to be a can of dynamite. To the eye of ordinary vigilance, the bundle is abandoned waste, which may be kicked or trod on with impunity. Is a passenger at the other end of the platform protected by the law against the unsuspected hazard concealed beneath the waste? If not, is the result to be any different, so far as the distant passenger is concerned, when the guard stumbles over a valise which a truckman or a porter has left upon the walk? The passenger far away, if the victim of a wrong at all, has a cause of action, not derivative, but original and primary. His claim to be protected against invasion of his bodily security is neither greater nor less because the act resulting in the invasion is a wrong to another far removed. In this case, the rights that are said to have been violated, the interests said to have been invaded, are not even of the same order. The man was not injured in his person nor even put in danger. The purpose of the act, as well as its effect, was to make his person safe. If there was a wrong to him at all, which may very well be doubted, it was a wrong to a property interest only, the safety of his package. Out of this wrong to property, which threatened injury to nothing else, there has passed, we are told, to the plaintiff by derivation or succession a right of action for the invasion of an interest of another order, the right to bodily security. The diversity of interests emphasizes the futility of the effort to build the plaintiff's right upon the basis of a wrong to someone else.* * *One who jostles one's neighbor in a crowd does not invade the rights of others standing at the outer fringe when the unintended contact casts a bomb upon the ground. The wrongdoer as to them is the man who carries the bomb, not the one who explodes it without suspicion of the danger. Life will have to be made over, and human nature transformed, before prevision so extravagant can be accepted as the norm of conduct, the customary standard to which behavior must conform.

The argument for the plaintiff is built upon the shifting meanings of such words as "wrong" and "wrongful," and shares their instability. What the plaintiff must show is "a wrong" to herself, i. e., a violation of her own right, and not merely a wrong to someone else, nor conduct "wrongful" because unsocial, but not "a wrong" to any one. We are told that one who drives at reckless speed through a crowded city street is guilty of a negligent act and, therefore, of a wrongful one irrespective of the consequences. Negligent the act is, and wrongful in the sense that it is unsocial, but wrongful and unsocial in relation to other travelers, only because the eye of vigilance perceives the risk of damage. If the same act were to be committed on a speedway or a race course, it would lose its wrongful quality. The risk reasonably to be perceived defines the duty to be obeyed, and risk imports relation; it is risk to another or to others within the range of apprehension. This does not mean, of course, that one who launches a destructive force is always relieved of liability if the force, though known to be destructive, pursues an unexpected path. "It was not necessary that the defendant should have had notice of the particular method in which an accident would occur, if the possibility of an accident was clear to the ordinarily prudent eye." Some acts, such as

shooting, are so imminently dangerous to any one who may come within reach of the missile, however unexpectedly, as to impose a duty of prevision not far from that of an insurer. Even today, and much oftener in earlier stages of the law, one acts sometimes at one's peril. Under this head, it may be, fall certain cases of what is known as transferred intent, an act willfully dangerous to A resulting by misadventure in injury to B. These cases aside, wrong is defined in terms of the natural or probable, at least when unintentional. The range of reasonable apprehension is at times a question for the court, and at times, if varying inferences are possible, a question for the jury. Here, by concession, there was nothing in the situation to suggest to the most cautious mind that the parcel wrapped in newspaper would spread wreckage through the station. If the guard had thrown it down knowingly and willfully, he would not have threatened the plaintiffs safety, so far as appearances could warn him. His conduct would not have involved, even then, an unreasonable probability of invasion of her bodily security. Liability can be no greater where the act is inadvertent.

* * *

The judgment of the Appellate Division and that of the Trial Term should be reversed, and the complaint dismissed, with costs in all courts.

CASE
17-4

Even if a plaintiff can show negligence, he may still lose the case if the defendant can prove that the plaintiff assumed the risk of harm or was contributorily negligent. This case considers the defense of assumption of risk and the question of whether plaintiff contributed to her own harm when she drank three beers before exiting from a bowling alley under icy conditions.

DUKAT v. LEISERV, INC.
Court of Appeal of Nebraska, 1998
6 Neb.App. 905, 578 N.W.2d 486, aff'd, 255 Neb. 750, 587 N.W.2d 96 (1998)

Sievers, J.

Introduction

We consider whether a jury should be instructed on the defense of assumption of risk when (1) the plaintiff slips and falls on an icy sidewalk outside of a bowling alley, (2) the property owner admits that the sidewalk was the only way in and out of the bowling alley, and (3) the injured plaintiff had prior knowledge of the sidewalk's icy condition.

Factual Background

Rebecca S. Dukat arrived at Mockingbird Lanes, a bowling alley in Omaha, Nebraska, at approximately 6 P.M. on Wednesday, February 2, 1994, to bowl in her league game. Witnesses described the night of February 2 as cold,* * *[and all agreed that] the conditions of the bowling alley's parking lot and adjacent sidewalk* * *were snow and ice covered.

Dukat proceeded to walk into the bowling alley on the only sidewalk provided in and out of the building. She testified that she noticed the sidewalk was icy. After bowling three games and drinking three beers, Dukat exited the bowling alley at approximately 9 P.M. She retraced her steps on the same sidewalk. The sidewalk was still ice covered and in a condition which, according to Frank Jameson, general manager of Mockingbird Lanes, was "unacceptable" if the bowling alley were open to customers. As Dukat proceeded along the sidewalk to her car, she slipped, attempted to catch herself by reaching toward a car, and fell. She suffered a fracture of both bones in her left ankle as well as a ruptured ligament.

Procedural Background

Dukat sued Leiserv, Inc., doing business as Mockingbird Lanes in Omaha * * * in the district court for Douglas County, Nebraska. Dukat alleged that Leiserv * * * were negligent in failing to keep the sidewalk in a reasonably safe condition, in failing to warn her of a dangerous condition, and in failing to take adequate and reasonable measures to protect her.

Leiserv * * * alleged two affirmative defenses: (1) Dukat was contributorily negligent (a) in failing to maintain a proper lookout and take notice of the condition of the sidewalk and (b) in consuming alcohol to the extent that it impaired her ability to walk and to take reasonable precautions, and (2) Dukat had assumed the risk of injury.

* * *

On September 9, 1996, the jury returned a general verdict for Leiserv. * * * Dukat appealed to this court.

* * *

Analysis

Assumption of Risk

Before the defense of assumption of risk may be submitted to a jury, the defendant has the burden to establish the elements of assumption of risk, which are that the plaintiff knew of the danger, understood the danger, and voluntarily exposed himself or herself to the danger which proximately caused the plaintiff's injury. [Citation.] Dukat argues that Leiserv failed to meet its burden of establishing the elements of assumption of risk. Specifically, she argues that Leiserv failed to prove that she knew, understood, and voluntarily exposed herself to the danger of walking unassisted on an icy sidewalk. Dukat's argument focuses primarily on the "voluntary" element of assumption of risk. She maintains that because the sidewalk was the only route into and out of the bowling alley, she did not "voluntarily" expose herself to the danger, rather, according to Nebraska case law, she merely "encountered" it.

Leiserv maintains that Dukat "knew full well that the sidewalk and parking lot were icy," because on her way into the bowling alley she had noticed the sidewalk was slippery. Leiserv contends that Dukat voluntarily exposed herself to the danger when she failed to (1) ask someone to assist her to her car or (2) tell a Mockingbird Lanes employee about the icy conditions and that the sidewalk needed sand or "ice melt."

The standard to be applied in determining whether a plaintiff has assumed the risk of injury is a subjective one based upon the particular facts and circumstances of the event. [Citation.] The subjective standard involves what "the particular plaintiff in fact sees, knows, understands and appreciates. In this it differs from the objective standard which is applied to contributory negligence." [Citation.] If one who knows and comprehends the danger chooses to expose himself or herself thereto, even though the choice is not negligent, he or she will be deemed to have assumed the risk of injury and be precluded from recovery. [Citations.] Thus, it was Leiserv's burden to show that Dukat knowingly and voluntarily exposed herself to the risk of walking on the sidewalk, but a subjective standard is employed.

* * *

In [citation], * * *[the plaintiff] argued that the court should have given the following instruction: "A plaintiff does not assume a risk of harm unless he or she voluntarily accepts the risk. A plaintiff's acceptance of a risk is not voluntary if the defendant's conduct has left plaintiff no reasonable alternative course of conduct in order to avert harm to plaintiff." [Citation.] The court, finding that [the plaintiff's] proposed instruction should have been given, stated:

> (1) A plaintiff does not assume a risk of harm unless he voluntarily accepts the risk. (2) The plaintiff's acceptance of a risk is not voluntary if the defendant's tortious conduct has left him no reasonable alternative course of conduct in order to (a) avert harm to himself or another, or (b) exercise or protect a right or privilege of which the defendant has no right to deprive him. [Citation], quoting the Restatement [(Second) of Torts] § 496E [(1965)].

* * *

The doctrine of a safer choice as used in [citation] and as illustrated by § 496E suggests something other than retreat from where a person needs to be or wants to be * * *. To further amplify our point, we quote two illustrations from the Restatement, supra, comment d. at 579:

> **8.** A illegally carries on blasting operations next to the public highway. B, approaching in a car, ignores a conspicuous warning sign and a flagman who tries to stop him and informs him that there will be a delay of five minutes. B insists upon proceeding along the highway, and is injured by the blasting. B assumes the risk.
>
> **9.** The A City clears the snow and ice from the sidewalk on one side of the street, leaving the sidewalk on the other side covered with ice, slippery, and visibly dangerous. B, having a free choice of either side, and fully understanding the risk, elects to walk on the icy sidewalk, slips, and is injured. B assumes the risk.

In each illustration, there is a reasonable safe choice readily available, and one which allows the "traveler" to reach his or her destination. When the "traveler" rejects the safe and reasonable choice, then there is assumption of risk. * * *

Contributory Negligence * * *

* * *

A plaintiff is contributorily negligent if (1) the plaintiff fails to protect himself or herself from injury; (2) the plaintiff's conduct concurs and cooperates with the defendant's actionable negligence; and (3) the plaintiff's conduct contributes to the plaintiff's injuries as a proximate cause. [Citation.] Contributory negligence is an affirmative defense which must be proved by the party asserting such defense. [Citation.] The distinction between assumption of risk and contributory negligence presents a difference which prevents interchangeable use of those defenses in a negligence action. [Citation.]

The Supreme Court of Nebraska has frequently held: "Where

different minds may reasonably draw different conclusions or inferences from the evidence adduced concerning the issues of negligence or contributory negligence and the degree thereof when one is compared with the other, such issues must be submitted to the jury." [Citations.]

Minds could reasonably differ on the evidence introduced with respect to Dukat's contributory negligence. It is a permissible inference from the record that the ice alone would not have caused the accident. It is clear from Dukat's testimony that she knew of the icy condition of the sidewalk as she entered the bowling alley and despite this knowledge may have done things a reasonably careful person might not have done. For example, the evidence shows that Dukat drank three beers while she was

at the bowling alley and that she did not recall eating dinner that night. Dukat also decided to navigate the same icy path she had come in on without asking the assistance of one of her friends who remained inside the bowling alley. A reasonable person might also have asked management to spread an ice-melting substance on the sidewalk and delayed their departure.

* * *

Conclusion

In view of our determination that the district court committed reversible error by submitting the defense of assumption of risk, the judgment of the district court is reversed, and the cause is remanded to the district court for a new trial.

CASE
17-5

Strict liability is liability based on the abnormally dangerous nature of the activity engaged in by the alleged tortfeasor. In this case, the court examines the issue of whether pyrotechnicians (those who display fireworks) should be subject to strict liability for their activities.

KLEIN v. PYRODYNE CORPORATION
Supreme Court of Washington, 1991
117 Wash.2d 1, 810 P.2d 917

Guy, J.

The plaintiffs in this case are persons injured when an aerial shell at a public fireworks exhibition went astray and exploded near them. The defendant is the pyrotechnic company hired to set up and discharge the fireworks. The issue before this court is whether pyrotechnicians are strictly liable for damages caused by fireworks displays. We hold that they are.

Defendant Pyrodyne Corporation (Pyrodyne) is a general contractor for aerial fireworks at public fireworks displays. Pyrodyne contracted to procure fireworks, to provide pyrotechnic operators, and to display the fireworks at the Western Washington State Fairgrounds in Puyallup, Washington on July 4, 1987. All operators of the fireworks display were Pyrodyne employees acting within the scope of their employment duties.

As required by Washington statute, Pyrodyne purchased a $1,000,000 insurance policy prior to the fireworks show. The policy provided $1,000,000 coverage for each occurrence of bodily injury or property damage liability. Plaintiffs allege that Pyrodyne failed to carry out a number of the other statutory and regulatory requirements in preparing for and setting off the fireworks. For example, they allege that Pyrodyne failed to properly bury the mortar tubes prior to detonation, failed to provide a diagram of the display and surrounding environment to the local government, failed to provide crowd control monitors, and failed to keep the invitees at the mandated safe distance.

During the fireworks display, one of the 5-inch mortars was knocked into a horizontal position. From this position a shell inside was ignited and discharged. The shell flew 500 feet in

a trajectory parallel to the earth and exploded near the crowd of onlookers. Plaintiffs Danny and Marion Klein were injured by the explosion. Mr. Klein's clothing was set on fire, and he suffered facial burns and serious injury to his eyes.

The parties provide conflicting explanations of the cause of the improper horizontal discharge of the shell. Pyrodyne argues that the accident was caused by a 5-inch shell detonating in its aboveground mortar tube without ever leaving the ground. Pyrodyne asserts that this detonation caused another mortar tube to be knocked over, ignited, and shot off horizontally. In contrast, the Kleins contend that the misdirected shell resulted because Pyrodyne's employees improperly set up the display. They further note that because all of the evidence exploded, there is no means of proving the cause of the misfire.

The Kleins brought suit against Pyrodyne under theories of products liability and strict liability. Pyrodyne filed a motion for summary judgment, which the trial court granted as to the products liability claim. The trial court denied Pyrodyne's summary judgment motion regarding the Kleins' strict liability claim, holding that Pyrodyne was strictly liable without fault and ordering summary judgment in favor of the Kleins on the issue of liability. Pyrodyne appealed the order of partial summary judgment to the Court of Appeals, which certified the case to this court. Pyrodyne is appealing solely as to the trial court's holding that strict liability is the appropriate standard of liability for pyrotechnicians. A strict liability claim against pyrotechnicians for damages caused by fireworks displays presents a case of first impression in Washington.

Analysis

Fireworks Displays as Abnormally Dangerous Activities

The Kleins contend that strict liability is the appropriate standard to determine the culpability of Pyrodyne because Pyrodyne was participating in an abnormally dangerous activity.* * *

The modern doctrine of strict liability for abnormally dangerous activities derives from *Fletcher v. Rylands*, [citation], in which the defendant's reservoir flooded mine shafts on the plaintiff's adjoining land. *Rylands v. Fletcher* has come to stand for the rule that "the defendant will be liable when he damages another by a thing or activity unduly dangerous and inappropriate to the place where it is maintained, in the light of the character of that place and its surroundings." [Citation.]

The basic principle of *Rylands v. Fletcher* has been accepted by the Restatement (Second) of Torts (1977). [Citation.] Section 519 of the Restatement provides that any party carrying on an "abnormally dangerous activity" is strictly liable for ensuing damages. The test for what constitutes such an activity is stated in section 520 of the Restatement. Both Restatement sections have been adopted by this court, and determination of whether an activity is an "abnormally dangerous activity" is a question of law. [Citations.]

Section 520 of the Restatement lists six factors that are to be considered in determining whether an activity is "abnormally dangerous." The factors are as follows: (a) existence of a high degree of risk of some harm to the person, land or chattels of others; (b) likelihood that the harm that results from it will be great; (c) inability to eliminate the risk by the exercise of reasonable care; (d) extent to which the activity is not a matter of common usage; (e) inappropriateness of the activity to the place where it is carried on; and (f) extent to which its value to the community is outweighed by its dangerous attributes. Restatement (Second) of Torts § 520 (1977). As we previously recognized in [citation], the comments to section 520 explain how these factors should be evaluated: Any one of them is not necessarily sufficient of itself in a particular case, and ordinarily several of them will be required for strict liability. On the other hand, it is not necessary that each of them be present, especially if others weigh heavily. Because of the interplay of these various factors, it is not possible to reduce abnormally dangerous activities to any definition. The essential question is whether the risk created is so unusual, either because of its magnitude or because of the circumstances surrounding it, as to justify the imposition of strict liability for the harm that results from it, even though it is carried on with all reasonable care. Restatement (Second) of Torts § 520, comment f (1977). Examination of these factors persuades us that fireworks displays are abnormally dangerous activities justifying the imposition of strict liability.

We find that the factors stated in clauses (a), (b), and (c) are all present in the case of fireworks displays. Any time a person ignites aerial shells or rockets with the intention of sending them aloft to explode in the presence of large crowds of people, a high risk of serious personal injury or property damage is created. That risk arises because of the possibility that a shell or rocket will malfunction or be misdirected. Furthermore, no matter how much care pyrotechnicians exercise, they cannot entirely eliminate the high risk inherent in setting off powerful explosives such as fireworks near crowds.

* * *

The factor expressed in clause (d) concerns the extent to which the activity is not a matter "of common usage." The Restatement explains that "[a]n activity is a matter of common usage if it is customarily carried on by the great mass of mankind or by many people in the community." Restatement (Second) of Torts § 520, comment i (1977). As examples of activities that are not matters of common usage, the Restatement comments offer driving a tank, blasting, the manufacture, storage, transportation, and use of high explosives, and drilling for oil. The deciding characteristic is that few persons engage in these activities. Likewise, relatively few persons conduct public fireworks displays. Therefore, presenting public fireworks displays is not a matter of common usage.

* * *

The factor stated in clause (e) requires analysis of the appropriateness of the activity to the place where it was carried on. In this case, the fireworks display was conducted at the Puyallup Fairgrounds. Although some locations—such as over water—may be safer, the Puyallup Fairgrounds is an appropriate place for a fireworks show because the audience can be seated at a reasonable distance from the display. Therefore, the clause (e) factor is not present in this case.

The factor stated in clause (f) requires analysis of the extent to which the value of fireworks to the community outweighs its dangerous attributes. We do not find that this factor is present here. This country has a long-standing tradition of fireworks on the 4th of July. That tradition suggests that we as a society have decided that the value of fireworks on the day celebrating our national independence and unity outweighs the risks of injuries and damage.

In sum, we find that setting off public fireworks displays satisfies four of the six conditions under the Restatement test; that is, it is an activity that is not "of common usage" and that presents an ineliminably high risk of serious bodily injury or property damage. We therefore hold that conducting public fireworks displays is an abnormally dangerous activity justifying the imposition of strict liability.

* * *

Conclusion

We hold that Pyrodyne Corporation is strictly liable for all damages suffered as a result of the July 1987 fireworks display. Detonating fireworks displays constitutes an abnormally dangerous activity warranting strict liability * * *. This establishes the standard of strict liability for pyrotechnicians. Therefore, we affirm the decision of the trial court.

QUESTIONS

1. List and briefly describe the three required elements of an action for negligence.
2. Explain the duty of care that is imposed upon (a) adults, (b) children, (c) persons with a physical disability, (d) persons with a mental deficiency, (e) persons with superior knowledge, and (f) persons acting in an emergency.

3. Differentiate among the duties that possessors of land owe to trespassers, licensees, and invitees.
4. Identify the defenses that are available to a tort action in negligence and those that are available to a tort action in strict liability.
5. Identify and discuss those activities giving rise to a tort action in strict liability.

PROBLEMS

1. A statute requiring railroads to fence their tracks is construed as intended solely to prevent animals that stray onto the right-of-way from being hit by trains. B & A Railroad Company fails to fence its tracks. Two of Calvin's cows wander onto the track. Nellie is hit by a train. Elsie is poisoned by weeds growing beside the track. For which cow(s), if any, is B & A Railroad Company liable to Calvin? Why?

2. Martha invites John to come to lunch. Though she knows that her private road is dangerous to travel, having been guttered by recent rains, Martha doesn't warn John of the condition, reasonably believing that he will notice the gutters and exercise sufficient care. While John is driving over, his attention is diverted from the road by the screaming of his child, who has been stung by a bee. He fails to notice the condition of the road, hits a gutter, and skids into a tree. If John is not contributorily negligent, is Martha liable to John?

3. Nathan is run over by a car and left lying in the street. Sam, seeing Nathan's helpless state, places him in his car for the purpose of taking him to the hospital. While on the way to the hospital, Sam drops his cell phone on to the floor of his car. Without stopping, Sam looks for the cell phone under his seat causing him to lose control of the car and to drive into a ditch resulting in additional injury to Nathan. Is Sam liable to Nathan?

4. Led Foot drives his car carelessly into another car driven by Marty. Marty's car contains dynamite, which Led had no way of knowing. The collision causes an explosion which shatters a window of a building half a block away on another street. The flying glass inflicts serious cuts on Sally, who is working at a desk near the window. The explosion seriously injures Marty and also harms Vic, who is walking on the sidewalk near the point of the collision. Toward whom is Led Foot negligent?

5. A statute requires all vessels traveling on the Great Lakes to provide lifeboats. One of Winston Steamship Company's boats is sent out of port without a lifeboat. Perry, a sailor, falls overboard in a storm so strong that had there been a lifeboat, it could not have been launched. Perry drowns. Is Winston liable to Perry's estate?

6. Lionel is negligently driving an automobile at excessive speed. Reginald's negligently driven car crosses the center line of the highway and scrapes the side of Lionel's car, damaging its fenders. As a result, Lionel loses control of his car, which goes into the ditch. Lionel's car is wrecked, and Lionel suffers personal injuries. What, if anything, can Lionel recover?

7. (a) Ellen, the owner of a baseball park, is under a duty to the entering public to provide a reasonably sufficient number of screened seats to protect those who desire such protection against the risk of being hit by batted balls. Ellen fails to do so. Frank, a customer entering the park, is unable to find a screened seat and, although fully aware of the risk, sits in an unscreened seat. Frank is struck and injured by a batted ball. Is Ellen liable?

(b) Gretchen, Frank's wife, has just arrived from Germany and is viewing baseball for the first time. Without asking any questions, she follows Frank to a seat. After the batted ball hits Frank, it caroms into Gretchen, injuring her. Is Ellen liable to Gretchen?

8. Negligent in failing to give warning of the approach of its train to a crossing, CC Railroad thereby endangers Larry, a blind man who is about to cross. Mildred, a bystander, in a reasonable effort to save Larry, rushes onto the track to push Larry out of danger. Although Mildred acts as carefully as possible, she is struck and injured by the train.

(a) Can Mildred recover from Larry?
(b) Can Mildred recover from CC Railroad?

9. Vance was served liquor while he was an intoxicated patron at a United States Air Force bar. He later injured himself as a result of his intoxication. An Alaska state statute makes it a crime to give or to sell liquor to intoxicated persons. Vance has brought an action seeking damages for the injuries he suffered. Could Vance successfully argue that the United States Air Force was negligent *per se* by its employee's violation of the statute?

10. Timothy keeps a pet chimpanzee, which is thoroughly tamed and accustomed to playing with its owner's children. The chimpanzee escapes, despite every precaution to keep it upon its owner's premises. It approaches a group of children. Wanda, the mother of one of the children, erroneously thinking the chimpanzee is about to attack the children, rushes to her child's assistance. In her hurry and excitement, she stumbles and falls, breaking her leg. Can Wanda recover for her personal injuries?

11. Hawkins slipped and fell on a puddle of water just inside the automatic door to the H. E. Butt Grocery Company's store. The water had been tracked into the store by customers and blown through the door by a strong wind. The store manager was aware of the puddle and had mopped it up several times earlier in the day. Still, no signs had been placed to warn store patrons of the danger. Hawkins brought an action to recover damages for injuries sustained in the fall. Was the store negligent in its conduct?

12. Escola, a waitress, was injured when a bottle of Coca-Cola exploded in her hand while she was putting it into the restaurant's cooler. The bottle came from a shipment that had remained under the counter for thirty-six hours after being delivered by the bottling company. The bottler had subjected the bottle to the method of testing for defects commonly used in the industry, and there is no evidence that Escola or anyone else did anything to damage the bottle between its delivery and the explosion. Escola brought an action against the

bottler for damages. As she is unable to show any specific acts of negligence on its part, she seeks to rely on the doctrine of *res ipsa loquitur*. Should she be able to recover on this theory? Explain.

13. Hunn injured herself when she slipped and fell on a loose plank while walking down some steps that the hotel had repaired the day before. The night before, while entering the hotel, she had noticed that the steps were dangerous, and although she knew from her earlier stays at the hotel that another exit was available, she chose that morning to leave via the dangerous steps. The hotel was aware of the hazard, as one of the other guests who had fallen that night had reported his accident to the desk clerk then on duty. Still, there were no cautionary signs on the steps to warn of the danger, and they were not roped off or otherwise excluded from use. Hunn brought an action against the hotel for injuries she sustained as a result of her fall. Should she recover? Explain.

14. Fredericks, a hotel owner, had a dog named "Sport" that he had trained as a watchdog. When Vincent Zarek, a guest at the hotel, leaned over to pet the dog, it bit him. Although Sport had never bitten anyone before, Fredericks was aware of the dog's violent tendencies and, therefore, did not allow it to roam around the hotel alone. Vincent brought an action for injuries sustained when the dog bit him. Is Fredericks' liable for the actions of his dog? Explain.

15. Two thugs in an alley in Manhattan held up an unidentified man. When the thieves departed with his possessions, the man quickly gave chase. He had almost caught one when the thief managed to force his way into an empty taxicab stopped at a traffic light. The thief pointed his gun at the driver's head and ordered him to drive on. The driver started to follow the directions while closely pursued by a posse of good citizens, but then suddenly jammed on the brakes and jumped out of the car to safety. The thief also jumped out, but the car traveled on, injuring Mrs. Cordas and her two children. The Cordases then brought an action for damages, claiming that the cab driver was negligent in jumping to safety and leaving the moving vehicle uncontrolled. Was the cab driver negligent? Explain.

16. A foul ball struck Marie Uzdavines on the head while she was watching the Metropolitan Baseball Club ("The Mets") play the Philadelphia Phillies at "The Mets" home stadium in New York. The ball came through a hole in a screen designed to protect spectators sitting behind home plate. The screen contained several holes that had been repaired with baling wire lighter in weight than the wire used in the original screen. Although the manager of the stadium makes no formal inspections of the screen, his employees do try to repair the holes as they find them. Weather conditions, rust deterioration, and baseballs hitting the screen are the chief causes of these holes. The owner of the stadium, the city of New York, leases the stadium to "The Mets" and replaces the entire screen every two years. Uzdavines sued "The Mets" for negligence under the doctrine of *res ipsa loquitur*. Is this an appropriate case for *res ipsa loquitur*? Explain.

17. Two-year-old David Allen was bitten by Joseph Whitehead's dog while he was playing on the porch at the Allen residence. Allen suffered facial cuts, a severed muscle in his left eye, a hole in his left ear, and scarring over his forehead. Through his father, David sued Whitehead, claiming that, as owner, Whitehead is responsible for his dog's actions. Whitehead admitted that (1) the dog was large, mean-looking, and frequently barked at neighbors; (2) the dog was allowed to roam wild; and (3) the dog frequently chased and barked at cars. He stated, however, that (1) the dog was friendly and often played

with his and neighbors' children; (2) he had not received previous complaints about the dog; (3) the dog was neither aggressive nor threatening; and (4) the dog had never bitten anyone before this incident. Is Whitehead liable?

18. Larry VanEgdom, in an intoxicated state, bought alcoholic beverages from the Hudson Municipal Liquor Store in Hudson, South Dakota. Immediately following the purchase, VanEgdom, while driving a car, struck and killed Guy William Ludwig, who was stopped on his motorcycle at a stop sign. Lela Walz, as special administrator of Ludwig's estate, brought an action against the city of Hudson, which operated the liquor store, for the wrongful death of Ludwig. Walz alleged that the store employee was negligent in selling intoxicating beverages to VanEgdom when he knew or could have observed that VanEgdom was drunk. Decision?

19. The *MacGilvray Shiras* was a ship owned by the Kinsman Transit Company. During the winter months, when Lake Erie was frozen, the ship and others moored at docks on the Buffalo River. As oftentimes happened, one night an ice jam disintegrated upstream, sending large chunks of ice downstream. Chunks of ice began to pile up against the *Shiras*, which at that time was without power and manned only by a shipman. The ship broke loose when a negligently constructed "deadman" to which one mooring cable was attached pulled out of the ground. The "deadman" was operated by Continental Grain Company. The ship began moving down the S-shaped river stern first and struck another ship, the *Tewksbury*. The *Tewksbury* also broke loose from its mooring, and the two ships floated down the river together. Although the crew manning the Michigan Avenue Bridge downstream had been notified of the runaway ships, they failed to raise the bridge in time to avoid a collision because of a mix-up in the shift changeover. As a result, both ships crashed into the bridge and were wedged against the bank of the river. The two vessels substantially dammed the flow of the river, causing ice and water to back up and flood installations as far as three miles upstream. The injured parties brought this action for damages against Kinsman, Continental, and the city of Buffalo. Who, if any, is liable? Explain.

20. Carolyn Falgout accompanied William Wardlaw as a social guest to Wardlaw's brother's camp. After both parties had consumed intoxicating beverages, Falgout walked onto a pier that was then only partially completed. Wardlaw had requested that she not go on the pier. Falgout said, "Don't tell me what to do," and proceeded to walk on the pier. Wardlaw then asked her not to walk past the completed portion of the pier. She ignored his warnings and walked to the pier's end. When returning to the shore, Falgout got her shoe caught between the boards. She fell, hanging by her foot, with her head and arms in the water. Wardlaw rescued Falgout, who had seriously injured her knee and leg. She sued Wardlaw for negligence. Decision?

21. Joseph Yania and Boyd Ross visited a coal strip-mining operation owned by John Bigan to discuss a business matter with Bigan. On Bigan's property there were several cuts and trenches he had dug to remove the coal underneath. While there, Bigan asked the two men to help him pump water from one of these cuts in the earth. This particular cut contained water eight to ten feet in depth with sidewalls or embankments sixteen to eighteen feet in height. The two men agreed, and the process began with Ross and Bigan entering the cut and standing at the point where the pump was located. Yania stood at the top of one of the cut's sidewalls. Apparently, Bigan taunted Yania into jumping into the water from the top of the sidewall—a height of sixteen to eighteen feet. As a result, Yania drowned. His widow brought a negligence action against Bigan. She claims that Bigan was negligent "(1) by urging, enticing, taunting, and inveigling Yania to jump into the water; (2) by failing to warn Yania of a dangerous condition on the land and (3) by failing to go to Yania's rescue after he jumped into the water." Was Bigan negligent?

22. Don Juan is so busy trying to get the attention of a young woman that he walks into a light pole and is knocked unconscious. Driver happens to be driving down the road and sees Don Juan's unfortunate incident. Driver is so amused by the incident that he takes his eyes off the road for a moment and nearly slams into the car ahead of him. Veering off the road to avoid an accident, Driver drives into a reataurant, breaking a large window. Noodle, who was enjoying a bowl of soup at that moment, is burned by the hot soup, which is knocked off the table and into Noodle's lap. Noodle sues the restaurant, Driver and Don Juan for negligence. As to each claim, what result? Explain.

http: **Internet Exercise** Find and review information about tort reform.

Appendix A

SELECTED NEW YORK STATE STATUTES
NEW YORK GENERAL OBLIGATIONS LAW

§ 1-202. Definition
As used in this chapter, the term "infant" or "minor" means a person who has not attained the age of eighteen years. (eff. Sept. 1, 1974)

§ 3-101. When contracts may not be disaffirmed on ground of infancy
1. A contract made on or after September first, nineteen hundred seventy-four by a person after he has attained the age of eighteen years may not be disaffirmed by him on the ground of infancy.

* * *

3. A husband and wife, with respect only to real property they occupy or which they affirm they are about to occupy as a home, regardless of the minority of either or both and without limitation of the powers of any such person who is of full age, shall each have power (a) to enter into and contract for a loan or loans with a bank, trust company, ... savings bank or savings and loan association whose home office is located in this state, with any insurance company authorized to do business in this state, with the United States government and its agencies, with respect to such real property and take any other action and execute any other document or instrument to the extent necessary or appropriate to effect any such loan, provide security therefor, carry out or modify the terms thereof, and effect any compromise or settlement of any such loan or of any claim with respect thereto; (b) to receive, hold and dispose of such real property, make and execute contracts, notes, deeds, mortgages, agreements and other instruments necessary and appropriate to acquire such property; and (c) to dispose of such real property so acquired, and make and execute contracts, deeds, agreements and other instruments necessary and appropriate to dispose of such property. Notwithstanding any contrary provision or rule of law, no such husband or wife shall have the power to disaffirm, because of minority, any act or transaction which he or she is hereinabove empowered to perform or engage in, nor shall any defense based upon minority be interposed in any action or proceeding arising out of any such act or transaction.

****

§ 3-102. Obligations of certain minors for hospital, medical and surgical treatment and care
An obligation incurred by a married minor for hospital, medical and surgical treatment and care for such minor or such minor's children shall not be voidable because of minority. For the purpose of this section only, subsequent judgment of divorce or annulment shall not alter the obligation previously incurred.

§ 3-112. Liability of parents and legal guardians having custody of an infant for certain damages caused by such infant
1. The parent or legal guardian, other than the state, a local social services department or a foster parent, of an infant over ten and less than eighteen years of age, shall be liable to any public officer, organization or authority, having by law the care and/or custody of any public property of the state or of any political subdivision thereof, or to any private individual or organization having by law the care, custody and/or ownership of any private property, for damages caused by such infant, where such infant has willfully, maliciously, or unlawfully damaged, defaced or destroyed such public or private property, whether real or personal, or, where such infant, with intent to deprive the owner and/or custodian of such property or to appropriate the same to himself or herself or to a third person, has knowingly entered or remained in a building and has wrongfully taken, obtained or withheld such public or private personal property from such building which personal property is owned or maintained by the state or any political subdivision thereof or which is owned or maintained by any individual, organization or authority, or where such infant has falsely reported an incident or placed a false bomb . . . . Such public officer, organization or authority, or private individual or organization, as the case may be, may bring an action for civil damages in a court of competent jurisdiction for a judgment to recover such damages from such parent or legal guardian other than the state or a local social services department or a foster parent. For the purposes of this subdivision, damages for falsely reporting an incident or placing a false bomb shall mean the funds reasonably expended by a victim in responding to such false

report...In no event shall such damages portion of a judgment authorized by this section, as described in this subdivision, exceed the sum of five thousand dollars.

2. Notwithstanding the provisions of subdivision one of this section, prior to the entering of a judgment under this section in the sum total of five hundred dollars or more, the court shall provide such parent or legal guardian of such infant with an opportunity to make an application to the court based upon such parent's or legal guardian's financial inability to pay any portion or all of the amount of such sum total which is in excess of five hundred dollars...

3. It shall be a defense to an action brought under this section that restitution has been paid... It shall also be a defense to an action brought under this section that such infant had voluntarily and without good cause abandoned the home of the parent or guardian and without good cause refused to submit to the guidance and control of the parent or guardian prior to and at the time of the occurrence of such damages or destruction. In no event shall it be a defense that the parent or legal guardian has exercised due diligent supervision over the activities of such infant, provided, however, that in the interests of justice, the court may consider mitigating circumstances that bear directly upon the actions of the parent or legal guardian in supervising such unemancipated infant.

§ 5-325. Garages and parking places

1. No person who conducts or maintains for hire or other consideration a garage, parking lot or other similar place which has the capacity for the housing, storage, parking, repair or servicing of four or more motor vehicles, as defined by the vehicle and traffic law, may exempt himself from liability for damages for injury to person or property resulting from the negligence of such person, his agents or employees, in the operation of any such vehicle, or in its housing, storage, parking, repair or servicing, or in the conduct or maintenance of such garage, parking lot or other similar place, and, except as hereinafter provided, any agreement so exempting such person shall be void.

2. Damages for loss or injury to property may be limited by a provision in the storage agreement limiting the liability in case of loss or damage by theft, fire or explosion and setting forth a specific liability per vehicle, which shall in no event be less than twenty-five thousand dollars, beyond which the person owning or operating such garage or lot shall not be liable; provided, however, that such liability may on request of the person delivering such vehicle be increased, in which event increased rates may be charged based on such increased liability.

§ 5-326. Agreements exempting pools, gymnasiums, places of public amusement or recreation and similar establishments from liability for negligence void and unenforceable

Every covenant, agreement or understanding in or in connection with, or collateral to, any contract, membership application, ticket of admission or similar writing, entered into between the owner or operator of any pool, gymnasium, place of amusement or recreation, or similar establishment and the user of such facilities, pursuant to which such owner or operator receives a fee or other compensation for the use of such facilities, which exempts the said owner or operator from liability for damages caused by or resulting from the negligence of the owner, operator or person in charge of such establishment, or their agents, servants or employees, shall be deemed to be void as against public policy and wholly unenforceable.

§ 5-332. Unsolicited and voluntarily sent merchandise deemed unconditional gift

1. No person, firm, partnership, association or corporation, or agent or employee thereof, shall, in any manner, or by any means, offer for sale goods, wares, or merchandise, where the offer includes the voluntary and unsolicited sending of such goods, wares, or merchandise not actually ordered or requested by the recipient, either orally or in writing. The receipt of any such goods, wares, or merchandise shall for all purposes be deemed an unconditional gift to the recipient who may use or dispose of such goods, wares, or merchandise in any manner he sees fit without any obligation on his part to the sender.

If after any such receipt deemed to be an unconditional gift under this section, the sender continues to send bill statements or requests for payment with respect thereto, an action may be brought by the recipient to enjoin such conduct, in which action there may also be awarded reasonable attorney's fees and costs to the prevailing party.

* * *

§ 5-401. Illegal wagers, bets and stakes

All wagers, bets or stakes, made to depend upon any race, or upon any gaming by lot or chance, or upon any lot, chance, casualty, or unknown or contingent event whatever, shall be unlawful.

§ 5-411. Contracts on account of money or property wagered, bet or staked are void

All contracts for or on account of any money or property, or thing in action wagered, bet or staked, as provided in section 5-401, shall be void.

[It should be noted that certain types of gambling and wagering are permissible, under government regulation and control. For example, casino gambling is licensed in Nevada and Atlantic City, N.J. In New York State, sections of the Racing, Pari-Mutuel, Wagering and Breeding Law license wagering at race tracks, and also provide for the New York City Off-Track Betting Corporation.]

§ 5-501. Rate of interest; usury forbidden

1. The rate of interest, as computed pursuant to this title, upon the loan or forbearance of any money, goods, or things in action, except as provided in subdivisions five and six of this section or as otherwise provided by law, shall be six per centum per annum unless a different rate is prescribed in section fourteen-a of the banking law... [See below.]

§ 5-511. Usurious contracts void

1. All bonds, bills, notes, assurances, conveyances, all other contracts or securities whatsoever, . . . and all deposits of goods or other things whatsoever, whereupon or whereby there shall be reserved or taken, or secured or agreed to be reserved or taken, any greater sum, or greater value, for the loan or forbearance of any money, goods or other things in action, than is prescribed in section 5-501, shall be void, except that the knowingly taking, receiving, reserving or charging such a greater sum or greater value by a savings bank, a savings and loan association or a federal savings and loan association shall only be held and adjudged a forfeiture of the entire interest which the loan or obligation carries with it or which has been agreed to be paid thereon. If a greater sum or greater value has been paid, the person paying the same or his legal representative may recover from the savings bank, the savings and loan association or the federal savings and loan association twice the entire amount of the interest thus paid.

2. Except as provided in subdivision one, whenever it shall satisfactorily appear by the admissions of the defendant, or by proof, that any bond, bill, note, assurance, pledge, conveyance, contract, security or any evidence of debt, has been taken or received in violation of the foregoing provisions, the court shall declare the same to be void, and enjoin any prosecution thereon, and order the same to be surrendered and cancelled.

§ 5-513. Recovery of excess

Every person who, for any such loan or forbearance, shall pay or deliver any greater sum or value than is allowed to be received pursuant to section 5-501, and his personal representatives, may recover in an action against the person who shall have taken or received the same, and his personal representatives, the amount of the money so paid or value delivered, above the rate aforesaid.

§ 5-515. Borrower bringing an action need not offer to repay

Whenever any borrower of money, goods or things in action, shall begin an action for the recovery of the money, goods or things in action taken in violation of the foregoing provisions of this title, it shall not be necessary for him to pay or offer to pay any interest or principal on the sum or thing loaned; nor shall any court require or compel the payment or deposit of the principal sum or interest, or any portion thereof, as a condition

of granting relief to the borrower in any case of usurious loans forbidden by the foregoing provisions of this title.

§ 5-519. Return of excess a bar to further penalties

Every person who shall repay or return the money, goods or other things so taken, accepted or received, or the value thereof, shall be discharged from any other or further forfeiture or penalty which he may have incurred under sections 5-511 or 5-513, by taking or receiving the money, goods or other thing so repaid, or returned, as aforesaid.

§ 5-521. Corporations prohibited from interposing defense of usury

1. No corporation shall hereafter interpose the defense of usury in any action . . . .

2. The provisions of subdivision one of this section shall not apply to a corporation, the principal asset of which shall be the ownership of a one or two family dwelling, where it appears either that the said corporation was organized and created, or that the controlling interest therein was acquired, within a period of six months prior to the execution, by said corporation of a bond or note evidencing indebtedness, and a mortgage creating a lien for said indebtedness on the said one or two family dwelling;...

Any provision of any contract, or any separate written instrument executed prior to, simultaneously with or within sixty days after the delivery of any moneys to any borrower in connection with such indebtedness, whereby the defense of usury is waived or any such corporation is estopped from asserting it, is hereby declared to be contrary to public policy and absolutely void....

§ 5-524. Taking security upon certain property for usurious loans

A person who takes security, upon any household furniture, sewing machines, plate or silverware in actual use, tools or implements of trade, wearing apparel or jewelry, for a loan or forbearance of money, or for the use or sale of his personal credit, conditioned upon the payment of a greater rate than the rate prescribed by the banking board pursuant to section four-teen-a of the banking law, or, if no rate has been so prescribed, six per centum per annum, or who as security for such loan, use or sale of personal credit as aforesaid, makes a pretended purchase of such property from any person, upon the like condition, and permits the pledgor to retain the possession thereof is guilty of a misdemeanor.

§ 5-701. Agreements required to be in writing

a. Every agreement, promise or undertaking is void, unless it or some note or memorandum thereof be in writing, and subscribed by the party to be charged therewith, or by his lawful agent, if such agreement, promise or undertaking:

1. By its terms is not to be performed within one year from the making thereof or the performance of which is not to be completed before the end of a lifetime;
2. Is a special promise to answer for the debt, default or miscarriage of another person;
3. Is made in consideration of marriage, except mutual promises to marry;

* * *

§ 5-703. Conveyances and contracts concerning real property required to be in writing

1. An estate or interest in real property, other than a lease for a term not exceeding one year, or any trust or power, over or concerning real property, or in any manner relating thereto, cannot be created, granted, assigned, surrendered or declared, unless by act or operation of law, or by a deed or conveyance in writing, subscribed by the person creating, granting, assigning, surrendering or declaring the same, or by his lawful agent, thereunto authorized by writing. But this subdivision does not affect the power of a testator in the disposition of his real property by will; nor prevent any trust from arising or being extinguished by implication or operation of law, nor any declaration of trust from being proved by a writing subscribed by the person declaring the same.
2. A contract for the leasing for a longer period than one year, or for the sale, of any real property, or an interest therein, is void unless the contract or some note or memorandum thereof, expressing the consideration, is in writing, subscribed by the party to be charged, or by his lawful agent thereunto authorized by writing.
3. A contract to devise real property or establish a trust of real property, or any interest therein or right with reference thereto, is void unless the contract or some note or memorandum thereof is in writing and subscribed by the party to be charged therewith, or by his lawfully authorized agent.
4. Nothing contained in this section abridges the powers of courts of equity to compel the specific performance of agreements in cases of part performance.

§ 5-1103. Written agreement for modification or discharge

An agreement, promise or undertaking to change or modify, or to discharge in whole or in part, any contract, obligation, or lease, or any mortgage or other security interest in personal or real property, shall not be invalid because of the absence of consideration, provided that the agreement, promise or undertaking changing, modifying, or discharging such contract, obligation, lease, mortgage or security interest, shall be in writing and signed by the party against whom it is sought to enforce the change, modification or discharge, or by his agent.

§ 5-1105. Written promise expressing past consideration

A promise in writing and signed by the promisor or by his agent shall not be denied effect as a valid contractual obligation on the ground that consideration for the promise is past or executed, if the consideration is expressed in the writing and is proved to have been given or performed and would be a valid consideration but for the time when it was given or performed.

§ 5-1107. Written assignment

An assignment shall not be denied the effect of irrevocably transferring the assignor's rights because of the absence of consideration, if such assignment is in writing and signed by the assignor, or by his agent.

§ 5-1109. Written irrevocable offer

Except as otherwise provided in section 2-205 of the uniform commercial code with respect to an offer by a merchant to buy or sell goods, when an offer to enter into a contract is made in a writing signed by the offeror, or by his agent, which states that the offer is irrevocable during a period set forth or until a time fixed, the offer shall not be revocable during such period or until such time because of the absence of consideration for the assurance of irrevocability. When such a writing states that the offer is irrevocable but does not state any period or time of irrevocability, it shall be construed to state that the offer is irrevocable for a reasonable time.

§ 5-1113. Written or published promise or reward

A promise to pay a reward for return of lost or mislaid property is not unenforceable because of absence of consideration if the promise was made in writing or the promisor caused it to be published.

§ 5-1301. How interest calculated

Whenever, in any statute, act, deed, written or verbal contract, or in any public or private instrument whatever, any certain rate of interest is or shall be mentioned, and no period of time is stated for which such rate is to be calculated, interest shall be calculated at the rate mentioned, by the year, in the same manner as if the words "per annum" or "by the year" had been added to such rate.

§ 13-101. Transfer of claims

Any claim or demand can be transferred, except in one of the following cases:
1. Where it is to recover damages for a personal injury;
2. Where it is founded upon a grant, which is made void by a statute of the state; or upon a claim to or interest in real property, a grant of which, by the transferrer, would be void by such a statute;

3. Where a transfer thereof is expressly forbidden by: (a) a statute of the state, or (b) a statute of the United States, or (c) would contravene public policy.

§ 15-301. When written agreement or other instrument cannot be changed by oral executory agreement, or discharged or terminated by oral executory agreement or oral consent or by oral notice

1. A written agreement or other written instrument which contains a provision to the effect that it cannot be changed orally, cannot be changed by an executory agreement unless such executory agreement is in writing and signed by the party against whom enforcement of the change is sought or by his agent.

2. A written agreement or other written instrument which contains a provision to the effect that it cannot be terminated orally, cannot be discharged by an executory agreement unless such executory agreement is in writing and signed by the party against whom enforcement of the discharge is sought, or by his agent, and cannot be terminated by mutual consent unless such termination is effected by an executed accord and satisfaction other than the substitution of one executory contract for another, or is evidenced by a writing signed by the party against whom it is sought to enforce the termination, or by his agent.

3. a. A discharge or partial discharge of obligations under a written agreement or other written instrument is a change of the agreement or instrument for the purpose of subdivision one of this section and is not a discharge or termination for the purpose of subdivision two, unless all executory obligations under the agreement or instrument are discharged or terminated.

b. A discharge or termination of all executory obligations under a written agreement or other written instrument is a discharge or termination for the purpose of subdivision two even though accrued obligations remaining unperformed at the date of the discharge or termination are not affected by it. c. If a written agreement or other written instrument containing a provision that it cannot be terminated orally also provides for termination or discharge on notice by one or either party, both subdivision two and subdivision four of this section apply whether or not the agreement or other instrument states specifically that the notice must be in writing.

4. If a written agreement or other written instrument contains a provision for termination or discharge on written notice by one or either party, the requirement that such notice be in writing cannot be waived except by a writing signed by the party against whom enforcement of the waiver is sought or by his agent.

5. If executed by an agent, any agreement, evidence of termination, notice of termination or waiver, required by this section to be in writing, which affects or relates to real property or an interest therein as defined in section 5-101 in any manner stated in subdivisions one or two of section 5-703 of this chapter shall be void unless such agent was thereunto authorized in writing.

6. As used in this section the term "agreement" includes promise and undertaking.

§ 15-303. Release in writing without consideration or seal

A written instrument which purports to be a total or partial release of all claims, debts, demands or obligations, or a total or partial release of any particular claim, debt, demand or obligation, or a release or discharge in whole or in part of a mortgage, lien, security interest or charge upon personal or real property, shall not be invalid because of the absence of consideration or of a seal.

§ 15-501. Executory accord

1. Executory accord as used in this section means an agreement embodying a promise express or implied to accept at some future time a stipulated performance in satisfaction or discharge in whole or in part of any present claim, cause of action, contract, obligation, or lease, or any mortgage or other security interest in personal or real property, and a promise express or implied to render such performance in satisfaction or in discharge of such claim, cause of action, contract, obligation, lease, mortgage or security interest.

2. An executory accord shall not be denied effect as a defense or as the basis of an action or counterclaim by reason of the fact that the satisfaction or discharge of the claim, cause of action, contract, obligation, lease, mortgage or other security interest which is the subject of the accord was to occur at a time after the making of the accord, provided the promise of the party against whom it is sought to enforce the accord is in writing and signed by such party or by his agent. If executed by an agent, any promise required by this section to be in writing which affects or relates to real property or an interest therein as defined in section 5-101 in any manner stated in subdivisions one or two of section 5-703 of this chapter shall be void unless such agent was thereunto authorized in writing.

3. If an executory accord is not performed according to its terms by one party, the other party shall be entitled either to assert his rights under the claim, cause of action, contract, obligation, lease, mortgage or other security interest which is the subject of the accord, or to assert his right under the accord.

§ 15-503. Offer of accord followed by tender

1. An offer in writing, signed by the offeror or by his agent, to accept a performance therein designated in satisfaction or discharge in whole or in part of any claim, cause of action, contract, obligation, or lease, or any mortgage or other security interest in personal or real property, followed by tender of such performance by the offeree or by his agent before revocation of

the offer, shall not be denied effect as a defense or as the basis of an action or counterclaim by reason of the fact that such tender was not accepted by the offeror or by his agent.

2. If executed by an agent, any offer required by this section to be in writing which affects or relates to real property or an interest therein as defined in section 5-101 in any manner stated in subdivisions one or two of section 5-703 of this chapter shall be void unless such agent was thereunto authorized in writing.

§ 17-101. Acknowledgment or new promise must be in writing

An acknowledgment or promise contained in a writing signed by the party to be charged thereby is the only competent evidence of a new or continuing contract whereby to take an action out of the operation of the provisions of limitations of time for commencing actions under the civil practice law and rules other than an action for the recovery of real property. This section does not alter the effect of a payment of principal or interest.

§ 17-103. Agreements waiving the statute of limitation

1. A promise to waive, to extend, or not to plead the statute of limitation applicable to an action arising out of a contract express or implied in fact or in law, if made after the accrual of the cause of action and made, either with or without consideration, in a writing signed by the promisor or his agent is effective, according to its terms, to prevent interposition of the defense of the statute of limitation in an action or proceeding commenced within the time that would be applicable if the cause of action had arisen at the date of the promise, or within such shorter time as may be provided in the promise.

2. A promise to waive, to extend, or not to plead the statute of limitation may be enforced as provided in this section by the person to whom the promise is made or for whose benefit it is expressed to be made or by any person who, after the making of the promise, succeeds or is subrogated to the interest of either of them.

3. A promise to waive, to extend, or not to plead the statute of limitation has no effect to extend the time limited by statute for commencement of an action or proceeding for any greater time or in any other manner than that provided in this section, or unless made as provided in this section.

4. This section

a. does not change the requirements or the effect with respect to the statute of limitation, of an acknowledgment or promise to pay, or a payment or part payment of principal or interest, or a stipulation made in an action or proceeding;

b. does not affect the power of the court to find that by reason of conduct of the party to be charged it is inequitable to permit him to interpose the defense of the statute of limitation; and

c. does not apply in any respect to a cause of action to fore close a mortgage of real property or a mortgage of a lease of real property, or to a cause of action to recover a judgment affecting the title to or the possession, use or enjoyment of real property, or a promise or waiver with respect to any statute of limitation applicable thereto.

NEW YORK BANKING LAW

§ 14-a. Rate of interest; banking board to adopt regulations

1. The maximum rate of interest provided for in section 5-501 of the general obligations law shall be sixteen per centum per annum.

2. The rate of interest as so prescribed under this section shall include as interest any and all amounts paid or payable, directly or indirectly, by any person, to or for the account of the lender in consideration for the making of a loan or forbearance as defined by the banking board pursuant to subdivision three of this section.

NEW YORK CIVIL PRACTICE LAW AND RULES (C.P.L.R)

§ 1411. Damages recoverable when contributory negligence or assumption of risk is established

In any action to recover damages for personal injury, injury to property, or wrongful death, the culpable conduct attributable to the claimant or to the decedent, including contributory negligence or assumption of risk, shall not bar recovery, but the amount of damages otherwise recoverable shall be diminished in the proportion which the culpable conduct attributable to the claimant or decedent bears to the culpable conduct which caused the damages.

§ 1412. Burden of pleading; burden of proof

Culpable conduct claimed in diminution of damages, in accordance with section fourteen hundred eleven, shall be an affirmative defense to be pleaded and proved by the party asserting the defense.

§ 1413. Applicability

This article shall apply to all causes of action accruing on or after September first, nineteen hundred seventy-five.

§ 3002. Actions and relief not barred for inconsistency
* * *

(d) Action on contract and to reform. A judgment denying recovery in an action upon an agreement in writing shall not be deemed to bar an action to reform such agreement and to enforce it as reformed.

(e) Claim for damages and rescission. A claim for damages sustained as a result of fraud or misrepresentation in the inducement of a contract or other transaction, shall not be deemed inconsistent with a claim for rescission or based upon rescission. In an action for rescission or based upon rescission the aggrieved party shall be allowed to obtain complete relief in one action, including rescission, restitution of the benefits, if any, conferred by him as a result of the transaction, and damages to which he is entitled because of such fraud or misrepresentation; but such complete relief shall not include duplication of items of recovery.

§ 3004. Where restoration of benefits before judgment unnecessary

A party who has received benefits by reason of a transaction that is void or voidable because of fraud, misrepresentation, mistake, duress, infancy or incompetency, and who, in an action or by way of defense or counterclaim, seeks rescission, restitution, a declaration or judgment that such transaction is void, or other relief, whether formerly denominated legal or equitable, dependent upon a determination that such transaction was void or voidable, shall not be denied relief because of a failure to tender before judgment restoration of such benefits; but the court may make a tender of restoration a condition of its judgment, and may otherwise in its judgment so adjust the equities between the parties that unjust enrichment is avoided.

§ 5230. Executions

(a) Form. An execution shall specify the date that the judgment or order was entered, the court in which it was entered, the amount of the judgment or order and the amount due thereon and it shall specify the names of the parties in whose favor and against whom the judgment or order was entered. An execution shall direct that only the property in which a named judgment debtor or obligor who is not deceased has an interest, or the debts owed to the named judgment debtor or obligor, be levied upon or sold thereunder and shall specify the last known address of that judgment debtor or obligor. . . .

§ 5231. Income execution

(a) Form. An income execution shall specify . . . the name and address of the person from whom the judgment debtor is receiving or will receive money; the amount of money, the frequency of its payment and the amount of the installments to be collected therefrom; and shall contain a notice to the judgment debtor that he shall commence payment of the installments specified to the sheriff forthwith and that, upon his default, the execution will be served upon the person from whom he is receiving or will receive money.

(b) Issuance. Where a judgment debtor is receiving or will receive money from any source, an income execution for installments therefrom of not more than ten percent thereof may be issued and delivered to the sheriff of the county in which the judgment debtor resides or, where the judgment debtor is a non- resident, the county in which he is employed ...

§ 5252. Discrimination against employees and prospective employees based upon wage assignment or income execution

1. No employer shall discharge, lay off, refuse to promote, or discipline an employee, or refuse to hire a prospective employee, because one or more wage assignments or income executions have been served upon such employer or a former employer against the employee's or prospective employee's wages or because of the pendency of any action or judgment against such employee or prospective employee for nonpayment of any alleged contractual obligation. In addition to being subject to the civil action authorized in subdivision two of this section, where any employer discharges, lays off, refuses to promote or disciplines an employee or refuses to hire a prospective employee because of the existence of one or more income executions and/or income deduction orders issued . . . the court may direct the payment of a civil penalty not to exceed five hundred dollars for the first instance and one thousand dollars per instance for the second and subsequent instances of employer or income payor discrimination.

2. An employee or prospective employee may institute a civil action for damages for wages lost as a result of a violation of this section within ninety days after such violation. Damages recoverable shall not exceed lost wages for six weeks and in such action the court also may order the reinstatement of such discharged employee or the hiring of such prospective employee. Except as provided for in subdivision (g) of section fifty-two hundred forty-one, not more than ten per centum of the damages recovered in such action shall be subject to any claims, attachments or executions by any creditors, judgment creditors or assignees of such employee or prospective employee. A violation of this section may also be punished as a contempt of court pursuant to the provisions of section seven hundred fifty-three of the judiciary law.

§ 5519. Stay of enforcement

(a) Stay without court order. Service upon the adverse party of a notice of appeal or an affidavit of intention to move for permission to appeal stays all proceedings to enforce the judgment or order appealed from pending the appeal or determination on the motion for permission to appeal where:

1. the appellant or moving party is the state or any political subdivision of the state or any officer or agency of the state or of any political subdivision of the state; . . . or

2. the judgment or order directs the payment of a sum of money, and an undertaking in that sum is given that if the

judgment or order appealed from, or any part of it, is affirmed, or the appeal is dismissed, the appellant or moving party shall pay the amount directed to be paid by the judgment or order, or the part of it as to which the judgment or order is affirmed; or

* * * (b) Stay in action defended by insurer. If an appeal is taken from a judgment or order entered against an insured in an action which is defended by an insurance corporation, or other insurer, on behalf of the insured under a policy of insurance the limit of liability of which is less than the amount of said judgment or order, all proceedings to enforce the judgment or order to the extent of the policy coverage shall be stayed pending the appeal, and no action shall be commenced or maintained against the insurer for payment under the policy pending the appeal . . . .

§ 7501. Effect of arbitration agreement

A written agreement to submit any controversy thereafter arising or any existing controversy to arbitration is enforceable without regard to the justiciable character of the controversy and confers jurisdiction on the courts of the state to enforce it and to enter judgment on an award. In determining any matter arising under this article, the court shall not consider whether the claim with respect to which arbitration is sought is tenable, or otherwise pass upon the merits of the dispute.

NEW YORK EDUCATION LAW

§ 281. Loans and extensions of credit to infants

A contract hereafter made by an infant after he has attained the age of sixteen years in relation to obtaining a loan or extension of credit from an institution of the university of the state of New York in connection with such infant's attendance upon a course of instruction offered by such institution, or from a bank, trust company, industrial bank or national bank whose principal office is in this state for the purpose of defraying all or a portion of the expenses of such infant's attendance upon a course of instruction in an institution of the university of the state of New York or any other institution for higher education without this state which is a member of or accredited by an accrediting agency recognized by the department, may not be disaffirmed by him on the ground of infancy.

§ 6501. Admission to a profession (licensing)

Admission to practice of a profession in this state is accomplished by a license being issued to a qualified applicant by the education department. To qualify for a license an applicant shall meet the requirements prescribed in the article for the particular profession...

§ 6503. Practice of a profession

Admission to the practice of a profession (1) entitles the licensee to practice the profession as defined in the article for the particular profession, (2) entitles the individual licensee to use the professional title as provided in the article for the particular profession, and (3) subjects the licensee to the procedures and penalties for professional misconduct as prescribed in this article...

§ 6512. Unauthorized practice a crime

1. Anyone not authorized to practice under this title who practices or offers to practice or holds himself out as being able to practice in any profession in which a license is a prerequisite to the practice of the acts, or who practices any profession as an exempt person during the time when his professional license is suspended, revoked or annulled, or who aids or abets an unlicensed person to practice a profession, or who fraudulently sells, files, furnishes, obtains, or who attempts fraudulently to sell, file, furnish or obtain any diploma, license, record or permit purporting to authorize the practice of a profession, shall be guilty of a class E felony. . . .

§ 6513. Unauthorized use of a professional title a crime

1. Anyone not authorized to use a professional title regulated by this title, and who uses such professional title, shall be guilty of a class A misdemeanor...

NEW YORK PENAL LAW

§ 180.00 Commercial bribing in the second degree

A person is guilty of commercial bribing in the second degree when he confers, or offers or agrees to confer, any benefit upon any employee, agent or fiduciary without the consent of the latter's employer or principal, with intent to influence his conduct in relation to his employer's or principal's affairs. Commercial bribing in the second degree is a class A misdemeanor.

§ 180.03 Commercial bribing in the first degree

A person is guilty of commercial bribing in the first degree when he confers, or offers or agrees to confer, any benefit upon any employee, agent or fiduciary without the consent of the latter's employer or principal, with intent to influence his conduct in relation to his employer's or principal's affairs, and when the value of the benefit conferred or offered or agreed to be conferred exceeds one thousand dollars and causes economic harm to the employer or principal in an amount exceeding two hundred fifty dollars. Commercial bribing in the first degree is a class E felony.

§ 180.08 Commercial bribe receiving in the first degree

An employee, agent or fiduciary is guilty of commercial bribe receiving in the first degree when, without the consent of his employer or principal, he solicits, accepts or agrees to accept any benefit from another person upon an agreement or understanding that such benefit will influence his conduct in relation to his employer's or principal's affairs, and when the value of the benefit solicited, accepted or agreed to be accepted exceeds one thousand dollars and causes economic harm to the employer or principal in an amount exceeding two hundred fifty dollars.

Commercial bribe receiving in the first degree is a class E felony.

§ 190.40 Criminal usury in the second degree

A person is guilty of criminal usury in the second degree when, not being authorized or permitted by law to do so, he knowingly charges, takes or receives any money or other property as interest on the loan or forbearance of any money or other property, at a rate exceeding twenty-five per centum per annum or the equivalent rate for a longer or shorter period. Criminal usury in the second degree is a class E felony.

NEW YORK ARTS AND CULTURAL AFFAIRS LAW

§ 35.03. Judicial approval of certain contracts for services of infants; ...

1. A contract made by an infant or made by a parent or guardian of an infant, or a contract proposed to be so made, under which (a) the infant is to perform or render services as an actor, actress, dancer, musician, vocalist or other performing artist, or as a participant or player in professional sports, or (b) a person is employed to render services to the infant in
connection with such services of the infant or in connection with contracts therefor, may be approved by the supreme court or the surrogate's court as provided in this section where the infant is a resident of this state or the services of the infant are to be performed or rendered in this state. If the contract is so approved the infant may not, either during his minority or upon reaching his majority, disaffirm the contract on the ground of infancy or assert that the parent or guardian lacked authority to make the contract. A contract modified, amended or assigned after its approval under this section shall be deemed a new contract.
2. (a) Approval of the contract pursuant to this section shall not exempt any person from any other law with respect to licenses, consents or authorizations required for any conduct, employment, use or exhibition of the infant in this state, nor limit in any manner the discretion of the licensing authority or other persons charged with the administration of such requirements, nor dispense with any other requirement of law relating to the infant.

(b) No contract shall be approved which provides for an employment, use or exhibition of the infant, within or without

the state, which is prohibited by law and could not be licensed to take place in this state.

(c) No contract shall be approved unless (i) the written acquiescence to such contract of the parent or parents having custody, or other person having custody of the infant, is filed in the proceeding or (ii) the court shall find that the infant is emancipated.

(d) No contract shall be approved if the term during which the infant is to perform or render services or during which a person is employed to render services to the infant, including any extensions thereof by option or otherwise, extends for a period of more than three years from the date of approval of the contract . . . .

NEW YORK CIVIL SERVICE LAW

§ 75-b. Retaliatory action by public employers
* * *

2. (a) A public employer shall not dismiss or take other disciplinary or other adverse personnel action against a public employee regarding the employee's employment because the employee discloses to a governmental body information: (i) regarding a violation of a law, rule or regulation which violation creates and presents a substantial and specific danger to the public health or safety; or (ii) which the employee reasonably believes to be true and reasonably believes constitutes an improper governmental action. "Improper governmental action" shall mean any action by a public employer or employee, or an agent of such employer or employee, which is undertaken in the performance of such agent's official duties, whether or not such action is within the scope of his employment, and which is in violation of any federal, state or local law, rule or regulation.

(b) Prior to disclosing information pursuant to paragraph (a) of this subdivision, an employee shall have made a good faith effort to provide the appointing authority or his or her designee the information to be disclosed and shall provide the appointing authority or designee a reasonable time to take appropriate action unless there is imminent and serious danger to public health or safety. For the purposes of this subdivision, an employee who acts pursuant to this paragraph shall be deemed to have disclosed information to a governmental body under paragraph (a) of this subdivision.

* * *

NEW YORK LABOR LAW

§ 201-d. Discrimination against the engagement in certain activities

1. Definitions. As used in this section:

a. "Political activities" shall mean (i) running for public office, (ii) campaigning for a candidate for public office, or (iii) participating in fund-raising activities for the benefit of a candidate, political party or political advocacy group;

b. "Recreational activities" shall mean any lawful, leisure-time activity, for which the employee receives no compensation and which is generally engaged in for recreational purposes, including but not limited to sports, games, hobbies, exercise, reading and the viewing of television, movies and similar material;

c. "Work hours" shall mean, for purposes of this section, all time, including paid and unpaid breaks and meal periods, that the employee is suffered, permitted or expected to be engaged in work, and all time the employee is actually engaged in work. This definition shall not be referred to in determining hours worked for which an employee is entitled to compensation under any law including article nineteen of this chapter.

2. Unless otherwise provided by law, it shall be unlawful for any employer or employment agency to refuse to hire, employ or license, or to discharge from employment or otherwise discriminate against an individual in compensation, promotion or terms, conditions or privileges of employment because of:

a. an individual's political activities outside of working hours, off of the employer's premises and without use of the employer's equipment or other property, if such activities are legal, provided, however, that this paragraph shall not apply to persons whose employment is defined in paragraph six of subdivision (a) of section seventy-nine-h of the civil rights law, and provided further that this paragraph shall not apply to persons who would otherwise be prohibited from engaging in political activity pursuant to chapter 15 of title 5 and subchapter III of chapter 73 of title 5 of the USCA;

b. an individual's legal use of consumable products prior to the beginning or after the conclusion of the employee's work hours, and off of the employer's premises and without use of the employer's equipment or other property;

c. an individual's legal recreational activities outside work hours, off of the employer's premises and without use of the employer's equipment or other property; or

d. an individual's membership in a union or any exercise of rights granted under Title 29, USCA, Chapter 7 or under article fourteen of the civil service law.

3. The provisions of subdivision two of this section shall not be deemed to protect activity which:

a. creates a material conflict of interest related to the employer's trade secrets, proprietary information or other proprietary or business interest;

b. with respect to employees of a state agency as defined in sections seventy-three and seventy-four of the public officers law respectively, is in knowing violation of subdivision two, three, four, five, seven, eight or twelve of section seventy-three or of section seventy-four of the public officers law, or of any executive order, policy, directive, or other rule which has been issued by the attorney general regulating outside employment or activities that could conflict with employees' performance of their official duties;

c. with respect to employees of any employer as defined in section twenty-seven-a of this chapter, is in knowing violation of a provision of a collective bargaining agreement concerning ethics, conflicts of interest, potential conflicts of interest, or the proper discharge of official duties;

d. with respect to employees of any employer as defined in section twenty-seven-a of this chapter who are not subject to section seventy-three or seventy-four of the public officers law, is in knowing violation of article eighteen of the general municipal law or any local law, administrative code provision, charter provision or rule or directive of the mayor or any agency head of a city having a population of one million or more, where such law, code provision, charter provision, rule or directive concerns ethics, conflicts of interest, potential conflicts of interest, or the proper discharge of official duties and otherwise covers such employees; and

e. with respect to employees other than those of any employer as defined in section twenty-seven-a of this chapter, violates a collective bargaining agreement or a certified or licensed professional's contractual obligation to devote his or her entire compensated working hours to a single employer, provided however that the provisions of this paragraph shall apply only to professionals whose compensation is at least fifty thousand dollars for the year nineteen hundred ninety-two and in subsequent years is an equivalent amount adjusted by the same percentage as the annual increase or decrease in the consumer price index.

4. Notwithstanding the provisions of subdivision three of this section, an employer shall not be in violation of this section where the employer takes action based on the belief either that: (i) the employer's actions were required by statute, regulation, ordinance or other governmental mandate, (ii) the employer's actions were permissible pursuant to an established substance abuse or alcohol program or workplace policy, professional contract or collective bargaining agreement, or (iii) the individual's actions were deemed by an employer or previous employer to be illegal or to constitute habitually poor performance, incompetency or misconduct.

5. Nothing in this section shall apply to persons who, on an individual basis, have a professional service contract with an employer and the unique nature of the services provided is such that the employer shall be permitted, as part of such professional service contract, to limit the off-duty activities which may be engaged in by such individual.

6. Nothing in this section shall prohibit an organization or employer from offering, imposing or having in effect a health, disability or life insurance policy that makes distinctions between employees for the type of coverage or the price of coverage based upon the employees' recreational activities or use of consumable products, provided that differential premium rates charged employees reflect a differential cost to the employer and that employers provide employees with a statement delineating the differential rates used by the carriers providing insurance for the employer, and provided further that such distinctions in type or price of coverage shall not be utilized to expand, limit or curtail the rights or liabilities of any party with regard to a civil cause of action.

7. a. Where a violation of this section is alleged to have occurred, the attorney general may apply in the name of the people of the state of New York for an order enjoining or restraining the commission or continuance of the alleged unlawful acts. In any such proceeding, the court may impose a civil penalty in the amount of three hundred dollars for the first violation and five hundred dollars for each subsequent violation.

b. In addition to any other penalties or actions otherwise applicable pursuant to this chapter, where a violation of this section is alleged to have occurred, an aggrieved individual may commence an action for equitable relief and damages.

§ 740. Retaliatory personnel action by employers; prohibition

* * *

2. Prohibitions. An employer shall not take any retaliatory personnel action against an employee because such employee does any of the following:
(a) discloses, or threatens to disclose to a supervisor or to a public body an activity, policy or practice of the employer that is in violation of law, rule or regulation which violation creates and presents a substantial and specific danger to the public health or safety; (b) provides information to, or testifies before, any public body conducting an investigation, hearing or inquiry into any such violation of a law, rule or regulation by such employer; or (c) objects to, or refuses to participate in any such activity, policy or practice in violation of a law, rule or regulation.

3. Application. The protection against retaliatory personnel action provided by paragraph (a) of subdivision two of this section pertaining to disclosure to a public body shall not apply to an employee who makes such disclosure to a public body unless the employee has brought the activity, policy or practice in violation of law, rule or regulation to the attention of a supervisor of the employer and has afforded such employer a reasonable opportunity to correct such activity, policy or practice.

4. Violation; remedy. (a) An employee who has been the subject of a retaliatory personnel action in violation of this section may institute a civil action in a court of competent jurisdic-

tion for relief as set forth in subdivision five of this section within one year after the alleged retaliatory personnel action was taken.

* * *

5. Relief. In any action brought pursuant to subdivision four of this section, the court may order relief as follows:
(a) an injunction to restrain continued violation of this section;
(b) the reinstatement of the employee to the same position held before the retaliatory personnel action, or to an equivalent position;
(c) the reinstatement of full fringe benefits and seniority rights;
(d) the compensation for lost wages, benefits and other remuneration; and
(e) the payment by the employer of reasonable costs, disbursements, and attorney's fees.

6. Employer relief. A court, in its discretion, may also order that reasonable attorneys' fees and court costs and disbursements be awarded to an employer if the court determines that an action brought by an employee under this section was without basis in law or in fact.

* * *

§ 741. Prohibition; health care employer who penalizes employees because of complaints of employer violations

1. Definitions. As used in this section, the following terms shall have the following meanings:
(a) "Employee" means any person who performs health care services for and under the control and direction of any public or private employer which provides health care services for wages or other remuneration.
(b) "Employer" means any partnership, association, corporation, the state, or any political subdivision of the state which: (i) provides health care services in a facility licensed pursuant to article twenty-eight or thirty-six of the public health law; (ii) provides health care services within a primary or secondary public or private school or public or private university setting; (iii) operates and provides health care services under the mental hygiene law or the correction law; or (iv) is registered with the department of education pursuant to section sixty-eight hundred eight of the education law.
(c) "Agent" means any individual, partnership, association, corporation, or group of persons acting on behalf of an employer.
(d) "Improper quality of patient care" means, with respect to patient care, any practice, procedure, action or failure to act of an employer which violates any law, rule, regulation or declaratory ruling adopted pursuant to law, where such violation relates to matters which may present a substantial and specific danger to public health or safety or a significant threat to the health of a specific patient.

(e) "Public body" means:

   (1) the United States Congress, any state legislature, or any elected local governmental body, or any member or employee thereof;

   (2) any federal, state or local court, or any member or employee thereof, any grand or petit jury;

   (3) any federal, state or local regulatory, administrative or public agency or authority, or instrumentality thereof;

   (4) any federal, state or local law enforcement agency, prosecutorial office, or police or peace officer;

   (5) any federal, state or local department of an executive branch of government; or

   (6) any division, board, bureau, office, committee or commission of any of the public bodies described in subparagraph one, two, three, four or five of this paragraph.

(f) "Retaliatory action" means the discharge, suspension, demotion, penalization or discrimination against an employee, or other adverse employment action taken against an employee in the terms and conditions of employment.

(g) "Supervisor" means any person within an employer's organization who has the authority to direct and control the work performance of an employee, or who has the authority to take corrective action regarding the violation of a law, rule or regulation to which an employee submits a complaint.

2. Retaliatory action prohibited. Notwithstanding any other provision of law, no employer shall take retaliatory action against any employee because the employee does any of the following:

   (a) discloses or threatens to disclose to a supervisor, or to a public body an activity, policy or practice of the employer or agent that the employee, in good faith, reasonably believes constitutes improper quality of patient care; or

   (b) objects to, or refuses to participate in any activity, policy or practice of the employer or agent that the employee, in good faith, reasonably believes constitutes improper quality of patient care.

3. Application. The protection against retaliatory personnel action provided by subdivision two of this section shall not apply unless the employee has brought the improper quality of patient care to the attention of a supervisor and has afforded the employer a reasonable opportunity to correct such activity, policy or practice. This subdivision shall not apply to an action or failure to act described in paragraph (a) of subdivision two of this section where the improper quality of patient care described therein presents an imminent threat to public health or safety or to the health of a specific patient and the employee reasonably believes in good faith that reporting to a supervisor would not result in corrective action.

4. Enforcement. A health care employee may seek enforcement of this section pursuant to paragraph (d) of subdivision four of section seven hundred forty of this article.

5. Relief. In any court action brought pursuant to this section it shall be a defense that the personnel action was predicated upon grounds other than the employee's exercise of any rights protected by this section.

APPENDIX B

Uniform Commercial Code

The Code consists of the following articles:

Art.

Article 1
GENERAL PROVISIONS

Part 1 Short Title, Construction, Application and Subject Matter of the Act

§ 1—101. Short Title.

This Act shall be known and may be cited as Uniform Commercial Code.

§ 1—102. Purposes; Rules of Construction; Variation by Agreement.

(1) This Act shall be liberally construed and applied to promote its underlying purposes and policies.

(2) Underlying purposes and policies of this Act are

(a) to simplify, clarify and modernize the law governing commercial transactions;

(b) to permit the continued expansion of commercial practices through custom, usage and agreement of the parties;

(c) to make uniform the law among the various jurisdictions.

(3) The effect of provisions of this Act may be varied by agreement, except as otherwise provided in this Act and except that the obligations of good faith, diligence, reasonableness and care prescribed by this Act may not be disclaimed by agreement but the parties may by agreement determine the standards by which the performance of such obligations is to be measured if such standards are not manifestly unreasonable.

(4) The presence in certain provisions of this Act of the words "unless otherwise agreed" or words of similar import does not imply that the effect of other provisions may not be varied by agreement under subsection (3).

(5) In this Act unless the context otherwise requires

(a) words in the singular number include the plural, and in the plural include the singular;

(b) words of the masculine gender include the feminine and the neuter, and when the sense so indicates words of the neuter gender may refer to any gender.

§ 1—103. Supplementary General Principles of Law Applicable.

Unless displaced by the particular provisions of this Act, the principles of law and equity, including the law merchant and the law relative to capacity to contract, principal and agent, estoppel, fraud, misrepresentation, duress, coercion, mistake, bankruptcy, or other validating or invalidating cause shall supplement its provisions.

§ 1—104. Construction Against Implicit Repeal.

This Act being a general act intended as a unified coverage of its subject matter, no part of it shall be deemed to be impliedly repealed by subsequent legislation if such construction can reasonably be avoided.

§ 1—105. Territorial Application of the Act; Parties' Power to Choose Applicable Law.

(1) Except as provided hereafter in this section, when a transaction

bears a reasonable relation to this state and also to another state or nation the parties may agree that the law either of this state or of such other state or nation shall govern their rights and duties. Failing such agreement this Act applies to transactions bearing an appropriate relation to this state.

(2) Where one of the following provisions of this Act specifies the applicable law, that provision governs and a contrary agreement is effective only to the extent permitted by the law (including the conflict of laws rules) so specified:

> Rights of creditors against sold goods. Section 2—402.
>
> Applicability of the Article on Leases. Sections 2A—105 and 2A—106.
>
> Applicability of the Article on Bank Deposits and Collections. Section 4—102.
>
> Governing law in the Article on Funds Transfers. Section 4A—507.
>
> Letters of Credit, Section 5—116.
>
> Bulk sales subject to the Article on Bulk Sales. Section 6—103.
>
> Applicability of the Article on Investment Securities. Section 8—106.
>
> Perfection provisions of the Article on Secured Transactions. Section 9—103.

§ 1—106. Remedies to Be Liberally Administered.

(1) The remedies provided by this Act shall be liberally administered to the end that the aggrieved party may be put in as good a position as if the other party had fully performed but neither consequential or special nor penal damages may be had except as specifically provided in this Act or by other rule of law.

(2) Any right or obligation declared by this Act is enforceable by action unless the provision declaring it specifies a different and limited effect.

§ 1—107. Waiver or Renunciation of Claim or Right After Breach.

Any claim or right arising out of an alleged breach can be discharged in whole or in part without consideration by a written waiver or renunciation signed and delivered by the aggrieved party.

§ 1—108. Severability.

If any provision or clause of this Act or application thereof to any person or circumstances is held invalid, such invalidity shall not affect other provisions or applications of the Act which can be given effect without the invalid provision or application, and to this end the provisions of this Act are declared to be severable.

§ 1—109. Section Captions.

Section captions are parts of this Act.

Part 2 General Definitions and Principles of Interpretation

§ 1—201. General Definitions.

Subject to additional definitions contained in the subsequent Articles of this Act which are applicable to specific Articles or Parts thereof, and unless the context otherwise requires, in this Act:

(1) "Action" in the sense of a judicial proceeding includes recoupment, counterclaim, set-off, suit in equity and any other proceedings in which rights are determined.

(2) "Aggrieved party" means a party entitled to resort to a remedy.

(3) "Agreement" means the bargain of the parties in fact as found in their language or by implication from other circumstances including course of dealing or usage of trade or course of performance as provided in this Act (Sections 1—205 and 2—208). Whether an agreement has legal consequences is determined by the provisions of this Act, if applicable; otherwise by the law of contracts (Section 1—103). (Compare "Contract".)

(4) "Bank" means any person engaged in the business of banking.

(5) "Bearer" means the person in possession of an instrument, document of title, or certificated security payable to bearer or indorsed in blank.

(6) "Bill of lading" means a document evidencing the receipt of goods for shipment issued by a person engaged in the business of transporting or forwarding goods, and includes an airbill. "Airbill" means a document serving for air transportation as a bill of lading does for marine or rail transportation, and includes an air consignment note or air waybill.

(7) "Branch" includes a separately incorporated foreign branch of a bank.

(8) "Burden of establishing" a fact means the burden of persuading the triers of fact that the existence of the fact is more probable than its non-existence.

(9) "Buyer in ordinary course of business" means a person who in good faith and without knowledge that the sale to him is in violation of the ownership rights or security interest of a third party in the goods buys in ordinary course from a person in the business of selling goods of that kind but does not include a pawnbroker. All persons who sell minerals or the like (including oil and gas) at wellhead or minehead shall be deemed to be persons in the business of selling goods of that kind. "Buying" may be for cash or by exchange of other property or on secured or unsecured credit and includes receiving goods or documents of title under a pre-existing contract for sale but does not include a transfer in bulk or as security for or in total or partial satisfaction of a money debt.

(10) "Conspicuous": A term or clause is conspicuous when it is so written that a reasonable person against whom it is to operate ought to have noticed it. A printed heading in capitals (as: NON-NEGOTIABLE BILL OF LADING) is conspicuous. Language in the body of a form is "conspicuous" if it is in larger or other contrasting type or color. But in a telegram any stated term is "conspicuous". Whether a term or clause is "conspicuous" or not is for decision by the court.

(11) "Contract" means the total legal obligation which results from the parties' agreement as affected by this Act and any other applicable rules of law. (Compare "Agreement".)

(12) "Creditor" includes a general creditor, a secured creditor, a lien creditor and any representative of creditors, including an assignee for the benefit of creditors, a trustee in bankruptcy, a receiver in equity and an executor or administrator of an insolvent debtor's or assignor's estate.

(13) "Defendant" includes a person in the position of defendant in a cross-action or counterclaim.

(14) "Delivery" with respect to instruments, documents of title, chattel paper, or certificated securities means voluntary transfer of possession.

(15) "Document of title" includes bill of lading, dock warrant, dock receipt, warehouse receipt or order for the delivery of goods, and also any other document which in the regular course of business or financing is treated as adequately evidencing that the person in possession of it is entitled to receive, hold and dispose of the document and the goods it covers. To be a document of title a document must purport to be issued by or addressed to a bailee and purport to cover goods in the bailee's possession which are either identified or are fungible portions of an identified mass.

(16) "Fault" means wrongful act, omission or breach.

(17) "Fungible" with respect to goods or securities means goods or securities of which any unit is, by nature or usage of trade, the equivalent of any other like unit. Goods which are not fungible shall be deemed fungible for the purposes of this Act to the extent that under a particular agreement or document unlike units are treated as equivalents.

(18) "Genuine" means free of forgery or counterfeiting.

(19) "Good faith" means honesty in fact in the conduct or transaction concerned.

(20) "Holder" with respect to a negotiable instrument, means the person in possession if the instrument is payable to bearer or, in the cases of an instrument payable to an identified person, if the identified person is in possession. "Holder" with respect to a document of title means the person in possession if the goods are deliverable to bearer or to the order of the person in possession.

(21) To "honor" is to pay or to accept and pay, or where a credit so engages to purchase or discount a draft complying with the terms of the credit.

(22) "Insolvency proceedings" includes any assignment for the benefit of creditors or other proceedings intended to liquidate or rehabilitate the estate of the person involved.

(23) A person is "insolvent" who either has ceased to pay his debts in the ordinary course of business or cannot pay his debts as they become due or is insolvent within the meaning of the federal bankruptcy law.

(24) "Money" means a medium of exchange authorized or adopted by a domestic or foreign government and includes a monetary unit of account established by an intergovernmental organization or by agreement between two or more nations.

(25) A person has "notice" of a fact when

(a) he has actual knowledge of it; or

(b) he has received a notice or notification of it; or

(c) from all the facts and circumstances known to him at the time in question he has reason to know that it exists.

A person "knows" or has "knowledge" of a fact when he has actual knowledge of it. "Discover" or "learn" or a word or phrase of similar import refers to knowledge rather than to reason to know. The time and circumstances under which a notice or notification may cease to be effective are not determined by this Act.

(26) A person "notifies" or "gives" a notice or notification to another by taking such steps as may be reasonably required to inform the other in ordinary course whether or not such other actually comes to know of it. A person "receives" a notice or notification when

(a) it comes to his attention; or

(b) it is duly delivered at the place of business through which the contract was made or at any other place held out by him as the place for receipt of such communications.

(27) Notice, knowledge or a notice or notification received by an organization is effective for a particular transaction from the time when it is brought to the attention of the individual conducting that transaction, and in any event from the time when it would have been brought to his attention if the organization had exercised due diligence. An organization exercises due diligence if it maintains reasonable routines for communicating significant information to the person conducting the transaction and there is reasonable compliance with the routines. Due diligence does not require an individual acting for the organization to communicate information unless such communication is part of his regular duties or unless he has reason to know of the transaction and that the transaction would be materially affected by the information.

(28) "Organization" includes a corporation, government or governmental subdivision or agency, business trust, estate, trust, partnership or association, two or more persons having a joint or common interest, or any other legal or commercial entity.

(29) "Party", as distinct from "third party", means a person who has engaged in a transaction or made an agreement within this Act.

(30) "Person" includes an individual or an organization (See Section 1—102).

(31) "Presumption" or "presumed" means that the trier of fact must find the existence of the fact presumed unless and until evidence is introduced which would support a finding of its non-existence.

(32) "Purchase" includes taking by sale, discount, negotiation, mortgage, pledge, lien, issue or re-issue, gift or any other voluntary transaction creating an interest in property.

(33) "Purchaser" means a person who takes by purchase.

(34) "Remedy" means any remedial right to which an aggrieved party is entitled with or without resort to a tribunal.

(35) "Representative" includes an agent, an officer of a corporation or association, and a trustee, executor or administrator of an estate, or any other person empowered to act for another.

(36) "Rights" includes remedies.

(37) "Security interest" means an interest in personal property or fixtures which secures payment or performance of an obligation. The retention or reservation of title by a seller of goods notwithstanding shipment or delivery to the buyer (Section 2—401) is limited in effect to a reservation of a "security interest". The term also includes any interest of a buyer of accounts or chattel paper which is subject to Article 9. The special property interest of a buyer of goods on identification of those goods to a contract for sale under Section 2—401 is not a "security interest", but a buyer may also acquire a "security interest" by complying with Article 9. Unless a consignment is intended as security, reservation of title thereunder is not a "security

interest," but a consignment is in any event subject to the provisions on consignment sales (Section 2—326).

Whether a transaction creates a lease or security interest is determined by the facts of each case; however, a transaction creates a security interest if the consideration the lessee is to pay the lessor for the right to possession and use of the goods is an obligation for the term of the lease not subject to termination by the lessee, and

(a) the original term of the lease is equal to or greater than the remaining economic life of the goods,

(b) the lessee is bound to renew the lease for the remaining economic life of the goods or is bound to become the owner of the goods,

(c) the lessee has an option to renew the lease for the remaining economic life of the goods for no additional consideration or nominal additional consideration upon compliance with the lease agreement, or

(d) the lessee has an option to become the owner of the goods for no additional consideration or nominal additional consideration upon compliance with the lease agreement.

A transaction does not create a security interest merely because it provides that

(a) the present value of the consideration the lessee is obligated to pay the lessor for the right to possession and use of the goods is substantially equal to or is greater than the fair market value of the goods at the time the lease is entered into,

(b) the lessee assumes risk of loss of the goods, or agrees to pay taxes, insurance, filing, recording, or registration fees, or service or maintenance costs with respect to the goods,

(c) the lessee has an option to renew the lease or to become the owner of the goods,

(d) the lessee has an option to renew the lease for a fixed rent that is equal to or greater than the reasonably predictable fair market rent for the use of the goods for the term of the renewal at the time the option is to be performed, or

(e) the lessee has an option to become the owner of the goods for a fixed price that is equal to or greater than the reasonably predictable fair market value of the goods at the time the option is to be performed.

For purposes of this subsection (37):

(x) Additional consideration is not nominal if (i) when the option to renew the lease is granted to the lessee the rent is stated to be the fair market rent for the use of the goods for the term of the renewal determined at the time the option is to be performed, or (ii) when the option to become the owner of the goods is granted to the lessee the price is stated to be the fair market value of the goods determined at the time the option is to be performed. Additional consideration is nominal if it is less than the lessee's reasonably predictable cost of performing under the lease agreement if the option is not exercised;

(y) "Reasonably predictable" and "remaining economic life of the goods" are to be determined with reference to the facts and circumstances at the time the transaction is entered into; and

(z) "Present value" means the amount as of a date certain of one

or more sums payable in the future, discounted to the date certain. The discount is determined by the interest rate specified by the parties if the rate is not manifestly unreasonable at the time the transaction is entered into; otherwise, the discount is determined by a commercially reasonable rate that takes into account the facts and circumstances of each case at the time the transaction was entered into.

(38) "Send" in connection with any writing or notice means to deposit in the mail or deliver for transmission by any other usual means of communication with postage or cost of transmission provided for and properly addressed and in the case of an instrument to an address specified thereon or otherwise agreed, or if there be none to any address reasonable under the circumstances. The receipt of any writing or notice within the time at which it would have arrived if properly sent has the effect of a proper sending.

(39) "Signed" includes any symbol executed or adopted by a party with present intention to authenticate a writing.

(40) "Surety" includes guarantor.

(41) "Telegram" includes a message transmitted by radio, teletype, cable, any mechanical method of transmission, or the like.

(42) "Term" means that portion of an agreement which relates to a particular matter.

(43) "Unauthorized" signature means one made without actual, implied or apparent authority and includes a forgery.

(44) "Value". Except as otherwise provided with respect to negotiable instruments and bank collections (Sections 3—303, 4—210 and 4—211) a person gives "value" for rights if he acquires them

(a) in return for a binding commitment to extend credit or for the extension of immediately available credit whether or not drawn upon and whether or not a chargeback is provided for in the event of difficulties in collection; or

(b) as security for or in total or partial satisfaction of a pre-existing claim; or

(c) by accepting delivery pursuant to a preexisting contract for purchase; or

(d) generally, in return for any consideration sufficient to support a simple contract.

(45) "Warehouse receipt" means a receipt issued by a person engaged in the business of storing goods for hire.

(46) "Written" or "writing" includes printing, typewriting or any other intentional reduction to tangible form.

§1—202. Prima Facie Evidence by Third Party Documents.

A document in due form purporting to be a bill of lading, policy or certificate of insurance, official weigher's or inspector's certificate, consular invoice, or any other document authorized or required by the contract to be issued by a third party shall be prima facie evidence of its own authenticity and genuineness and of the facts stated in the document by the third party.

§ 1—203. Obligation of Good Faith.

Every contract or duty within this Act imposes an obligation of good faith in its performance or enforcement.

§ 1—204. Time; Reasonable Time; "Seasonably".

(1) Whenever this Act requires any action to be taken within a reasonable time, any time which is not manifestly unreasonable may be fixed by agreement.

(2) What is a reasonable time for taking any action depends on the nature, purpose and circumstances of such action.

(3) An action is taken "seasonably" when it is taken at or within the time agreed or if no time is agreed at or within a reasonable time.

§ 1—205. Course of Dealing and Usage of Trade.

(1) A course of dealing is a sequence of previous conduct between the parties to a particular transaction which is fairly to be regarded as establishing a common basis of understanding for interpreting their expressions and other conduct.

(2) A usage of trade is any practice or method of dealing having such regularity of observance in a place, vocation or trade as to justify an expectation that it will be observed with respect to the transaction in question. The existence and scope of such a usage are to be proved as facts. If it is established that such a usage is embodied in a written trade code or similar writing the interpretation of the writing is for the court.

(3) A course of dealing between parties and any usage of trade in the vocation or trade in which they are engaged or of which they are or should be aware give particular meaning to and supplement or qualify terms of an agreement.

(4) The express terms of an agreement and an applicable course of dealing or usage of trade shall be construed wherever reasonable as consistent with each other; but when such construction is unreasonable express terms control both course of dealing and usage of trade and course of dealing controls usage trade.

(5) An applicable usage of trade in the place where any part of performance is to occur shall be used in interpreting the agreement as to that part of the performance.

(6) Evidence of a relevant usage of trade offered by one party is not admissible unless and until he has given the other party such notice as the court finds sufficient to prevent unfair surprise to the latter.

§ 1—206. Statute of Frauds for Kinds of Personal Property Not Otherwise Covered.

(1) Except in the cases described in subsection (2) of this section a contract for the sale of personal property is not enforceable by way of action or defense beyond five thousand dollars in amount or value of remedy unless there is some writing which indicates that a contract for sale has been made between the parties at a defined or stated price, reasonably identifies the subject matter, and is signed by the party against whom enforcement is sought or by his authorized agent.

(2) Subsection (1) of this section does not apply to contracts for the sale of goods (Section 2—201) nor of securities (Section 8—113) nor to security agreements (Section 9—203).

§ 1—207. Performance or Acceptance Under Reservation of Rights.

(1) A party who with explicit reservation of rights performs or promises performance or assents to performance in a manner demanded or offered by the other party does not thereby prejudice the rights reserved. Such words as "without prejudice", "under protest" or the like are sufficient.

(2) Subsection (1) does not apply to an accord and satisfaction.

§ 1—208. Option to Accelerate at Will.

A term providing that one party or his successor in interest may accelerate payment or performance or require collateral or additional collateral "at will" or "when he deems himself insecure" or in words of similar import shall be construed to mean that he shall have power to do so only if he in good faith believes that the prospect of payment or performance is impaired. The burden of establishing lack of good faith is on the party against whom the power has been exercised.

§ 1—209. Subordinated Obligations.

An obligation may be issued as subordinated to payment of another obligation of the person obligated, or a creditor may subordinate his right to payment of an obligation by agreement with either the person obligated or another creditor of the person obligated. Such a subordination does not create a security interest as against either the common debtor or a subordinated creditor. This section shall be construed as declaring the law as it existed prior to the enactment of this section and not as modifying it. Added 1966.

Note: This new section is proposed as an optional provision to make it clear that a subordination agreement does not create a security interest unless so intended.

Article 2
SALES

Part 1 Short Title, General Construction and Subject Matter

§ 2—101. Short Title.

This Article shall be known and may be cited as Uniform Commercial Code—Sales.

§ 2—102. Scope; Certain Security and Other Transactions Excluded From This Article.

Unless the context otherwise requires, this Article applies to transactions in goods; it does not apply to any transaction which although in the form of an unconditional contract to sell or present sale is intended to operate only as a security transaction nor does this Article impair or repeal any statute regulating sales to consumers, farmers or other specified classes of buyers.

§ 2—103. Definitions and Index of Definitions.

(1) In this Article unless the context otherwise requires

(a) "Buyer" means a person who buys or contracts to buy goods.

(b) "Good faith" in the case of a merchant means honesty in fact and the observance of reasonable commercial standards of fair dealing in the trade.

(c) "Receipt" of goods means taking physical possession of them.

(d) "Seller" means a person who sells or contracts to sell goods.

(2) Other definitions applying to this Article or to specified Parts thereof, and the sections in which they appear are:

"Acceptance". Section 2—606.
"Banker's credit". Section 2—325.
"Between merchants". Section 2—104.
"Cancellation". Section 2—106(4).
"Commercial unit". Section 2—105.
"Confirmed credit". Section 2—325.
"Conforming to contract". Section 2—106.
"Contract for sale". Section 2—106.
"Cover". Section 2—712.
"Entrusting". Section 2—403.
"Financing agency". Section 2—104.
"Future goods". Section 2—105.
"Goods". Section 2—105.
"Identification". Section 2—501.
"Installment contract". Section 2—612.
"Letter of Credit". Section 2—325.
"Lot". Section 2—105.
"Merchant". Section 2—104.
"Overseas". Section 2—323.
"Person in position of seller". Section 2—707.
"Present sale". Section 2—106.
"Sale". Section 2—106.
"Sale on approval". Section 2—326.
"Sale or return". Section 2—326.
"Termination". Section 2—106.

(3) The following definitions in other Articles apply to this Article:

"Check". Section 3—104.
"Consignee". Section 7—102.
"Consignor". Section 7—102.
"Consumer goods". Section 9—109.
"Dishonor". Section 3—507.
"Draft". Section 3—104.

(4) In addition Article 1 contains general definitions and principles of construction and interpretation applicable throughout this Article.

§ 2—104. Definitions: "Merchant"; "Between Merchants"; "Financing Agency".

(1) "Merchant" means a person who deals in goods of the kind or otherwise by his occupation holds himself out as having knowledge or skill peculiar to the practices or goods involved in the transaction or to whom such knowledge or skill may be attributed by his employment of an agent or broker or other intermediary who by his occupation holds himself out as having such knowledge or skill.

(2) "Financing agency" means a bank, finance company or other person who in the ordinary course of business makes advances against goods or documents of title or who by arrangement with either the seller or the buyer intervenes in ordinary course to make or collect payment due or claimed under the contract for sale, as by purchasing or paying the seller's draft or making advances against it or by merely taking it for collection whether or not documents of title accompany the draft. "Financing agency" includes also a bank or other person who similarly intervenes between persons who are in the position of seller and buyer in respect to the goods (Section 2—707).

(3) "Between merchants" means in any transaction with respect to which both parties are chargeable with the knowledge or skill of merchants.

§ 2—105. Definitions: Transferability; "Goods"; "Future" Goods; "Lot"; "Commercial Unit".

(1) "Goods" means all things (including specially manufactured goods) which are movable at the time of identification to the contract for sale other than the money in which the price is to be paid, investment securities (Article 8) and things in action. "Goods" also includes the unborn young of animals and growing crops and other identified things attached to realty as described in the section on goods to be severed from realty (Section 2—107).

(2) Goods must be both existing and identified before any interest in them can pass. Goods which are not both existing and identified are "future" goods. A purported present sale of future goods or of any interest therein operates as a contract to sell.

(3) There may be a sale of a part interest in existing identified goods.

(4) An undivided share in an identified bulk of fungible goods is sufficiently identified to be sold although the quantity of the bulk is not determined. Any agreed proportion of such a bulk or any quantity thereof agreed upon by number, weight or other measure may to the extent of the seller's interest in the bulk be sold to the buyer who then becomes an owner in common.

(5) "Lot" means a parcel or a single article which is the subject matter of a separate sale or delivery, whether or not it is sufficient to perform the contract.

(6) "Commercial unit" means such a unit of goods as by commercial usage is a single whole for purposes of sale and division of which materially impairs its character or value on the market or in use. A commercial unit may be a single article (as a machine) or a set of articles (as a suite of furniture or an assortment of sizes) or a quantity (as a bale, gross, or carload) or any other unit treated in use or in the relevant market as a single whole.

§ 2—106. Definitions: "Contract"; "Agreement"; "Contract for Sale"; "Sale"; "Present Sale"; "Conforming" to Contract; "Termination"; "Cancellation".

(1) In this Article unless the context otherwise requires "contract" and "agreement" are limited to those relating to the present or future sale of goods. "Contract for sale" includes both a present sale of goods and a contract to sell goods at a future time. A "sale" consists in the passing of title from the seller to the buyer for a price (Section 2—401). A "present sale" means a sale which is accomplished by the making of the contract.

(2) Goods or conduct including any part of a performance are "conforming" or conform to the contract when they are in accordance with the obligations under the contract.

(3) "Termination" occurs when either party pursuant to a power created by agreement or law puts an end to the contract otherwise than for its breach. On "termination" all obligations which are still executory on both sides are discharged but any right based on prior breach or performance survives.

(4) "Cancellation" occurs when either party puts an end to the contract for breach by the other and its effect is the same as that of "termination" except that the cancelling party also retains any remedy for breach of the whole contract or any unperformed balance.

§ 2—107. Goods to Be Severed From Realty: Recording.

(1) A contract for the sale of minerals or the like (including oil and gas) or a structure or its materials to be removed from realty is a contract for the sale of goods within this Article if they are to be severed by the seller but until severance a purported present sale thereof which is not effective as a transfer of an interest in land is effective only as a contract to sell.

(2) A contract for the sale apart from the land of growing crops or other things attached to realty and capable of severance without material harm thereto but not described in subsection (1) or of timber to be cut is a contract for the sale of goods within this Article whether the subject matter is to be severed by the buyer or by the seller even though it forms part of the realty at the time of contracting, and the parties can by identification effect a present sale before severance.

(3) The provisions of this section are subject to any third party rights provided by the law relating to realty records, and the contract for sale may be executed and recorded as a document transferring an interest in land and shall then constitute notice to third parties of the buyer's rights under the contract for sale.

Part 2 Form, Formation and Readjustment of Contract

§ 2—201. Formal Requirements; Statute of Frauds.

(1) Except as otherwise provided in this section a contract for the sale of goods for the price of $500 or more is not enforceable by way of action or defense unless there is some writing sufficient to indicate that a contract for sale has been made between the parties and signed by the party against whom enforcement is sought or by his authorized agent or broker. A writing is not insufficient because it omits or incorrectly states a term agreed upon but the contract is not enforceable under this paragraph beyond the quantity of goods shown in such writing.

(2) Between merchants if within a reasonable time a writing in confirmation of the contract and sufficient against the sender is received and the party receiving it has reason to know its contents, its satisfies the requirements of subsection (1) against such party unless written notice of objection to its contents is given within ten days after it is received.

(3) A contract which does not satisfy the requirements of subsection (1) but which is valid in other respects is enforceable

(a) if the goods are to be specially manufactured for the buyer and are not suitable for sale to others in the ordinary course of the seller's business and the seller, before notice of repudiation is received and under circumstances which reasonably indicate that the goods are for the buyer, has made either a substantial beginning of their manufacture or commitments for their procurement; or

(b) if the party against whom enforcement is sought admits in his pleading, testimony or otherwise in court that a contract for sale was made, but the contract is not enforceable under this provision beyond the quantity of goods admitted; or

(c) with respect to goods for which payment has been made and accepted or which have been received and accepted (Sec. 2—606).

§ 2—202. Final Written Expression: Parol or Extrinsic Evidence.

Terms with respect to which the confirmatory memoranda of the parties agree or which are otherwise set forth in a writing intended by the parties as a final expression of their agreement with respect to such terms as are included therein may not be contradicted by evidence of any prior agreement or of a contemporaneous oral agreement but may be explained or supplemented

(a) by course of dealing or usage of trade (Section 1—205) or by course of performance (Section 2—208); and

(b) by evidence of consistent additional terms unless the court finds the writing to have been intended also as a complete and exclusive statement of the terms of the agreement.

§ 2—203. Seals Inoperative.

The affixing of a seal to a writing evidencing a contract for sale or an offer to buy or sell goods does not constitute the writing a sealed instrument and the law with respect to sealed instruments does not apply to such a contract or offer.

§ 2—204. Formation in General.

(1) A contract for sale of goods may be made in any manner sufficient to show agreement, including conduct by both parties which recognizes the existence of such a contract.

(2) An agreement sufficient to constitute a contract for sale may be found even though the moment of its making is undetermined.

(3) Even though one or more terms are left open a contract for sale does not fail for indefiniteness if the parties have intended to make a contract and there is a reasonably certain basis for giving an appropriate remedy.

§ 2—205. Firm Offers.

An offer by a merchant to buy or sell goods in a signed writing which by its terms gives assurance that it will be held open is not revocable, for lack of consideration, during the time stated or if no time is stated for a reasonable time, but in no event may such period of irrevocability exceed three months; but any such term of assurance on a form supplied by the offeree must be separately signed by the offeror.

§ 2—206. Offer and Acceptance in Formation of Contract.

(1) Unless otherwise unambiguously indicated by the language or circumstances

(a) an offer to make a contract shall be construed as inviting acceptance in any manner and by any medium reasonable in the circumstances;

(b) an order or other offer to buy goods for prompt or current shipment shall be construed as inviting acceptance either by a prompt promise to ship or by the prompt or current shipment of conforming or nonconforming goods, but such a shipment of nonconforming goods does not constitute an acceptance if the seller seasonably notifies the buyer that the shipment is offered only as an accommodation to the buyer.

(2) Where the beginning of a requested performance is a reasonable mode of acceptance an offeror who is not notified of acceptance within a reasonable time may treat the offer as having lapsed before acceptance.

§ 2—207. Additional Terms in Acceptance or Confirmation.

(1) A definite and seasonable expression of acceptance or a written confirmation which is sent within a reasonable time operates as an acceptance even though it states terms additional to or different from those offered or agreed upon, unless acceptance is expressly made conditional on assent to the additional or different terms.

(2) The additional terms are to be construed as proposals for addition to the contract. Between merchants such terms become part of the contract unless:

> (a) the offer expressly limits acceptance to the terms of the offer;
>
> (b) they materially alter it; or
>
> (c) notification of objection to them has already been given or is given within a reasonable time after notice of them is received.

(3) Conduct by both parties which recognizes the existence of a contract is sufficient to establish a contract for sale although the writings of the parties do not otherwise establish a contract. In such case the terms of the particular contract consist of those terms on which the writings of the parties agree, together with any supplementary terms incorporated under any other provisions of this Act.

§ 2—208. Course of Performance or Practical Construction.

(1) Where the contract for sale involves repeated occasions for performance by either party with knowledge of the nature of the performance and opportunity for objection to it by the other, any course of performance accepted or acquiesced in without objection shall be relevant to determine the meaning of the agreement.

(2) The express terms of the agreement and any such course of performance, as well as any course of dealing and usage of trade, shall be construed whenever reasonable as consistent with each other; but when such construction is unreasonable, express terms shall control course of performance and course of performance shall control both course of dealing and usage of trade (Section 1—205).

(3) Subject to the provisions of the next section on modification and waiver, such course of performance shall be relevant to show a waiver or modification of any term inconsistent with such course of performance.

§ 2—209. Modification, Rescission and Waiver.

(1) An agreement modifying a contract within this Article needs no consideration to be binding.

(2) A signed agreement which excludes modification or rescission except by a signed writing cannot be otherwise modified or rescinded, but except as between merchants such a requirement on a form supplied by the merchant must be separately signed by the other party.

(3) The requirements of the statute of frauds section of this Article (Section 2—201) must be satisfied if the contract as modified is within its provisions.

(4) Although an attempt at modification or rescission does not satisfy the requirements of subsection (2) or (3) it can operate as a waiver.

(5) A party who has made a waiver affecting an executory portion of the contract may retract the waiver by reasonable notification received by the other party that strict performance will be required of any term waived, unless the retraction would be unjust in view of a material change of position in reliance on the waiver.

§ 2—210. Delegation of Performance; Assignment of Rights.

(1) A party may perform his duty through a delegate unless otherwise agreed or unless the other party has a substantial interest in having his original promisor perform or control the acts required by the contract. No delegation of performance relieves the party delegating of any duty to perform or any liability for breach.

(2) Unless otherwise agreed all rights of either seller or buyer can be assigned except where the assignment would materially change the duty of the other party, or increase materially the burden or risk imposed on him by his contract, or impair materially his chance of obtaining return performance. A right to damages for breach of the whole contract or a right arising out of the assignor's due performance of his entire obligation can be assigned despite agreement otherwise.

(3) Unless the circumstances indicate the contrary a prohibition of assignment of "the contract" is to be construed as barring only the delegation to the assignee of the assignor's performance.

(4) An assignment of "the contract" or of "all my rights under the contract" or an assignment in similar general terms is an assignment of rights and unless the language or the circumstances (as in an assignment for security) indicate the contrary, it is a delegation of performance of the duties of the assignor and its acceptance by the assignee constitutes a promise by him to perform those duties. This promise is enforceable by either the assignor or the other party to the original contract.

(5) The other party may treat any assignment which delegates performance as creating reasonable grounds for insecurity and may without prejudice to his rights against the assignor demand assurances from the assignee (Section 2—609).

Part 3 General Obligation and Construction of Contract

§ 2—301. General Obligations of Parties.

The obligation of the seller is to transfer and deliver and that of the buyer is to accept and pay in accordance with the contract.

§ 2—302. Unconscionable Contract or Clause.

(1) If the court as a matter of law finds the contract or any clause of the contract to have been unconscionable at the time it was made the court may refuse to enforce the contract, or it may enforce the remainder of the contract without the unconscionable clause, or it may so limit the application of any unconscionable clause as to avoid any unconscionable result.

(2) When it is claimed or appears to the court that the contract or any clause thereof may be unconscionable the parties shall be afforded a reasonable opportunity to present evidence as to its commercial set-

ting, purpose and effect to aid the court in making the determination.

§ 2—303. Allocations or Division of Risks.

Where this Article allocates a risk or a burden as between the parties "unless otherwise agreed", the agreement may not only shift the allocation but may also divide the risk or burden.

§ 2—304. Price Payable in Money, Goods, Realty, or Otherwise.

(1) The price can be made payable in money or otherwise. If it is payable in whole or in part in goods each party is a seller of the goods which he is to transfer.

(2) Even though all or part of the price is payable in an interest in realty the transfer of the goods and the seller's obligations with reference to them are subject to this Article, but not the transfer of the interest in realty or the transferor's obligations in connection therewith.

§ 2—305. Open Price Term.

(1) The parties if they so intend can conclude a contract for sale even though the price is not settled. In such a case the price is a reasonable price at the time for delivery if

(a) nothing is said as to price; or

(b) the price is left to be agreed by the parties and they fail to agree; or

(c) the price is to be fixed in terms of some agreed market or other standard as set or recorded by a third person or agency and it is not so set or recorded.

(2) A price to be fixed by the seller or by the buyer means a price for him to fix in good faith.

(3) When a price left to be fixed otherwise than by agreement of the parties fails to be fixed through fault of one party the other may at his option treat the contract as cancelled or himself fix a reasonable price.

(4) Where, however, the parties intend not to be bound unless the price be fixed or agreed and it is not fixed or agreed there is no contract. In such a case the buyer must return any goods already received or if unable so to do must pay their reasonable value at the time of delivery and the seller must return any portion of the price paid on account.

§ 2—306. Output, Requirements and Exclusive Dealings.

(1) A term which measures the quantity by the output of the seller or the requirements of the buyer means such actual output or requirements as may occur in good faith, except that no quantity unreasonably disproportionate to any stated estimate or in the absence of a stated estimate to any normal or otherwise comparable prior output or requirements may be tendered or demanded.

(2) A lawful agreement by either the seller or the buyer for exclusive dealing in the kind of goods concerned imposes unless otherwise agreed an obligation by the seller to use best efforts to supply the goods and by the buyer to use best efforts to promote their sale.

§ 2—307. Delivery in Single Lot or Several Lots.

Unless otherwise agreed all goods called for by a contract for sale must be tendered in a single delivery and payment is due only on such tender but where the circumstances give either party the right to make or demand delivery in lots the price if it can be apportioned may be demanded for each lot.

§ 2—308. Absence of Specified Place for Delivery.

Unless otherwise agreed

(a) the place for delivery of goods is the seller's place of business or if he has none his residence; but

(b) in a contract for sale of identified goods which to the knowledge of the parties at the time of contracting are in some other place, that place is the place for their delivery; and

(c) documents of title may be delivered through customary banking channels.

§ 2—309. Absence of Specific Time Provisions; Notice of Termination.

(1) The time for shipment or delivery or any other action under a contract if not provided in this Article or agreed upon shall be a reasonable time.

(2) Where the contract provides for successive performances but is indefinite in duration it is valid for a reasonable time but unless otherwise agreed may be terminated at any time by either party.

(3) Termination of a contract by one party except on the happening of an agreed event requires that reasonable notification be received by the other party and an agreement dispensing with notification is invalid if its operation would be unconscionable.

§ 2—310. Open Time for Payment or Running of Credit; Authority to Ship Under Reservation.

Unless otherwise agreed

(a) payment is due at the time and place at which the buyer is to receive the goods even though the place of shipment is the place of delivery; and

(b) if the seller is authorized to send the goods he may ship them under reservation, and may tender the documents of title, but the buyer may inspect the goods after their arrival before payment is due unless such inspection is inconsistent with the terms of the contract (Section 2—513); and

(c) if delivery is authorized and made by way of documents of title otherwise than by subsection (b) then payment is due at the time and place at which the buyer is to receive the documents regardless of where the goods are to be received; and

(d) where the seller is required or authorized to ship the goods on credit the credit period runs from the time of shipment but post-dating the invoice or delaying its dispatch will correspondingly delay the starting of the credit period.

§ 2—311. Options and Cooperation Respecting Performance.

(1) An agreement for sale which is otherwise sufficiently definite (subsection (3) of Section 2—204) to be a contract is not made invalid by the fact that it leaves particulars of performance to be specified by one of the parties. Any such specification must be made in good faith and within limits set by commercial reasonableness.

(2) Unless otherwise agreed specifications relating to assortment of the goods are at the buyer's option and except as otherwise provided in subsections (1)(c) and (3) of Section 2—319 specifications or arrangements relating to shipment are at the seller's option.

(3) Where such specification would materially affect the other party's performance but is not seasonably made or where one party's cooperation is necessary to the agreed performance of the other but is not seasonably forthcoming, the other party in addition to all other remedies

(a) is excused for any resulting delay in his own performance; and

(b) may also either proceed to perform in any reasonable manner or after the time for a material part of his own performance treat the failure to specify or to cooperate as a breach by failure to deliver or accept the goods.

§ 2—312. Warranty of Title and Against Infringement; Buyer's Obligation Against Infringement.

(1) Subject to subsection (2) there is in a contract for sale a warranty by the seller that

(a) the title conveyed shall be good, and its transfer rightful; and

(b) the goods shall be delivered free from any security interest or other lien or encumbrance of which the buyer at the time of contracting has no knowledge.

(2) A warranty under subsection (1) will be excluded or modified only by specific language or by circumstances which give the buyer reason to know that the person selling does not claim title in himself or that he is purporting to sell only such right or title as he or a third person may have.

(3) Unless otherwise agreed a seller who is a merchant regularly dealing in goods of the kind warrants that the goods shall be delivered free of the rightful claim of any third person by way of infringement or the like but a buyer who furnishes specifications to the seller must hold the seller harmless against any such claim which arises out of compliance with the specifications.

§ 2—313. Express Warranties by Affirmation, Promise, Description, Sample.

(1) Express warranties by the seller are created as follows:

(a) Any affirmation of fact or promise made by the seller to the buyer which relates to the goods and becomes part of the basis of the bargain creates an express warranty that the goods shall conform to the affirmation or promise.

(b) Any description of the goods which is made part of the basis of the bargain creates an express warranty that the goods shall conform to the description.

(c) Any sample or model which is made part of the basis of the bargain creates an express warranty that the whole of the goods shall conform to the sample or model.

(2) It is not necessary to the creation of an express warranty that the seller use formal words such as "warrant" or "guarantee" or that he have a specific intention to make a warranty, but an affirmation merely of the value of the goods or a statement purporting to be merely the seller's opinion or commendation of the goods does not

create a warranty.

§ 2—314. Implied Warranty: Merchantability; Usage of Trade.

(1) Unless excluded or modified (Section 2—316), a warranty that the goods shall be merchantable is implied in a contract for their sale if the seller is a merchant with respect to goods of that kind. Under this section the serving for value of food or drink to be consumed either on the premises or elsewhere is a sale.

(2) Goods to be merchantable must be at least such as

(a) pass without objection in the trade under the contract description; and

(b) in the case of fungible goods, are of fair average quality within the description; and

(c) are fit for the ordinary purposes for which such goods are used; and

(d) run, within the variations permitted by the agreement, of even kind, quality and quantity within each unit and among all units involved; and

(e) are adequately contained, packaged, and labeled as the agreement may require; and

(f) conform to the promises or affirmations of fact made on the container or label if any.

(3) Unless excluded or modified (Section 2—316) other implied warranties may arise from course of dealing or usage of trade.

§ 2—315. Implied Warranty: Fitness for Particular Purpose.

Where the seller at the time of contracting has reason to know any particular purpose for which the goods are required and that the buyer is relying on the seller's skill or judgment to select or furnish suitable goods, there is unless excluded or modified under the next section an implied warranty that the goods shall be fit for such purpose.

§ 2—316. Exclusion or Modification of Warranties.

(1) Words or conduct relevant to the creation of an express warranty and words or conduct tending to negate or limit warranty shall be construed wherever reasonable as consistent with each other; but subject to the provisions of this Article on parol or extrinsic evidence (Section 2—202) negation or limitation is inoperative to the extent that such construction is unreasonable.

(2) Subject to subsection (3), to exclude or modify the implied warranty of merchantability or any part of it the language must mention merchantability and in case of a writing must be conspicuous, and to exclude or modify any implied warranty of fitness the exclusion must be by a writing and conspicuous. Language to exclude all implied warranties of fitness is sufficient if it states, for example, that "There are no warranties which extend beyond the description on the face hereof."

(3) Notwithstanding subsection (2)

(a) unless the circumstances indicate otherwise, all implied warranties are excluded by expressions like "as is", "with all faults" or other language which in common understanding calls the buyer's attention to the exclusion of warranties and makes plain that there is no implied warranty; and

(b) when the buyer before entering into the contract has examined the goods or the sample or model as fully as he desired or has refused to examine the goods there is no implied warranty with regard to defects which an examination ought in the circumstances to have revealed to him; and

(c) an implied warranty can also be excluded or modified by course of dealing or course of performance or usage of trade.

(4) Remedies for breach of warranty can be limited in accordance with the provisions of this Article on liquidation or limitation of damages and on contractual modification of remedy (Sections 2—718 and 2—719).

§ 2—317. Cumulation and Conflict of Warranties Express or Implied.

Warranties whether express or implied shall be construed as consistent with each other and as cumulative, but if such construction is unreasonable the intention of the parties shall determine which warranty is dominant. In ascertaining that intention the following rules apply:

(a) Exact or technical specifications displace an inconsistent sample or model or general language of description.

(b) A sample from an existing bulk displaces inconsistent general language of description.

(c) Express warranties displace inconsistent implied warranties other than an implied warranty of fitness for a particular purpose.

§ 2—318. Third Party Beneficiaries of Warranties Express or Implied.

Note: If this Act is introduced in the Congress of the United States this section should be omitted. (States to select one alternative.)

Alternative A

A seller's warranty whether express or implied extends to any natural person who is in the family or household of his buyer or who is a guest in his home if it is reasonable to expect that such person may use, consume or be affected by the goods and who is injured in person by breach of the warranty. A seller may not exclude or limit the operation of this section.

Alternative B

A seller's warranty whether express or implied extends to any natural person who may reasonably be expected to use, consume or be affected by the goods and who is injured in person by breach of the warranty. A seller may not exclude or limit the operation of this section.

Alternative C

A seller's warranty whether express or implied extends to any person who may reasonably be expected to use, consume or be affected by the goods and who is injured by breach of the warranty. A seller may not exclude or limit the operation of this section with respect to injury to the person of an individual to whom the warranty extends. As amended 1966.

§ 2—319. F.O.B. and F.A.S. Terms.

(1) Unless otherwise agreed the term F.O.B. (which means "free on board") at a named place, even though used only in connection with the stated price, is a delivery term under which

(a) when the term is F.O.B. the place of shipment, the seller must at that place ship the goods in the manner provided in this Article (Section 2—504) and bear the expense and risk of putting them into the possession of the carrier; or

(b) when the term is F.O.B. the place of destination, the seller must at his own expense and risk transport the goods to that place and there tender delivery of them in the manner provided in this Article (Section 2—503);

(c) when under either (a) or (b) the term is also F.O.B. vessel, car or other vehicle, the seller must in addition at his own expense and risk load the goods on board. If the term is F.O.B. vessel the buyer must name the vessel and in an appropriate case the seller must comply with the provisions of this Article on the form of bill of lading (Section 2—323).

(2) Unless otherwise agreed the term F.A.S. vessel (which means "free alongside") at a named port, even though used only in connection with the stated price, is a delivery term under which the seller must

(a) at his own expense and risk deliver the goods alongside the vessel in the manner usual in that port or on a dock designated and provided by the buyer; and

(b) obtain and tender a receipt for the goods in exchange for which the carrier is under a duty to issue a bill of lading.

(3) Unless otherwise agreed in any case falling within subsection (1)(a) or (c) or subsection (2) the buyer must seasonably give any needed instructions for making delivery, including when the term is F.A.S. or F.O.B. the loading berth of the vessel and in an appropriate case its name and sailing date. The seller may treat the failure of needed instructions as a failure of cooperation under this Article (Section 2—311). He may also at his option move the goods in any reasonable manner preparatory to delivery or shipment.

(4) Under the term F.O.B. vessel or F.A.S. unless otherwise agreed the buyer must make payment against tender of the required documents and the seller may not tender nor the buyer demand delivery of the goods in substitution for the documents.

§ 2—320. C.I.F. and C. & F. Terms.

(1) The term C.I.F. means that the price includes in a lump sum the cost of the goods and the insurance and freight to the named destination. The term C. & F. or C.F. means that the price so includes cost and freight to the named destination.

(2) Unless otherwise agreed and even though used only in connection with the stated price and destination, the term C.I.F. destination or its equivalent requires the seller at his own expense and risk to

(a) put the goods into the possession of a carrier at the port for shipment and obtain a negotiable bill or bills of lading covering the entire transportation to the named destination; and

(b) load the goods and obtain a receipt from the carrier (which may be contained in the bill of lading) showing that the freight has been paid or provided for; and

(c) obtain a policy or certificate of insurance, including any war risk insurance, of a kind and on terms then current at the port of shipment in the usual amount, in the currency of the contract, shown to cover the same goods covered by the bill of lading and providing for payment of loss to the order of the buyer or for the account of whom it may concern; but the seller may add to the price the amount of the premium for any such war risk insurance; and

(d) prepare an invoice of the goods and procure any other documents required to effect shipment or to comply with the contract; and

(e) forward and tender with commercial promptness all the documents in due form and with any indorsement necessary to perfect the buyer's rights.

(3) Unless otherwise agreed the term C. & F. or its equivalent has the same effect and imposes upon the seller the same obligations and risks as a C.I.F. term except the obligation as to insurance.

(4) Under the term C.I.F. or C. & F. unless otherwise agreed the buyer must make payment against tender of the required documents and the seller may not tender nor the buyer demand delivery of the goods in substitution for the documents.

§ 2—321. C.I.F. or C. & F.: "Net Landed Weights"; "Payment on Arrival"; Warranty of Condition on Arrival.

Under a contract containing a term C.I.F. or C. & F.

(1) Where the price is based on or is to be adjusted according to "net landed weights", "delivered weights", "out turn" quantity or quality or the like, unless otherwise agreed the seller must reasonably estimate the price. The payment due on tender of the documents called for by the contract is the amount so estimated, but after final adjustment of the price a settlement must be made with commercial promptness.

(2) An agreement described in subsection (1) or any warranty of quality or condition of the goods on arrival places upon the seller the risk of ordinary deterioration, shrinkage and the like in transportation but has no effect on the place or time of identification to the contract for sale or delivery or on the passing of the risk of loss.

(3) Unless otherwise agreed where the contract provides for payment on or after arrival of the goods the seller must before payment allow such preliminary inspection as is feasible; but if the goods are lost delivery of the documents and payment are due when the goods should have arrived.

§ 2—322. Delivery "Ex-Ship".

(1) Unless otherwise agreed a term for delivery of goods "ex-ship" (which means from the carrying vessel) or in equivalent language is not restricted to a particular ship and requires delivery from a ship which has reached a place at the named port of destination where goods of the kind are usually discharged.

(2) Under such a term unless otherwise agreed

(a) the seller must discharge all liens arising out of the carriage and furnish the buyer with a direction which puts the carrier under a duty to deliver the goods; and

(b) the risk of loss does not pass to the buyer until the goods leave the ship's tackle or are otherwise properly unloaded.

§ 2—323. Form of Bill of Lading Required in Overseas Shipment; "Overseas".

(1) Where the contract contemplates overseas shipment and contains a term C.I.F. or C. & F. or F.O.B. vessel, the seller unless otherwise agreed must obtain a negotiable bill of lading stating that the goods have been loaded on board or, in the case of a term C.I.F. or C. & F., received for shipment.

(2) Where in a case within subsection (1) a bill of lading has been issued in a set of parts, unless otherwise agreed if the documents are not to be sent from abroad the buyer may demand tender of the full set; otherwise only one part of the bill of lading need be tendered. Even if the agreement expressly requires a full set

(a) due tender of a single part is acceptable within the provisions of this Article on cure of improper delivery (subsection (1) of Section 2—508); and

(b) even though the full set is demanded, if the documents are sent from abroad the person tendering an incomplete set may nevertheless require payment upon furnishing an indemnity which the buyer in good faith deems adequate.

(3) A shipment by water or by air or a contract contemplating such shipment is "overseas" insofar as by usage of trade or agreement it is subject to the commercial, financing or shipping practices characteristic of international deep water commerce.

§ 2—324. "No Arrival, No Sale" Term.

Under a term "no arrival, no sale" or terms of like meaning, unless otherwise agreed,

(a) the seller must properly ship conforming goods and if they arrive by any means he must tender them on arrival but he assumes no obligation that the goods will arrive unless he has caused the non-arrival; and

(b) where without fault of the seller the goods are in part lost or have so deteriorated as no longer to conform to the contract or arrive after the contract time, the buyer may proceed as if there had been casualty to identified goods (Section 2—613).

§ 2—325. "Letter of Credit" Term; "Confirmed Credit".

(1) Failure of the buyer seasonably to furnish an agreed letter of credit is a breach of the contract for sale.

(2) The delivery to seller of a proper letter of credit suspends the buyer's obligation to pay. If the letter of credit is dishonored, the seller may on seasonable notification to the buyer require payment directly from him.

(3) Unless otherwise agreed the term "letter of credit" or "banker's credit" in a contract for sale means an irrevocable credit issued by a financing agency of good repute and, where the shipment is overseas, of good international repute. The term "confirmed credit" means that the credit must also carry the direct obligation of such an agency which does business in the seller's financial market.

§ 2—326. Sale on Approval and Sale or Return; Consignment Sales and Rights of Creditors.

(1) Unless otherwise agreed, if delivered goods may be returned by the buyer even though they conform to the contract, the transaction is

(a) a "sale on approval" if the goods are delivered primarily for use, and

(b) a "sale or return" if the goods are delivered primarily for resale.

(2) Except as provided in subsection (3), goods held on approval are not subject to the claims of the buyer's creditors until acceptance; goods held on sale or return are subject to such claims while in the buyer's possession.

(3) Where goods are delivered to a person for sale and such person maintains a place of business at which he deals in goods of the kind involved, under a name other than the name of the person making delivery, then with respect to claims of creditors of the person conducting the business the goods are deemed to be on sale or return. The provisions of this subsection are applicable even though an agreement purports to reserve title to the person making delivery until payment or resale or uses such words as "on consignment" or "on memorandum". However, this subsection is not applicable if the person making delivery

(a) complies with an applicable law providing for a consignor's interest or the like to be evidenced by a sign, or

(b) establishes that the person conducting the business is generally known by his creditors to be substantially engaged in selling the goods of others, or

(c) complies with the filing provisions of the Article on Secured Transactions (Article 9).

(4) Any "or return" term of a contract for sale is to be treated as a separate contract for sale within the statute of frauds section of this Article (Section 2—201) and as contradicting the sale aspect of the contract within the provisions of this Article on parol or extrinsic evidence (Section 2—202).

§ 2—327. Special Incidents of Sale on Approval and Sale or Return.

(1) Under a sale on approval unless otherwise agreed

(a) although the goods are identified to the contract the risk of loss and the title do not pass to the buyer until acceptance; and

(b) use of the goods consistent with the purpose of trial is not acceptance but failure seasonably to notify the seller of election to return the goods is acceptance, and if the goods conform to the contract acceptance of any part is acceptance of the whole; and

(c) after due notification of election to return, the return is at the seller's risk and expense but a merchant buyer must follow any reasonable instructions.

(2) Under a sale or return unless otherwise agreed

(a) the option to return extends to the whole or any commercial unit of the goods while in substantially their original condition, but must be exercised seasonably; and

(b) the return is at the buyer's risk and expense.

§ 2—328. Sale by Auction.

(1) In a sale by auction if goods are put up in lots each lot is the subject of a separate sale.

(2) A sale by auction is complete when the auctioneer so announces by the fall of the hammer or in other customary manner. Where a bid is made while the hammer is falling in acceptance of a prior bid the auctioneer may in his discretion reopen the bidding or declare the goods sold under the bid on which the hammer was falling.

(3) Such a sale is with reserve unless the goods are in explicit terms put up without reserve. In an auction with reserve the auctioneer may withdraw the goods at any time until he announces completion of the sale. In an auction without reserve, after the auctioneer calls for bids on an article or lot, that article or lot cannot be withdrawn unless no bid is made within a reasonable time. In either case a bidder may retract his bid until the auctioneer's announcement of completion of the sale, but a bidder's retraction does not revive any previous bid.

(4) If the auctioneer knowingly receives a bid on the seller's behalf or the seller makes or procures such as bid, and notice has not been given that liberty for such bidding is reserved, the buyer may at his option avoid the sale or take the goods at the price of the last good faith bid prior to the completion of the sale. This subsection shall not apply to any bid at a forced sale.

Part 4 Title, Creditors and Good Faith Purchasers

§ 2—401. Passing of Title; Reservation for Security; Limited Application of This Section.

Each provision of this Article with regard to the rights, obligations and remedies of the seller, the buyer, purchasers or other third parties applies irrespective of title to the goods except where the provision refers to such title. Insofar as situations are not covered by the other provisions of this Article and matters concerning title became material the following rules apply:

(1) Title to goods cannot pass under a contract for sale prior to their identification to the contract (Section 2—501), and unless otherwise explicitly agreed the buyer acquires by their identification a special property as limited by this Act. Any retention or reservation by the seller of the title (property) in goods shipped or delivered to the buyer is limited in effect to a reservation of a security interest. Subject to these provisions and to the provisions of the Article on Secured Transactions (Article 9), title to goods passes from the seller to the buyer in any manner and on any conditions explicitly agreed on by the parties.

(2) Unless otherwise explicitly agreed title passes to the buyer at the time and place at which the seller completes his performance with reference to the physical delivery of the goods, despite any reservation of a security interest and even though a document of title is to be delivered at a different time or place; and in particular and despite any reservation of a security interest by the bill of lading

(a) if the contract requires or authorizes the seller to send the goods to the buyer but does not require him to deliver them at destination, title passes to the buyer at the time and place of shipment; but

(b) if the contract requires delivery at destination, title passes on tender there.

(3) Unless otherwise explicitly agreed where delivery is to be made without moving the goods,

(a) if the seller is to deliver a document of title, title passes at the time when and the place where he delivers such documents; or

(b) if the goods are at the time of contracting already identified and no documents are to be delivered, title passes at the time and place of contracting.

(4) A rejection or other refusal by the buyer to receive or retain the goods, whether or not justified, or a justified revocation of acceptance revests title to the goods in the seller. Such revesting occurs by operation of law and is not a "sale".

§ 2—402. Rights of Seller's Creditors Against Sold Goods.

(1) Except as provided in subsections (2) and (3), rights of unsecured creditors of the seller with respect to goods which have been identified to a contract for sale are subject to the buyer's rights to recover the goods under this Article (Sections 2—502 and 2—716).

(2) A creditor of the seller may treat a sale or an identification of goods to a contract for sale as void if as against him a retention of possession by the seller is fraudulent under any rule of law of the state where the goods are situated, except that retention of possession in good faith and current course of trade by a merchant-seller for a commercially reasonable time after a sale or identification is not fraudulent.

(3) Nothing in this Article shall be deemed to impair the rights of creditors of the seller

(a) under the provisions of the Article on Secured Transactions (Article 9); or

(b) where identification to the contract or delivery is made not in current course of trade but in satisfaction of or as security for a pre-existing claim for money, security or the like and is made under circumstances which under any rule of law of the state where the goods are situated would apart from this Article constitute the transaction a fraudulent transfer or voidable preference.

§ 2—403. Power to Transfer; Good Faith Purchase of Goods; "Entrusting".

(1) A purchaser of goods acquires all title which his transferor had or had power to transfer except that a purchaser of a limited interest acquires rights only to the extent of the interest purchased. A person with voidable title has power to transfer a good title to a good faith purchaser for value. When goods have been delivered under a transaction of purchase the purchaser has such power even though

(a) the transferor was deceived as to the identity of the purchaser, or

(b) the delivery was in exchange for a check which is later dishonored, or

(c) it was agreed that the transaction was to be a "cash sale", or

(d) the delivery was procured through fraud punishable as larcenous under the criminal law.

(2) Any entrusting of possession of goods to a merchant who deals in goods of that kind gives him power to transfer all rights of the entruster to a buyer in ordinary course of business.

(3) "Entrusting" includes any delivery and any acquiescence in retention of possession regardless of any condition expressed between the parties to the delivery or acquiescence and regardless of whether the procurement of the entrusting or the possessor's disposition of the goods have been such as to be larcenous under the criminal law.

(4) The rights of other purchasers of goods and of lien creditors are governed by the Articles on Secured Transactions (Article 9), Bulk Transfers (Article 6) and Documents of Title (Article 7).

Part 5 Performance

§ 2—501. Insurable Interest in Goods; Manner of Identification of Goods.

(1) The buyer obtains a special property and an insurable interest in goods by identification of existing goods as goods to which the contract refers even though the goods so identified are non-conforming and he has an option to return or reject them. Such identification can be made at any time and in any manner explicitly agreed to by the parties. In the absence of explicit agreement identification occurs

(a) when the contract is made if it is for the sale of goods already existing and identified;

(b) if the contract is for the sale of future goods other than those described in paragraph (c), when goods are shipped, marked or otherwise designated by the seller as goods to which the contract refers;

(c) when the crops are planted or otherwise become growing crops or the young are conceived if the contract is for the sale of unborn young to be born within twelve months after contracting or for the sale of crops to be harvested within twelve months or the next normal harvest season after contracting whichever is longer.

(2) The seller retains an insurable interest in goods so long as title to or any security interest in the goods remains in him and where the identification is by the seller alone he may until default or insolvency or notification to the buyer that the identification is final substitute other goods for those identified.

(3) Nothing in this section impairs any insurable interest recognized under any other statute or rule of law.

§ 2—502. Buyer's Right to Goods on Seller's Insolvency.

(1) Subject to subsection (2) and even though the goods have not been shipped a buyer who has paid a part or all of the price of goods in which he has a special property under the provisions of the immediately preceding section may on making and keeping good a tender of any unpaid portion of their price recover them from the seller if the seller becomes insolvent within ten days after receipt of the first installment on their price.

(2) If the identification creating his special property has been made by the buyer he acquires the right to recover the goods only if they conform to the contract for sale.

§ 2—503. Manner of Seller's Tender of Delivery.

(1) Tender of delivery requires that the seller put and hold conforming goods at the buyer's disposition and give the buyer any notification reasonably necessary to enable him to take delivery. The manner, time and place for tender are determined by the agreement and this Article, and in particular

(a) tender must be at a reasonable hour, and if it is of goods they must be kept available for the period reasonably necessary to enable the buyer to take possession; but

(b) unless otherwise agreed the buyer must furnish facilities reasonably suited to the receipt of the goods.

(2) Where the case is within the next section respecting shipment tender requires that the seller comply with its provisions.

(3) Where the seller is required to deliver at a particular destination tender requires that he comply with subsection (1) and also in any appropriate case tender documents as described in subsections (4) and (5) of this section.

(4) Where goods are in the possession of a bailee and are to be delivered without being moved

(a) tender requires that the seller either tender a negotiable document of title covering such goods or procure acknowledgment by the bailee of the buyer's right to possession of the goods; but

(b) tender to the buyer of a non-negotiable document of title or of a written direction to the bailee to deliver is sufficient tender unless the buyer seasonably objects, and receipt by the bailee of notification of the buyer's rights fixes those rights as against the bailee and all third persons; but risk of loss of the goods and of any failure by the bailee to honor the non-negotiable document of title or to obey the direction remains on the seller until the buyer has had a reasonable time to present the document or direction, and a refusal by the bailee to honor the document or to obey the direction defeats the tender.

(5) Where the contract requires the seller to deliver documents

(a) he must tender all such documents in correct form, except as provided in this Article with respect to bills of lading in a set (subsection (2) of Section 2—323); and

(b) tender through customary banking channels is sufficient and dishonor of a draft accompanying the documents constitutes non-acceptance or rejection.

§ 2—504. Shipment by Seller.

Where the seller is required or authorized to send the goods to the buyer and the contract does not require him to deliver them at a particular destination, then unless otherwise agreed he must

(a) put the goods in the possession of such a carrier and make such a contract for their transportation as may be reasonable having regard to the nature of the goods and other circumstances of the case; and

(b) obtain and promptly deliver or tender in due form any document necessary to enable the buyer to obtain possession of the goods or otherwise required by the agreement or by usage of trade; and

(c) promptly notify the buyer of the shipment.

Failure to notify the buyer under paragraph (c) or to make a proper contract under paragraph (a) is a ground for rejection only if material delay or loss ensues.

§ 2—505. Seller's Shipment under Reservation.

(1) Where the seller has identified goods to the contract by or before

shipment:

(a) his procurement of a negotiable bill of lading to his own order or otherwise reserves in him a security interest in the goods. His procurement of the bill to the order of a financing agency or of the buyer indicates in addition only the seller's expectation of transferring that interest to the person named.

(b) a non-negotiable bill of lading to himself or his nominee reserves possession of the goods as security but except in a case of conditional delivery (subsection (2) of Section 2—507) a non-negotiable bill of lading naming the buyer as consignee reserves no security interest even though the seller retains possession of the bill of lading.

(2) When shipment by the seller with reservation of a security interest is in violation of the contract for sale it constitutes an improper contract for transportation within the preceding section but impairs neither the rights given to the buyer by shipment and identification of the goods to the contract nor the seller's powers as a holder of a negotiable document.

§ 2—506. Rights of Financing Agency.

(1) A financing agency by paying or purchasing for value a draft which relates to a shipment of goods acquires to the extent of the payment or purchase and in addition to its own rights under the draft and any document of title securing it any rights of the shipper in the goods including the right to stop delivery and the shipper's right to have the draft honored by the buyer.

(2) The right to reimbursement of a financing agency which has in good faith honored or purchased the draft under commitment to or authority from the buyer is not impaired by subsequent discovery of defects with reference to any relevant document which was apparently regular on its face.

§ 2—507. Effect of Seller's Tender; Delivery on Condition.

(1) Tender of delivery is a condition to the buyer's duty to accept the goods and, unless otherwise agreed, to his duty to pay for them. Tender entitles the seller to acceptance of the goods and to payment according to the contract.

(2) Where payment is due and demanded on the delivery to the buyer of goods or documents of title, his right as against the seller to retain or dispose of them is conditional upon his making the payment due.

§ 2—508. Cure by Seller of Improper Tender or Delivery; Replacement.

(1) Where any tender or delivery by the seller is rejected because non-conforming and the time for performance has not yet expired, the seller may seasonably notify the buyer of his intention to cure and may then within the contract time make a conforming delivery.

(2) Where the buyer rejects a non-conforming tender which the seller had reasonable grounds to believe would be acceptable with or without money allowance the seller may if he seasonably notifies the buyer have a further reasonable time to substitute a conforming tender.

§ 2—509. Risk of Loss in the Absence of Breach.

(1) Where the contract requires or authorizes the seller to ship the

goods by carrier

(a) if it does not require him to deliver them at a particular destination, the risk of loss passes to the buyer when the goods are duly delivered to the carrier even though the shipment is under reservation (Section 2—505); but

(b) if it does require him to deliver them at a particular destination and the goods are there duly tendered while in the possession of the carrier, the risk of loss passes to the buyer when the goods are there duly so tendered as to enable the buyer to take delivery.

(2) Where the goods are held by a bailee to be delivered without being moved, the risk of loss passes to the buyer

(a) on his receipt of a negotiable document of title covering the goods; or

(b) on acknowledgment by the bailee of the buyer's right to possession of the goods; or

(c) after his receipt of a non-negotiable document of title or other written direction to deliver, as provided in subsection (4)(b) of Section 2—503.

(3) In any case not within subsection (1) or (2), the risk of loss passes to the buyer on his receipt of the goods if the seller is a merchant; otherwise the risk passes to the buyer on tender of delivery.

(4) The provisions of this section are subject to contrary agreement of the parties and to the provisions of this Article on sale on approval (Section 2—327) and on effect of breach on risk of loss (Section 2—510).

§ 2—510. Effect of Breach on Risk of Loss.

(1) Where a tender or delivery of goods so fails to conform to the contract as to give a right of rejection the risk of their loss remains on the seller until cure or acceptance.

(2) Where the buyer rightfully revokes acceptance he may to the extent of any deficiency in his effective insurance coverage treat the risk of loss as having rested on the seller from the beginning.

(3) Where the buyer as to conforming goods already identified to the contract for sale repudiates or is otherwise in breach before risk of their loss has passed to him, the seller may to the extent of any deficiency in his effective insurance coverage treat the risk of loss as resting on the buyer for a commercially reasonable time.

§ 2—511. Tender of Payment by Buyer; Payment by Check.

(1) Unless otherwise agreed tender of payment is a condition to the seller's duty to tender and complete any delivery.

(2) Tender of payment is sufficient when made by any means or in any manner current in the ordinary course of business unless the seller demands payment in legal tender and gives any extension of time reasonably necessary to procure it.

(3) Subject to the provisions of this Act on the effect of an instrument on an obligation (Section 3—310), payment by check is conditional and is defeated as between the parties by dishonor of the check on due presentment.

§ 2—512. Payment by Buyer Before Inspection.

(1) Where the contract requires payment before inspection non-conformity of the goods does not excuse the buyer from so making payment unless

(a) the non-conformity appears without inspection; or

(b) despite tender of the required documents the circumstances would justify injunction against honor under the provisions of this Act (Section 5—114).

(2) Payment pursuant to subsection (1) does not constitute an acceptance of goods or impair the buyer's right to inspect or any of his remedies.

§ 2—513. Buyer's Right to Inspection of Goods.

(1) Unless otherwise agreed and subject to subsection (3), where goods are tendered or delivered or identified to the contract for sale, the buyer has a right before payment or acceptance to inspect them at any reasonable place and time and in any reasonable manner. When the seller is required or authorized to send the goods to the buyer, the inspection may be after their arrival.

(2) Expenses of inspection must be borne by the buyer but may be recovered from the seller if the goods do not conform and are rejected.

(3) Unless otherwise agreed and subject to the provisions of this Article on C.I.F. contracts (subsection (3) of Section 2—321), the buyer is not entitled to inspect the goods before payment of the price when the contract provides

(a) for delivery "C.O.D." or on other like terms; or

(b) for payment against documents of title, except where such payment is due only after the goods are to become available for inspection.

(4) A place or method of inspection fixed by the parties is presumed to be exclusive but unless otherwise expressly agreed it does not postpone identification or shift the place for delivery or for passing the risk of loss. If compliance becomes impossible, inspection shall be as provided in this section unless the place or method fixed was clearly intended as an indispensable condition failure of which avoids the contract.

§ 2—514. When Documents Deliverable on Acceptance; When on Payment.

Unless otherwise agreed documents against which a draft is drawn are to be delivered to the drawee on acceptance of the draft if it is payable more than three days after presentment; otherwise, only on payment.

§ 2—515. Preserving Evidence of Goods in Dispute.

In furtherance of the adjustment of any claim or dispute

(a) either party on reasonable notification to the other and for the purpose of ascertaining the facts and preserving evidence has the right to inspect, test and sample the goods including such of them as may be in the possession or control of the other; and

(b) the parties may agree to a third party inspection or survey to determine the conformity or condition of the goods and may agree that the findings shall be binding upon them in any subsequent litigation or adjustment.

Part 6 Breach, Repudiation and Excuse

§ 2—601. Buyer's Rights on Improper Delivery.

Subject to the provisions of this Article on breach in installment contracts (Section 2—612) and unless otherwise agreed under the sections on contractual limitations of remedy (Sections 2—718 and 2—719), if the goods or the tender of delivery fail in any respect to conform to the contract, the buyer may

    (a) reject the whole; or

    (b) accept the whole; or

    (c) accept any commercial unit or units and reject the rest.

§ 2—602. Manner and Effect of Rightful Rejection.

(1) Rejection of goods must be within a reasonable time after their delivery or tender. It is ineffective unless the buyer seasonably notifies the seller.

(2) Subject to the provisions of the two following sections on rejected goods (Sections 2—603 and 2—604),

    (a) after rejection any exercise of ownership by the buyer with respect to any commercial unit is wrongful as against the seller; and

    (b) if the buyer has before rejection taken physical possession of goods in which he does not have a security interest under the provisions of this Article (subsection (3) of Section 2—711), he is under a duty after rejection to hold them with reasonable care at the seller's disposition for a time sufficient to permit the seller to remove them; but

    (c) the buyer has no further obligations with regard to goods rightfully rejected.

(3) The seller's rights with respect to goods wrongfully rejected are governed by the provisions of this Article on Seller's remedies in general (Section 2—703).

§ 2—603. Merchant Buyer's Duties as to Rightfully Rejected Goods.

(1) Subject to any security interest in the buyer (subsection (3) of Section 2—711), when the seller has no agent or place of business at the market of rejection a merchant buyer is under a duty after rejection of goods in his possession or control to follow any reasonable instructions received from the seller with respect to the goods and in the absence of such instructions to make reasonable efforts to sell them for the seller's account if they are perishable or threaten to decline in value speedily. Instructions are not reasonable if on demand indemnity for expenses is not forthcoming.

(2) When the buyer sells goods under subsection (1), he is entitled to reimbursement from the seller or out of the proceeds for reasonable expenses of caring for and selling them, and if the expenses include no selling commission then to such commission as is usual in the trade or if there is none to a reasonable sum not exceeding ten per cent on the gross proceeds.

(3) In complying with this section the buyer is held only to good faith and good faith conduct hereunder is neither acceptance nor conversion nor the basis of an action for damages.

§ 2—604. Buyer's Options as to Salvage of Rightfully Rejected Goods.

Subject to the provisions of the immediately preceding section on perishables if the seller gives no instructions within a reasonable time after notification of rejection the buyer may store the rejected goods for the seller's account or reship them to him or resell them for the seller's account with reimbursement as provided in the preceding section. Such action is not acceptance or conversion.

§ 2—605. Waiver of Buyer's Objections by Failure to Particularize.

(1) The buyer's failure to state in connection with rejection a particular defect which is ascertainable by reasonable inspection precludes him from relying on the unstated defect to justify rejection or to establish breach

    (a) where the seller could have cured it if stated seasonally; or

    (b) between merchants when the seller has after rejection made a request in writing for a full and final written statement of all defects on which the buyer proposes to rely.

(2) Payment against documents made without reservation of rights precludes recovery of the payment for defects apparent on the face of the documents.

§ 2—606. What Constitutes Acceptance of Goods.

(1) Acceptance of goods occurs when the buyer

    (a) after a reasonable opportunity to inspect the goods signifies to the seller that the goods are conforming or that he will take or retain them in spite of their nonconformity; or

    (b) fails to make an effective rejection (subsection (1) of Section 2—602), but such acceptance does not occur until the buyer has had a reasonable opportunity to inspect them; or

    (c) does any act inconsistent with the seller's ownership; but if such act is wrongful as against the seller it is an acceptance only if ratified by him.

(2) Acceptance of a part of any commercial unit is acceptance of that entire unit.

§ 2—607. Effect of Acceptance; Notice of Breach; Burden of Establishing Breach After Acceptance; Notice of Claim or Litigation to Person Answerable Over.

(1) The buyer must pay at the contract rate for any goods accepted.

(2) Acceptance of goods by the buyer precludes rejection of the goods accepted and if made with knowledge of a non-conformity cannot be revoked because of it unless the acceptance was on the reasonable assumption that the non-conformity would be seasonably cured but acceptance does not of itself impair any other remedy provided by this Article for non-conformity.

(3) Where a tender has been accepted

    (a) the buyer must within a reasonable time after he discovers or should have discovered any breach notify the seller of breach or be barred from any remedy; and

    (b) if the claim is one for infringement or the like (subsection (3) of Section 2—312) and the buyer is sued as a result of such a breach he must so notify the seller within a reasonable time after he receives notice of the litigation or be barred from any remedy over for liability established by the litigation.

(4) The burden is on the buyer to establish any breach with respect to the goods accepted.

(5) Where the buyer is sued for breach of a warranty or other obligation for which his seller is answerable over

(a) he may give his seller written notice of the litigation. If the notice states that the seller may come in and defend and that if the seller does not do so he will be bound in any action against him by his buyer by any determination of fact common to the two litigations, then unless the seller after seasonable receipt of the notice does come in and defend he is so bound.

(b) if the claim is one for infringement or the like (subsection (3) of Section 2—312) the original seller may demand in writing that his buyer turn over to him control of the litigation including settlement or else be barred from any remedy over and if he also agrees to bear all expense and to satisfy any adverse judgment, then unless the buyer after seasonable receipt of the demand does turn over control the buyer is so barred.

(6) The provisions of subsections (3), (4) and (5) apply to any obligation of a buyer to hold the seller harmless against infringement or the like (subsection (3) of Section 2—312).

§ 2—608. Revocation of Acceptance in Whole or in Part.

(1) The buyer may revoke his acceptance of a lot or commercial unit whose non-conformity substantially impairs its value to him if he has accepted it

(a) on the reasonable assumption that its nonconformity would be cured and it has not been seasonably cured; or

(b) without discovery of such non-conformity if his acceptance was reasonably induced either by the difficulty of discovery before acceptance or by the seller's assurances.

(2) Revocation of acceptance must occur within a reasonable time after the buyer discovers or should have discovered the ground for it and before any substantial change in condition of the goods which is not caused by their own defects. It is not effective until the buyer notifies the seller of it.

(3) A buyer who so revokes has the same rights and duties with regard to the goods involved as if he had rejected them.

§ 2—609. Right to Adequate Assurance of Performance.

(1) A contract for sale imposes an obligation on each party that the other's expectation of receiving due performance will not be impaired. When reasonable grounds for insecurity arise with respect to the performance of either party the other may in writing demand adequate assurance of due performance and until he receives such assurance may if commercially reasonable suspend any performance for which he has not already received the agreed return.

(2) Between merchants the reasonableness of grounds for insecurity and the adequacy of any assurance offered shall be determined according to commercial standards.

(3) Acceptance of any improper delivery or payment does not preju-

dice the party's right to demand adequate assurance of future performance.

(4) After receipt of a justified demand failure to provide within a reasonable time not exceeding thirty days such assurance of due performance as is adequate under the circumstances of the particular case is a repudiation of the contract.

§ 2—610. Anticipatory Repudiation.

When either party repudiates the contract with respect to a performance not yet due the loss of which will substantially impair the value of the contract to the other, the aggrieved party may

(a) for a commercially reasonable time await performance by the repudiating party; or

(b) resort to any remedy for breach (Section 2—703 or Section 2—711), even though he has notified the repudiating party that he would await the latter's performance and has urged retraction; and

(c) in either case suspend his own performance or proceed in accordance with the provisions of this Article on the seller's right to identify goods to the contract notwithstanding breach or to salvage unfinished goods (Section 2—704).

§ 2—611. Retraction of Anticipatory Repudiation.

(1) Until the repudiating party's next performance is due he can retract his repudiation unless the aggrieved party has since the repudiation cancelled or materially changed his position or otherwise indicated that he considers the repudiation final.

(2) Retraction may be by any method which clearly indicates to the aggrieved party that the repudiating party intends to perform, but must include any assurance justifiably demanded under the provisions of this Article (Section 2—609).

(3) Retraction reinstates the repudiating party's rights under the contract with due excuse and allowance to the aggrieved party for any delay occasioned by the repudiation.

§ 2—612. "Installment Contract"; Breach.

(1) An "installment contract" is one which requires or authorizes the delivery of goods in separate lots to be separately accepted, even though the contract contains a clause "each delivery is a separate contract" or its equivalent.

(2) The buyer may reject any installment which is non-conforming if the non-conformity substantially impairs the value of that installment and cannot be cured or if the non-conformity is a defect in the required documents; but if the non-conformity does not fall within subsection (3) and the seller gives adequate assurance of its cure the buyer must accept that installment.

(3) Whenever non-conformity or default with respect to one or more installments substantially impairs the value of the whole contract there is a breach of the whole. But the aggrieved party reinstates the contract if he accepts a non-conforming installment without seasonably notifying of cancellation or if he brings an action with respect only to past installments or demands performance as to future installments.

§ 2—613. Casualty to Identified Goods.

Where the contract requires for its performance goods identified when the contract is made, and the goods suffer casualty without fault of either party before the risk of loss passes to the buyer, or in a proper case under a "no arrival, no sale" term (Section 2—324) then

(a) if the loss is total the contract is avoided; and

(b) if the loss is partial or the goods have so deteriorated as no longer to conform to the contract the buyer may nevertheless demand inspection and at his option either treat the contract as voided or accept the goods with due allowance from the contract price for the deterioration or the deficiency in quantity but without further right against the seller.

§ 2—614. Substituted Performance.

(1) Where without fault of either party the agreed berthing, loading, or unloading facilities fail or an agreed type of carrier becomes unavailable or the agreed manner of delivery otherwise becomes commercially impracticable but a commercially reasonable substitute is available, such substitute performance must be tendered and accepted.

(2) If the agreed means or manner of payment fails because of domestic or foreign governmental regulation, the seller may withhold or stop delivery unless the buyer provides a means or manner of payment which is commercially a substantial equivalent. If delivery has already been taken, payment by the means or in the manner provided by the regulation discharges the buyer's obligation unless the regulation is discriminatory, oppressive or predatory.

§ 2—615. Excuse by Failure of Presupposed Conditions.

Except so far as a seller may have assumed a greater obligation and subject to the preceding section on substituted performance:

(a) Delay in delivery or non-delivery in whole or in part by a seller who complies with paragraphs (b) and (c) is not a breach of his duty under a contract for sale if performance as agreed has been made impracticable by the occurrence of a contingency the nonoccurrence of which was a basic assumption on which the contract was made or by compliance in good faith with any applicable foreign or domestic governmental regulation or order whether or not it later proves to be invalid.

(b) Where the causes mentioned in paragraph (a) affect only a part of the seller's capacity to perform, he must allocate production and deliveries among his customers but may at his option include regular customers not then under contract as well as his own requirements for further manufacture. He may so allocate in any manner which is fair and reasonable.

(c) The seller must notify the buyer seasonably that there will be delay or non-delivery and, when allocation is required under paragraph (b), of the estimated quota thus made available for the buyer.

§ 2—616. Procedure on Notice Claiming Excuse.

(1) Where the buyer receives notification of a material or indefinite delay or an allocation justified under the preceding section he may by written notification to the seller as to any delivery concerned, and where the prospective deficiency substantially impairs the value of the whole contract under the provisions of this Article relating to breach of installment contracts (Section 2—612), then also as to the whole,

(a) terminate and thereby discharge any unexecuted portion of the contract; or

(b) modify the contract by agreeing to take his available quota in substitution.

(2) If after receipt of such notification from the seller the buyer fails so to modify the contract within a reasonable time not exceeding thirty days the contract lapses with respect to any deliveries affected.

(3) The provisions of this section may not be negated by agreement except in so far as the seller has assumed a greater obligation under the preceding section.

Part 7 Remedies

§ 2—701. Remedies for Breach of Collateral Contracts Not Impaired.

Remedies for breach of any obligation or promise collateral or ancillary to a contract for sale are not impaired by the provisions of this Article.

§ 2—702. Seller's Remedies on Discovery of Buyer's Insolvency.

(1) Where the seller discovers the buyer to be insolvent he may refuse delivery except for cash including payment for all goods theretofore delivered under the contract, and stop delivery under this Article (Section 2—705).

(2) Where the seller discovers that the buyer has received goods on credit while insolvent he may reclaim the goods upon demand made within ten days after the receipt, but if misrepresentation of solvency has been made to the particular seller in writing within three months before delivery the ten day limitation does not apply. Except as provided in this subsection the seller may not base a right to reclaim goods on the buyer's fraudulent or innocent misrepresentation of solvency or of intent to pay.

(3) The seller's right to reclaim under subsection (2) is subject to the rights of a buyer in ordinary course or other good faith purchaser under this Article (Section 2—403). Successful reclamation of goods excludes all other remedies with respect to them.

§ 2—703. Seller's Remedies in General.

Where the buyer wrongfully rejects or revokes acceptance of goods or fails to make a payment due on or before delivery or repudiates with respect to a part or the whole, then with respect to any goods directly affected and, if the breach is of the whole contract (Section 2—612), then also with respect to the whole undelivered balance, the aggrieved seller may

(a) withhold delivery of such goods;

(b) stop delivery by any bailee as hereafter provided (Section 2—705);

(c) proceed under the next section respecting goods still unidentified to the contract;

(d) resell and recover damages as hereafter provided (Section 2—706);

(e) recover damages for non-acceptance (Section 2—708) or in a proper case the price (Section 2—709);

(f) cancel.

§ 2—704. Seller's Right to Identify Goods to the Contract Notwithstanding Breach or to Salvage Unfinished Goods.

(1) An aggrieved seller under the preceding section may

(a) identify to the contract conforming goods not already identified if at the time he learned of the breach they are in his possession or control;

(b) treat as the subject of resale goods which have demonstrably been intended for the particular contract even though those goods are unfinished.

(2) Where the goods are unfinished an aggrieved seller may in the exercise of reasonable commercial judgment for the purposes of avoiding loss and of effective realization either complete the manufacture and wholly identify the goods to the contract or cease manufacture and resell for scrap or salvage value or proceed in any other reasonable manner.

§ 2—705. Seller's Stoppage of Delivery in Transit or Otherwise.

(1) The seller may stop delivery of goods in the possession of a carrier or other bailee when he discovers the buyer to be insolvent (Section 2—702) and may stop delivery of carload, truckload, planeload or larger shipments of express or freight when the buyer repudiates or fails to make a payment due before delivery or if for any other reason the seller has a right to withhold or reclaim the goods.

(2) As against such buyer the seller may stop delivery until

(a) receipt of the goods by the buyer; or

(b) acknowledgment to the buyer by any bailee of the goods except a carrier that the bailee holds the goods for the buyer; or

(c) such acknowledgment to the buyer by a carrier by reshipment or as warehouseman; or

(d) negotiation to the buyer of any negotiable document of title covering the goods.

(3) (a) To stop delivery the seller must so notify as to enable the bailee by reasonable diligence to prevent delivery of the goods.

(b) After such notification the bailee must hold and deliver the goods according to the directions of the seller but the seller is liable to the bailee for any ensuing charges or damages.

(c) If a negotiable document of title has been issued for goods the bailee is not obliged to obey a notification to stop until surrender of the document.

(d) A carrier who has issued a non-negotiable bill of lading is not obliged to obey a notification to stop received from a person other than the consignor.

§ 2—706. Seller's Resale Including Contract for Resale.

(1) Under the conditions stated in Section 2—703 on seller's remedies, the seller may resell the goods concerned or the undelivered balance thereof. Where the resale is made in good faith and in a commercially reasonable manner the seller may recover the difference between the resale price and the contract price together with any

incidental damages allowed under the provisions of this Article (Section 2—710), but less expenses saved in consequence of the buyer's breach.

(2) Except as otherwise provided in subsection (3) or unless otherwise agreed resale may be at public or private sale including sale by way of one or more contracts to sell or of identification to an existing contract of the seller. Sale may be as a unit or in parcels and at any time and place and on any terms but every aspect of the sale including the method, manner, time, place and terms must be commercially reasonable. The resale must be reasonably identified as referring to the broken contract, but it is not necessary that the goods be in existence or that any or all of them have been identified to the contract before the breach.

(3) Where the resale is at private sale the seller must give the buyer reasonable notification of his intention to resell.

(4) Where the resale is at public sale

(a) only identified goods can be sold except where there is a recognized market for a public sale of futures in goods of the kind; and

(b) it must be made at a usual place or market for public sale if one is reasonably available and except in the case of goods which are perishable or threaten to decline in value speedily the seller must give the buyer reasonable notice of the time and place of the resale; and

(c) if the goods are not to be within the view of those attending the sale the notification of sale must state the place where the goods are located and provide for their reasonable inspection by prospective bidders; and

(d) the seller may buy.

(5) A purchaser who buys in good faith at a resale takes the goods free of any rights of the original buyer even though the seller fails to comply with one or more of the requirements of this section.

(6) The seller is not accountable to the buyer for any profit made on any resale. A person in the position of a seller (Section 2—707) or a buyer who has rightfully rejected or justifiably revoked acceptance must account for any excess over the amount of his security interest, as hereinafter defined (subsection (3) of Section 2—711).

§ 2—707. "Person in the Position of a Seller".

(1) A "person in the position of a seller" includes as against a principal an agent who has paid or become responsible for the price of goods on behalf of his principal or anyone who otherwise holds a security interest or other right in goods similar to that of a seller.

(2) A person in the position of a seller may as provided in this Article withhold or stop delivery (Section 2—705) and resell (Section 2—706) and recover incidental damages (Section 2—710).

§ 2—708. Seller's Damages for Non-Acceptance or Repudiation.

(1) Subject to subsection (2) and to the provisions of this Article with respect to proof of market price (Section 2—723), the measure of damages for non-acceptance or repudiation by the buyer is the difference between the market price at the time and place for tender and the unpaid contract price together with any incidental damages pro-

vided in this Article (Section 2—710), but less expenses saved in consequence of the buyer's breach.

(2) If the measure of damages provided in subsection (1) is inadequate to put the seller in as good a position as performance would have done then the measure of damages is the profit (including reasonable overhead) which the seller would have made from full performance by the buyer, together with any incidental damages provided in this Article (Section 2—710), due allowance for costs reasonably incurred and due credit for payments or proceeds of resale.

§ 2—709. Action for the Price.

(1) When the buyer fails to pay the price as it becomes due the seller may recover, together with any incidental damages under the next section, the price

>   (a) of goods accepted or of conforming goods lost or damaged within a commercially reasonable time after risk of their loss has passed to the buyer; and

>   (b) of goods identified to the contract if the seller is unable after reasonable effort to resell them at a reasonable price or the circumstances reasonably indicate that such effort will be unavailing.

(2) Where the seller sues for the price he must hold for the buyer any goods which have been identified to the contract and are still in his control except that if resale becomes possible he may resell them at any time prior to the collection of the judgment. The net proceeds of any such resale must be credited to the buyer and payment of the judgment entitles him to any goods not resold.

(3) After the buyer has wrongfully rejected or revoked acceptance of the goods or has failed to make a payment due or has repudiated (Section 2—610), a seller who is held not entitled to the price under this section shall nevertheless be awarded damages for non-acceptance under the preceding section.

§ 2—710. Seller's Incidental Damages.

Incidental damages to an aggrieved seller include any commercially reasonable charges, expenses or commissions incurred in stopping delivery, in the transportation, care and custody of goods after the buyer's breach, in connection with return or resale of the goods or otherwise resulting from the breach.

§ 2—711. Buyer's Remedies in General; Buyer's Security Interest in Rejected Goods.

(1) Where the seller fails to make delivery or repudiates or the buyer rightfully rejects or justifiably revokes acceptance then with respect to any goods involved, and with respect to the whole if the breach goes to the whole contract (Section 2—612), the buyer may cancel and whether or not he has done so may in addition to recovering so much of the price as has been paid

>   (a) "cover" and have damages under the next section as to all the goods affected whether or not they have been identified to the contract; or

>   (b) recover damages for non-delivery as provided in this Article (Section 2—713).

(2) Where the seller fails to deliver or repudiates the buyer may also

>   (a) if the goods have been identified recover them as provided in this Article (Section 2—502); or

>   (b) in a proper case obtain specific performance or replevy the goods as provided in this Article (Section 2—716).

(3) On rightful rejection or justifiable revocation of acceptance a buyer has a security interest in goods in his possession or control for any payments made on their price and any expenses reasonably incurred in their inspection, receipt, transportation, care and custody and may hold such goods and resell them in like manner as an aggrieved seller (Section 2—706).

§ 2—712. "Cover"; Buyer's Procurement of Substitute Goods.

(1) After a breach within the preceding section the buyer may "cover" by making in good faith and without unreasonable delay any reasonable purchase of or contract to purchase goods in substitution for those due from the seller.

(2) The buyer may recover from the seller as damages the difference between the cost of cover and the contract price together with any incidental or consequential damages as hereinafter defined (Section 2—715), but less expenses saved in consequence of the seller's breach.

(3) Failure of the buyer to effect cover within this section does not bar him from any other remedy.

§ 2—713. Buyer's Damages for Non-Delivery or Repudiation.

(1) Subject to the provisions of this Article with respect to proof of market price (Section 2—723), the measure of damages for non-delivery or repudiation by the seller is the difference between the market price at the time when the buyer learned of the breach and the contract price together with any incidental and consequential damages provided in this Article (Section 2—715), but less expenses saved in consequence of the seller's breach.

(2) Market price is to be determined as of the place for tender or, in cases of rejection after arrival or revocation of acceptance, as of the place of arrival.

§ 2—714. Buyer's Damages for Breach in Regard to Accepted Goods.

(1) Where the buyer has accepted goods and given notification (subsection (3) of Section 2—607) he may recover as damages for any nonconformity of tender the loss resulting in the ordinary course of events from the seller's breach as determined in any manner which is reasonable.

(2) The measure of damages for breach of warranty is the difference at the time and place of acceptance between the value of the goods accepted and the value they would have had if they had been as warranted, unless special circumstances show proximate damages of a different amount.

(3) In a proper case any incidental and consequential damages under the next section may also be recovered.

§ 2—715. Buyer's Incidental and Consequential Damages.

(1) Incidental damages resulting from the seller's breach include expenses reasonably incurred in inspection, receipt, transportation

and care and custody of goods rightfully rejected, any commercially reasonable charges, expenses or commissions in connection with effecting cover and any other reasonable expense incident to the delay or other breach.

(2) Consequential damages resulting from the seller's breach include

(a) any loss resulting from general or particular requirements and needs of which the seller at the time of contracting had reason to know and which could not reasonably be prevented by cover or otherwise; and

(b) injury to person or property proximately resulting from any breach of warranty.

§ 2—716. Buyer's Right to Specific Performance or Replevin.

(1) Specific performance may be decreed where the goods are unique or in other proper circumstances.

(2) The decree for specific performance may include such terms and conditions as to payment of the price, damages, or other relief as the court may deem just.

(3) The buyer has a right of replevin for goods identified to the contract if after reasonable effort he is unable to effect cover for such goods or the circumstances reasonably indicate that such effort will be unavailing or if the goods have been shipped under reservation and satisfaction of the security interest in them has been made or tendered.

§ 2—717. Deduction of Damages From the Price.

The buyer on notifying the seller of his intention to do so may deduct all or any part of the damages resulting from any breach of the contract from any part of the price still due under the same contract.

§ 2—718. Liquidation or Limitation of Damages; Deposits.

(1) Damages for breach by either party may be liquidated in the agreement but only at an amount which is reasonable in the light of the anticipated or actual harm caused by the breach, the difficulties of proof of loss, and the inconvenience or nonfeasibility of otherwise obtaining an adequate remedy. A term fixing unreasonably large liquidated damages is void as a penalty.

(2) Where the seller justifiably withholds delivery of goods because of the buyer's breach, the buyer is entitled to restitution of any amount by which the sum of his payments exceeds

(a) the amount to which the seller is entitled by virtue of terms liquidating the seller's damages in accordance with subsection (1), or

(b) in the absence of such terms, twenty per cent of the value of the total performance for which the buyer is obligated under the contract or $500, whichever is smaller.

(3) The buyer's right to restitution under subsection (2) is subject to offset to the extent that the seller establishes

(a) a right to recover damages under the provisions of this Article other than subsection (1), and

(b) the amount or value of any benefits received by the buyer directly or indirectly by reason of the contract.

(4) Where a seller has received payment in goods their reasonable value or the proceeds of their resale shall be treated as payments for

the purposes of subsection (2); but if the seller has notice of the buyer's breach before reselling goods received in part performance, his resale is subject to the conditions laid down in this Article on resale by an aggrieved seller (Section 2—706).

§ 2—719. Contractual Modification or Limitation of Remedy.

(1) Subject to the provisions of subsections (2) and (3) of this section and of the preceding section on liquidation and limitation of damages,

(a) the agreement may provide for remedies in addition to or in substitution for those provided in this Article and may limit or alter the measure of damages recoverable under this Article, as by limiting the buyer's remedies to return of the goods and repayment of the price or to repair and replacement of nonconforming goods or parts; and

(b) resort to a remedy as provided is optional unless the remedy is expressly agreed to be exclusive, in which case it is the sole remedy.

(2) Where circumstances cause an exclusive or limited remedy to fail of its essential purpose, remedy may be had as provided in this Act.

(3) Consequential damages may be limited or excluded unless the limitation or exclusion is unconscionable. Limitation of consequential damages for injury to the person in the case of consumer goods is prima facie unconscionable but limitation of damages where the loss is commercial is not.

§ 2—720. Effect of "Cancellation" or "Rescission" on Claims for Antecedent Breach.

Unless the contrary intention clearly appears, expressions of "cancellation" or "rescission" of the contract or the like shall not be construed as a renunciation or discharge of any claim in damages for an antecedent breach.

§ 2—721. Remedies for Fraud.

Remedies for material misrepresentation or fraud include all remedies available under this Article for non-fraudulent breach. Neither rescission or a claim for rescission of the contract for sale nor rejection or return of the goods shall bar or be deemed inconsistent with a claim for damages or other remedy.

§ 2—722. Who Can Sue Third Parties for Injury to Goods.

Where a third party so deals with goods which have been identified to a contract for sale as to cause actionable injury to a party to that contract

(a) a right of action against the third party is in either party to the contract for sale who has title to or a security interest or a special property or an insurable interest in the goods; and if the goods have been destroyed or converted a right of action is also in the party who either bore the risk of loss under the contract for sale or has since the injury assumed that risk as against the other;

(b) if at the time of the injury the party plaintiff did not bear the risk of loss as against the other party to the contract for sale and there is no arrangement between them for disposition of the recovery, his suit or settlement is, subject to his own interest, as a fiduciary for the other party to the contract;

(c) either party may with the consent of the other sue for the benefit of whom it may concern.

§ 2—723. Proof of Market Price: Time and Place.

(1) If an action based on anticipatory repudiation comes to trial before the time for performance with respect to some or all of the goods, any damages based on market price (Section 2—708 or Section 2—713) shall be determined according to the price of such goods prevailing at the time when the aggrieved party learned of the repudiation.

(2) If evidence of a price prevailing at the times or places described in this Article is not readily available the price prevailing within any reasonable time before or after the time described or at any other place which in commercial judgment or under usage of trade would serve as a reasonable substitute for the one described may be used, making any proper allowance for the cost of transporting the goods to or from such other place.

(3) Evidence of a relevant price prevailing at a time or place other than the one described in this Article offered by one party is not admissible unless and until he has given the other party such notice as the court finds sufficient to prevent unfair surprise.

§ 2—724. Admissibility of Market Quotations.

Whenever the prevailing price or value of any goods regularly bought and sold in any established commodity market is in issue, reports in official publications or trade journals or in newspapers or periodicals of general circulation published as the reports of such market shall be admissible in evidence. The circumstances of the preparation of such a report may be shown to affect its weight but not its admissibility.

§ 2—725. Statute of Limitations in Contracts for Sale.

(1) An action for breach of any contract for sale must be commenced within four years after the cause of action has accrued. By the original agreement the parties may reduce the period of limitation to not less than one year but may not extend it.

(2) A cause of action accrues when the breach occurs, regardless of the aggrieved party's lack of knowledge of the breach. A breach of warranty occurs when tender of delivery is made, except that where a warranty explicitly extends to future performance of the goods and discovery of the breach must await the time of such performance the cause of action accrues when the breach is or should have been discovered.

(3) Where an action commenced within the time limited by subsection (1) is so terminated as to leave available a remedy by another action for the same breach such other action may be commenced after the expiration of the time limited and within six months after the termination of the first action unless the termination resulted from voluntary discontinuance or from dismissal for failure or neglect to prosecute.

(4) This section does not alter the law on tolling of the statute of limitations nor does it apply to causes of action which have accrued before this Act becomes effective.

Article 2A
LEASES

Part 1 General Provisions

§ 2A—101. Short Title.

This Article shall be known and may be cited as the Uniform Commercial Code—Leases.

§ 2A—102. Scope.

This Article applies to any transaction, regardless of form, that creates a lease.

§ 2A—103. Definitions and Index of Definitions.

(1) In this Article unless the context otherwise requires:

(a) "Buyer in ordinary course of business" means a person who in good faith and without knowledge that the sale to him [or her] is in violation of the ownership rights or security interest or leasehold interest of a third party in the goods buys in ordinary course from a person in the business of selling goods of that kind but does not include a pawnbroker. "Buying" may be for cash or by exchange of other property or on secured or unsecured credit and includes receiving goods or documents of title under a preexisting contract for sale but does not include a transfer in bulk or as security for or in total or partial satisfaction of a money debt.

(b) "Cancellation" occurs when either party puts an end to the lease contract for default by the other party.

(c) "Commercial unit" means such a unit of goods as by commercial usage is a single whole for purposes of lease and division of which materially impairs its character or value on the market or in use. A commercial unit may be a single article, as a machine, or a set of articles, as a suite of furniture or a line of machinery, or a quantity, as a gross or carload, or any other unit treated in use or in the relevant market as a single whole.

(d) "Conforming" goods or performance under a lease contract means goods or performance that are in accordance with the obligations under the lease contract.

(e) "Consumer lease" means a lease that a lessor regularly engaged in the business of leasing or selling makes to a lessee who is an individual and who takes under the lease primarily for a personal, family, or household "purpose [, if" the total payments to be made under the lease contract, excluding payments for options to renew or buy, do not exceed. . . .

(f) "Fault" means wrongful act, omission, breach, or default.

(g) "Finance lease" means a lease with respect to which:

(i) the lessor does not select, manufacture or supply the goods;

(ii) the lessor acquires the goods or the right to possession and use of the goods in connection with the lease; and

(iii) one of the following occurs:

(A) the lessee receives a copy of the contract by which the lessor acquired the goods or the right to possession and use of the goods before signing the lease contract;

(B) the lessee's approval of the contract by which the lessor acquired the goods or the right to possession and use of the goods is a condition to effectiveness of the lease contract;

(C) the lessee, before signing the lease contract, receives an accurate and complete statement designating the promises and warranties, and any disclaimers of warranties, limitations or modifications of remedies, or liquidated damages, including those of a third party, such as the manufacturer of the goods, provided to the lessor by the person supplying the goods in connection with or as part of the contract by which the lessor acquired the goods or the right to possession and use of the goods; or

(D) if the lease is not a consumer lease, the lessor, before the lessee signs the lease contract, informs the lessee in writing (a) of the identity of the person supplying the goods to the lessor, unless the lessee has selected that person and directed the lessor to acquire the goods or the right to possession and use of the goods from that person, (b) that the lessee is entitled under this Article to any promises and warranties, including those of any third party, provided to the lessor by the person supplying the goods in connection with or as part of the contract by which the lessor acquired the goods or the right to possession and use of the goods, and (c) that the lessee may communicate with the person supplying the goods to the lessor and receive an accurate and complete statement of those promises and warranties, including any disclaimers and limitations of them or of remedies.

(h) "Goods" means all things that are movable at the time of identification to the lease contract, or are fixtures (Section 2A—309), but the term does not include money, documents, instruments, accounts, chattel paper, general intangibles, or minerals or the like, including oil and gas, before extraction. The term also includes the unborn young of animals.

(i) "Installment lease contract" means a lease contract that authorizes or requires the delivery of goods in separate lots to be separately accepted, even though the lease contract contains a clause "each delivery is a separate lease" or its equivalent.

(j) "Lease" means a transfer of the right to possession and use of goods for a term in return for consideration, but a sale, including a sale on approval or a sale or return, or retention or creation of a security interest is not a lease. Unless the context clearly indicates otherwise, the term includes a sublease.

(k) "Lease agreement" means the bargain, with respect to the lease, of the lessor and the lessee in fact as found in their language or by implication from other circumstances including course of dealing or usage of trade or course of performance as provided in this Article. Unless the context clearly indicates otherwise, the term includes a sublease agreement.

(l) "Lease contract" means the total legal obligation that results from the lease agreement as affected by this Article and any other applicable rules of law. Unless the context clearly indicates otherwise, the term includes a sublease contract.

(m) "Leasehold interest" means the interest of the lessor or the lessee under a lease contract.

(n) "Lessee" means a person who acquires the right to possession and use of goods under a lease. Unless the context clearly indicates otherwise, the term includes a sublessee.

(o) "Lessee in ordinary course of business" means a person who in good faith and without knowledge that the lease to him [or her] is in violation of the ownership rights or security interest or leasehold interest of a third party in the goods, leases in ordinary course from a person in the business of selling or leasing goods of that kind but does not include a pawnbroker. "Leasing" may be for cash or by exchange of other property or on secured or unsecured credit and includes receiving goods or documents of title under a pre-existing lease contract but does not include a transfer in bulk or as security for or in total or partial satisfaction of a money debt.

(p) "Lessor" means a person who transfers the right to possession and use of goods under a lease. Unless the context clearly indicates otherwise, the term includes a sublessor.

(q) "Lessor's residual interest" means the lessor's interest in the goods after expiration, termination, or cancellation of the lease contract.

(r) "Lien" means a charge against or interest in goods to secure payment of a debt or performance of an obligation, but the term does not include a security interest.

(s) "Lot" means a parcel or a single article that is the subject matter of a separate lease or delivery, whether or not it is sufficient to perform the lease contract.

(t) "Merchant lessee" means a lessee that is a merchant with respect to goods of the kind subject to the lease.

(u) "Present value" means the amount as of a date certain of one or more sums payable in the future, discounted to the date certain. The discount is determined by the interest rate specified by the parties if the rate was not manifestly unreasonable at the time the transaction was entered into; otherwise, the discount is determined by a commercially reasonable rate that takes into account the facts and circumstances of each case at the time the transaction was entered into.

(v) "Purchase" includes taking by sale, lease, mortgage, security interest, pledge, gift, or any other voluntary transaction creating an interest in goods.

(w) "Sublease" means a lease of goods the right to possession and use of which was acquired by the lessor as a lessee under an existing lease.

(x) "Supplier" means a person from whom a lessor buys or leases goods to be leased under a finance lease.

(y) "Supply contract" means a contract under which a lessor buys or leases goods to be leased.

(z) "Termination" occurs when either party pursuant to a power created by agreement or law puts an end to the lease contract otherwise than for default.

(2) Other definitions applying to this Article and the sections in which they appear are:

"Accessions". Section 2A—310(1).
"Construction mortgage". Section 2A—309(1)(d).
"Encumbrance". Section 2A—309(1)(e).

"Fixtures". Section 2A—309(1)(a).

"Fixture filing". Section 2A—309(1)(b).

"Purchase money lease". Section 2A—309(1)(c).

(3) The following definitions in other Articles apply to this Article:

"Accounts". Section 9—106.

"Between merchants". Section 2—104(3).

"Buyer". Section 2—103(1)(a).

"Chattel paper". Section 9—105(1)(b).

"Consumer goods". Section 9—109(1).

"Document". Section 9—105(1)(f).

"Entrusting". Section 2—403(3).

"General intangibles". Section 9—106.

"Good faith". Section 2—103(1)(b).

"Instrument". Section 9—105(1)(i).

"Merchant". Section 2—104(1).

"Mortgage". Section 9—105(1)(j).

"Pursuant to commitment". Section 9—105(1)(k).

"Receipt". Section 2—103(1)(c).

"Sale". Section 2—106(1).

"Sale on approval". Section 2—326.

"Sale or return". Section 2—326.

"Seller". Section 2—103(1)(d).

(4) In addition Article 1 contains general definitions and principles of construction and interpretation applicable throughout this Article.

As amended in 1990.

§ 2A—104. Leases Subject to Other Law.

(1) A lease, although subject to this Article, is also subject to any applicable:

   (a) certificate of title statute of this State: (list any certificate of title statutes covering automobiles, trailers, mobile homes, boats, farm tractors, and the like);

   (b) certificate of title statute of another jurisdiction (Section 2A—105); or

   (c) consumer protection statute of this State, or final consumer protection decision of a court of this State existing on the effective date of this Article.

(2) In case of conflict between this Article, other than Sections 2A—105, 2A—304(3), and 2A—305(3), and a statute or decision referred to in subsection (1), the statute or decision controls.

(3) Failure to comply with an applicable law has only the effect specified therein.

As amended in 1990.

§ 2A—105. Territorial Application of Article to Goods Covered by Certificate of Title.

Subject to the provisions of Sections 2A—304(3) and 2A—305(3), with respect to goods covered by a certificate of title issued under a statute of this State or of another jurisdiction, compliance and the effect of compliance or noncompliance with a certificate of title statute are governed by the law (including the conflict of laws rules) of the jurisdiction issuing the certificate until the earlier of (a) surrender of the certificate, or (b) four months after the goods are removed from that jurisdiction and thereafter until a new certificate of title is issued by another jurisdiction.

§ 2A—106. Limitation on Power of Parties to Consumer Lease to Choose Applicable Law and Judicial Forum.

(1) If the law chosen by the parties to a consumer lease is that of a jurisdiction other than a jurisdiction in which the lessee resides at the time the lease agreement becomes enforceable or within 30 days thereafter or in which the goods are to be used, the choice is not enforceable.

(2) If the judicial forum chosen by the parties to a consumer lease is a forum that would not otherwise have jurisdiction over the lessee, the choice is not enforceable.

§ 2A—107. Waiver or Renunciation of Claim or Right After Default.

Any claim or right arising out of an alleged default or breach of warranty may be discharged in whole or in part without consideration by a written waiver or renunciation signed and delivered by the aggrieved party.

§ 2A—108. Unconscionability.

(1) If the court as a matter of law finds a lease contract or any clause of a lease contract to have been unconscionable at the time it was made the court may refuse to enforce the lease contract, or it may enforce the remainder of the lease contract without the unconscionable clause, or it may so limit the application of any unconscionable clause as to avoid any unconscionable result.

(2) With respect to a consumer lease, if the court as a matter of law finds that a lease contract or any clause of a lease contract has been induced by unconscionable conduct or that unconscionable conduct has occurred in the collection of a claim arising from a lease contract, the court may grant appropriate relief.

(3) Before making a finding of unconscionability under subsection (1) or (2), the court, on its own motion or that of a party, shall afford the parties a reasonable opportunity to present evidence as to the setting, purpose, and effect of the lease contract or clause thereof, or of the conduct.

(4) In an action in which the lessee claims unconscionability with respect to a consumer lease:

   (a) If the court finds unconscionability under subsection (1) or (2), the court shall award reasonable attorney's fees to the lessee.

   (b) If the court does not find unconscionability and the lessee claiming unconscionability has brought or maintained an action he [or she] knew to be groundless, the court shall award reasonable attorney's fees to the party against whom the claim is made.

   (c) In determining attorney's fees, the amount of the recovery on behalf of the claimant under subsections (1) and (2) is not controlling.

§ 2A—109. Option to Accelerate at Will.

(1) A term providing that one party or his [or her] successor in interest may accelerate payment or performance or require collateral or additional collateral "at will" or "when he [or she] deems himself [or herself] insecure" or in words of similar import must be construed to mean that he [or she] has power to do so only if he [or she] in good faith believes that the prospect of payment or performance is impaired.

(2) With respect to a consumer lease, the burden of establishing good faith under subsection (1) is on the party who exercised the power; otherwise the burden of establishing lack of good faith is on the party against whom the power has been exercised.

Part 2 Formation and Construction of Lease Contract

§ 2A—201. Statute of Frauds.

(1) A lease contract is not enforceable by way of action or defense unless:

(a) the total payments to be made under the lease contract, excluding payments for options to renew or buy, are less than $1,000; or

(b) there is a writing, signed by the party against whom enforcement is sought or by that party's authorized agent, sufficient to indicate that a lease contract has been made between the parties and to describe the goods leased and the lease term.

(2) Any description of leased goods or of the lease term is sufficient and satisfies subsection (1)(b), whether or not it is specific, if it reasonably identifies what is described.

(3) A writing is not insufficient because it omits or incorrectly states a term agreed upon, but the lease contract is not enforceable under subsection (1)(b) beyond the lease term and the quantity of goods shown in the writing.

(4) A lease contract that does not satisfy the requirements of subsection (1), but which is valid in other respects, is enforceable:

(a) if the goods are to be specially manufactured or obtained for the lessee and are not suitable for lease or sale to others in the ordinary course of the lessor's business, and the lessor, before notice of repudiation is received and under circumstances that reasonably indicate that the goods are for the lessee, has made either a substantial beginning of their manufacture or commitments for their procurement;

(b) if the party against whom enforcement is sought admits in that party's pleading, testimony or otherwise in court that a lease contract was made, but the lease contract is not enforceable under this provision beyond the quantity of goods admitted; or

(c) with respect to goods that have been received and accepted by the lessee.

(5) The lease term under a lease contract referred to in subsection (4) is:

(a) if there is a writing signed by the party against whom enforcement is sought or by that party's authorized agent specifying the lease term, the term so specified;

(b) if the party against whom enforcement is sought admits in that party's pleading, testimony, or otherwise in court a lease term, the term so admitted; or

(c) a reasonable lease term.

§ 2A—202. Final Written Expression: Parol or Extrinsic Evidence.

Terms with respect to which the confirmatory memoranda of the parties agree or which are otherwise set forth in a writing intended by the parties as a final expression of their agreement with respect to such terms as are included therein may not be contradicted by evidence of any prior agreement or of a contemporaneous oral agreement but may be explained or supplemented:

(a) by course of dealing or usage of trade or by course of performance; and

(b) by evidence of consistent additional terms unless the court finds the writing to have been intended also as a complete and exclusive statement of the terms of the agreement.

§ 2A—203. Seals Inoperative.

The affixing of a seal to a writing evidencing a lease contract or an offer to enter into a lease contract does not render the writing a sealed instrument and the law with respect to sealed instruments does not apply to the lease contract or offer.

§ 2A—204. Formation in General.

(1) A lease contract may be made in any manner sufficient to show agreement, including conduct by both parties which recognizes the existence of a lease contract.

(2) An agreement sufficient to constitute a lease contract may be found although the moment of its making is undetermined.

(3) Although one or more terms are left open, a lease contract does not fail for indefiniteness if the parties have intended to make a lease contract and there is a reasonably certain basis for giving an appropriate remedy.

§ 2A—205. Firm Offers.

An offer by a merchant to lease goods to or from another person in a signed writing that by its terms gives assurance it will be held open is not revocable, for lack of consideration, during the time stated or, if no time is stated, for a reasonable time, but in no event may the period of irrevocability exceed 3 months. Any such term of assurance on a form supplied by the offeree must be separately signed by the offeror.

§ 2A—206. Offer and Acceptance in Formation of Lease Contract.

(1) Unless otherwise unambiguously indicated by the language or circumstances, an offer to make a lease contract must be construed as inviting acceptance in any manner and by any medium reasonable in the circumstances.

(2) If the beginning of a requested performance is a reasonable mode of acceptance, an offeror who is not notified of acceptance within a reasonable time may treat the offer as having lapsed before acceptance.

§ 2A—207. Course of Performance or Practical Construction.

(1) If a lease contract involves repeated occasions for performance by either party with knowledge of the nature of the performance and opportunity for objection to it by the other, any course of performance accepted or acquiesced in without objection is relevant to determine the meaning of the lease agreement.

(2) The express terms of a lease agreement and any course of perfor-

mance, as well as any course of dealing and usage of trade, must be construed whenever reasonable as consistent with each other; but if that construction is unreasonable, express terms control course of performance, course of performance controls both course of dealing and usage of trade, and course of dealing controls usage of trade.

(3) Subject to the provisions of Section 2A—208 on modification and waiver, course of performance is relevant to show a waiver or modification of any term inconsistent with the course of performance.

§ 2A—208. Modification, Rescission and Waiver.

(1) An agreement modifying a lease contract needs no consideration to be binding.

(2) A signed lease agreement that excludes modification or rescission except by a signed writing may not be otherwise modified or rescinded, but, except as between merchants, such a requirement on a form supplied by a merchant must be separately signed by the other party.

(3) Although an attempt at modification or rescission does not satisfy the requirements of subsection (2), it may operate as a waiver.

(4) A party who has made a waiver affecting an executory portion of a lease contract may retract the waiver by reasonable notification received by the other party that strict performance will be required of any term waived, unless the retraction would be unjust in view of a material change of position in reliance on the waiver.

§ 2A—209. Lessee under Finance Lease as Beneficiary of Supply Contract.

(1) The benefit of the supplier's promises to the lessor under the supply contract and of all warranties, whether express or implied, including those of any third party provided in connection with or as part of the supply contract, extends to the lessee to the extent of the lessee's leasehold interest under a finance lease related to the supply contract, but is subject to the terms warranty and of the supply contract and all defenses or claims arising therefrom.

(2) The extension of the benefit of supplier's promises and of warranties to the lessee (Section 2A–209(1)) does not: (i) modify the rights and obligations of the parties to the supply contract, whether arising therefrom or otherwise, or (ii) impose any duty or liability under the supply contract on the lessee.

(3) Any modification or rescission of the supply contract by the supplier and the lessor is effective between the supplier and the lessee unless, before the modification or rescission, the supplier has received notice that the lessee has entered into a finance lease related to the supply contract. If the modification or rescission is effective between the supplier and the lessee, the lessor is deemed to have assumed, in addition to the obligations of the lessor to the lessee under the lease contract, promises of the supplier to the lessor and warranties that were so modified or rescinded as they existed and were available to the lessee before modification or rescission.

(4) In addition to the extension of the benefit of the supplier's promises and of warranties to the lessee under subsection (1), the lessee retains all rights that the lessee may have against the supplier which arise from an agreement between the lessee and the supplier or under other law.

As amended in 1990.

§ 2A—210. Express Warranties.

(1) Express warranties by the lessor are created as follows:

(a) Any affirmation of fact or promise made by the lessor to the lessee which relates to the goods and becomes part of the basis of the bargain creates an express warranty that the goods will conform to the affirmation or promise.

(b) Any description of the goods which is made part of the basis of the bargain creates an express warranty that the goods will conform to the description.

(c) Any sample or model that is made part of the basis of the bargain creates an express warranty that the whole of the goods will conform to the sample or model.

(2) It is not necessary to the creation of an express warranty that the lessor use formal words, such as "warrant" or "guarantee," or that the lessor have a specific intention to make a warranty, but an affirmation merely of the value of the goods or a statement purporting to be merely the lessor's opinion or commendation of the goods does not create a warranty.

§ 2A—211. Warranties Against Interference and Against Infringement; Lessee's Obligation Against Infringement.

(1) There is in a lease contract a warranty that for the lease term no person holds a claim to or interest in the goods that arose from an act or omission of the lessor, other than a claim by way of infringement or the like, which will interfere with the lessee's enjoyment of its leasehold interest.

(2) Except in a finance lease there is in a lease contract by a lessor who is a merchant regularly dealing in goods of the kind a warranty that the goods are delivered free of the rightful claim of any person by way of infringement or the like.

(3) A lessee who furnishes specifications to a lessor or a supplier shall hold the lessor and the supplier harmless against any claim by way of infringement or the like that arises out of compliance with the specifications.

§ 2A—212. Implied Warranty of Merchantability.

(1) Except in a finance lease, a warranty that the goods will be merchantable is implied in a lease contract if the lessor is a merchant with respect to goods of that kind.

(2) Goods to be merchantable must be at least such as

(a) pass without objection in the trade under the description in the lease agreement;

(b) in the case of fungible goods, are of fair average quality within the description;

(c) are fit for the ordinary purposes for which goods of that type are used;

(d) run, within the variation permitted by the lease agreement, of even kind, quality, and quantity within each unit and among all units involved;

(e) are adequately contained, packaged, and labeled as the lease agreement may require; and

(f) conform to any promises or affirmations of fact made on the container or label.

(3) Other implied warranties may arise from course of dealing or usage of trade.

§ 2A—213. Implied Warranty of Fitness for Particular Purpose.

Except in a finance of lease, if the lessor at the time the lease contract is made has reason to know of any particular purpose for which the goods are required and that the lessee is relying on the lessor's skill or judgment to select or furnish suitable goods, there is in the lease contract an implied warranty that the goods will be fit for that purpose.

§ 2A—214. Exclusion or Modification of Warranties.

(1) Words or conduct relevant to the creation of an express warranty and words or conduct tending to negate or limit a warranty must be construed wherever reasonable as consistent with each other; but, subject to the provisions of Section 2A—202 on parol or extrinsic evidence, negation or limitation is inoperative to the extent that the construction is unreasonable.

(2) Subject to subsection (3), to exclude or modify the implied warranty of merchantability or any part of it the language must mention "merchantability", be by a writing, and be conspicuous. Subject to subsection (3), to exclude or modify any implied warranty of fitness the exclusion must be by a writing and be conspicuous. Language to exclude all implied warranties of fitness is sufficient if it is in writing, is conspicuous and states, for example, "There is no warranty that the goods will be fit for a particular purpose".

(3) Notwithstanding subsection (2), but subject to subsection (4),

(a) unless the circumstances indicate otherwise, all implied warranties are excluded by expressions like "as is" or "with all faults" or by other language that in common understanding calls the lessee's attention to the exclusion of warranties and makes plain that there is no implied warranty, if in writing and conspicuous;

(b) if the lessee before entering into the lease contract has examined the goods or the sample or model as fully as desired or has refused to examine the goods, there is no implied warranty with regard to defects that an examination ought in the circumstances to have revealed; and

(c) an implied warranty may also be excluded or modified by course of dealing, course of performance, or usage of trade.

(4) To exclude or modify a warranty against interference or against infringement (Section 2A—211) or any part of it, the language must be specific, be by a writing, and be conspicuous, unless the circumstances, including course of performance, course of dealing, or usage of trade, give the lessee reason to know that the goods are being leased subject to a claim or interest of any person.

§ 2A—215. Cumulation and Conflict of Warranties Express or Implied.

Warranties, whether express or implied, must be construed as consistent with each other and as cumulative, but if that construction is unreasonable, the intention of the parties determines which warranty is dominant. In ascertaining that intention the following rules apply:

(a) Exact or technical specifications displace an inconsistent sample or model or general language of description.

(b) A sample from an existing bulk displaces inconsistent general language of description.

(c) Express warranties displace inconsistent implied warranties other than an implied warranty of fitness for a particular purpose.

§ 2A—216. Third-Party Beneficiaries of Express and Implied Warranties.

Alternative A

A warranty to or for the benefit of a lessee under this Article, whether express or implied, extends to any natural person who is in the family or household of the lessee or who is a guest in the lessee's home if it is reasonable to expect that such person may use, consume, or be affected by the goods and who is injured in person by breach of the warranty. This section does not displace principles of law and equity that extend a warranty to or for the benefit of a lessee to other persons. The operation of this section may not be excluded, modified, or limited, but an exclusion, modification, or limitation of the warranty, including any with respect to rights and remedies, effective against the lessee is also effective against any beneficiary designated under this section.

Alternative B

A warranty to or for the benefit of a lessee under this Article, whether express or implied, extends to any natural person who may reasonably be expected to use, consume, or be affected by the goods and who is injured in person by breach of the warranty. This section does not displace principles of law and equity that extend a warranty to or for the benefit of a lessee to other persons. The operation of this section may not be excluded, modified, or limited, but an exclusion, modification, or limitation of the warranty, including any with respect to rights and remedies, effective against the lessee is also effective against the beneficiary designated under this section.

Alternative C

A warranty to or for the benefit of a lessee under this Article, whether express or implied, extends to any person who may reasonably be expected to use, consume, or be affected by the goods and who is injured by breach of the warranty. The operation of this section may not be excluded, modified, or limited with respect to injury to the person of an individual to whom the warranty extends, but an exclusion, modification, or limitation of the warranty, including any with respect to rights and remedies, effective against the lessee is also effective against the beneficiary designated under this section.

§ 2A—217. Identification.

Identification of goods as goods to which a lease contract refers may be made at any time and in any manner explicitly agreed to by the parties. In the absence of explicit agreement, identification occurs:

(a) when the lease contract is made if the lease contract is for a lease of goods that are existing and identified;

(b) when the goods are shipped, marked, or otherwise designated by the lessor as goods to which the lease contract refers, if the lease contract is for a lease of goods that are not existing and identified; or

(c) when the young are conceived, if the lease contract is for a lease of unborn young of animals.

§ 2A—218. Insurance and Proceeds.

(1) A lessee obtains an insurable interest when existing goods are identified to the lease contract even though the goods identified are nonconforming and the lessee has an option to reject them.

(2) If a lessee has an insurable interest only by reason of the lessor's identification of the goods, the lessor, until default or insolvency or notification to the lessee that identification is final, may substitute other goods for those identified.

(3) Notwithstanding a lessee's insurable interest under subsections (1) and (2), the lessor retains an insurable interest until an option to buy has been exercised by the lessee and risk of loss has passed to the lessee.

(4) Nothing in this section impairs any insurable interest recognized under any other statute or rule of law.

(5) The parties by agreement may determine that one or more parties have an obligation to obtain and pay for insurance covering the goods and by agreement may determine the beneficiary of the proceeds of the insurance.

§ 2A—219. Risk of Loss.

(1) Except in the case of a finance lease, risk of loss is retained by the lessor and does not pass to the lessee. In the case of a finance lease, risk of loss passes to the lessee.

(2) Subject to the provisions of this Article on the effect of default on risk of loss (Section 2A—220), if risk of loss is to pass to the lessee and the time of passage is not stated, the following rules apply:

(a) If the lease contract requires or authorizes the goods to be shipped by carrier

(i) and it does not require delivery at a particular destination, the risk of loss passes to the lessee when the goods are duly delivered to the carrier; but

(ii) if it does require delivery at a particular destination and the goods are there duly tendered while in the possession of the carrier, the risk of loss passes to the lessee when the goods are there duly so tendered as to enable the lessee to take delivery.

(b) If the goods are held by a bailee to be delivered without being moved, the risk of loss passes to the lessee on acknowledgment by the bailee of the lessee's right to possession of the goods.

(c) In any case not within subsection (a) or (b), the risk of loss passes to the lessee on the lessee's receipt of the goods if the lessor, or, in the case of a finance lease, the supplier, is a merchant; otherwise the risk passes to the lessee on tender of delivery.

§ 2A—220. Effect of Default on Risk of Loss.

(1) Where risk of loss is to pass to the lessee and the time of passage is not stated:

(a) If a tender or delivery of goods so fails to conform to the lease contract as to give a right of rejection, the risk of their loss remains with the lessor, or, in the case of a finance lease, the supplier, until cure or acceptance.

(b) If the lessee rightfully revokes acceptance, he [or she], to the extent of any deficiency in his [or her] effective insurance coverage, may treat the risk of loss as having remained with the lessor from the beginning.

(2) Whether or not risk of loss is to pass to the lessee, if the lessee as to conforming goods already identified to a lease contract repudiates or is otherwise in default under the lease contract, the lessor, or, in the case of a finance lease, the supplier, to the extent of any deficiency in his [or her] effective insurance coverage may treat the risk of loss as resting on the lessee for a commercially reasonable time.

§ 2A—221. Casualty to Identified Goods.

If a lease contract requires goods identified when the lease contract is made, and the goods suffer casualty without fault of the lessee, the lessor or the supplier before delivery, or the goods suffer casualty before risk of loss passes to the lessee pursuant to the lease agreement or Section 2A—219, then:

(a) if the loss is total, the lease contract is avoided; and

(b) if the loss is partial or the goods have so deteriorated as to no longer conform to the lease contract, the lessee may nevertheless demand inspection and at his [or her] option either treat the lease contract as avoided or, except in a finance lease that is not a consumer lease, accept the goods with due allowance from the rent payable for the balance of the lease term for the deterioration or the deficiency in quantity but without further right against the lessor.

Part 3 Effect Of Lease Contract

§ 2A—301. Enforceability of Lease Contract.

Except as otherwise provided in this Article, a lease contract is effective and enforceable according to its terms between the parties, against purchasers of the goods and against creditors of the parties.

§ 2A—302. Title to and Possession of Goods.

Except as otherwise provided in this Article, each provision of this Article applies whether the lessor or a third party has title to the goods, and whether the lessor, the lessee, or a third party has possession of the goods, notwithstanding any statute or rule of law that possession or the absence of possession is fraudulent.

§ 2A—303. Alienability of Party's Interest Under Lease Contract or of Lessor's Residual Interest in Goods; Delegation of Performance; Transfer of Rights.

(1) As used in this section, "creation of a security interest" includes the sale of a lease contract that is subject to Article 9, Secured Transactions, by reason of Section 9—102(1)(b).

(2) Except as provided in subsections (3) and (4), a provision in a lease agreement which (i) prohibits the voluntary or involuntary transfer, including a transfer by sale, sublease, creation or enforcement of a security interest, or attachment, levy, or other judicial process, of an interest of a party under the lease contract or of the

lessor's residual interest in the goods, or (ii) makes such a transfer an event of default, gives rise to the rights and remedies provided in subsection (5), but a transfer that is prohibited or is an event of default under the lease agreement is otherwise effective.

(3) A provision in a lease agreement which (i) prohibits the creation or enforcement of a security interest in an interest of a party under the lease contract or in the lessor's residual interest in the goods, or (ii) makes such a transfer an event of default, is not enforceable unless, and then only to the extent that, there is an actual transfer by the lessee of the lessee's right of possession or use of the goods in violation of the provision or an actual delegation of a material performance of either party to the lease contract in violation of the provision. Neither the granting nor the enforcement of a security interest in (i) the lessor's interest under the lease contract or (ii) the lessor's residual interest in the goods is a transfer that materially impairs the prospect of obtaining return performance by, materially changes the duty of, or materially increases the burden or risk imposed on, the lessee within the purview of subsection (5) unless, and then only to the extent that, there is an actual delegation of a material performance of the lessor.

(4) A provision in a lease agreement which (i) prohibits a transfer of a right to damages for default with respect to the whole lease contract or of a right to payment arising out of the transferor's due performance of the transferor's entire obligation, or (ii) makes such a transfer an event of default, is not enforceable, and such a transfer is not a transfer that materially impairs the prospect of obtaining return performance by, materially changes the duty of, or materially increases the burden or risk imposed on, the other party to the lease contract within the purview of subsection (5).

(5) Subject to subsections (3) and (4):

(a) if a transfer is made which is made an event of default under a lease agreement, the party to the lease contract not making the transfer, unless that party waives the default or otherwise agrees, has the rights and remedies described in Section 2A—501(2);

(b) if paragraph (a) is not applicable and if a transfer is made that (i) is prohibited under a lease agreement or (ii) materially impairs the prospect of obtaining return performance by, materially changes the duty of, or materially increases the burden or risk imposed on, the other party to the lease contract, unless the party not making the transfer agrees at any time to the transfer in the lease contract or otherwise, then, except as limited by contract, (i) the transferor is liable to the party not making the transfer for damages caused by the transfer to the extent that the damages could not reasonably be prevented by the party not making the transfer and (ii) a court having jurisdiction may grant other appropriate relief, including cancellation of the lease contract or an injunction against the transfer.

(6) A transfer of "the lease" or of "all my rights under the lease," or a transfer in similar general terms, is a transfer of rights and, unless the language or the circumstances, as in a transfer for security, indicate the contrary, the transfer is a delegation of duties by the transferor to the transferee. Acceptance by the transferee constitutes a promise by the transferee to perform those duties. The promise is enforceable by either the transferor or the other party to the lease contract.

(7) Unless otherwise agreed by the lessor and the lessee, a delegation of performance does not relieve the transferor as against the other party of any duty to perform or of any liability for default.

(8) In a consumer lease, to prohibit the transfer of an interest of a party under the lease contract or to make a transfer an event of default, the language must be specific, by a writing, and conspicuous.

As amended in 1990.

§ 2A—304. Subsequent Lease of Goods by Lessor.

(1) Subject to Section 2A—303, a subsequent lessee from a lessor of goods under an existing lease contract obtains, to the extent of the leasehold interest transferred, the leasehold interest in the goods that the lessor had or had power to transfer, and except as provided in subsection (2) and Section 2A—527(4), takes subject to the existing lease contract. A lessor with voidable title has power to transfer a good leasehold interest to a good faith subsequent lessee for value, but only to the extent set forth in the preceding sentence. If goods have been delivered under a transaction of purchase the lessor has that power even though:

(a) the lessor's transferor was deceived as to the identity of the lessor;

(b) the delivery was in exchange for a check which is later dishonored;

(c) it was agreed that the transaction was to be a "cash sale"; or

(d) the delivery was procured through fraud punishable as larcenous under the criminal law.

(2) A subsequent lessee in the ordinary course of business from a lessor who is a merchant dealing in goods of that kind to whom the goods were entrusted by the existing lessee of that lessor before the interest of the subsequent lessee became enforceable against that lessor obtains, to the extent of the leasehold interest transferred, all of that lessor's and the existing lessee's rights to the goods, and takes free of the existing lease contract.

(3) A subsequent lessee from the lessor of goods that are subject to an existing lease contract and are covered by a certificate of title issued under a statute of this State or of another jurisdiction takes no greater rights than those provided both by this section and by the certificate of title statute.

As amended in 1990.

§ 2A—305. Sale or Sublease of Goods by Lessee.

(1) Subject to the provisions of Section 2A—303, a buyer or sublessee from the lessee of goods under an existing lease contract obtains, to the extent of the interest transferred, the leasehold interest in the goods that the lessee had or had power to transfer, and except as provided in subsection (2) and Section 2A—511(4), takes subject to the existing lease contract. A lessee with a voidable leasehold interest has power to transfer a good leasehold interest to a good faith buyer for value or a good faith sublessee for value, but only to the extent set forth in the preceding sentence. When goods have been delivered under a transaction of lease the lessee has that power even though:

(a) the lessor was deceived as to the identity of the lessee;

(b) the delivery was in exchange for a check which is later dishonored; or

(c) the delivery was procured through fraud punishable as larcenous under the criminal law.

(2) A buyer in the ordinary course of business or a sublessee in the ordinary course of business from a lessee who is a merchant dealing in goods of that kind to whom the goods were entrusted by the lessor obtains, to the extent of the interest transferred, all of the lessor's and lessee's rights to the goods, and takes free of the existing lease contract.

(3) A buyer or sublessee from the lessee of goods that are subject to an existing lease contract and are covered by a certificate of title issued under a statute of this State or of another jurisdiction takes no greater rights than those provided both by this section and by the certificate of title statute.

§ 2A—306. Priority of Certain Liens Arising by Operation of Law.

If a person in the ordinary course of his [or her] business furnishes services or materials with respect to goods subject to a lease contract, a lien upon those goods in the possession of that person given by statute or rule of law for those materials or services takes priority over any interest of the lessor or lessee under the lease contract or this Article unless the lien is created by statute and the statute provides otherwise or unless the lien is created by rule of law and the rule of law provides otherwise.

§ 2A—307. Priority of Liens Arising by Attachment or Levy on, Security Interests in, and Other Claims to Goods.

(1) Except as otherwise provided in Section 2A—306, a creditor of a lessee takes subject to the lease contract.

(2) Except as otherwise provided in subsections (3) and (4) and in Sections 2A—306 and 2A—308, a creditor of a lessor takes subject to the lease contract unless:

(a) the creditor holds a lien that attached to the goods before the lease contract became enforceable,

(b) the creditor holds a security interest in the goods and the lessee did not give value and receive delivery of the goods without knowledge of the security interest; or

(c) the creditor holds a security interest in the goods which was perfected (Section 9—303) before the lease contract became enforceable.

(3) A lessee in the ordinary course of business takes the leasehold interest free of a security interest in the goods created by the lessor even though the security interest is perfected (Section 9—303) and the lessee knows of its existence.

(4) A lessee other than a lessee in the ordinary course of business takes the leasehold interest free of a security interest to the extent that it secures future advances made after the secured party acquires knowledge of the lease or more than 45 days after the lease contract becomes enforceable, whichever first occurs, unless the future advances are made pursuant to a commitment entered into without knowledge of the lease and before the expiration of the 45-day period.

§ 2A—308. Special Rights of Creditors.

(1) A creditor of a lessor in possession of goods subject to a lease contract may treat the lease contract as void if as against the creditor retention of possession by the lessor is fraudulent under any statute or rule of law, but retention of possession in good faith and current course of trade by the lessor for a commercially reasonable time after the lease contract becomes enforceable is not fraudulent.

(2) Nothing in this Article impairs the rights of creditors of a lessor if the lease contract (a) becomes enforceable, not in current course of trade but in satisfaction of or as security for a pre-existing claim for money, security, or the like, and (b) is made under circumstances which under any statute or rule of law apart from this Article would constitute the transaction a fraudulent transfer or voidable preference.

(3) A creditor of a seller may treat a sale or an identification of goods to a contract for sale as void if as against the creditor retention of possession by the seller is fraudulent under any statute or rule of law, but retention of possession of the goods pursuant to a lease contract entered into by the seller as lessee and the buyer as lessor in connection with the sale or identification of the goods is not fraudulent if the buyer bought for value and in good faith.

§ 2A—309. Lessor's and Lessee's Rights When Goods Become Fixtures.

(1) In this section:

(a) goods are "fixtures" when they become so related to particular real estate that an interest in them arises under real estate law;

(b) a "fixture filing" is the filing, in the office where a mortgage on the real estate would be filed or recorded, of a financing statement covering goods that are or are to become fixtures and conforming to the requirements of Section 9—402(5);

(c) a lease is a "purchase money lease" unless the lessee has possession or use of the goods or the right to possession or use of the goods before the lease agreement is enforceable;

(d) a mortgage is a "construction mortgage" to the extent it secures an obligation incurred for the construction of an improvement on land including the acquisition cost of the land, if the recorded writing so indicates; and

(e) "encumbrance" includes real estate mortgages and other liens on real estate and all other rights in real estate that are not ownership interests.

(2) Under this Article a lease may be of goods that are fixtures or may continue in goods that become fixtures, but no lease exists under this Article of ordinary building materials incorporated into an improvement on land.

(3) This Article does not prevent creation of a lease of fixtures pursuant to real estate law.

(4) The perfected interest of a lessor of fixtures has priority over a conflicting interest of an encumbrancer or owner of the real estate if:

(a) the lease is a purchase money lease, the conflicting interest of the encumbrancer or owner arises before the goods become fixtures, the interest of the lessor is perfected by a fixture filing before the goods become fixtures or within ten days thereafter, and the lessee has an interest of record in the real estate or is in possession of the real estate; or

(b) the interest of the lessor is perfected by a fixture filing before the interest of the encumbrancer or owner is of record, the lessor's interest has priority over any conflicting interest of a predecessor in title of the encumbrancer or owner, and the lessee has an interest of record in the real estate or is in possession of the real estate.

(5) The interest of a lessor of fixtures, whether or not perfected, has priority over the conflicting interest of an encumbrancer or owner of the real estate if:

(a) the fixtures are readily removable factory or office machines, readily removable equipment that is not primarily used or leased for use in the operation of the real estate, or readily removable replacements of domestic appliances that are goods subject to a consumer lease, and before the goods become fixtures the lease contract is enforceable; or

(b) the conflicting interest is a lien on the real estate obtained by legal or equitable proceedings after the lease contract is enforceable; or

(c) the encumbrancer or owner has consented in writing to the lease or has disclaimed an interest in the goods as fixtures; or

(d) the lessee has a right to remove the goods as against the encumbrancer or owner. If the lessee's right to remove terminates, the priority of the interest of the lessor continues for a reasonable time.

(6) Notwithstanding paragraph (4)(a) but otherwise subject to subsections (4) and (5), the interest of a lessor of fixtures, including the lessor's residual interest, is subordinate to the conflicting interest of an encumbrancer of the real estate under a construction mortgage recorded before the goods become fixtures if the goods become fixtures before the completion of the construction. To the extent given to refinance a construction mortgage, the conflicting interest of an encumbrancer of the real estate under a mortgage has this priority to the same extent as the encumbrancer of the real estate under the construction mortgage.

(7) In cases not within the preceding subsections, priority between the interest of a lessor of fixtures, including the lessor's residual interest, and the conflicting interest of an encumbrancer or owner of the real estate who is not the lessee is determined by the priority rules governing conflicting interests in real estate.

(8) If the interest of a lessor of fixtures, including the lessor's residual interest, has priority over all conflicting interests of all owners and encumbrancers of the real estate, the lessor or the lessee may (i) on default, expiration, termination, or cancellation of the lease agreement but subject to the agreement and this Article, or (ii) if necessary to enforce other rights and remedies of the lessor or lessee under this Article, remove the goods from the real estate, free and clear of all conflicting interests of all owners and encumbrancers of the real estate, but the lessor or lessee must reimburse any encumbrancer or owner of the real estate who is not the lessee and who has not otherwise agreed for the cost of repair of any physical injury, but not for any diminution in value of the real estate caused by the absence of the goods removed or by any necessity of replacing them. A person entitled to reimbursement may refuse permission to remove until the party seeking removal gives adequate security for the performance of this obligation.

(9) Even though the lease agreement does not create a security interest, the interest of a lessor of fixtures, including the lessor's residual interest, is perfected by filing a financing statement as a fixture filing for leased goods that are or are to become fixtures in accordance with the relevant provisions of the Article on Secured Transactions (Article 9).

As amended in 1990.

§ 2A—310. Lessor's and Lessee's Rights When Goods Become Accessions.

(1) Goods are "accessions" when they are installed in or affixed to other goods.

(2) The interest of a lessor or a lessee under a lease contract entered into before the goods became accessions is superior to all interests in the whole except as stated in subsection (4).

(3) The interest of a lessor or a lessee under a lease contract entered into at the time or after the goods became accessions is superior to all subsequently acquired interests in the whole except as stated in subsection (4) but is subordinate to interests in the whole existing at the time the lease contract was made unless the holders of such interests in the whole have in writing consented to the lease or disclaimed an interest in the goods as part of the whole.

(4) The interest of a lessor or a lessee under a lease contract described in subsection (2) or (3) is subordinate to the interest of

(a) a buyer in the ordinary course of business or a lessee in the ordinary course of business of any interest in the whole acquired after the goods became accessions; or

(b) a creditor with a security interest in the whole perfected before the lease contract was made to the extent that the creditor makes subsequent advances without knowledge of the lease contract.

(5) When under subsections (2) or (3) and (4) a lessor or a lessee of accessions holds an interest that is superior to all interests in the whole, the lessor or the lessee may (a) on default, expiration, termination, or cancellation of the lease contract by the other party but subject to the provisions of the lease contract and this Article, or (b) if necessary to enforce his [or her] other rights and remedies under this Article, remove the goods from the whole, free and clear of all interests in the whole, but he [or she] must reimburse any holder of an interest in the whole who is not the lessee and who has not otherwise agreed for the cost of repair of any physical injury but not for any diminution in value of the whole caused by the absence of the goods removed or by any necessity for replacing them. A person entitled to reimbursement may refuse permission to remove until the party seeking removal gives adequate security for the performance of this obligation.

§ 2A—311. Priority Subject to Subordination.

Nothing in this Article prevents subordination by agreement by any person entitled to priority.

As added in 1990.

Part 4 Performance Of Lease Contract: Repudiated, Substituted And Excused

§ 2A—401. Insecurity: Adequate Assurance of Performance.

(1) A lease contract imposes an obligation on each party that the other's expectation of receiving due performance will not be impaired.

(2) If reasonable grounds for insecurity arise with respect to the performance of either party, the insecure party may demand in writing adequate assurance of due performance. Until the insecure party receives that assurance, if commercially reasonable the insecure party may suspend any performance for which he [or she] has not already received the agreed return.

(3) A repudiation of the lease contract occurs if assurance of due performance adequate under the circumstances of the particular case is not provided to the insecure party within a reasonable time, not to exceed 30 days after receipt of a demand by the other party.

(4) Between merchants, the reasonableness of grounds for insecurity and the adequacy of any assurance offered must be determined according to commercial standards.

(5) Acceptance of any nonconforming delivery or payment does not prejudice the aggrieved party's right to demand adequate assurance of future performance.

§ 2A—402. Anticipatory Repudiation.

If either party repudiates a lease contract with respect to a performance not yet due under the lease contract, the loss of which performance will substantially impair the value of the lease contract to the other, the aggrieved party may:

(a) for a commercially reasonable time, await retraction of repudiation and performance by the repudiating party;

(b) make demand pursuant to Section 2A—401 and await assurance of future performance adequate under the circumstances of the particular case; or

(c) resort to any right or remedy upon default under the lease contract or this Article, even though the aggrieved party has notified the repudiating party that the aggrieved party would await the repudiating party's performance and assurance and has urged retraction. In addition, whether or not the aggrieved party is pursuing one of the foregoing remedies, the aggrieved party may suspend performance or, if the aggrieved party is the lessor, proceed in accordance with the provisions of this Article on the lessor's right to identify goods to the lease contract notwithstanding default or to salvage unfinished goods (Section 2A—524).

§ 2A—403. Retraction of Anticipatory Repudiation.

(1) Until the repudiating party's next performance is due, the repudiating party can retract the repudiation unless, since the repudiation, the aggrieved party has cancelled the lease contract or materially changed the aggrieved party's position or otherwise indicated that the aggrieved party considers the repudiation final.

(2) Retraction may be by any method that clearly indicates to the aggrieved party that the repudiating party intends to perform under the lease contract and includes any assurance demanded under Section 2A—401.

(3) Retraction reinstates a repudiating party's rights under a lease contract with due excuse and allowance to the aggrieved party for any delay occasioned by the repudiation.

§ 2A—404. Substituted Performance.

(1) If without fault of the lessee, the lessor and the supplier, the agreed berthing, loading, or unloading facilities fail or the agreed type of carrier becomes unavailable or the agreed manner of delivery otherwise becomes commercially impracticable, but a commercially reasonable substitute is available, the substitute performance must be tendered and accepted.

(2) If the agreed means or manner of payment fails because of domestic or foreign governmental regulation:

(a) the lessor may withhold or stop delivery or cause the supplier to withhold or stop delivery unless the lessee provides a means or manner of payment that is commercially a substantial equivalent; and

(b) if delivery has already been taken, payment by the means or in the manner provided by the regulation discharges the lessee's obligation unless the regulation is discriminatory, oppressive, or predatory.

§ 2A—405. Excused Performance.

Subject to Section 2A—404 on substituted performance, the following rules apply:

(a) Delay in delivery or nondelivery in whole or in part by a lessor or a supplier who complies with paragraphs (b) and (c) is not a default under the lease contract if performance as agreed has been made impracticable by the occurrence of a contingency the nonoccurrence of which was a basic assumption on which the lease contract was made or by compliance in good faith with any applicable foreign or domestic governmental regulation or order, whether or not the regulation or order later proves to be invalid.

(b) If the causes mentioned in paragraph (a) affect only part of the lessor's or the supplier's capacity to perform, he [or she] shall allocate production and deliveries among his [or her] customers but at his [or her] option may include regular customers not then under contract for sale or lease as well as his [or her] own requirements for further manufacture. He [or she] may so allocate in any manner that is fair and reasonable.

(c) The lessor seasonably shall notify the lessee and in the case of a finance lease the supplier seasonably shall notify the lessor and the lessee, if known, that there will be delay or nondelivery and, if allocation is required under paragraph (b), of the estimated quota thus made available for the lessee.

§ 2A—406. Procedure on Excused Performance.

(1) If the lessee receives notification of a material or indefinite delay or an allocation justified under Section 2A—405, the lessee may by written notification to the lessor as to any goods involved, and with respect to all of the goods if under an installment lease contract the value of the whole lease contract is substantially impaired (Section 2A—510):

(a) terminate the lease contract (Section 2A—505(2)); or

(b) except in a finance lease that is not a consumer lease, modify the lease contract by accepting the available quota in substitution, with due allowance from the rent payable for the balance of the lease term for the deficiency but without further right against the lessor.

(2) If, after receipt of a notification from the lessor under Section 2A—405, the lessee fails so to modify the lease agreement within a reasonable time not exceeding 30 days, the lease contract lapses with respect to any deliveries affected.

§ 2A—407. Irrevocable Promises: Finance Leases.

(1) In the case of a finance lease that is not a consumer lease the lessee's promises under the lease contract become irrevocable and independent upon the lessee's acceptance of the goods.

(2) A promise that has become irrevocable and independent under subsection (1):

(a) is effective and enforceable between the parties, and by or against third parties including assignees of the parties, and

(b) is not subject to cancellation, termination, modification, repudiation, excuse, or substitution without the consent of the party to whom the promise runs.

(3) This section does not affect the validity under any other law of a covenant in any lease contract making the lessee's promises irrevocable and independent upon the lessee's acceptance of the goods.

As amended in 1990.

Part 5 Default

A. In General

§ 2A—501. Default: Procedure.

(1) Whether the lessor or the lessee is in default under a lease contract is determined by the lease agreement and this Article.

(2) If the lessor or the lessee is in default under the lease contract, the party seeking enforcement has rights and remedies as provided in this Article and, except as limited by this Article, as provided in the lease agreement.

(3) If the lessor or the lessee is in default under the lease contract, the party seeking enforcement may reduce the party's claim to judgment, or otherwise enforce the lease contract by self-help or any available judicial procedure or nonjudicial procedure, including administrative proceeding, arbitration, or the like, in accordance with this Article.

(4) Except as otherwise provided in Section 1–106(1) or this Article or the lease agreement, the rights and remedies referred to in subsections (2) and (3) are cumulative.

(5) If the lease agreement covers both real property and goods, the party seeking enforcement may proceed under this Part as to the goods, or under other applicable law as to both the real property and the goods in accordance with that party's rights and remedies in respect of the real property, in which case this Part does not apply.

As amended in 1990.

§ 2A—502. Notice After Default.

Except as otherwise provided in this Article or the lease agreement, the lessor or lessee in default under the lease contract is not entitled to notice of default or notice of enforcement from the other party to the lease agreement.

§ 2A—503. Modification or Impairment of Rights and Remedies.

(1) Except as otherwise provided in this Article, the lease agreement may include rights and remedies for default in addition to or in substitution for those provided in this Article and may limit or alter the measure of damages recoverable under this Article.

(2) Resort to a remedy provided under this Article or in the lease agreement is optional unless the remedy is expressly agreed to be exclusive. If circumstances cause an exclusive or limited remedy to fail of its essential purpose, or provision for an exclusive remedy is unconscionable, remedy may be had as provided in this Article.

(3) Consequential damages may be liquidated under Section 2A—504, or may otherwise be limited, altered, or excluded unless the limitation, alteration, or exclusion is unconscionable. Limitation, alteration, or exclusion of consequential damages for injury to the person in the case of consumer goods is prima facie unconscionable but limitation, alteration, or exclusion of damages where the loss is commercial is not prima facie unconscionable.

(4) Rights and remedies on default by the lessor or the lessee with respect to any obligation or promise collateral or ancillary to the lease contract are not impaired by this Article.

As amended in 1990.

§ 2A—504. Liquidation of Damages.

(1) Damages payable by either party for default, or any other act or omission, including indemnity for loss or diminution of anticipated tax benefits or loss or damage to lessor's residual interest, may be liquidated in the lease agreement but only at an amount or by a formula that is reasonable in light of the then anticipated harm caused by the default or other act or omission.

(2) If the lease agreement provides for liquidation of damages, and such provision does not comply with subsection (1), or such provision is an exclusive or limited remedy that circumstances cause to fail of its essential purpose, remedy may be had as provided in this Article.

(3) If the lessor justifiably withholds or stops delivery of goods because of the lessee's default or insolvency (Section 2A—525 or 2A—526), the lessee is entitled to restitution of any amount by which the sum of his [or her] payments exceeds:

(a) the amount to which the lessor is entitled by virtue of terms liquidating the lessor's damages in accordance with subsection (1); or

(b) in the absence of those terms, 20 percent of the then present value of the total rent the lessee was obligated to pay for the balance of the lease term, or, in the case of a consumer lease, the lesser of such amount or $500.

(4) A lessee's right to restitution under subsection (3) is subject to offset to the extent the lessor establishes:

(a) a right to recover damages under the provisions of this Article other than subsection (1); and

(b) the amount or value of any benefits received by the lessee directly or indirectly by reason of the lease contract.

§ 2A—505. Cancellation and Termination and Effect of Cancellation, Termination, Rescission, or Fraud on Rights and Remedies.

(1) On cancellation of the lease contract, all obligations that are still executory on both sides are discharged, but any right based on prior default or performance survives, and the cancelling party also retains any remedy for default of the whole lease contract or any unperformed balance.

(2) On termination of the lease contract, all obligations that are still executory on both sides are discharged but any right based on prior default or performance survives.

(3) Unless the contrary intention clearly appears, expressions of "cancellation," "rescission," or the like of the lease contract may not be construed as a renunciation or discharge of any claim in damages for an antecedent default.

(4) Rights and remedies for material misrepresentation or fraud include all rights and remedies available under this Article for default.

(5) Neither rescission nor a claim for rescission of the lease contract nor rejection or return of the goods may bar or be deemed inconsistent with a claim for damages or other right or remedy.

§ 2A—506. Statute of Limitations.

(1) An action for default under a lease contract, including breach of warranty or indemnity, must be commenced within 4 years after the cause of action accrued. By the original lease contract the parties may reduce the period of limitation to not less than one year.

(2) A cause of action for default accrues when the act or omission on which the default or breach of warranty is based is or should have been discovered by the aggrieved party, or when the default occurs, whichever is later. A cause of action for indemnity accrues when the act or omission on which the claim for indemnity is based is or should have been discovered by the indemnified party, whichever is later.

(3) If an action commenced within the time limited by subsection (1) is so terminated as to leave available a remedy by another action for the same default or breach of warranty or indemnity, the other action may be commenced after the expiration of the time limited and within 6 months after the termination of the first action unless the termination resulted from voluntary discontinuance or from dismissal for failure or neglect to prosecute.

(4) This section does not alter the law on tolling of the statute of limitations nor does it apply to causes of action that have accrued before this Article becomes effective.

§ 2A—507. Proof of Market Rent: Time and Place.

(1) Damages based on market rent (Section 2A—519 or 2A—528) are determined according to the rent for the use of the goods concerned for a lease term identical to the remaining lease term of the original lease agreement and prevailing at the times specified in Sections 2A–519 and 2A–528.

(2) If evidence of rent for the use of the goods concerned for a lease term identical to the remaining lease term of the original lease agreement and prevailing at the times or places described in this Article is not readily available, the rent prevailing within any reasonable time before or after the time described or at any other place or for a different lease term which in commercial judgment or under usage of trade would serve as a reasonable substitute for the one described may be used, making any proper allowance for the difference, including the cost of transporting the goods to or from the other place.

(3) Evidence of a relevant rent prevailing at a time or place or for a lease term other than the one described in this Article offered by one party is not admissible unless and until he [or she] has given the other party notice the court finds sufficient to prevent unfair surprise.

(4) If the prevailing rent or value of any goods regularly leased in any established market is in issue, reports in official publications or trade journals or in newspapers or periodicals of general circulation published as the reports of that market are admissible in evidence. The circumstances of the preparation of the report may be shown to affect its weight but not its admissibility.

As amended in 1990.

B. Default by Lessor

§ 2A—508. Lessee's Remedies.

(1) If a lessor fails to deliver the goods in conformity to the lease contract (Section 2A—509) or repudiates the lease contract (Section 2A—402), or a lessee rightfully rejects the goods (Section 2A—509) or justifiably revokes acceptance of the goods (Section 2A—517), then with respect to any goods involved, and with respect to all of the goods if under an installment lease contract the value of the whole lease contract is substantially impaired (Section 2A—510), the lessor is in default under the lease contract and the lessee may:

    (a) cancel the lease contract (Section 2A—505(1));

    (b) recover so much of the rent and security as has been paid and is just under the circumstances;

    (c) cover and recover damages as to all goods affected whether or not they have been identified to the lease contract (Sections 2A—518 and 2A—520), or recover damages for nondelivery (Sections 2A—519 and 2A—520);

    (d) exercise any other rights or pursue any other remedies provided in the lease contract..

(2) If a lessor fails to deliver the goods in conformity to the lease contract or repudiates the lease contract, the lessee may also:

    (a) if the goods have been identified, recover them (Section 2A—522); or

    (b) in a proper case, obtain specific performance or replevy the goods (Section 2A—521).

(3) If a lessor is otherwise in default under a lease contract, the lessee may exercise the rights and pursue the remedies provided in the lease contract, which may include a right to cancel the lease, and in Section 2A–519(3).

(4) If a lessor has breached a warranty, whether express or implied, the lessee may recover damages (Section 2A—519(4)).

(5) On rightful rejection or justifiable revocation of acceptance, a lessee has a security interest in goods in the lessee's possession or control for any rent and security that has been paid and any expenses reasonably incurred in their inspection, receipt, transportation, and

care and custody and may hold those goods and dispose of them in good faith and in a commercially reasonable manner, subject to Section 2A—527(5).

(6) Subject to the provisions of Section 2A—407, a lessee, on notifying the lessor of the lessee's intention to do so, may deduct all or any part of the damages resulting from any default under the lease contract from any part of the rent still due under the same lease contract.

As amended in 1990.

§ 2A—509. Lessee's Rights on Improper Delivery; Rightful Rejection.

(1) Subject to the provisions of Section 2A—510 on default in installment lease contracts, if the goods or the tender or delivery fail in any respect to conform to the lease contract, the lessee may reject or accept the goods or accept any commercial unit or units and reject the rest of the goods.

(2) Rejection of goods is ineffective unless it is within a reasonable time after tender or delivery of the goods and the lessee seasonably notifies the lessor.

§ 2A—510. Installment Lease Contracts: Rejection and Default.

(1) Under an installment lease contract a lessee may reject any delivery that is nonconforming if the nonconformity substantially impairs the value of that delivery and cannot be cured or the nonconformity is a defect in the required documents; but if the nonconformity does not fall within subsection (2) and the lessor or the supplier gives adequate assurance of its cure, the lessee must accept that delivery.

(2) Whenever nonconformity or default with respect to one or more deliveries substantially impairs the value of the installment lease contract as a whole there is a default with respect to the whole. But, the aggrieved party reinstates the installment lease contract as a whole if the aggrieved party accepts a nonconforming delivery without seasonably notifying of cancellation or brings an action with respect only to past deliveries or demands performance as to future deliveries.

§ 2A—511. Merchant Lessee's Duties as to Rightfully Rejected Goods.

(1) Subject to any security interest of a lessee (Section 2A—508(5)), if a lessor or a supplier has no agent or place of business at the market of rejection, a merchant lessee, after rejection of goods in his [or her] possession or control, shall follow any reasonable instructions received from the lessor or the supplier with respect to the goods. In the absence of those instructions, a merchant lessee shall make reasonable efforts to sell, lease, or otherwise dispose of the goods for the lessor's account if they threaten to decline in value speedily. Instructions are not reasonable if on demand indemnity for expenses is not forthcoming.

(2) If a merchant lessee (subsection (1)) or any other lessee (Section 2A—512) disposes of goods, he [or she] is entitled to reimbursement either from the lessor or the supplier or out of the proceeds for reasonable expenses of caring for and disposing of the goods and, if the expenses include no disposition commission, to such commission as

is usual in the trade, or if there is none, to a reasonable sum not exceeding 10 percent of the gross proceeds.

(3) In complying with this section or Section 2A—512, the lessee is held only to good faith. Good faith conduct hereunder is neither acceptance or conversion nor the basis of an action for damages.

(4) A purchaser who purchases in good faith from a lessee pursuant to this section or Section 2A—512 takes the goods free of any rights of the lessor and the supplier even though the lessee fails to comply with one or more of the requirements of this Article.

§ 2A—512. Lessee's Duties as to Rightfully Rejected Goods.

(1) Except as otherwise provided with respect to goods that threaten to decline in value speedily (Section 2A—511) and subject to any security interest of a lessee (Section 2A—508(5)):

(a) the lessee, after rejection of goods in the lessee's possession, shall hold them with reasonable care at the lessor's or the supplier's disposition for a reasonable time after the lessee's seasonable notification of rejection;

(b) if the lessor or the supplier gives no instructions within a reasonable time after notification of rejection, the lessee may store the rejected goods for the lessor's or the supplier's account or ship them to the lessor or the supplier or dispose of them for the lessor's or the supplier's account with reimbursement in the manner provided in Section 2A—511; but

(c) the lessee has no further obligations with regard to goods rightfully rejected.

(2) Action by the lessee pursuant to subsection (1) is not acceptance or conversion.

§ 2A—513. Cure by Lessor of Improper Tender or Delivery; Replacement.

(1) If any tender or delivery by the lessor or the supplier is rejected because nonconforming and the time for performance has not yet expired, the lessor or the supplier may seasonably notify the lessee of the lessor's or the supplier's intention to cure and may then make a conforming delivery within the time provided in the lease contract.

(2) If the lessee rejects a nonconforming tender that the lessor or the supplier had reasonable grounds to believe would be acceptable with or without money allowance, the lessor or the supplier may have a further reasonable time to substitute a conforming tender if he [or she] seasonably notifies the lessee.

§ 2A—514. Waiver of Lessee's Objections.

(1) In rejecting goods, a lessee's failure to state a particular defect that is ascertainable by reasonable inspection precludes the lessee from relying on the defect to justify rejection or to establish default:

(a) if, stated seasonably, the lessor or the supplier could have cured it (Section 2A—513); or

(b) between merchants if the lessor or the supplier after rejection has made a request in writing for a full and final written statement of all defects on which the lessee proposes to rely.

(2) A lessee's failure to reserve rights when paying rent or other consideration against documents precludes recovery of the payment for defects apparent on the face of the documents.

§ 2A—515. Acceptance of Goods.

(1) Acceptance of goods occurs after the lessee has had a reasonable opportunity to inspect the goods and

(a) the lessee signifies or acts with respect to the goods in a manner that signifies to the lessor or the supplier that the goods are conforming or that the lessee will take or retain them in spite of their nonconformity; or

(b) the lessee fails to make an effective rejection of the goods (Section 2A—509(2)).

(2) Acceptance of a part of any commercial unit is acceptance of that entire unit.

§ 2A—516. Effect of Acceptance of Goods; Notice of Default; Burden of Establishing Default after Acceptance; Notice of Claim or Litigation to Person Answerable Over.

(1) A lessee must pay rent for any goods accepted in accordance with the lease contract, with due allowance for goods rightfully rejected or not delivered.

(2) A lessee's acceptance of goods precludes rejection of the goods accepted. In the case of a finance lease, if made with knowledge of a nonconformity, acceptance cannot be revoked because of it. In any other case, if made with knowledge of a nonconformity, acceptance cannot be revoked because of it unless the acceptance was on the reasonable assumption that the nonconformity would be seasonably cured. Acceptance does not of itself impair any other remedy provided by this Article or the lease agreement for nonconformity.

(3) If a tender has been accepted:

(a) within a reasonable time after the lessee discovers or should have discovered any default, the lessee shall notify the lessor and the supplier, if any, or be barred from any remedy against the party notified;

(b) except in the case of a consumer lease, within a reasonable time after the lessee receives notice of litigation for infringement or the like (Section 2A—211) the lessee shall notify the lessor or be barred from any remedy over for liability established by the litigation; and

(c) the burden is on the lessee to establish any default.

(4) If a lessee is sued for breach of a warranty or other obligation for which a lessor or a supplier is answerable over the following apply:

(a) The lessee may give the lessor or the supplier, or both, written notice of the litigation. If the notice states that the person notified may come in and defend and that if the person notified does not do so that person will be bound in any action against that person by the lessee by any determination of fact common to the two litigations, then unless the person notified after seasonable receipt of the notice does come in and defend that person is so bound.

(b) The lessor or the supplier may demand in writing that the lessee turn over control of the litigation including settlement if the claim is one for infringement or the like (Section 2A—211) or else be barred from any remedy over. If the demand states that the lessor or the supplier agrees to bear all expense and to satisfy any adverse judgment, then unless the lessee after seasonable receipt of the demand does turn over control the lessee is so barred.

(5) Subsections (3) and (4) apply to any obligation of a lessee to hold the lessor or the supplier harmless against infringement or the like (Section 2A—211).

As amended in 1990.

§ 2A—517. Revocation of Acceptance of Goods.

(1) A lessee may revoke acceptance of a lot or commercial unit whose nonconformity substantially impairs its value to the lessee if the lessee has accepted it:

(a) except in the case of a finance lease, on the reasonable assumption that its nonconformity would be cured and it has not been seasonably cured; or

(b) without discovery of the nonconformity if the lessee's acceptance was reasonably induced either by the lessor's assurances or, except in the case of a finance lease, by the difficulty of discovery before acceptance.

(2) Except in the case of a finance lease that is not a consumer lease, a lessee may revoke acceptance of a lot or commercial unit if the lessor defaults under the lease contract and the default substantially impairs the value of that lot or commercial unit to the lessee.

(3) If the lease agreement so provides, the lessee may revoke acceptance of a lot or commercial unit because of other defaults by the lessor.

(4) Revocation of acceptance must occur within a reasonable time after the lessee discovers or should have discovered the ground for it and before any substantial change in condition of the goods which is not caused by the nonconformity. Revocation is not effective until the lessee notifies the lessor.

(5) A lessee who so revokes has the same rights and duties with regard to the goods involved as if the lessee had rejected them.

As amended in 1990.

§ 2A—518. Cover; Substitute Goods.

(1) After a default by a lessor under the lease contract of the type described in Section 2A—508(1), or, if agreed, after other default by the lessor, the lessee may cover by making any purchase or lease of or contract to purchase or lease goods in substitution for those due from the lessor.

(2) Except as otherwise provided with respect to damages liquidated in the lease agreement (Section 2A—504) or otherwise determined pursuant to agreement of the parties (Sections 1—102(3) and 2A—503), if a lessee's cover is by lease agreement substantially similar to the original lease agreement and the new lease agreement is made in good faith and in a commercially reasonable manner, the lessee may recover from the lessor as damages (i) the present value, as of the date of the commencement of the term of the new lease agreement, of the rent under the new lease agreement applicable to that period of the new lease term which is comparable to the then remaining term of the original lease agreement minus the present value as of the same date of the total rent for the then remaining lease term of the original lease agreement, and (ii) any incidental or consequential damages, less expenses saved in consequence of the lessor's default.

(3) If a lessee's cover is by lease agreement that for any reason does not qualify for treatment under subsection (2), or is by purchase or

otherwise, the lessee may recover from the lessor as if the lessee had elected not to cover and Section 2A—519 governs.

As amended in 1990.

§ 2A—519. Lessee's Damages for Non-Delivery, Repudiation, Default, and Breach of Warranty in Regard to Accepted Goods.

(1) Except as otherwise provided with respect to damages liquidated in the lease agreement (Section 2A—504) or otherwise determined pursuant to agreement of the parties (Sections 1—102(3) and 2A—503), if a lessee elects not to cover or a lessee elects to cover and the cover is by lease agreement that for any reason does not qualify for treatment under Section 2A—518(2), or is by purchase or otherwise, the measure of damages for non-delivery or repudiation by the lessor or for rejection or revocation of acceptance by the lessee is the present value, as of the date of the default, of the then market rent minus the present value as of the same date of the original rent, computed for the remaining lease term of the original lease agreement, together with incidental and consequential damages, less expenses saved in consequence of the lessor's default.

(2) Market rent is to be determined as of the place for tender or, in cases of rejection after arrival or revocation of acceptance, as of the place of arrival.

(3) Except as otherwise agreed, if the lessee has accepted goods and given notification (Section 2A—516(3)), the measure of damages for non-conforming tender or delivery or other default by a lessor is the loss resulting in the ordinary course of events from the lessor's default as determined in any manner that is reasonable together with incidental and consequential damages, less expenses saved in consequence of the lessor's default.

(4) Except as otherwise agreed, the measure of damages for breach of warranty is the present value at the time and place of acceptance of the difference between the value of the use of the goods accepted and the value if they had been as warranted for the lease term, unless special circumstances show proximate damages of a different amount, together with incidental and consequential damages, less expenses saved in consequence of the lessor's default or breach of warranty.

As amended in 1990.

§ 2A—520. Lessee's Incidental and Consequential Damages.

(1) Incidental damages resulting from a lessor's default include expenses reasonably incurred in inspection, receipt, transportation, and care and custody of goods rightfully rejected or goods the acceptance of which is justifiably revoked, any commercially reasonable charges, expenses or commissions in connection with effecting cover, and any other reasonable expense incident to the default.

(2) Consequential damages resulting from a lessor's default include:

(a) any loss resulting from general or particular requirements and needs of which the lessor at the time of contracting had reason to know and which could not reasonably be prevented by cover or otherwise; and

(b) injury to person or property proximately resulting from any breach of warranty.

§ 2A—521. Lessee's Right to Specific Performance or Replevin.

(1) Specific performance may be decreed if the goods are unique or in other proper circumstances.

(2) A decree for specific performance may include any terms and conditions as to payment of the rent, damages, or other relief that the court deems just.

(3) A lessee has a right of replevin, detinue, sequestration, claim and delivery, or the like for goods identified to the lease contract if after reasonable effort the lessee is unable to effect cover for those goods or the circumstances reasonably indicate that the effort will be unavailing.

§ 2A—522. Lessee's Right to Goods on Lessor's Insolvency.

(1) Subject to subsection (2) and even though the goods have not been shipped, a lessee who has paid a part or all of the rent and security for goods identified to a lease contract (Section 2A—217) on making and keeping good a tender of any unpaid portion of the rent and security due under the lease contract may recover the goods identified from the lessor if the lessor becomes insolvent within 10 days after receipt of the first installment of rent and security.

(2) A lessee acquires the right to recover goods identified to a lease contract only if they conform to the lease contract.

C. Default by Lessee

§ 2A—523. Lessor's Remedies.

(1) If a lessee wrongfully rejects or revokes acceptance of goods or fails to make a payment when due or repudiates with respect to a part or the whole, then, with respect to any goods involved, and with respect to all of the goods if under an installment lease contract the value of the whole lease contract is substantially impaired (Section 2A—510), the lessee is in default under the lease contract and the lessor may:

(a) cancel the lease contract (Section 2A—505(1));

(b) proceed respecting goods not identified to the lease contract (Section 2A—524);

(c) withhold delivery of the goods and take possession of goods previously delivered (Section 2A—525);

(d) stop delivery of the goods by any bailee (Section 2A—526);

(e) dispose of the goods and recover damages (Section 2A—527), or retain the goods and recover damages (Section 2A—528), or in a proper case recover rent (Section 2A—529)

(f) exercise any other rights or pursue any other remedies provided in the lease contract.

(2) If a lessor does not fully exercise a right or obtain a remedy to which the lessor is entitled under subsection (1), the lessor may recover the loss resulting in the ordinary course of events from the lessee's default as determined in any reasonable manner, together with incidental damages, less expenses saved in consequence of the lessee's default.

(3) If a lessee is otherwise in default under a lease contract, the lessor may exercise the rights and pursue the remedies provided in the lease contract, which may include a right to cancel the lease. In addition, unless otherwise provided in the lease contract:

(a) if the default substantially impairs the value of the lease contract to the lessor, the lessor may exercise the rights and pursue the remedies provided in subsections (1) or (2); or

(b) if the default does not substantially impair the value of the lease contract to the lessor, the lessor may recover as provided in subsection (2).

As amended in 1990.

§ 2A—524. Lessor's Right to Identify Goods to Lease Contract.

(1) After default by the lessee under the lease contract of the type described in Section 2A—523(1) or 2A—523(3)(a) or, if agreed, after other default by the lessee, the lessor may:

(a) identify to the lease contract conforming goods not already identified if at the time the lessor learned of the default they were in the lessor's or the supplier's possession or control; and

(b) dispose of goods (Section 2A—527(1)) that demonstrably have been intended for the particular lease contract even though those goods are unfinished.

(2) If the goods are unfinished, in the exercise of reasonable commercial judgment for the purposes of avoiding loss and of effective realization, an aggrieved lessor or the supplier may either complete manufacture and wholly identify the goods to the lease contract or cease manufacture and lease, sell, or otherwise dispose of the goods for scrap or salvage value or proceed in any other reasonable manner.

As amended in 1990.

§ 2A—525. Lessor's Right to Possession of Goods.

(1) If a lessor discovers the lessee to be insolvent, the lessor may refuse to deliver the goods.

(2) After a default by the lessee under the lease contract of the type described in Section 2A—523(1) or 2A—523(3)(a) or, if agreed, after other default by the lessee, the lessor has the right to take possession of the goods. If the lease contract so provides, the lessor may require the lessee to assemble the goods and make them available to the lessor at a place to be designated by the lessor which is reasonably convenient to both parties. Without removal, the lessor may render unusable any goods employed in trade or business, and may dispose of goods on the lessee's premises (Section 2A—527).

(3) The lessor may proceed under subsection (2) without judicial process if that can be done without breach of the peace or the lessor may proceed by action.

As amended in 1990.

§ 2A—526. Lessor's Stoppage of Delivery in Transit or Otherwise.

(1) A lessor may stop delivery of goods in the possession of a carrier or other bailee if the lessor discovers the lessee to be insolvent and may stop delivery of carload, truckload, planeload, or larger shipments of express or freight if the lessee repudiates or fails to make a payment due before delivery, whether for rent, security or otherwise under the lease contract, or for any other reason the lessor has a right to withhold or take possession of the goods.

(2) In pursuing its remedies under subsection (1), the lessor may stop delivery until

(a) receipt of the goods by the lessee;

(b) acknowledgment to the lessee by any bailee of the goods,

except a carrier, that the bailee holds the goods for the lessee; or

(c) such an acknowledgment to the lessee by a carrier via reshipment or as warehouseman.

(3) (a) To stop delivery, a lessor shall so notify as to enable the bailee by reasonable diligence to prevent delivery of the goods.

(b) After notification, the bailee shall hold and deliver the goods according to the directions of the lessor, but the lessor is liable to the bailee for any ensuing charges or damages.

(c) A carrier who has issued a nonnegotiable bill of lading is not obliged to obey a notification to stop received from a person other than the consignor.

§ 2A—527. Lessor's Rights to Dispose of Goods.

(1) After a default by a lessee under the lease contract of the type described in Section 2A—523(1) or 2A–523(3)(a) or after the lessor refuses to deliver or takes possession of goods (Section 2A—525 or 2A—526), or, if agreed, after other default by a lessee, the lessor may dispose of the goods concerned or the undelivered balance thereof by lease, sale, or otherwise.

(2) Except as otherwise provided with respect to damages liquidated in the lease agreement (Section 2A—504) or otherwise determined pursuant to agreement of the parties (Sections 1—102(3) and 2A—503), if the disposition is by lease agreement substantially similar to the original lease agreement and the new lease agreement is made in good faith and in a commercially reasonable manner, the lessor may recover from the lessee as damages (i) accrued and unpaid rent as of the date of the commencement of the term of the new lease agreement, (ii) the present value, as of the same date, of the total rent for the then remaining lease term of the original lease agreement minus the present value, as of the same date, of the rent under the new lease agreement applicable to that period of the new lease term which is comparable to the then remaining term of the original lease agreement, and (iii) any incidental damages allowed under Section 2A—530, less expenses saved in consequence of the lessee's default.

(3) If the lessor's disposition is by lease agreement that for any reason does not qualify for treatment under subsection (2), or is by sale or otherwise, the lessor may recover from the lessee as if the lessor had elected not to dispose of the goods and Section 2A—528 governs.

(4) A subsequent buyer or lessee who buys or leases from the lessor in good faith for value as a result of a disposition under this section takes the goods free of the original lease contract and any rights of the original lessee even though the lessor fails to comply with one or more of the requirements of this Article.

(5) The lessor is not accountable to the lessee for any profit made on any disposition. A lessee who has rightfully rejected or justifiably revoked acceptance shall account to the lessor for any excess over the amount of the lessee's security interest (Section 2A—508(5)).

As amended in 1990.

§ 2A—528. Lessor's Damages for Non-acceptance, Failure to Pay, Repudiation, or Other Default.

(1) Except as otherwise provided with respect to damages liquidated

in the lease agreement (Section 2A—504) or otherwise determined pursuant to agreement of the parties (Section 1—102(3) and 2A—503), if a lessor elects to retain the goods or a lessor elects to dispose of the goods and the disposition is by lease agreement that for any reason does not qualify for treatment under Section 2A—527(2), or is by sale or otherwise, the lessor may recover from the lessee as damages for a default of the type described in Section 2A—523(1) or 2A—523(3)(a), or if agreed, for other default of the lessee, (i) accrued and unpaid rent as of the date of the default if the lessee has never taken possession of the goods, or, if the lessee has taken possession of the goods, as of the date the lessor repossesses the goods or an earlier date on which the lessee makes a tender of the goods to the lessor, (ii) the present value as of the date determined under clause (i) of the total rent for the then remaining lease term of the original lease agreement minus the present value as of the same date of the market rent as the place where the goods are located computed for the same lease term, and (iii) any incidental damages allowed under Section 2A—530, less expenses saved in consequence of the lessee's default.

(2) If the measure of damages provided in subsection (1) is inadequate to put a lessor in as good a position as performance would have, the measure of damages is the present value of the profit, including reasonable overhead, the lessor would have made from full performance by the lessee, together with any incidental damages allowed under Section 2A—530, due allowance for costs reasonably incurred and due credit for payments or proceeds of disposition.

As amended in 1990.

§ 2A—529. Lessor's Action for the Rent.

(1) After default by the lessee under the lease contract of the type described in Section 2A—523(1) or 2A—523(3)(a) or, if agreed, after other default by the lessee, if the lessor complies with subsection (2), the lessor may recover from the lessee as damages:

(a) for goods accepted by the lessee and not repossessed by or tendered to the lessor, and for conforming goods lost or damaged within a commercially reasonable time after risk of loss passes to the lessee (Section 2A—219), (i) accrued and unpaid rent as of the date of entry of judgment in favor of the lessor (ii) the present value as of the same date of the rent for the then remaining lease term of the lease agreement, and (iii) any incidental damages allowed under Section 2A—530, less expenses saved in consequence of the lessee's default; and

(b) for goods identified to the lease contract if the lessor is unable after reasonable effort to dispose of them at a reasonable price or the circumstances reasonably indicate that effort will be unavailing, (i) accrued and unpaid rent as of the date of entry of judgment in favor of the lessor, (ii) the present value as of the same date of the rent for the then remaining lease term of the lease agreement, and (iii) any incidental damages allowed under Section 2A—530, less expenses saved in consequence of the lessee's default.

(2) Except as provided in subsection (3), the lessor shall hold for the lessee for the remaining lease term of the lease agreement any goods that have been identified to the lease contract and are in the lessor's control.

(3) The lessor may dispose of the goods at any time before collection of the judgment for damages obtained pursuant to subsection (1). If the disposition is before the end of the remaining lease term of the lease agreement, the lessor's recovery against the lessee for damages is governed by Section 2A—527 or Section 2A—528, and the lessor will cause an appropriate credit to be provided against a judgment for damages to the extent that the amount of the judgment exceeds the recovery available pursuant to Section 2A—527 or 2A—528.

(4) Payment of the judgment for damages obtained pursuant to subsection (1) entitles the lessee to the use and possession of the goods not then disposed of for the remaining lease term of and in accordance with the lease agreement.

(5) After default by the lessee under the lease contract of the type described in Section 2A—523(1) or Section 2A—523(3)(a) or, if agreed, after other default by the lessee, a lessor who is held not entitled to rent under this section must nevertheless be awarded damages for non-acceptance under Sections 2A—527 and 2A—528.

As amended in 1990.

§ 2A—530. Lessor's Incidental Damages.

Incidental damages to an aggrieved lessor include any commercially reasonable charges, expenses, or commissions incurred in stopping delivery, in the transportation, care and custody of goods after the lessee's default, in connection with return or disposition of the goods, or otherwise resulting from the default.

§ 2A—531. Standing to Sue Third Parties for Injury to Goods.

(1) If a third party so deals with goods that have been identified to a lease contract as to cause actionable injury to a party to the lease contract (a) the lessor has a right of action against the third party, and (b) the lessee also has a right of action against the third party if the lessee:

(i) has a security interest in the goods;

(ii) has an insurable interest in the goods; or

(iii) bears the risk of loss under the lease contract or has since the injury assumed that risk as against the lessor and the goods have been converted or destroyed.

(2) If at the time of the injury the party plaintiff did not bear the risk of loss as against the other party to the lease contract and there is no arrangement between them for disposition of the recovery, his [or her] suit or settlement, subject to his [or her] own interest, is as a fiduciary for the other party to the lease contract.

(3) Either party with the consent of the other may sue for the benefit of whom it may concern.

§ 2A—532. Lessor's Rights to Residual Interest.

In addition to any other recovery permitted by this Article or other law, the lessor may recover from the lessee an amount that will fully compensate the lessor for any loss of or damage to the lessor's residual interest in the goods caused by the default of the lessee.

As added in 1990.

(b) If the signature of the issuer of an instrument is made by automated means, such as a check-writing machine, the payee of the instrument is determined by the intent of the person who supplied the name or identification of the payee, whether or not authorized to do so.

(c) A person to whom an instrument is payable may be identified in any way, including by name, identifying number, office, or account number. For the purpose of determining the holder of an instrument, the following rules apply:

(1) If an instrument is payable to an account and the account is identified only by number, the instrument is payable to the person to whom the account is payable. If an instrument is payable to an account identified by number and by the name of a person, the instrument is payable to the named person, whether or not that person is the owner of the account identified by number.

(2) If an instrument is payable to:

(i) a trust, an estate, or a person described as trustee or representative of a trust or estate, the instrument is payable to the trustee, the representative, or a successor of either, whether or not the beneficiary or estate is also named;

(ii) a person described as agent or similar representative of a named or identified person, the instrument is payable to the represented person, the representative, or a successor of the representative;

(iii) a fund or organization that is not a legal entity, the instrument is payable to a representative of the members of the fund or organization; or

(iv) an office or to a person described as holding an office, the instrument is payable to the named person, the incumbent of the office, or a successor to the incumbent.

(d) If an instrument is payable to two or more persons alternatively, it is payable to any of them and may be negotiated, discharged, or enforced by any or all of them in possession of the instrument. If an instrument is payable to two or more persons not alternatively, it is payable to all of them and may be negotiated, discharged, or enforced only by all of them. If an instrument payable to two or more persons is ambiguous as to whether it is payable to the persons alternatively, the instrument is payable to the persons alternatively.

APPENDIX C

Dictionary of Legal Terms

abatement Reduction or elimination of gifts by category upon the reduction in value of the estate.

absolute surety Surety liable to a creditor immediately upon the default of the principal debtor.

acceptance *Commercial paper* Acceptance is the drawee's signed engagement to honor the draft as presented. It becomes operative when completed by delivery or notification. UCC § 3–410.

    Contracts Compliance by offeree with terms and conditions of offer.

    Sale of goods UCC § 2–606 provides three ways a buyer can accept goods: (1) by signifying to the seller that the goods are conforming or that he will accept them in spite of their nonconformity, (2) by failing to make an effective rejection, and (3) by doing an act inconsistent with the seller's ownership.

acceptor Drawee who has accepted an instrument.

accession An addition to one's property by increase of the original property or by production from such property. *E.g.,* A innocently converts the wheat of B into bread. UCC § 9–315 changes the common law where a perfected security interest is involved.

accident and health insurance Provides protection from losses due to accident or sickness.

accommodation An arrangement made as a favor to another, usually involving a loan of money or commercial paper. While a party's intent may be to aid a maker of a note by lending his credit, if he seeks to accomplish thereby legitimate objects of his own and not simply to aid the maker, the act is not for accommodation.

accommodation indorser Signer not in the chain of title.

accommodation party A person who signs commercial paper in any capacity for the purpose of lending his name to another party to an instrument. UCC § 3–415.

accord and satisfaction A method of discharging a claim whereby the parties agree to accept something in settlement, the "accord" being the agreement and the "satisfaction" its execution or performance. It is a new contract that is substituted for an old contract, which is thereby discharged, or for an obligation or cause of action and that must have all of the elements of a valid contract.

account Any account with a bank, including a checking, time, interest or savings account. UCC § 4–194. Also, any right to payment, for goods or services, that is not evidenced by an instrument or chattel paper. *E.g.,* account receivable.

accounting Equitable proceeding for a complete settlement of all partnership affairs.

Many of the definitions are abridged and adapted from *Black's Law Dictionary*, 5th edition, West Publishing Company, 1979.

act of state doctrine Rule that a court should not question the validity of actions taken by a foreign government in its own country.

actual authority Power conferred upon agent by actual consent given by principal.

actual express authority Actual authority derived from written or spoken words of principal.

actual implied authority Actual authority inferred from words or conduct manifested to agent by principal.

actual notice Knowledge actually and expressly communicated.

actus reas Wrongful or overt act.

ademption The removal or extinction of a devise by act of the testator.

adequacy of consideration Not required where parties have freely agreed to the exchange.

adhesion contract Standard "form" contract, usually between a large retailer and a consumer, in which the weaker party has no realistic choice or opportunity to bargain.

adjudication The giving or pronouncing of a judgment in a case; also, the judgment given.

administrative agency Governmental entity (other than courts and legislatures) having authority to affect the rights of private parties.

administrative law Law dealing with the establishment, duties, and powers of agencies in the executive branch of government.

administrative process Entire set of activities engaged in by administrative agencies while carrying out their rulemaking, enforcement, and adjudicative functions.

administrator A person appointed by the court to manage the assets and liabilities of an intestate (a person dying without a will). A person named in the will of a testator (a person dying with a will) is called the executor. Female designations are administratrix and executrix.

adversary system System in which opposing parties initiate and present their cases.

adverse possession A method of acquiring title to real property by possession for a statutory period under certain conditions. The periods of time may differ, depending on whether the adverse possessor has color of title.

affidavit A written statement of facts, made voluntarily, confirmed by oath or affirmation of the party making it, and taken before an authorized officer.

affiliate Person who controls, is controlled by, or is under common control with the issuer.

affirm Uphold the lower court's judgment.

affirmative action Active recruitment of minority applicants.

affirmative defense A response that attacks the plaintiff's legal right to bring an action as opposed to attacking the truth of the claim. *E.g.,* accord and satisfaction; assumption of risk; contributory negligence; duress; estoppel.

affirmative disclosure Requirement that an advertiser include certain information in its advertisement so that the ad is not deceptive.

after-acquired property Property the debtor may acquire at some time after the security interest attaches.

agency Relation in which one person acts for or represents another by the latter's authority.

Actual agency Exists where the agent is really employed by the principal.

Agency by estoppel One created by operation of law and established by proof of such acts of the principal as reasonably lead to the conclusion of its existence.

Implied agency One created by acts of the parties and deduced from proof of other facts.

agent Person authorized to act on another's behalf.

allegation A statement of a party setting out what he expects to prove.

allonge Piece of paper firmly affixed to the instrument.

annuity contract Agreement to pay periodic sums to insured upon reaching a designated age.

annul To annul a judgment or judicial proceeding is to deprive it of all force and operation.

answer The answer is the formal written statement made by a defendant setting forth the ground of his defense.

antecedent debt Preexisting obligation.

anticipatory breach of contract (or **anticipatory repudiation**) The unjustified assertion by a party that he will not perform an obligation that he is contractually obligated to perform at a future time. See UCC §§ 610 & 611.

apparent authority Such principal power that a reasonable person would assume an agent has in light of the principal's conduct.

appeal Resort to a superior (appellate) court to review the decision of an inferior (trial) court or administrative agency.

appeal by right Mandatory review by a higher court.

appellant A party who takes an appeal from one court to another. He may be either the plaintiff or defendant in the original court proceeding.

appellee The party in a cause against whom an appeal is taken; that is, the party who has an interest adverse to setting aside or reversing the judgment. Sometimes also called the "respondent."

appropriation Unauthorized use of another person's name or likeness for one's own benefit.

appurtenances Things appurtenant pass as incident to the principal thing. Sometimes an easement consisting of a right of way over one piece of land will pass with another piece of land as being appurtenant to it.

APR Annual percentage rate.

arbitration The reference of a dispute to an impartial (third) person chosen by the parties, who agree in advance to abide by the arbitrator's award issued after a hearing at which both parties have an opportunity to be heard.

arraignment Accused is informed of the crime against him and enters a plea.

articles of incorporation (or **certificate of incorporation**) The instrument under which a corporation is formed. The contents are prescribed in the particular state's general incorporation statute.

articles of partnership A written agreement by which parties enter into a partnership, to be governed by the terms set forth therein.

as is Disclaimer of implied warranties.

assault Unlawful attempted battery; intentional infliction of apprehension of immediate bodily harm or offensive contact.

assignee Party to whom contract rights are assigned.

assignment A transfer of the rights to real or personal property, usually intangible property such as rights in a lease, mortgage, sale agreement, or partnership.

assignment of rights Voluntary transfer to a third party of the rights arising from a contract.

assignor Party making an assignment.

assumes Delegatee agrees to perform the contractual obligation of the delegator.

assumes the mortgage Purchaser of mortgaged property becomes personally liable to pay the debt.

assumption of risk Plaintiff's express or implied consent to encounter a known danger.

attachment The process of seizing property, by virtue of a writ, summons, or other judicial order, and bringing the same into the custody of the court for the purpose of securing satisfaction of the judgment ultimately to be entered in the action. While formerly the main objective was to coerce the defendant debtor to appear in court, today the writ of attachment is used primarily to seize the debtor's property in the event a judgment is rendered.

Distinguished from execution See **execution**.

Also, the process by which a security interest becomes enforceable. Attachment may occur upon the taking of possession or upon the signing of a security agreement by the person who is pledging the property as collateral.

authority Power of an agent to change the legal status of his principal.

authorized means Any reasonable means of communication.

automatic perfection Perfection upon attachment.

award The decision of an arbitrator.

bad checks Issuing a check with funds insufficient to cover it.

bailee The party to whom personal property is delivered under a contract of bailment.

Extraordinary bailee Absolutely liable for the safety of the bailed property without regard to the cause of loss.

Ordinary bailee Must exercise due care.

bailment A delivery of personal property in trust for the execution of a special object in relation to such goods, beneficial either to the bailor or bailee or both, and upon a contract to either redeliver the goods to the bailor or otherwise dispose of the same in conformity with the purpose of the trust.

bailor The party who delivers goods to another in the contract of bailment.

bankrupt The state or condition of one who is unable to pay his debts as they are, or become, due.

Bankruptcy Code The Act was substantially revised in 1978, effective October 1, 1979. Straight bankruptcy is in the nature of a liquidation proceeding and involves the collection and distribution to creditors of all the bankrupt's nonexempt property by the trustee in the manner provided by the Act. The debtor rehabilitation provisions of the Act (Chapters 11 and 13) differ from straight bankruptcy in that the debtor looks to rehabilitation and reorganization, rather than liquidation, and the creditors look to future earnings of the bankrupt, rather than to property held by the bankrupt, to satisfy their claims.

bargain Negotiated exchange.

bargained exchange Mutually agreed-upon exchange.

basis of the bargain Part of the buyer's assumption underlying the sale.

battery Unlawful touching of another; intentional infliction of harmful or offensive bodily contact.

bearer Person in possession of an instrument.

bearer paper Payable to holder of the instrument.

beneficiary One who benefits from act of another. See also **third-party beneficiary**.

Incidental A person who may derive benefit from performance on contract, though he is neither the promisee nor the one to whom performance is to be rendered. Since the incidental beneficiary is not a donee or creditor beneficiary (see **third-party beneficiary**), he has no right to enforce the contract.

Intended beneficiary Third party intended by the two contracted parties to receive a benefit from their contract.

Trust As it relates to trust beneficiaries, includes a person who has any present or future interest, vested or contingent, and also includes the owner of an interest by assignment or other transfer and, as it relates to a charitable trust, includes any person entitled to enforce the trust.

bequeath to give or leave to by will

beyond a reasonable doubt Proof that is entirely convincing and satisfying to a moral certainty; criminal law standard.

bilateral contract Contract in which both parties exchange promises.

bill of lading Document evidencing receipt of goods for shipment issued by person engaged in business of transporting or forwarding goods; includes airbill. UCC § 1–201(6).

   Through bill of lading A bill of lading which specifies at least one connecting carrier.

bill of sale A written agreement, formerly limited to one under seal, by which one person assigns or transfers his right to or interest in goods and personal chattels to another.

binder A written memorandum of the important terms of a contract of insurance which gives temporary protection to an insured pending investigation of risk by the insurance company or until a formal policy is issued.

blue law Prohibition of certain types of commercial activity on Sunday.

blue sky laws A popular name for state statutes providing for the regulation and supervision of securities offerings and sales, to protect citizen-investors from investing in fraudulent companies.

bona fide Latin. In good faith.

bond A certificate or evidence of a debt on which the issuing company or governmental body promises to pay the bondholders a specified amount of interest for a specified length of time and to repay the loan on the expiration date. In every case, a bond represents debt—its holder is a creditor of the corporation, not a part owner, as the shareholder is.

boycott Agreement among parties not to deal with a third party.

breach Wrongful failure to perform the terms of a contract.

   Material breach Nonperformance which significantly impairs the aggrieved party's rights under the contract.

bribery Offering property to a public official to influence the official's decision.

bulk transfer Transfer not in the ordinary course of the transferor's business of a major part of his inventory.

burglary Breaking and entering the home of another at night with intent to commit a felony.

business judgment rule Protects directors from liability for honest mistakes of judgment.

business trust A trust (managed by a trustee for the benefit of a beneficiary) established to conduct a business for a profit.

but for rule Person's negligent conduct is a cause of an event if the event would not have occurred in the absence of that conduct.

buyer in ordinary course of business Person who buys in ordinary course, in good faith, and without knowledge that the sale to him is in violation of anyone's ownership rights or of a security interest.

by-laws Regulations, ordinances, rules, or laws adopted by an association or corporation for its government.

callable bond Bond that is subject to redemption (reacquisition) by the corporation.

cancellation One party's putting an end to a contract because of a breach by other party.

capital Accumulated goods, possessions, and assets, used for the production of profits and wealth. Owners' equity in a business. Also used to refer to the total assets of a business or to capital assets.

capital surplus Surplus other than earned surplus.

carrier Transporter of goods.

casualty insurance Covers property loss due to causes other than fire or the elements.

cause of action The ground on which an action may be sustained.

caveat emptor Latin. Let the buyer beware. This maxim is more applicable to judicial sales, auctions, and the like than to sales of consumer goods, where strict liability, warranty, and other laws protect.

certificate of deposit A written acknowledgment by a bank or banker of a deposit with promise to pay to depositor, to his order, or to some other person or to his order. UCC § 3–104(2)(c).

certificate of title Official representation of ownership.

certification Acceptance of a check by a drawee bank.

certification of incorporation See **articles of incorporation**.

certification mark Distinctive symbol, word, or design used with goods or services to certify specific characteristics.

certiorari Latin. To be informed of. A writ of common law origin issued by a superior to an inferior court requiring the latter to produce a certified record of a particular case tried therein. It is most commonly used to refer to the Supreme Court of the United States, which uses the writ of certiorari as a discretionary device to choose the cases it wishes to hear.

chancery Equity; equitable jurisdiction; a court of equity; the system of jurisprudence administered in courts of equity.

charging order Judicial lien against a partner's interest in the partnership.

charter An instrument emanating from the sovereign power, in the nature of a grant. A charter differs from a constitution in that the former is granted by the sovereign, while the latter is established by the people themselves.

   Corporate law An act of a legislature creating a corporation or creating and defining the franchise of a corporation. Also a corporation's constitution or organic law; that is to say, the articles of incorporation taken in connection with the law under which the corporation was organized.

chattel mortgage A pre-Uniform Commercial Code security device whereby the mortgagee took a security interest in personal property of the mortgagor. Such security device has generally been superseded by other types of security agreements under UCC Article 9 (Secured Transactions).

chattel paper Writings that evidence both a debt and a security interest.

check A draft drawn upon a bank and payable on demand, signed by the maker or drawer, containing an unconditional promise to pay a sum certain in money to the order of the payee. UCC § 3–104(2)(b).

   Cashier's check A bank's own check drawn on itself and signed by the cashier or other authorized official. It is a direct obligation of the bank.

C. & F. Cost and freight; a shipping contract.

C.I.F. Cost, insurance, and freight; a shipping contract.

civil law Laws concerned with civil or private rights and remedies, as contrasted with criminal laws.

   The system of jurisprudence administered in the Roman empire, particularly as set forth in the compilation of Justinian and his successors, as distinguished from the common law of England and the canon law. The civil law (Civil Code) is followed by Louisiana.

claim A right to payment.

clearinghouse An association of banks for the purpose of settling accounts on a daily basis.

close corporation See **corporation**.

closed-ended credit Credit extended to debtor for a specific period of time.

closed shop Employer can only hire union members.

C.O.D. Collect on delivery; generally a shipping contract.

code A compilation of all permanent laws in force consolidated and classified according to subject matter. Many states have published official codes of all laws in force, including the common law and statutes as judicially interpreted, which have been compiled by code commissions and enacted by the legislatures.

codicil A supplement or an addition to a will; it may explain, modify, add to, subtract from, qualify, alter, restrain, or revoke provisions in an existing will. It must be executed with the same formalities as a will.

cognovit judgment Written authority by debtor for entry of judgment against him in the event he defaults in payment. Such provision in a debt instrument on default confers judgment against the debtor.

collateral Secondarily liable; liable only if the party with primary liability does not perform.

collateral (security) Personal property subject to security interest.

   Banking Some form of security in addition to the personal obligation of the borrower.

collateral promise Undertaking to be secondarily liable, that is, liable if the principal debtor does not perform.

collecting bank Any bank, except the payor bank, handling the item for collection. UCC § 4–105(d).

collective mark Distinctive symbol used to indicate membership in an organization.

collision insurance Protects the owner of an automobile against damage due to contact with other vehicles or objects.

commerce power Exclusive power granted by the U.S. Constitution to the federal government to regulate commerce with foreign countries and among the states.

commercial bailment   Bailment in which parties derive a mutual benefit.

commercial impracticability   Performance can only be accomplished with unforeseen and unjust hardship.

commercial law   A phrase used to designate the whole body of substantive jurisprudence (*e.g.,* Uniform Commercial Code; Truth in Lending Act) applicable to the rights, intercourse, and relations of persons engaged in commerce, trade, or mercantile pursuits. See **Uniform Commercial Code**.

commercial paper   Bills of exchange (*i.e.,* drafts), promissory notes, bank checks, and other negotiable instruments for the payment of money, which, by their form and on their face, purport to be such instruments. UCC Article 3 is the general law governing commercial paper.

commercial reasonableness   Judgment of reasonable persons familiar with the business transaction.

commercial speech   Expression related to the economic interests of the speaker and its audience.

common carrier   Carrier open to the general public.

common law   Body of law originating in England and derived from judicial decisions. As distinguished from statutory law created by the enactment of legislatures, the common law comprises the judgments and decrees of the courts recognizing, affirming, and enforcing usages and customs of immemorial antiquity.

community property   Rights of a spouse in property acquired by the other during marriage.

comparable worth   Equal pay for jobs of equal value to the employer.

comparative negligence   Under comparative negligence statutes or doctrines, negligence is measured in terms of percentage, and any damages allowed shall be diminished in proportion to amount of negligence attributable to the person for whose injury, damage, or death recovery is sought.

complainant   One who applies to the courts for legal redress by filing a complaint (*i.e.,* plaintiff).

complaint   The pleading which sets forth a claim for relief. Such complaint (whether it be the original claim, counterclaim, cross-claim, or third-party claim) shall contain (1) a short, plain statement of the grounds upon which the court's jurisdiction depends, unless the court already has jurisdiction and the claim needs no new grounds of jurisdiction to support it, (2) a short, plain statement of the claim showing that the pleader is entitled to relief, and (3) a demand for judgment for the relief to which he deems himself entitled. Fed.R. Civil P. 8(a). The complaint, together with the summons, is required to be served on the defendant. Rule 4.

composition   Agreement between debtor and two or more of her creditors that each will take a portion of his claim as full payment.

compulsory arbitration   Arbitration required by statute for specific types of disputes.

computer crime   Crime committed against or through the use of a computer or computer/services.

concealment   Fraudulent failure to disclose a material fact.

conciliation   Nonbinding process in which a third party acts as an intermediary between disputing parties.

concurrent jurisdiction   Authority of more than one court to hear the same case.

condition   An uncertain event which affects the duty of performance.

   Concurrent conditions   The parties are to perform simultaneously.

   Express condition   Performance is contingent on the happening or non-happening of a stated event.

condition precedent   An event which must occur or not occur before performance is due; event or events (presentment, dishonor, notice of dishonor) which must occur to hold a secondary party liable to commercial paper.

condition subsequent   An event which terminates a duty of performance.

conditional acceptance   An acceptance of an offer contingent upon the acceptance of an additional or different term.

conditional contract   Obligations are contingent upon a stated event.

conditional guarantor of collection   Surety liable to creditor only after cred-

itor exhausts his legal remedies against the principal debtor.

confession of judgment   Written agreement by debtor authorizing creditor to obtain a court judgment in the event debtor defaults. See also **cognovit judgment**.

confiscation   Governmental taking of foreign-owned property without payment.

conflict of laws   That branch of jurisprudence, arising from the diversity of the laws of different nations, states, or jurisdictions, that reconciles the inconsistencies, or decides which law is to govern in a particular case.

confusion   Results when goods belonging to two or more owners become so intermixed that the property of any of them no longer can be identified except as part of a mass of like goods.

consanguinity   Kinship; blood relationship; the connection or relation of persons descended from the same stock or common ancestor.

consensual arbitration   Arbitration voluntarily entered into by the parties.

consent   Voluntary and knowing willingness that an act should be done.

conservator   Appointed by court to manage affairs of incompetent or to liquidate business.

consideration   The cause, motive, price, or impelling influence which induces a contracting party to enter into a contract. Some right, interest, profit, or benefit accruing to one party or some forbearance, detriment, loss, or responsibility given, suffered, or undertaken by the other.

consignee   One to whom a consignment is made. Person named in bill of lading to whom or to whose order the bill promises delivery. UCC § 7–102(b).

consignment   Ordinarily implies an agency; denotes that property is committed to the consignee for care or sale.

consignor   One who sends or makes a consignment; a shipper of goods. The person named in a bill of lading as the person from whom the goods have been received for shipment. UCC § 7–102(c).

consolidation   In *corporate law*, the combination of two or more corporations into a newly created corporation. Thus, A Corporation and B Corporation consolidate to form C Corporation.

constitution   Fundamental law of a government establishing its powers and limitations.

constructive   That which is established by the mind of the law in its act of *construing* facts, conduct, circumstances, or instruments. That which has not in its essential nature the character assigned to it, but acquires such character in consequence of the way in which it is regarded by a rule or policy of law; hence, inferred, implied, or made out by legal interpretation; the word "legal" being sometimes used here in lieu of "constructive."

constructive assent   An assent or consent imputed to a party from a construction or interpretation of his conduct; as distinguished from one which he actually expresses.

constructive conditions   Conditions in contracts which are neither expressed nor implied but rather are imposed by law to meet the ends of justice.

constructive delivery   Term comprehending all those acts which, although not truly conferring a real possession of the vendee, have been held by construction of law to be equivalent to acts of real delivery.

constructive eviction   Failure by the landlord in any obligation under the lease that causes a substantial and lasting injury to the tenant's enjoyment of the premises.

constructive notice   Knowledge imputed by law.

constructive trust   Arising by operation of law to prevent unjust enrichment. See also **trustee**.

consumer goods   Goods bought or used for personal, family, or household purposes.

consumer product   Tangible personal property normally used for family, household, or personal purposes.

contingent remainder   Remainder interest, conditional upon the happening of an event in addition to the termination of the preceding estate.

contract   An agreement between two or more persons which creates an obligation to do or not to do a particular thing. Its essentials are competent parties, subject matter, a legal consideration, mutuality of agreement, and mutuality of obligation.

   Destination contract   Seller is required to tender delivery of the goods at a particular destination; seller bears the expense and risk of loss.

Executed contract Fully performed by all of the parties.

Executory contract Contract partially or entirely unperformed by one or more of the parties.

Express contract Agreement of parties that is expressed in words either in writing or orally.

Formal contract Agreement which is legally binding because of its particular form or mode or expression.

Implied-in-fact contract Contract where agreement of the parties is inferred from their conduct.

Informal contract All oral or written contracts other than formal contracts.

Installment contract Goods are delivered in separate lots.

Integrated contract Complete and total agreement.

Output contract A contract in which one party agrees to sell his entire output and the other agrees to buy it; it is not illusory, though it may be indefinite.

Quasi contract Obligation not based upon contract that is imposed to avoid injustice.

Requirements contract A contract in which one party agrees to purchase his total requirements from the other party; hence, such a contract is binding, not illusory.

Substituted contract An agreement between the parties to rescind their old contract and replace it with a new contract.

Unconscionable contract One which no sensible person not under delusion, duress, or in distress would make, and such as no honest and fair person would accept. A contract the terms of which are excessively unreasonable, overreaching, and one-sided.

Unenforceable contract Contract for the breach of which the law does not provide a remedy.

Unilateral and bilateral A unilateral contract is one in which one party makes an express engagement or undertakes a performance, without receiving in return any express engagement or promise of performance from the other. Bilateral (or reciprocal) contracts are those by which the parties expressly enter into mutual engagements.

contract clause Prohibition against the states' retroactively modifying public and private contracts.

contractual liability Obligation on a negotiable instrument, based upon signing the instrument.

contribution Payment from cosureties of their proportionate share.

contributory negligence An act or omission amounting to a want of ordinary care on the part of the complaining party, which, concurring with defendant's negligence, is proximate cause of injury.

The defense of contributory negligence is an absolute bar to any recovery in some states; because of this, it has been replaced by the doctrine of comparative negligence in many other states.

conversion Unauthorized and wrongful exercise of dominion and control over another's personal property, to exclusion of or inconsistent with rights of the owner.

convertible bond Bond that may be exchanged for other securities of the corporation.

copyright Exclusive right granted by federal government to authors of original works including literary, musical, dramatic, pictorial, graphic, sculptural, and film works.

corporation A legal entity ordinarily consisting of an association of numerous individuals. Such entity is regarded as having a personality and existence distinct from that of its several members and is vested with the capacity of continuous succession, irrespective of changes in its membership, either in perpetuity or for a limited term of years.

Closely held or close corporation Corporation that is owned by few shareholders and whose shares are not actively traded.

Corporation de facto One existing under color of law and in pursuance of an effort made in good faith to organize a corporation under the statute. Such a corporation is not subject to collateral attack.

Corporation de jure That which exists by reason of full compliance with

requirements of an existing law permitting organization of such corporation.

Domestic corporation Corporation created under the laws of a given state.

Foreign corporation Corporation created under the laws of any other state, government, or country.

Publicly held corporation Corporation whose shares are owned by a large number of people and are widely traded.

Subchapter S corporation A small business corporation which, under certain conditions, may elect to have its undistributed taxable income taxed to its shareholders. I.R.C. § 1371 et seq. Of major significance is the fact that Subchapter S status usually avoids the corporate income tax, and corporate losses can be claimed by the shareholders.

Subsidiary and parent Subsidiary corporation is one in which another corporation (called parent corporation) owns at least a majority of the shares and over which it thus has control.

corrective advertising Disclosure in an advertisement that previous ads were deceptive.

costs A pecuniary allowance, made to the successful party (and recoverable from the losing party), for his expenses in prosecuting or defending an action or a distinct proceeding within an action. Generally, "costs" do not include attorneys' fees unless such fees are by a statute denominated costs or are by statute allowed to be recovered as costs in the case.

cosureties Two or more sureties bound for the same debt of a principal debtor.

co-tenants Persons who hold title concurrently.

counterclaim A claim presented by a defendant in opposition to or deduction from the claim of the plaintiff.

counteroffer A statement by the offeree which has the legal effect of rejecting the offer and of proposing a new offer to the offeror. However, the provisions of UCC § 2–207(2) modify this principle by providing that the "additional terms are to be construed as proposals for addition to the contract."

course of dealing A sequence of previous acts and conduct between the parties to a particular transaction which is fairly to be regarded as establishing a common basis of understanding for interpreting their expressions and other conduct. UCC § 1–205(1).

course of performance Conduct between the parties concerning performance of the particular contract.

court above—court below In appellate practice, the "court above" is the one to which a cause is removed for review, whether by appeal, writ of error, or certiorari, while the "court below" is the one from which the case is being removed.

covenant Used primarily with respect to promises in conveyances or other instruments dealing with real estate.

Covenants against encumbrances A stipulation against all rights to or interests in the land which may subsist in third persons to the diminution of the value of the estate granted.

Covenant appurtenant A covenant which is connected with land of the grantor, not in gross. A covenant running with the land and binding heirs, executors, and assigns of the immediate parties.

Covenant for further assurance An undertaking, in the form of a covenant, on the part of the vendor of real estate to do such further acts for the purpose of perfecting the purchaser's title as the latter may reasonably require.

Covenant for possession A covenant by which the grantee or lessee is granted possession.

Covenant for quiet enjoyment An assurance against the consequences of a defective title, and against any disturbances thereupon.

Covenants for title Covenants usually inserted in a conveyance of land, on the part of the grantor, and binding him for the completeness, security, and continuance of the title transferred to the grantee. They comprise covenants for seisin, for right to convey, against encumbrances, or quiet enjoyment, sometimes for further assurance, and almost always of warranty.

Covenant in gross Such as do not run with the land.

Covenant of right to convey An assurance by the covenantor that the grantor has sufficient capacity and title to convey the estate which he by his deed undertakes to convey.

Covenant of seisin An assurance to the purchaser that the grantor has the very estate in quantity and quality which he purports to convey.

Covenant of warranty An assurance by the grantor of an estate that the grantee shall enjoy the same without interruption by virtue of paramount title.

Covenant running with land A covenant which goes with the land, as being annexed to the estate, and which cannot be separated from the land or transferred without it. A covenant is said to run with the land when not only the original parties or their representatives, but each successive owner of the land, will be entitled to its benefit, or be liable (as the case may be) to its obligation. Such a covenant is said to be one which "touches and concerns" the land itself, so that its benefit or obligation passes with the ownership. Essentials are that the grantor and grantee must have intended that the covenant run with the land, the covenant must affect or concern the land with which it runs, and there must be privity of estate between the party claiming the benefit and the party who rests under the burden.

covenant not to compete Agreement to refrain from entering into a competing trade, profession, or business.

cover Buyer's purchase of goods in substitution for those not delivered by breaching seller.

credit beneficiary See **third-party beneficiary**.

creditor Any entity having a claim against the debtor.

crime An act or omission in violation of a public law and punishable by the government.

criminal duress Coercion by threat of serious bodily injury.

criminal intent Desired or virtually certain consequences of one's conduct.

criminal law The law that involves offenses against the entire community.

cure The right of a seller under the UCC to correct a nonconforming delivery of goods to buyer within the contract period. § 2–508.

curtesy Husband's estate in the real property of his wife.

cy-pres As near (as possible). Rule for the construction of instruments in equity, by which the intention of the party is carried out *as near as may be*, when it would be impossible or illegal to give it literal effect.

damage Loss, injury, or deterioration caused by the negligence, design, or accident of one person, with respect to another's person or property. The word is to be distinguished from its plural, "damages," which means a compensation in money for a loss or damage.

damages Money sought as a remedy for breach of contract or for tortious acts.

Actual damages Real, substantial, and just damages, or the amount awarded to a complainant in compensation for his actual and real loss or injury, as opposed, on the one hand, to "nominal" damages and, on the other, to "exemplary" or "punitive" damages. Synonymous with "compensatory damages" and "general damages."

Benefit-of-the-bargain damages Difference between the value received and the value of the fraudulent party's performance as represented.

Compensatory damages Compensatory damages are such as will compensate the injured party for the injury sustained, and nothing more; such as will simply make good or replace the loss caused by the wrong or injury.

Consequential damages Such damage, loss, or injury as does not flow directly and immediately from the act of the party, but only from some of the consequences or results of such act. Consequential damages resulting from a seller's breach of contract include any loss resulting from general or particular requirements and needs of which the seller at the time of contracting had reason to know and which could not reasonably be prevented by cover or otherwise, and injury to person or property proximately resulting from any breach of warranty. UCC § 2–715(2).

Exemplary or punitive damages Damages other than compensatory damages which may be awarded against a person to punish him for outrageous conduct.

Expectancy damages Calculable by subtracting the injured party's actual dollar position as a result of the breach from that party's projected dollar

position had performance occurred.

Foreseeable damages Loss of which the party in breach had reason to know when the contract was made.

Incidental damages Under UCC § 2–710, such damages include any commercially reasonable charges, expenses, or commissions incurred in stopping delivery, in the transportation, care, and custody of goods after the buyer's breach, in connection with the return or resale of the goods, or otherwise resulting from the breach. Also, such damages, resulting from a seller's breach of contract, include expenses reasonably incurred in inspection, receipt, transportation, and care and custody of goods rightfully rejected, any commercially reasonable charges, expenses, or commissions in connection with effecting cover, and any other reasonable expense incident to the delay or other breach. UCC § 2–715(1).

Irreparable damages In the law pertaining to injunctions, damages for which no certain pecuniary standard exists for measurement.

Liquidated damages and penalties Damages for breach by either party may be liquidated in the agreement but only at an amount which is reasonable in the light of the anticipated or actual harm caused by the breach, the difficulties of proof of loss, and the inconvenience or nonfeasibility of otherwise obtaining an adequate remedy. A term fixing unreasonably large liquidated damages is void as a penalty. UCC § 2–718(1).

Mitigation of damages A plaintiff may not recover damages for the effects of an injury which she reasonably could have avoided or substantially ameliorated. This limitation on recovery is generally denominated as "mitigation of damages" or "avoidance of consequences."

Nominal damages A small sum awarded where a contract has been breached but the loss is negligible or unproven.

Out-of-pocket damages Difference between the value received and the value given.

Reliance damages Contract damages placing the injured party in as good a position as he would have been in had the contract not been made.

Treble damages Three times actual loss.

de facto In fact, in deed, actually. This phrase is used to characterize an officer, a government, a past action, or a state of affairs which must be accepted for all practical purposes but which is illegal or illegitimate. See also **corporation**, *corporation de facto*.

de jure Descriptive of a condition in which there has been total compliance with all requirements of law. In this sense it is the contrary of *de facto*. See also **corporation**, *corporation de jure*.

de novo Anew; afresh; a second time.

debenture Unsecured bond.

debt security Any form of corporate security reflected as debt on the books of the corporation in contrast to equity securities such as stock; *e.g.*, bonds, notes, and debentures are debt securities.

debtor Person who owes payment or performance of an obligation.

deceit A fraudulent and cheating misrepresentation, artifice, or device used to deceive and trick one who is ignorant of the true facts, to the prejudice and damage of the party imposed upon. See also **fraud; misrepresentation.**

decree Decision of a court of equity.

deed A conveyance of realty; a writing, signed by a grantor, whereby title to realty is transferred from one party to another.

deed of trust Interest in real property which is conveyed to a third person as trustee for the creditor.

defamation Injury of a person's reputation by publication of false statements.

default judgment Judgment against a defendant who fails to respond to a complaint.

defendant The party against whom legal action is sought.

definite term Lease that automatically expires at end of the term.

delectus personae Partner's right to choose who may become a member of the partnership.

delegatee Third party to whom the delegator's duty is delegated.

delegation of duties Transferring to another all or part of one's duties arising under a contract.

delegator Party delegating his duty to a third party.

delivery The physical or constructive transfer of an instrument or of goods from one person to another. See also **constructive delivery.**

demand Request for payment made by the holder of the instrument.

demand paper Payable on request.

demurrer An allegation of a defendant that even if the facts as stated in the pleading to which objection is taken be true, their legal consequences are not such as to require the demurring party to answer them or to proceed further with the cause.

The Federal Rules of Civil Procedure do not provide for the use of a demurrer, but provide an equivalent to a general demurrer in the motion to dismiss for failure to state a claim on which relief may be granted. Fed.R. Civil P. 12(b).

deposition The testimony of a witness taken upon interrogatories, not in court, but intended to be used in court. See also **discovery.**

depository bank The first bank to which an item is transferred for collection even though it may also be the payor bank. UCC § 4–105(a).

descent Succession to the ownership of an estate by inheritance or by any act of law, as distinguished from "purchase."

Descents are of two sorts, *lineal* and *collateral.* Lineal descent is descent in a direct or right line, as from father or grandfather to son or grandson. Collateral descent is descent in a collateral or oblique line, that is, up to the common ancestor and then down from him, as from brother to brother, or between cousins.

design defect Plans or specifications inadequate to ensure the product's safety.

devise A testamentary disposition of land or realty; a gift of real property by the last will and testament of the donor. When used as a noun, means a testamentary disposition of real or personal property; when used as a verb, means to dispose of real or personal property by will.

dictum Generally used as an abbreviated form of *obiter dictum,* "a remark by the way"; that is, an observation or remark made by a judge which does not embody the resolution or determination of the court and which is made without argument or full consideration of the point.

directed verdict In a case in which the party with the burden of proof has failed to present a prima facie case for jury consideration, the trial judge may order the entry of a verdict without allowing the jury to consider it because, as a matter of law, there can be only one such verdict. Fed.R. Civil P. 50(a).

disaffirmance Avoidance of a contract.

discharge Termination of certain allowed claims against a debtor.

disclaimer Negation of warranty.

discount A discount by a bank means a drawback or deduction made upon its advances or loans of money, upon negotiable paper or other evidences of debt payable at a future day, which are transferred to the bank.

discovery The pretrial devices that can be used by one party to obtain facts and information about the case from the other party in order to assist the party's preparation for trial. Under the Federal Rules of Civil Procedure, tools of discovery include depositions upon oral and written questions, written interrogatories, production of documents or things, permission to enter upon land or other property, physical and mental examinations, and requests for admission. Rules 26–37.

dishonor To refuse to accept or pay a draft or to pay a promissory note when duly presented. UCC § 3–507(1); § 4–210. See also **protest.**

disparagement Publication of false statements resulting in harm to another's monetary interests.

disputed debt Obligation whose existence or amount is contested.

dissenting shareholder One who opposes a fundamental change and has the right to receive the fair value of her shares.

dissolution The dissolution of a partnership is the change in the relation of the partners caused by any partner's ceasing to be associated with the carrying on, as distinguished from the winding up, of the business. See also **winding up.**

distribution Transfer of partnership property from the partnership to a partner; transfer of property from a corporation to any of its shareholders.

dividend The payment designated by the board of directors of a corporation to be distributed pro rata among a class or classes of the shares outstanding.

document Document of title.

document of title Instrument evidencing ownership of the document and the goods it covers.

domicile That place where a person has his true, fixed, and permanent home and principal establishment, and to which whenever he is absent he has the intention of returning.

dominant Land whose owner has rights in other land.

donee Recipient of a gift.

donee beneficiary See **third-party beneficiary.**

donor Maker of a gift.

dormant partner One who is both a silent and a secret partner.

dower A species of life-estate which a woman is, by law, entitled to claim on the death of her husband, in the lands and tenements of which he was seised in fee during the marriage, and which her issue, if any, might by possibility have inherited.

Dower has been abolished in the majority of the states and materially altered in most of the others.

draft A written order by the first party, called the drawer, instructing a second party, called the drawee (such as a bank), to pay a third party, called the payee. An order to pay a sum certain in money, signed by a drawer, payable on demand or at a definite time, and to order or bearer. UCC § 3–104.

drawee A person to whom a bill of exchange or draft is directed, and who is requested to pay the amount of money therein mentioned. The drawee of a check is the bank on which it is drawn.

When a drawee accepts, he engages that he will pay the instrument according to its tenor at the time of his engagement or as completed. UCC § 3–413(1).

drawer The person who draws a bill or draft. The drawer of a check is the person who signs it.

The drawer engages that upon dishonor of the draft and any necessary notice of dishonor or protest, he will pay the amount of the draft to the holder or to any indorser who takes it up. The drawer may disclaim this liability by drawing without recourse. UCC § 3–413(2).

due negotiation Transfer of a negotiable document in the regular course of business to a holder, who takes in good faith, without notice of any defense or claim, and for value.

duress Unlawful constraint exercised upon a person, whereby he is forced to do some act against his will.

Physical duress Coercion involving physical force or the threat of physical force.

duty Legal obligation requiring a person to perform or refrain from performing an act.

earned surplus Undistributed net profits, income, gains, and losses.

earnest The payment of a part of the price of goods sold, or the delivery of part of such goods, for the purpose of binding the contract.

easement A right in the owner of one parcel of land, by reason of such ownership, to use the land of another for a special purpose not inconsistent with a general property right in the owner. This right is distinguishable from a "license," which merely confers a personal privilege to do some act on the land.

Affirmative easement One where the servient estate must permit something to be done thereon, as to pass over it, or to discharge water on it.

Appurtenant easement An incorporeal right which is attached to a superior right and inheres in land to which it is attached and is in the nature of a covenant running with the land.

Easement by necessity Such arises by operation of law when land conveyed is completely shut off from access to any road by land retained by the grantor or by land of the grantor and that of a stranger.

Easement by prescription A mode of acquiring title to property by immemorial or long-continued enjoyment; refers to personal usage restricted to claimant and his ancestors or grantors.

Easement in gross An easement in gross is not appurtenant to any estate in land or does not belong to any person by virtue of ownership of an estate in other land but is a mere personal interest in or a right to use the land of another; it is purely personal and usually ends with death of grantee.

Easement of access Right of ingress and egress to and from the premises of a lot owner to a street appurtenant to the land of the lot owner.

ejectment An action to determine whether the title to certain land is in the plaintiff or is in the defendant.

electronic funds transfer A transaction with a financial institution by means of computer, telephone, or other electronic instrument.

emancipation The act by which an infant is liberated from the control of a parent or guardian and made his own master.

embezzlement The taking, in violation of a trust, of the property of one's employer.

emergency Sudden, unexpected event calling for immediate action.

eminent domain Right of the people or government to take private property for public use upon giving fair consideration.

employment discrimination Hiring, firing, compensating, promoting, or training of employees based on race, color, sex, religion, or national origin.

employment relationship One in which employer has right to control the physical conduct of employee.

endowment contract Agreement to pay insured a lump sum upon reaching a specified age or in event of death.

entirety Used to designate that which the law considers as a single whole incapable of being divided into parts.

entrapment Induced by a government official into committing a crime.

entrusting Transfer of possession of goods to a merchant who deals in goods of that kind and who may in turn transfer valid title to a buyer in the ordinary course of business.

equal pay Equivalent pay for the same work.

equal protection Requirement that similarly situated persons be treated similarly by government action.

equipment Goods used primarily in business.

equitable Just, fair, and right. Existing in equity; available or sustainable only in equity, or only upon the rules and principles of equity.

equity Justice administered according to fairness, as contrasted with the strictly formulated rules of common law. It is based on a system of rules and principles which originated in England as an alternative to the harsh rules of common law and which were based on what was fair in a particular situation.

equity of redemption The right of the mortgagor of an estate to redeem the same after it has been forfeited, at law, by a breach of the condition of the mortgage, upon paying the amount of debt, interest, and costs.

equity securities Stock or similar security, in contrast to debt securities such as bonds, notes, and debentures.

error A mistake of law, or a false or irregular application of it, such as vitiates legal proceedings and warrants reversal of the judgment.

Harmless error In appellate practice, an error committed in the progress of the trial below which was not prejudicial to the rights of the party assigning it and for which, therefore, the appellate court will not reverse the judgment.

Reversible error In appellate practice, such an error as warrants the appellate court's reversal of the judgment before it.

escrow A system of document transfer in which a deed, bond, or funds is or are delivered to a third person to hold until all conditions in a contract are fulfilled; *e.g.*, delivery of deed to escrow agent under installment land sale contract until full payment for land is made.

estate The degree, quantity, nature, and extent of interest which a person has in real and personal property. An estate in lands, tenements, and hereditaments signifies such interest as the tenant has therein.

Also, the total property of whatever kind that is owned by a decedent prior to the distribution of that property in accordance with the terms of a will or, when there is no will, by the laws of inheritance in the state of domicile of the decedent.

Future estate An estate limited to commence in possession at a future day, either without the intervention of a precedent estate or on the determination by lapse of time, or otherwise, of a precedent estate created at the same time. Examples include reversions and remainders.

estoppel A bar or impediment raised by the law which precludes a person from alleging or from denying a certain fact or state of facts, in consequence of his or her previous allegation, denial, conduct, or admission, or in consequence of a final adjudication of the matter in a court of law. See also **waiver**.

eviction Dispossession by process of law; the act of depriving a person of the possession of lands which he has held, pursuant to the judgment of a court.

evidence Any species of proof or probative matter legally presented at the trial of an issue by the act of the parties and through the medium of witnesses, records, documents, concrete objects, etc., for the purpose of inducing belief in the minds of the court or jury as to the parties' contention.

exception A formal objection to the action of the court, during the trial of a cause, in refusing a request or overruling an objection; implying that the party excepting does not acquiesce in the decision of the court but will seek to procure its reversal, and that he means to save the benefit of his request or objection in some future proceeding.

exclusionary rule Prohibition of illegally obtained evidence.

exclusive dealing Sole right to sell goods in a defined market.

exclusive jurisdiction Such jurisdiction that permits only one court (state or federal) to hear a case.

exculpatory clause Excusing oneself from fault or liability.

execution *Execution of contract* includes performance of all acts necessary to render it complete as an instrument; implies that nothing more need be done to make the contract complete and effective.

Execution upon a money judgment is the legal process of enforcing the judgment, usually by seizing and selling property of the debtor.

executive order Legislation issued by the president or a governor.

executor A person appointed by a testator to carry out the directions and requests in his will and to dispose of the property according to his testamentary provisions after his decease. The female designation is executrix. A person appointed by the court in an intestacy situation is called the administrator(rix).

executory That which is yet to be executed or performed; that which remains to be carried into operation or effect; incomplete; depending upon a future performance or event. The opposite of executed.

executory contract See **contracts**.

executory promise Unperformed obligation.

exemplary damages See **damages**.

exoneration Relieved of liability.

express Manifested by direct and appropriate language, as distinguished from that which is inferred from conduct. The word is usually contrasted with "implied."

express warranty Explicitly made contractual promise regarding property or contract rights transferred; in a sale of goods, an affirmation of fact or a promise about the goods or a description, including a sample, of goods which becomes part of the basis of the bargain.

expropriation Governmental taking of foreign-owned property for a public purpose and with payment.

ex-ship Risk of loss passes to buyer when the goods leaving the ship. See UCC § 2–322. See also **F.A.S.**

extortion Making threats to obtain property.

fact An event that took place or a thing that exists.

false imprisonment Intentional interference with a person's freedom of movement by unlawful confinement.

false light Offensive publicity placing another in a false light.

false pretenses Intentional misrepresentation of fact in order to cheat another.

farm products Crops, livestock, or stock used or produced in farming.

F.A.S. Free alongside. Term used in sales price quotations indicating that the price includes all costs of transportation and delivery of the goods alongside the ship. See UCC § 2–319(2).

federal preemption First right of the federal government to regulate matters within its powers to the possible exclusion of state regulation.

federal question Any case arising under the Constitution, statutes, or treaties of the United States.

fee simple

Absolute A fee simple absolute is an estate that is unlimited as to duration, disposition, and descendibility. It is the largest estate and most extensive interest that can be enjoyed in land.

Conditional Type of transfer in which grantor conveys fee simple on condition that something be done or not done.

Defeasible Type of fee grant which may be defeated on the happening of an event. An estate which may last forever, but which may end upon the happening of a specified event, is a "fee simple defeasible."

Determinable Created by conveyance which contains words effective to create a fee simple and, in addition, a provision for automatic expiration of the estate on occurrence of stated event.

fee tail An estate of inheritance, descending only to a certain class or classes of heirs; *e.g.*, an estate is conveyed or devised "to A. and the heirs of his body," or "to A. and the heirs male of his body," or "to A., and the heirs female of his body."

fellow servant rule Common law defense relieving employer from liability to an employee for injuries caused by negligence of fellow employee.

felony Serious crime.

fiduciary A person or institution who manages money or property for another and who must exercise in such management activity a standard of care imposed by law or contract; *e.g.*, executor of estate; receiver in bankruptcy; trustee.

fiduciary duty Duty of utmost loyalty and good faith, such as that owed by a fiduciary such as an agent to her principal.

field warehouse Secured party takes possession of the goods but the debtor has access to the goods.

final credit Payment of the instrument by the payor bank.

financing statement Under the Uniform Commercial Code, a financing statement is used under Article 9 to reflect a public record that there is a security interest or claim to the goods in question to secure a debt. The financing statement is filed by the security holder with the secretary of state or with a similar public body; thus filed, it becomes public record. See also **secured transaction**.

fire (property) insurance Provides protection against loss due to fire or other related perils.

firm offer Irrevocable offer to sell or buy goods by a merchant in a signed writing which gives assurance that it will not be rescinded for up to three months.

fitness for a particular purpose Goods are fit for a stated purpose, provided that the seller selects the product knowing the buyer's intended use and that the buyer is relying on the seller's judgment.

fixture An article in the nature of personal property which has been so annexed to realty that it is regarded as a part of the land. Examples include a furnace affixed to a house or other building, counters permanently affixed to the floor of a store, and a sprinkler system installed in a building. UCC § 9–313(1)(a).

Trade fixtures Such chattels as merchants usually possess and annex to the premises occupied by them to enable them to store, handle, and display their goods, which generally are removable without material injury to the premises.

F.O.B. Free on board at some location (for example, F.O.B shipping point; F.O.B destination); the invoice price includes delivery at seller's expense to that location. Title to goods usually passes from seller to buyer at the F.O.B location. UCC § 2–319(1).

foreclosure Procedure by which mortgaged property is sold on default of mortgagor in satisfaction of mortgage debt.

forgery Intentional falsification of a document with intent to defraud.

four unities Time, title, interest, and possession.

franchise A privilege granted or sold, such as to use a name or to sell products or services. The right given by a manufacturer or supplier to a retailer to use his products and name on terms and conditions mutually agreed upon.

fraud Elements include false representation; of a present or past fact; made by defendant; action in reliance thereon by plaintiff; and damage resulting to plaintiff from such misrepresentation.

fraud in the execution Misrepresentation that deceives the other party as to the nature of a document evidencing the contract.

fraud in the inducement Misrepresentation regarding the subject matter of a contract that induces the other party to enter into the contract.

fraudulent misrepresentation False statement made with knowledge of its falsity and intent to mislead.

freehold An estate for life or in fee. It must possess two qualities: (1) immobility, that is, the property must be either land or some interest issuing out of or annexed to land; and (2) indeterminate duration.

friendly fire Fire contained where it is intended to be.

frustration of purpose doctrine Excuses a promisor in certain situations when the objectives of contract have been utterly defeated by circumstances arising after formation of the agreement, and performance is excused under this rule even though there is no impediment to actual performance.

full warranty One under which warrantor will repair the product and, if unsuccessful, will replace it or refund its cost.

fungibles With respect to goods or securities, those of which any unit is, by nature or usage of trade, the equivalent of any other like unit. UCC § 1–201(17); *e.g.*, a bushel of wheat or other grain.

future estate See **estate**.

garnishment A statutory proceeding whereby a person's property, money, or credits in the possession or control of another are applied to payment of the former's debt to a third person.

general intangible Catchall category for collateral not otherwise covered.

general partner Member of either a general or limited partnership with unlimited liability for its debts, full management powers, and a right to share in the profits.

gift A voluntary transfer of property to another made gratuitously and without consideration. Essential requisites of "gift" are capacity of donor, intention of donor to make gift, completed delivery to or for donee, and acceptance of gift by donee.

gift causa mortis A gift in view of death is one which is made in contemplation, fear, or peril of death and with the intent that it shall take effect only in case of the death of the giver.

good faith Honesty in fact in conduct or in a transaction.

good faith purchaser Buyer who acts honestly, gives value, and takes the goods without notice or knowledge of any defect in the title of his transferor.

goods A term of variable content and meaning. It may include every species of personal property, or it may be given a very restricted meaning. Sometimes the meaning of "goods" is extended to include all tangible items, as in the phrase "goods and services."

All things (including specially manufactured goods) which are movable at the time of identification to a contract for sale other than the money in which the price is to be paid, investment securities, and things in action. UCC § 2–105(1).

grantee Transferee of property.

grantor A transferor of property. The creator of a trust is usually designated as the grantor of the trust.

gratuitous promise Promise made without consideration.

group insurance Covers a number of individuals.

guaranty A promise to answer for the payment of some debt, or the performance of some duty, in case of the failure of another person who, in the first instance, is liable for such payment or performance.

The terms *guaranty* and *suretyship* are sometimes used interchangeably; but they should not be confounded. The distinction between contract of suretyship and contract of guaranty is whether or not the undertaking is a joint undertaking with the principal or a separate and distinct contract; if it is the former, it is one of "suretyship," and if the latter, it is one of "guaranty." See also **surety**.

guardianship The relationship under which a person (the guardian) is appointed by a court to preserve and control the property of another (the ward).

heir A person who succeeds, by the rules of law, to an estate in lands, tenements, or hereditaments, upon the death of his ancestor, by descent and right of relationship.

holder Person who is in possession of a document of title or an instrument or an investment security drawn, issued, or indorsed to him or to his order, or to bearer, or in blank. UCC § 1–201(20).

holder in due course A holder who takes an instrument for value, in good faith, and without notice that it is overdue or has been dishonored or of any defense against or claim to it on the part of any person.

holograph A will or deed written entirely by the testator or grantor with his own hand and not witnessed (attested). State laws vary with respect to the validity of the holographic will.

homicide Unlawful taking of another's life.

horizontal privity Who may bring a cause of action.

horizontal restraints Agreements among competitors.

hostile fire Any fire outside its intended or usual place.

identified goods Designated goods as a part of a particular contract.

illegal per se Conclusively presumed unreasonable and therefore illegal.

illusory promise Promise imposing no obligation on the promisor.

implied-in-fact condition Contingencies understood but not expressed by the parties.

implied-in-law condition Contingency that arises from operation of law.

implied warranty Obligation imposed by law upon the transferor of property or contract rights; implicit in the sale arising out of certain circumstances.

implied warranty of habitability Leased premises are fit for ordinary residential purposes.

impossibility Performance that cannot be done.

in personam Against the person. Action seeking judgment against a person involving his personal rights and based on jurisdiction of his person, as distinguished from a judgment against property (*i.e.*, in rem).

in personam jurisdiction Jurisdiction based on claims against a person, in contrast to jurisdiction over his property.

in re In the affair; in the matter of; concerning; regarding. This is the usual method of entitling a judicial proceeding in which there are no adversary parties, but merely some res concerning which judicial action is to be taken, such as a bankrupt's estate, an estate in the probate court, a proposed public highway, etc.

in rem A technical term used to designate proceedings or actions instituted *against the thing*, in contradistinction to personal actions, which are said to be *in personam*.

> *Quasi in rem* A term applied to proceedings which are not strictly and purely *in rem*, but are brought against the defendant personally, though the real object is to deal with particular property or subject property to the discharge of claims asserted; for example, foreign attachment, or proceedings to foreclose a mortgage, remove a cloud from title, or effect a partition.

in rem jurisdiction Jurisdiction based on claims against property.

incidental beneficiary Third party whom the two parties to a contract have no intention of benefiting by their contract.

income bond Bond that conditions payment of interest on corporate earnings.

incontestability clause The prohibition of an insurer to avoid an insurance policy after a specified period of time.

indemnification Duty owed by principal to agent to pay agent for losses incurred while acting as directed by principal.

indemnify To reimburse one for a loss already incurred.

indenture A written agreement under which bonds and debentures are issued, setting forth maturity date, interest rate, and other terms.

independent contractor Person who contracts with another to do a particular job and who is not subject to the control of the other.

indicia Signs; indications. Circumstances which point to the existence of a given fact as probable, but not certain.

indictment Grand jury charge that the defendant should stand trial.

indispensable paper Chattel paper, instruments, and documents.

indorsee The person to whom a negotiable instrument, promissory note, bill of lading, etc., is assigned by indorsement.

indorsement The act of a payee, drawee, accommodation indorser, or holder of a bill, note, check, or other negotiable instrument, in writing his name upon the back of the same, with or without further or qualifying words, whereby the property in the same is assigned and transferred to another. UCC § 3–202 *et seq.*

> *Blank indorsement* No indorsee is specified.
>
> *Qualified indorsement* Without recourse, limiting one's liability on the instrument.
>
> *Restrictive indorsement* Limits the rights of the indorser in some manner.
>
> *Special indorsement* Designates an indorsee to be paid.

infliction of emotional distress Extreme and outrageous conduct intentionally or recklessly causing severe emotional distress.

information Formal accusation of a crime brought by a prosecutor.

infringement Unauthorized use.

injunction An equitable remedy forbidding the party defendant from doing some act which he is threatening or attempting to commit, or restraining him in the continuance thereof, such act being unjust and inequitable, injurious to the plaintiff, and not such as can be adequately redressed by an action at law.

innkeeper Hotel or motel operator.

inquisitorial system System in which the judiciary initiates, conducts, and decides cases.

insider Relative or general partner of debtor, partnership in which debtor is a partner, or corporation in which debtor is an officer, director, or controlling person.

insiders Directors, officers, employees, and agents of the issuer as well as those the issuer has entrusted with information solely for corporate purposes.

insolvency Under the UCC, a person is insolvent who either has ceased to pay his debts in the ordinary course of business or cannot pay his debts as they fall due or is insolvent within the meaning of the Federal Bankruptcy Law. UCC § 1–201(23).

> *Insolvency (bankruptcy)* Total liabilities exceed total value of assets.
>
> *Insolvency (equity)* Inability to pay debts in ordinary course of business or as they become due.

inspection Examination of goods to determine whether they conform to a contract.

instrument Negotiable instruments, stocks, bonds, and other investment securities.

insurable interest Exists where insured derives pecuniary benefit or advantage by preservation and continued existence of property or would sustain pecuniary loss from its destruction.

insurance A contract whereby, for a stipulated consideration, one party undertakes to compensate the other for loss on a specified subject by specified perils. The party agreeing to make the compensation is usually called the "insurer" or "underwriter"; the other, the "insured" or "assured"; the written contract, a "policy"; the events insured against, "risks" or "perils"; and the subject, right, or interest to be protected, the "insurable interest." Insurance is a contract whereby one undertakes to indemnify another against loss, damage, or liability arising from an unknown or contingent event.

> *Co-insurance* A form of insurance in which a person insures property for less than its full or stated value and agrees to share the risk of loss.
>
> *Life insurance* Payment of a specific sum of money to a designated beneficiary upon the death of the insured.
>
> *Ordinary life* Life insurance with a savings component that runs for the life of the insured.
>
> *Term life* Life insurance issued for a limited number of years that does not have a savings component.

intangible property Protected interests that are not physical.

intangibles Accounts and general intangibles.

intent Desire to cause the consequences of an act or knowledge that the consequences are substantially certain to result from the act.

inter alia Among other things.

inter se or **inter sese** Latin. Among or between themselves; used to distinguish rights or duties between two or more parties from their rights or duties to others.

interest in land Any right, privilege, power, or immunity in real property.

interest in partnership Partner's share in the partnership's profits and surplus.

interference with contractual relations Intentionally causing one of the parties to a contract not to perform the contract.

intermediary bank Any bank, except the depositary or payor bank, to which an item is transferred in the course of collection. UCC § 4–105(c).

intermediate test Requirement that legislation have a substantial relationship to an important governmental objective.

international law Deals with the conduct and relations of nation-states and international organizations.

interpretation Construction or meaning of a contract.

interpretative rules Statements issued by an administrative agency indicating its construction of its governing statute.

intestate A person is said to die intestate when he dies without making a will. The word is also often used to signify the person himself. *Compare* **testator**.

intrusion Unreasonable and highly offensive interference with the seclusion of another.

inventory Goods held for sale or lease or consumed in a business.

invitee A person is an "invitee" on land of another if (1) he enters by invitation, express or implied, (2) his entry is connected with the owner's business or with an activity the owner conducts or permits to be conducted on his land, and (3) there is mutual benefit or a benefit to the owner.

joint liability Liability where creditor must sue all of the partners as a group.

joint and several liability Liability where creditor may sue partners jointly as a group or separately as individuals.

joint stock company A general partnership with some corporate attributes.

joint tenancy See **tenancy**.

joint venture An association of two or more persons to carry on a single business transaction for profit.

judgment The official and authentic decision of a court of justice upon the respective rights and claims of the parties to an action or suit therein litigated and submitted to its determination.

judgment in personam A judgment against a particular person, as distinguished from a judgment against a thing or a right or *status*.

judgment in rem An adjudication pronounced upon the status of some particular thing or subject matter, by a tribunal having competent authority.

judgment n. o. v. Judgment non obstante veredicto in its broadest sense is a judgment rendered in favor of one party notwithstanding the finding of a verdict in favor of the other party.

judgment notwithstanding the verdict A final binding determination on the merits made by the judge after and contrary to the jury's verdict.

judgment on the pleadings Final binding determination on the merits made by the judge after the pleadings.

judicial lien Interest in property that is obtained by court action to secure payment of a debt.

judicial review Power of the courts to determine the constitutionality of legislative and executive acts.

jurisdiction The right and power of a court to adjudicate concerning the subject matter in a given case.

jurisdiction over the parties Power of a court to bind the parties to a suit.

jury A body of persons selected and summoned by law and sworn to try the facts of a case and to find according to the law and the evidence. In general, the province of the jury is to find the facts in a case, while the judge passes upon pure questions of law. As a matter of fact, however, the jury must often pass upon mixed questions of law and fact in determining the case, and in all such cases the instructions of the judge as to the law become very important.

justifiable reliance Reasonably influenced by a misrepresentation.

labor dispute Any controversy concerning terms or conditions of employment or union representation.

laches Based upon maxim that equity aids the vigilant and not those who slumber on their rights. It is defined as neglect to assert a right or claim which, taken together with a lapse of time and other circumstances causing prejudice to the adverse party, operates as a bar in a court of equity.

landlord The owner of an estate in land, or a rental property, who has leased it to another person, called the "tenant." Also called "lessor."

larceny Trespassory taking and carrying away of the goods of another with the intent to permanently deprive.

last clear chance Final opportunity to avoid an injury.

lease Any agreement which gives rise to relationship of landlord and tenant (real property) or lessor and lessee (real or personal property).

The person who conveys is termed the "lessor," and the person to whom conveyed, the "lessee"; and when the lessor conveys land or tenements to a lessee, he is said to lease, demise, or let them.

Sublease, or *underlease* One executed by the lessee of an estate to a third person, conveying the same estate for a shorter term than that for which the lessee holds it.

leasehold An estate in realty held under a lease. The four principal types of leasehold estates are the estate for years, periodic tenancy, tenancy at will, and tenancy at sufferance.

leasehold estate Right to possess real property.

legacy "Legacy" is a gift or bequest by will of personal property, whereas a "devise" is a testamentary disposition of real estate.

Demonstrative legacy A bequest of a certain sum of money, with a direction that it shall be paid out of a particular fund. It differs from a specific legacy in this respect: that, if the fund out of which it is payable fails for any cause, it is nevertheless entitled to come on the estate as a general legacy. And it differs from a general legacy in this: that it does not abate in that class, but in the class of specific legacies.

General legacy A pecuniary legacy, payable out of the general assets of a testator.

Residuary legacy A bequest of all the testator's personal estate not otherwise effectually disposed of by his will.

Specific legacy One which operates on property particularly designated. A legacy or gift by will of a particular specified thing, as of a horse, a piece of furniture, a term of years, and the like.

legal aggregate A group of individuals not having a legal existence separate from its members.

legal benefit Obtaining something to which one had no legal right.

legal detriment Doing an act one is not legally obligated to do or not doing an act one has a legal right to do.

legal entity An organization having a legal existence separate from that of its members.

legal sufficiency Benefit to promisor or detriment to promisee.

legislative rules Substantive rules issued by an administrative agency under the authority delegated to it by the legislature.

letter of credit An engagement by a bank or other person made at the request of a customer that the issuer will honor drafts or other demands for payment upon compliance with the conditions specified in the credit.

letters of administration Formal document issued by probate court appointing one an administrator of an estate.

letters testamentary The formal instrument of authority and appointment given to an executor by the proper court, empowering him to enter upon the discharge of his office as executor. It corresponds to letters of administration granted to an administrator.

levy To assess; raise; execute; exact; tax; collect; gather; take up; seize. Thus, to levy (assess, exact, raise, or collect) a tax; to levy an execution, *i.e.*, to levy or collect a sum of money on an execution.

liability insurance Covers liability to others by reason of damage resulting from injuries to another's person or property.

liability without fault Crime to do a specific act or cause a certain result without regard to the care exercised.

libel Defamation communicated by writing, television, radio, or the like.

liberty Ability of individuals to engage in freedom of action and choice regarding their personal lives.

license License with respect to real property is a privilege to go on premises for a certain purpose, but does not operate to confer on or vest in the licensee any title, interest, or estate in such property.

licensee Person privileged to enter or remain on land by virtue of the consent of the lawful possessor.

lien A qualified right of property which a creditor has in or over specific property of his debtor, as security for the debt or charge or for performance of some act.

lien creditor A creditor who has acquired a lien on the property by attachment.

life estate An estate whose duration is limited to the life of the party holding it or of some other person. Upon the death of the life tenant, the property will go to the holder of the remainder interest or to the grantor by reversion.

limited liability Liability limited to amount invested in a business enterprise.

limited partner Member of a limited partnership with liability for its debts only to the extent of her capital contribution.

limited partnership See **partnership.**

limited partnership association A partnership which closely resembles a corporation.

liquidated Ascertained; determined; fixed; settled; made clear or manifest. Cleared away; paid; discharged.

liquidated damages See **damages.**

liquidated debt Obligation that is certain in amount.

liquidation The settling of financial affairs of a business or individual, usually by liquidating (turning to cash) all assets for distribution to creditors, heirs, etc. To be distinguished from dissolution.

loss of value Value of promised performance minus value of actual performance.

lost property Property with which the owner has involuntarily parted and which she does not know where to find or recover, not including property which she has intentionally concealed or deposited in a secret place for safekeeping. Distinguishable from mislaid property, which has been deliberately placed somewhere and forgotten.

main purpose rule Where object of promisor/surety is to provide an economic benefit for herself, the promise is considered outside of the statute of frauds.

maker One who makes or executes; as the maker of a promissory note. One who signs a check; in this context, synonymous with drawer. See **draft.**

mala in se Morally wrong.

mala prohibita Wrong by law.

mandamus Latin, we command. A legal writ compelling the defendant to do an official duty.

manslaughter Unlawful taking of another's life without malice.

Involuntary manslaughter Taking the life of another by criminal negligence or during the course of a misdemeanor.

Voluntary manslaughter Intentional killing of another under extenuating circumstances.

manufacturing defect Not produced according to specifications.

mark Trade symbol.

market allocations Division of market by customers, geographic location, or products.

marketable title Free from any defects, encumbrances, or reasonable objections to one's ownership.

marshaling of assets Segregating the assets and liabilities of a partnership from the assets and liabilities of the individual partners.

master See **principal.**

material Matters to which a reasonable investor would attach importance in deciding whether to purchase a security.

material alteration Any change that changes the contract of any party to an instrument.

maturity The date at which an obligation, such as the principal of a bond or a note, becomes due.

maxim A general legal principle.

mechanic's lien A claim created by state statutes for the purpose of securing priority of payment of the price or value of work performed and materials furnished in erecting or repairing a building or other structure; as such, attaches to the land as well as buildings and improvements erected thereon.

mediation Nonbinding process in which a third party acts as an intermediary between the disputing parties and proposes solutions for them to consider.

mens rea Criminal intent.

mentally incompetent Unable to understand the nature and effect of one's acts.

mercantile law An expression substantially equivalent to commercial law. It designates the system of rules, customs, and usages generally recognized and adopted by merchants and traders that, either in its simplicity or as modified by common law or statutes, constitutes the law for the regulation of their transactions and the solution of their controversies. The Uniform Commercial Code is the general body of law governing commercial or mercantile transactions.

merchant A person who deals in goods of the kind involved in a transaction or who otherwise by his occupation holds himself out as having knowledge or skill peculiar to the practices or goods involved in the transaction or to whom such knowledge or skill may be attributed by his employment of an agent or broker or other intermediary who by his occupation holds himself out as having such knowledge or skill. UCC § 2–104(1).

merchantability Merchant seller guarantees that the goods are fit for their ordinary purpose.

merger The fusion or absorption of one thing or right into another. In corporate law, the absorption of one company by another, the latter retaining its own name and identity and acquiring the assets, liabilities, franchises, and powers of the former, which ceases to exist as separate business entity. It differs from a consolidation, wherein all the corporations terminate their separate existences and become parties to a new one.

Conglomerate merger An acquisition, which is not horizontal or vertical, by one company of another.

Horizontal merger Merger between business competitors, such as manufacturers of the same type of products or distributors selling competing products in the same market area.

Short-form merger Merger of a 90 percent subsidiary into its parent.

Vertical merger Union with corporate customer or supplier.

midnight deadline Midnight of the next banking day after receiving an item.

mining partnership A specific type of partnership for the purpose of extracting raw minerals.

minor Under the age of legal majority (usually eighteen).

mirror image rule An acceptance cannot deviate from the terms of the offer.

misdemeanor Less serious crime.

mislaid property Property which an owner has put deliberately in a certain place that she is unable to remember, as distinguished from lost property, which the owner has left unwittingly in a location she has forgotten. See also **lost property.**

misrepresentation Any manifestation by words or other conduct by one person to another that, under the circumstances, amounts to an assertion not in accordance with the facts. A "misrepresentation" that justifies the rescission of a contract is a false statement of a substantive fact, or any conduct which leads to a belief of a substantive fact material to proper understanding of the matter in hand. See also **deceit; fraud.**

Fraudulent misrepresentation False statement made with knowledge of its falsity and intent to mislead.

Innocent misrepresentation Misrepresentation made without knowledge of its falsity but with due care.

Negligent misrepresentation Misrepresentation made without due care in ascertaining its falsity.

M'Naughten Rule Right/wrong test for criminal insanity.

modify Change the lower court's judgment.

money Medium of exchange issued by a government body.

monopoly Ability to control price or exclude others from the marketplace.

mortgage A mortgage is an interest in land created by a written instrument providing security for the performance of a duty or the payment of a debt.

mortgagor Debtor who uses real estate to secure an obligation.

multinational enterprise Business that engages in transactions involving the movement of goods, information, money, people, or services across national borders.

multiple product order Order requiring an advertiser to cease and desist from deceptive statements on all products it sells.

murder Unlawful and premeditated taking of another's life.

mutual mistake Where the common but erroneous belief of both parties forms the basis of a contract.

necessaries Items needed to maintain a person's station in life.

negligence The omission to do something which a reasonable person, guided by those ordinary considerations which ordinarily regulate human affairs, would do, or the doing of something which a reasonable and prudent person would not do.

> *Culpable negligence* Greater than ordinary negligence but less than gross negligence.

negligence *per se* Conclusive on the issue of negligence (duty of care and breach).

negotiable Legally capable of being transferred by indorsement or delivery. Usually said of checks and notes and sometimes of stocks and bearer bonds.

negotiable instrument Signed document (such as a check or promissory note) containing an unconditional promise to pay a "sum certain" of money at a definite time to order or bearer.

negotiation Transferee becomes a holder.

net assets Total assets minus total debts.

no arrival, no sale A destination contract, but if goods do not arrive, seller is excused from liability unless such is due to the seller's fault.

no-fault insurance Compensates victims of automobile accidents regardless of fault.

nonconforming use Preexisting use not in accordance with a zoning ordinance.

nonprofit corporation One whose profits must be used exclusively for the charitable, educational, or scientific purpose for which it was formed.

nonsuit Action in form of a judgment taken against a plaintiff who has failed to appear to prosecute his action or failed to prove his case.

note See **promissory note**.

novation A novation substitutes a new party and discharges one of the original parties to a contract by agreement of all three parties. A new contract is created with the same terms as the original one; only the parties have changed.

nuisance Nuisance is that activity which arises from the unreasonable, unwarranted, or unlawful use by a person of his own property, working obstruction or injury to the right of another or to the public, and producing such material annoyance, inconvenience, and discomfort that law will presume resulting damage.

obiter dictum See **dictum**.

objective fault Gross deviation from reasonable conduct.

objective manifestation What a reasonable person under the circumstances would believe.

objective satisfaction Approval based upon whether a reasonable person would be satisfied.

objective standard What a reasonable person under the circumstances would reasonably believe or do.

obligee Party to whom a duty of performance is owed (by delegator and delegatee).

obligor Party owing a duty (to the assignor).

offer A manifestation of willingness to enter into a bargain, so made as to justify another person in understanding that his assent to that bargain is invited and will conclude it. Restatement, Second, Contracts, § 24

offeree Recipient of the offer.

offeror Person making the offer.

open-ended credit Credit arrangement under which debtor has rights to enter into a series of credit transactions.

opinion Belief in the existence of a fact or a judgment as to value.

option Contract providing that an offer will stay open for a specified period of time.

order A final disposition made by an agency.

order paper Payable to a named person or to anyone designated by that person.

order to pay Direction or command to pay.

original promise Promise to become primarily liable.

output contract See **contracts.**

palpable unilateral mistake Erroneous belief by one party that is recognized by the other.

parent corporation Corporation which controls another corporation.

parol evidence Literally oral evidence, but now includes prior to and contemporaneous, oral, and written evidence.

parol evidence rule Under this rule, when parties put their agreement in writing, all previous oral agreements merge in the writing and the contract as written cannot be modified or changed by parol evidence, in the absence of a plea of mistake or fraud in the preparation of the writing. But the rule does not forbid a resort to parol evidence not inconsistent with the matters stated in the writing. Also, as regards sales of goods, such written agreement may be explained or supplemented by course of dealing, usage of trade, or course of conduct, and by evidence of consistent additional terms, unless the court finds the writing to have been intended also as a complete and exclusive statement of the terms of the agreement. UCC § 2–202.

part performance In order to establish part performance taking an oral contract for the sale of realty out of the statute of frauds, the acts relied upon as part performance must be of such a character that they reasonably can be naturally accounted for in no other way than that they were performed in pursuance of the contract, and they must be in conformity with its provisions. See UCC § 2–201(3).

partial assignment Transfer of a portion of contractual rights to one or more assignees.

partition The dividing of lands held by joint tenants, copartners, or tenants in common into distinct portions, so that the parties may hold those lands in severalty.

partnership An association of two or more persons to carry on, as co-owners, a business for profit.

Partnerships are treated as a conduit and are, therefore, not subject to taxation. The various items of partnership income (gains and losses, etc.) flow through to the individual partners and are reported on their personal income tax returns.

> *Limited partnership* Type of partnership comprised of one or more general partners who manage business and who are personally liable for partnership debts, and one or more limited partners who contribute capital and share in profits but who take no part in running business and incur no liability with respect to partnership obligations beyond contribution.

> *Partnership at will* One with no definite term or specific undertaking.

partnership capital Total money and property contributed by partners for permanent use by the partnership.

partnership property Sum of all of the partnership's assets.

past consideration An act done before the contract is made.

patent Exclusive right to an invention.

payee The person in whose favor a bill of exchange, promissory note, or check is made or drawn.

payer or **payor** One who pays or who is to make a payment, particularly the person who is to make payment of a check, bill, or note. Correlative to "payee."

payor bank A bank by which an item is payable as drawn or accepted. UCC § 4–105(b). Correlative to "Drawee bank."

per capita This term, derived from the civil law and much used in the law of descent and distribution, denotes that method of dividing an intestate estate by which an equal share is given to each of a number of persons, all of whom stand in equal degree to the decedent, without reference to their stocks or the right of representation. The opposite of *per stirpes*.

per stirpes This term, derived from the civil law and much used in the law of descent and distribution, denotes that method of dividing an intestate estate where a class or group of distributees takes the share to which its deceased would have been entitled, taking thus by its right of representing such ancestor and not as so many individuals. The opposite of *per capita*.

perfect tender rule Seller's tender of delivery must conform exactly to the contract.

perfection of security interest Acts required of a secured party in the way of giving at least constructive notice so as to make his security interest effective at least against lien creditors of the debtor. See UCC §§ 9–302 through 9–306. In most cases, the secured party may obtain perfection either by filing with the secretary of state or by taking possession of the collateral.

performance Fulfillment of one's contractual obligations. See also **part performance**; **specific performance**.

periodic tenancy Lease with a definite term that is to be continued.

personal defenses Contractual defenses which are good against holders but not holders in due course.

personal property Any property other than an interest in land.

petty crime Misdemeanor punishable by imprisonment of six months or less.

plaintiff The party who initiates a civil suit.

pleadings The formal allegations by the parties of their respective claims and defenses.

> *Rules or codes of civil procedure* Unlike the rigid technical system of common law pleading, pleadings under federal and state rules or codes of civil procedure have a far more limited function, with determination and narrowing of facts and issues being left to discovery devices and pretrial conferences. In addition, the rules and codes permit liberal amendment and supplementation of pleadings.
>
> Under rules of civil procedure, the pleadings consist of a complaint, an answer, a reply to a counterclaim, an answer to a cross-claim, a third-party complaint, and a third-party answer.

pledge A bailment of goods to a creditor as security for some debt or engagement.

> Much of the law of pledges has been replaced by the provisions for secured transactions in Article 9 of the UCC.

possibility of reverter The interest which remains in a grantor or testator after the conveyance or devise of a fee simple determinable and which permits the grantor to be revested automatically of his estate on breach of the condition.

possibility test Under the statute of frauds, asks whether performance could possibly be completed within one year.

power of appointment A power of authority conferred by one person by deed or will upon another (called the "donee") to appoint, that is, to select and nominate, the person or persons who is or are to receive and enjoy an estate or an income therefrom or from a fund, after the testator's death, or the donee's death, or after the termination of an existing right or interest.

power of attorney An instrument authorizing a person to act as the agent or attorney of the person granting it.

power of termination The interest left in the grantor or testator after the conveyance or devise of a fee simple on condition subsequent or conditional fee.

precatory Expressing a wish.

precedent An adjudged case or decision of a court, considered as furnishing an example or authority for an identical or similar case afterwards arising or a similar question of law. See also **stare decisis**.

preemptive right The privilege of a stockholder to maintain a proportionate share of ownership by purchasing a proportionate share of any new stock issues.

preference The act of an insolvent debtor who, in distributing his property or in assigning it for the benefit of his creditors, pays or secures to one or more creditors the full amount of their claims or a larger amount than they would be entitled to receive on a *pro rata* distribution. The treatment of such preferential payments in bankruptcy is governed by the Bankruptcy Act, § 547.

preliminary hearing Determines whether there is probable cause.

premium The price for insurance protection for a specified period of exposure.

preponderance of the evidence Greater weight of the evidence; standard used in civil cases.

prescription Acquisition of a personal right to use a way, water, light, and air by reason of continuous usage. See also **easement**.

presenter's warranty Warranty given to any payor or acceptor of an instrument.

presentment The production of a negotiable instrument to the drawee for his acceptance, or to the drawer or acceptor for payment; or of a promissory note to the party liable, for payment of the same. UCC § 3–504(1).

presumption A presumption is a rule of law, statutory or judicial, by which a finding of a basic fact gives rise to the existence of presumed fact, until presumption is rebutted. A presumption imposes on the party against whom it is directed the burden of going forward with evidence to rebut or meet the presumption, but does not shift to such party the burden of proof in the sense of the risk of nonpersuasion, which remains throughout the trial upon the party on whom it was originally cast.

price discrimination Price differential.

price fixing Any agreement for the purpose and effect of raising, depressing, fixing, pegging, or stabilizing prices.

prima facie Latin. At first sight; on the first appearance; on the face of it; so far as can be judged from the first disclosure; presumably; a fact presumed to be true unless disproved by some evidence to the contrary.

primary liability Absolute obligation to pay a negotiable instrument.

principal *Law of agency* The term "principal" describes one who has permitted or directed another (*i.e.*, an agent or a servant) to act for his benefit and subject to his direction and control. Principal includes in its meaning the term "master" or employer, a species of principal who, in addition to other control, has a right to control the physical conduct of the species of agents known as servants or employees, as to whom special rules are applicable with reference to harm caused by their physical acts.

> *Disclosed principal* One whose existence and identity are known.
> *Partially disclosed principal* One whose existence is known but whose identity is not known.
> *Undisclosed principal* One whose existence and identity are not known.

principal debtor Person whose debt is being supported by a surety.

priority Precedence in order of right.

private carrier Carrier which limits its service and is not open to the general public.

private corporation One organized to conduct either a privately owned business enterprise for profit or a nonprofit corporation.

private law The law involving relationships among individuals and legal entities.

privilege Immunity from tort liability.

privity Contractual relationship.

privity of contract That connection or relationship which exists between two or more contracting parties. The absence of privity as a defense in actions for damages in contract and tort actions is generally no longer viable with the enactment of warranty statutes (*e.g.*, UCC § 2–318), acceptance by states of the doctrine of strict liability, and court decisions which have extended the right to sue to third-party beneficiaries and even innocent bystanders.

probable cause Reasonable belief of the offense charged.

probate Court procedure by which a will is proved to be valid or invalid, though in current usage this term has been expanded to include generally all matters and proceedings pertaining to administration of estates, guardianships, etc.

procedural due process Requirement that governmental action depriving a person of life, liberty, or property be done through a fair procedure.

procedural law Rules for enforcing substantive law.

procedural rules Rules issued by an administrative agency establishing its organization, method of operation, and rules of conduct for practice before it.

procedural unconscionability Unfair or irregular bargaining.

proceeds Consideration for the sale, exchange, or other disposition of collateral.

process *Judicial process* In a wide sense, this term may include all the acts of a court from the beginning to the end of its proceedings in a given cause; more specifically, it means the writ, summons, mandate, or other process which is used to inform the defendant of the institution of proceedings against him and to compel his appearance, in either civil or criminal cases.

   Legal process This term is sometimes used as equivalent to "lawful process." Thus, it is said that legal process means process not merely fair on its face but valid in fact. But properly it means a summons, writ, warrant, mandate, or other process issuing from a court.

profit corporation One founded for the purpose of operating a business for profit.

profit à prendre Right to make some use of the soil of another, such as a right to mine metals; carries with it the right of entry and the right to remove.

promise to pay Undertaking to pay an existing obligation.

promisee Person to whom a promise is made.

promisor Person making a promise.

promissory estoppel Arises where there is a promise which promisor should reasonably expect to induce action or forbearance on part of promisee and which does induce such action or forbearance, and where injustice can be avoided only by enforcement of the promise.

promissory note An unconditional written promise to pay a specified sum of money on demand or at a specified date. Such a note is negotiable if signed by the maker and containing an unconditional promise to pay a sum certain in money either on demand or at a definite time and payable to order or bearer. UCC § 3–104.

promoters In the law relating to corporations, those persons who first associate themselves for the purpose of organizing a company, issuing its prospectus, procuring subscriptions to the stock, securing a charter, etc.

property Interest that is legally protected.

   Abandoned property Intentionally disposed of by the owner.

   Lost property Unintentionally left by the owner.

   Mislaid property Intentionally placed by the owner but unintentionally left.

prosecute To bring a criminal proceeding.

protest A formal declaration made by a person interested or concerned in some act about to be done, or already performed, whereby he expresses his dissent or disapproval or affirms the act against his will. The object of such a declaration usually is to preserve some right which would be lost to the protester if his assent could be implied, or to exonerate him from some responsibility which would attach to him unless he expressly negatived his assent.

   Notice of protest A notice given by the holder of a bill or note to the drawer or indorser that the bill has been protested for refusal of payment or acceptance. UCC § 3–509.

provisional credit Tentative credit for the deposit of an instrument until final credit is given.

proximate cause Where the act or omission played a substantial part in bringing about or actually causing the injury or damage and where the injury or damage was either a direct result or a reasonably probable consequence of the act or omission.

proxy (Contracted from "procuracy.") Written authorization given by one person to another so that the second person can act for the first, such as that given by a shareholder to someone else to represent him and vote his shares at a shareholders' meeting.

public corporation One created to administer a unit of local civil government or one created by the United States to conduct public business.

public disclosure of private facts Offensive publicity given to private information about another person.

public law The law dealing with the relationship between government and individuals.

puffery Sales talk that is considered general bragging or overstatement.

punitive damages Damages awarded in excess of normal compensation to punish a defendant for a serious civil wrong.

purchase money security interest Security interest retained by a seller of goods in goods purchased with the loaned money.

qualified fee Ownership subject to its being taken away upon the happening of an event.

quantum meruit Expression "quantum meruit" means "as much as he deserves"; describes the extent of liability on a contract implied by law. Elements essential to recovery under quantum meruit are (1) valuable services rendered or materials furnished (2) for the person sought to be charged, (3) which services and materials such person accepted, used, and enjoyed, (4) under such circumstances as reasonably notified her that plaintiff, in performing such services, was expected to be paid by the person sought to be charged.

quasi Latin. As if; almost as it were; analogous to. Negatives the idea of identity but points out that the conceptions are sufficiently similar to be classed as equals of one another.

quasi contract Legal fiction invented by common law courts to permit recovery by contractual remedy in cases where, in fact, there is no contract, but where circumstances are such that justice warrants a recovery as though a promise had been made.

quasi in rem See **in rem**.

quasi in rem jurisdiction Jurisdiction over property not based on claims against it.

quiet enjoyment Right of a tenant not to have his physical possession of premises interfered with by the landlord.

quitclaim deed A deed of conveyance operating by way of release; that is, intended to pass any title, interest, or claim which the grantor may have in the premises but neither professing that such title is valid nor containing any warranty or covenants for title.

quorum When a committee, board of directors, meeting of shareholders, legislature, or other body of persons cannot act unless at least a certain number of them are present.

rape Unlawful, nonconsensual sexual intercourse.

ratification In a broad sense, the confirmation of a previous act done either by the party himself or by another; as, for example, confirmation of a voidable act.

   In the law of principal and agent, the adoption and confirmation by one person, with knowledge of all material facts, of an act or contract performed or entered into in his behalf by another who at the time assumed without authority to act as his agent.

rational relationship test Requirement that legislation bear a rational relationship to a legitimate governmental interest.

real defenses Defenses that are valid against all holders, including holders in due course.

real property Land, and generally whatever is erected or growing upon or affixed to land. Also, rights issuing out of, annexed to, and exercisable within or about land. See also **fixture**.

reasonable man standard Duty of care required to avoid being negligent; one who is careful, diligent, and prudent.

receiver A fiduciary of the court, whose appointment is incident to other proceedings wherein certain ultimate relief is prayed. He is a trustee or ministerial officer representing the court, all parties in interest in the litigation, and the property or funds entrusted to him.

recognizance Formal acknowledgment of indebtedness made in court.

redemption The realization of a right to have the title of property restored free and clear of a mortgage, performance of the mortgage obligation being essential for such purpose. (b) Repurchase by corporation of its own shares.

reformation Equitable remedy used to reframe written contracts to reflect accurately real agreement between contracting parties when, either through mutual mistake or unilateral mistake coupled with actual or equitable fraud by the other party, the writing does not embody the contract as actually made.

regulatory license Requirement to protect the public interest.

reimbursement Duty owed by principal to pay back authorized payments agent has made on principal's behalf. Duty owed by a principal debtor to repay surety who pays principal debtor's obligation.

rejection The refusal to accept an offer; manifestation of an unwillingness to accept the goods (sales).

release The relinquishment, concession, or giving up of a right, claim, or privilege, by the person in whom it exists or to whom it accrues, to the person against whom it might have been demanded or enforced.

remainder An estate limited to take effect and be enjoyed after another estate is determined.

remand To send back. The sending by the appellate court of a cause back to the same court out of which it came, for the purpose of having some further action taken on it there.

remedy The means by which the violation of a right is prevented, redressed, or compensated. Though a remedy may be by the act of the party injured, by operation of law, or by agreement between the injurer and the injured, we are chiefly concerned with one kind of remedy, the judicial remedy, which is by action or suit.

rent Consideration paid for use or occupation of property. In a broader sense, it is the compensation or fee paid, usually periodically, for the use of any property, land, buildings, equipment, etc.

replevin An action whereby the owner or person entitled to repossession of goods or chattels may recover those goods or chattels from one who has wrongfully distrained or taken such goods or chattels or who wrongfully detains them.

reply Plaintiff's pleading in response to the defendant's answer.

repudiation Repudiation of a contract means refusal to perform duty or obligation owed to other party.

requirements contract See **contracts**.

res ipsa loquitur "The thing speaks for itself"; permits the jury to infer both negligent conduct and causation.

rescission An equitable action in which a party seeks to be relieved of his obligations under a contract on the grounds of mutual mistake, fraud, impossibility, etc.

residuary Pertaining to the residue; constituting the residue; giving or bequeathing the residue; receiving or entitled to the residue. See also **legacy**, **residuary legacy**.

respondeat superior Latin. Let the master answer. This maxim means that a master or employer is liable in certain cases for the wrongful acts of his servant or employee, and a principal for those of his agent.

respondent In equity practice, the party who makes an answer to a bill or other proceeding. In appellate practice, the party who contends against an appeal; *i.e.*, the appellee. The party who appeals is called the "appellant."

restitution An equitable remedy under which a person who has rendered services to another seeks to be reimbursed for the costs of his acts (but not his profits) even though there was never a contract between the parties.

restraint on alienation A provision in an instrument of conveyance which prohibits the grantee from selling or transferring the property which is the subject of the conveyance. Many such restraints are unenforceable as against public policy and the law's policy of free alienability of land.

restraint of trade Agreement that eliminates or tends to eliminate competition.

restrictive covenant Private restriction on property contained in a conveyance.

revenue license Measure to raise money.

reverse An appellate court uses the term "reversed" to indicate that it annuls or avoids the judgment, or vacates the decree, of the trial court.

reverse discrimination Employment decisions taking into account race or gender in order to remedy past discrimination.

reversion The term reversion has two meanings. First, it designates the estate left in the grantor during the continuance of a particular estate; second, it denotes the residue left in grantor or his heirs after termination of a particular estate. It differs from a remainder in that it arises by an act of law, whereas a remainder arises by an act of the parties. A reversion, moreover, is the remnant left in the grantor, while a remainder is the remnant of the whole estate disposed of after a preceding part of the same has been given away.

revocation The recall of some power, authority, or thing granted, or a destroying or making void of some deed that had existence until the act of revocation made it void.

revocation of acceptance Rescission of one's acceptance of goods based upon a nonconformity of the goods which substantially impairs their value.

right Legal capacity to require another person to perform or refrain from performing an act.

right of entry The right to take or resume possession of land by entering on it in a peaceable manner.

right of redemption The right (granted by statute only) to free property from the encumbrance of a foreclosure or other judicial sale, or to recover the title passing thereby, by paying what is due, with interest, costs, etc. Not to be confounded with the "equity of redemption," which exists independently of statute but must be exercised before sale. See also **equity of redemption**.

right to work law State statute that prohibits union shop contracts.

rights in collateral Personal property the debtor owns, possesses, or is in the process of acquiring.

risk of loss Allocation of loss between seller and buyer where the goods have been damaged, destroyed, or lost.

robbery Larceny from a person by force or threat of force.

rule Agency statement of general or particular applicability designed to implement, interpret, or process law or policy.

rule against perpetuities Principle that no interest in property is good unless it must vest, if at all, not later than twenty-one years, plus period of gestation, after some life or lives in being at time of creation of interest.

rule of reason Balancing the anticompetitive effects of a restraint against its procompetitive effects.

sale Transfer of title to goods from seller to buyer for a price.

sale on approval Transfer of possession without title to buyer for trial period.

sale or return Sale where buyer has option to return goods to seller.

sanction Means of enforcing legal judgments.

satisfaction The discharge of an obligation by paying a party what is due to him (as on a mortgage, lien, or contract) or what has been awarded to him by the judgment of a court or otherwise. Thus, a judgment is satisfied by the payment of the amount due to the party who has recovered such judgment, or by his levying the amount. See also **accord and satisfaction**.

scienter Latin. Knowingly.

seal Symbol that authenticates a document.

secondary liability Obligation to pay is subject to the conditions of presentment, dishonor, notice of dishonor, and sometimes protest.

secret partner Partner whose membership in the partnership is not disclosed.

Section 402A Strict liability in tort.

secured bond A bond having a lien on specific property.

secured claim Claim with a lien on property of the debtor.

secured party Creditor who possesses a security interest in collateral.

secured transaction A transaction founded on a security agreement. Such agreement creates or provides for a security interest. UCC § 9–105(h).

securities Stocks, bonds, notes, convertible debentures, warrants, or other documents that represent a share in a company or a debt owed by a company.

Certificated security Security represented by a certificate.

Exempt security Security not subject to registration requirements of 1933 Act.

Exempt transaction Issuance of securities not subject to the registration requirements of 1933 Act.

Restricted securities Securities issued under an exempt transaction.

Uncertificated security Security not represented by a certificate.

security agreement Agreement that grants a security interest.

security interest Right in personal property securing payment or performance of an obligation.

seisin Possession with an intent on the part of him who holds it to claim a freehold interest.

self-defense Force to protect oneself against attack.

separation of powers Allocation of powers among the legislative, executive, and judicial branches of government.

service mark Distinctive symbol, word, or design that is used to identify the services of a provider.

servient Land subject to an easement.

setoff A counterclaim demand which defendant holds against plaintiff, arising out of a transaction extrinsic to plaintiff's cause of action.

settlor Creator of a trust.

severance The destruction of any one of the unities of a joint tenancy. It is so called because the estate is no longer a joint tenancy, but is severed.

Term may also refer to the cutting of crops, such as corn, wheat, etc., or to the separation of anything from realty.

share A proportionate ownership interest in a corporation.

Shelley's case, rule in Where a person takes an estate of freehold, legally or equitably, under a deed, will, or other writing, and in the same instrument there is a limitation by way of remainder of any interest of the same legal or equitable quality to his heirs, or heirs of his body, as a class of persons to take in succession from generation to generation, the limitation to the heirs entitles the ancestor to the whole estate.

The rule was adopted as a part of the common law of this country, though it has long since been abolished by most states.

shelter rule Transferee gets rights of transferor.

shipment contract Seller is authorized or required only to bear the expense of placing goods with the common carrier and bears the risk of loss only up to such point.

short-swing profits Profits made by insider through sale or other disposition of corporate stock within six months after purchase.

sight draft An instrument payable on presentment.

signature Any symbol executed with intent to validate a writing.

silent partner Partner who takes no part in the partnership business.

slander Oral defamation.

small claims courts Inferior civil courts with jurisdiction limited by dollar amount.

social security Measures by which the government provides economic assistance to disabled or retired employees and their dependents.

sole proprietorship A form of business in which one person owns all the assets of the business, in contrast to a partnership or a corporation.

sovereign immunity Foreign country's freedom from a host country's laws.

special warranty deed Seller promises that he has not impaired title.

specific performance The doctrine of specific performance is that where damages would compensate inadequately for the breach of an agreement, the contractor or vendor will be compelled to perform specifically what he has agreed to do; *e.g.,* ordered to execute a specific conveyance of land.

With respect to the sale of goods, specific performance may be decreed where the goods are unique or in other proper circumstances. The decree for specific performance may include such terms and conditions as to payment of the price, damages, or other relief as the court may deem just. UCC §§ 2–711(2)(b), 2–716.

standardized business form A preprinted contract.

stare decisis Doctrine that once a court has laid down a principle of law as applicable to a certain state of facts, it will adhere to that principle and apply it to all future cases having substantially the same facts, regardless of whether the parties and property are the same or not.

state action Actions by governments, as opposed to actions taken by private individuals.

state-of-the-art Made in accordance with the level of technology at the time the product is made.

stated capital Consideration, other than that allocated to capital surplus, received for issued stock.

statute of frauds A celebrated English statute, passed in 1677, which has been adopted, in a more or less modified form, in nearly all of the United States. Its chief characteristic is the provision that no action shall be brought on certain contracts unless there be a note or memorandum thereof in writing, signed by the party to be charged or by his authorized agent.

statute of limitation A statute prescribing limitations to the right of action on certain described causes of action; that is, declaring that no suit shall be maintained on such causes of action unless brought within a specified period after the right accrued.

statutory lien Interest in property, arising solely by statute, to secure payment of a debt.

stock "Stock" is distinguished from "bonds" and, ordinarily, from "debentures" in that it gives a right of ownership in part of the assets of a corporation and a right to interest in any surplus after the payment of debt. "Stock" in a corporation is an equity, representing an ownership interest. It is to be distinguished from obligations such as notes or bonds, which are not equities and represent no ownership interest.

Capital stock See **capital**.

Common stock Securities which represent an ownership interest in a corporation. If the company has also issued preferred stock, both common and preferred have ownership rights. Claims of both common and preferred stockholders are junior to claims of bondholders or other creditors of the company. Common stockholders assume the greater risk, but generally exercise the greater control and may gain the greater reward in the form of dividends and capital appreciation.

Convertible stock Stock which may be changed or converted into common stock.

Cumulative preferred Stock having a provision that if one or more dividends are omitted, the omitted dividends must be paid before dividends may be paid on the company's common stock.

Preferred stock is a separate portion or class of the stock of a corporation that is accorded, by the charter or by-laws, a preference or priority in respect to dividends, over the remainder of the stock of the corporation, which in that case is called *common stock*.

Stock warrant A certificate entitling the owner to buy a specified amount of stock at a specified time(s) for a specified price. Differs from a stock option only in that options are granted to employees and warrants are sold to the public.

Treasury stock Shares reacquired by a corporation.

stock option Contractual right to purchase stock from a corporation.

stop payment Order for a drawee not to pay an instrument.

strict liability A concept applied by the courts in product liability cases in which a seller is liable for any and all defective or hazardous products which unduly threaten a consumer's personal safety. This concept applies to all members involved in the manufacture and sale of any facet of the product.

strict scrutiny test Requirement that legislation be necessary to promote a compelling governmental interest.

subagent Person appointed by agent to perform agent's duties.

subject matter jurisdiction Authority of a court to decide a particular kind of case.

subject to the mortgage Purchaser is not personally obligated to pay the debt, but the property remains subject to the mortgage.

subjective fault Desired or virtually certain consequences of one's conduct.

subjective satisfaction Approval based upon a party's honestly held opinion.

sublease Transfer of less than all of a tenant's interest in a leasehold.

subpoena A subpoena is a command to appear at a certain time and place to give testimony upon a certain matter. A subpoena duces tecum requires production of books, papers, and other things.

subrogation The substitution of one thing for another, or of one person into the place of another with respect to rights, claims, or securities.

Subrogation denotes the putting of a third person who has paid a debt in the place of the creditor to whom he has paid it, so that he may exercise against the debtor all the rights which the creditor, if unpaid, might have exercised.

subscribe Literally, to write underneath, as one's name. To sign at the end of a document. Also, to agree in writing to furnish money or its equivalent, or to agree to purchase some initial stock in a corporation.

subscriber Person who agrees to purchase initial stock in a corporation.

subsidiary corporation Corporation controlled by another corporation.

substantial performance Equitable doctrine protects against forfeiture for technical inadvertence, trivial variations, or omissions in performance.

substantive due process Requirement that governmental action be compatible with individual liberties.

substantive law The basic law of rights and duties (contract law, criminal law, tort law, law of wills, etc.), as opposed to procedural law (law of pleading, law of evidence, law of jurisdiction, etc.).

substantive unconscionability Oppressive or grossly unfair contractual terms.

sue To begin a lawsuit in a court.

suit "Suit" is a generic term of comprehensive signification that applies to any proceeding in a court of justice in which the plaintiff pursues, in such court, the remedy which the law affords him for the redress of an injury or the recovery of a right.

Derivative suit Suit brought by a shareholder on behalf of a corporation to enforce a right belonging to the corporation.

Direct suit Suit brought by a shareholder against a corporation based upon his ownership of shares.

summary judgment Rule of Civil Procedure 56 permits any party to a civil action to move for a summary judgment on a claim, counterclaim, or cross-claim when he believes that there is no genuine issue of material fact and that he is entitled to prevail as a matter of law.

summons Writ or process directed to the sheriff or other proper officer, requiring him to notify the person named that an action has been commenced against him in the court from which the process has issued and that he is required to appear, on a day named, and answer the complaint in such action.

superseding cause Intervening event that occurs after the defendant's negligent conduct and relieves him of liability.

supreme law Law that takes precedence over all conflicting laws.

surety One who undertakes to pay money or to do any other act in event that his principal debtor fails therein.

suretyship A guarantee of debts of another.

surplus Excess of net assets over stated capital.

tangible property Physical objects.

tariff Duty or tax imposed on goods moving into or out of a country.

tenancy Possession or occupancy of land or premises under lease.

Joint tenancy Joint tenants have one and the same interest, accruing by one and the same conveyance, commencing at one and the same time, and held by one and the same undivided possession. The primary incident of joint tenancy is survivorship, by which the entire tenancy on the decease of any joint tenant remains to the survivors, and at length to the last survivor.

Tenancy at sufferance Only naked possession which continues after tenant's right of possession has terminated.

Tenancy at will Possession of premises by permission of owner or landlord, but without a fixed term.

Tenancy by the entirety A tenancy which is created between a husband and wife and by which together they hold title to the whole with right of survivorship so that, upon death of either, the other takes the whole to the exclusion of the deceased's heirs. It is essentially a "joint tenancy," modified by the common law theory that husband and wife are one person.

Tenancy for a period A tenancy for years or for some fixed period.

Tenancy in common A form of ownership whereby each tenant (*i.e.*, owner) holds an undivided interest in property. Unlike the interest of a joint tenant or a tenant by the entirety, the interest of a tenant in common does not terminate upon his or her prior death (*i.e.*, there is no right of survivorship).

tenancy in partnership Type of joint ownership that determines partners' rights in specific partnership property.

tenant Possessor of a leasehold interest.

tender An offer of money; the act by which one produces and offers to a person holding a claim or demand against him the amount of money which he considers and admits to be due, in satisfaction of such claim or demand, without any stipulation or condition.

Also, there may be a tender of performance of a duty other than the payment of money.

tender of delivery Seller makes available to buyer goods conforming to the contract and so notifies the buyer.

tender offer General invitation to all shareholders to purchase their shares at a specified price.

testament Will.

testator One who makes or has made a testament or will; one who dies leaving a will.

third-party beneficiary One for whose benefit a promise is made in a contract but who is not a party to the contract.

Creditor beneficiary Where performance of a promise in a contract will benefit a person other than the promisee, that person is a creditor beneficiary if no purpose to make a gift appears from the terms of the promise, in view of the accompanying circumstances, and performance of the promise will satisfy an actual, supposed, or asserted duty of the promisee to the beneficiary.

Donee beneficiary The person who takes the benefit of the contract even though there is no privity between him and the contracting parties. A third-party beneficiary who is not a creditor beneficiary. See also **beneficiary**.

time paper Payable at definite time.

time-price doctrine Permits sellers to have different prices for cash sales and credit sales.

title The means whereby the owner of lands or of personalty has the just possession of his property.

title insurance Provides protection against defect in title to real property.

tort A private or civil wrong or injury, other than breach of contract, for which a court will provide a remedy in the form of an action for damages.

Three elements of every tort action are the existence of a legal duty from defendant to plaintiff, breach of that duty, and damage as proximate result.

tortfeasor One who commits a tort.

trade acceptance A draft drawn by a seller which is presented for signature (acceptance) to the buyer at the time goods are purchased and which then becomes the equivalent of a note receivable of the seller and the note payable of the buyer.

trade name Name used in trade or business to identify a particular business or manufacturer.

trade secrets Private business information.

trademark Distinctive insignia, word, or design of a good that is used to identify the manufacturer.

transferor's warranty Warranty given by any person who transfers an instrument and receives consideration.

treaty An agreement between or among independent nations.

treble damages Three times actual loss.

trespass At common law, trespass was a form of action brought to recover damages for any injury to one's person or property or relationship with another.

Trespass to chattels or personal property An unlawful and serious interference with the possessory rights of another to personal property.

Trespass to land At common law, every unauthorized and direct breach of the boundaries of another's land was an actionable trespass. The present prevailing position of the courts finds liability for trespass only in the case of intentional intrusion, or negligence, or some "abnormally dangerous activity" on the part of the defendant. *Compare* **nuisance**.

trespasser Person who enters or remains on the land of another without permission or privilege to do so.

trust Any arrangement whereby property is transferred with the intention that it be administered by a trustee for another's benefit.

A trust, as the term is used in the Restatement, when not qualified by the word "charitable," "resulting," or "constructive," is a fiduciary relationship with respect to property, subjecting the person by whom the title to the property is held to equitable duties to deal with the property for the benefit of another person, which arises through a manifestation of an intention to create such benefit. Restatement, Second, Trusts § 2.

Charitable trust To benefit humankind.

Constructive trust Wherever the circumstances of a transaction are such that the person who takes the legal estate in property cannot also enjoy the beneficial interest without necessarily violating some established principle of equity, the court will immediately raise a *constructive trust* and fasten it upon the conscience of the legal owner, so as to convert him into a trustee for the parties who in equity are entitled to the beneficial enjoyment.

Inter vivos trust Established during the settlor's lifetime.

Resulting trust One that arises by implication of law, where the legal estate in property is disposed of, conveyed, or transferred, but the intent appears or is inferred from the terms of the disposition, or from the accompanying facts and circumstances, that the beneficial interest is not to go or be enjoyed with the legal title.

Spendthrift trust Removal of the trust estate from the beneficiary's control.

Testamentary trust Established by a will.

Totten trust A tentative trust which is a joint bank account opened by the settlor.

Voting trust A trust which holds the voting rights to stock in a corporation. It is a useful device when a majority of the shareholders in a corporation cannot agree on corporate policy.

trustee In a strict sense, a "trustee" is one who holds the legal title to property for the benefit of another, while, in a broad sense, the term is sometimes applied to anyone standing in a fiduciary or confidential relation to another, such as agent, attorney, bailee, etc.

trustee in bankruptcy Representative of the estate in bankruptcy who is responsible for collecting, liquidating, and distributing the debtor's assets.

tying arrangement Conditioning a sale of a desired product (tying product) on the buyer's purchasing a second product (tied product).

ultra vires Acts beyond the scope of the powers of a corporation, as defined by its charter or by the laws of its state of incorporation. By the doctrine of ultra vires, a contract made by a corporation beyond the scope of its corporate powers is unlawful.

unconscionable Unfair or unduly harsh.

unconscionable contract See **contracts**.

underwriter Any person, banker, or syndicate that guarantees to furnish a definite sum of money by a definite date to a business or government in return for an issue of bonds or stock. In insurance, the one assuming a risk in return for the payment of a premium.

undisputed debt Obligation whose existence and amount are not contested.

undue influence Term refers to conduct by which a person, through his power over the mind of a testator, makes the latter's desires conform to his own, thereby overmastering the volition of the testator.

unemployment compensation Compensation awarded to workers who have lost their jobs and cannot find other employment.

unenforceable Contract under which neither party can recover.

unfair employer practice Conduct in which an employer is prohibited from engaging.

unfair labor practice Conduct in which an employer or union is prohibited from engaging.

unfair union practice Conduct in which a union is prohibited from engaging.

Uniform Commercial Code One of the Uniform Laws, drafted by the National Conference of Commissioners on Uniform State Laws, governing commercial transactions (sales of goods, commercial paper, bank deposits and collections, letters of credit, bulk transfers, warehouse receipts, bills of lading,

investment securities, and secured transactions).

unilateral mistake Erroneous belief on the part of only one of the parties to a contract.

union shop Employer can hire nonunion members, but such employees must then join the union.

universal life Ordinary life divided into two components, a renewable term insurance policy and an investment portfolio.

unliquidated debt Obligation that is uncertain or contested in amount.

unqualified indorsement (see **indorsement**) One that imposes liability upon the indorser.

unreasonably dangerous Danger beyond that which the ordinary consumer contemplates.

unrestrictive indorsement (see **indorsement**) One that does not attempt to restrict the rights of the indorsee.

usage of trade Any practice or method of dealing having such regularity of observance in a place, vocation, or trade as to justify an expectation that it will be observed with respect to the transaction in question.

usury Collectively, the laws of a jurisdiction regulating the charging of interest rates. A usurious loan is one whose interest rates are determined to be in excess of those permitted by the usury laws.

value The performance of legal consideration, the forgiveness of an antecedent debt, the giving of a negotiable instrument, or the giving of an irrevocable commitment to a third party. UCC § 1–201(44).

variance A use differing from that provided in a zoning ordinance in order to avoid undue hardship.

vendee A purchaser or buyer; one to whom anything is sold. See also **vendor**.

vendor The person who transfers property by sale, particularly real estate; "seller" being more commonly used for one who sells personalty. See also **vendee**.

venue "Jurisdiction" of the court means the inherent power to decide a case, whereas "venue" designates the particular county or city in which a court with jurisdiction may hear and determine the case.

verdict The formal and unanimous decision or finding of a jury, impaneled and sworn for the trial of a cause, upon the matters or questions duly submitted to it upon the trial.

vertical privity Who is liable to the plaintiff.

vertical restraints Agreements among parties at different levels of the distribution chain.

vested Fixed; accrued; settled; absolute. To be "vested," a right must be more than a mere expectation based on an anticipation of the continuance of an existing law; it must have become a title, legal or equitable, to the present or future enforcement of a demand, or a legal exemption from the demand of another.

vested remainder Unconditional remainder that is a fixed present interest to be enjoyed in the future.

vicarious liability Indirect legal responsibility; for example, the liability of an employer for the acts of an employee or that of a principal for the torts and contracts of an agent.

vitiate to make ineffective

void Null; ineffectual; nugatory; having no legal force or binding effect; unable, in law, to support the purpose for which it was intended.

This difference separates the words "void" and "voidable": *void* in the strict sense means that an instrument or transaction is nugatory and ineffectual, so that nothing can cure it; *voidable* exists when an imperfection or defect can be cured by the act or confirmation of the person who could take advantage of it.

Frequently, the word "void" is used and construed as having the more liberal meaning of "voidable."

voidable Capable of being made void. See also **void**.

voir dire Preliminary examination of potential jurors.

voluntary Resulting from free choice. The word, especially in statutes, often implies knowledge of essential facts.

voting trust Transfer of corporate shares' voting rights to a trustee.

wager (gambling) Agreement that one party will win or lose depending upon the outcome of an event in which the only interest is the gain or loss.

waiver Terms "estoppel" and "waiver" are not synonymous; "waiver" means the voluntary, intentional relinquishment of a known right, and "estoppel" rests upon principle that, where anyone has done an act or made a statement that would be a fraud on his part to controvert or impair, because the other party has acted upon it in belief that what was done or said was true, conscience and honest dealing require that he not be permitted to repudiate his act or gainsay his statement. See also **estoppel**.

ward An infant or insane person placed by authority of law under the care of a guardian.

warehouse receipt Receipt issued by a person storing goods.

warehouser Storer of goods for compensation.

warrant, *v.* In contracts, to engage or promise that a certain fact or state of facts, in relation to the subject matter, is, or shall be, as it is represented to be.

In conveyancing, to assure the title to property sold, by an express covenant to that effect in the deed of conveyance.

warranty A warranty is a statement or representation made by a seller of goods, contemporaneously with and as a part of a contract of sale, though collateral to express the object of the sale, having reference to the character, quality, or title of goods, and by which the seller promises or undertakes to ensure that certain facts are or shall be as he then represents them.

The general statutory law governing warranties on sales of goods is provided in UCC § 2–312 *et seq.* The three main types of warranties are (1) express warranty; (2) implied warranty of fitness; (3) implied warranty of merchantability.

warranty deed Deed in which grantor warrants good clear title. The usual covenants of title are warranties of seisin, quiet enjoyment, right to convey, freedom from encumbrances, and defense of title as to all claims.

Special warranty deed Seller warrants that he has not impaired title.

warranty liability Applies to persons who transfer an instrument or receive payment or acceptance.

warranty of title Obligation to convey the right to ownership without any lien.

waste Any act or omission that does permanent injury to the realty or unreasonably changes its value.

white-collar crime Corporate crime.

will A written instrument executed with the formalities required by statutes, whereby a person makes a disposition of his property to take effect after his death.

winding up To settle the accounts and liquidate the assets of a partnership or corporation, for the purpose of making distribution and terminating the concern.

without reserve Auctioneer may not withdraw the goods from the auction.

workers' compensation Compensation awarded to an employee who is injured, when the injury arose out of and in the course of his employment.

writ of certiorari Discretionary review by a higher court. See also **certiorari**.

writ of execution Order served by sheriff upon debtor demanding payment of a court judgment against debtor.

zoning Public control over land use.

Index

D

Damages